HANDBOOK FOR SUSTAINABLE TOURISM PRACTITIONERS

RESEARCH HANDBOOKS IN TOURISM

Series Editor: Robin Nunkoo, *University of Mauritius*

This timely series brings together critical and thought-provoking contributions on key topics and issues in tourism and hospitality research from a range of management and social science perspectives. Comprising specially-commissioned chapters from leading academics these comprehensive *Research Handbooks* feature cutting-edge research and are written with a global readership in mind. Equally useful as reference tools or high-level introductions to specific topics, issues, methods and debates, these *Research Handbooks* will be an essential resource for academic researchers and postgraduate students.

Titles in this series include:

Handbook of Social Tourism
Edited by Anya Diekmann and Scott McCabe

Handbook for Sustainable Tourism Practitioners
The Essential Toolbox
Edited by Anna Spenceley

Handbook for Sustainable Tourism Practitioners

The Essential Toolbox

Edited by

Anna Spenceley

Independent consultant, Chair of the IUCN WCPA Tourism and Protected Areas Specialist Group, Director of the Global Sustainable Tourism Council, Independent Advisory Panel member of Travelyst, Honorary Fellow, University of Brighton, UK and Senior Research Fellow, University of Johannesburg, South Africa

RESEARCH HANDBOOKS IN TOURISM

 Edward Elgar
PUBLISHING

Cheltenham, UK • Northampton, MA, USA

Published by
Edward Elgar Publishing Limited
The Lypiatts
15 Lansdown Road
Cheltenham
Glos GL50 2JA
UK

Edward Elgar Publishing, Inc.
William Pratt House
9 Dewey Court
Northampton
Massachusetts 01060
USA

Paperback edition 2022

A catalogue record for this book
is available from the British Library

Library of Congress Control Number: 2021932285

This book is available electronically in the **Elgar**online
Geography, Planning and Tourism subject collection
http://dx.doi.org/10.4337/9781839100895

ISBN 978 1 83910 088 8 (cased)
ISBN 978 1 83910 089 5 (eBook)
ISBN 978 1 0353 0815 6 (paperback)
Printed and bound by CPI Group (UK) Ltd, Croydon, CR0 4YY

This book is dedicated to my daughter, Emma, in anticipation of her future travels across the world.

Contents

Contributors

Elena A. Bigart

Since 2006, Elena A. Bigart has been working with protected areas around the world to increase their capacity in visitor management and environmental education. She developed and led more than 50 trainings and study tours for park managers, and visited a variety of national parks in different countries. In 2013–2016, Elena served in the Steering Committee of the World Commission on Protected Areas. In 2019, she received her PhD and is now teaching at the University of Montana.

William T. Borrie

William T. Borrie is with the School of Life & Environmental Sciences at Deakin University, Australia. His research interests are the values, experiences, and management of parks and protected areas. Dr Borrie worked on research in Yellowstone National Park; the Bob Marshall Wilderness complex; the Arctic National Wildlife Refuge; the Okefenokee National Wildlife Refuge; the Selway-Bitterroot Wilderness and the Flathead Wild & Scenic River. His PhD is from Virginia Tech and his BS and MS are from the University of Melbourne.

Wen-Huei Chang

Dr Wen-Huei Chang is a Senior Economist with the US Army Corps of Engineers Institute for Water Resources, where he leads the Natural Resources Management Support Program that provides support for the agency's 12 million acres of lands and waters and 260 million annual visitors. He also manages the Value to the Nation program that documents and communicates the benefits delivered through the Corps' Civil Works Program and provides a foundation to effectively manage the capital and natural resources.

Alex Chidakel

Dr Alex Chidakel received his PhD in Interdisciplinary Ecology from the University of Florida. His research explores the potential strategic, management and academic roles for the economic monitoring of protected areas.

Brian Child

Brian Child, Associate Professor, University of Florida has been involved in wildlife economics and governance in southern Africa for 35 years as a practitioner, project manager, and scholar. He obtained his PhD from Oxford (Rhodes Scholar) working on the comparative economics of wildlife and livestock. He supported the private conservation sector and coordinated Zimbabwe's CAMPFIRE program. In Zambia, he managed community programs, restructured South Luangwa National Park as a financially viable cost centre, and tested performance-based anti-poaching in Kafue National Park. At Florida, he has led over 150 students in the field, established Higher Education for Development Projects including co-developing a Masters in Sustainable Development practice, and published a number of books, papers and reports, many with his graduate students. He chaired the IUCN-Southern African Sustainable Use Specialist Group, and was the Biodiversity Panel Member for the Scientific and Technical Advisory Panel of the GEF.

Nicholas Coetzer
Associate Professor Nicholas Coetzer teaches architectural design and history at the University of Cape Town and has a PhD from the Bartlett School of Architecture, University College, London. He has published *Building Apartheid* through Routledge with a follow-up commission to write An Architecture of Care: A Genealogy of Moral Instrumentality from Arts and Crafts to South Africa. He has published extensive reviews and articles for *Architecture SA* journal and has a research interest in vernacular architecture, sustainability and ecotourism.

Randy Durband
Randy Durband is CEO of the Global Sustainable Tourism Council (GSTC), a UN-created NGO managing global sustainable tourism standards. His 40 years in tourism include senior leadership positions with major tour operators – President of Travcoa and Clipper Cruise Lines, Executive Vice President of Tauck – plus a second career in sustainable tourism. He is a frequent adviser to governments and businesses on sustainable tourism policies and has served on many tourism boards, committees, and awards juries.

Paul F. J. Eagles, PhD, RPP, MCIP
Paul F. J. Eagles is a Distinguished Professor Emeritus at the University of Waterloo, Waterloo, Canada. His primary appointment was to the Department of Recreation and Leisure Studies, with cross appointment to the School of Planning. He specializes in environmental, recreation and tourism planning, with 45 years of planning experience. He undertook planning and research in these fields in over 40 countries and has 410 publications, of which 142 are refereed. He was involved, in various ways, in each of the case studies outlined in his book chapter.

Joel Erkkonen
Joel Erkkonen is a development manager at Metsähallitus, Parks & Wildlife Finland, Rovaniemi. He has a long domestic and international career on sustainability and management of recreation and tourism. He has a solid experience about several development projects focusing on visitor monitoring, sustainable nature-based tourism, developing visitor centres, service design and customer experience, branding of national parks and health benefits of protected areas. He is a pioneer of harmonized visitor monitoring in Finland.

Mike Fabricius
Mike Fabricius (PhD) is an experienced tourism policy analyst and strategist, with a tourism career that spans 30 years. He has been consulting globally in the area of tourism destination management since 2005 and has worked extensively in Africa, the Middle East, Asia, Europe and the Caribbean. Having spearheaded the adoption of South Africa's tourism policy in the late 1990s and as co-signatory of the Cape Town Declaration on Responsible Tourism, Mike is a passionate proponent of sustainable tourism development.

Shane Feyers
Shane Feyers is a PhD candidate in Interdisciplinary Ecology and a Biodiversity Institute Fellow at the University of Florida. Specializing in Urban and Regional Planning, Shane studies conservation land use and the geography of responsible nature-based tourism (i.e. ecotourism) on private property in the United States and beyond. Shane holds a Master of Environmental Management degree in Human Dimensions from Yale School of the

Environment and a Bachelor of Science in Natural Resource Management from the University of Connecticut.

Roger Goodacre

Roger is an experienced tourism planning and development consultant who has widespread experience of drafting tourism master plans, particularly in emerging markets. He is employed regularly as a technical expert and team leader by UNWTO and other international organizations, government development agencies and consultancy firms, and has carried out multiple assignments in eastern Europe, east, west and southern Africa, the Mediterranean and Middle East, and South Asia. His career in tourism began as a graduate trainee with the British Tourist Authority in London, where he trained in all aspects of destination marketing before postings to Amsterdam and Paris. Roger is a Fellow of the Tourism Society, and since 2012 has been Chairman of the Tourism Consultants Network, Europe's leading professional association of tourism consultants.

Virginia Gorsevski

Dr Virginia Gorsevski is a Program Manager for biodiversity at the Scientific and Technical Advisory Panel, which is responsible for providing independent scientific and technical advice to the Global Environment Facility. Virginia has a background in international development and earned her PhD in Geographical Sciences from the University of Maryland, where she focused on the impact of conflict on forest cover in South Sudan.

Amran Hamzah

Dr Amran Hamzah is an academic-practitioner who specializes in tourism policy planning and the interface between tourism and conservation. Besides his academic duties, Amran is equally active as a tourism consultant for international clients such as APEC, the ASEAN Secretariat, IUCN and UNESCO as well as national agencies, notably the Ministry of Tourism, Arts and Culture Malaysia (MOTAC) and Tourism Malaysia. Amran was the lead consultant for Malaysia's National Ecotourism Plan (2016–2025) and the National Tourism Policy (2020–2030).

Vanessa Hull

Vanessa Hull is an Assistant Professor in the Department of Wildlife Ecology and Conservation at the University of Florida. She studies coupled human and natural systems, wildlife ecology and management, and conservation biology around the world, especially in protected areas in China. Vanessa obtained MS and PhD degrees from the Department of Fisheries and Wildlife at Michigan State University and a BS in Animal Behavior from Bucknell University.

Liisa Kajala

Liisa Kajala is a senior adviser in Metsähallitus, Parks & Wildlife Finland. She has a long international career on protected area management, with focus on visitor monitoring, outdoor recreation, tourism and wilderness management. Her special interest is in making visitor information widely available, accessible and efficiently used by managers and decision makers.

Jacqueline N. Kariithi

Jacqueline Kariithi is an environmental scientist passionate about conservation, tourism and development issues. She holds a PhD in Environmental and Geographical Science and her thesis was titled 'Developing Responsible Nature Based Tourism at the Mount Elgon region of Kenya: Integrated Approaches'. She is currently a postdoctoral researcher in the department of Ecology and Evolutionary Biology at Princeton University. Her main research interests lie in the intersection between cultural heritage, biodiversity conservation and sustainable livelihoods for community stakeholders living adjacent to parks and protected areas.

Lynne Koontz

Dr Lynne Koontz is an Economist with the National Park Service Social Science Program located in Fort Collins, Colorado. Lynne provides economic expertise and technical support to parks and leadership on a variety of issues. She is a co-author of the annual Visitor Spending Effects analysis which measures how park visitor spending cycles through local economies, generating business sales and supporting jobs and income.

Wayne L. Linklater

Wayne trained as an ecologist and then wildlife biologist in New Zealand, working in freshwater systems and then with wild horses. After his PhD he worked with a variety of mammals in Australia, North America and South Africa before developing a long-term interest in the behaviour, ecology and management of large mammals, especially rhinoceros. Over time his interests have diversified to include many human dimensions of wildlife management such as wildlife crime, conflict and policy.

Carolin Lusby

Carolin Lusby Pereira holds a PhD in Tourism and Natural Resources from the University of Florida. She was a Fulbright Scholar in Brazil, where she consulted in community-based tourism and collaborated in various research projects. She is an Assistant Professor in Tourism at Florida International University's Chaplin School of Hospitality and Tourism Management where she oversees the tourism program. She is passionate about travel and connecting people to people while preserving natural and cultural resources.

Ante Mandić

Dr Ante Mandić is an Assistant Professor at the University of Split, Faculty of Economics, Business and Tourism – Department of Tourism and Economy, Croatia. His research focuses on destination management, nature-based tourism and smart tourism. He has a wide experience in tourism-related projects and has worked as an expert on EU funded projects (ERDF MED, INTERREG, CBC, and Horizon 2020), regional and local tourism destination strategies and integrated coastal zone management plans. He is a member of the IUCN World Commission on Protected Areas (WCPA), Tourism and Protected Areas Specialist Group (TAPAS Group), and Europarc Federation.

Edward W. (Ted) Manning

Edward W. (Ted) Manning is President of Tourisk Inc., based in Ottawa Canada and providing integrated planning for heritage sites and tourism destinations worldwide. He has worked in over 50 countries in Asia, Europe, Africa and the Americas focused on protecting the world's special places. He has led the development of indicators of sustainability for the global tourism sector and currently advises the UNWTO and the Global Sustainable Tourism Council. He has published 23 books and over 100 articles on development, tourism and environmental management topics. He is an Associate Member of the Club of Rome, former President Canadian Association of Geographers and Adjunct Professor of Geography and Environmental Studies at Carleton University.

P. J. Massyn
P. J. Massyn is currently chief executive and co-owner of RETURNAfrica, a tourism company operating in the Western Cape and the Kruger National Park. Previously, he managed the African Safari Foundation, a not-for-profit initiative to improve linkages between the tourism industry and local economies. He has done tourism research, planning and project management across Africa, and published widely on topics in tourism planning, concessions, land reform, economics, world heritage and public–private partnerships. He continues to act as a tourism specialist advising public agencies.

Stephen F. McCool
Steve believes that societies flourish when they are connected with and bond to their heritage. His research has involved understanding and enhancing that connection through principally tourism in natural settings. He is Professor Emeritus at the University of Montana, USA. Since retirement in that position he has emphasized building capacity of natural heritage managers and scientists to apply contemporary visitor management concepts to planning, management and research. In 2019, he co-edited (with Keith Bosak) *A Research Agenda for Sustainable Tourism*.

Hannah R. Messerli
Hannah is dedicated to using tourism as an economic development tool for emerging economies. As a senior private sector development specialist in tourism at the World Bank, she supports government initiatives to develop private sector capacity in emerging markets. Working across the public and private sectors in tourism policy, planning and development, she has crafted solutions for countries in every region worldwide. Previously, she was a faculty member at New York University and The George Washington University and management consultant in Asia and Australia. Dr Messerli has a master's and doctorate degree in hotel administration and tourism planning from Cornell University and a master's degree in tourism planning and development from The George Washington University.

Monica Mic
Monica is a multilingual tourism professional and founder of Monecolodge International, a branding firm she established in 2017. She is also a doctoral candidate in Sustainable Business at Waterloo University, Ontario, Canada, working on the issue of ecolodge branding. Previously, Monica worked as a brand manager for Starwood Hotels & Resorts and graduated from Waterloo University with an MES degree in Tourism Geography.

Jonathan Mitchell
Jonathan has 30 years of economic development experience, working with donors (World Bank, Department for International Development and European Commission), consultancies (Ove Arup, Coffey International and Oxford Policy Management) and a 'think tank' (Overseas Development Institute) in more than 30 countries. He is a published author in inclusive economic growth and development impact assessment with interests in market systems development and private sector development with sector expertise in agriculture and tourism. He currently manages the private sector programme at Oxford Policy Management.

Jeff R. Muntifering
Since 1999, Dr Jeff Muntifering has applied an interdisciplinary approach to provide science leadership and share technical expertise within multi-stakeholder groups to improve conservation impact. His applied research on black rhinoceros in Namibia with Save the Rhino Trust has informed innovative management policies and practice including community-based monitoring, ecotourism protocols, outreach campaigns and re-introduction strategies. He lectures at Beijing Forestry University and holds an adjunct position at Namibia University of Science and Technology.

Regis Musavengane
Regis Musavengane (PhD) is a Research Fellow at the School of Ecological and Human Sustainability, Department of Environmental Sciences, University of South Africa (UNISA) and Faculty member at the Midlands State University, Zimbabwe. His research focuses on political ecology in sub-Saharan African contexts, with particular interest in co-management of natural resources, conservation, environmental governance and tourism systems that promote stakeholder participation. He is a member of the IUCN's World Commission on Protected Areas (WCPA) Tourism and Protected Areas Specialist Group (TAPAS Group).

Darlington Muzeza
Darlington Muzeza (PhD) is a multidisciplinary researcher and development expert. His interests cover social ecology, transboundary biodiversity governance, inclusive participatory conservation management, tourism, capacity building, and conflict management and resolution. He served in various governmental and non-governmental capacities including having served as the Southern African Development Community (SADC) Technical Advisory Committee Member from 2007–2011. He has experience working in diplomacy, agriculture and wildlife value chains, human and social development, humanitarian aid and training institutions in Africa.

Marina Novelli
Professor Marina Novelli (PhD) is a human geographer with a background in economics and a keen interest in international cooperation for development. She is an internationally renowned tourism and sustainable development expert. At the University of Brighton (UK), she is Professor of Tourism and International Development and Academic Lead for the Responsible Futures Research and Enterprise Agenda. As an academic applied researcher and a practitioner she has worked extensively in Africa, Europe and Asia and advised on projects funded by the World Bank, the EU, the UN, the Commonwealth Secretariat, national ministries and tourism boards, regional development agencies, private sector organizations and NGOs. Her work is globally recognized for contributing to the identification of tourism-related interventions that generate more sustainable economic development, improved environments and more inclusive societies.

Andjelko Novosel
Andjelko Novosel is a geologist and geographer specialized in protected area management and a professional underwater filmmaker. For two years he was the Director of Plitvice Lakes National Park and for four years was the head of Nature Conservation Department at the same park. As Park Director, he started the process of developing the new management plan and was involved as part of the planning team. Now he is an independent consultant.

Amit Sharma
Amit Sharma is Professor and Associate Director of School of Hospitality Management at Penn State University, Director of Food Decisions Research Laboratory, and Senior Research Associate at University of Johannesburg. Dr Sharma teaches finance and economics. His interdisciplinary research focuses on decision-making, cost–benefit analysis, and small business financing, in local food system contexts. He was President (2017–2018) of International Council of Hotel, Restaurant, and Institutional Education, and President of International Association of Hospitality Financial Management Educators (iAHFME) (2019–2020).

Ognjen Škunca
Ognjen Škunca has 20 years of experience working as consultant and team leader on a wide array of subjects in areas of sustainable development, environmental and nature protection. A major project was the UNDP project supporting development of nature-based tourism in the Croatian coastal area and on the preparation of the Croatian Green Tourism Plan. In the development of the Management Plan for Plitvice lakes National Park he participated as the team coordinator and an expert for visitor use management and nature-based sustainable rural development.

Liandi Slabbert
Liandi has almost 20 years' collective experience working as a researcher and consultant supporting strategic, tactical and operational initiatives for large enterprises in various sectors. At the South African National Parks, she overseas tourism research for its 19 national parks and is currently pursuing a PhD in Tourism Management. Her research interests include protected areas tourism, visitor research, visitor management, human–nature interactions, strategic market development and knowledge utilization.

Susan Snyman
Susan Snyman, PhD, is the Director of Research at the African Leadership University's School of Wildlife Conservation. Previously, Sue worked for Wilderness Safaris, a private sector ecotourism operator, for 10 years in various roles, including as Group Sustainability Manager. She is vice-chair of the IUCN WCPA Tourism and Protected Areas Specialist Group and recently managed the Biodiversity and Protected Areas Management Programme for IUCN in 24 countries in Africa. Her research focus is on sustainable, diversified wildlife economies in Africa.

Thiago do Val Simardi Beraldo Souza
Dr Thiago Beraldo Souza is the Economics Coordinator of the Tourism and Protected Areas Working Group (TAPAS/IUCN). For the last 18 years, Thiago worked for the Chico Mendes Institute for Biodiversity Conservation (ICMBio) – Federal Protected Areas Agency of Brazil developing agendas such as capacity building, ecotourism planning, community-based tourism, wildlife tourism, long distance trails, visitor monitoring, recreation concessions and economic impacts of tourism. Thiago has a PhD in Interdisciplinary Ecology from the University of Florida, USA and is currently the International Technical Adviser for the BIOTUR – Biodiversity and Tourism Project funded by UNDP/GEF in Cape Verde.

Anna Spenceley
Dr Anna Spenceley is a sustainable tourism consultant with over 20 years' international experience. She has an extensive publication record, rich diversity of project experience, and an

extensive international network. She is Chair of the IUCN World Commission on Protected Areas (WCPA) Tourism and Protected Areas Specialist Group (TAPAS Group), and she sits on the board of Global Sustainable Tourism Council, and the Advisory Panel of Travalyst. She is an Honorary Fellow in the School of Sport and Service Management at the University of Brighton, UK and Senior Research Fellow in the School of Tourism and Hospitality at the University of Johannesburg, South Africa.

Jos van der Sterren

Jos van der Sterren is an international economist with experience in financial inclusion, tourism destination management, value chain development and the informal economy. His background allows him to apply financial inclusion to business environments in tourism destinations. Specializations include investment fund design and management and institutional governance of (micro)finance institutions. Since 2003 he has extended his field of experience to higher tourism education, and works as a lecturer, researcher and consultant at Breda University of Applied Sciences.

Gretchen Stokes

Gretchen Stokes is a National Science Foundation Graduate Research Fellow and PhD candidate in Ecology at the University of Florida. With a focus on geospatial analysis and modelling, Gretchen is developing a global assessment framework to evaluate threats to freshwater fisheries. Gretchen holds a MS in Fish and Wildlife Conservation from Virginia Polytechnic Institute and State University and a BS in Fisheries, Wildlife and Conservation Biology from North Carolina State University, and is a certified Associate Wildlife Biologist.

Cathy Cullinane Thomas

Cathy Cullinane Thomas is a natural resource economist with the US Geological Survey and has specialized in developing regional economic models to address social and economic issues related to protected area management and visitation. Cathy is the lead modeller for the US National Park Service Visitor Spending Effects Model and produces annual estimates of the economic contributions of tourism to US National Parks.

Louise Twining-Ward

Dr Twining-Ward is a Senior Private Sector Specialist at the World Bank, with more than 20 years' experience in the design, implementation, and monitoring of tourism development projects in Latin America, South Asia, and sub-Saharan Africa. Louise has a PhD in Sustainable Tourism Monitoring and an MSc in Tourism Management from the University of Surrey in the UK. She also works on gender equality, environmental sustainability and digital tourism projects. Louise previously led the NGO Sustainable Travel International (STI).

Jose Miguel Villascusa

Jose Miguel Villascusa is as a Private Sector Development Consultant for the World Bank where he works in the design and implementation of tourism projects. He also conducts research in tourism, specifically in institutional appraisal, private sector assessment and M&E. He holds an MA in International Business by the Spanish Institute of Foreign Trade and is an MBA candidate at Georgetown University. He has been a member of the World Bank Global Tourism Team of tourism specialists since 2016.

Vesna Vukadin
Vesna Vukadin is a biologist who specializes in participatory management planning for protected areas and Natura 2000 sites. She has 13 years of experience in the field, gained by working in both the public and private nature conservation sector in Croatia. Her role in the development of the Management Plan for Plitvice Lakes National Park was as an expert for participatory management planning. She is employed in her own small limited company Park Bureau.

Michael Wright
With 18 years' experience in ecotourism and environmental consulting, lodge development and tour guiding, Michael Wright loves to provide solutions to projects that enhance ecotourism potential and offer optimal environmental outcomes. Michael seeks to ensure biodiversity conservation through sustainable development and responsible enterprise. He owns Sustain, a consulting and tour operating company, and is a registered professional natural scientist and nature tour guide. Most of his work has found him adventuring in or near protected areas and other conserved spaces.

Acknowledgements

I would like to sincerely thank all of the authors for their tremendous contributions in this handbook, and to Professor Marina Novelli, Dr Susan Snyman, and Dr Louise Twining-Ward for their efforts to review the manuscript and provide valuable feedback.

Notably, the book compilation period has overlapped with the onset and emergence of the coronavirus COVID-19 pandemic, which continues to be an immense challenge. It is a testament to the contributors' resolve, and a credit to their professionalism, that they have been able to continue during this time and enable completion of this volume.

Foreword

The *Handbook for Sustainable Tourism Practitioners* is a pleasure to read, and a great tool to refer to. Written by world experts in their fields, it fills a gap in the market for sustainable tourism research that is helpful and practical. It is gratifying to read all these chapters from consultants and practice-oriented academics that I have admired for years, which allow us an insight into the experience they have gained over decades of working for some of the most influential international organizations, overseas development agencies, governments and protected areas.

The authors have summarized a number of tools and techniques that are relevant to address some of today's most urgent and important challenges: balancing commercialization interests of businesses with the loss of biodiversity and wildlife, poverty and inclusivity, inequity and gender disparity, and of course the health and economic implications of the spread of COVID-19.

The first section on planning and designing sustainable tourism covers essential topics on policy formation, tourism planning, protected area management, commercialization strategies, development of feasibility plans and risk management, and the preparation of funding proposals. This is then followed by a number of chapters outlining key operational management tools, including practical advice on community and infrastructure development, stakeholder consultation, market research, value chain analysis, indicator design, standard setting and auditing. The third section of the book focuses on visitor management in practice, in order to achieve a balance of overtourism and undertourism, including management strategies to set and achieve desirable levels of tourism. The final section of the book brings together experience in methods to monitor and evaluate sustainable tourism, which includes chapters outlining the concepts and examples on visitor counting, options for the economic analysis of visitation, biological impacts, social and cultural assessment, and the use of certification and case studies to establish sustainability.

Whereas some of these topics have been covered in publications before, the novelty here is that the book is unashamedly not theoretical, but applied. The writing style is agile, yet this does not take away from the rigour applied. The book is teeming with case studies and examples, many of which have not been in the academic domain previously. The book provides a wealth of relevant information that allows the reader to understand key concepts, with a 'how to' emphasis and the depth of field experience necessary to focus on the key points.

This book is full of practical knowledge that is immediately relevant. It will hold a treasured place on my bookshelf, and I already know it will come out to help me from time to time get a reality check.

Dr Xavier Font
Professor of Sustainability Marketing, School of Hospitality and Tourism Management,
University of Surrey, UK
Professor ll, School of Business and Economics, UiT. The Arctic University of Norway,
Tromsø, Norway
Co-editor of the *Journal of Sustainable Tourism*

1. Introduction to the *Handbook for Sustainable Tourism Practitioners: The Essential Toolbox*
Anna Spenceley

ORIGINS OF THE BOOK

This book emerged from the sustainable tourism research and consulting work I have undertaken over the past 20 or so years. During this time I have had the good fortune to collaborate with many highly skilled consultants and foresighted clients. Coming originally from an academic background, with a doctorate and postdoctoral fellowships, I developed a strong desire to translate academic methods into streamlined reliable and practical tools. These are essentially approaches that can be applied within shorter time frames than academic research in order to generate meaningful answers to complex questions. Transferring knowledge and research methods from the academic realm into practical assignment approaches for clients – whether government, development agency, academic, private sector, or non-governmental organization – is a multi-faceted challenge. Scott and Ding (2005) note that knowledge is embedded within people, and it either accumulates with experience or is created by thinking or reasoning. Furthermore, knowledge uses skills and experience to add intelligence to information and data, in order to inform reliable decision-making (Cooper, 2015). One of several methods of knowledge transfer is by translating it into a readily understandable form (Nonaka, 1991), and that is what this volume aspires to achieve.

Starting out in the field of sustainable tourism as a practitioner can be difficult. In reality, there is a great deal of 'learning by doing', and practitioners need to balance a series of challenges: ambitious and sometimes ambiguous terms of reference for tasks; high expectations of clients; limited time by which to undertake the research and deliver meaningful answers; collaboration with team members who have different expectations and ways of working; and also budgets that are rarely expandable. From every assignment I undertake, I learn something useful that can be transferred on to the next – whether it is something that worked well, or something that could have been improved. Another route of my own learning has been through doing project design work and project evaluations for development agencies (e.g. the European Union, the World Bank Group, USAID, the International Labour Organization, UN World Tourism Organization, United Nations Development Programme and others), and through reviewing design and evaluation reports compiled by others. This has taught me a great deal about approaches that work, those that do not, and a daunting array of 'landmines' to be avoided along the way. In my experience, good deliverables are produced by practitioners where they have (a) clear and specific terms of reference and an approved inception report that establishes a common understanding of the tasks, approach, and outputs, (b) an endorsed contract prior to starting work (which sounds obvious, but often there is time pressure to begin before this is in place), (c) adequate budget to cover both the time and expenses required to deliver, (d) sufficient time and resources for data collection, including from field observations, consultation with key stakeholders, and literature review, (e) agreement on any adjustments and changes to adapt the assignment along the way, and (f) a pragmatic review of draft deliverables prior to finalizing them. In my experience, if one or more of these elements is missing, or inadequate, then the task becomes more challenging for all parties concerned. What would have been helpful for me, particularly in the early years of my work, would have been access to a suite of good practices that address different approaches and techniques in sustainable tourism.

This comprehensive Handbook brings together practical advice from leading international practitioners in sustainable tourism. This book is not designed as a guide for long-term academic projects, but instead applies good research design principles within the parameters of modest time frames and resources, to provide workable and rational step-by-step approaches to researching real-life challenges. Until now, there has been no comprehensive handbook written by practitioners – and available to practitioners and their clients – on best practices for an array of tasks needed to inform sustainable tourism work. The book also provides a useful suite of resources for those that aspire to become sustainable tourism practitioners in the future, and want practical guidance from experts on how to do so. So, the chapters in this volume move beyond traditional research approaches in the academic arena, and towards approaches that can be applied in practical situations.

Taking multi-faceted topics – researching them well – and translating the highly technical concepts into easily digestible form and understandable by decision-makers – is no easy task. Successful approaches to the challenges are shared by the many contributors to this volume; the Handbook aims to shine light on tools and techniques, by drawing together decades of collective knowledge from an outstanding suite of authors, and explain them clearly to readers.

The timing of this book is highly opportune. We live in unprecedented times with daunting global challenges: global climate change, waste plastic in our oceans, dramatic declines in wildlife, the coronavirus COVID-19 pandemic (see Box 1.1), poverty and gender disparity. Tourism can either exacerbate these, or can promote sustainable development practices as part of the solution to ameliorating and resolving them. Several of the book's contributors have reflected on this situation, making their experience all the more relevant to readers. Now, more than ever, practitioners need to use the best available knowledge to provide information to decision-makers that allows them to map the best way forward.

BOX 1.1   THE CORONAVIRUS COVID-19 PANDEMIC AND SUSTAINABLE TOURISM

COVID-19 is an infectious disease created by a newly discovered coronavirus, for which there are no specific vaccines or treatments. The disease first emerged in China at the end of 2019 (Readfearn, 2020), and by 22 January 2021 there were 96.3 million confirmed cases and over 2 million deaths (WHO, 2021). The virus spreads from person to person through respiratory droplets produced when an infected person sneezes, coughs, or talks – and can be spread by people who are not showing symptoms (CDC, 2020). The coronavirus COVID-19 pandemic has had a global impact on the travel sector. Between January and May 2020, 100% of global destinations imposed travel restrictions, and 45% had totally or partially closed their borders for tourists (UNWTO, 2020a). The World Travel and Tourism Council (WTTC) has estimated a global loss of 100.8 million jobs in 2020 and USD 2.7 trillion in revenue due to the pandemic. There are grave concerns that with the tourism sector suspended, millions of jobs could be lost, and progress made in equality and sustainable economic growth could be rolled back (UNWTO, 2020b).

ABOUT THE CONTRIBUTORS

The book contributors have endeavoured to unpack how to undertake environmental, socio-cultural and economic assessments that establish the feasibility for new tourism ventures, or ascertain what impacts they have had over time. They are people that have spent their careers working in the practice of these techniques, and are experts in their respective fields. I am truly humbled that so many people I have collaborated with in the past, and those who I have great admiration for, agreed to contribute to this volume, and that they have been so generous in sharing their insights and expertise with readers. Also I'm very thankful for the constructive and insightful reviews provided by Dr Susan Snyman, Professor Marina Novelli and Dr Louise Twining-Ward on the volume. As three leaders in both the academic and practitioner worlds of sustainable tourism, their perspectives are highly pertinent. Biographical notes for all of the contributors can be found in the notes on contributors, in case you want more insights into their work.

WHO SHOULD READ THIS BOOK

This Handbook is useful for researchers at all levels, and particularly to those working within government institutions responsible for tourism and private tourism businesses. It is also a resource for practitioners, not-for-profit organizations and consultants that provide technical support in the planning, feasibility, development, operation and evaluation of sustainable tourism. The book may also provide useful insights for university students – including at masters, doctoral and postdoctoral levels – as an additional resource that can supplement more traditional research literature. This may further help them to make transitions from academic to practitioner realms. Furthermore, the book also provides important insights that can inform the agencies that commission, finance and coordinate sustainable tourism assignments (e.g. development agencies, non-governmental organizations, tourism destinations and governments). This not only includes important techniques that are recommended for use (and which can be incorporated in terms of reference), but also highlighting the work of leading individuals who are contributing to success in this field through their work. The book will also certainly be of value to those who are the recipients – or beneficiaries – of these approaches, as it provides guidance on what good practices look like.

BOOK STRUCTURE

Each contributor was invited to submit a chapter on a key topic for the book. In order to shape the guidance that they provided, they were challenged to describe:

- Key issues that the research approach addresses, and when or where it could be used in practice

- Major areas of research, literature or their previous work that has informed the approach
- A step-by-step approach for others wishing to apply the approach, explaining any specific tools required
- Any potential challenges, limitations, or issues for troubleshooting
- Implications of the approach.

The chapters in this book have been divided into four parts, which are outlined below.

Part I: Planning and Designing Sustainable Tourism

The chapters in Part I consider the tools and techniques required to create the right conditions for sustainable tourism to take place. These include the policy framework, master planning, and strategies for commercialization. For enterprises themselves, there are chapters on feasibility studies and funding proposals, coupled with guidance on environmental and social impact assessments and indicators. Getting the right foundations in place can be critical in destinations in order that the basis for sustainable tourism is in place. For example, Bhutan has the concept of sustainable development deeply embedded within its policies and strategies, including using 'Gross National Happiness' rather than Gross National Product to describe success; and Botswana's 'high value, low impact' strategy underpins the success of the luxury safari tourism segment in iconic destinations such as the Okavango Delta. Destinations that have established indicators for sustainable tourism have been able to measure their progress, and check that their policies and strategies are on track.

To begin with, Louise Twining-Ward, Hannah R. Messerli, Jose Miguel Villascusa and Amit Sharma explain how to use a Theory of Change to map connections between development challenges, interventions and outcomes (Chapter 2). Based on an international World Bank publication by the same authors, they explain the principles of Theory of Change and then describe a simple five-step process to prepare one. Examples from World Bank projects are used to illustrate how to establish a clear connection between development challenges and desired impacts. With Theory of Change increasingly used by development agencies and within funding proposals including the Global Environment Facility, this chapter provides practical advice to help practitioners address donor expectations.

Next, Mike Fabricius sets out guidelines for tourism policy formulation in developing countries (Chapter 3). He clarifies the differences between policy, strategy and tactics in relation to enabling legislation and regulations, and outlines frameworks for formulating policies. Using an example from South Africa – and a process that Mike coordinated – the policy development process is described along with the structure of a typical policy. He provides detailed information on policy components relating to tourist access, sustainable development, visitor welfare, infrastructure, human resources, marketing and promotion, and institutional and financial arrangements.

Roger Goodacre then outlines key steps and fundamental considerations for tourism master planning in destinations (Chapter 4). His chapter explains the value of comprehensive master plans in delivering economic growth, job creation, and sustainable use of natural and cultural resources, providing an example from Rwanda where he led a UN World Tourism Organization planning process. Of immense value to those both commissioning master plans and compiling them, he describes how terms of reference are compiled, commissioned and funded, the skills and qualifications required on the teams, and their recruitment. He continues to describe the process of researching and writing the plan, and outlines the structure and content that can be used.

Focusing on protected areas, Paul F. J. Eagles explains what is required for protected area authorities to establish commercialization strategies, and to help decide whether to insource or outsource tourism services (Chapter 5). With a series of real-world illustrations, he describes how outsourcing can take place with for-profit companies, non-profit and community organizations, government departments and joint ventures. He outlines elements that should be included in procurement prospectuses used in competitive bidding processes, and characteristics of success and guidance to help managers make decisions on the range of partnership types. Given Paul's extensive practical experience on concessions systems in Canada and elsewhere in the world, this is a chapter based in the practical realities encountered by protected area managers.

Next, P. J. Massyn unpacks how to test the feasibility of ideas for new lodging facilities in relation to technical, legal, environmental, social and economic elements (Chapter 6). The chapter provides guidance on how to evaluate project risks, and step-by-step guidance on the preparation of business plans as road maps for implementation. The chapter gives clear instructions and examples on the preparation of financial models that can predict cash flows and returns on investment, both for investors and land-rights holders. These approaches have been applied in several protected area systems over the years, including in Bhutan, Madagascar, Rwanda, and South Africa, and provide a robust process.

Following neatly from this, in the following chapter Michael Wright describes how to compile a funding proposal for a tourism venture (Chapter 7). He explains that the nature of proposals differ depending on whether they are for new facilities, or existing businesses seeking support for expansion or refurbishment. This has implications for the level of supporting information that can be shared in a persuasive proposal. The types of finance (e.g. grants, equity, debt etc.), sources of finance for tourism ventures, along with their advantages and disadvantages of different types of funder are described. Michael explains how to craft an enticing funding proposal and also how a funder will evaluate it. He explains why sustainable tourism ventures are of particular interest to funders, particularly in relation to concerns about the sector and the UN Sustainable Development Goals. I recall a presentation that Michael gave several years ago at a workshop on transboundary tourism concessions, where he and his colleagues described the challenges of obtaining funding from various sources due to the requirements they placed on applicants. His advice on how to create proposals is highly practical.

A critical aspect of sustainable tourism ventures is the level of local involvement. Amran Hamzah draws on over 30 years' experience researching community-based tourism (CBT) to explain nine steps that should guide its development (Chapter 8). These steps integrate participatory processes, consensus building, and conflict resolution with people both within and outside the communities. The chapter leads readers from the initial step of assessing whether a community is ready for tourism, through raising awareness, identifying champions, developing community organizations and partnerships, using integrated approaches, planning and design, marketing and promotion, through to monitoring its performance. Now, more than ever, communities need resilient models to sustain their livelihoods, including through domestic clients.

Creating tourism infrastructure – such as accommodation and visitor centres – with sustainable design can have substantial implications for their operational efficiency and the procurement of materials for their construction. Nicholas Coetzer explains that buildings, particularly in nature-based or ecotourism spaces, often lack the ethos of their conservation settings (Chapter 9). He emphasizes that vernacular architecture offers clues as to how to mitigate weather and climatic challenges, how to build settlements with local resources, and also how to engage local communities. Then, where vernacular architecture does not exist in the area the ethos of 'touching the earth lightly' should be pursued. As a counter to this, a strategy of 'touching the earth heavily' raises the challenge to developers, practitioners and architects to approach the design as an emergent response to local ecologies – as an evolutionary *process*. Nicholas guides readers through a series of steps such as: do nothing; know your vernacular; and touch the earth lightly. He explains how to establish an experts map and assist the architect in defining the brief and site *before* the design work proceeds.

The author of the UN World Tourism Organization's 'Indicators of sustainable development for tourism destinations', Ted Manning, gives an insightful account into their development, and how they have been used in practice since then (Chapter 10). He explains the origins of the programme and how the indicators were developed by experts, tested in 14 destinations, and discussed in a series of workshops and conferences. Ted stresses the importance of using a participatory approach to indicator development, and how there have been further advances through the Global Sustainable Tourism Council (GSTC) and Observatories of Sustainable Tourism (INSTO). The application of indicators in broader sustainable destination projects and certification is explained, as are some of the challenges associated with their use.

Part II: Enhancing the Sustainability of Existing Tourism

Part II of this volume explains how to boost the sustainability of operational tourism facilities. This includes through supply and value chain analysis, establishing sustainability standards, designing protocols for wildlife viewing, audits of social and environmental performance, consultation approaches and market research.

First looking at supply chain analysis, Jos van der Sterren considers a circular approach (Chapter 11). The chapter shares a method that allows researchers to understand inefficiencies and spillovers in tourism supply chains and proposes solutions through a circular economy approach. Jos describes how supply chains can be composed while using options to reduce waste, reuse resources and recycle valuable materials.

Next, Jonathan Mitchell examines how value chain analysis (VCA) can be used to map and quantify the benefits that accrue to local communities from tourism in destinations (Chapter 12). Jon's paper demystifies the process of undertaking a VCA, and shares a practical process that can be undertaken within 10–20 days of fieldwork. Drawing on his extensive global experience, he shares examples, practical hints and guidance, and explains the implications of VCA results for economic development and tourism practitioners.

Randy Durband, Chief Executive Officer of the GSTC explains the importance of sustainability standards, their role, and how they are established and applied (Chapter 13). Using two GSTC standards to illustrate, namely the GSTC Industry and Destination criteria, Randy explains how they are used and by whom, and how they are developed and maintained over time. The process of using standards in certification with tiered levels of assurance and the importance of continual improvement are described. The chapter also illustrates some of the beneficial impacts that certification can have for hotels and tour operators and destinations.

Furthermore, he explains how those who operating sustainably are increasingly benefiting from improved market access.

Looking specifically at wildlife viewing, researchers Jeff R. Muntifering and Wayne L. Linklater demonstrate how the development of wildlife protocols through statistical analysis and modelling can help to: (1) identify the characteristics of human–wildlife encounters that cause disturbance and displacement; and (2) design encounter guidelines that improve sustainability (Chapter 14). They draw from a real-world case in north-west Namibia, where paying tourists have an opportunity to encounter the critically endangered black rhinoceros (*Diceros bicornis*) on foot. The authors explain step-by-step how they researched the situation in Namibia, and used the findings to establish good wildlife viewing scenarios – in terms of duration and distance from the rhinos.

Next, Carolin Lusby describes consultation approaches for sustainable tourism (Chapter 15). She summarizes the main approaches that practitioners can use (e.g. certification/auditing, workshops and seminars, case studies, hands-on training, website analysis, data collection and analysis), giving special attention to the applicability of each approach to specific projects and circumstances. Providing guidance on the steps that each technique requires, she also introduces a number of examples and case studies to illustrate.

Part III: Balancing Overtourism and Undertourism: Visitor Management in Practice

Part III of the book deals with approaches to balancing levels of visitors, and managing them, in tourism destinations. Some destinations have tourism at its infancy, and employ techniques to attract visitors, encourage them to stay a while, spend some money, and have a minimal environmental impact during their trip. Other destinations and sites are more established, and can become very popular. In some instances the level of popularity is described as overtourism, where visitation exceeds physical, environmental, social, economic, psychological, and/or political capacity thresholds. Uncontrolled tourism development can cause substantial damage to landscapes, seascapes, air and water quality, as well as the living conditions of residents, causing economic inequalities and social exclusion, amongst many other issues (Peeters et al., 2018). The purpose of visitor management is to find the right balance between visitor levels, systems and infrastructure to support them, and the lives of people, wildlife and habitats that reside there.

Introducing this section of the book, Stephen F. McCool outlines a research strategy of acceptable biophysical and social conditions for sustainable tourism (Chapter 16). He highlights challenges that protected area and destination managers have with trade-offs in balancing quality of visitor access and experiences with the protection of natural and cultural heritage. Steve's chapter proposes a holistic research strategy to develop the knowledge and understanding at the foundation of more effective and equitable destination management. This is a thought-provoking chapter underpinned by many years of experience on these complex 'wicked problems', using a systems approach.

The Visitor Use Management (VUM) framework is a tool used by US national parks and other protected areas to improve the quality of visitor experiences and to protect the resources upon which they are based. William T. Borrie and Elena A. Bigart explain how this tool is used to identify the social, biophysical, and managerial conditions desired, in addition to meaningful and measurable indicators related to management actions (Chapter 17). Step by step, they take readers through four stages of (1) building foundations, (2) defining VUM direction, (3) identifying management strategies, and (4) implementing, monitoring, evaluating and adjustment. Usefully, they also describe other frameworks used in visitor management, such as the Recreation Opportunity Spectrum, and Limits of Acceptable Change.

Next, Paul F. J. Eagles, Andjelko Novosel, Ognjen Škunca and Vesna Vukadin deal with the challenging issue of establishing reasonable visitor targets that support sustainability (Chapter 18). They unpick the challenges of the 'carrying capacity' concept, such as the difficulties for public institutions in establishing minimum and maximum use levels. They explain that conflicts may arise between influential interest groups resulting in political gridlock. They explain concepts of peak load management and standards development, with practical illustrations and lessons learned from Pinery Provincial Park and Point Pelee National Park in Ontario, Canada and also Plitvica National Park in Croatia.

A detailed destination approach to addressing overtourism is proposed by Ante Mandić (Chapter 19). This approach adapts a Driver–Pressure–State–Impact–Response (DPSIR) framework to analyse potential and currently applied responses aiming to optimize tourism development. The step-by-step approach is described based on its application within the Mediterranean region, and specifically describes DPSIR elements in Split, Croatia. Ante describes how the structured-thinking approach is cognizant of context, data, participation, cooperation, monitoring and complexity.

Readers of this book should note that two further chapters were originally planned for this section, on sustainable tourism in an era of climate change, and carbon offsetting for tourism and travellers. However, due to pressures of the COVID-19 pandemic during 2020, the authors were unable to supply manuscripts in time for publication. I hope that further editions of this book will be able to rectify this gap, but in the meantime some links to resources on climate change and tourism are indicated in Box 1.2 below.

BOX 1.2   SUSTAINABLE TOURISM AND CLIMATE CHANGE

Climate change is the existential crisis of our time. Numerous resources on sustainable tourism and climate change are available to guide practitioners. These include materials from United Nations agencies (e.g. UNWTO and UNEP, 2008; UNWTO, 2019) and also companies providing guidance on how to decarbonise or offset travel emissions (e.g. Intrepid Travel, 2020; Cho, 2018). Tourism professionals and companies can also form their own commitment and plan to address climate change using the 'Tourism Declares a Climate Emergency' platform (Tourism Declares, 2021).

Part IV: Monitoring and Evaluation

Monitoring and evaluation are crucial elements of sustainable tourism. Once we have our policy frameworks established, our tourism services operating, our visitor management in place, we need to ascertain whether we are actually achieving our objective of sustainable development. This part of the book examines visitor counting, options for the economic analysis of visitation, biological impacts, social and cultural assessment, and the use of certification and case studies to establish sustainability. An example of how to design a sustainable tourism research programme for institutions that manage tourism is also shared.

Joel Erkkonen and Liisa Kajala draw on their extensive work across Finland's protected areas to provide guidance on visitor counting and surveys (Chapter 20). They explain the entire visitor monitoring process, including data collection and using the data in reporting. Joel and Liisa highlight how the combination of systematic visitor counts and surveys can be used to establish a diverse picture of protected area visitation. The application of findings to decision-making and policy is also explained.

Next, looking at economic impacts and contributions of visitation, Cathy Cullinane Thomas and Lynne Koontz offer insights into the methods used by the US National Park Service (Chapter 21) based on the Money Generation Model (MGM2). After explaining the economic models that underpin their work, they share guidance on data required (including the visitation data, and survey data explained in the previous chapter along with multipliers). Cathy and Lynne explain how this information is used to estimate visitor spending and economic effects, and also how the results can be used. Using the example of Yosemite National Park to illustrate trip characteristics such as spending patterns and visitor segment variations, the chapter demonstrates how park level data can be combined to estimate state and national level visitor spending effects. Powerfully, they highlight how three decades of annual NPS reports have become well-recognized, respected indicators of how protected areas contribute to the national economy.

Along similar lines, Chapter 22 shares other approaches used for economic assessment of visitation. Thiago do Val Simardi Beraldo Souza, Alex Chidakel, Brian Child, Wen-Huei Chang, and Virginia Gorsevski explain how the Tourism Economic Model for Protected Areas (TEMPA) has been modified from the MGM2 approach described in the previous chapter. The TEMPA is applicable to managers of protected areas in developing countries where there are different levels of information available – due to budget, time, and capacity constraints. They share examples of economic assessment – using the TEMPA and other approaches – in Brazil's protected areas, the Kruger National Park in South Africa, and the Luangwa National Park in Zambia.

Focusing next on environmental and biodiversity elements, and taking a step-by-step approach, Shane Feyers, Gretchen Stokes and Vanessa Hull describe Rapid Biological Assessments as standardized procedures that tourism operators can use to assess the baseline biological conditions of sites (Chapter 23). They explain how to establish objectives and priorities for the use of biodiversity, and monitor the resulting impacts. Leaving aside issues of ethics and theory, they provide guidance on the evaluation techniques and identification of stressors. They also share some of the limitations, applications and benefits of the approach.

Jacqueline N. Kariithi completes this 'triple bottom line' picture of economic, environmental and social monitoring and evaluation, with a chapter on the social and cultural impact assessment of sustainable tourism (Chapter 24). Jackie presents the phases and steps used in the application of social and cultural impact assessment tools, and describes the complexities of cultural and social dimensions. She also recognizes that the identification and standardization of tools for cultural and social impact assessment remains elusive, and qualitative, rather than highly technical.

Certification is a tool that provides independent verification of sustainability claims by tourism enterprises and destinations. Building on the background of Chapter 10 on indicators, and Chapter 13 on sustainability standards, Monica Mic provides an evaluation of some of the most popular tourism certification audits and investigates successful cases and best practice while also recognising failures (Chapter 25). In doing so, this chapter looks at the specific steps in the audit process, the different tools and approaches available to auditors, and compliance challenges among auditing participants in ensuring a good level of effectiveness and efficiency from audit activities.

Case studies provide a research tool for evaluating sustainable tourism in real-life contexts in depth. Regis Musavengane and Darlington Muzeza explain the steps that researchers can apply to develop case studies (Chapter 26). Using the example of case study research in Somkhanda Game Reserve in South Africa, they explain how to plan, design, prepare, collect data, analyse findings, and share the results.

Concluding the book, Liandi Slabbert describes how research programmes can be established and managed in tourism destinations, using the example of South African National Parks (Chapter 27). Her chapter is particularly notable as it draws together concepts from a number of other chapters in this book, including underlying policies on sustainable tourism and consultation processes. Particularly interesting is the challenge of combining academic interests of universities and their students, with the practical requirements for market intelligence needed for operational decision-making. She outlines the process and evolution of the research programme and protocols for this protected area authority, and describes the research cycle, how proposed research projects are rated and reviewed, and also partnerships with universities that have been established.

REFERENCES

CDC (2020) How COVID-19 is spread. https://www.cdc.gov/media/releases/2020/s1005-how-spread -covd.html. Accessed 27 July 2020.

Cho, R. (2018) The 35 easiest ways to reduce your carbon footprint, State of the Planet, Earth Institute, Columbia University. Available at: https://blogs.ei.columbia.edu/2018/12/27/35-ways-reduce-carbon -footprint/. Accessed 23 January 2021.

Cooper, C. (2015) Managing tourism knowledge. *Tourism Recreation Research*, 40, 107–119.

Intrepid Travel (2020) A 10 step guide to decarbonising your travel business. Available at: https://www .intrepidtravel.com/adventures/decarbonise-travel/. Accessed 23 January 2021.

Nonaka, L. (1991) The knowledge creating company. *Harvard Business Review*, 69, 96–104.

Peeters, P., Gössling, S., Klijs, J., Milano, C., Novelli, M., Dijkmans, C., Eijgelaar, E., Hartman, S., Heslinga, J., Isaac, R., Mitas, O., Moretti, S., Nawijn, J., Papp, B. and Postma, A. (2018) Research for TRAN Committee – Overtourism: impact and possible policy responses. European Parliament, Policy Department for Structural and Cohesion Policies, Brussels.

Readfearn, G. (2020) How did coronavirus start and where did it come from? Was it really Wuhan's animal market? *The Guardian*, 15 April.

Scott, N. and Ding, P. (2005) Management of tourism research knowledge in Australia and China. *Current Issues in Tourism*, 11, 514–528.

Tourism Declares a Climate Emergency (2021) Tourism Declares a Climate Emergency, Available at: https://www.tourismdeclares.com, Accessed 23 January 2021.

UNWTO and UNEP (2008) Climate change and tourism – Responding to global challenges, World Tourism Organisation and United Nations Environment Program. Available at: https://www.e-unwto .org/doi/pdf/10.18111/9789284412341. Accessed 23 January 2021.

UNWTO (2019) Transport-related CO2 emissions of the tourism sector – modelling results, UNWTO: Madrid. Available at https://www.e-unwto.org/doi/book/10.18111/9789284416660. Accessed 23 January 2021.

UN World Tourism Organization (UNWTO) (2020a) 100% of global destinations now have COVID-19 travel restrictions. UNWTO reports.

UNWTO (2020b) COVID-19 response: 96% of global destinations impose travel restrictions. UNWTO reports.

World Health Organization (WHO) (2021) WHO Coronavirus Disease (COVID-19) Dashboard. https://covid19.who.int. Accessed 23 January 2021.

World Travel and Tourism Council (WTTC) (2020) WTTC members COVID-19 hub. https://wttc.org/COVID-19. Accessed 7 May 2020.

PART I

PLANNING AND DESIGNING SUSTAINABLE TOURISM

2. Tourism Theory of Change: a tool for planners and developers

Louise Twining-Ward, Hannah R. Messerli, Jose Miguel Villascusa and Amit Sharma

WHAT IS A THEORY OF CHANGE? ORIGINS AND APPLICATIONS

Every project design contains assumptions about how change happens, for example, that developing a tourism plan will result in more coordinated and sustainable development. When these beliefs are incorrect, incomplete, or the assumptions on which they are based are not fully explored, projects may fail to achieve their desired outcome. Theory of Change (ToC) is a simple tool to map the connections between development challenges, interventions and outcomes. It originated in the 1990s in the field of community-based social change initiatives in the United States. The concept is described as "the pathways of change that lead to the long-term goal and the connections between activities, outputs, and outcomes that occur at each step along the way" in a given project or intervention programme (Taplin et al., 2013; see also Taplin and Clark, 2012).

ToC involves the virtual mapping of a project from the underlying problem all the way to the long-term desired outcomes at the end of the project period. Project activities can then be assessed for their ability to create a pathway of change from the problem towards the outcomes. As development projects and non-profit organizations have been called upon to become more transparent about their methods and the development challenges they are addressing, ToC has become a recurrent tool of choice; in project scoping, design, and strategy development, right through implementation, evaluation, and impact assessment. Preparing a ToC does not require any specialist skills except knowledge of the tool, a questioning mindset, a dynamic team, and an ability to see the big picture. It can usually be completed by a team in two half-day brainstorming sessions.

ToC builds on the foundation provided by the Logical Framework Approach and Results Frameworks. The Logical Framework Approach (LFA) was developed in the late 1960s to support planning and evaluation systems using a matrix or logframe. LFA uses a matrix to help map the connection between project inputs, activities and outcomes, to improve project planning. Results Framework (RF) (also referred to as Results Chain) is a similar planning, management, and communications tool that has been used since the mid-1990s to anticipate results from specific interventions.

The main difference between LFA, RF and ToC is the starting point. Whereas ToC starts by developing an understanding of the long-term desired outcome and roots of the problems to be solved, LFA and Results Chains start with the intervention and map its connection to the outcome. A ToC therefore provides a much broader context and involves understanding the underlying assumptions that connect interventions (project activities) and outcomes. ToC's advantage is, first, that it requires clarity on the problem to be solved and the underlying causes

Table 2.1   *Comparison of change measurement tools*

Logical Framework	Results Framework	Theory of Change
Is a linear representation of change, from activity to result.	The objectives and interventions provide the base for its design.	Is about critical thinking, and has room for complexity and deep questioning.
Descriptive in approach; logframes only state what is believed will happen or will be achieved.	Descriptive in approach; oriented towards describing the sequence of activities leading up to expected results.	Explanatory in approach; ToC articulates and explains the what, how, and why of the change sought and the contribution of the project or programme.
Has three results levels (output, outcome, and impact).	Is focused on articulating different levels of results expected from an intervention.	The paths of change are unlimited and parallel results chains or webs, and feedback mechanisms.
Provides a simplified explanation of causal relations between result levels.	It does not allow causality between outcomes to be explained.	Involves deeper explanation of causal relationships within the theory (rationales).
Focuses only on assumptions about external conditions.	Focuses only on assumptions about external conditions.	Articulates and explains three levels of assumptions (from context to causal relations).

Sources: van Es et al. (2015); James (2011); World Bank (2012); Wigodzky and Farmelo (2014).

of those problems. Second, it requires project teams to question and articulate the assumptions about causality; the relationship between the problems and the interventions. Third, the ToC is not descriptive but explanatory, articulating how change happens and why it is needed. This helps avoid the tendency to jump to a solution before the problem is fully understood. Consequently, the ToC approach allows teams to build more robust projects and more realistic results chains, which is why the World Bank Group has adopted ToC as its prevailing change management framework. A comparison of the three tools is shown in Table 2.1.

Theory of Change has multiple applications, from planning to evaluation, and can be used at various levels, from understanding why change occurs in society to specifically understanding why changes happen in a particular setting or project. Three important applications are noted:

- **Strategic planning:** frequently used in conjunction with logical framework approaches, a ToC can help map the process of change and expected outcomes to facilitate project design. It can help reinforce partnerships, streamline communication, and support organizational development (Taplin et al., 2013).
- **Communication:** a ToC can be used to communicate an organization's chosen *path of change* (the articulation of assumptions, outcomes and activities and the connections between them) or to explain the underlying theory of an organization, project or programme. This application is popular with non-profit and civil society organizations.
- **Evaluation and assessment:** ToC can be used to evaluate or assess a project's contribution to change. When used at the start of the project it can help organizations to establish attribution (Taplin et al., 2013). When used at project completion, it can help to explain the successes and failures of the programme or project.

Finally, a ToC can be used at four different levels:

- **Macro-level:** these are "worldview theories of change" (van Es et al., 2015). Examples include political change, economic growth, empowerment of individuals or strengthening of civil society.

- **Organizational level:** these theories frame the understanding of change held by a given organization: What needs to change, why does it need to change, how can it change and what is the organization's role and practices to bring about change? (e.g. World Bank's ToC).
- **Thematic policy:** these theories go a step further to focus on areas or topics where an organization is working to bring change. They are critical to understanding and justifying what a department or policy is and what change it is working to achieve (e.g. World Bank's Tourism Thematic ToC).
- **Project level theories of change:** these go deepest to analyse the specific *path of change* for a specific project in a country or destination (e.g. ToC of a tourism project in Peru).

WHY A THEORY OF CHANGE IN TOURISM?

While the ToC tool has been used widely in international development, it has not been systematically adopted by academics or consultants. As a result, there are few examples in the literature of ToC applied to tourism. ToC is also typically absent from strategic planning, communication or project design and evaluation. Therefore, this chapter has two objectives. First, it attempts to address this gap through defining and illustrating a Tourism Theory of Change. Second, it aims to provide tourism practitioners with a guide and a set of tools for applying the ToC to specific tourism interventions, whether in design, evaluation or communication. The chapter draws on the experience of tourism as an engine for development in World Bank projects.

A Tourism Theory of Change is developed to help understand why and how change happens. To be successful, tourism programmes and projects need to take the entire tourism landscape into consideration and leverage insights from theoretical research, experience, and empirical evidence. The thematic Tourism ToC presented here provides a framework for the planning, execution and evaluation of tourism projects. It connects project goals and development objectives to project outcomes and therefore helps maximize tourism's potential. The methodology used to develop this theory of change involved: (i) analysis of tourism projects and lessons learned from World Bank Group (WBG) tourism operations, (ii) research of academic work on tourism as a tool for development and (iii) study of ToC as a tool for project design and evaluation. The results of these three steps were white-boarded, reviewed and considered by practitioners. The final product is shown in Figure 2.1. It illustrates the most common development challenges identified across World Bank tourism projects and the most used interventions to address them. The next section explains how to develop a ToC.

DEVELOPING A TOURISM THEORY OF CHANGE

Step 1. Stakeholder Identification

Step 1 in developing a ToC is to identify the main stakeholders for a particular project or programme. Identifying and including stakeholders in the process is a key part of developing an effective ToC. Developing a ToC independently is very difficult and not recommended. Stakeholder participation increases the likelihood of correctly mapping existing

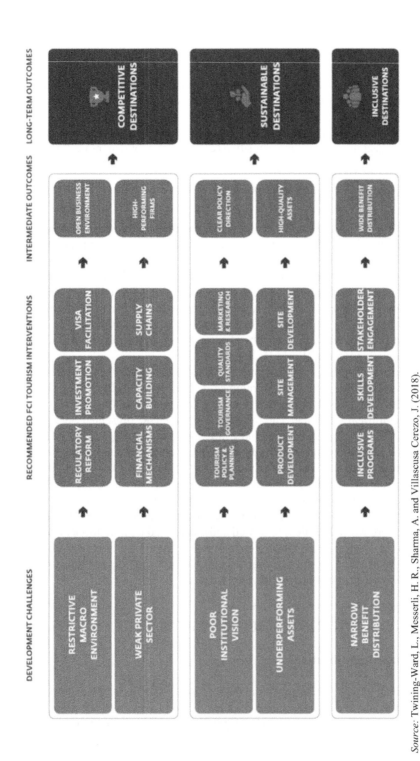

Source: Twining-Ward, L., Messerli, H. R., Sharma, A. and Villascusa Cerezo, J. (2018).

Figure 2.1   A big picture Tourism Theory of Change

development challenges to their underlying causes and boosts the chances of developing the right activities to tackle the barriers within the paths of change. Effective stakeholder participation involves: (i) identifying all actors that may have influence or interest and/or may be affected by the project; (ii) mapping the relationship between the power they hold and the interest they have in the project; and (iii) developing measures to engage them at different project stages. In tourism, this might include the following:

- **Private sector:** consider consulting businesses along the tourism value chain and include both local and international providers of goods, services, and investment capital (foreign, national, and diaspora investors). Often private sector organizations in tourism can be consulted through a tourism business association.
- **Public sector:** there are many public and governmental institutions that are involved in tourism. Actors specific to this group include the Ministry of Tourism or tourism board, municipality, park authority, and other regional or local government entities.
- **Individuals and civil society:** this group includes community groups, non-profit associations, and online interest groups. Tourists (national, regional, and international, including diaspora) are included here as well.
- **Other institutions:** this group includes all institutional actors with variable influence, power, and interests in the development of the tourism industry. It includes international donors, such as the World Bank, thought-leadership organizations such as the UN World Tourism Organization (UNWTO), as well as destination management organizations, which are usually made up of a variety of private and public participants, and scientific and research communities.

Step 2. Long-Term Outcomes and Assumptions

Step 2 of developing a ToC is to discuss and identify long-term outcomes and assumptions together with the key stakeholders. The most important element of a ToC is defining the long-term outcome – the goal that the project is designed to achieve. This outcome must be attributable by project and inside the project 'accountability ceiling', meaning that it can be achieved within the life of, and be attributed to, the project. Based on review of World Bank tourism research, there are three common long-term desired outcomes:

1. *Competitiveness:* to improve the economic performance of the tourism sector by enhancing the destination's ability to attract and satisfy tourists. The competitiveness of a destination depends on: (i) the competitiveness of the firms that supply services in the destination and (ii) the supply-side factors that must exist at a destination that determine its image and attractiveness (Enright and Newton, 2004).
2. *Sustainability:* to ensure tourism takes full account of its current and future economic, social and environmental impacts; and addresses the needs of visitors, the sector, the environment and host communities (UNWTO, 2016).
3. *Inclusiveness:* to ensure tourism development brings broad benefits across the population, including women, youth, indigenous groups, and those marginalized particularly through geography, conflict or climate-related events (Bakker and Messerli, 2015).

Attribution can be problematic in tourism where there is rarely a linear relationship between action and outcome, but project teams can define the boundary of the project sphere of influence and develop realistic outcomes. Clarifying the assumptions made by the team can help with this process. Assumptions, in this case, refers to the assumed conditions necessary for the intermediate outcomes to connect to the long-term outcomes – the conditions needed for the project to succeed. There are three main types of assumptions: (i) assumptions about the relationship between activities and outcomes, (ii) assumptions about the political, social, cultural or economic environment in which the project takes place (externalities), and (iii) assumptions about the outcome framework, the relevance of the outcomes, and the order in which they are likely to occur. The process of exposing, articulating and questioning assumptions is a critical element of a ToC (Vogel, 2012).

Step 3. Challenges and Intermediate Outcomes

Step 3 in the development of a TOC is to identify challenges and establish intermediate outcomes. Intermediate outcomes are milestones on the path to achieving the long-term outcome. They usually note the changes (political, social, economic, behavioural, etc.) that need to occur for the long-term outcome to be achieved. Challenges are the problems the project is trying to solve; the issues currently standing in the way of outcomes being achieved. These may be related to, among other factors, capacity, budget, or enabling environment.

   While each project may have specific intermediate outcomes, based on a review of World Bank tourism projects, the five intermediate outcomes listed in the left-hand column of Table 2.2 are the most likely intermediate steps to create competitive, sustainable, and inclusive destinations. The challenges standing in the way of the achievement of the outcomes are listed on the right. The evidence base for the relationship between the challenges and the outcomes are listed in parenthesis. The table can be used as a checklist or template when using ToC while designing or evaluating a project.

Step 4. Interventions

Step 4 in the development of a good ToC involves designing 'intervention pathways', to address the challenges outlined in the previous section. Intervention pathways are the project's activities, such as training, investment promotion, and marketing, that are designed to directly address the challenges and help achieve intermediate and long-term outcomes. This section provides some ideas about the types of interventions that can be used to achieve each of the intermediate outcomes in Table 2.2.

Table 2.2   Common tourism development challenges and intermediate outcomes

Intermediate Outcomes	Challenges
1. Open business environment Business-environment reforms help attract foreign and domestic investment (Gatsinzi and Donaldson, 2010); allow domestic, foreign, and joint-venture companies to establish or expand; create new jobs (Chao et al., 2005); and improve efficiency at the firm level (Turco et al., 2003).	• Inconsistent and burdensome licensing, regulatory, and legal frameworks • Outdated and contradictory laws • Unattractive tourism investment environment • Ineffective incentives for tourism • Visa/access cost and burden • Poor public–private dialogue (PPD) • Low security and visitor safety
2. High-performing firms Access to finance is fundamental for growing firms and one of the primary factors of private sector development, especially for SMEs (Holden and Howell, 2009). Improving linkages between the tourism sector and other industries has been found to enhance firm competitiveness and boost employment generation (OECD, 2001).	• Difficulty in accessing finance • Lack of access to land • Lack of legal, business, market research know-how • Poor marketing and market access • Poor working conditions • Weak SME support and incentives • Low management and business development capacity • Lack of available training • Weak understanding of gender issues
3. Clear policy direction and management Sustainable destinations do not happen on their own. They require a deliberate, clear policy direction and leadership. Sustainable destinations are a result of many management factors working together, including proper planning, good policy, reliable data and research, high standards, good governance and coordination, capacity, and site development. Clear policy direction has numerous benefits, such as better tourism planning, improved market positioning, better tourism infrastructure, and enhanced security.	• Lack of clear direction • Lack of consultation during policy development • Poor prioritization and vision • Lack of integrated destination planning • Lack of data on demand • Limited public sector capacity • Poor service quality • Lack of public sector investment • Poor marketing and promotion • Lack of infrastructure • Lack of implementation of policy • Incongruent policies • Lack of allocation of roles and responsibilities/buy-in to policy implementation

Intermediate Outcomes	Challenges
4. High-quality assets The quality of a destination's tourism assets and experiences, and their alignment with market demand, has a significant impact on the competitiveness and sustainability of the destination (Blazeska et al., 2015). Tourism assets include natural features, landscapes, cultural sites, unique culinary traditions, resorts, convention centres and cities. Enhancing the quality of tourism assets improves visitor yield (spending per visitor), protects the destination's assets, and boosts the overall economic impact from tourism.	• Poor interagency coordination • Poor visitor management • Limited revenue capture (rent, entrance fees, etc.) • Lack of environmental and heritage regulations • Poor heritage, culture and natural asset management • Outdated and undifferentiated product(s) • Overcrowding and degradation • Lack of interpretation
5. Wide benefit distribution Inclusive destinations have been found to be more competitive in the long term (McKinsey, 2015). They also demonstrate a deep, well-connected tourism value chain, which links related suppliers, such as agriculture, food producers, and service providers. The development of these linkages is essential for tourism to maximize its potential for poverty reduction, economic growth, and employment generation (Munjal, 2013). Key barriers to inclusion are lack of tourism skills and knowhow at varying levels. This can result in delays in the development of products and services, destination stagnation, and leakage of benefits from the local communities (Koutra, 2007; Moscardo, 2008). Investing in skills can also bring other benefits, such as improved health, better opportunities for women and young people, and greater productivity, which is closely linked to the capacity of tourism to reduce poverty (Koutra, 2007).	• Lack of community involvement and consultation mechanisms • Weak supply chain • Low youth involvement • Low community involvement • High geographic concentration (e.g. all tourism occurs in a specific location or area) • Low tourism awareness • High degree of informality • Low female inclusion

Open business environment

Creating an open, business-friendly environment helps the private sector thrive (see Box 2.1). Improving the business environment for tourism can involve property rights, business registration, contract compliance, stability and security, rule of law, appropriate labour costs, access, visas, political stability and an innovation framework (Cárdenas-Garcia et al., 2013). At the micro-level the significance of the business environment is evident by its impact on tourism business performance (Sharma and Upneja, 2005; Huang et al., 2019). While the macro-level interventions that address challenges in this category are many, World Bank tourism projects tend to identify three main areas that address the need for a more open business environment:

1. *Regulatory reform.* Regulations relating to tourism, such as business licensing, construction permitting, taxes and aviation policy, can be overly burdensome and negatively impact tourism growth. This intervention path involves identifying the opportunity costs of these policies and facilitates a way to improve policies and tourism outcomes. Regulatory reforms are also critical as tourism activity expands into non-traditional areas such as medical tourism (Labonté et al., 2018). Often such regulatory reforms are essential to also ensure tourism impact outcomes are sustainable, and in the interest of the local population's health and well-being.
2. *Investment promotion.* Investment promotion can help attract airlines, hotels and travel companies, to invest in the destination, driving visitor demand and creating jobs. This may involve reviews and improvements to the investment climate, incentives, identification of development zones, and investor pre- and after-care. However, an important element of investment promotion is also tourism readiness, the idea that there are appropriate products and experiences to offer tourists to ensure tourist satisfaction, and truly tourism-led economic development (Okoye, 2017).
3. *Visa facilitation.* Research reveals that visa facilitation can increase international tourist arrivals of affected markets by 5 to 25 per cent whether this be by introduction of 'visa on arrival' systems or e-visa platforms (UNWTO and WTTC, 2012). This intervention path involves identifying the cost–benefit analysis of current visa procedures and helps facilitate easier access. Additionally, visa policies that are aligned with the overall tourism marketing strategies of the country, and policies that facilitate visas for visitors (such as e-visas), have been found to have similar positive impacts despite a diverse approach to such outcomes (Bilbil, 2017).

BOX 2.1 PERU CASE STUDY

In Peru in 2010, a WBG team was asked to analyse issues related to the business climate for tourism in Cusco. The team explored key development challenges and found that the tourism private sector was affected by cumbersome procedures and lack of articulation among entities affecting cultural protected assets. In addition, it was identified that tourism was highly geographically concentrated and not inclusive. Cusco had the highest tourism growth in the country, but it continued to be one of the poorest regions of Peru. A ToC helped to map the connections between the excessive and inadequate bureaucratic procedures, inadequate training, and limited use of technology, which all resulted in high transaction costs for tourism operators. An Investment Climate Tourism Project was then designed for Cusco to reduce transaction costs affecting tourism sector entrepreneurs by streamlining procedures for obtaining licences and permits needed for the start-up and operation of tourism businesses in Cusco. Following this intervention, the time to obtain licences and permits decreased by 1,130 days, a saving of 75 per cent. A total of 750 public servants were trained in 37 training events (46 per cent women), and two new IT systems were put in place to issue and track licences. A total of USD 760,000 of compliance cost savings to the private sector was achieved within eight months of reform implementation.

High-performing firms

Analysis shows competitive destinations are characterized by high-performing tourism firms, and a more competitive private sector promotes job creation and economic growth (World Bank, 2015). This intervention pathway comprises activities that aim to enhance tourism's private sector performance at the firm level. While there are many interventions that could be included here, such as regulations that address poor working conditions, gender inequality, or incentives or access to land, three main intervention categories for high-performing firms have been identified:

1. *Financial mechanisms.* Access to finance is often a significant constraint to firm competitiveness particularly for women-owned or led firms. Research shows access to finance, combined with the ability of firms to create fixed capital, determines their capital productivity. Interventions to improve firm performance may include matching grants or concessionary loans in conjunction with business training and mentorship. Diverse approaches that reduce information asymmetry to provide access to finance for tourism businesses are particularly critical as traditional mechanisms such as fixed asset based financing may be restrictive, especially for tourism and hospitality small and medium enterprises (SMEs) (Sharma, 2007; Motta and Sharma, 2020).
2. *Capacity building.* Skills are vitally important to all tourism interventions because they can result in improved management, higher revenue, increased customer satisfaction, better perception of the destination brand, and better policy planning and destination management. Skills interventions can include training or capacity building in business, management, marketing, customer service, and guiding. Enhanced skills can increase employability in the tourism sector (and beyond). Such employment capabilities can also be associated with creation of empowerment, particularly in women (Butler, 2017). Therefore the positive impact of capacity building in tourism can have positive spillover effects into community life.
3. *Supply-chain development.* This intervention is about strengthening linkages between the tourism sector and potential and actual suppliers of goods and services to the tourism value chain (see Box 2.2). The development of these linkages is essential for tourism to maximize its potential on poverty reduction, economic growth, and employment generation. Tourism value chains also need to emphasize sustainability in all aspects of tourism activity; not just in areas such as ecotourism (Watanabe and Patitad, 2020). This ensures a holistic approach to tourism value chain development.

BOX 2.2 GHANA CASE STUDY

In Ghana, a WB team was asked to analyse barriers to tourism competitiveness. The team found that the SMEs sector contributed only around 6 per cent of the GDP, despite representing about 30 per cent of the workforce. Making up most of the tourism sector, this group of enterprises faced numerous constraints. These included cumbersome and ineffective administrative procedures, lack of capacity in public agencies to implement and enforce regulations, and the high cost of doing business that prevented SMEs from expanding and reaching a size sufficient to compete in both domestic and world markets. Potentially bankable SMEs lacked the management capacity, entrepreneurial appetite, business planning and financial skills to develop into attractive propositions for banks. They did not have sufficient access to land, labour, information, updated equipment, or research and development to innovate and remain competitive. Their access to public contracts and subcontracts was limited, arising from cumbersome bidding procedures. The team mapped these constraints using a ToC as the framework for a new tourism project. The Ghana Micro, Small and Medium Enterprise Project aimed to enhance the competitiveness and employment levels of Ghanaian SMEs. Particularly, it was designed to address these constraints with three main components: (i) increasing access to commercially viable SME credit operations in locally based commercial banks; (ii) facilitating access to markets, trade facilitation, and entrepreneurship development to help SMEs overcome technical barriers to their expansion in the domestic and foreign markets; and (iii) improving the business environment to make it easier to register and start a business. Indicators selected included the number of banks participating, number of SMEs reporting improved operational efficiencies, and percentage of SMEs applying new management techniques.

Clear policy direction

Strong leadership and clear policy direction are the foundation of all successful tourism destinations and can improve the sustainability of a destination or a tourism product. Sustainability is indicated by the destination's ability to address the needs of visitors, the industry, the environment, and host communities in the long term. In addition, a clear policy direction can also improve and address challenges such as lack of infrastructure, poor prioritization, absence of vision or lack of public sector investment. In this context, planning for sustainable development of tourism can and should be better aligned to sustainable development goals (Christie and Sharma, 2008; Adu-Ampong and Kimbu, 2019), to ensure a comprehensive and holistic approach to tourism development.

There are four recommended intervention categories for policy direction:

1. *Tourism policy and planning.* Having a clear policy direction helps support the growth of tourism and ensure interventions enable a long-term view. Tourism policies clarify the high-level tourism vision and the role and responsibilities of different institutions. Tourism plans provide the roadmap for how to achieve the vision sustainably and equitably. Policy and planning interventions include tourism master plans, strategic plans and policies to support investment and product development.
2. *Tourism governance.* Strengthening the institutions involved in tourism is critical to long-term success and helps provide a platform for collaboration between the public and private sectors. Effective governance involves entities at the local/municipal, province/

state and national levels. Interventions may include training, organizational planning, association support, and public–private dialogue facilitation through a federation, tourism council or other cross-cutting agency.

3. *Tourism marketing and research.* High-quality, targeted marketing is critical to the achievement of the destination's goals and vision. Research and data collection help both inform marketing and promotion and monitor its effectiveness. This intervention can include improving tourism data collection, market research and destination marketing strategies.

4. *Tourism standards and capacity.* Managing the growth of tourism businesses and ensuring visitors' health and safety are at the core of this category. The establishment of tourism industry standards and licensing for different tourism suppliers, such as accommodation, tour guides, and SMEs are key as well.

High-quality assets
High-quality assets are key attractors for visitors and investors to most destinations. Asset development includes diversifying tourism product offerings, improving last-mile access, and upgrading tourism-related infrastructure.

There are three common interventions to achieve high-quality assets:

1. *Product development.* Tourism products include the sites, services and resources that attract tourists to the destination. Product development involves enhancing the quality tourism experiences by creating tourism routes, new attractions, and improving interpretation.

2. *Site development.* Attraction sites tailored to keeping visitors safe also require management to ensure the sustainability of the site. Interventions include upgraded infrastructure to provide easy access, the development of onsite facilities, site rehabilitation, signage and interpretation.

3. *Site management.* Tourism brings much-needed attention and revenue to natural and cultural sites and the communities that surround them, but increased visitation can place pressure on tourism assets. Sites need ongoing investment and management to mitigate damage and support preservation, while also generating needed revenue from ticket sales. Site management includes ticketing systems, visitor service plans, restoration and maintenance plans, and visitor impact assessments (see Box 2.3).

BOX 2.3   ETHIOPIA CASE STUDY

Ethiopia's rich array of cultural, historic and natural sites that set it apart from its neighbours, provided the destination with a strong base to increase the development and economic potential of tourism through the country's offering. However, in the early 2000s, Ethiopia approached the WB to help address its tourism challenges. These included how to capture a larger share of the tourism market in the region and transform cultural and natural assets into economic value. Ethiopia's World Heritage Sites, as well as many others of equal (though unrecognized) significance and beauty, had been neglected. There had been minimal public investment in site maintenance, interpretation for visitors, and access infrastructure. Investments in infrastructure (e.g. airports, roads, telecommunications, water supply, and sanitation), accommodation, and human resources remained insufficient to meet the growing sector's needs. International visitors generally expected high-quality services and well-preserved, well-presented sites. This fundamental mismatch was the core challenge. Both in the administration and private sector, there was a growing recognition of this problem and broad commitment to addressing it. The Ethiopia Sustainable Tourism Development Project supported by the World Bank, aimed to contribute to the enhancement of the quality and variety of tourism products and services in targeted destinations, in order to increase the volume of tourism, foreign exchange earnings, and jobs. There were four components to the project, the first component being destination development, particularly the rehabilitation and enhancement of basic infrastructure in key historic sites, visitor services and tourism product development. The second focused on market development, utilizing a matching grant scheme and providing support to communities. The third component addressed institutional development and capacity building. Guided by the development of a ToC, implementation of the project was designed to yield the following key outcomes, in key destinations: (i) an annual increase of international visitors; (ii) increased average spending by visitors; and (iii) an increased number of direct and indirect tourism-related jobs.

Wide benefit distribution

Inclusion or inclusiveness is the third long-term outcome of a Tourism Theory of Change. This pathway is focused on the inclusion of marginalized groups in the tourism value chain through targeted interventions, skills development, and stakeholder engagement.

Empowering individuals and communities with new training and skill sets may enable them to take new jobs, advance their careers or improve their business ventures. Tourism skills have also been shown to lead to increased customer satisfaction, higher visitor numbers, higher sales, better perception of the destination's brand, and/or better policy planning and destination management, which are necessary for the success of that tourism venture (Cater et al., 2015).

Four interventions for inclusive tourism value chains are:

1. *Inclusion.* Tourism must be designed inclusively to maximize its development potential. Inclusion is about more than just consulting or considering women, vulnerable groups, rural populations and those who are living in poverty. It is about taking proactive steps to reduce the gaps felt by typically excluded groups. Programmes for inclusion can include specific awareness training, grants or loans.
2. *Local linkages development.* Tourism interventions must be designed to include activities that allow local communities to gain market access across the tourism value chain. These include suppliers of food and vegetables, artists and artisans, laundry services, etc. Unlike interventions that focus exclusively on the attributes of the supplier's firm and workers, such as the ones under High Performing Firms, these can focus on addressing issues in the regulatory framework, or on the buyer's side (e.g. matchmaking events). Research suggests that such approaches to sourcing local products and services positively contribute to sustainable long-term economic development at the community level (Yodsuwan et al., 2019).
3. *Skills development.* Skills are the capacities needed to be successful in a particular line of work. Skills development can include both 'soft' and 'hard' skills. Soft skills include per-

sonal initiative, informal training, awareness programmes, and community management, which contrasts with formally accredited skills provided by capacity building interventions in the High Performing Firms section.

4. *Stakeholder engagement.* As has been pointed out before, tourism is a cross-cutting area with many stakeholders. Engaging tourism stakeholders helps to ensure that interventions have local ownership, benefits of tourism are broadly distributed, and tourism grows sustainably. Stakeholder engagement should go beyond regular meetings, town halls and other forms of community outreach to include meaningful roles in project design, monitoring and decision-making. Meaningful stakeholder engagement can lead to resilient tourism development, one where stakeholders are able to anticipate vulnerabilities in tourism development, prevent downside risks, and even learn from local knowledge to ensure sustainable development of tourism activity (Pyke et al., 2018).

Step 5. Selection of Indicators

Monitoring progress towards outcomes is a key component (and the final step) of a ToC. The indicators are markers that determine when an outcome, immediate or long-term, has been achieved. Development of proper indicators is critical, so that progress can be assessed and measured for the established outcomes (or preconditions). ToC indicators are different to sustainable tourism monitoring indicators as they are designed to monitor the particular relationship between project interventions and intermediate outcomes rather than monitor tourism performance in general. The following indicators are not exhaustive but based on World Bank and International Finance Corporation (IFC) project experience and linked to the five intermediate TOC areas explained in the earlier section.

There are two types of indicators used in a ToC: output and outcome indicators. Output indicators are generally used for things that are done and can be counted and they are used to measure the immediate results of the interventions (number of reports written, people trained, sites upgraded, etc.). Outcome indicators generally measure the result of the output, that is they are used to measure the change represented by intermediate or long-term outcomes (LTOs) (i.e. laws changed, sales increased, and visitor spending change). Table 2.3 provides some general indicators that can be used for the WB thematic ToC. Each project will need specific indicators aligned to its intermediate outcomes and interventions. Table 2.4 gives an example for the Ethiopia project.

Table 2.3   LTOs and suggested indicators

Long-term outcome	Suggested indicators
Open business environment The state of the business environment in a destination is usually measured by the time and cost to start, operate and close a business.	**Intermediate outcome indicators:** Number of investment restrictions removed Number of licences needed to start a business Number of updated laws Number of new incentives **Long-term outcome indicators:** Days needed to start a business Cost to start a business Number of new firms registered Time/cost necessary to obtain a visa/construction permit Value of new investment generated
High-firm performance High-firm performance is usually measured by increases in the firm's people, products, and processes. In a tourism context this includes jobs, market share, sales and contracts. Investment would also be an indicator, but it is rarely measured, due to difficulties with attribution.	**Intermediate outcome indicators:** Number of firms trained Number of workshop participants **Long-term outcome indicators:** Number of project-supported/trained firms with online presence as a result of the training Number of project-supported/trained firms certified by a quality standard Number of project-supported firms with increased sales Number of new contracts signed by project supported firms Number of project-supported/trained firms with improved management qualifications
Clear policy direction Clear policy direction can be measured by outputs (plans, policies, etc.), implementation (timely data collection), and outcomes (visitor arrivals, satisfaction, and spending).	**Intermediate outcome indicators:** Increase in budget for tourism institutions Number of plans, policies and new laws adopted Number of development plans budgeted under tourism institutions Tourism plan in place, up to date and implemented Number of tourism agencies/destination management organizations (DMOs) established and operationalized Number of tourism campaigns conducted annually Number of coordination and public–private dialogue processes held **Long-term outcome indicators:** Number/change tourists (domestic and international) Increased/Overall tourist satisfaction Improved dissemination of regular tourism statistics Increased/Overall residents' satisfaction Increased country-brand recognition
High-quality assets Changes in the asset base of the tourism sector and its impact can be monitored by physical improvements but also by changes in the people who use or visit the assets.	**Intermediate outcome indicators:** Number of sites upgraded Number of kilometres of road improved Percentage of sites with visitor management plans in place Number of site destination information and guidance tools developed Number of trails with signage in selected destinations Investment in cultural/natural heritage upgrading **Long-term outcome indicators:** Visitor satisfaction with upgraded sites Change in average visitor spending at upgraded sites/surrounding destinations Increased revenue from tickets Number of visitors to identified upgraded sites (by market)
Wide-reaching benefits Inclusiveness is about closing the gaps between men and women, rural and urban, disabled and youth groups. The gap should be identified and measured, interventions designed to close the gaps, e.g. training and financial services and indicators developed to measure progress. For specific indicators related to the gender gap the World Bank paper *Women and Tourism: Designing for Inclusion* suggests some that can be integrated into tourism projects and go beyond mainstreaming and disaggregation of conventional indicator data (Twining-Ward and Zhou, 2017).	**Intermediate outcome indicators:** Number of workshop participants (of which % are women) Number of supplier/buyer matchmaking events **Long-term outcome indicators:** Percentage of female professional and technical employees Percentage of women business owners (rural/urban) Percentage of women in leadership positions in companies and tourism institutions New jobs in targeted areas Resident satisfaction Resident access to services Number of contracts signed Amount of local produce purchased

Table 2.4   Selected indicators for Ethiopia's project

Long-term outcome	LTO indicators	Selected intermediate outcomes	Intermediate outcome indicators
To contribute to enhancement of the quality and variety of tourism products and services in targeted destinations so as to increase the volume of tourism, foreign exchange earnings and jobs	(i) Average % increase in the number of international tourist arrivals in targeted destinations (ii) Average expenditure by tourists in targeted destinations (iii) Number of new tourism-related jobs created in targeted destinations	(i) Historic sites in key destinations rehabilitated and enhanced (ii) Enhanced visitor centres in operation (iii) Increased cultural offerings in targeted destinations (iv) Tourism products improved at emerging destinations	(i) Number of historic monuments rehabilitated in key destinations/Number of kilometres of secondary roads rehabilitated (ii) Number of enhanced visitor centres in operation in key destinations/Number of trails with signage in selected destinations (iii) Number of emerging destinations with tourism development plans

COMMON MISTAKES IN PROJECT MONITORING AND EVALUATION

Accurate and timely monitoring and evaluation (M&E) is critical to understanding if a particular project is successful. Even the best indicators are not useful if they are not directly connected to the interventions or outcomes. Below are a few of the most common mistakes made in ToC monitoring and project indicators.

Mismatched Indicators

It is important that indicators measure progress towards the desired LTO of the project. Though this may seem obvious, it is all too common for development projects to have mismatched LTOs and indicators. For example, if a project has an objective of facilitating 'increased private sector investment' private sector investment must be measured in the project indicators. Similarly, if a project is designed to improve competitiveness of a destination, visitation numbers might not be the best way to show this.

Poor Attribution

Attribution is critical to the robustness of an indicator framework. As evident in the above examples and noted earlier, it can be difficult to find direct attribution and causality between the project activities and the observed results. For example, 'Number of hospitality workers in the tourism value chain' would be very difficult to attribute to the activities of a particular project even if capacity building was an intervention. It is good practice to align indicators to actual activities; for example, in this case, 'number of hospitality workers trained under the project who are able to demonstrate level 2 customer service skills'. It is important to understand and be transparent about attribution.

Lack of Baseline Data and Timelines

Without baseline data, it is very difficult to establish if change has occurred. Lack of baseline data is common, especially in instances where the destination has no means for measuring or has not measured indicators previously. For example, if a project seeks to diversify marketing, without a baseline, the indicator 'Number of tourism arrivals from non-traditional markets' is not helpful. Often percentage change is preferred over actual number. But either way, baseline data must be established at the outset of the project to accurately measure development impacts.

Low Budget

Some indicators require rigorous baseline or exit surveys, tourism satellite accounting, or formalized methods to gather information, which might not be included in the project budget. For example, indicators that look to measure resident satisfaction with tourism such as 'Share of local residents that are satisfied with tourism development in the destinations' will need a clearly defined budget for this activity and a consistent methodology will need to be established to gather the data.

Overly Simplistic Volume versus Value

Historically, there has been an over-reliance on tourist arrivals as an indicator in tourism development projects. This is problematic for a few reasons. First, it encourages volume growth, which may not be what the destination needs (depending on the stage of development) especially in a post-COVID-19 world. Second, arrival numbers can be affected by many external factors, such as currency fluctuations and political unrest, so it has poor attribution qualities. Third, arrivals are typically tracked at a national level and are difficult to apply to regional or municipal projects without thorough systems in place. Expenditure data per tourist (yield), or change in length of stay, gives more indication of the change in value of the sector, and attribution needs to be clearly delineated. If volume needs to be used, it is sensible to focus on a particular market segment such as business or leisure travellers, rather than all arrivals. It is vital to be critical when selecting indicator segments to increase attribution.

CONCLUSION

ToC can and should be a team leader's go-to tool after initial scoping of a project. What does the client want to achieve? What is the challenge that is holding them back? Will these activities really address the challenge and, if so, how will we monitor this? Brainstorming a ToC at the end of an initial scoping can be an excellent way to build a team and to set a project on a firm foundation. ToC can reduce risks, enhance project design, and improve results. It helps ensure that the project addresses the root causes of the identified development problems. It elevates a standard report to a tool that clearly connects to a development project. Finally, it is important to note that no ToC is permanent. Tourism is a complex and dynamic system. Change continues, assumptions evolve, and solutions and projects improve over time. Teams should come back to their ToC on a regular basis, question the assumptions, and review the indicators. This will help keep the team laser-focused on the desired outcomes and help ensure the project really does address the underlying development challenges.

REFERENCES

Adu-Ampong, E. A. and Kimbu, A. N. (2019) The past, present and future of sustainability in tourism policy and planning in sub-Saharan Africa. *Tourism Planning & Development*, 16(2), 119–123.

Bakker, M. and Messerli, H. (2015) Inclusive growth versus pro-poor growth: Implications for tourism development. *Tourism and Hospitality Research*, 17(4), 384–391.

Bilbil, E. T. (2017) The Role of the UNWTO in visa facilitation: The diverse impacts on tourism industries of China, Russia and Turkey. *International Journal of Tourism and Hospitality Management in the Digital Age*, 1(1), 17–35.

Blazeska, D., Milenkovski, A. and Gramatnikovski, S. (2015) The quality of the tourist destination is a key factor for increasing their attractiveness. *UTMS Journal of Economics*, 6(2), 341–353.

Butler, G. (2017) Fostering community empowerment and capacity building through tourism: Perspectives from Dullstroom, South Africa. *Journal of Tourism and Cultural Change*, 15(3), 199–212.

Cárdenas-García, P. J., Sánchez-Rivero, M. and Pulido-Fernández, J. I. (2013) Does tourism growth influence economic development? *Journal of Travel Research*, 54(2), 206–221.

Cater, C., Garrod, B. and Low, T. (eds.) (2015) *The Encyclopaedia of Sustainable Tourism*. Wallingford: CABI.

Chao, C., Hazari, B. R., Laffargue, J. P., Sgro, P. M., Laffargue, J. and Yu, E. S. H. (2005) Tourism, jobs, capital accumulation and the economy: A dynamic analysis. *Nota di Lavoro, Fondazione Eni Enrico Mattei*, No. 136.

Christie, I. T. and Sharma, A. (2008) Research note: Millennium Development Goals – What is tourism's place? *Tourism Economics*, 14(2), 427–430.

Enright, M. and Newton, J. (2004) Tourism destination competitiveness: A quantitative approach. *Tourism Management*, 25, 777–788.

Gatsinzi, J. and Donaldson, R. (2010) Investment challenges in the hotel industry in Kigali, Rwanda: Hotel managers' perspectives. *Development Southern Africa*, 27(2), 225–240.

Holden, P. and Howell, H. (2009) *Enhancing Access to Finance in the Caribbean: Private Sector Development*. Discussion paper #4. Washington, DC: Inter-American Development Bank.

Huang, Q., Li, X. Y., Jia, X. J. and Li, H. (2019) Global hospitality growth and institutional quality. *Journal of Hospitality and Tourism Management*, 41, 117–128.

James, C. (2011) *Theory of Change Review: A Report Commissioned by Comic Relief*. London. Accessed 2 July 2020 at https://www.actknowledge.org/resources/documents/James_ToC.pdf.

Koutra, C. (2007) Building capacities for tourism development and poverty reduction. Brighton, UK: University of Brighton.

Labonté, R., Crooks, V. A., Valdés, A. C., Runnels, V. and Snyder, J. (2018) Government roles in regulating medical tourism: Evidence from Guatemala. *International Journal for Equity in Health*, 17(1), 1–10.

McKinsey & Company (2015) *The Power of Parity: How Advancing Women's Equality Can Add $12 Trillion to Global Growth*. Washington, DC: McKinsey Global Institute.

Moscardo, G. (ed.) (2008) *Building Community Capacity for Tourism Development*. Wallingford: CABI.

Motta, V. and Sharma, A. (2020) Lending technologies and access to finance for SMEs in the hospitality industry. *International Journal of Hospitality Management*, 86, 102371.

Munjal, P. (2013) Measuring the economic impact of the tourism industry in India using the tourism satellite account and input–output analysis. *Tourism Economics*, 19(6), 1345–1359.

Okoye, C. U. (2017) Tourism readiness, investment promotion, economic growth and development in South East Nigeria: An expose and proposal. *Journal of Tourism and Heritage Studies*, 6(1), 51–87.

Organisation for Economic Co-operation and Development (2001) *Enhancing SME Competitiveness: The OECD Bologna Ministerial Conference*. Paris: OECD.

Pyke, J., Law, A., Jiang, M. and de Lacy, T. (2018) Learning from the locals: The role of stakeholder engagement in building tourism and community resilience. *Journal of Ecotourism*, 17(3), 206–219.

Sharma, A. (2007) Small hotel financing in sub-Saharan Africa: Evidence from Tanzania. *The Journal of Hospitality Financial Management*, 15(2), 25–38.

Sharma, A. and Upneja, A. (2005) Factors influencing financial performance of small hotels in Tanzania. *International Journal of Contemporary Hospitality Management*, 17, 504–515.

Taplin, D. and Clark, H. (2012) *Theory of Change Basics: A Primer on Theory of Change*. New York: ActKnowledge. Accessed 2 July 2020 at http://www.theoryofchange.org/wp-content/uploads/toco _library/pdf/ToCBasics.pdf.

Taplin, D., Clark, H., Collins, E. and Colby, D. (2013) *Theory of Change Technical Papers: A series of papers to support development of Theories of Change based on practice in the field*. New York: ActKnowledge. Accessed 2 July 2020 at http://www.theoryofchange.org/wp-content/uploads/toco _library/pdf/ToC-Tech-Papers.pdf.

Turco, D. M., Swart, K., Bob, U. and Moodley, V. (2003) Socio-economic impacts of sport tourism in the Durban Unicity, South Africa. *Journal of Sport Tourism*, 8(4), 223–239.

Twining-Ward, L., Messerli, H. R., Sharma, A. and Villascusa Cerezo, J. (2018) *Tourism Theory of Change*. Tourism for Development Knowledge Series. Washington, DC: The World Bank.

Twining-Ward, L. and Zhou, V. (2017) *Women and Tourism: Designing for Inclusion*. Washington, DC: World Bank Group. Accessed 2 July 2020 at https://openknowledge.worldbank.org/handle/10986/ 28535.

van Es, M., Vogel, I. and Guijt, I. (2015) *Theory of Change in Practice: A Stepwise Approach*. The Hague: HIVO. Accessed 2 July 2020 at http://www.theoryofchange.nl/sites/default/files/resource/ hivos_toc_guidelines_final_nov_2015.pdf.

Vogel, I. (2012) *Review of the use of "Theory of Change" in international development*. London: DFID. Accessed 2 July 2020 at https://assets.publishing.service.gov.uk/media/57a08a5ded915d3cfd00071a/ DFID_ToC_Review_VogelV7.pdf.

Watanabe, W. C. and Patitad, P. (2020) A study of tourism supply chain by using sustainability aspect of the GMS economic corridors: Case study of Lower North Provincial Cluster 1 of Thailand and Sichuan Province of PR China. In *2020 IEEE 7th International Conference on Industrial Engineering and Applications (ICIEA)* (pp. 454–458). IEEE.

Wigodzky, V. and Farmelo, M. (2014) *Developing a Useful Strategic Plan: Practical Advice before Starting the Process*. Menlo Park, CA. Accessed 2 July 2020 at http://effectiveorgs.org/wp-content/ uploads/sites/2/2015/04/DevelopingUsefulStrategicPlanFeb2015.pdf.

World Bank (2012) *Designing a Results Framework for Achieving Results: A How-To Guide*. Washington, DC: The World Bank. Accessed 2 July 2020 at https://siteresources.worldbank.org/ EXTEVACAPDEV/Resources/designing_results_framework.pdf.

World Bank (2015) *Trade & Competitiveness Global Practice: Expanding Market Opportunity & Enabling Private Initiative for Dynamic Economies*. Washington, DC: World Bank.

World Tourism Organization (UNWTO) (2016) International year of sustainable tourism for development 2017. Accessed 2 July 2020 at http://www.tourism4development2017.org/about/.

World Tourism Organization (UNWTO) and World Travel and Tourism Council (WTTC) (2012) The Impact of Visa Facilitation on Job Creation in the G20 Economies. Madrid, Spain. Accessed 2 July 2020 at https://www.wttc.org/-/media/files/reports/policy%20research/visa_facilitation%20g20.pdf.

Yodsuwan, C., Intralawan, A., Manomaivibool, P., Dokmaingam, P., Prapattong, P., Vititanon, N. and Diez, J. (2019) Local economic linkage between private enterprises and local communities: A comparative case study of Thailand tourism business developments. *MFU Connexion: Journal of Humanities and Social Sciences*, 8(2), 19–35.

3. Guidelines for tourism policy formulation in developing countries

Mike Fabricius

INTRODUCTION

The United Nations World Tourism Organization (UNWTO) identifies effective policy formulation as a key success factor for sustainable tourism development (UNWTO, 2019). Tourism is one of the fastest growing economic sectors and an important driver of economic growth and development with a significant impact on trade, job creation, investment, infrastructure development, and the promotion of social inclusion.

Most emerging economies have overall economic development policies that provide the guidelines by which a nation aims to improve the economic, political, and social well-being of its people. Economic, environmental and social sustainability are usually key underlying principles of national development policies.

Due to its many advantages tourism is often included as a priority sector in economic development policies of emerging economies. As such, tourism's contribution to sustainable development is increasingly recognized by national and international policy makers showing the importance of aligning tourism with national and global policies. Tourism is included in the United Nations' Sustainable Development Goals (SDGs) (United Nations, 2020) as a target in Goals 8, 12 and 14:

- Goal 8, target 8.9: "By 2030, devise and implement policies to promote sustainable tourism that creates jobs and promotes local culture and products".
- Goal 12, target 12.B: "Develop and implement tools to monitor sustainable development impacts for sustainable tourism that creates jobs and promotes local culture and products".
- Goal 14, target 14.7: "By 2030, increase the economic benefits to Small Island developing States and least developed countries from the sustainable use of marine resources, including through sustainable management of fisheries, aquaculture and tourism".

The increasing recognition of tourism in sustainable development and in the achievement of the 2030 Agenda brings a unique opportunity for governments to become actively involved in national tourism planning for the SDGs. Thus, the formulation of national tourism policies, strategies and action plans should be fully aligned with national SDG planning.

According to the UNWTO and United Nations Environment Programme (UNEP) *Baseline Report on the Integration of Sustainable Consumption and Production* [SCP] *Patterns into Tourism Policies* (UNWTO and UNEP, 2019), the following aspects deserve special attention:

- Tourism policy makers appear to be fully aware of the need to sustainably develop the tourism sector;
- There is a good awareness of the main environmental areas of concern for the tourism sector or 'SCP impact areas' as these are frequently mentioned in national tourism policies;

- The references to policy instruments with potential to transform commitments into action are still not comprehensive enough and thus call for enhancing the environmental components of national tourism policies;
- National governments which have proactively engaged in the implementation of Agenda 2030 at the national level appear to regard tourism as a sector with the potential to contribute to advancing the SDGs, but the direct connection between tourism and SDG 12 is not yet widely acknowledged; and
- Although the findings suggest that there is a good level of awareness among tourism policy makers of the need to ensure that policies on SCP are implemented, the findings also suggest the existence of an implementation gap between the formulation of national tourism policies and action on the ground.

The following section provides an overview of tourism policy formulation methods and contents, including:

- Distinction between policy, strategy and tactical action.
- Frameworks for guiding tourism policy formulation.
- The policy development process.
- Typical structure of a tourism policy.
- Key elements of the tourism value chain that require policy guidance, as well as the main issues confronting each element, typical policy considerations and specific policy guidelines to consider in addressing each issue.

THE DEFINITION AND PURPOSE OF A GOVERNMENT TOURISM POLICY

A short definition of public policy is: "a set of *ideas* or *plans* that is used as a *basis* for making *decisions* and on which laws rest" (Collins, 2020).
   The implications of this definition include the following:

- Public policy is decided by specific organs of government through established procedures.
- Planning as a basis for decision-making suggests goals and the absence of logical contradictions.
- Public policy implies that government is *responsive* to its citizens and voters.
- Before a policy is made, a public debate over an *issue* should be held.
- The policy should result in actions that must be administered, implemented and put into practice in a manner consistent with the stated intentions, something that is often sorely neglected.
- The action that might bring about a public policy must *go somewhere* – and we need to identify which organization(s) has jurisdiction and might feasibly respond.
- Usually, a policy statement is followed by legislation, executive order, or administrative rule-making, all of which becomes legally binding.

POLICY, STRATEGY AND TACTICS

Public agencies often confuse tourism policy, strategy and tactics as these are closely related. Essentially tourism destination strategy provides a 'game plan' or decision-making guide for ensuring that the policy is implemented optimally. It is a general, undetailed plan of action, encompassing a long period of time, to achieve the policy goals. As there is always an element of uncertainty about the future, strategy is more about a set of options ('strategic considerations') than a fixed plan.

Two elements underpin the rationale for strategy, namely:

1. It guides (often tough) considerations in allocating finances and manpower for implementing the policy because the available resources are seldom adequate.
2. It is all about gaining (or being prepared to gain) a position of advantage over adversaries or best exploiting emerging possibilities.

Tactics are usually contained in short-term action plans or business plans. They provide the tools to implement strategy and are subordinated to the main goal of strategy. Tactics are the actual means used to gain an objective, while strategy is the overall directional plan, which may involve complex operational consultation and decision-making that lead to tactical execution.

As indicated in Figure 3.1:

- The policy is a longer-term statement of government intent and approach to tourism and is typically contained in a formal policy document, White Paper or similar document. Once adopted it will normally be followed by legislation that will enable and ensure adherence to the policy directives.
- The strategy is typically contained in one or more medium-term strategic plans, formulated by the institutions that are mandated to ensure implementation of the policy.
- The strategy execution tactics are usually contained in the annual action or business plans of the various parties and partner organizations involved in implementing the strategy.
- Policies, strategies and tactical plans are underpinned by enabling legislation (usually the Tourism Act) and accompanied regulations. Appropriate legislative frameworks are extremely important for giving policies 'teeth', without adding unnecessary controls and red tape that could stifle business growth and innovation.
- Challenges and opportunities encountered during tactical implementation should be monitored and fed back into the medium-term strategy and eventually into policy and legislation.

For example, consider a hypothetical destination with a rich and interesting cultural diversity and heritage as its main tourism draw-card.

The policy core goal is to attract high-value tourism through responsible and sustainable development of sensitive cultural resources. The policy includes key principles that underpin the vision (e.g. local community involvement, a focus on small business development, an emphasis on local job creation, etc.). It also sets long-term targets for tourism growth and establishes the cultural positioning upon which the destination will differentiate itself from other cultural tourism destinations. The policy provides a range of statements to voice the government's intent regarding cultural preservation, development of arts, community-based

Source: Author.

Figure 3.1   *Relationship between policy, legislation, strategy and tactics*

tourism advancement, small business stimulation, training for cultural enterprises, attracting and hosting cultural tourism markets, etc. It clarifies the roles of the various agencies involved in cultural tourism and develops an institutional framework for advancing the policy.

The strategic plan (strategy) provides specific, actionable guidelines for achieving the policy goals and statements over the next three to five years. This would typically include measurable growth targets, a brand identity for communicating the cultural market positioning, and a target market strategy (e.g. touring segments, specific cultural niche markets, etc.). In addition strategic programmes could relate to product development (priority cultural product development initiatives, incentives for small business development in tourism-related arts and cultural industries, pilot community-based tourism projects), human resources development (outline of training and entrepreneurship mentoring programmes and initiatives), suggested marketing thrusts and campaigns, partnership opportunities with the private sector, statistical measurement and market research, etc. There should ideally be a single destination strategy, with all public and private partners following and supporting the same strategic guidelines and reviewing these regularly to ensure they remain in tune with macroeconomic and social events. The strategic plan should include an outline implementation plan over the lifespan of the strategy indicating programmes, priorities, outline budgets, indicative time frames and parties involved.

Various tactical, immediate actions emanating from the destination strategy will be included in the annual implementation plans (usually called action or business plans) of parties involved in tactical implementation. These usually include a variety of government ministries (e.g. Culture, Transport, Commerce, Immigration, etc.), the Tourism Board and other govern-ment agencies, private sector associations and companies, non-governmental organizations (NGOs), community based organizations (CBOs), etc. In some cases, the tourism aspects will form a small part of a partner's overall business plan. The implementation plans will contain detailed actions for implementing and monitoring the tourism strategic plan over a short time span (e.g. a financial year) with clear actions, time frames, responsible parties, budgets, etc. Ideally, the plans of the various implementing partners should be regularly coordinated based on the strategy, with the Tourism Ministry or Authority being the coordinator in this regard.

SUSTAINABLE TOURISM AS KEY FACTOR IN TOURISM POLICY FORMULATION

As indicated in the introductory section of this chapter, tourism's contribution to sustainable development and to the achievement of the 2030 Agenda is increasingly being recognized at global and national levels. According to the United Nations Environment Programme (UNEP) and United Nations World Tourism Organization (UNWTO) (UNEP and UNWTO, 2005) sustainable tourism can be defined as:

> Tourism that takes full account of its current and future economic, social and environmental impacts, addressing the needs of visitors, the industry, the environment and host communities.

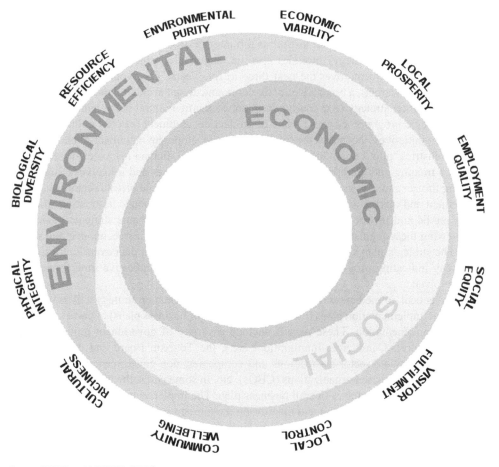

Source: UNEP and UNWTO (2005).

Figure 3.2   Three pillars and twelve aims of sustainable tourism

Sustainability principles refer to the environmental, economic, and socio-cultural aspects of tourism development, and a suitable balance must be established between these three dimensions to guarantee its long-term sustainability (see Figure 3.2).

From a policy perspective sustainable tourism should:

- Make optimal use of environmental resources that constitute a key element in tourism development, maintaining essential ecological processes and helping to conserve natural heritage and biodiversity.
- Respect the socio-cultural authenticity of host communities, conserve their built and living cultural heritage and traditional values, and contribute to inter-cultural understanding and tolerance.
- Ensure viable, long-term economic operations, providing socio-economic benefits to all stakeholders that are fairly distributed, including stable employment and income-earning opportunities and social services to host communities, and contributing to poverty alleviation.

The 12 aims of sustainable tourism (see Figure 3.2) identified by UNWTO are:

1. *Economic Viability:* To ensure the viability and competitiveness of tourism destinations and enterprises, so that they are able to continue to prosper and deliver benefits in the long term.
2. *Local Prosperity:* To maximize the contribution of tourism to the economic prosperity of the host destination, including the proportion of visitor spending that is retained locally.
3. *Employment Quality:* To strengthen the number and quality of local jobs created and supported by tourism, including the level of pay, conditions of service and availability to all without discrimination by gender, race, disability or in other ways.
4. *Social Equity:* To seek a widespread and fair distribution of economic and social benefits from tourism throughout the recipient community, including improving opportunities, income and services available to the poor.
5. *Visitor Fulfilment:* To provide a safe, satisfying and fulfilling experience for visitors, available to all without discrimination by gender, race, disability or in other ways.
6. *Local Control:* To engage and empower local communities in planning and decision-making about the management and future development of tourism in their area, in consultation with other stakeholders.
7. *Community Well-being:* To maintain and strengthen the quality of life in local communities, including social structures and access to resources, amenities and life support systems, avoiding any form of social degradation or exploitation.
8. *Cultural Richness:* To respect and enhance the historic heritage, authentic culture, traditions and distinctiveness of host communities.
9. *Physical Integrity:* To maintain and enhance the quality of landscapes, both urban and rural, and avoid the physical and visual degradation of the environment.
10. *Biological Diversity:* To support the conservation of natural areas, habitats and wildlife, and minimize damage to them.
11. *Resource Efficiency:* To minimize the use of scarce and non-renewable resources in the development and operation of tourism facilities and services.
12. *Environmental Purity:* To minimize the pollution of air, water and land and the generation of waste by tourism enterprises and visitors.

These aims imply a holistic approach to sustainable tourism development with the principles of sustainable management underpinning an integrated tourism development plan.

POLICY DEVELOPMENT PROCESS

The process that is used to develop a policy that supports sustainable tourism is vitally important – and sometimes can be as important as the actual content of the policy or strategy itself. Different countries have their own protocols on how policies should be designed, but in general terms, they should incorporate the following:

- Establishment of a working group that applies a consensus-building method to the development. The political leadership responsible for tourism (e.g. the Tourism Ministry) usually takes the lead in mandating the establishment of a working group. It should comprise representatives of all major parties involved in tourism such as those government ministries that play important roles in creating a favourable tourism environment, private sector tourism organization, relevant labour unions and community-based (non-governmental) tourism organizations.
- Background research and fieldwork on underlying conditions, including other compatible (or incongruent) policies and legal instruments, tourism statistics, the status of sustainable tourism.
- Consultation with key stakeholders and the public including representatives from the private sector, government, communities and others. This could be done through surveys, one-on-one interviews, stakeholder workshops and other suitable consultative methods.
- Use of national tourism expertise and knowledge to shape the policy, complemented by international technical assistance if necessary.
- Opportunity for key stakeholders and the public to review draft policies, and for their comments to be used in finalizing the text.
- Written in simple language, and no longer than necessary, and if possible in an attractive, user-friendly format. It should be translated in all official languages to ensure the broadest possible reach and clear understanding.
- A process for institutional endorsement of the policy, usually through a validation process that involves the major stakeholder groups mentioned above, and finally formally endorsed by the relevant political decision-making structure (e.g. Cabinet, Council of Ministers, Parliament, etc.).
- Integration of the policy into plans, and legal instruments such as regulations and laws that follow. Ensconcing policy in legislations usually follows the prescribed legislative processes laid down in the country's Constitution.

For example, South Africa's White Paper on the Development and Promotion of Tourism (Government of South Africa, 1996) was established through an extensive participatory process. A two-year development process incorporated:

- Establishment of an Interim Tourism Task Force (ITTF), with the mandate of drafting a discussion paper – a green paper – to inform the tourism policy, and representing business, labour, government, and community organizations.

- Circulation of the green paper for comment across South Africa, through the relevant provincial and local tourism organizations, private sector tourism councils and associations, media, etc.
- Establishment of an international tourism specialist team to develop a tourism White Paper.
- Meetings of the ITTF to monitor progress and provide comment on the process and White Paper content.
- A series of 10 workshops across the country, with more than 500 participants, funded by the Ministry of Environmental Affairs and Tourism.
- Nearly 100 expert interviews and one-on-one consultations with key stakeholders.
- Consideration of more than 100 written submissions.
- Strategic meetings of notable groups, including of ministers, hotel industry, tourism security, and a national tourism workshop.
- Recruitment of local consultants for secondary research and analysis of the tourism industry and to develop strategies and implementation programmes.
- Review of reports by the national tourism board, government departments and others.

This White Paper was notable because it was the first globally to promote a 'responsible' approach to tourism, translating strategies on the empowerment of those who had been historically disadvantaged during apartheid into policy, while conserving South Africa's rich cultural and natural heritage. Its solid foundations ultimately led to the development of national Responsible Tourism Guidelines, and the Cape Town Declaration (see Spenceley, 2008 for an overview). These also underpin other processes, such as the development of a responsible tourism policy and research strategy for South African National Parks (see Chapter 27).

TYPICAL POLICY STRUCTURE

Public policy making has three key components: taking stock of the problem or challenge facing the society and its environment, setting the policy, i.e. a standing decision by government to address it, and following a suitable process that involves multiple participants to ensure the policy is executed effectively.

This essentially means involving partners and stakeholders in (a) defining the policy problem, purpose and key issues that underpin the problem, (b) setting a future vision, goals and policy guidelines to address these, and (c) devising an institutional framework for affecting the policy.

The typical outline structure of a tourism policy is shown in Table 3.1.

Table 3.1   *Outline structure for a tourism policy*

Section	Contents
Background	Foreword
	Definitions and abbreviations
	Policy formulation process and partners
Policy Context	Role and performance of tourism (economic contribution, benefits, growth performance and trends, etc.)
	Tourism potential (contribution to national economic agenda, demand potential, comparative advantages, etc.)
	The problem (performance and opportunity gap)
	Key issues and challenges (specific factors and constraints that inhibit tourism from reaching its potential)
Future Approach	Vision
	Tourism positioning (type of tourism to best address the vision and issues, competitive direction, etc.)
	Goals and principles
	Policy guidelines (specific policy statements with regard to key issues identified)
	Stakeholder roles (outlining the relationships and roles of the Government, private sector, civil society and other stakeholder sectors in addressing the policy)
Implementation	Organizational structure
	Financial arrangements
	Way forward

GUIDING FRAMEWORKS FOR DESTINATION POLICY FORMULATION

Two frameworks are particularly useful in serving as reference frameworks for destination tourism policy formulation (UNWTO, 2007), namely:

1. *Competitiveness*: Tourism is becoming increasingly competitive as countries realize the value of the world's largest economic force and the power and value of their comparative natural, cultural and man-made resources. In addition to supporting the national economic development agenda, the tourism policy should aim at ensconcing and improving the country's tourism competitiveness.

   Porter's 'National Diamond Framework' was adapted by Fabricius (2001) as a basis for plotting aspects of destination competitiveness (see Figure 3.3) and the policy interventions required to make the destination more competitive.

   As can be seen from the figure the four pillars that should be assessed and covered in the tourism policy for assessing and addressing destination competitiveness are:

   (a) Resources: These are the comparative assets that form the basis of a destination's tourism attractiveness. They include natural and cultural features, man-made attractions, human resources, land availability and security and intangible resources such as brand reputation, a welcoming and hospitable culture, perceptions of personal safety, etc.

   (b) Demand conditions: These are market conditions that indicate the market growth potential and destination readiness for attracting visitors, including the size and growth of the domestic travel market, historical tourism growth trends, tourism yield (e.g. visitor expenditure and length of stay), market accessibility and connectedness (e.g. visa conditions, air access) and the affinity and power of intermediary partners and technology systems.

(c) Related and supporting industries that make it possible for visitors to experience a destination including hospitality services (accommodation and catering), airports and airlift, tour and travel services, transport and other infrastructure, heritage services, information and signage, etc.

(d) Industry structure and rivalry, i.e. conditions that allow private business growth and innovation, quality and standards measures and controls, stakeholder collaboration in the interest of destination competitiveness, strategic management of the destination, etc.

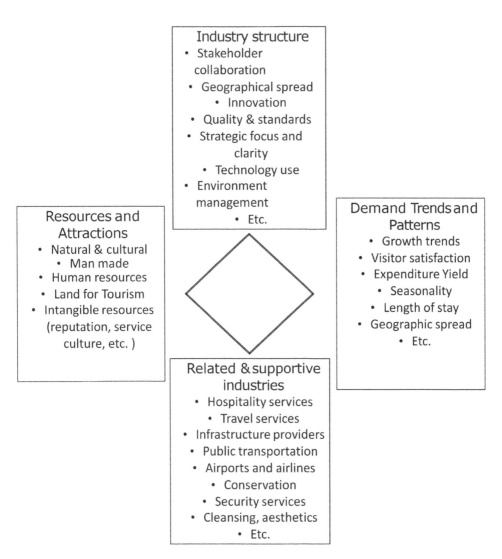

Source: Fabricius (2001).

Figure 3.3   *Porter's National Diamond Framework adapted to a tourism destination*

2. *Destination value chain*: The tourism experience comprises a combination or 'chain' of required, value-adding activities that add up to produce the overall experience. Value is added to the customer experience at each point along the destination value chain. The primary elements of the destination value chain include:

   (a) The conceptualization and planning of the destination experience and all its components.
   (b) Development and packaging of attractions and services (facilities, activities, services, etc.).
   (c) In- and outbound visitor logistics (visas, flights, immigration, transport to arrive at and depart from the destination).
   (d) Promotion of the destination and experiences.
   (e) Distribution and sales channels for purchasing the tourism experience.
   (f) Provision and management of visitor facilities and services.
   (g) Constant improvement of the experience.

These value chain elements add to the cost of the experience and depending on their complexity each element is underpinned by a range of value-adding components that spread the value through the tourism economy. The primary value chain is supported by secondary value chain elements including destination planning and infrastructure provision, human resource development, technology and systems development and procurement from related industries.

KEY ELEMENTS OF DEVELOPING COUNTRY TOURISM POLICIES

Based on the above-mentioned frameworks for ensuring destination competitiveness and addressing all aspects of the tourism destination value chain, the following policy elements are usually relevant and should be considered when formulating tourism policies for tourism destinations (UNWTO, 2011), especially those that are in the exploratory and developmental stages of the tourism life cycle (OECD, 2010).

Tourist Access

Air access
Inadequate and expensive air access from target markets is often a major barrier to tourism growth. The majority of developing destinations are significant distances away from their core generating markets and many foreign visitors are able to reach these destinations only by air. With flights comprising a significant share of travel costs and time, convenient, affordable air access is often a critical tourism success factor.

   Key guidelines for developing destinations are:

- Have progressive, market related plans for airport expansion – airport investments can be catalysts for airline expansion – be careful to avoid white elephants.
- Liberalize the airspace responsibly – avoid protecting the national flag carrier at the expense of tourism growth and strike up alliances with global airlines.
- Be careful about charter subsidies and developments that rely heavily on charter business – volumes may be substantial but local benefits and quality should be watched.

- Promote competition among domestic airlines and consider limited support for new entrants.

Immigration and visas

Visa restrictions, visitor taxes and cumbersome immigration procedures often deter potential visitors. Government officials for various reasons often favour strict visa requirements: as a negotiating tool with other states, as a source of foreign revenue or as a state security mechanism. The tourism consequences and implications of such restrictions are seldom considered. Tourism is regularly viewed as a 'soft' revenue target and airport and entry taxes, bed levies and other forms of taxation are used to supplement government coffers. The immigration service is the first point of contact with the host country and insensitive, cumbersome and corrupt immigration processes can be a major tourism deterrent. In addition, there is ample evidence from the research that gains from tourism expenditure under a liberalized visa regime far outweigh revenues earned from visas.

Key guidelines for developing destinations are:

- Consider waiving visa reciprocity principles for lucrative target markets with tight visa conditions, given the potentially huge tourism benefits for the developing destination.
- Prioritize visa on arrival arrangements where possible.
- Work in tandem with immigration authorities to ensure immigration staff and processes are geared towards receiving visitors in the most convenient manner without prejudicing international safety and immigration protocols.
- Reduce tourist taxes as much as possible as these affect price competitiveness. Where taxes or levies are required, consolidate them as a single entry/exit tax (e.g. as part of the air ticket) and earmark them to accrue to a special tourism fund/account with clear and strategic application. In addition, any changes in taxes should allow for a lead-in time of at least nine months to allow tourism operators to factor these into their contracted rates.

Sustainable Development

Natural and cultural resource management

Sensitive natural and cultural resources are often the main tourist attractors and the effective management and sustainable leveraging of these resources is at the core of tourism growth. Governments often face tough considerations regarding the exploitation and protection of valuable natural and cultural heritage. With political success often depending on the votes of citizens in need of immediate incomes and jobs, the considerations between economic development (e.g. mining in sensitive habitats or constructing a road or port in a protected area) and long-term conservation and sustainable resource use need to be guided by clear and responsible policies.

Key guidelines for developing destinations are:

- Integrated economic planning and proper land use planning are at the heart of sustainable tourism expansion – tourism authorities should strike up alliances with local authorities and land use agencies to ensure appropriate planning.
- While environmental impact assessments (EIAs) are critical components of development applications, the EIA processes should be streamlined to avoid deterring developers.

- Destinations should take a clear view on their approaches to sustainable tourism – sustainability should be non-negotiable in tourism advancement; however, the level of social and environmental enforcement (waste management, water and energy management, recycling, etc.) will differ depending on the environmental and social sensitivity and management capacity of the destination. Since government capacity is often inadequate to monitor and enforce compulsory systems, voluntary industry certification schemes should be encouraged.
- Parks and conservation areas should be differentiated and carrying capacity approaches should be diversified. While high value-low volume tourism may be suitable for sensitive ecosystems it may not be appropriate for others.
- Heritage conservation often does not receive a fair share of resources and adequate priority in developing country tourism policies, even though such resources may be highly valuable for tourism. Close cooperation should be forged with heritage management authorities.

Investment

Private investors are the driving forces of successful tourism destinations and industries; however, government processes for land allocation, licensing and investment incentives are often cumbersome or outright obstructive. Private investors are always looking for competitive advantages through exploiting market gaps, moving first to take up land concessions, generating cash flows as early as possible, etc. Unfortunately government processes are often slow and cumbersome, whether it be tendering out public development opportunities, approving development concepts and licences, processing financial assistance and incentive schemes, etc. This may result in investors losing interest or missing a window of access to capital.

Key guidelines for developing destinations are:

- Acquiring state land for tourism development should be as streamlined and transparent as possible. Land inventories and/or land banks could be considered if the state is able to acquire substantial land parcels for tourism development.
- Suitable public–private partnership models have become the preferred avenue of many governments for leveraging and adding value to government tourism assets in a viable and sustainable manner, e.g. build, own, operate, transfer.
- Transparency should be non-negotiable and bidding processes should be clearly laid down without being overly cumbersome.
- Investment incentives (tax benefits and exemptions, cash subsidies, preferential concessions, etc.) should be geared at assisting developers and operators (especially where there is market failure), e.g. opening up new areas for tourism, innovation and launching of new products, technology start-ups, etc. Incentives should not become long-term 'crutches' for non-viable enterprises.

Business development

Tourism is touted as an excellent vehicle for small and medium business advancement; however, small and medium enterprises (SMEs) often find it difficult to survive the start-up stages due to factors such as cumbersome business process, limited access to tourism markets, and cash flow requirements. SMEs are mostly managed and operated by small teams with limited cash resources. Having to deal with costly and time-consuming legal and administrative requirements can easily break a start-up business. SMEs also find it extremely difficult to access travel markets, especially where established companies have strong brand identities and long-standing relationships in such markets.

Key guidelines for developing destinations are:

- Where special financing schemes are instituted, finance providers such as banks and small business development corporations should be engaged as partners in approving and disbursing finance for small business development.
- SME incentive schemes should address market failure and should be performance linked and of limited duration.
- Every effort should be made to streamline and simplify cumbersome licensing and business approval processes and a consolidated, one-stop facility should be considered for processing approvals.
- SMEs should be provided with special assistance to access (especially foreign) tourism markets, through financial subsidies, access to international exhibitions, mentoring and coaching, alliances with established entrepreneurs, etc.

Quality and standards

Given that most visitors travel to a destination once-off or irregularly, consumer loyalty and demand forces are often unable to duly influence product quality and eliminate poor products. The tourism industry in many developing countries comprises large numbers of small and medium sized businesses (e.g. guest houses, bed-and-breakfast establishments, apartments, independent hotels, tour operators, etc.) without known brands and with a lack of credibility. With growing trends towards direct bookings and independent travel, visitor considerations are dependent upon credible quality indicators.

Key guidelines for developing destinations are:

- Tourism licensing requirements and processes should be made easy, accessible and equitable and foreign operators should not be discriminated against.
- Special consideration should be given to regulate the growth of accommodation in the sharing economy (e.g. Airbnb, Uber, etc.) to prevent distortion and displacement of the residential property market, without curbing tourism growth and entrepreneurship.
- A clear distinction should be drawn between compulsory, entry level standards and requirements for registering and operating a tourism business (e.g. hygiene, safety, legal compliance, etc.) and aspirational quality improvement systems such as grading schemes. The latter standards should be developed in close collaboration with the private operators and where possible should be managed on a voluntary basis.
- While common regional standards could play an important role in improving standards across borders, these should be applied with discretion and flexibility as capacity and conditions often differ substantially among countries in the same region.

Visitor Welfare

Health, safety, security and crisis management

Tourism destinations all over the world, and especially developing destinations are increasingly confronted with health, safety and security challenges. Recent outbreaks of COVID-19,

MERS, SARS, Ebola and other diseases pose grave threats to the sustainability of the industry. Tourists are often regarded by criminal elements as affluent, soft targets. In addition, the growing threat of terrorism cannot be ignored. Tourism authorities need to work in partnership with relevant authorities to prevent or mitigate health, safety and security incidents and deal with crises when they arise.

Key guidelines for developing destinations are:

- Collaboration between health, security and tourism agencies is key to effective management and communication of safety and security incidents and incidences of disease outbreaks.
- Crisis communication plans and formal crisis communication mechanisms should be established and practised on a regular basis.
- Safe tourist 'hot spots' should be identified and hygiene and security should be improved in such areas, e.g. health screening and hygiene measures, improved lighting and spatial design, introducing tourist police, on-street camera systems, etc.
- Where tourist safety risks prevail, tourists should be provided with guidance and information regarding suitable areas and behaviour for reducing such risks.

Visitor services and amenities
An enjoyable visitor experience will ensure visitors visit more places, stay longer and become ambassadors of a destination. Good variety and quality of accommodation is paramount. In addition, basic visitor facilities like toilets and washrooms, rest areas, visitor information points, adequate parking, landscaping of key tourist areas, etc. are all important aspects that could make a visitor's experience either enjoyable or miserable.

Key guidelines for developing destinations are:

- Key natural and cultural sites (including UNESCO World Heritage Sites) are the major tourism draw-cards for developing destinations; growth catalysts and policy measures for consistent improvement and adequate maintenance of these should receive priority.
- A 'bottom-up' approach to tourism advancement, involving local authorities and communities and having them take responsibility for local hygiene, waste management, publicity and visitor amenities is an important tourism success factor for many destinations.
- Local government agencies should be made responsible for providing and maintaining suitable visitor amenities.

Transacting, foreign exchange and pricing
Tourist expenditure should be maximized at local shops, eateries, accommodation establishments and other services that are not in a position to accept credit cards and travellers cheques. Fair pricing policies should be promoted for locals and foreigners. Many developing country currencies are not traded in developed source market countries and secure provision of credible foreign exchange facilities and expansion of credit card usage are important success factors for stimulating tourism expenditure. Allowing foreigners and locals fair access to tourism resources requires suitable pricing policies.

Key guidelines for developing destinations are:

- Developing country tourism policies should promote practical tourism foreign exchange policies. While destinations should avoid, as far as possible, differential tourism pricing, some destinations suffer from high inflation conditions and their currencies are not traded on international platforms, resulting in a need for trading in hard currencies.
- Visitors should be informed about currency conditions and rates and legitimate foreign exchange facilities should be provided.
- Foreign tourists are sensitive to being 'ripped off' by having to pay inflated prices for tourism goods, entrances and services. Policies should promote equitable pricing while ensuring affordable access for locals to natural and cultural resources.

Infrastructure

Public transport and taxi services
Independent travellers depend heavily on reliable and convenient public transport when deciding on, and experiencing, destinations. While developing destinations may not be in a position to provide state-of-the art public transport networks, the available taxi, bus, ship and rail services should be operated as conveniently and safely as possible.
   Key guidelines for developing destinations are:

- Tourism policies should link up with public transport policies to ensure that tourism is acknowledged and integrated in public transport provision. Public transport to, and between, major tourism locations should receive special attention.
- While regulatory mechanisms to ensure convenient and safe public transport services (such as public transport permits, operating licences, roadworthy permits, public transport speed limits, etc.) are important requirements, such systems should be appropriate to local conditions and should not be obstacles to entrepreneurship.

Roads and road signs
Roads are the fundamental links for tourism travel and few destinations are able to grow and expand without improved road access that links access points to main tourist attractions. Road access with effective signage is the one of the most important instruments for unlocking underdeveloped tourism areas.
   Key guidelines for developing destinations are:

- Tourism policies should promote alignment of national and local transport plans with tourism growth requirements – road access is essential for opening up attractive natural and cultural tourism potential and government should realize that tourism will not be able to flourish without targeted investment in good quality road infrastructure.
- Destinations aiming to attract independent travel should pay particular attention to providing internationally recognized, efficient road signage.

Human Resources

Education and training

Tourism is all about personal services – tourists pay to have a break from their usual environments and the enjoyment and value of such experiences depends heavily on the human interactions, whether at hospitality enterprises, public facilities and services, general retail facilities, etc.

Developing countries often do not have the benefit of having developed a tourism and hospitality 'culture' over many decades and even ages. Fortunately, hospitality is an inherent value of many societies around the world; however, citizens need to be trained in applying such inherent friendliness and hospitality to the satisfaction of travellers of other cultures and backgrounds who are paying for such services.

Key guidelines for developing destinations are:

- Every effort should be made to promote quality skills development based on a national qualifications standards and accreditation system.
- Policies for rapid development of scarce skills should be considered.
- Care should be taken to match the development of new training facilities with suitable quality lecturing staff and management. International cooperation may be valuable in this regard.
- Raising awareness of the benefits and responsibilities associated with tourism growth and instilling a 'tourism culture' is of utmost importance in developing tourism destinations, and policies should be considered for introducing tourism in school curricula.
- Tour guiding could be a major tourism job creator and a standardized and quality-controlled tour guide system is an important contributor to tourist knowledge and proper understanding of history, heritage and lifestyle conditions in developing countries.

Community-based tourism

Tourism happens at the local level where tourists move around and interact to experience the destination's attractions. Local communities, who often have a direct influence over the quality and sustainability of cultural and natural heritage, are able to extract tourism benefits (income, jobs, business prospects) in return for services. Communities need to be organized, trained and advised to make the most of their tourism assets and their engagement with visitors, private sector partners and government processes, and officials should be well informed.

Key guidelines for developing destinations are:

- 'Bottom-up' tourism development should be encouraged, and special provision should be made for tourism capacity building, including related to the business of tourism, and entrepreneurship development at community and individual level.
- Where tourism is managed through community organizations (e.g. trusts, associations, etc.) government should consider checks and balances to ensure transparency and good corporate and financial governance.

Marketing and Promotion

Strategic marketing approach
Tourism is highly competitive and developing destinations often have limited financial and human marketing resources. Breaking into tourism markets in the face of established competition is not easy. To compete effectively, destinations have to be strategic and focused. Targeted marketing, brand differentiation, intelligent decision-making and impact measurement are keys to market growth.

Key guidelines for developing destinations are:

- The saying 'if you can't measure it you can't manage it' is highly relevant to destination management and effective and efficient statistical management should be a cornerstone of tourism policies.
- The growing importance and effectiveness of online communication, promotion and transitioning and associated possibilities for sustainable tourism promotion should be recognized and supported.
- Targeted marketing, based on adequate market research should be ensconced in the tourism policy.
- The value, importance and management implications of a strong destination brand should be emphasized.

Product and market focus
Developing destinations have to make specific considerations with regard to the market and product segments they intend focusing on and that best complement their competitive positioning. Trying to be 'everything to everyone' is not advisable in the face of competition and limited resources.

Key guidelines for developing destinations are:

- Destinations need to identify and promote their Unique Selling Point (USP). Strategies to maintain this USP should also be developed.
- Market-related product development should be encouraged – a 'build it and they will come' approach seldom works for developing destinations and private sector investor appetite is the acid test for tourism product ideas.

Institutional and Financial Arrangements

Roles and responsibilities
Successful tourism growth depends on buy-in and partnerships between public sector agencies (cross-sector and at all tiers) and a multi-partner destination strategy is required to make tourism policies work.

Key guidelines for developing destinations are:

- Inter-ministerial policy coordination should be mandated at the highest level and inter-ministerial tourism structures (e.g. tourism cluster committee) should be set up with senior level attendance, for example engaging with safety, immigration, etc.

- Tourism agency structures such as Tourism Boards, Tourism Authorities and other institutions should have substantial private sector representation, preferably at least 50 per cent of members.
- Local tourism associations should be established as public–private partnerships with local, both government and private business, members contributing.
- The Tourism Ministry and its agencies should set up formal, practical partnerships with private sector tourism bodies and the private sector should be encouraged to establish a single 'voice' umbrella body to engage with the government.

Financing tourism destination management and promotion
Destination promotion and development in developing destinations requires substantial government funding for creating brand awareness and preparing the destination to receive travellers.
    Key guidelines for developing destinations are:

- Solid arguments should be put forward for canvassing for a larger share of the budget for tourism – satellite accounting to show the impact of tourism and focused, measurable marketing and product development could be key instruments in this regard.
- Private sector companies spend substantial funds on promoting their individual companies and destination marketing should leverage on such efforts through e.g. co-branding, joint marketing campaigns, etc.

POTENTIAL CHALLENGES AND TROUBLESHOOTING

While policy formulation and promulgation are often well managed, transparent and highly consultative, successful tourism policy-making has been proven to face some steep challenges. Amongst others, these have been related to:

- The lack of implementation, or slow implementation of policies adopted. All too often governments pay lip-service to policies that look impressive on paper, but with implementation being either disregarded or under-resourced. Formulating and adopting tourism policies is a battle half won – only when this is followed by successful execution, monitoring and evaluation, can policies be regarded as successful.
- Changing circumstances and events in the broader economic and socio-political environment can lead to governments and private businesses deviating from sound and sustainable tourism policies and implementing policies inconsistently. While the concept of sustainability is usually embedded in public policies, sustainable tourism principles and practices often come under severe pressure when there is quick money to be made or votes to be won. Tensions can also develop between tourism authorities that promote a longer term, sustainable growth vision and other sectors and leaders in government and private sector, who cite and support rapid increases in arrivals. Such populist approaches could result in 'overtourism' and reduction in yields per visitor.
- Tourism policy formulation and execution require active commitment from a broad range of private entities and public sector ministries and agencies that provide critical services along the tourism value chain. These include airlines and aviation regulators, immigration

authorities, transport providers and regulators, the security fraternity, the health sector, conservation authorities, and utilities providers to name but a few. Relevant tourism policy directives should not only be embedded in the policies of such players but should also be reflected in their budgetary and capacity plans. This requires support for tourism policy execution from the highest levels in government and business, something that is absent in many countries.

IMPLICATIONS

Sound and successful tourism policies form the bedrock of sustainable tourism development. Tourism sustainability has received much focus and attention at national and international levels during the past two decades and the importance of sustainable tourism development is broadly accepted among tourism leaders globally. Yet, the integration and execution of sound and sustainable tourism policies have sadly been lacking in many destinations.

Giving effect to vibrant and sustainable tourism policies requires a bold and consistent policy-making approach that:

- Advances competitiveness across the entire tourism value chain, while ensuring the long-term sustainability of destinations.
- Ensures policy ownership of execution vests with all key institutions and players that play a part in tourism value creation.
- Empowers tourism ministries and authorities to play a critical leadership and coordination role in sustainable policy execution, i.e. to be empowered as conductors of the tourism 'orchestra' towards delivering a seamless and harmonious tourism performance.

REFERENCES

Collins (2020) *COBUILD Advanced English Dictionary*, accessed 10 April 2020 at https://www .collinsdictionary.com/dictionary/english/public-policy.
Fabricius, M. (2001) Competitive strategies for tourism destination. Dissertation in partial fulfilment of the master's degree in business leadership, University of South Africa.
Government of South Africa (1996) *White Paper on the Development and Promotion of Tourism in South Africa*. Government Printer.
OECD (2010). Tourism 2020, policies to promote competitive and sustainable tourism. In *OECD Tourism Trends and Policies 2010*. Paris: OECD Publishing.
Spenceley, A. (2008) Responsible tourism in Southern Africa. In A. Spenceley (ed.), *Responsible Tourism: Critical Issues for Conservation and Development*. London: Earthscan, 1–24.
United Nations (2020) *Sustainable Development Goals*, accessed 10 April 2020 at https://sdgs.un.org/.
UNEP and UNWTO (2005) *Making Tourism More Sustainable: A Guide for Policy Makers*. Madrid: UNWTO.
UNWTO (2007) *Policies, Strategies and Tools for the Sustainable Development of Tourism*. Madrid: UNWTO.
UNWTO (2011) *Policy and Practice for Global Tourism*. Madrid: UNWTO.
UNWTO (2019) *Position Paper on Tourism Policy and Strategic Planning*. UNWTO Committee on Tourism and Competitiveness (CTC), final version, 3 September. Madrid: UNWTO.
UNWTO and UNEP (2019) *Baseline Report on the Integration of Sustainable Consumption and Production Patterns into Tourism Policies*. Madrid: UNWTO.

4. Tourism master planning: the key to sustainable long-term growth

Roger Goodacre

INTRODUCTION

What Is the Purpose of a Tourism Master Plan?

Since the early 1960s, tourism in its many forms has expanded rapidly and continuously, spreading gradually to most parts of the world, bringing with it blessings and blight, challenges and opportunities. As has been seen in many tourism hotspots, without adequate controls tourism can too easily have serious negative impacts, whether on the natural environment, local culture or community life. With this growth has spread the realization that good forward planning and active and adaptive management are essential if tourism is to be harnessed to optimize the benefits and minimize the negative impacts.

A medium- to long-term planning framework, in the form of a tourism development master plan, has thus come to be widely accepted as a key tool for stimulating and managing demand in ways that are economically, socially and environmentally sustainable. Master plans generally have a lifespan of 10 years (occasionally 15 or even 20 years), and can be employed at national, regional or local level (although local plans, which are less complex, usually take the form of a Destination Management Plan): this chapter discusses the main objectives and characteristics of a typical national master plan, based primarily on experience gained in emerging markets around the world.

Unlike most industries, tourism is intricately linked to many other sectors of the economy, including transport, services, manufacturing, agriculture and education. It is a complex and fragmented business, whose benefits are widely distributed through the multiplier effect and along myriad value chains, creating sources of income for many small businesses and marginalized communities. Development planning therefore has to take into account the demands and impacts that policies and strategies may have on many other sectors over which tourism authorities have no control. It is difficult, for example, to channel traffic towards areas with spare capacity, however attractive, if the transport ministry is unwilling or unable to fund the new roads or access links needed.

Tourism is also a valuable mechanism for addressing some of the most pressing issues facing society, including poverty, marginalization of rural communities, lack of economic competitiveness, environmental and heritage degradation and eroding of cultural traditions. The funding provided by some national development agencies – whether to commission a master plan or to support tourism development projects – is often tied specifically to addressing one or more of these issues.

These many issues, based on the fundamental imperative to balance demand and supply, come together in a comprehensive and flexible tourism master plan, that must be regularly reviewed and adjusted according to changing circumstances in order to deliver the key aims desired.

Content: What Does a Tourism Master Plan Cover?

A master plan is a term most commonly associated with urban or land planning, where it is a long-term planning document in the form of a conceptual layout designed to guide future development.

A tourism master plan shares these essential characteristics and constitutes a comprehensive framework for development in the medium to long-term, generally for a country or region. Its main purpose is to provide a detailed roadmap for all stakeholders, setting out a vision and key objectives for future development and defining the policies, strategy, actions and resources to be employed to achieve those objectives. As an official document usually with legal status, it provides stakeholders, whether investors, operators or government authorities, with the necessary basis on which to make planning and investment decisions.

In its most comprehensive form a master plan addresses every aspect of the development, management, regulation and functioning of the tourism sector. It prescribes the appropriate institutional structure for the governance and regulation of the sector, for marketing the destination, for ensuring the supply of adequately skilled human resources, and for attracting the investment needed to drive growth.

A master plan must ensure that capacity is sufficient to accommodate forecast demand. Spatial planning in the form of designated 'Tourism Development Areas' and hubs is used to focus resources on strategic locations. The product development strategy will identify the services (e.g. accommodation, restaurants, information services, guides, etc.) and essential support infrastructure (e.g. airports, roads, utilities, etc.) needed to attract new markets. It will include outline designs or templates (e.g. detailed plans and drawings) for recommended flagship developments, whether a resort, a building conversion or a new attraction.

To be successful a master plan should be the outcome of widespread consultation, where the final draft is widely accepted by stakeholders from every part of the tourism sector. Its effectiveness should be measured by a range of performance indicators and allow for adjustments to be made to reflect changing circumstances.

The drafting of a master plan requires the involvement of a range of technical experts with specialist skills, who can bring first-hand experience of best practice from around the world. It should normally take from four to twelve months in preparation, depending on the scope specified in the Terms of Reference.

CONTEXT

Tourism's Relentless Growth: The Need for Strategic Planning

Policy makers and planners involved in making long-term decisions need to have a broad awareness of international tourism trends and the underlying drivers of growth. Over the six decades from 1960 and prior to COVID-19, tourism had experienced virtually continuous growth, expanding and diversifying, despite the occasional hiatus, to become one of the largest economic sectors in the world. It is now the third largest export category in the world, after chemicals and fuels and ahead of automotive products and food. International tourist arrivals have increased from 25 million in 1950 to 278 million in 1980, 674 million in 2000, and 1.5 billion in 2019 (UNWTO, 2019). Tourism is also one of the biggest revenue-generating industries in the world. In this same period, international tourism receipts earned by destinations worldwide have surged from USD 2 billion in 1950 to USD 104 billion in 1980, USD 495 billion in 2000, and USD 1.7 trillion (including passenger transport) in 2018 (UNWTO, 2019).

Five other characteristics differentiate tourism and make it particularly attractive as a force for economic growth and societal benefit, especially in developing nations: (1) tourism is labour intensive, cannot easily be automated (other than in areas such as information distribution and travel booking), and employs a higher proportion of women than other sectors, (2) it has low barriers to entry, offering opportunities to entrepreneurs and people with limited skills, (3) unlike most businesses, the tourism product (its natural assets, built heritage, culture, etc.) cannot be relocated – it can only be consumed on the spot, (4) tourism can bring revenue earning opportunities to remote or marginalized communities where opportunities are limited, and (5) can have multiplier values across the broader economy through value chains.

As a consequence, more and more emerging economies around the world have looked to develop their tourism assets and exploit their potential as a generator of export revenues and driver of socio-economic change. As tourism has grown, the need for better planning has become more widely recognized, not just to stimulate growth but increasingly to manage and channel demand.

The Benefits and Risks of Tourism Development

Tourism development needs to be sensitively managed. Growth of the magnitude experienced in recent decades can bring significant economic benefits but also have serious negative impacts on communities, cultures and the environment if inadequately planned.

Properly planned and managed, tourism can deliver a multitude of benefits for both urban and rural communities, from the creation of jobs and enterprises to investment in better transport infrastructure, cultural attractions and leisure facilities. Tourism can also stimulate stronger measures for protection of the natural environment, biodiversity and wildlife, the conservation of built heritage and protection of intangible heritage, which become better appreciated as valuable resources. Economic diversification, poverty alleviation and women's empowerment are other desirable outcomes of good tourism planning.

However, inadequate planning or poor management can have serious deleterious impacts, on the environment, habitat or culture, and arouse strong opposition to tourism. The so-called 'overtourism' phenomenon is only one well-publicized manifestation of inadequate management of tourism demand. The concreting of vast stretches of the Mediterranean coast is a visible example of poor short-term policy-making, allowing greed and criminality to flourish to the long-term detriment of the natural environment.

Good planning and good management are essential in avoiding the consequences of uncontrolled development and, just as importantly, in ensuring growth based on a sustainable use of resources.

THE PLANNING PROCESS

Researching and Drafting the Terms of Reference

The decision to commission a national tourism master plan is almost invariably taken by a government department with procurement authority (most often the Ministry or Department of Tourism). In developing countries it may also be decided following consultation with a multilateral or bilateral organization that is able to facilitate or provide the necessary funding support for the master plan project.

The principal desired outputs and broad scope of the master plan will first be agreed in discussion between the client and the sponsoring/facilitating agency involved. These will be articulated in the Terms of Reference (TOR) for the master plan, which will specify in detail the precise activities that each expert in the team is expected to undertake, and the deliverables (draft and final reports, etc.) that are required.

The drafting of the TOR should be done on the basis of an informed up-to-date understanding of the tourism situation and the issues involved in the client country or region. Poorly drafted TORs are a recipe for confusion and unsatisfactory outcomes, not to say unwelcome complications for the master plan team.

Scoping the Project

The drafting of the TOR is often preceded by a scoping (or mapping) mission, which will provide a detailed and up-to-date evaluation of the tourism situation, give an understanding of key issues, and allow an assessment to be made of the expertise needed to deliver the desired outputs. The scoping mission will be carried out by a suitably qualified technical expert, who should have adequate first-hand experience of working on master plans and a broad understanding of the realities and technicalities of tourism development. This mission will usually demand a field visit of at least two weeks, with a further ten to fifteen working days required for desk research and the drafting of the scoping report.

During the field visit, the expert should consult with key public and private sector stakeholders, principally senior officials in the Tourism Ministry or Department, the National Tourist Organization and leading industry representatives, and make a broad evaluation of the country's major tourism assets and infrastructure. The desk research should involve reviewing relevant policies, strategies, statistical data and research studies, and identifying any important gaps in intelligence.

The scoping report that will be delivered should generally comprise (1) a broad profile of the country or region, summarizing its salient characteristics (population size, notable geographical and cultural features), economic situation and outlook and its prime tourism assets, etc., (2) an assessment of the tourism situation, including the latest visitor statistics and market trends (numbers, source markets, revenues etc.), and identifying the key issues needing to be addressed, (3) a recommendation for the technical expertise needed to deliver the master plan, specifying the skills and experience required, with suggested timeframes for delivery.

Drafting the Terms of Reference

Using the conclusions of the scoping report, if one is available, the commissioning agency will then draft the detailed TOR for the preparation of the master plan. These will describe the nature of the project, the timeframe to be covered by the master plan, the key outputs required and any special factors to be taken into account.

The TOR will specify the precise technical expertise required (number and type of experts), the time (in working days or weeks) allotted to each expert, the 'deliverables' (draft and final reports, etc.) to be produced with dates for submission, and the financial terms offered. Individual TORs will be prepared for each consultant in the team, specifying their main duties and responsibilities, the scope of research and consultation to be undertaken, the deliverables and the financial terms offered.

Delivery of a master plan that not merely adheres to the TOR but satisfies the expectations of the client can only be achieved if the TOR offers a judicious balance between the outputs demanded and the time and budget allowed. The very minimum timeframe within which a master plan can be delivered with a realistic expectation of a quality output is probably four months. Detailed plans that cover a wide range of issues need to be given adequate time, to allow for research, consultation, analysis and revision: national master plans that involve extensive research and consultation can take up to twelve months to be delivered.

One tendency of TORs is to over-specify, in terms of demanding too much ground to cover in too much detail in relation to the time allowed, or available budget, with the inevitable result that consultants take short cuts and quality is compromised. Some of these issues or excessive expectations may be resolved satisfactorily during the inception phase.

COMMISSIONING THE MASTER PLAN

Who Commissions and Funds Tourism Master Plans?

In the developing world, national or regional tourism master plans are almost invariably commissioned and/or sponsored by an international organization or development agency. Very often the funding support for a tourism master plan forms part of the sponsoring institution's own broader development policy agenda in developing nations, such as achieving the UN's Sustainable Development Goals. Funding may be tied to specific multi-sectoral objectives, such as improving economic competitiveness, fostering economic or environmental sustainability, alleviating poverty, empowering women, protecting biodiversity, etc.

International organizations and agencies[1] that are, or have been, involved in commissioning or sponsoring tourism master plans fall into one of two categories:

- **Multilateral organizations**: For example the African Development Bank (AfDB), Asian Development Bank (ADB), Commonwealth Secretariat, European Union (EU), European Bank for Reconstruction and Development, Inter-American Development Bank, United Nations Development Programme (UNDP), UN World Tourism Organization (UNWTO), World Bank, etc.

- **Bilateral organizations**: AFD (Agence Française pour le Développement, France), DfID (Department for International Development, UK), GIZ (Gesellschaft für Internationale Zusammenarbeit, Germany), USAID (US Agency for International Development), etc.

Most of these institutions have a record of funding or contributing as a partner to tourism development strategies. The list is purely indicative: national development agencies in particular change their policies regularly in line with their government's priorities, and their interest in tourism as a vehicle for development policy therefore also changes regularly. The Dutch development agency SNV, for example, was once very active in tourism development but eventually switched its support to other sectors (currently agriculture, water and energy, sanitation and hygiene).

The budget for commissioning a tourism master plan should be based on the key issues needing to be addressed and key outputs desired, identified through a scoping mission and/ or in discussion between the funding agency and the client. The budget needs to cover the experts' fees, their transport and subsistence, transport in the field, the fees of any local experts engaged, administrative costs and a contingency allowance to meet the costs of unforeseen expenditures or additional requirements such as bespoke research surveys. All project management firms and some international organizations such as UNWTO charge a management fee for delivering the project.

Deciding the Composition of the Master Plan Team

Once the budget and TOR have been settled and agreed with the client, the composition of the team needed to deliver the key outputs will be determined: the size of the team and number of experts included will depend directly on the agreed budget for the project. A standard master planning team would normally be built around a core group of experts in most of the following areas:

- Strategy, policy, sustainable development (often the team leader)
- Research and statistics
- Destination marketing (often with a requirement for branding expertise)
- Tourism legislation and regulation
- Capacity building (human resources, training, etc.)
- Product development (sometimes included in the physical planning or marketing brief)
- Physical planning (also covering spatial planning, and sometimes transport planning)
- Tourism economics (including funding and investment)

Depending on the project scope and budget, the team may be smaller, with experts asked to take on additional responsibilities, or bigger, and include specialists in particular fields (e.g. cultural heritage, adventure tourism, ecotourism/environmental sustainability, wellness/health tourism, accommodation classification systems, quality standards, etc.). In most instances, one or more local tourism experts will be included, either as specialists in their own right or as special advisers to team members (for example, bringing detailed knowledge of local tourism legislation and regulations). This is important to ensure that the planning is grounded in local knowledge and expertise.

What Qualifications Are Needed to Work on a Tourism Master Plan?

The key qualification needed for a consultant to be considered for a master planning assignment, in addition to demonstrable professional, and ideally practical, expertise in one or more aspects of tourism development, is experience, both in the consultant's own field and of previous master planning assignments. Most TORs demand a minimum number of years' experience of master plan projects. Degree or postgraduate level qualifications from a university or recognized higher education institution that offer relevant tourism training are a valuable asset and are often specified in TORs. Master planning is not, generally speaking, a field of activity for tourism professionals in the early stages of their career, unless they have a very specialized technical skill that is in short supply.

All team members will be expected to have certain core skills and languages, including the ability to draft a report clearly in the formal style appropriate to an official document that may have legal status. Research and analytical skills are essential, as also the ability to present and justify findings and recommendations to stakeholder audiences. It goes without saying that the ability to adjust to the cultural norms, etiquette and business practices that apply in different parts of the world, and to work as part of a team in occasionally less than ideal working conditions, is a fundamental requirement.

The core members of a well-equipped multi-disciplinary team for a large country with a complex tourism sector would be expected to bring the following basic experience or qualifications (with smaller simpler teams for less complicated projects):

- **Team leader** (aka Chief Technical Adviser): substantial experience of master planning or strategic development assignments in relevant markets; expertise in tourism policy, governance, planning and sustainable development; project and team management experience; see below for more detail.
- **Governance expert**: expertise in institutional reform and governance structures in the tourism sector, with specific regard to government institutions and National Tourism Offices; ability to advise on streamlining management systems based on international best practice, and on establishing mechanisms to ensure cross-departmental collaboration and communication.
- **Research and statistics expert**: good understanding of international tourism statistics and trends, familiarity with statistical measurement tools such as the Tourism Satellite Account, ability to analyse and forecast trends, ability to design and manage or commission qualitative or quantitative research (such as customer satisfaction or exit surveys).
- **Destination marketing expert**: expertise in researching and designing destination marketing strategy for National Tourist Organizations, based on ability to evaluate, forecast and stimulate demand; excellent understanding of how to use modern online distribution channels and e-marketing techniques to reach target markets; expertise in destination branding often desired.
- **Tourism legislation expert**: preferably a legal qualification and/or regulatory experience in the tourism sector, with awareness of international best practice (including for some regions knowledge of EU tourism regulations); experience in amending or drafting legislation or regulations appropriate to all areas of the tourism sector (services, planning, heritage, human resources, etc.).

- **Capacity building expert**: expertise in tourism and hospitality training best practice; ability to evaluate effectiveness of vocational and academic training institutions and recommend appropriate improvements; experience in assessing tourism management skills of public sector officials and identifying capacity building needs; ability to draft human resource development strategy and devise suitable interventions for SMEs; ability to forecast future manpower demand in tourism and hospitality sectors based on growth projections.

- **Product development expert** (sometimes included in the physical planning or marketing brief): experience in analysing and identifying product development opportunities and developing a product development strategy. Awareness of international best practice and product development trends in the tourism, hospitality and leisure sectors, especially in emerging markets; experience in preparing product concepts (physical, thematic, etc.) corresponding to market growth or diversification strategies.

- **Physical planning expert** (also covering spatial planning, sometimes infrastructure or transport planning): a professional qualification in planning or architecture with experience in all aspects of spatial, land use and town planning in a tourism context; experience in evaluating and planning tourism hubs and Tourism Development Areas; ability to design concept proposals for 'demonstration projects' – product developments or templates that can enhance or differentiate the tourism offer.

- **Infrastructure expert**: a planning expert with a relevant professional qualification and with experience in analysing and forecasting future capacity needs in every area of the tourism sector (air and land transport, roads, accommodation, utilities, etc.). Experience in planning an infrastructure development strategy in the tourism sector, especially in the developing world.

- **Funding and investment expert**: a qualification in economics or financial management, with experience in economic and financial analysis in the tourism sector; awareness of best practice in national tourism economic policy, sustainable development, business planning and enterprise legislation; ability to research and prepare revenue projections based on different visitor growth scenarios; experience in drafting an investment strategy, including the use of public–private partnerships, and identifying potential sources of investment, to drive product development; experience in devising recommendations for enhancing small business development opportunities through business support schemes and mechanisms to encourage small business growth and sustainable development.

Selection of experts is always done on the basis of the candidate's Curriculum Vitae (CV), which occasionally but not commonly may be followed by a telephone or online interview. A consultant wishing to apply for a position on a master plan team must therefore have a professionally presented CV, adapted where necessary to a prescribed standard format (such as for all EU-funded projects). Prospective consultants should register their CVs with as many consultancy and recruitment firms as possible and have a presence on online professional forums such as LinkedIn. The key requirement of a successful CV is an established project track record, in addition to relevant professional skills. This creates a classic chicken and egg situation for consultants at the outset of a career. The longer the track record, the greater the chance of the consultant being selected.

Getting started in tourism master planning is far from straightforward. Seeking advice from established consultants, registering with project management and consultancy firms, networking in appropriate circles and active self-promotion are all necessary steps to get a foot in the door. Searching for opportunities, submitting expressions of interest, preparing a project bid, and patiently following up enquiries and submissions are a time-consuming, frustrating but inherent element of the life of a consultant.

The manner in which a master plan team is assembled will depend entirely on the type of commissioning agency.

Role of the team leader

The team leader is responsible for the following tasks and activities:

- Day-to-day liaison with the client in the field, working through a local 'counterpart' (generally a senior official from the Tourism Ministry/Department).
- Management of the project programme, planning the team schedule (usually in the form of a Gantt chart).
- Organizing logistics including office and hotel accommodation as necessary.
- Providing a style guide so that all inputs are delivered in the same format, font, etc.
- Ensuring that experts' inputs are delivered on schedule.
- Organizing consultation meetings and workshops, in collaboration with the counterpart.
- Communicating with and leading presentations to ministers, senior government officials and the steering committee.
- Preparing and presenting the inception report to the steering committee at the end of the inception phase, in which the methodologies to be employed and the workplan will be presented, raising any unforeseen issues that need to be considered, and requesting any additional resources or support that may be needed.
- General troubleshooting, resolving any team or individual concerns or issues arising during the course of the mission, where necessary in consultation with the project manager.
- Reviewing and editing team members' inputs.
- Formally presenting the draft final report to the steering committee.
- Editing and delivering the final report.

How Are Tourism Master Planning Consultants Recruited?

Tourism master plan projects are generally either put out to tender or directly managed by the commissioning agency. Multilateral organizations, with the exception of UNWTO, tend to invite bids from consultancy or project management firms. The contract is usually awarded according to specified criteria, often using a points-based formula: so many points awarded for proposed methodology, for experts' qualifications, for budget cost, etc. Some of the big international consulting firms have their own in-house experts but most project management firms tend to prepare a bid by assembling a team of invited independent experts.

To prepare a bid, contractors must first put together a team of experts as specified in the project TOR, which in practice means that an expert may well receive invitations to join a bid from more than one contractor. This leaves the expert in the invidious position of having to guess which contractor is more likely to win the tender, with little information (such as the contractor's record in winning bids, who else is in the team, or who offers the lowest budget) on how best to decide. It is standard practice for contractors to require a signed statement of exclusivity, which means that the expert cannot then change allegiance should a more attractive or suitable proposition be made by a rival contractor.

UNWTO and the World Bank post both project tenders and/or individual consultancy opportunities on their websites, so it is wise to check for new postings on a regular basis. All institutions that commission master plan projects and consultancy firms that bid for projects tend to maintain a database of consultants that they build up over time, from which they source as much of the expertise required to make up a team as possible.

Much recruitment of experts is done by word-of-mouth: established consultants are regularly asked if they can suggest or recommend suitable candidates. Positions are regularly advertised online through international development platforms such as Devex and DevelopmentAid, or occasionally are put out to recruitment firms. From the perspective of a consultant, direct invitations to be part of a project team are the most desirable procedure but tend to happen only after a suitable track record has been acquired.

THE MASTER PLANNING PROCESS

Inception Phase

Once a master plan team has been appointed, an outline schedule will be planned by the project manager and/or team leader, setting out the deployment programme for each member of the team together with delivery deadlines for draft and final reports.

The field research and most of the drafting of the master plan takes place in the country or region concerned, although some desk research and final editing may be carried out at the experts' home base.

The project will start with a first visit to the client destination by the team leader (TL), possibly accompanied by other key experts, for the inception phase, during which the TL will make practical preparations for the master planning process. These involve reviewing preliminary arrangements for deployment of the full team in the light of actual conditions, assessing the resources needed and available, and working with a local counterpart (usually a senior official from the Tourism Ministry or other government department) to plan key events such as field visits and consultation workshops.

Following this ground-laying process, generally taking two or more weeks, a formal meeting will be held with the Steering Committee, a group of senior stakeholders from the public and private sectors appointed by the government to monitor the project's progress, at which the Inception Report will be presented. This will contain the detailed project schedule with any suggested modifications to the proposal or TOR, the research and planning methodologies to be used, and will be the occasion for requesting any additional support or resources required. Key objectives and issues will be outlined and discussed so that all parties are clear about processes and deliverables. As this becomes the roadmap to the assignment, it is very important to have this agreed by the client before moving forward.

Master Plan Team Deployment

Following presentation of the Inception Report, the master planning process will begin in earnest, with the arrival on the ground of the core team. Team members will usually be recruited for differing lengths of time, generally expressed in working days (or man days), according to the inputs required, so experts are likely to come and go over the course of the project.

Master Planning Approach

The plan should be based on desk and field research and extensive consultation with all stakeholders. The research should involve the review of all relevant policies, legislation, studies and statistical data, supplemented where necessary and feasible by tailor-made qualitative or quantitative surveys.

Widespread consultation with stakeholders is essential, not least in ensuring that local communities feel that their concerns and needs are being taken into account. Experts need to source their information from one-to-one meetings with senior officials in all relevant departments of government (Ministries of Tourism, Transport, Education, Finance, Culture, etc. and National Statistics Office) or local authority, and from prominent private sector stakeholders. Formal meetings and focus groups with industry associations (such as hotel owners/managers, tour operators, tour guides, etc.) and stakeholder workshops in key tourist areas around the country should be organized, so that all interested parties, including regional authorities and small businesses, are able to share information directly with the master plan team and express their views.

Once the research has been completed and the necessary information and data gathered, analysed and shaped into a draft plan, the first outline – containing the team's key findings and recommendations – will be presented at a meeting with the Steering Committee and/or at a stakeholders' workshop, usually in PowerPoint format, for comment and validation. The draft plan will then be revised to take account of the comments made and the print version submitted to the client for approval. A further exchange of comments and revisions may follow before final acceptance of the master plan.

Master Plan Structure and Content

Tourism master plans generally follow a standard structure, with variations, although in some cases a local official template, common to all of a country's sectorial development strategies, may be prescribed by the host government.

To achieve the desired aims, the master plan needs to articulate a clear vision and way forward that will be widely endorsed by stakeholders from across the tourism sector. It must show where development will be concentrated and why, where growth will come from and how, what tools and resources will be needed, what benefits will result, and how an integrated plan will ensure long-term sustainable development.

A full master plan involving the inputs of several experts is likely to be a substantial document that can run to 300–500 pages. Therefore, there is always a need for an executive summary to give a concise overview of the detailed plan, in order to make it more practical and usable by policy makers.

Structure

A standard tourism master plan should be organized along the following lines:

- **Introduction and Executive Summary**: the Introduction should provide the context for the master plan, describing the destination's geophysical, historical and social features, the general evolution and present situation of its tourism sector, and key economic and employment data. A list of contents, acronyms used and definition of key terms (including the UN definition of tourism and the different categories of visitor) should be provided. The Executive Summary should describe the methodology used in the master plan, its key aims and the issues it addresses, and summarize its key recommendations for how to deliver those aims, with an indication of the resources needed.
- **Situation Assessment**: should provide a detailed forensic analysis of every aspect of the tourism sector and its performance, highlighting key trends and identifying the key issues that need to be addressed in the master plan.
- **SWOT analysis (Strengths, Weaknesses, Opportunities, Threats)**: the assessment phase will allow the formulation of a SWOT analysis, which should identify in tabular form the key strengths, weaknesses, opportunities and threats most relevant to tourism development, arranged by sector (governance, legislation, research/statistics, products/ attractions, natural assets, infrastructure, marketing, human resources, funding, etc.).
- **Vision Statement**: should articulate concisely, in two or three sentences, the position and situation that the destination aspires to have achieved following implementation of the master plan. Vision statements should be bold and ambitious but avoid being either too bland and formulaic or wildly unrealistic. The workshop consultation process should be used to gather suggestions and obtain broad consensus on the vision to be adopted.
- **Key Aims**: should state the key economic, social and environmental benefits that the master plan is designed to deliver. These might include, for example, an increase in the overall contribution of the tourism sector to GDP by a certain proportion within a given timeframe; the wider spread of tourism revenues and supply chains, notably to rural/ disadvantaged communities; or measures to ensure that tourism development adheres to international sustainable development principles, with minimal negative impacts on local culture, natural and built heritage; etc.
- **Tourism Development Strategy**: the core section of the master plan should articulate in detail, across every specialist area, how the key issues that have been identified in the Situation Assessment are to be addressed. Each section should define the specific objectives that need to be achieved in order to deliver the strategy, and describe the strategic approach, tools and mechanisms that will be employed to do so. See below for a broad description of the principal components of the development strategy.
- **Action Plan and Key Performance Indicators**: the action plan should describe in detail the actions that need to be implemented over the first three years following the client's acceptance of the final master plan report. It should indicate the sequence and years in which actions must take place, the department or entity responsible for delivery, Key Performance Indicators (KPIs) to measure progress, and wherever possible give an indicative budget cost for the action.

Components of the master plan development strategy

This core section of the master plan should set out, in each specialist area to be covered by the plan, the Key Objectives that need to be achieved in order to deliver the master plan's Key Aims and to address the issues identified in the Situation Assessment. The aim of increasing tourism revenues, for example, might be achieved in part by setting as an objective an increase in visitors' average length-of-stay within a given timeframe, or attracting new markets by opening new air links.

The strategy should always take account of the likely availability of the human and financial resources needed to implement recommended activities, particularly in emerging markets where funding may be severely limited.

The following activities are likely to form the basis of the different components of the master plan development strategy, enhanced or modified according to the project TORs:

Governance

A suitable framework for administration and development of the tourism sector should be agreed, ensuring separation of policy/strategy formulation and regulation from marketing and strategy implementation. Organograms should be provided as necessary for the key institutions – generally the Ministry or Department of Tourism and the National Tourism organization – illustrating the departmental hierarchical structure, showing key posts and responsibilities.

Mechanisms should be put into place where appropriate to ensure coordination, at ministerial and other levels, of tourism-related policy across all government departments. Responsibility for implementing and delivering key strategic initiatives such as a tourism master plan should be allocated to a nominated senior post-holder; and mechanisms should be defined for monitoring and managing tourism traffic flows, to forestall potential problems of overtourism at iconic tourism or heritage sites.

Legislation and regulation

Legislation that should be introduced or modified as necessary in line with issues identified in the situation assessment. It should as a minimum requirement ensure protection for visitors, the natural, built and cultural heritage, wildlife, etc. Regulations should be introduced as necessary to ensure basic quality standards in tourism and hospitality services; and to provide an attractive and secure investment environment, including building and land use planning regulations to ensure a specified basic quality of development in designated Tourism Development Areas. The TOR may require the legislative expert either to identify/recommend the legislative and regulatory amendments and additions required or to draft a new legislative white paper, possibly in collaboration with a local expert.

Research and statistics

Measures should be recommended for improving the system of tourism statistics, as necessary, including the adoption where possible of the Tourism Satellite Account to measure tourism's contribution to GDP more accurately.

Recommendations should be made to improve market intelligence and better understand visitor behaviour and characteristics, for example through regular exit and visitor satisfaction surveys.

In consultation with the project team, projections for future tourist arrivals should be agreed, showing the potential impacts on infrastructure, product development and human resource requirements.

A forecast of the contribution of tourism to GDP, foreign exchange earnings, government revenues and the creation of employment (direct and indirect) should be produced.

Visitor and revenue growth forecasts should be made, showing three potential scenarios: (1) forecast trend if current marketing activity and levels of investment are left largely unchanged, (2) forecast growth if master plan minimal recommendations are implemented, (3) forecast growth if master plan full promotional and investment recommendations are implemented.

Marketing and branding
Naturally all destinations would like to attract the ideal high-spend low-impact segments of the travel market, but clearly not every destination has the quality of attractions and services to do so. The marketing strategy should take a realistic view of how to brand and position the destination, based on plausible demand forecasts and in relation to direct competition from rival destinations.

The strategy should quantify future demand and clearly identify key source markets, taking into account ease of accessibility and illustrated in a product/market-fit matrix. It should define the tools/mechanisms best suited to enter or expand the selected source markets, using a cost-effective mix of distribution channels, social media, e-marketing and traditional promotional tools to deliver growth targets. Where possible, promotional campaigns should be co-funded by the private sector partners (hotels, airlines, tour operators, etc.) who will benefit directly from the investment. Information distribution both for foreign and domestic visitors should be optimized, using traditional and electronic tools (e.g. printed maps/guides, apps, to satisfy the preferences of different markets).

A brand image should be developed or refreshed as necessary, following the necessary consultation process, that reflects and communicates the distinctive features of the destination. Given the cost of brand promotion activity, which needs to be sustained over years to have real impact, it may be more appropriate in some instances to develop or adopt a country's national brand, with suitable modifications, so that costs are more widely spread.

Physical planning and product development
A spatial plan should be developed in map form showing the selected Tourism Development Areas (TDAs) and hubs where product development should be focused, so that resources are invested cost-efficiently. The plan should also identify key areas, in town centres or around major attractions, where tourist facilities and services should be clustered in order to optimize tourist visitation. The product development strategy should always be drafted in close consultation with the project team, notably the marketing expert, to ensure that product supply matches identified existing or potential demand.

The plan should contain graphic designs for physical developments in the TDAs, supported by basic economic justifications, as part of a product or market diversification strategy. These might include, for example, a template for a high-end resort in an under-exploited wildlife park or area of natural beauty; hiking trails to open up little-known areas and provide links to rural communities; conference or exhibition facilities to attract high-spending business visitors; or a visitor centre in a key location offering space for local handicrafts vendors and tourism services.

Note: Golf course projects (a too-common proposal for attracting high-end tourists) should generally be avoided unless sufficient local support is available to provide year-round utilization and ensure financial viability. Golf projects based on real estate sales too often fail through unrealistic expectations or market fluctuations. Golf courses are expensive to design, build and maintain, use large amounts of land and water, and need to offer high quality standards to attract/satisfy regular golfers; furthermore, tourists on a golfing holiday will seek a destination that offers a choice of at least two courses to play. Cable cars (popular in the Middle East) are another project best rejected unless they provide a useful link between two places that will attract constant repeat business: besides their environmental and aesthetic impact, they rarely generate enough usage to operate sustainably other than in ski resorts or hilly urban environments.

Infrastructure development
The infrastructure strategy should help to facilitate and stimulate visitor demand, ensure good accessibility and efficient movement between key tourist areas, and provide the capacity and services needed to handle projected visitor growth.

Based on the master plan's visitor growth objectives, the strategy should identify opportunities for improving air transport accessibility from key growth markets, through an Open Skies policy and appropriate incentives if justified; it should highlight essential road improvements needed to provide good access, or remove bottlenecks, to key tourist attractions and TDAs; and make provision for the basic utilities (i.e. water, electricity, telecommunications) needed to allow accommodation developments in key areas with good tourism development potential. Standardized road signage to key attractions, both in rural and urban areas, should be introduced or extended as required. Recommendations should be made for essential improvements to public or private transport services that can be expected to generate additional visitor traffic.

Capacity building
Based on identified shortcomings in tourism and hospitality skills and shortages of trained manpower, the strategy should outline a capacity building programme to ensure an adequate supply of key skills in every sector of the industry to meet actual and projected future needs.

It should make recommendations for the strengthening of tourism/hospitality training programmes. Specific proposals should be formulated for the development of industry programmes, training support for SMEs, establishment of funding support initiatives, and graduate and management training.

Recommendations should also be made for a continuous process of specialized training and capacity strengthening of government and public sector officials in their respective areas of specialization (policy, development, management, marketing and promotion, conservation, etc.).

Funding and investment
A strategy should be developed, identifying ways of improving the economic impact of tourism (such as increasing the length of stay; targeting new markets; improving linkages between sectors, etc.).

Recommendations should be made for enhancing small business development opportunities through business support schemes. These could include incentives and initiatives by government to strengthen the local tourism supply chain and encourage hospitality and tourism enterprises to purchase goods and services from local suppliers; providing business start-up advice for entrepreneurs, and training in key skills such as e-marketing and yield/revenue management systems for local businesses.

An investment strategy should be prepared, containing recommendations for facilitating and simplifying procedures to encourage investment in the sector. A guide should be produced in consultation with the project team describing investment opportunities, and incentives if available, in the selected Tourism Development Areas.

Action plan and master plan implementation

The action plan normally covers the first three years from the launch of implementation of the master plan (very occasionally five). It itemizes in tabular form all the actions recommended in the tourism development strategy and can be used by the client and implementation team as a checklist to measure implementation progress.

The action plan format is variable but should normally include the following:

- Brief description of the action: e.g. Design and launch an e-marketing campaign; Introduce minimum quality standards regulation; Publish a map of TDAs, etc.
- Year(s) in which the action is to be implemented
- Delivery deadline
- Entity or department responsible for delivery
- Indicative budget cost, where applicable
- Success criteria and performance indicators to be used

The way in which the master plan is to be implemented varies from country to country. Some prefer to do it with their own resources; some request the assistance of a small team of experienced experts for at least a part of the implementation phase (often the first year or two), the funding for which may be provided by an international organization.

KEYS TO SUCCESS AND FAILURE

It is not unheard of for master plans and other strategic studies to lie on a shelf gathering dust for a number of years following delivery; only for a new or revised master plan to be commissioned when a new administration comes into office. Sometimes the minister who commissioned the master plan may lose office or be moved to another department before being able to initiate action on implementation.

The tendency in some administrations is to pick and choose elements of the master plan that may be easier or less contentious to implement, possibly because of budget constraints: but the inevitable result is that the impetus that the master plan is designed to drive will be compromised. Vital elements fall by the wayside, the links between capacity supply and market demand are broken, and the master plan's key economic and other aims become impossible to achieve. Of course, one reason why specific elements of the master plan may be favoured is that external funding from a donor agency may be available only for specific actions that correspond to that agency's goals.

The most reliable guarantee for successful implementation of a master plan is a tourism champion – someone in a senior position of authority who is fully persuaded of the economic and other benefits that a flourishing tourism sector can bring, such as a president or government minister who has the power to make available the resources needed. But the first priority is to ensure that the consultation process is seen to be broad and thorough and that widespread agreement is achieved among both private and public sector stakeholders for the key aims and strategy articulated in the master plan.

A SUCCESS STORY: RWANDA

In 2008, the Rwanda government commissioned a tourism master plan through UNWTO. At that time Rwanda was a small country in East Africa of which the world had only become widely aware as a result of the horrific genocide of 1994, in which some 800,000 people were massacred in about 100 days.

Fourteen years after the catastrophe, Rwanda's tourism sector was beginning to recover but still suffered from significant constraints: a large proportion of the wildlife in its national parks had been killed for food during the crisis, investment had dried up, it had few direct international flight connections, and the country's image was primarily associated with violence. In addition, its regional neighbours were three of Africa's best-established tourist destinations – Uganda, Kenya and Tanzania – all of which offered a similar wildlife-based product and competed for the same markets. Rwanda was also landlocked which drove up the cost of imported goods.

Rwanda, however, did have one iconic product that differentiated it from most of its rivals and proved to have international appeal – its mountain gorillas. Publicity for the gorillas, notably by Dian Fossey, and popular films such as *Gorillas in the Mist* helped stimulate widespread interest in the destination. It also had three national parks each with different natural characteristics, a distinctive landscape (Land of a Thousand Hills) and one of the beautiful Great Lakes along its border with the Democratic Republic of Congo (DRC). It has a good road network and all its main attractions can be reached easily from Kigali in the centre.

Rwanda's urgent priorities in 2008 were the need to differentiate the product in order to reduce reliance on the gorillas; and to increase foreign revenues, by extending the average length of stay and attracting more high-end visitors: too many visitors would spend just two or three days in the country, essentially to see the gorillas, before crossing the border to Uganda or Tanzania on a multi-destination tour. A key aim also was to spread the benefits of tourism more widely, to marginalized communities such as the Batwa pygmy tribes that inhabit the Virunga mountains.

The master plan included a number of key product development recommendations, including the building of a major conference and exhibition complex in the capital, Kigali, on the basis that this type of facility was lacking in the East Africa region and offered an opportunity to attract valuable high-spending 'MICE' markets (meetings, incentives, conferences, and exhibitions). By good fortune, the president was persuaded to take an interest in tourism and subsequently gave the master plan the essential support it needed.

By 2018, the Kigali Conference and Exhibition Village was attracting nearly 40,000 delegates and USD 56m in MICE revenues, and was ranked the second most popular destination in Africa, after Cape Town, in the ICCA ratings for international meetings and events. This development has stimulated the arrival of a number of high-profile international brand hotels in Kigali and helped drive the growth in visitor expenditures.

Over the same period, much has been done to rehabilitate the national parks. Major re-stocking of Akagera National Park , a savannah and wetland landscape, with lion and rhino among other species, has transformed its fortunes and significantly driven up visitor numbers. In recent years, the bold decision was taken to double the fees for viewing the mountain gorillas in the Virunga National Park from USD 750 to USD 1,500, an interesting and so far successful use of price controls to manage numbers.

The statistics illustrate Rwanda tourism's remarkable story of growth since 2008, and the value of pursuing a coordinated development strategy. From 508,000 foreign arrivals in 2008, numbers had risen to 1,135m by 2018, and foreign revenues from USD 224m to USD 616m by 2017. The total contribution of tourism to the economy was estimated at USD 1,129m, representing 12.7 per cent of GDP. Tourism was responsible for 11.1 per cent of employment and 30.5% of export revenues (*sources:* World Bank and WTTC).

NOTE

1. UNWTO publish a directory of multilateral and bilateral organizations that sponsor tourism development, including the availability of funding, and terms and conditions of each organization – see: https://www.e-unwto.org/doi/pdf/10.18111/9789284401345.

REFERENCES AND SOURCES

Selected Handbooks

Dredge, D. and Jenkins, J. (2007) *Tourism Policy and Planning*. Brisbane: John Wiley & Sons.
Hall, C. M. (2000) *Tourism Planning: Policies, Processes and Relationships*. Harlow: Prentice Hall.
Inskeep, E. (1991) *Tourism Planning: An Integrated and Sustainable Approach*. New York: John Wiley & Sons.
Veal, A. J. (2002) *Leisure and Tourism Policy and Planning*. Wallingford: CABI Publishing.

Online Handbook

GIZ (German international development agency) (n.d.) *Tourism Planning in Development Cooperation: A Handbook*. https://www.mascontour.info/images/PDF/2_GIZ-Handbook_Tourism_Development _Cooperation.pdf.

International Tourism Statistics and Research

European Commission: Eurostat – Tourism Statistics (monthly and annual). https:/ec.europa.eu/eurostat/ web/tourism/data/database.
UNWTO (Madrid) Annual visitor numbers and foreign revenues reports, regular research studies. https:/ www.e-unwto.org/toc/unwtotfb/current.
UNWTO (2019) UNWTO Tourism Highlights.
UNWTO (n.d.) *Glossary of Tourism Terms*. unwto.org.
World Economic Forum. *The Travel and Tourism Competitiveness Report and Index* (bi-annual): 'Benchmarks the T&T competitiveness of 140 economies and measures the set of factors and policies that enable the sustainable development of the Travel & Tourism (T&T) sector, which in turn contributes to the development and competitiveness of a country'.
WTTC: Economic Impact Country Reports (annual). www.wttc.org.

5. Commercialization strategies for tourism within parks and protected areas

Paul F. J. Eagles

INTRODUCTION

Parks and protected areas normally provide some level of tourism services to visitors. There are both direct tourism services and indirect tourism services in parks.

The direct tourism services include:

1. Recreation service fees, special events and services
2. Accommodation
3. Equipment rental
4. Food sales (restaurants and stores)
5. Parking
6. Merchandise sales (equipment, clothing, souvenirs)

The indirect tourism services include:

1. Roads, rail lines, aircraft landing strips
2. Electrical distribution
3. Water supply
4. Sewage and waste management
5. Policing and security

The direct tourism services are those provided directly to the visitor, such as accommodation and food sales. The indirect tourism services are all those that support the tourism infrastructure and visitor experience, such as roads and water supplies. All of these services must work within an integrated management structure for tourism services to be effectively delivered. For all such services, a decision must be made on what approach will be used; either provided by the park itself or provided by an outside body through a contractual arrangement.

This chapter outlines the options available to managers for the delivery of such services. It will attempt to provide a background for decision-makers on choosing the most appropriate service delivery approach.

INSOURCING VERSUS OUTSOURCING

There are two major options for the provision of all direct and indirect tourism services; insourcing and outsourcing. Insourcing involves the park management body providing those services with its own staff, facilities, and equipment. This can involve two forms of governance; (1) the fully public model, and (2) the public utility, parastatal model. Outsourcing involves the park management body contracting the provision of services to some form of outside body. The decision of which option to use must be done carefully with a full understanding of the current legal situation, the policy environment, and the implications of the choice.

The ideology of government provides a policy direction within which the manager must work. Some governments tend to prefer the use of the private, for-profit companies for the delivery of services. Others prefer the use of government administration for the delivery of services, such as the fully public model. This chapter will assume that the manager has the flexibility to choose a management option based on an independent analysis of the pros and cons of each model, irrespective of government ideology.

There are several papers that provide useful background to this chapter. Eagles (2008, 2009) provides a conceptual background for the governance models applicable in parks; finding eight management models that most commonly underpin recreation and tourism partnerships in parks and protected areas. More (2005) proposed governance models for parks, which he called: (1) fully public model; (2) public utility, parastatal model; (3) outsourcing; (4) private, non-profit ownership; and (5) private, for-profit ownership. The fully public model has a government agency operating all services. The public utility model is a government agency functioning like a private corporation; also known as a parastatal. Within this chapter the public utility, parastatal model is emphasized. Spenceley et al. (2017, 2019) provide a fulsome approach to understanding the advantages and disadvantages of using the insourcing and outsourcing options, based on a thorough analysis of the current experience of the national parks of Southern Africa. These papers are a good starting point for any major procurement exercise.

INSOURCING

Policy Background

Insourcing involves the park management body providing those services with its own staff, facilities, and equipment. Two of More's (2005) models are relevant here: (1) the fully public model; and (2) the public utility, parastatal model. The fully public model has the park agency as an expenditure agency; with all budgets coming from government, all income being returned to government, and all expenditures based on the budget provided by government. The fully public model has major disadvantages in tourism management, as budgets are fixed yearly with no ability to change with changing tourism volumes. In this model, increasing visitor use often becomes a threat to the park due to lack of ability to respond quickly to the changes. It is this model that forces many park agencies to outsource many park tourism functions. The public utility, parastatal model has the park operating as a company, retaining all income, which removes most of the disadvantages of the fully public model, as the park can retain income and fund those services directly from this income. Eagles (2014) describes one agency, Ontario Parks, moving from a fully public model to a public utility model in the mid-1990s. For the remainder of this chapter the phrase insourcing refers to the public utility, parastatal model of operation.

For insourcing to be effective, the park management structure must be capable of undertaking all of the functions necessary for effective operation. Four questions need to be answered by managers.

Question 1: Does the park have the capital needed to purchase, construct, and manage the facilities and the equipment needed for operation?

For example, a restaurant will require a building with all the necessary food storage, preparation and consumption facilities. This building will normally require electrical provision, water sources, sewage sources and waste services. There must be transportation access for both the restaurant employees and the clients. It may be necessary to provide accommodation for the employees. The upfront capital requirements will be large for just this one service; food provision (see Figure 5.1).

Figure 5.1   Concession restaurant operated in park-owned facility in Kruger National Park

Question 2: Does the park have the staff members that are qualified to deliver specialized services, such as food provision, recreation services, and sales?

If the answer is no, can the park hire people with the required skills? Can the park re-train current staff members for these services?

Question 3: In the case of service and product sales, does the park have an efficient manner of purchasing the required materials?

Many government agencies must use complicated and expensive tendering (procurement) procedures for all purchases. This can be very unwieldy for consumer goods, food, and ongoing consumables.

Question 4: In the case of service and product sales, does the park have an efficient manner of setting prices and collecting funds?

Many parks must obtain high level permission to set all prices, such as by the Minister, causing inefficient price setting. Many parks cannot retain all income; being required by policy to send this income to another government body. Many parks cannot retain income over the end of the fiscal year; making prebooking and payment impossible if the operation extends across the date of the end of the fiscal year.

If the park is unable to deal with all these questions, then outsourcing must be the chosen approach. If the park is able to deal with all the issues outlined in this section, there are advantages for insourcing of all tourism services.

One of the best examples of insourcing involves Canada's oldest park management agency: The Niagara Parks Commission. This body was established by provincial statute in 1885 with the express purpose of developing and managing the tourism activities on the Canadian side of Niagara Falls and the Niagara River. Niagara Parks owns and maintains over 1,325 hectares (3,274 acres) of parkland along the length of the Niagara River, stretching 56 kilometres (36 miles) from Fort Erie in the south to Niagara-on-the-Lake in the north (Niagara Parks Commission, 2019). Capital monies for the initial purchase of lands and the creation of parkland came from the provincial government in 1885. From the very beginning the agency was required to earn all operational funds from tourism fees and services. It has been successful in this regard during almost its entire 135 years of existence. The Niagara Parks Commission operates virtually all of the direct and indirect tourism services with its own staff; insourcing. This includes restaurants, souvenir stores, recreation facilities, parking facilities, a bank and money exchange office, transportation facilities, including a bus operation, and policing (see Figure 5.2). The only outsourced activity is a boat tour operation in the river near the falls. Niagara Parks employs over 1,700 staff; approximately 300 full-time and 1,400 seasonal employees. Given the seasonal nature of the operations, with highest visitation in the warm summer months, seasonal employment is high. The Niagara Parks Commission receives no government financing and raises its own revenues through various fees and charges levied on its visitors. This is an excellent example of insourcing. It shows that a park agency can operate effectively as a tourism delivery agency.

Pros of Insourcing

The pros of insourcing for a protected area authority include:

1. Income to the park could be from 30% to 50% higher than earned from concessionaires.
2. No costs of tendering for concessionaires.
3. No costs of contract monitoring and enforcement.
4. Lower potential risk exposure to the park from poor operators.
5. Lower risks to the park from bankruptcy of private concessionaires and contractors.
6. Ability to deal with staff issues more quickly than working through a contractor.

*Figure 5.2   Tourist activities at the lip of Niagara Falls, Canada. The viewing platform
                under the falls is one of many tourist facilities operated directly by the
                Niagara Parks Commission*

7. Contact between visitors and park staff maintained.
8. High levels of control of all aspects of tourism service management.
9. Reduced problem with reassigning tourism staff from elsewhere in the park due to unfore-
    seen or emergency demands.
10. Heightened ability to build a non-profit organization into the tourism service delivery
    system as park concessionaires often lobby against NGO operation of tourism services.
11. Heightened ability of park to obtain donations of time and money from visitors.
12. Development of higher levels of staff qualifications and expertise in hospitality and
    tourism.
13. Ability of managers to have rapid detection of service quality problems.

14. With good management, the park can move quickly to deal with changing tourism demands.

Cons of Insourcing

The cons of insourcing include:

1. Often there is little access to private capital monies for tourism infrastructure creation and renewal; capital monies must come from government, private sector, or donations.
2. Increased power transferred to public sector unions.
3. Slow decision-making due to complex public sector decision flows.
4. The park must have full administrative and business capabilities, such as the ability to retain income, set prices, set hours of operation, and set service delivery levels.
5. The park must have, or be able to obtain and retain, staff with qualifications and expertise in hospitality and tourism.
6. The park must have the ability to reward employees for exceptional work and deal with under-performing staff.
7. The park or park agency must have its own human resources office and staff.
8. The management authority may concentrate only on conservation, with little or no capability to undertake tourism management.

OUTSOURCING

Outsourcing involves the park management body contracting the provision of services to some form of outside body. There are many options for the outsourcing of tourism services, both direct and indirect. There are at least five options available for service delivery through outsourcing (Spenceley et al., 2017, 2019). These include:

1. Using for-profit, private companies
2. Using non-profit organizations
3. Using local community organizations
4. Using another government department
5. Using a joint-venture company (i.e. public–private, private–community, public–community or public–private–community)

Each of these five options is discussed below. Thompson et al. (2014) provide a thorough review of the various approaches to concessioning tourism services through outsourcing. Outsourcing is complex, as illustrated by the following example. The author of this chapter once provided a day-long seminar to the staff of a major Canadian park agency on the issue of outsourcing and concessions. The Director of the Agency sat through the entire day, and commented at the end: "I had no idea of the complexity of the management issues that I was asking my staff to tackle."

For-Profit, Private Companies

The most-used outsourcing option is that of for-profit, private companies. These entities have many advantages. The pros of outsourcing to a for-profit, private company include:

1. Access to specialized expertise
2. Access to capital needed for major construction and maintenance
3. Use of existing brand and market profile
4. The capability to adapt to changing market needs
5. Freedom on setting prices
6. The capability of rewarding employees for exceptional work, through incentives
7. Providing less exposure to public sector union demands

Private, for-profit companies are able to secure and provide capital monies for the construction and maintenance of facilities (see Figure 5.3). Once they obtain a contract from the park agency, they can obtain loans against the expectation of return from the contract. They usually provide specialized expertise and equipment. They may bring brand recognition, such as that of a hotel chain or a bus tour company.

Figure 5.3   Outfitter operation on a long-term lease within park-owned building on Lake Opeongo, Algonquin Provincial Park

The largest concession operation in national parks of the world is that of the National Park Service (NPS) of the USA. This park agency "administers nearly 500 concession contracts that, in total, gross over $1 billion annually. NPS concessioners employ more than 25,000 people in a variety of jobs during peak seasons, providing services ranging from food and lodging, to white water rafting adventures and motor coach tours" (NPS Concessions, 2019). The first director of the National Park Service, Stephen Mather, established the precedent of using private, for-profit concessionaires to provide many visitor services in the first decade of NPS operation after 1916. This approach became embedded in this park system and continues to the present (Mantell, 1979). It is also the approach of those park agencies that follow the American model of tourism delivery services, such as those of Brazil.

Highly specialized services are often operated by specialist companies. Kruger National Park has a small airport that was long used by park management for light aircraft for patrol across this vast park. After a lengthy process of bidding, evaluation and adjudication of offers, SANParks gave the Skukuza Airport Management Company the authority in 2013 to renovate and operate this airport to enable scheduled passenger services on airline aircraft (see Figure 5.4). This contract is a 10-year public–private agreement (Aviation News South Africa, 2019; Skukuza Airport, 2019).

Figure 5.4   Lounge built and managed by a contractor in Skukuza Airport in Kruger National Park

Non-Profit Companies and Organizations

A few parks, with the support of park agencies, use non-profit companies and organizations for the provision of direct tourism services, such as information programmes and retail sales. These are usually designed as a monopoly contract between the park and a dedicated non-profit company. Often these organizations are encouraged and designed with the park agency to involve local and public individuals in management. These are often known as Friends Organizations. An example of such an organization is the Friends of Algonquin Park (see Figure 5.5).

Figure 5.5   Store operated by the Friends of Algonquin Park in a park-owned facility

This organization describes its involvement as follows:

> The Friends of Algonquin Park (FOAP) is a non-profit Canadian registered charity for people passionate about Algonquin Park. We dedicate our resources to furthering the educational and interpretive programs to develop current and future stewards of Algonquin Park. We do this through research, the development and delivery of programs, workshops, and events, plus the production of educational materials. (FOAP, 2019)

These are normally membership organizations, to which people pay a yearly fee. They often concentrate on direct tourism services such as information provision, retail sales, equipment rental, and special events. They stimulate the donation of money and time for park-related activities.

Non-profits typically function in parks that have sufficient levels of public use to enable a pool of potential volunteers. The visitor experience to the parks stimulates some people to join and volunteer for a non-government organization. For example, Ontario Parks manages a system of 340 provincial parks, of which 110 are operating parks, and 295 conservation reserves. Only 27 provincial parks have Friends Groups operating (Friends of Ontario Parks, 2019). These are parks with substantial visitor flows.

Cherng and Heaney (2005) provide best practices for Friends Groups and national parks. Friends Groups can provide a valuable public voice on park management issues. They can often raise policy issues that park managers are reluctant to raise. Some park managers work with the Friends Group to raise policy issues. However, park managers are often cautious of the high public profile of such groups.

A few parks are operated almost entirely by Friends Groups. For example, the very active Friends of Misery Bay operate the Misery Bay Nature Reserve Provincial Park in Ontario (Friends of Misery Bay, 2019). This park is largely the creation of local community members who wished to preserve a unique limestone alvar ecosystem on Manitoulin Island on the shore of Lake Huron (see Figure 5.6). With the help of the Nature Conservancy of Canada they purchased shore lands. These people later coalesced into an NGO capable of managing the lands they had purchased. They supported the designation of the site as a Provincial Park due to the powerful legal framework available for management. The Gulf of Georgia Cannery Society operates the Georgia Cannery National Historic Site on behalf of Parks Canada (Gulf of Georgia Cannery, 2019); another example of an active NGO operating a public heritage site.

Figure 5.6   Misery Bay Nature Reserve Provincial Park is operated by the Friends of Misery Bay

Friends Groups in a region may band together to provide mutual support. For example, the Friends of Parks Inc. is an organization established to protect and represent the interests of the many individual Friends of Parks groups and affiliated groups in the State of South Australia. Together these groups, over 113 in 2016, represent a membership of over 5,000 volunteers whose common interest is the protection and enhancement of South Australia's natural and cultural heritage (Friends of Parks Inc., 2019). In South Australia, each group operates in parks and cultural sites through a Memorandum of Understanding with a government park agency.

These non-government organizations are usually given rights of operation in parks without a tender or bidding process. They often have monopoly rights to provide services. Park agencies may have staff dedicated to the encouragement of Friends Groups; including providing start-up funds and management advice. The services provided by Friends Groups may be restricted by the contract stipulations given to concessionaires. This occurs in US national parks where the Friends Groups can only provide services that do not compete with the for-profit concessionaire companies.

Local Community Organizations

Some parks involve local community organizations in various aspects of tourism service delivery. A local community is a social group whose members reside in a specific locality and have a common cultural and historic heritage. It can also refer to a group of individuals who interact within their immediate surroundings, such as a community of shared interest. A typical local community consists of business operators, public agency staff and residents, and their interactions can include sharing of resources, information and support as well as establishing commercial relationships between local businesses and consumers (Spenceley et al., 2017). In areas adjacent to parks, there may be several identifiable local communities, based on language, ethnicity, and place of residence. For large parks, there may be many local communities. For example, Algonquin Provincial Park in Ontario, Canada has 22 municipalities immediately adjacent to the park boundary. The second tier of municipalities that abut these 22 includes many more cities and major towns. Therefore, in large, complex parks there will be many local community organizations with an interest in the park.

These local community organizations are typically given rights of operation in parks without a tender or bidding process. They often have monopoly rights to provide services. Park agencies may have staff dedicated to help and encourage local community organizations.

Another Government Department

Outsourcing to another government department is a specialized activity, such as working with a local hospital for medical care, a transportation agency for road maintenance, or the military for security. In India, some national parks use the state tourist department to provide accommodation and food provision in the park. It is common for parks to maintain policy and contract relationships with other government agencies and bodies. The complex issue of search and rescue of park visitors often necessitates such arrangements. This may involve the military, the local search, rescue and ambulance service, the local police, the local medical personnel and facilities, and the media. A similar arrangement occurs where the park has undertaken preparation for a disaster, such a plane crash or major storm event. These arrangements with other government departments can involve a contract or a simple verbal agreement of cooperation.

Joint Venture Company

A joint venture partnership involves a contractual relationship amongst community partners, a private company, and possibly the park management. Joint ventures are typically undertaken to ensure that local community organizations have an identified stake in tourism operations. A joint venture company can involve a variety of partnerships, such as public–private, private–community, public–community or public–private–community (Spenceley et al., 2017). These are often designed to fulfil a specific political situation, such as a land claim agreement or the involvement of an indigenous people that gives preferential access to tourism programme delivery.

Snyman and Spenceley (2019) provide a fulsome set of examples of joint venture tourism partnership options and examples from Africa. These include a joint venture involving ownership of a lodge on government land. Another example is a joint venture lodge on community-owned land. A third option is a community-owned lodge on government land but with a private management company. There are many examples of privately owned lodges on community lands. And there is one example of a tripartite venture involving a local community, a private tourism company and a government park agency. Each of these joint ventures is designed to build on the strengths of each of the partners.

The Complications of Outsourcing

Outsourcing is a complicated and expensive management activity. This section of the chapter will discuss many of the issues involved with outsourcing. All outsourcing will involve some combination of licence, permit, lease and/or concession (see Table 5.1) (Spenceley et al., 2017).

A concession involves a special purpose contract providing a right to use public land for a commercial operation. The contracts can be from 10 to 50 years long. A lease involves a contract where the park allows an operation to use public land and facilities for a specified time period, such as a concessionaire using a park-owned building. A licence involves an authority giving a privilege of operation according to some level of quality control, such as a licence to operate a recreational activity. A permit is permission to operate for a short length of time, such as providing a bus tour.

There are many types of permits. Some parks allow tourist facilities through land use permits. This occurs when a company owns and operates facilities on park land. Camp Ahmek, one of seven children's camps in Algonquin Provincial Park, was established in 1921 and operates on parkland through a land use permit (see Figure 5.7). The camp owns facilities and operates programmes on park land and waters. This camp has had immense social impact in Canada as it has three Canadian Prime Ministers amongst its alumni, Pierre Trudeau, John Turner, and Justin Trudeau. Pierre Trudeau's government created more national parks than any other Canadian Prime Minister in history, and his son Justin is promoting the doubling of Canada's park estate. These camps were all created in the first decades of the last century and continue to operate through land use permits.

Table 5.1   Legal instruments for outsourcing

Type of legal instrument	Description	Length	Examples
Concession	A concession is the right to use land or other property for a specified purpose, granted by a government, company, or other controlling body. It can include a commercial operation and/or a piece of land. A tourism concession could provide accommodation, food and beverages, recreation, education, retail, and interpretive services.	10 to 40 years	Accommodation, restaurant, or retail facilities
Lease	A contractual agreement in which one party conveys an estate (i.e. land and facilities) to another party for a specified, limited time period. The lessor retains ownership in the property while the lessee obtains rights to use the property. Typically a lease is paid for.	5 to 30 years	Use of fixed infrastructure such as accommodation, airports, restaurants, shops, etc. for a rental fee
Licence	Gives permission to a legally competent authority to exercise a certain privilege that, without such authorization, would constitute an illegal act. Often seen by the public as a form of quality control and requires due diligence by the competent authority, in contrast to a permit. Possession of the land is not granted through the licence. Licences give protected area authorities the ability to screen applicants to ensure that they fulfil a set of conditions.	Up to 10 years	Vehicle-based tours (e.g. game drives, hot-air ballooning, white-water rafting, boat cruise) using operator's own equipment
Permit	A temporary form of permission giving the recipient approval to do a lawful activity within the protected area. Permits normally expire within a short length of time. Usually the number of permits is large and limited by social or environmental considerations. In most cases, permits are given to anyone who pays the corresponding fee.	Up to 10 years	Activities such as guiding, canoeing, hunting, and climbing using operator's own equipment

Figure 5.7   Camp Ahmek, a children's camp in Algonquin Provincial Park, operates through a land use permit

For the first 124 years of operation of Ontario Provincial Parks, land use permits were the primary legal mechanism to allow private use of land in provincial parks. These permits were used for private cottages and children's camps. After 31 December 2017, cottage land use permit holders were offered a licence of occupation (Ontario Parks, 2019). An important point of this discussion is that each park agency will operate within its own government legal structure for concessions, licences, permits and leases.

Thompson et al. (2014) outline the necessary components of the legal framework required for concessions in protected areas:

1. The park must have clear foundational laws and regulations.
2. The public must support and have input into the types of concessions permitted in protected areas.
3. Concession law should be drafted with input from potential concessionaires, environmental groups, the general public and other stakeholders.
4. The law must include only the most important general provisions relating to concessions and allow the implementing agency the flexibility to establish the details through regulations and policy.
5. The law must be implemented through thorough regulations and policies.
6. The implementation of concession law, regulations, and policies must be regularly evaluated and modified when necessary.
7. Provision must be made for oversight and monitoring of concession activities.

The park manager must be familiar with the legal and policy issues involved with each of these legal instruments; concession, lease, licence and permit. All stipulations contained within these instruments must be monitored to ensure that the contractor and contractee are doing what was agreed upon.

A contractee is the project owner (also called client or principal) that enters into a contract with a contractor or vendor and receives specified goods and services under the terms of the contract. The contractee has duties and responsibilities dictated under the contract. Contract disputes can occur when the contractor feels that the contractee has not fulfilled his or her responsibility or vice versa. An example includes a dispute where the contractor operating a tourist lodge at the end of a park road feels that the park is not fulfilling its commitment to keep the access road in good condition.

If the contract requirements are not being followed, then a dispute mechanism is triggered. Depending on the contract and the willingness of both sides to cooperate, dispute resolution can occur in different ways:

1. Resolving dispute through negotiation
2. Alternative dispute resolution such as mediation and arbitration
3. Litigation in court

The resolution of compliance disputes is time consuming and expensive. The ultimate arbitrator will be the courts, and court actions can take many years for resolution.

Outsourcing management can be fraught with political interference; as the contractor uses political contacts inside and outside the park management to influence contract implementation. Contractors may use their political contacts to force park managers to agree to their demands, including deviations from contract stipulations. The author of this chapter was told personally by five directors of state park systems in the USA that their number one management problem was political interference by park concessionaires who went directly to the governor's office over contract administration issues. These contractors signed their contracts; then deviated from some of the contract stipulations. They subsequently went to the governor's office in an attempt to stop the park managers from enforcing the agreed upon contract stipulations.

When a body outside the park administration is involved in the delivery of service, there is a loss of contact between the park visitor and the park employees. The visitor is more likely to see the contract employee, rather than the park employee. This may be confusing to the visitor who usually will not understand the contract arrangements. For example, the US National Park System employed approximately 27,000 people in 2018, while the concessionaires employed more than 25,000 people (NPS Concessions, 2019). Since the vast majority of the concession employees have front line responsibilities in serving the public, the visitor is more likely to encounter a concession employee rather than a park service employee during their recreation activities. This can become a problem when that employee is not fully aware of park management policies.

When an outside body earns the income from the provision of a service the park will lose from 30% to 50% of the cash flow that could have been earned by the park (Lohuis, pers. comm.). Therefore, the provision of visitor services with concessionaires and contractors is not a good way for the park to earn income. In the National Park Service the average franchise fee in 2014 was 6.9% of gross income, earning the park service $85.4 million (McDowall, 2015). This is a very modest return to the park service when considering the gross concessionaire income was $1.3 billion in 2014.

Park concessionaires will only operate programmes which provide a financial return. Park operations that normally do not provide a financial return include: (1) education programmes for schools, (2) resource management, (3) policing, (4) resource inventory, and (5) search and rescue operations. The park management must operate such programmes. If the park turns park facilities over to concessionaires then the income the park earns from the concessionaires must be devoted to all operations including those listed above. The phrase 'tourism vulture' has been applied to park concessionaires who take over all the programmes that can earn income, leaving the park with only the programmes that cannot earn income.

The staffing of outsourced operations may involve problems. In first world park systems, many concession staff members are paid the lowest possible wage; typically the minimum wage of the responsible jurisdictions. This may create a cadre of individuals in a park with very low incomes and the incentive to obtain benefits from illegal or alternative means. Park managers have reported that concession employees sometimes resort to petty crime due to their low incomes. Concession operations may involve the rapid turnover of staff; with several concurrent problems, including the constant need for retraining. In Africa, many concession employees earn higher salaries than park staff; reducing staff turnover.

Even though the contracts may stipulate that employees of the contractors must have certain levels of education and training, this is difficult to monitor and police. Many contract staff may have no knowledge or sympathy for park conservation objectives. Their primary field of training may not involve knowledge of park objectives.

One of the major issues involved with contracting out services is answering the question, often posed by the late Australian scholar Dr Elery Hamilton Smith, namely "Who picks up the broken glass?" Any contractor has specific duties outlined in the contract. For example, a contractor who cuts the grass in a park will only cut the grass; he or she will not accept responsibilities outside the contract, such as picking up broken glass. Therefore, all management responsibilities outside those specified in the contract must be assumed by park staff or volunteers. The contractor will not be available for a search and rescue effort, for fighting a forest fire, or to deal with a rogue animal. Contractors may be asked to provide such services, but this is difficult to place into a contract due to their open-ended status.

One of the goals for all staff is to create a positive image for the park and for the park management. Park visitors often do not discriminate between staff who work for a concessionaire and those who work for the park. For example, poor service quality by concession staff impacts directly on the visitor's overall view of the park's management and vice versa. The park visitor will naturally ask the contract employee questions concerning a whole suite of park-related issues. The contract employee may not know the answers to many of those questions, and may inadvertently provide inaccurate information. Therefore careful training of all concessionaire staff in park policies is essential.

One of the major reasons for moving from park-owned and operated operations of facilities to park-owned but privately operated operations is due to the high cost of facility renovation and upkeep. Contractors may be willing to invest large sums of money into public facilities if they are given long contract periods and are assured that they can earn a profit. This forces the park to give long-term contracts, greater than 10 years and possibly up to 50 years. Long-term contracts mean that park control over facilities and programmes is lost for long periods. The managers may not have access to these facilities to monitor their condition. Contractors typically stop repairing facilities in the last five years of a contract, unless there is a good likelihood of renewal of the contract.

What happens when the contractor is unable to earn the money they anticipated in their financial predictions? They may demand contract changes. And there are examples of contractors taking legal actions against a park under the concept that the park prospectus was misleading which led them into a situation for which they were unprepared. They might simply drop the contract and suddenly cease operation.

The issue of capital maintenance of facilities that are owned by the park but used by contractors is very important, and fraught with expensive complications. The example of the USA national parks is illustrative. Under the 1965 law covering concessions "at the end of a concessions contract the improvements completed over the life of that contract are valued by taking reconstruction costs and subtracting depreciation to come up with a dollar value that does not exceed fair market value. That amount was known as 'possessory interest'" (Repanshek, 2015). Contractors were owed the value of the possessory interest if another contractor takes over; a figure that could be millions of dollars. Over time the value of possessory interest owed became so large that it stymied new bidders from being able to take over the contract. In 1998 the US Congress changed the possessory interest formula, but this new formula did not encourage increased competition in bidding when contracts were up for renewal. This example shows that the need to deal with the ongoing costs of capital maintenance remains a controversial issue in national park management in the USA and elsewhere.

There is a major problem for the park when a contractor goes bankrupt. Spenceley et al. (2017) detail the outcome of the bankruptcy of a contractor in a national park in Canada. Glacier Park Lodge operated a hotel, two restaurants, and an auto service station near the TransCanada Highway in Glacier National Park in Canada under a concession contract. In 2008 the facility concessionaire sold the business to another concessionaire. In 2012 Parks

Canada declined to renew the lease on the land and buildings, causing the new owners to shut down the business. Multiple lawsuits resulted involving the initial owners, the new owners, and Parks Canada. The major outcome is that this facility is now empty, derelict, and declining rapidly. With failure of the business, the protected area authorities ultimately must assume capital costs, including those of reclamation of the facilities and lands. The bankruptcy of a sole-source operation, such as a company providing tourist booking services, can be very problematic. The park must scramble to try to restore this service. The issue of bankruptcy of a contractor has received scant attention in the park management literature.

The right to transfer or sell the concession contract to another party must be stipulated in the contract. This right is often demanded by contractors as it increases the value of the contract. Any new contractor must assume all the rights and responsibilities of the contract. Transfer can involve a high degree of training and monitoring by the park staff to ensure that the new contractor understands the full implications of all contract stipulations. From the point of view of the park managers, the change to a new contractor will involve much work in ensuring that all the contract arrangements are understood and implemented.

The contractor may suddenly change key contract stipulations, such as hours of operations, prices, or service levels, without park approval. In the absence of ongoing contract monitoring, these facts may not be known to the park managers. This can have implications for the visiting public and for the park management.

Monitoring all the stipulations in the various legal instruments can be expensive and time consuming. Since most parks have low staff numbers, parks may not properly fulfil their contract monitoring responsibilities. They may not be proactive through systematic monitoring; relying only on visitor complaints to stimulate action.

Contracts with for-profit companies will normally stipulate the level of competition allowed. Many contractors demand monopolies, to ensure adequate financial return. This may limit the ability of the park to utilize non-profit service operations, such as Friends Groups or Community Groups.

It is often difficult to include in concession contracts demands for levels of education of staff, local employment, and local sourcing of products. Even if they are included in the contract, it is difficult and expensive for the park managers to monitor such contractual elements.

An important issue is the policy of setting prices for concession products or services. The simplest approach for the park manager is to let the contractors set prices according to what the market can bear. However, since many contracts are monopolies in remote areas where there is no nearby competition to constrain prices, there is no competitive market. This can lead to very high prices. One response to such a situation is for the park agency to regulate all prices. The National Park Service of the USA regulates the prices of all the services and products within 500 concession contracts in the system. There are thousands of products in 27 categories of products, varying from cigarettes to food services, each with a different level of markup from cost. Cigarettes are allowed an 18% markup, while ice is allowed 161% (NPS Commercial Services Program, 2019). The cost of administration of this rate management programme is not published, but it must be large.

Mantell (1979) argued that the concessions approach in the USA national parks gave the contractors too much protection. It enabled them to wield an unjustifiable degree of influence over management. They may become so powerful as to dictate the policies under which they work and prosper. Mantell (1979, p. 52) cautions "Policies need to be devised which will not only reduce the influence of concessioners, but also free the Park Service from excessive management burdens." The issue of understanding the cost of administration of contracts and concessions in parks has received scant attention in the park management literature.

Typically, the contracts between the parks and the contractors are secret documents that are not open to public scrutiny (Frost and Laing, 2018). Over many years of research in this field, the author of this chapter has only been able to obtain one copy of a concession contract out of the hundreds requested. This makes the analysis of such contracts very challenging for scholars; it also raises suspicions in the public's mind. Thompson et al. (2014) maintained that one basic principle of outsourcing was that the public must support and have input into the types of concessions permitted in protected areas. This principle cannot be fulfilled when concession contracts are secret and not available for public review.

The issue of insourcing and outsourcing is strongly politicized, with some governments prone to encourage the use of profit-making private companies to the exclusion of other options. Cole (2018) warns against procurement decisions being made by political ideology. Such a plea is desirable, but not realistic in many situations.

Cole (2018) maintains there are three main reasons for failures of outsourcing:

1. The client is totally unable to manage the contract (for whatever reasons) and thinks that bringing it in-house will solve the problem.
2. The specification was flawed from the outset which meant that failure was always the most likely outcome.
3. The business case was flawed and the service should never have been outsourced in the first place.

Schniederjans et al. (2005) provide a thorough review of the concepts and methodologies that can help managers understand and use outsourcing strategies. Bourbeau (2004) found that the evidence regarding the effectiveness of outsourcing is minimal, confusing, and highly subjective. He also maintains that outsourcing can save money, but usually at the expense of service quality.

ELEMENTS OF A PROSPECTUS

The provision of contracts within a park is typically governed by government procurement policies. For the use of for-profit companies applying for a concession this usually involves competitive bidding through a tendering procedure. There are fundamental issues that must be included in a concession bidding, granting, monitoring, and enforcement programme (Eagles et al., 2009; Thompson, et al., 2014) listed below:

1. A comprehensive business plan
2. The regulatory obligations of concessionaires
3. All relevant laws, regulations and policies
4. The environmental policies and practices
5. Product selections
6. Pricing
7. Payment systems for contracts
8. Insurance requirements
9. Staff qualifications

10. Education and cultural education of visitors
11. Customer service programmes
12. Reporting and record keeping requirements
13. Human resource management
14. Staff housing and incentives
15. Utilities and services

Not only must all these issues be understood by park managers and potential concessionaires before contractor selection begins, they must be fully outlined in contracts. Park agencies are typically not staffed with personnel that have formal training in tender policies, procedures and laws. Such people must be hired or obtained from other government agencies. The tendering process is complicated, takes a long time, and is expensive for a park and a park agency. Of course, park agencies can hire people with specialized expertise in business management if it is deemed to be necessary.

Frost and Laing (2018) describe the legal problems involved with one public–private partnership on Phillip Island, Australia. Soon after the contract was given, it was beset by problems. A long court action found in favour of the private developer, who was awarded $A37 million in damages, with ownership of the centre returning to the state. This court decision revealed the complexity of legal issues that arise from contracts for public–private partnerships. It further revealed that advanced legal advice is necessary in the development and administration of all such contracts. "The Seal Rocks case does not invalidate the whole issue of public–private partnerships for tourism services within national parks, but it does highlight that parks agencies must have sufficient capability and expertise to effectively manage complex contracts and relationships" (Frost and Laing, 2018, p. 954).

To the knowledge of the author of this chapter, there are no educational courses available for park staff on the issue of concessions specifically and commercialization of tourism in parks more generally. This is a major deficiency in park management education worldwide.

CHARACTERISTICS OF SUCCESSFUL TOURISM CONCESSIONING

Spenceley et al. (2016) outline 14 characteristics of successful programmes for outsourcing tourism services through concessions:

1. For all tourism and concession programmes, the conservation objectives of the park must be recognized and all programmes must adhere to conservation regulations. Some parks may not be attractive for tourism and some may be too sensitive for recreational activities.
2. Successful tourism programmes should help achieve the conservation goals of parks.
3. Tourism programmes in parks must be as sustainable as possible.
4. Local community participation is essential for public acceptance and support of tourism.
5. The market viability must be firmly established early in the planning process.
6. There must be stakeholder awareness and strong engagement of those parties.
7. There must be a concession framework for successful concession agreements.
8. The concessions must be in agreement with, and supported by, a management plan.
9. The most appropriate concession model must be chosen.
10. The procurement procedures must be transparent and clearly stated.

11. The contracts must be effective and protect the interests of all parties.
12. Long-term contract management must be systematically undertaken.
13. Risks occur with all concessions programmes. Successful concessions manage risk by identifying, mitigating, and monitoring risk through stakeholder engagement, site assessments, regular reporting, adequate due diligence, and employing experienced, and reputable, technical personnel.
14. All concession programmes must be monitored and evaluated in order to understand the impact and performance of all contracts.

The 14 valuable principles reveal the complexity of programmes for outsourcing tourism services through concessions. It also argues for specialized staff in park agencies with professional level training in concessions, licences and permits.

MAKING A DECISION

Ultimately the manager must choose the management model that is most appropriate. This chapter has provided information to assist with the decision process. Spenceley et al. (2017, 2019) provided a table of relative benefits of each of the five main management options (see Table 5.2). This table does not include the use of other government bodies since each of these are individually negotiated and operated, making it difficult to discern generalizable principles.

The contents of this table provide a framework to help decision-makers determine which management model is most appropriate for their context.

IMPLICATIONS

This chapter concludes that all five options available for service delivery of tourism services through outsourcing are valid and currently in practice. Additionally, insourcing of the delivery of tourism services is also valid, and used (Spenceley et al., 2017). Insourcing is best done within a parastatal model of governance (Eagles, 2008). Therefore, the senior policy makers and managers must carefully evaluate all six options and choose the one that is most suitable within the legal, policy, and financial environment that is currently in the park system.

Typically, a park may use several of these options. For example, the food services may be provided by a private concessionaire while the information service may be provided by a Friends Group. Table 5.3 outlines the varied options used for some of the direct and indirect tourist services operated within Algonquin Provincial Park in Canada. The decision for each of these activities was made by a suite of managers over the 127 years of operation of this park. Once a precedent was made, it then became the de facto method of operation from then on.

National parks in Africa are unique in that one service may be divided amongst several different management options in a park. For example, in Kruger National Park the accommodation services are provided in some camps by the park itself (see Figure 5.8), in other locales by private concessionaires, and in another locale by a local Community Group.

Table 5.2   Relative benefits of five management options for tourism services

Theme	Criteria for choosing partnership type	Outsource: For-profit	Outsource: Community	Outsource: NGO	Outsource: Joint venture	Insource: PA Authority
Financial issues	Protected area (PA) and government costs	Low cost to PA	Variable costs to PA	Low cost to PA	Moderate cost to PA	High cost to PA
	Gaining income for the PA	Moderate	Low	Moderate	Moderate	Moderate, depends on policy
	Expense of contract management, monitoring	High	High	Moderate	High	Low
	Expense of tendering procedures	High	High, variable	High	High	None
	Difficulty and expense of monitoring finance	High	High	Low	High	Low
	Ability of the PA to function like a business	Needed	Needed	Needed	Needed	Needed
	Expense of resolving conflicts	High	High, variable	High, variable	High	Low
Tourism operations	Quality of visitor services	High	Low (unless managed by for-profit sub-contractor)	Moderate, variable	High	Moderate, depends on tourism policy
	Specialized tourism expertise	High	Low	Hired by NGO	High	Hired by PA
	PA seen as competing with private enterprise	No	Low	Low	No	High
	Access to new tourist markets	More access	Low access	More access	More access	Depends on PA policy
	Tourism workable with low visitor numbers	No	No	Yes	No	No
	Direct contact of PA staff with PA visitors	Low	Low	Low	Low	High
Socio-economic impact	Opportunity for community equity	Depends on contracts	High	High	High	High
	Business and job creation for local population	Moderate, variable	High	Moderate	High	High
	Flexibility in purchasing	High	High	High	High	Low
	Concession selection process open and transparent	High	High	Low	High	None
Governance	Control of services by PA	Moderate	Low	Low	Moderate	High
	Potential source of corruption during procurement	Moderate	Moderate	Moderate	Moderate	Moderate
	Concessionaire influence PA authority policy	Moderate	Low	Low	High	None
	Concessionaires gain political power	Moderate	Yes	Moderate	Moderate	Not a problem
	Power of public sector unions	Low	Low	Low	High, variable	High

Theme	Criteria for choosing partnership type	Outsource: For-profit	Outsource: Community	Outsource: NGO	Outsource: Joint venture	Insource: PA Authority
	Political influences on PA management by concessionaire	High potential	Moderate potential	Moderate potential	High potential	None, no concessionaire
	Liability exposure	Concessionaire	Concessionaire	Concessionaire	Concessionaire	Protected Area
	Conflict over PA objectives	Moderate	High	Moderate	High	None
Risk	Reversibility of decisions	Low	Low	High	Low	High
	Transaction costs to establish partnership	Moderate	High	Moderate	High	None
	Difficulty of removing a bad concessionaire	High	High	Moderate	High	None, no concessionaire
	Bankruptcy of the concessionaire	Problem	Problem	Problem	Problem	Not a problem
	Public sector union contracts	None	None	None	None	Full
	Employment rules and regulations	Company rules	Government rules	Company rules	Company rules	Government rules
	Staff working on all PA needs	Seldom	Sometimes	Sometimes	Sometimes	Not a problem
Human resources	Contract management expertise needed in protected area	Yes	Yes	Yes	Yes	Somewhat true
	Ability to use volunteers	Moderate	High	High	Moderate	Moderate
	Ability to obtain donations of money and time	Moderate	High	High	High	Low
	Likelihood of contributing to biodiversity conservation	Moderate	Low	High	Moderate	High
Environment and conservation	Likelihood of applying an environmental management system (e.g. renewable energy, water conservation, recycling)	Moderate	Low	High	High	Low
	Likelihood of using of third party certification to demonstrate 'sustainability'	High	Moderate	Moderate	High	Low

Table 5.3   Complexity of tourism services in Algonquin Provincial Park

Activity	Manager	Structure
Children's camps	Private companies	Land lease
Campgrounds	Park agency	Agency operation
Food and souvenir stores	Private companies	Concessions
Educational programme	Friends of Algonquin	Contract
Picnic sites	Park agency	Agency operation
Lodges	Private companies	Land lease
Highway 60	Ministry of Transport	Agency operation
Trails	Friends of Algonquin	Contract
Bus tours	Private companies	Permit and agency operation
Cottages	Private individuals	Licence of occupation
Wilderness canoeing	Park agency	Permit and agency operation

Figure 5.8   Rondovel operated by park agency and park staff in Kruger National Park

This system of setting up internal competition amongst the service delivery options is unique and worthy of emulation.

Thompson et al. (2014) describe the complexities of outsourcing through concessions within parks and protected areas. Eagles (2014) provided an analysis of a park agency, Ontario Parks, which moved from government funding of operations to tourism funding starting in 1996. This park system moved from 32% cost recovery to 90% cost recovery through the judicious use of both outsourcing and insourcing of tourism services. Basically, if the park could make money from the service it was operated internally.

There is a major concern in most park management agencies in that very few employees have formal training in the field of contracts and concessions. This lack of in-depth understanding makes the process fraught with danger for the park and the park agency. Most current employees have learned this field through on the job experience.

Reviewers of this chapter consistently reported that through much of Africa the private, for-profit tourism operators consistently provide higher levels of service quality to the tourists than does the park agency staff. This is to be expected when the park staff members are hired for resource and conservation management, with little or no training or reward systems for tourism delivery. However, such problems can be solved with tourism operations within parks being operated in such a way that staff are hired for their expertise in business and tourism management, and are rewarded accordingly. There is nothing fundamental in park management that stops park management agencies from operating tourism effectively, as revealed by the examples in this chapter from the Niagara Parks Commission and Ontario Parks, both in Canada. Park agencies only need to be designed so that they can operate both conservation programmes and tourism services.

It is very important that conservationists understand that effective resource management requires sufficient levels of financial and human resources. Such resources can be had through effective utilization of the income from sustainable tourism activities through the most appropriate management delivery system.

The majority of the literature dealing with commercialization of tourism in parks favours outsourcing of tourism services; essentially giving money and control to private companies. The advantages of insourcing have been underestimated and poorly documented. This chapter attempts to better balance this discussion.

It is clear that financial sustainability of the park is enhanced when the park owns and operates the tourism facilities directly and operates like a tourism company. When the park does not control the hotels and restaurants, it will lose future income and some level of control. This reduces the financial resources available for nature conservation. The income from the hotels, restaurants and stores can be important income sources for nature conservation management.

The decision on which management approach to use in the operation of direct and indirect tourism services is complex and important. It is one of the most critical decisions in park and sustainable tourism management.

REFERENCES

Aviation News South Africa (2019) Skukuza Airport Management Company wins bid, accessed 19 August 2019 at http://www.bizcommunity.com/Article/196/583/99553.html.

Bourbeau, J. A. (2004) Has outsourcing/contracting out saved money and/or improved service quality? A vote-counting analysis. PhD thesis, Virginia Polytechnic Institute and State University.

Cherng, M. and Heaney, M. (2005) *Friends Group Best Practices Report*. Washington, DC: Center for Park Management, National Parks and Conservation Association.

Cole, K. (2018) Insourcing and outsourcing: No place for political ideology. *The Catalyst*, 18, accessed 17 August 2019 at http://library.sps-consultancy.co.uk/documents/newsletter-archive/the-catalyst-autumn-2018.pdf.

Eagles, P. F. J. (2008) Governance models for parks, recreation and tourism. In K. S. Hanna, D. A. Clark and D. S. Slocombe (eds.), *Transforming Parks: Protected Area Policy and Management in a Changing World*. London: Routledge, 39–61.

Eagles, P. F. J. (2009) Governance criteria in parks and protected areas. *Journal of Sustainable Tourism*, 17(1), 1–18.

Eagles, P. F. J. (2014) Fiscal implications of moving to tourism finance for parks: Ontario Provincial Parks. *Managing Leisure*, 19(1), 1–17.

Eagles, P. F. J., Baycetich, C. M., Chen, X., Dong, L., Halpenny, E., Kwan, P. B., Lenuzzi, J. J., Wang, X., Xiao, H. and Zhang, Y. (2009) *Guidelines for Planning and Management of Concessions, Licenses and Permits for Tourism in Protected Areas*. Waterloo, ON: University of Waterloo.

Friends of Algonquin Park (2019) *Friends of Algonquin Park*, accessed 16 August 2019 at http://www.algonquinpark.on.ca/foap/.

Friends of Misery Bay (2019) *Come and visit the park*, accessed 18 August 2019 at http://www.miserybay.ca/index.php.

Friends of Ontario Parks (2019) *Ontario Parks is proud to be supported by 27 Friends organizations*, accessed 17 August 2019 at http://www.ontarioparks.com/friends.

Friends of Parks Inc. (2019) *About us*, accessed 18 August 2019 at http://www.friendsofparkssa.org.au/about-us.

Frost, W. and Laing, J. (2018) Public–private partnerships for nature-based tourist attractions: The failure of Seal Rocks. *Journal of Sustainable Tourism*, 26(6), 942–956.

Gulf of Georgia Cannery (2019) *Our Mission*, accessed 17 August 2019 at http://gulfofgeorgiacannery.org/about.

Lohuis, J. (pers. comm.) Personal communication on the issue of concession finance.

Mantell, M. (1979) Preservation and use: Concessions in the National Parks. *Ecology Law Quarterly*, 8(1), 1–54.

McDowall, L. (2015) *Modernizing the National Park Service Concession Program*. Office of the Congressional and Legislative Affairs, U.S. Department of the Interior, accessed 17 August 2019 at http://www.doi.gov/ocl/modernizing-national-park-service-concession-program.

More, T. (2005) From public to private: Five concepts of park management and their consequences. *The George Wright Forum*, 22(2), 12–20.

National Park Services Concessions (2019) *Ensuring High Quality Visitor Services*, accessed 17 August 2019 at http://nps.gov/subjects/concessions/index.htm.

Niagara Parks Commission (2019) *About Niagara Parks*, accessed 17 August 2019 at https://www.niagaraparks.com/corporate/about-us/#:~:text=In%20its%20long%20history%2C%20Niagara,the%2DLake%20in%20the%20north.

NPS Commercial Services Program (2019) *2019 Convenience Item and Fuel Markup Percentages*. National Park Service Technical Bulletin C3823, accessed 17 August 2019 at http://nps.gov/subjects/concessions/upload/2019-Convenience-Store-and-Fuel-Markup-TB.pdf.

Ontario Parks (2019) *Algonquin Cottage Lot Transfer Fact Sheet*, accessed 19 August 2019 at www.ontarioparks.com/documents/content/12/176.

Repanshek, K. (2015) National Park Service sitting on half-a-billion dollars of Concession Obligations. *National Parks Traveler*, accessed 17 August 2019 at http://www.nationalparkstraveler.org/2015/03/national-park-service-sitting-half-billion-dollars-concessions-obligations26283.

Schniederjans, M. J., Schniederjans, A. M. and Schniederjans, D. G. (2005) *Outsourcing and Insourcing in an International Context*. London: Routledge.

Skukuza Airport (2019) *Skukuza Airport*, accessed 19 August 2019 at http://skukuzaairport.com.

Snyman, S. and Spenceley, A. (2019) *Private Sector Tourism in Conservation Areas in Africa*. Wallingford: CABI.

Spenceley, A., Nevill, H., Coelho, C. F. and Souto, M. (2016) *An Introduction to Tourism Concessioning: 14 Characteristics of Successful Programs*. Washington, DC: World Bank Group.

Spenceley, A., Snyman, S. and Eagles, P. (2017) *Guidelines for Tourism Partnerships and Concessions for Protected Areas: Generating Sustainable Revenues for Conservation and Development*. Report to the Secretariat of the Convention on Biological Diversity and IUCN.

Spenceley, A., Snyman, S. and Eagles, P. (2019) A decision framework on the choice of management models for park and protected area tourism services. *Journal of Outdoor Recreation and Tourism*, 25, 72–90.

Thompson, A., Massyn, P. J., Pendry, J. and Pastorelli, J. (2014) *Tourism Concessions in Protected Natural Areas: Guidelines for Managers*. New York: United Nations Development Programme.

6. Feasibility studies, business plans and predicting returns for new lodging facilities

P. J. Massyn

INTRODUCTION

Tourism today is competitive, diverse and globally integrated. It is a volatile industry facing tough competition and increasingly selective customers that are able to assess attractions and experiences through instant access to information about alternative destinations and comparative products. Planning lodging facilities – the focus of this chapter – must take these complexities into account if new investments are to be made with any degree of confidence.

This chapter is being written at a time of extreme disruption in global and national economies. The COVID-19 pandemic, currently ravaging the world, has dramatically highlighted the unique risks facing tourism in an age of global interconnectivity. In good times, the travel industry benefited enormously from the increased integration of the contemporary world. As people, goods, services and information flowed around the globe with ever greater ease, tourism flourished. New ventures, including high-end lodging facilities, developed in places hitherto outside the reach of the global economy. They drew travellers to some of the world's most remote areas bringing jobs, spending and other benefits to the wider communities within which they operated. In many places, local economies thrived, sometimes becoming dependent on such businesses and the ease of movement that underpinned them. But the very interconnectivity that allowed these ventures to flourish also made them particularly vulnerable to a global pandemic – an external event wholly beyond the control of local actors – that abruptly severed the flow of people, goods and services, closing individual businesses and plunging the sector as a whole into deep crisis. At the time of writing, we do not yet know what the long-term effect of the COVID-19 pandemic will be. It seems certain though that travel will remain curtailed for a long time; tourism, particularly cross-border travel, is likely to be one of the last sectors of the economy to revive, and in ways that are currently impossible to predict.

Was the pandemic a "'Black Swan' hence something so unexpected not planning for it is excusable" (Taleb and Spitznagel, 2020) or was it foreseeable and should developers and operators have assessed it as a predictable risk when they planned – and subsequently managed – new tourism ventures? Even if a global pandemic were not foreseeable as a specific adverse event, should planners and managers have built contingency into their business models to buffer against large external shocks such as pandemics, terrorist attacks or climate change? Has the interconnectivity of the world – and the threats that come with it – made such buffering more necessary than ever? This chapter will return to these questions as it considers how to go about assessing the feasibility of new investment in lodging facilities.

Lodges are complex businesses. They typically provide not only overnight accommodation but also a range of related services such as food, drinks, retail and activities. Many facilities offer their guests much more than a bed. They feature in-house restaurants, bars, shops, transfers and activities. In addition to their internal complexity, these businesses also operate in intricate ecosystems, relying on networks of suppliers that stretch far beyond local economies. They buy goods and services from a range of providers, rely on multi-skilled workforces and draw diverse, well-informed, often international, travellers via multiple channels. New ventures frequently involve large investments and require state-of-the-art know-how. They face strong competition from established rivals and an array of risks. Given these characteristics, proposed new lodges require careful consideration to test feasibility, assess risk and predict returns before decisions are made to proceed. The absence of careful initial investigation of business potential greatly increases the risk of project failure; conversely, a rigorous assessment designed to test the feasibility of a proposed venture at the concept stage substantially enhances the likelihood of success.

This chapter sets out the steps involved in testing the likely success of proposed new lodges across technical, legal, environmental, social and financial dimensions. It provides guidelines for practitioners to assess and answer each of these questions in turn. For projects that meet minimum feasibility criteria with acceptable levels of risk, the chapter also provides guidance on the preparation of business plans that function as road maps for project implementation. At the heart of the business plan is the assessment of demand and likely financial yields. Predicting returns involves financial analysis via a project financial model that checks cash flows, returns and financial robustness.

Feasibility studies allow investors to make informed decisions before committing capital to new projects. "Conducting a feasibility study is all about minimizing risk. It is testing the idea or concept for viability, before making a financial commitment" (Tonge, 1983, p. 6). Often, these studies do not just inform the decisions of project promoters but are also used to support applications for finance from third parties. Feasibility assessments must stand up to robust interrogation if they are to attract external finance. The chapter provides an overview of financial models that cover income statements, cash flows and balance sheets as well as the key indicators of project bankability typically required by third-party financiers.

THE PRE-FEASIBILITY SCREENING

There are generally two stages in assessing whether a proposed project makes sense: an initial 'pre-feasibility' or first-level screening that identifies a possible project, defines a business concept and tests its likely success (or failure) at an indicative level. If the project appears viable, it is then subjected to a full feasibility study involving more detailed scrutiny.

"A pre-feasibility is an initial overview of the project, and on the basis of preliminary market and other research, should give an initial indication if it is likely to be a feasible proposition" (Tonge, 1983, p. 7). As the name suggests, pre-feasibility screening is done before committing to a full feasibility study, which is typically time consuming and expensive, and often requires professional, third-party expertise. If the concept passes the first hurdle – if it does not contain any fatal flaws and appears indicatively viable – a more detailed appraisal or full feasibility study generally follows. A pre-feasibility assessment is thus an intermediate step – often conducted in-house – to rule out fatally flawed or clearly unviable business concepts and to identify specific issues that require further study. It is sometimes also used to select the most promising of multiple project options for more detailed assessment.

Pre-feasibility screenings usually start by identifying a possible project and outlining an associated business concept. New project ideas may emerge from the vision of entrepreneurs seeking to enter the market for the first time. In such instances, a promoter identifies a novel project and defines a new business concept, which is then subjected to an initial viability assessment. Alternatively, projects may be pre-identified and the basic parameters – including location, size and product offering – specified, whether by external authorities such as state agencies bringing predefined opportunities to potential investors or by the business models of established private firms seeking to add additional products to existing portfolios. The former is often the case where conservation or other public bodies make concessions, leases or public–private partnerships available in parks or other land under their management. In the latter case, a firm's existing product portfolio and business model may determine the broad outlines of proposed new ventures. Many companies already operate collections of lodges that target specific markets and form coherent interlinking circuits. In such cases, new project concepts are likely to be predetermined by the operator's existing product and client profile.

Depending upon project origin, scale, location, business environment and other factors, pre-feasibility screenings should review the following aspects:

- **A preliminary assessment of the physical characteristics of the proposed site/s** including availability, access, infrastructure, topography and environmental sensitivity. This involves a rapid scoping to screen for fatal flaws and to identify any specific issues requiring further assessment during the feasibility study. It might also involve a comparative ranking to identify the most attractive of several possible development sites, which is then subjected to further scrutiny during the feasibility stage.
- **An indicative market review** to build a brief profile of the potential markets for the proposed investment, segmented by factors such as size, demographics, interests, preferences, price sensitivity, levels of education, time availability and seasonality. At the pre-feasibility level, market reviews typically draw on existing secondary information and analysis. They may also involve an initial 'test-the-water' exercise to identify and assess the interest of potential sales partners such as tour operators and destination marketing companies.
- **The quality and uniqueness of the attraction and the mix of experiences and services to be offered** relative to the interests/preferences of the targeted markets.
- **A pricing strategy** including price point/s for each of the proposed products.
- **An initial design concept and list of required equipment**, including the size, layout and characteristics of the proposed facilities (including 'front-of-house' and support infrastructure) and the equipment required to implement the project.
- **An initial order-of-magnitude estimate of development, provisioning and pre-opening costs**.
- **An overview of potential project partners** in ownership, finance, marketing, design, construction and operations.
- **A competitor analysis** including an overview of rival tourism products and an initial assessment of supply and demand conditions at the national, regional and local scales as they affect the proposed product. At this level, competitor analyses use mostly published information from government agencies or trade associations. Internet resources such as booking.com or tripadvisor.com also provide useful information because almost all potential competitors are likely registered on these platforms.
- **A first-level revenue and expenditure analysis** including a preliminary cash flow, break-even and return on investment analysis.

Taking all these factors into account, the pre-feasibility study should conclude by:

- Recommending that a project concept initially appears viable and should be subjected to detailed feasibility study.
- Demonstrating that the project suffers from obvious or fatal impediments and should be abandoned.
- Recommending that the project lacks indicative viability and should either be redefined or abandoned.

If the pre-feasibility assessment indicates probable viability, it should provide a checklist of all aspects of the proposed business that require more detailed scrutiny during the next (feasibility) stage of study.

THE FEASIBILITY STUDY AND BUSINESS PLAN

If initial research rules out fatal flaws and indicates likely viability, the aspects reviewed during the preliminary screening – or at least those flagged for further study – are typically subjected to more rigorous appraisal in the form of a detailed feasibility study. At the conclusion of this next assessment stage, project proponents should have a detailed grasp of the proposed venture and a high degree of confidence that it is workable, that the associated risks can be mitigated and that it will make a reasonable profit.

The requirements for the completion of individual feasibility studies vary depending on factors such as the complexity, capital cost, financial structure and risk profile of the proposed project. Simple, low-cost projects often require little more than basic business plans that draw on work done during the pre-feasibility screening. By contrast, complex high-cost projects require much more detailed study, often involving external advice in the form of financial specialists, architects, lawyers and other professional experts. This process typically involves appraising a proposed project across several dimensions. Each aspect can be approached by answering a series of questions typically asked by promoters when testing the feasibility of proposed projects.

Before continuing, it is worth distinguishing between feasibility studies and business plans. The two concepts are closely related but not identical. A feasibility study is a prior step that tests a business concept for feasibility across several dimensions. According to Bean-Mellinger (2019), "A business plan details how the business will operate. It assumes your feasibility study has been completed and it was determined the idea is viable. Now you're going to spell out your financial and other objectives, the methods you plan to use to achieve them, and your proposed organizational structure." The feasibility study and business plan are therefore two sequential stages in the project planning cycle: "Feasibility studies determine whether to go ahead with the business or with another idea, whereas business plans are designed after the decision to go ahead has already been made" (Bean-Mellinger, 2019). Feasibility studies often form the basis of subsequent business plans: "a feasibility study can readily be converted to a business plan" (Hamilton, 2020). The former are research projects, conducted to check the feasibility of a proposed future business; the latter provide step-by-step guidance to managers for the implementation of projects that have passed prior viability tests. In practice, the two stages – although distinct in theory – cover much the same terrain and are often – but not always – combined. State agencies seeking to procure investors in concessions or public–private partnerships will generally conduct feasibility studies, but not detailed business plans (which are left to the project implementers), when preparing projects for offer to private firms via concession, lease or other form of public–private partnership. Entrepreneurs, on the other hand, will typically assess a proposed project's feasibility and, if satisfied, convert the feasibility study into an implementation or business plan.

This chapter will treat feasibility study and business planning as a sequential process that first tests the various dimensions of a project concept for feasibility and then, if deemed workable, converts the insights into a practical plan to guide implementation.

Legal Feasibility

What are the legal requirements for project implementation? Are there any legal barriers to the project and, if so, are they surmountable?

Answering these questions include assessing, amongst other things, the availability of the proposed development site and activities area, whether via freehold, leasehold or other mechanism; any impediments, restrictions or other registered rights over the site (such as servitudes or easements); any zoning and other planning restrictions or requirements affecting the project; any formal or informal community or other claims to the site that may impede or affect the proposed business; any other relevant legal requirements such as labour, safety or health regulations, limitations on foreign ownership, foreign exchange restrictions, limitations on the repatriation of profits, etc.

The feasibility study identifies the legal issues affecting the project and takes a view on the feasibility of compliance and risk mitigation. If the project clears this hurdle and moves to implementation, the business plan sets out the steps required to ensure compliance across all the identified legal requirements.

Site Feasibility

Is the identified development site suitable for the project? Can the site be serviced at a reasonable cost?

Depending on the characteristics of the individual project, answering these questions may require a survey of the site boundaries, topography and other characteristics including, if necessary, slope and soil analyses to identify areas suitable for development. It will also require an infrastructure and services assessment to identify, design and cost road and, where applicable, air or boat access, water supply, electricity provisioning, sewerage treatment, telecommunications and waste removal.

Again, the feasibility study confirms the feasibility of developing and servicing the proposed site; the business plan sets out the detailed designs and a roadmap for the implementation of the identified solutions.

Environmental and Social Sustainability

What are the environmental and social risks associated with the project? Can they feasibly be minimized and mitigated? Can the project comply with the minimum requirements of applicable national law and planning standards? What additional environmental or social standards may be required by investors, other financing agencies or major suppliers (such as international tour operators), and can the project comply?

When testing for feasibility, project planners will seek positive answers to these questions; at the implementation stage, managers will set out the individual steps to achieve compliance and mitigate risks. Depending on the size and complexity of the project, the latter may require a full environmental impact assessment, which could, in the case of large investments, take considerable time, cost and professional expertise.

MARKET FEASIBILITY

What is the existing and expected future competition for the project? What are the target markets for the project? What is the likely future level of demand per market segment? What is the pricing strategy for the proposed products? What are the marketing networks and distribution channels? What marketing infrastructure and collateral does the project need to reach its target markets? How long will it take to establish a firm market presence?

The feasibility study extends the initial market review by conducting in-depth research into the full range of potential markets, supply channels, risks and competitors. "While travellers can connect with destinations and attractions through a variety of channels, the dominant channel particularly for the world's largest outbound travel market, Europe, and long haul travel from North America, is through inbound or ground operators, tour operations, and travel agents" (Phillips et al., 2020, p. 42). In addition to these traditional channels, travellers today also use the internet to conduct comparative research and make reservations, whether on the supplier's own website, on social media platforms, or via intermediaries in the form of web-based niche agencies, large booking engines such as booking.com or expedia.com, or travel review sites such as TripAdvisor.

Primary research is expensive and time consuming but essential for estimating market demand, which, together with financial viability, lies at the heart of any feasibility assessment or business plan. Depending on the type and scale of the project, in-depth research should focus on identifying and interviewing key travel trade suppliers (including inbound, outbound and ground operators). It should also review potential competitors via web research and in-person interviews. "A detailed understanding of the competitive context and the characteristics of potential competitors provides a great deal more information and insight than simply an estimate of potential demand. Each potential competitor can also provide valuable information about customer preferences, pricing, management, design, financing strategies and other variables" (Phillips et al., 2020, p. 45). The review should not be restricted to competitors but include complementary facilities and attractions that could benefit the proposed project by, for example, combined offerings or shared infrastructure. Research should also include surveys that seek direct information about the preferences and other characteristics of travellers. Such consumer research traditionally takes the form of personal interviews or online surveys of guests in the targeted markets but access to statistically significant samples is often difficult and surveys generally offer mostly qualitative insights into consumer profiles, preferences and price expectations. Today, much information about guest profiles and preferences can be drawn from internet sources, particularly comments on individual company websites or, more often, on review sites such as TripAdvisor.

The purpose of market research is to gain a clear understanding of potential demand, competition, pricing and required marketing infrastructure. It uses the gathered information to:

- Delineate target markets including the key characteristics of each identified segment in terms of national, demographic and psychographic characteristics, seasonal trends, sources, spending patterns and price sensitivities.
- Identify and evaluate existing and expected future competition as well as complementary facilities and attractions.
- Quantify likely consumer demand, typically in the form of projected occupancies over the project period and, where more than one market segment is targeted, estimating the market mix, growth patterns and penetration rates.
- Describe and evaluate the marketing networks and channels for the project as well as the relative contribution and cost of each channel.
- Define and motivate the pricing strategy through a breakdown of expected rates per product including retail tariffs, discounts and projected yield rates (taking into account the mix and cost of the various marketing channels).
- Identify and describe the marketing infrastructure and collateral required to achieve the projected demand including internet presence, search engine optimization, reservation systems, payment mechanisms, sales staff, selling tools, trade show attendance, trade association memberships, etc.
- Analyse and project the period expected to attract a mature share of each targeted segment; identify related risks to demand and develop a sensitivity analysis that quantifies risk and estimates a range of possible outcomes, usually in the form of low, medium and high growth scenarios.

The outcome of the market assessment is critical for the appraisal of project feasibility. "Identifying, assessing, and quantifying potential market support is undoubtedly on the most important steps in the investment process. Without sufficient market support the project will likely fail, regardless of how well designed or financed" (Phillips et al., 2020, p. 48). The market analysis informs all the other aspects of the project, including facility design, product offering, pricing and, most notably, financial feasibility. Occupancy, price and growth projections developed during the market appraisal provide critical inputs for the models that test financial viability discussed in a later section.

Design and Development Feasibility

What is the design of the proposed lodging facility and its associated service infrastructure? What are the furnishing, fitting and equipment needs of the project? What are the estimated costs, and what is the anticipated construction time?

When appraising feasibility, the initial design concept – covering the size, layout and characteristics of the proposed facilities and support infrastructure – is elaborated, usually with the assistance of professional design services from architects and landscape planners; "these services can sometimes be secured on a success-fee basis, where planners and architects prepare drawings and renderings to promote investment (to give potential investors a visual sense of the project) and get compensated after the project acquires its funding" (Phillips et al., 2020, p. 57).

At the feasibility stage, the designs take the form of professionally prepared drawings and costings (including schedules of furniture, fittings and equipment), which are used to check overall feasibility and cost-effectiveness; during the implementation stage, designs are converted into technical drawings, professional costings and associated project management schedules.

Operational Feasibility

What legal form will the project take and how will it be structured? What is the proposed business concept and model? Does the proposed operator have the necessary experience in developing, managing and marketing similar facilities? What are the management structure, reporting lines and staffing requirements of the proposed project? Does the operator have the ability to recruit key business partners, service providers and personnel?

During the feasibility study, these questions are assessed and, if the outcome is positive, the business plan provides the implementation details. The latter will, for example, set out the relationships between the various partners in the project. These may include promoters, owners, lenders, operators, marketers, community partners and other service providers. It will develop an employment plan detailing the number, positions and conditions of service of staff as well as the proposed management structure and reporting lines of the project. It will specify which services and other activities will be offered in-house and which will be outsourced.

Risk Assessment

Project planners often use a matrix to summarize and assess the project-specific risks identified during appraisal of the various project dimensions. The risk matrix presented in Table 6.1 is adapted from the South African Treasury's manual on public–private partnerships in tourism. It provides a summary of typical tourism-related risks, which can be elaborated depending on the characteristics of individual projects.

Financial Feasibility

Is the proposed project likely to provide an attractive return to investors? Are the risks associated with the project reasonable and are the probable returns robust enough to offset the risks?

Assessing financial potential and related project risk lies at the core of feasibility analysis. Before committing capital, investors and lenders require realistic assessment of the risks and financial prospects of proposed projects. An important tool to assess commercial viability is a financial model that simulates cash flows to check returns and financial robustness under different scenarios. This section gives an overview of such predictive models. It covers income statements, cash flows and balance sheets, and provides guidance on using the results to draw out the key indicators of project bankability required by investors and third-party financiers.

Before proceeding a caution is in order. To counter what might be termed 'promoter's bias' – the tendency of project proponents to underestimate risk, exaggerate demand and inflate returns – it is vital to employ sober professional expertise when preparing or assessing financial models, particularly for complex, high-cost projects. "Predicting the future is at best always uncertain, without the added complications of adjusting for expected inflation, rates of market penetration, currency fluctuations, operating costs and development cost, etc.

Table 6.1   Sample tourism risk matrix

Risk	General description	Project-specific description	Probability of risk (high/ medium/low)	Mitigation measures
Financing	The raising of capital for capital expenditure and operating expenditure, tax, inflation, interest rate, and currency risks			
Supporting infrastructure	The risk that supporting infrastructure may be inadequate or too costly to sustain the enterprise			
Planning, design and construction	The possibility that planning consents are not obtained; that the design is not fit for the purpose; and that construction is not completed on time and on budget			
Utilities	The risk that utilities may not be fully available or may cause delays			
Environment and heritage	The possibility of liability for losses caused by environmental or heritage damage or delays			
Maintenance	The possibility that the costs of maintenance to required standards may vary from projections or that maintenance is not carried out			
Operations	The possibility of any factors (other than force majeure) impacting on operations			
Market, demand, volume	The possibility that demand for the product is less than projected			
Political	The possibility of unforeseeable conduct by any government institution adversely affecting the project or expropriation of private assets			
Force majeure	The possibility of the occurrence of unexpected events beyond the parties' control adversely affecting the project (such as COVID-19)			

Source: SA National Treasury (2005).

The tendency to plan without professional help is to overestimate potential market demand (income) and underestimate operating and development costs (operating expenses and capital investment required)" (Phillips et al., 2020, p. 53).

Financial models are typically prepared in the form of spreadsheets (such as Excel) consisting of a number of worksheets.

Inputs and assumptions
This sheet summarizes the assumptions underpinning the project in the form of a set of inputs that can be varied to create a dynamic model capable of simulating the impact of changes in

the fundamentals of the project. By varying the inputs, planners can use the model to assess changes in economic fundamentals, pricing, financing terms, capital costs, project delays, subsidy levels, demand fluctuations and operating costs. The initial set of inputs are drawn from the results of the feasibility analysis to create a base case scenario and are then varied to test financial robustness under changing conditions. Figure 6.1 illustrates an inputs sheet prepared for a generic midmarket lodging facility developed under a public–private partnership with a state agency. This type of sheet allows project planners to vary inputs that carry through the model, thus creating a dynamic tool that enables sensitivity analysis and continual assessment of changed project fundamentals.

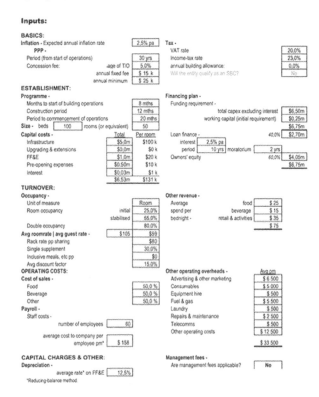

Figure 6.1   Inputs sheet for a generic midmarket lodging facility

Income statements, cash flow statements and balance sheets

These sheets project financial flows across a defined period based on the input assumptions, typically in the form of annual statements for periods that allow decision makers to measure expected returns (see Figures 6.2–6.4). For small, low-cost projects, the period covered by statements is usually fairly short (say, five years); for complex, high-cost projects, the period is generally longer (say, 10 to 20 years). In high risk environments, investors or lenders may require shorter time horizons to recover capital and make acceptable returns; in such cases, even high-cost projects may be required to show reasonable returns over shorter periods.

INCOME STATEMENT:	Yr# 0	Yr# 1	Yr# 2	Yr# 3	Yr# 4	Yr# 5
Inflation @ 3% pa						
Average room occupancy		25,0%	40,0%	55,0%	55,0%	55,0%
Average bed occupancy		22,5%	36,0%	49,5%	49,5%	49,5%
Average room rate		$ 110	$ 113	$ 115	$ 118	$ 121
Average guest rate		$ 61	$ 63	$ 64	$ 66	$ 67
Turnover -		$'000	$'000	$'000	$'000	$'000
Accommodation		501	822	1 158	1 187	1 217
Food, beverage & other		642	1 053	1 483	1 521	1 559
Total turnover		1 143	1 874	2 642	2 708	2 775
Operating costs & expenses -						
Cost of sales		321	526	742	760	779
Payroll		119	122	125	128	131
Other operating costs		483	562	576	590	605
Total operating costs		923	1 210	1 442	1 478	1 515
Gross operating profit		220	665	1 199	1 229	1 260
		19,2 %	35,5 %	45,4 %	45,4 %	45,4 %
Capital charges:						
Amortisation of buildings over 30 yrs		167	167	167	167	167
PPP fee @ $15,0k + 5% of turnover		83	120	159	163	168
Depreciation of FF&E @ 1.3% pa		129	125	125	126	128
Interest on loan @ 3% pa		68	68	68	59	50
Interest paid/(earned) on						
overdraft/(surplus funds) @ 4%/(0%) pa		0	0	0	0	0
Management fees (not applicable in this case)		0	0	0	0	0
Pre-opening expenses		500				
Total capital charges		947	480	520	516	512
Profit/(loss) before tax		(727)	185	680	714	748
Tax		0	0	139	202	210
			0	139	342	552
Net profit		(727)	185	540	511	538
		(63,6)%	9,8 %	20,5 %	18,9 %	19,4 %

Figure 6.2   Five-year profit and loss account for a generic midmarket lodging facility

CASHFLOW STATEMENT:	Yr# 0	Yr# 1	Yr# 2	Yr# 3	Yr# 4	Yr# 5
	$'000	$'000	$'000	$'000	$'000	$'000
Operations -						
Gross operating profit as above		220	665	1 199	1 229	1 260
PPP fees		(83)	(120)	(159)	(163)	(168)
Management fees		0	0	0	0	0
Total cashflow from operations	0	137	544	1 040	1 066	1 093
Capital expenditure -						
Initial capital costs	(6 000)					
Pre-opening expenses	(500)					
Ongoing replacements of FF&E		(63)	(128)	(131)	(135)	(138)
Total capex	(6 500)	(63)	(128)	(131)	(135)	(138)
Cashflow before financing & debt	(6 500)	74	416	909	931	955
Financing -						
Owners' equity	4 050					
Loan received/(repaid)	2 700	(68)	(68)	(430)	(430)	(430)
Interest earned/(paid)		0	0	0	0	0
Total cashflow from financing	6 750	(68)	(68)	(430)	(430)	(430)
Tax		0	0	(139)	(202)	(210)
Net cash in/(out)-flow for year	250	6	348	339	299	314
Net cash & equivalents from prior year		250	256	604	943	1 242
Net cash & equivalents end of year	250	256	604	943	1 242	1 556

Figure 6.3   Five-year cash flow statement for a generic midmarket lodging facility

BALANCE SHEET (ABRIDGED):	Yr# 0 $'000	Yr# 1 $'001	Yr# 2 $'002	Yr# 3 $'003	Yr# 4 $'004	Yr# 5 $'005
Non-current assets -						
Buildings	5 031	4 864	4 698	4 531	4 364	4 198
Furniture, fittings & equipment	1 000	934	937	943	951	962
Total non-current assets	6 031	5 798	5 635	5 474	5 316	5 160
Current assets -						
Pre-opening expenses	500	0	0	0	0	0
Cash & equivalents	250	256	604	943	1 242	1 556
Total current assets	750	256	604	943	1 242	1 556
Total assets	6 781	6 054	6 239	6 417	6 557	6 715
Equity -						
Owner's original equity	4 050	4 050	4 050	4 050	4 050	4 050
Retained earnings		(727)	(543)	(2)	509	1 047
Total equity	4 050	3 323	3 507	4 048	4 559	5 097
Non-current liabilities -						
Loans	2 731	2 731	2 731	2 369	1 998	1 618
Less: Current portion	0	0	(362)	(371)	(380)	(390)
Total non-current liabilities	2 731	2 731	2 369	1 998	1 618	1 229
Current liabilities -						
Current portion of loan	0	0	362	371	380	390
Bank overdraft	0	0	0	0	0	0
Total current liabilities	0	0	362	371	380	390
Total equity & liabilities	6 781	6 054	6 239	6 417	6 557	6 715
Current ratio	~	~	1,7	2,5	3,3	4,0
Debt ratio	~	~	~	~	~	~
Interest cover	~	(0.0)	3,7	11,0	13,0	16,0

Figure 6.4   Five-year balance sheet for a generic midmarket lodging facility

Results and key indicators

The results of the model are usually presented as a set of financial metrics, often illustrated by graphs. In dynamic models, the results will vary as assumptions are changed to illustrate the impact of shifts in project fundamentals. This is particularly useful to model different risk scenarios and thus to check the robustness of the project. The financial metric most used by project planners is the Internal Rate of Return (IRR), which can assess returns to the project as a whole or to individual equity investors.

Project IRR measures returns regardless of the financing structure. What is considered an attractive IRR depends on the risk profile of the project and the tolerance level of the investor. It is usually presented as a range, varied to assess changed risk assumptions (often in the form of base, high and low scenarios). Project IRR is therefore a key high-level metric to measure the overall attractiveness – both in terms of absolute returns and robustness – of a proposed project.

Geared or *Equity* IRR measures returns to individual equity investors after debt servicing. It is typically used to assess individual investment cases; potential investors will assess their own predicted returns measured against their unique risk appetite. So, for example, some development finance institutions may have higher, and certain social impact investors yet higher, risk tolerance than private equity or other commercial investors. The latter would typically require higher Equity IRRs and greater project robustness.

For example, the base scenario modelled in the sample spreadsheets above yielded a project IRR of 12.0%, and an investor IRR of 10.4%. When varied to test below anticipated performance, both the project and investor IRRs fell below 10%, which suggested that the project was vulnerable given its risk profile.

Other widely used metrics include liquidity and solvency ratios that measure the project's ability to service its debt and unexpected costs without having to raise additional capital. Liquidity ratios assess the project's ability to cover short-term obligations while solvency ratios measure longer-term ability to cover debt and other costs. Again, minimum expected ratios will depend on project fundamentals and the risk tolerance of individual investors.

CONCLUSION

By way of conclusion, a final caveat is in order. The COVID-19 pandemic has dramatically highlighted the risks faced by the travel and tourism economy. Tourism across the globe has been hit by a near total collapse in demand due to external factors entirely beyond the control of the industry and its individual actors. Many tourism firms have abruptly lost their revenue streams and only the most robust are likely to survive the crisis. Moreover, travel habits are likely to change in unforeseeable ways once the pandemic eases. Appraising feasibility and planning new ventures in such circumstances will be more difficult than ever. Given the recent memory of sudden, dramatic collapse and the unpredictability of future travel patterns, investors will be more risk-averse, demanding robust projects with high margins and returns. In the aftermath of the pandemic, investors are likely to require greater returns and higher liquidity and solvency ratios than before. Under such circumstances, many projects that were previously deemed feasible face rejection as too vulnerable. It is also likely that business managers will run their firms with greater caution, reducing costs and building cash reserves as buffers against future shocks. For the foreseeable future, there are likely to be fewer of the pioneering projects that brought jobs, opportunities and prosperity to developing economies in recent decades. This is one of the many unfortunate consequences of the current upheaval. The basic principles set out in this chapter remain applicable but, until travel resumes – in whatever form – and the global tourism economy settles, appraising the feasibility of new lodging facilities is likely to be fraught by unprecedented levels of uncertainty.

REFERENCES

Bean-Mellinger, B. (2019) Business Plan vs. Feasibility Study. Accessed 28 March 2020 at https://smallbusiness.chron.com/business-plan-vs-feasibility-study-43382.html.

Hamilton, D. (2020) Difference between Feasibility Study and Business Plan. Accessed 28 March 2020 at https://drdianehamilton.com/difference-between-feasibility-study-and-business-plan/.

National Treasury, Government of South Africa (2005) *National Treasury PPP Practice Note Number 01 of 2005*. Pretoria.

Phillips, P., Faulkner, J. and Solimar International (2020) *Tourism Investment and Finance: Accessing Sustainable Funding and Social Impact Capital*. Washington, DC: US Agency for International Development.

Taleb, N. T. and Spitznagel, M. (2020) Corporate socialism: The government is bailing out investors & managers not you. Accessed 28 March 2020 at https://medium.com/incerto/corporate-socialism -the-government-is-bailing-out-investors-managers-not-you-3b31a67bff4a.

Tonge, R. (1983) *How to Conduct Feasibility Studies for Tourism Projects*. Coolum Beach, Queensland: Gull Publishing.

7. Funding proposals for new tourism ventures
Michael Wright

INTRODUCTION

Tourism is big business. The travel and tourism sector plays a vital role in the global economy and community. In 2019, the industry helped generate 10.4 per cent of world gross domestic product (GDP) and a similar share of employment, and has shown enormous resilience over the last decade, until COVID-19 struck (World Tourism Organization (UNWTO), 2020). In 2019, there were 1.5 billion international tourist arrivals worldwide, with a growth of 4 per cent as compared to 6 per cent in 2018 and 7 per cent in 2017 (World Economic Forum, 2019): 2019 was the tenth consecutive year of sustained growth (World Tourism Organization (UNWTO), 2019). Export earnings generated by tourism in 2018 grew to USD 1.7 trillion. Furthermore, tourism remained the world's third largest export category after fuels and chemicals, and ahead of automotive products and food. International tourism accounts for 29 per cent of the world's services exports and 7 per cent of overall exports. In some regions these proportions exceed the world average, especially the Middle East and Africa where tourism represents over 50 per cent of services exports and about 9 per cent of exports overall (World Tourism Organization (UNWTO), 2019). In addition, these figures only refer to international tourism; the significant influence of domestic tourism must also be considered. It is clear from the above statistics that the tourism industry is a major economic and job creation sector in many developed nations, and a high potential growth sector and/or priority sector for many developing nations. When considering sustainable tourism, the benefits of the sector are often even more significant for those countries that possess greater natural beauty, biodiversity and/or cultural diversity.

All countries benefit from the tourism industry's positive economic, environmental and social impacts, through the creation of jobs, preservation and celebration of indigenous culture, reduction of poverty, and promotion of environmental conservation. Furthermore, developing countries in particular, and the international development agencies that support them, have recognized the numerous positive impacts of tourism and actively pursue tourism development to promote economic growth and development assistance objectives (adapted from Phillips et al., 2013).

Hence, interest and demand are high for businesses to obtain funding to undertake new tourism ventures, or to expand existing ventures. To obtain this greatly sought-after funding, tourism ventures are typically required to prepare an attractive funding proposal. The goal of doing so is obviously to provide the business with the highest probability of success in securing that funding. The previous chapter in this volume spoke to the need for an aspiring tourism business owner to first undertake a feasibility study, a business plan and to predict returns. So, on the assumption that this exercise has already been undertaken, and that a quality business plan has been prepared, we will undertake the next step in the process – to secure funding in line with the business plan. With this in mind, this chapter will focus on developing funding proposals that should be well received and favourably prioritized by funding institutions, and that will hopefully be offered favourable funding terms.

However, before even commencing with preparing a funding application, one first needs to appreciate that undertaking this exercise will demand significant investment from the applicant, vis-à-vis: time, effort, research, skill, finances and patience. Crafting an attractive proposal is an art, and involves a lot more than what is simply written on paper. Before getting into it, let us first discuss the typical stages of any tourism project or business start-up. Doing so will hopefully provide you with better insight into this chapter, and the great volume of work required before proceeding with a funding application.

STAGES OF A TOURISM PROJECT

Before commencing with operating a new tourism business or project there are five stages within the project cycle that need to be undertaken. The funding and financial closure stage is the fourth stage in this cycle. It is also important to realize that as a project progresses through each of these stages, so the value of your project, and the degree of confidence you can have in it, increases. This is due to the fact that a more complete and robust product has been developed, supported by a great deal of information and evidence. In doing so, you would have spent more time, money and effort, which amounts to 'sweat equity' that has a real value in financial terms. Figure 7.1 illustrates the full tourism project cycle up to commencement of operation.

THE NATURE OF A FUNDING PROPOSAL

The nature of a funding proposal may differ depending on its sector category, and whether or not it is purposed for a new start-up venture, or an existing business seeking either expansion or refurbishment and support. Importantly, before writing the proposal, one needs to clearly define why you are writing it, what you are asking for, and for whom it is intended. This is essential to directing your efforts and saving you a great deal of time and money. So, ensure the business is well considered and well planned and know who it needs to be sold to: for example, a government financial institution versus a small corporate funder.

As mentioned earlier, we are assuming upfront that your funding proposal is being backed by information obtained through your own process of research, which commenced with a scoping or concept study, and proceeded to a pre-feasibility study, and then ended with a bankable feasibility study. One of the main products of this exercise will have been a robust business plan, which includes a robust and industry specific financial model that proves commercial viability. It is also assumed that the business will follow this business plan precisely to achieve its predicted outcomes. Why the assumption? This is what the funder will require, and this is what they will base their initial decision-making on. They will understand that if the plan is not followed exactly, then the predicted returns will differ and the risk factor will change. However, do not make the mistake of assuming the funder is going to take the assumptions and predictions presented to them for granted. Any decent and experienced funder will utilize the information provided, and will rationalize it by devising their own financial model before making any serious decisions. In addition, they will require evidence of at least a large portion

Scoping or Concept Study

Stage 1

• The objective of this phase is to generate and refine ideas of the tourism product into a commercially viable business model.

Pre-feasibility Study (PFS)

Stage 2

• The objective of this phase is to assess the business model generated during the scoping phase and select the most commercially viable and executable business model.
• The selected business model is then developed in more detail so that all assumptions are qualified.
• This will then confirm the viability of the project and identify key risks, as well as define possible mitigants.
• The end product will be a business plan.

Bankable Feasibility Study (BFS)

Stage 3

• This is a key step in the development of the project. The objectives of the BFS are to execute material contracts that will minimise the project's uncertainty.
• Examples include:
  • Concluding a lump sum turn-key contract for the construction of a themepark;
  • Concluding a supply contract for the regular supply of arts and crafts stock;
  • Concluding an international management agreement with a hotel management company;
  • Receiving a positive environmental authorisation
  • On the basis of the terms in these material contracts, the project promoters will finalise the funding proposal and approach financiers (funders) to raise the full capital to execute the project.

Fund Raising and Financial Closure (FC)

Stage 4

• This involves the raising of capital as determined by the BFS and once all financing agreements have been effected, the project will have reached financial closure.
• The financier (funder), at this stage, will elect to play a further role by providing private equity and/or project finance depending on the size and nature of the project.

Construction and Technical Completion

Stage 5

• This is the stage at which capital is deployed to execute the project.
• At the completion of this stage the project will be able to operate as an independent company.

Source: Adapted from National Empowerment Fund (2020).

Figure 7.1   *The tourism project cycle up to operational commencement*

of the other supporting documentation that adds to the bankability of the plan. Only upon the thorough evaluation of this information will they be in a position to decide whether or not they are willing to draft a funding term sheet. A term sheet is a non-binding agreement setting forth the basic terms and conditions under which an investment will be made. It serves as a template to develop more detailed legally binding documents. Once the parties involved reach an agreement on the details laid out in the term sheet, a binding agreement or contract that conforms to the term sheet details is then drawn up (Ganti, 2019).

At all times, it is vital to remember that you are crafting a funding proposal in order to persuade someone, or a group of people, to give your organization and/or your project money. The chief purpose of a funding proposal is persuasion, and not detail and description. So, while you do need to describe the business and project adequately, you need to do so in a way that 'sells it' and convinces the funder to give you all the money you are asking for. In 'selling it', be sure to remain realistic by stating achievable targets and projected earnings.

Now, a business plan for a new start-up venture will naturally differ significantly from that of an existing business seeking either expansion or refurbishment and support. With a start-up, the plan will talk to intended actions, the predicted outcomes to these, and a set of assumptions upon which the plan is based. While a plan to expand a business, or to refurbish a major asset, will also need to present a track record of prior performance to better inform the predicted outcomes, and will be based on fewer assumptions that are easier to gauge. So, good record keeping (accounting, asset management, human resources, maintenance, etc.) and presenting these records well is very important. You will notice that the word 'assumptions' has been used several times already. Assumptions will be made about factors like market demand and supply, occupancy, seasonality, exchange rates, human resources, etc. The reasonableness of the assumptions will be important for funders and their willingness to believe and trust what is presented to them. Should the assumptions presented be reasonable, they will have a greater degree of confidence and willingness to entertain the proposal. Should the assumptions be lofty and unrealistic, they will be circumspect. In order to ensure that these assumptions are reliable, one must attempt to qualify them as much as possible by providing research evidence to justify them. On the subject of trustworthiness, the funder will need to be convinced that the business owners, directors and managers possess the requisite skills, experience, technical competence, and ability to enact the plan. More importantly though, they will need to demonstrate that they have the will to do so. Sometimes the business plan is prepared by a consultant and not the directors of an institution, and should this be the case, the funders will need to believe that the directors fully understand, buy into, and have confidence in the plan. There is no point in a business being funded on the strength of a plan that is poor quality or not followed closely. The degree to which the plan is weak, or is not followed, is the degree to which risks escalate in the mind of the funder.

Another important matter is to demonstrate that you know your own ability, and your business and industry sector very well. This will require you to clearly articulate:

- Your business vision and objectives.
- The processes and procedures you are instituting.
- Your personal SWOT (strengths, weaknesses, opportunities and threats).
- Your track record in business, in the tourism industry, and especially in the sector you are intending to build a business around.
- The business vehicle you are proposing to use (new or existing, special purpose vehicle, public company, private company, non-profit organization, non-governmental organization, trust, cooperative, etc.).

All of these elements have a strong bearing on your likelihood of securing funding, and it is important to present these in a convincing manner.

A further significant factor during this process will be the quality of the relationship and trust formed between the two negotiating parties. What we have addressed so far has focused on what the funder requires to learn about you and your business. However, just as important is for you to learn about your funder. So, learning about the funder, on both an individual and organizational level, and their funding mandate is equally vital. The more you understand about them beforehand, the more confidence you will have in them being the right funding partner before even approaching them. This may require meeting with others who have dealt with the particular funding party/ies and the representatives within these parties (the decision-maker(s) and/or technical expert(s)), and obtaining useful information about them. Remember that writing a funding proposal is a 'selling' process, and in this instance the funder is the prospective 'buyer'. So, what do funders want? Most funders want a range of things (adapted from Shapiro, 2011), including:

• To make an impact or a difference – they want their money to count, they want the work they fund to be successful, and they want to be seen to be successful.
• To acquire knowledge, understanding and information.
• To share knowledge, understanding and information in their area of specialization, and, in so doing, add value to their chosen interventions.
• To increase their influence in addressing what they consider to be the challenges of the world, the region, the country, or a particular area.

An applicant needs to understand this, and must ensure that their own business agenda meets the agenda of the funder as closely as possible. They must convince the funder that their business or project will achieve many of the funder's hopes and objectives as well, and that the funder will be proud to have played a meaningful part in it. Funders would like applicants to believe that their funding decisions are purely based on the numbers, but they are human beings too, and can also be appealed to, and influenced, on an emotional level.

Hopefully what has been addressed so far has helped to provide some insight into how important the nature of the proposal is to your prospects of success.

FUNDING AVENUES TO PURSUE

Identifying which funding avenues to pursue depends on your business. Your particular business needs must be correlated with your business venture's goals and objectives, and this will necessitate understanding the investment mandate and criteria of the funder(s).

It is vital that the tourism venture's goals and objectives were succinctly defined during the business planning phase. It is now your job to communicate these to prospective funders in an effective manner. The first task is to identify and target a funder who marries well with your goals and objectives, and who can provide the requisite funds, over the required period, and according to your preferred funding mix. If this is possible, it becomes easier to craft a funding proposal that matches your business needs. However, it is not a perfect world, and there are often myriad factors at play, both known and unknown to you, that determine the outcome of an application. In addition, funding processes and negotiations can sometimes take several months before you can have any confidence that a decision will be made soon. So, do not 'place all your eggs in one basket', and be prepared to approach more than just one or two interested funders. Consequently, when seeking funding for a tourism business it is important to research and analyse each funder upfront, and to prioritize them based on relevant criteria (much of this information will be available on the internet). Hence, one does not want to simply create a generic proposal that is shared with each funder, as this is likely to lessen one's chance with all of them. Instead, tweak and tailor-make each proposal with a specific emphasis on that funder's mandate. This could involve subtle changes in emphasis and prioritization of information shared, and need not necessitate changing the fundamentals of the business. Funders all have defined mandates and industry sectors and concerns they focus on. If you are going to have any reasonable chance of success, it is important to research these mandates and to be sure that your business proposition meets their criteria as closely as possible. Catering towards the respective funder's mandates will greatly improve your chance of success. Funding institutions may, for example:

- Only offer funding quantums between a particular range (e.g. $3m and $20m), i.e. a minimum and maximum funding threshold.
- Only offer certain categories of financing (e.g. debt and quasi-equity).
- Prefer to develop, promote and implement responsible tourism initiatives.
- Have job creation and employment equity targets.
- Have conservation objectives and commitments.
- Have social impact targets.
- Have climate change goals and obligations.
- Have a particular geographical development preference at that time.
- Only be willing to take a view over a particular term.
- Offer reduced interest rates subject to certain criteria being met.
- Provide particular incentives for interventions such as: green design, cleaner and more resource efficient technologies, greening tourism products at destination level, restoring and renovating old tourism sites, etc.

Table 7.1   Different types of funders

Type of funder	Advantages	Disadvantages
Government Government agencies Development finance institutions	• Often have a lot of money • May be useful on issues of policy, access, etc. • If project fits government strategy, this increases possibility of meaningful impact • May offer incentives – tax breaks, subsidies, guarantees, or infrastructure	• Process of application is often bureaucratic and long-winded • Payment is often delayed and there is very little flexibility • Application requirements can be complex • Political motives and agendas can be influential
Major corporate funding	• Have large sums of money to give • Often have professional, accessible staff • Usually clear on what they want from the arrangement • No hidden agenda	• Change priorities quite often • Sometimes want direct representation on the board • Often very sensitive to anything that might alienate other stakeholders
Small corporate funding	• Informal approach • Interested in local projects • Personal connections very helpful • Agenda usually clear	• Not that much money • Interests limited • If no personal connections, funding is very unlikely
General foundations Large family foundations	• Have large sums of money to give • Staff are professional, understand the issues and civil society concerns • Clear guidelines on what is funded and the process for getting funding usually provided • Willing to share international experience	• Process for application can be lengthy • Requirements for applications can be complex • Priorities may change
Small family foundations	• Often form close relationships and have a personal commitment to an organization • More flexible on format and process • More flexible on what they fund	• Staff not always as professional as that of bigger foundations • May not have much money • Personal contacts very important (can also be an advantage)

Source: Adapted from Shapiro (2011).

Types of Funders

At a high level, the funding options available, and the general advantages and disadvantages of each, are outlined in Table 7.1.

From the types of funders identified in Table 7.1, you would need to identify and prioritize which ones you prefer, and then identify the individual entities that fall into these categories. It will be those select institutions that become the ones that must be researched in greater detail.

CRAFTING AN ENTICING FUNDING PROPOSAL

Crafting an enticing funding proposal will necessitate several key ingredients, namely: thorough planning, research, good structure, quality content, rapport with the funder(s), presentation and follow-up. Some of these ingredients have already been addressed at a high level in the above sections. So, what specifically will the funder require? The funder will want to receive a well-packaged and well-presented funding proposal. Often funders will provide a particular set of guidelines or a template that specifies the format they want to receive the proposal in. Thus, if multiple funders are approached (which is advisable), it will require tailoring each proposal accordingly. Most importantly, the funder will want to receive a funding proposal that is accompanied by a business plan as well as any other relevant and related information. This is what is termed a 'bankable feasibility study'. The nature of this information will, however, naturally differ depending on the nature of the tourism venture. As you can imagine, the factors affecting a hotel or lodge development will differ significantly from those affecting a tour operating business, travel agency, theme park, restaurant or museum. In the tourism sector, especially when it comes to any projects involving infrastructure build, this will necessitate far more than just a business plan. In addition, it will require more commitment in the way of time, cost, and assessment. When preparing your funding proposal, you will need to also complete and submit a signed application form. Table 7.2 provides an example of a list of information that may be required to accompany this application form.

It is evident from this list that the additional requirements are often numerous, and could prove onerous and out of reach for some businesses, especially start-ups. Although one can also understand and appreciate why a funder would require this information before being willing to lend millions of dollars to what is merely a business proposition at the time. Hopefully it is now becoming apparent that undertaking a tourism venture will require significant planning, time, money and technical experience to achieve 'bankability'.

We will now explore some of the steps involved in this process in greater detail.

Planning

Hopefully you now realize that planning is a big factor. Before approaching the funder, the promoter(s) of the business will need to systematically and concurrently attend to a plethora of tasks. This may necessitate dealing with, and appointing, numerous other parties to the process, sometimes months and years in advance. In addition, it may require having to appoint and pay numerous service providers and professionals in order to obtain the necessary information. For example, in the case of a lodge or theme park development it may require appointing environmental assessment practitioners, town planners, architects, engineers and/

Table 7.2   *List of information required to accompany a signed funding application form*

No.	Item	Start-up business	Existing business
1	Business plan (inclusive of much of the information listed below)	Yes (or an information memorandum detailing the nature of the business as a minimum)	Yes (or an information memorandum detailing the nature of the business as a minimum)
2	Affidavit from other directors or members of the company that they are aware of the contents of the application form	Yes	Yes
3	Right of use – title deed, lease agreement, concession agreement, public–private partnership agreement	Yes	Yes
4	Company registration documents and all legal documents relevant to the entity	Yes (if available)	Yes
5	Company financial records/statements	Yes, whatever is available. Include shareholder and/ or promoter loan accounts detailing financial (cash equity) and time (sweat equity) spend	Yes, three years of records (if the business has operated for that long) – balance sheet, income statement, and cash flow statement. Last six months of management accounts (if available)
6	Financial projections – five-year forecast balance sheet, income statement, and cash flow statement. First year projections should be reflected on a monthly basis, and annually thereafter	Yes	Yes
7	Shareholding structure, including shareholders agreement, shareholders' certified identity documents, and shareholders' personal statement of assets and liabilities (including spouses' if married in community of property)	Yes (if available)	Yes
8	List of directors, directors' certified identity documents, and directors' personal statement of assets and liabilities (including spouses' if married in community of property)	Yes (if available)	Yes
9	A business bank account in the name of the applicant, including bank statements	Yes, for as many months as is available	Yes, for the past twelve months (if available)
10	Town planning approvals – zoning, building plans, services agreements or evidence of availability of services (water and power)	Yes	Yes
11	Environmental authorizations – environmental impact assessment (including environmental management programme), water use licences, threatened and protected species permits	Yes (if applicable)	Yes (if applicable)
12	Architectural concept designs	Yes (if applicable)	Yes (if applicable)
13	Engineering concept designs and reports	Yes (if applicable)	Yes (if applicable)
14	Project construction preliminary cost estimate	Yes (if applicable)	Yes (if applicable)
15	Capital expenditure requirements	Yes	Yes
16	Market assessment – tourism market analysis, market surveys and demand analysis	Yes	Yes
17	Proposed gearing (overall debt:equity ratio)	Yes	Yes
18	Loan repayment schedule	Yes	Yes
19	The proposed management and marketing company(ies) or operator(s) – include the management and marketing strategy, and evidence of track record	Yes	Yes
20	The proposed organizational plan and professional team members	Yes (if applicable)	Yes (if applicable)
21	Evidence of community consultation (particularly in or near protected areas)	Yes (if applicable)	Yes (if applicable)

or quantity surveyors to obtain the necessary approvals, designs and cost estimates. It would also require acquiring a right of use of the property in question, and obtaining written commitment from a managing agent. In the case of a restaurateur, it may require obtaining a lease on a property, appointing an architect and interior decorator to provide concept drawings, and a designer to create relevant marketing material.

Research

The research phase cannot be stressed enough, especially if you are fairly new to the tourism industry. Earlier we spoke of the need to research the different types of finance, the different types of funders, and the different types of funds they each offer. In addition, it is important to research and understand your market, your competitors, your industry service providers, your suppliers, the design and technological options available to you, the best systems to serve your business, the routes to promote, etc. A valuable exercise you should also undertake (if relevant) is to review publications such as the national, provincial and local tourism development strategies and plans; the local Integrated Development Plan and Spatial Development Framework; and the Local Economic Development strategy for your regions of operation. These will serve to provide you with great insight into the intents of government and industry, and will help you determine the chance of your business developing successfully in these regions. Furthermore, ensuring your business matches the intents of these plans and strategies will go a long way to obtaining support from key stakeholders, and will serve to strengthen your cause with the funders.

Good Structure and Quality Content

Once you have undertaken the necessary planning and research, the applicant must ensure that the proposal offers pertinent and accurate information that meets the criteria and expectations of the funder. It will require applying the information in the most succinct, effective and convincing way possible. Furthermore, it needs to be presented in an impactful manner and packaged professionally. Before submitting the application, however, if your business proposition is novel and innovative, containing valuable intellectual property, it would be wise to require the funder(s) to first sign a non-circumvention non-disclosure (NCND) agreement to safeguard your ideas. The funder will also probably require the information in electronic format, and the financial model in a usable format in order to insert the figures directly into their own financial models.

Rapport with the Funder(s)

Earlier, we spoke about the need to research and learn about the funder on both an individual and organizational level. This will set a good base from which to develop a relationship with the funders. It is vital that an applicant becomes very intentional about developing a strong rapport with both the funding entity as a whole, and more specifically with the individual organizational representative that you have direct interaction with. Remember that you are trying to 'sell' your business to them, and you are hoping to enter into a short- to long-term contractual relationship with them. So, ensure you are friendly, courteous, respectful and professional in your conduct at all times. Respect their time, and do not overburden them with your needs. In addition, be sure to respond to their correspondence in a timely manner.

Possible Challenges

Challenges that may be experienced in developing a bankable tourism funding proposal could include several risk factors listed in Table 7.3.

Table 7.3   List of possible challenges before being able to submit a funding application

Regulatory and planning risk	Suitability of land for the proposed development and onerous planning approval process
Environmental risk	Onerous environmental impact assessment requirements
Bulk infrastructure	Availability and access to bulk infrastructural services
Affordability risk	Challenges in raising the required equity contributions and paying the necessary professional service providers beforehand
Market demand or supply risk	Access to key demand and supply markets
Socio-political risk	Support and buy-in from affected communities and relevant stakeholders

Source: Debedu (2017).

Sources of Support

Should you require support with your application, require tourism marketing and investment facilitation, and require access to basic services and regulatory compliance issues, it is advisable for you to approach national, provincial/state, district and local tourism authorities and development agencies.

FORMS OF FUNDING TO PURSUE

Funding can comprise several forms, and applying the correct combination or ratio of these will be vital to achieving profitability in the shortest possible timeframe. In addition, funding for tourism can be sourced from numerous different avenues, and knowing the appropriate avenue to approach, and prioritizing these will save you a lot of time and effort. First, we will focus on the types of finance that can be secured, and the best combination of these to provide your business with the best chance of growth and success. The best type(s) of finance for your business will depend on the nature of your tourism business, its sector, its scale, the size of your vision and your risk appetite.

Types of Finance

For the most part, the different types of funding relevant to the gross majority of tourism business ventures include:

- *Grant* – non-repayable funds or products given by one party to a recipient.
- *Equity* – capital provided for shares in the business.

- *Debt* – obtaining a secured or unsecured loan for working capital or capital expenditure that requires repayment over a set period of time at a set rate of interest.
- *Quasi-equity* – a form of capital with debt-like properties and equity-like functionality (e.g. mezzanine loan).
- *Takeover finance or refinancing* – a form of loan finance offered to well-established concerns with a number of years of satisfactory credit records.

The ideal funding ratio (gearing) may also differ depending on the nature of your tourism business and the interest rate secured on the loan (determined by your credit scoring). For example, it is generally believed, if equity and debt funding can both be obtained, that a good debt:equity ratio (calculated by dividing a company's total liabilities by its shareholder equity) for a viable hotel or lodging business is between 50:50 and 65:35. Adding any more debt will decrease liquidity and would generally be considered over-gearing.

In addition, it will be very important to get the right balance between the types of finance. This may actually be provided by the funder, but the project owner will need to consider the implications before accepting the funder's proposal, particularly with regard to cash flow and cost of funding. Before the funding is accepted in a proposed format, the financial feasibility study of the business plan will have to be altered to reflect the actual funding structure agreed upon, and management will need to assess the implications of the revised financial structure (Wright, 2020). It is also important to differentiate between national and international sources of funding. International funding introduces the prospect of exchange rate complications, combined with more limited chance of success due to the much wider geographical options open to the funder (Wright, 2020).

Grant funding
It is without question that the best type of finance is grant funding, if you are able to obtain it. Grants, whether from public or private sources, may come in the form of cash and/or tax credits for start-up or expanding businesses. However, receiving the grant will come with particular terms and conditions, and with accountability. It also may restrict your business vision to the objectives of the grant. Grants are also often only supplied to disadvantaged individuals, community trusts or non-profit organizations (NPOs). Furthermore, if you require more funding than the grant offers, then you will need to investigate the other sources as well. In the case where a project is considered ready for investment, the applicant may request grant funding in support of long-term financing from participating lenders. The different forms of eligible grant support may include (DBSA, 2020):

- Technical assistance, to support the management or implementation of the project.
- Direct grant, to finance a specific part of the investment (for example: soft components).
- Interest rate subsidies.
- Loan guarantee cost financing and insurance premiums.

Equity funding
The next form of funding to consider is equity finance. Equity comes with a great deal of benefit, but too much of it can also be unhelpful. To obtain equity you need to give away shares in your company to partners. Giving away more than you need to can be disadvantageous and can result in a large number of other problems. Partners will have different ideas and opinions,

which could at times prove either helpful or unhelpful. The great benefit of equity funding is that it financially resources the company, and equity partners share the risk and provide added support and skills. The risks come in, however, when partners have a different level of business and tourism industry experience than you do, do not fully buy into the business vision that you created, or have an unethical motive. Generally, the fewer partners the better, although the best situation is to have the fewest number of unrelated minority partners possible. Equity funding is usually the most expensive funding option, as it will water down your own returns on your already considerable investment. If taking on an equity partner is a consideration, it is preferable that you retain a controlling shareholder interest, so as to avoid the possibility that the business will not adhere to the business plan once implemented. The importance of the new partner possessing the same values, vision and business objectives as your own needs to be carefully evaluated (Wright, 2020).

Debt funding
The term of a loan can differ between short-, medium- and long-term. Generally short-term is considered less than 3 years, medium-term is considered 3 to 5 years, and long-term is considered more than 5 years. However, it is not uncommon for funding institutions to provide loans for periods extending up to as much as 12 years. Importantly, however, there are also different types of debt that could be applied for, even within the same application, depending on the items needing to be financed. These will have different term durations, funding amounts and interest rates. For example: funding for a hotel building may be treated differently to funding for vehicles and golf carts, which may be treated differently to funding for working capital. Furthermore, one can also secure debt from more than one lender. The first lender will be termed the principal debtor, who holds the senior debt, with the first claim on securities offered. The second lender will be the subordinate debtor, holding the junior debt.

Quasi-equity
Quasi-equity provides a more equal sharing of risk and reward between investor and investee. Quasi-equity fills the gap between debt and equity, and aims to reflect some of the characteristics of both. It is usually structured as investments where the financial return is calculated as a percentage of the investee's future revenue streams. A quasi-equity investment can be a useful source of finance when debt financing is inappropriate or too onerous, or where share capital may not be possible due to the investee's legal structure. Unlike a loan, this investment is dependent on the financial performance of the organization. If future expected financial performance is not achieved, a lower or possibly zero financial return is paid to the investor. Conversely, if performance is better than expected, then a higher financial return may be payable. A quasi-equity investment may be structured so that its return is capped (e.g. revenue participation payments cannot exceed double the original investment size), or be limited in duration (e.g. the right to revenue participation is extinguished after a specified period of time) (NCVO Knowhow, 2015).

Takeover finance or refinancing
Takeover finance or refinancing is a form of loan finance offered to well-established concerns with a number of years of satisfactory credit records.

Sources of Finance

The potential sources of finance that could be targeted for tourism ventures include:

- *Government* – Can offer grant finance, often based on certain incentive schemes.
- *Institutional funders* – A highly diversified mutual fund for high net worth investors (pension funds, governments, not-for-profit organizations, companies), with substantial amounts of capital to invest. They offer a high minimum investment, and their loans are typically secured, at low interest rates, and over longer terms. The investment could be in the form of equity, quasi-equity or debt finance.
- *Banks* – Offer debt finance and asset finance, generally at moderate interest rates over short- to medium-terms, and on the strength of a company's balance sheet and track record, and secured by collateral.
- *Venture capitalist* – Start-up or growth equity (for shares) or secured loan capital (at higher than market interest rates) provided by private investors or specialized financial institutions to businesses with high potential, but with the expectation of high financial returns over shorter terms.
- *Angel investor* – A high net worth individual or very small group (to spread risk or increase available funds) who provide start-up or growth capital in promising ventures, either in exchange for convertible debt or equity, and help indirectly with advice and contacts.
- *Small business lenders* – Organizations that offer secured loans to small businesses, over short- to medium-terms, at moderate to high interest rates.
- *Donors* – A person or institution who gives assets to another person or institution, either directly or through a trust (local or foreign aid assistance).
- *Crowdfunding* – Using an internet-based platform to pitch a business proposition to a great multiple of investors who contribute funds in their individual capacities, but cumulatively as a crowd. Investments can be debt, equity or rewards-based.
- *Peer-to-peer lending (P2P) platforms* – These match small businesses directly with individuals or organizations who are willing to lend money. Loans tend to be short-term, made up of many small investments, and easy and quick to access.
- *Family and friends* – Can provide either equity or debt (sometimes unsecured), usually in small increments, and on variable and flexible terms to either kickstart or expand a business. This, however, can prove very risky for relationships.
- *Initial public offering* (IPO) – An IPO is when a company that has decided to 'go public' (to transition to a publicly traded company) offers up initial shares on a publicly traded market such as a stock exchange.

Assessing the Funder and Applying for Funds

Having researched and understood how the funder is structured to assist businesses, the next step would be to undertake a self-needs analysis to see how the funder is able to assist you and your business needs. If and when you are ready to engage with them, the first step would be to complete and submit an application form that will present your business case for assessment. Ensure that your proposal contains comprehensive information to support the commercial viability and the financial position of your business. In a typical funding process the following course of events should apply:

- Once your application is received it will be evaluated.
- Should it fulfil the mandatory requirements, it will enter into an evaluation process towards final approval and disbursement of the funds.
- If you do not submit all of the necessary documents together there will likely be a delay in processing your application form.
- The period of time for the funder to process your application from receipt to approval stage may take between one and two months, or longer depending on the funder.
- If it is approved, then (providing there are no untoward delays from your side) it will likely take the funder a further one to two months to complete their process and to be in a position to disburse funds.

Application and Assessment Process

The funding application and assessment process performed by the financier will likely involve the procedure outlined in Figure 7.2.

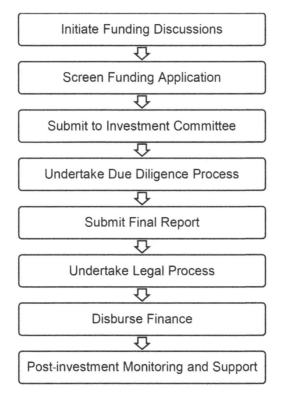

Source: Adapted from National Empowerment Fund (2020).

Figure 7.2　*Funding application and assessment process*

Negotiating Funding

When being furnished with a funding term sheet, followed by a funding agreement, one must be mindful of several critical factors to negotiate. These may include:

- *Project lifecycle* – Some tourism businesses only have a finite period of time in which to succeed, such as a concession or a public–private partnership, which may only last between 5 and 30 years. Hence negotiating terms based on this finite lifecycle becomes even more critical;
- *Moratorium on interest* – Should the date of commencement of commercial operations only be 2 or 3 years after agreement signing, due to time being required for a period of construction, then you should request a moratorium on commencement of making the first repayment;
- *Minimum core promoter contributions* – Funders will likely require a minimum equity contribution from promoters into the business. This could be anything from 40 per cent to 50 per cent of the equity, depending on the total capital cost. Alternatively, they could require 20 per cent to 30 per cent of the equity, exclusive of the land cost for the project. This will be viewed as seed (start-up) capital – an 'at risk' investment by the promoters of a new venture, which represents a meaningful and tangible commitment on their part to making the business a success;
- *Loan duration and repayment schedule* – This is the period over which the loan is granted, and is to be repaid according to an agreed debt interest rate. The longer the term of the loan, the less the quantum of each monthly repayment. However, the sooner the loan can be repaid by the investee the better so it does not continue to accrue interest. Lenders may not want early repayment of the loan, however, and may include penalties for such an eventuality;
- *Security* – The funder will want to secure their investment with collateral from the business and the business owners, such as bonds over fixed and movable assets of the business. The investor (creditor) will also likely require suretyships from the shareholders (debtors) in the way of personal guarantees of the promoters and corporate guarantees of the shareholding group concerned. The creditor may also bind the surety as the co-principal debtor, which means that the surety's obligations are equivalent to those of the principal debtor and he or she is jointly and severally liable to the creditor. This is often the highest risk element and the most deterring aspect of borrowing funds. In addition, the funder may require a first charge on movable and immovable fixed assets, as well as a pledge of the promoters' shareholding;
- *Guarantee of deferred payments* – The funder issues a guarantee, on your request, when goods are purchased from a creditor on terms, after a specified time, in lump sum or in instalments. The creditor requires such deferred payment terms to be guaranteed by the bankers of the principal debtor;
- *Financing fees* – Funders may want to charge a funding application appraisal fee as a percentage of the loan, legal fees for their due-diligence process, as well as administrative fees over the tie of the funding. These could potentially be negotiated; and
- Other matters that could potentially be negotiated include: 'tax holidays' in the formative years; labour or training subsidies; tariff exemptions on imported materials and supplies; or special depreciation allowances (Houston, 2013).

Once Funds Are Secured

If and when you are fortunate enough to secure funding from a financier, and sign a funding agreement, the first thing you should do is to celebrate! The next thing to do is to appreciate that you are now in a funding contract that has significant terms and conditions, and comes with enormous responsibility and liability. Thus, these funds need to be managed with great care and responsibility. Without going into detail, there will be a continual monitoring and evaluation process to be followed with the funder for the full duration of the contract. This process will necessitate regular reporting and the provision of supporting evidence throughout. Without getting prescriptive when it comes to managing the use of these new funds, one very important piece of advice is to manage your business' cashflow requirements very carefully, as these are crucial to avoiding the drawing down of funds not yet needed (Wright, 2020).

REQUIREMENTS FOR OBTAINING FUNDING FOR SUSTAINABLE TOURISM

Sustainable tourism is the future of tourism, and hence understanding the particular requirements for obtaining funding for this type of tourism is becoming increasingly important where either the funder or applicant values a 'triple bottom line' approach.

Concerns about the Tourism Industry

A key challenge on the part of companies of all sizes, large and small, and regardless of industry, stems from the fact that they often fail to account for the impact of their actions on the environment, and society as a whole. If there is a cheaper way to operate, companies will choose that option, unless they are better informed about the business case for adopting sustainable practices, are provided with financial incentives to move towards sustainable practices, and face regulatory constraints to limit unsustainable actions.

Tourism can also have negative impacts. Tourism firms regularly encounter conflicts in balancing economic growth and environmental impact (Wu et al., 2019). Particular attention must be paid to environmental and social concerns, as well as pressure placed on non-renewable resources and infrastructure. Assessing and managing these impacts is a core function of the investment promotion process (Phillips et al., 2013). The rapid growth of tourism in many developing countries also introduces new threats to the environment. Water and energy consumption, utilization of natural resources, and increased waste are just some potential negative environmental impacts. Through sustainable forms of tourism development many of these impacts can be mitigated (Phillips et al., 2013). Tourism marketing has often been seen as exploitative and fuelling hedonistic consumerism. Sustainability marketing can, however, use marketing skills and techniques to good purpose, by understanding market needs, designing more sustainable products and identifying more persuasive methods of communication to bring behavioural change (Font and McCabe, 2017).

Fortunately, more and more financiers have started to appreciate the risks and harm that many unscrupulous industries create on an environmental and social level. To deter this, many are now offering financial disincentives for unsustainable actions, and incentives for companies to adopt more sustainable practices. These disincentive and incentive schemes are generally applied across all industries, including the tourism industry. A good and welcome example of the collective action and responsibility being taken by many responsible tourism companies within the tourism industry is the movement being promoted by an organization called 'Tourism Declares a Climate Emergency', which is a collective of 78 travel and tourism businesses, organizations and individual professionals declaring a climate emergency and taking purposeful action to reduce their carbon emissions. They are coming together to find solutions to this challenge, as they acknowledge the science stating we have 10 years to address this crisis, and they accept their responsibility to tell the truth, act now, and work together to help turn it around (Tourism Declares, 2020).

The Case for Financing Sustainable Tourism

Sustainability is the backbone of business – this has always been true and for largely obvious reasons, whether business owners realize it or not. Any organization which is absent of sustainability is destined to, at some point or another, fail. Typically, this is not a desirable outcome for an organization. So, sustainability is the name of the game (Broadstock, 2016). Sustainability and competitiveness go hand in hand as both destinations and businesses can become more competitive through the efficient use of resources, the promotion of biodiversity conservation and actions to tackle climate change. Sustainability forms a key part of tourism policies in 101 United Nations World Tourism Organization (UNWTO) member states surveyed in 2019 (UNWTO, 2019):

- 100 per cent refer to sustainability as an objective.
- 67 per cent refer to resource efficiency.
- 64 per cent connect sustainability and competitiveness.
- 55 per cent refer to sustainability extensively.
- 10 years is the average duration of tourism policies.

The United Nations designated 2017 as the International Year of Sustainable Tourism for Development, recognizing, in its resolution, "the important role of sustainable tourism as a positive instrument towards the eradication of poverty, the protection of the environment, the improvement of quality of life and the economic empowerment of women and youth and its contribution to … sustainable development, especially in developing countries" (United Nations General Assembly, 2016). Today sustainability – environmental, social, and economic – is increasingly recognized as the benchmark for all tourism business, of all sizes, in all destinations, and across all sectors of the industry.

Tourism, as one of the most promising drivers of growth for the world economy, can play an important role in driving the transition to a green economy, and contributing to more sustainable and inclusive growth (Center for Responsible Travel, 2017). Investment and financing are an essential part of this. The possibilities are wide-ranging, and include public and private investment in low carbon transport options and the construction of resource efficient tourism infrastructure, as well as initiatives to support innovation, promote the adoption of responsible business practices and encourage the integration of tourism businesses into low carbon and sustainable tourism supply chains.

The 2030 Agenda for Sustainable Development sets out a broad and ambitious global poverty reduction strategy involving both advanced and emerging economies. Tourism has the potential to contribute, directly or indirectly, to all of the Sustainable Development Goals (SDGs), but has been particularly included as targets in Goals 8, 12, and 14 on inclusive and sustainable economic growth, sustainable consumption and production, and the sustainable use of oceans and marine resources. Tourism-related targets in the SDGs include:

- **Goal 8:** Promote sustained, inclusive and sustainable economic growth, full and productive employment and decent work for all.
  - *Target 8.9: By 2030, devise and implement policies to promote sustainable tourism that creates jobs and promotes local culture and products.*
- **Goal 12:** Ensure sustainable consumption and production patterns.
  - *Target 12b: Develop and implement tools to monitor sustainable development impacts for sustainable tourism that creates jobs and promotes local culture and products.*
- **Goal 14:** Conserve and sustainably use the oceans, seas and marine resources for sustainable development.
  - *Target 14.7: By 2030, increase the economic benefits to small islands developing states and least developed countries from the sustainable use of marine resources, including through sustainable management of fisheries, aquaculture and tourism (OECD, 2018).*

Attracting Funding for Sustainable Tourism

One of the most important trends shaping tourism-related investment, and investment in developing countries in general, is investment in projects using a 'triple bottom line' approach, which seeks returns on investment that are financial, social, and environmental. The overarching term for investing in this category is 'sustainable investing'. It is becoming an increasingly popular way for investors to evaluate companies in which they want to invest. Those tourism companies that have implemented sustainable procurement practices through the use of third-party certification schemes are deriving meaningful benefits across a range of factors. For example, TUI Group found: "Sustainability certifications for hotels help to drive sustainability performance and continuous environmental and socio-economic improvements. Analysing the data of the certification schemes can also support hotels to monitor their business performance, and identify where improvements are required in specific destinations" (TUI Group, 2018). A category of sustainable investing is 'socially responsible investing' (SRI), which is any investment strategy which seeks to consider both financial return and social/environmental good by bringing about positive and long-term impact on society, the environment and the performance of the business. Within SRI are two subsets, namely:

- 'Impact investing' – This is investing devoted to the conscious creation of social impact through investment. In general, it is project- or venture capital-focused. Impact investing blends philanthropy and private equity to more sustainably achieve philanthropic objectives through the development of self-financing initiatives and enterprises that generate triple bottom line returns.

- 'ESG investing' – This is investing based on environmental, social and governance (ESG) criteria. These criteria act as a set of standards for a company's operations, and socially conscious investors use them to screen potential investments. Environmental criteria consider how a company performs as a steward of nature. Social criteria examine how it manages relationships with employees, suppliers, customers, and the communities where it operates. Governance deals with a company's leadership, executive pay, audits, internal controls, and shareholder rights (Cohen and Scott, 2020).

Sustainable tourism is smart business – not only is it seen as more attractive; it is increasingly providing businesses in the industry with a competitive edge. Growing numbers of travellers are increasingly seeking environmentally friendly vacation destinations and operators that commit to sustainable and responsible business practices. Importantly, international donors, finance institutions, and private sector funders are increasingly supporting this trend. Obtaining funding for sustainable tourism requires not only a feasible business proposition, but a strong commitment to socio-cultural and environmental objectives as well. Demonstrating dedication and commitment to these elements may prove the key to being offered an attractive funding agreement. Moreover, if you can demonstrate continual commitment to these throughout the term of the agreement, it will help maintain your relationship with the funder in good stead. So, when promoting a tourism venture to funders be sure to incorporate as many sustainability attributes into your business case as possible. For example, it would be helpful to include the following:

- Highlight all the aspects of your business that have genuine environmental and socio-cultural benefits, such as reducing waste, supporting biodiversity conservation, and promoting inclusive growth and cultural heritage.
- Identify where your business will act to tackle climate change, resource efficiency, lower carbon emissions, and social inclusivity.
- Commit to procure as many of the goods and services during the periods of both construction and operation from sources as near to your business location as possible.
- Commit to market your business as a sustainable business by mentioning all of its sustainability attributes. Why is this important? Funders will understand that businesses with a sustainability ethos are more likely to be supported by the market.

CONCLUSION

Throughout this chapter we have endeavoured to provide you with a full appreciation of the many factors that influence funding for tourism ventures. We have explored a range of aspects, and trust that in doing so we have provided you with a greater depth of understanding of the many elements involved. We hope that this will assist to guide you on your journey towards successfully securing finance for your business venture, whether it is for a new endeavour or for the expansion of an existing business. We also hope that you will incorporate sustainability into your business case to provide your business with the greatest probability of funding success.

REFERENCES

Broadstock, D. (2016) Finding a balance between economic and environmental: Entrepreneurial finance could play a key role in funding environmentally sustainable investments that help generate economic value for organisations. Accessed 27 February 2020 at https://www.scmp .com/business/global-economy/article/1956350/finding-balance-between-economic-and -environmental.

Center for Responsible Travel (2017) *The Case for Responsible Travel: Trends & Statistics 2017.* Washington, DC: Center for Responsible Travel.

Cohen, J. and Scott, G. (2020) Environmental, Social, and Governance (ESG) criteria. Accessed 2 March 2020 at https://www.investopedia.com/terms/e/environmental-social-and-governance-esg -criteria.asp.

DBSA (2020) Grant funding. Accessed 29 February 2020 at https://www.dbsa.org/EN/prodserv/ IIPSA/Pages/Grant-Funding.aspx.

Debedu, J. (2017) Developing a bankable tourism project funding proposal. Paper presented at the National Department of Tourism Local Government Tourism Conference 2017, Grant Thornton International Ltd.

Font, X. and McCabe, S. (2017) Sustainability and marketing in tourism: Its contexts, paradoxes, approaches, challenges and potential. *Journal of Sustainable Tourism* 25(7), 869–883.

Ganti, A. (2019) Term Sheet. Accessed 5 March 2020 at https://www.investopedia.com/terms/t/ termsheet.asp.

Houston, K. (2013) Finance & Funding in Travel and Tourism – sources of funding. Accessed 11 September 2019 at https://www.slideshare.net/karenhouston125/unit-2-learning-outcome-4-v1.

National Empowerment Fund (2020) Strategic Projects Fund. Accessed 29 February 2020 at https:// www.nefcorp.co.za/products-services/strategic-projects-fund/.

NCVO Knowhow (2015) Quasi-Equity / Revenue Participation. Accessed 27 February 2020 at https://knowhow.ncvo.org.uk/funding/social-investment-1/investment-types/quasi-equity -revenue-participation.

OECD (2018) *OECD Tourism Trends and Policies 2018: Towards Investment and Financing for Sustainable Tourism.* Paris: OECD Publishing. DOI: https://doi.org/10.1787/tour-2018-7-en.

Phillips, J., Faulkner, J. and Solimar International (2013) US Agency for International Development. Sustainable Tourism: International Cooperation for Development Online Tool Kit and Resource Series. Tourism Investment and Finance Accessing: Sustainable Funding and Social Impact Capital. Accessed 26 February 2020 at https://www.solimarinternational.com/toolkit/tourism -investment-and-finance-accessing-sustainable-funding-and-social-impact-capital/.

Shapiro, J. (2011) Writing a Funding Proposal. Civicus. Accessed 26 February 2020 at https://www .civicus.org/index.php/media-resources/resources/toolkits/618-writing-a-funding-proposal.

Tourism Declares (2020) Tourism declares a climate emergency. Accessed 26 February 2020 at https://www.tourismdeclares.com/.

TUI Group (2018) Certification: Encouraging sustainable procurement practices through the use of third-party certification schemes. Accessed 26 February 2020 at https://www.oneplanetnetwork .org/sites/default/files/encouraging_sustainable_procurement_through_the_use_of_third-party _certification_schemes.pdf.

United Nations General Assembly (2016) Resolution adopted by the General Assembly on 22 December 2015: 70/193. International Year of Sustainable Tourism for Development, 2017. Accessed 29 February 2020 at http://www.un.org/en/ga/search/view_doc.asp?symbol=A/RES/ 70/193&referer=/english/&Lang=E.

UNWTO (2019) *UNWTO Baseline Report on the Integration of Sustainable Consumption and Production Patterns into Tourism Policies, 2019.*

World Economic Forum (2019) *The Travel & Tourism Competitiveness Report 2019.* http://reports .weforum.org/ttcr.

World Tourism Organization (UNWTO) (2019) *International Tourism Highlights 2019 Edition.* Accessed 28 February 2020 at https://www.e-unwto.org/doi/book/10.18111/9789284421152.

World Tourism Organization (UNWTO) (2020) *UNWTO World Tourism Barometer*, Volume 18, Issue 1. https://www.e-unwto.org/loi/wtobarometereng.

Wright, P. (2020) Pers. Comms.

Wu, K. J., Zhu, Y., Chen, Q. and Tseng, M. L. (2019) Building sustainable tourism hierarchical framework: Coordinated triple bottom line approach in linguistic preferences. *Journal of Cleaner Production* 229, 157–168.

8. Planning for optimal local involvement in tourism and partnership development

Amran Hamzah

INTRODUCTION

The involvement of local communities in tourism development has been a subject of interest for scholars since the 1970s. The commonly held view shared by early scholars was that local communities were often displaced and marginalized by tourism development due to their lack of capital, business skills and exposure. However, the earlier body of work was mainly shaped by sociological case studies and post-positivistic research that were devoid of a strong theoretical foundation. Smith's (1977) seminal book on the anthropology of tourism was an exception, which contained 16 scholarly papers that investigated the intricacies of the relationship between 'hosts' and 'guests'. Britton (1982) was one of the early scholars to approach the subject matter from a wider political economy perspective, by proposing that a structural dependency is imposed on peripheral destinations due to the predominance of foreign ownership in the tourism industry. By the 1990s the view that local communities were merely bystanders due to their lack of capacity had been replaced by the recognition of local responses that predominantly took the form of the organic growth of small-scale and family owned tourism enterprises, parallel with the growth of the formal tourism sector along coastal areas (Cohen, 1982). Subsequently the body of work around the Social Exchange Theory (SET) (Ap, 1992; Choi and Sirakaya-Turk, 2005; Andereck et al., 2006; Ward and Berno, 2011; Nunkoo, 2016) became pronounced and led to a dynamic discourse based on the proposition that the attitude and support for tourism development by the local community is dependent on the exchange of resources; and that positive support will occur if the perceived benefits are higher than the perceived costs.

In essence the research and discourse on local involvement and support for tourism had been largely approached in the context of tourism development at destinations that were being driven by outside investors. Taking an alternative pathway, Murphy (1988) argued that the community's role is central and not peripheral in shaping the form, spirit and appropriateness of tourism development at the destination level. As such a community-based approach could maximize local ownership, control and benefits. Instead of relegating the role of the local community in the search of an advantageous position in tandem with a positive social exchange – with the advent of formal tourism development – Murphy's alternative pathway was prescriptive rather than descriptive, by way of seeking to empower the local community in the decision-making process to collectively determine and co-create the form of tourism that they would embrace to suit the local aspirations and values. It is widely acknowledged that Murphy's model provided the foundation for the emergence of Community-Based Tourism (CBT), both as a concept and practice.

It is not the aim of this chapter to pursue the theoretical discourse on local involvement and partnerships in tourism. Instead this chapter will attempt to provide a practical guide in optimizing local involvement and partnerships in tourism by referring to best practices in CBT. This is in line with the overall content and purpose of the book as well as the intended readers (practitioners). CBT is a subset of rural tourism which is increasingly popular in developing countries as a vehicle for revitalizing as well as stimulating the rural economy (Hjalager, 1996; Tooman, 1997; Sharpley, 2002; MacDonald and Joliffe, 2003). More importantly local involvement and control remain central to the spirit and characteristics of CBT (Tosun, 2000; Scheyvens, 2002; Mitchell and Ashley, 2010). The use of CBT as a rural development tool is favoured by most developing countries because of its low start-up capital and ease of implementation (Swarbrooke, 1999; Timothy, 2002). The reason why CBT is often favoured over other sources of livelihood in rural areas is its perceived image as being small-scale, low density and low impact as well as being able to optimize local involvement and empowerment (Hamzah and Khalifah, 2009). In addition, CBT has been fully embraced by donors and governments in developing countries due to its inherent compatibility with the poverty reduction agenda (Mitchell and Ashley, 2010). CBT is often regarded as a panacea for rural development despite the fact that local communities frequently lack the capacity to operate a tourism business (Telfer and Sharpley, 2008). In addition to being an effective economic and rural development tool, the drive to provide high-quality tourism experiences has led to greater awareness and protection among local communities (Lee et al., 2018) as well as furnishing opportunities for cultural interaction and awareness between local guides, community members and visitors (Lemelin et al., 2015).

The materials in this chapter are mainly based on the author's experience as an academic-practitioner who has spent more than 30 years researching CBT. Although dated, the chapter mainly refers to the *Handbook on Community-Based Tourism* (Hamzah and Khalifah, 2009) which is based on a one-year research study on the sustainability of CBT projects in 10 APEC economies. The CBT case studies in the handbook cover the whole spectrum ranging from tourism accommodation to services. Many of them provide tourism accommodation and services such as wildlife watching and 'voluntourism' activities but several offer only activities and services with minimal accommodation facilities. More importantly the principles used in the planning and sustaining of CBT as prescribed in the handbook are still relevant to this day. Additionally, this chapter refers to the main findings from a longitudinal study at Miso Walai Homestay in Sabah, Malaysia which is one of the 10 APEC case studies. Although there is a bias in this writing towards the success stories of CBT in the APEC economies, notably Miso Walai Homestay, it is meant to enhance the illustrative nature of the narrative to suit the readers while ensuring relevance to the universal understanding of local involvement and partnerships in tourism. It should also be stressed that there is no one size that fits all in CBT development. CBT located in remote areas, for instance, is mostly challenged by the lack of local capacity and access to markets hence forging strong partnerships with tourism industry players is critical. Despite the regional variations in the implementation of CBT its guiding principles are universal in nature.

The following nine steps are recommended to guide the development of CBT so as to optimize local involvement and empowerment as well as partnerships with key tourism stakeholders. Central to the nine steps is a participatory process that requires not only consensus building and conflict resolution within the CBT community but also engagement with outside stakeholders. Essentially the nine steps are intended to demonstrate the need for systematic planning of CBT but they should not be cast in stone. Readers and practitioners may skip a few of the steps or rearrange their sequence to suit the local context and conditions, as long as a logical sequence is achieved.

STEP 1: ASSESS COMMUNITY NEEDS AND READINESS FOR TOURISM

In rural and remote areas, the local communities, especially indigenous communities, often lack formal education and tourism core skills that are essential for the tourism business. More often than not, during the inception of CBT initiated by NGOs and the government, it is assumed that the local community understands and wants to embrace tourism as a source of livelihood. The reality is less rosy given that communities are entering into a totally different environment from what they are accustomed to, which is likely to bring about major changes to their way of life, values and relationship with the outside world. In this light it is crucial to ask the community five main questions before proceeding with the CBT project, namely:

1. What is the community's existing source of livelihood?
2. What are the long-term prospects of their current source of livelihood?
3. Are they happy with their current socio-economic condition?
4. What are their shared values related to community empowerment?
5. Do they want change?

Asking the right questions could be regarded as an essential part of a screening process, and if there is a consensus among the community for change, they should then be asked why should tourism be the agent for change, instead of other economic sectors? In most instances, support for CBT among rural and remote communities was mainly influenced by outsiders (government officials and NGOs). The proponents of CBT rightly assert that it involves a low level of start-up capital besides being able to generate supplementary income, diversifying the local economy, preserving culture, conserving the environment and providing educational opportunities (MacDonald and Jolliffe, 2003; Briedenhann and Wickens, 2004; Harrison and Schipani, 2007). What is seldom communicated to the local community is the failure of up to 90 per cent of CBT projects in the developing world (Goodwin and Santilli, 2009; Mitchell and Muckosy, 2008) as well as the challenges in sustaining the economic viability of CBT despite its relatively easy start.

This has often resulted in unrealistic expectations followed by disappointment and disillusionment when the CBT projects initiated by the government and NGOs became stagnant or were not generating the expected outcome. Even the most successful CBT project in Laos in terms of economic return, the Nam Ha Ecotourism Project, was almost totally dependent on the technical advisers appointed by the donor, and the expected knowledge transfer from the technical advisers to the local community did not materialize for the latter to optimize their involvement and empowerment. Instead the local community succumbed to the dependency trap based on the preconceived idea that tourism could be the panacea to move them out of poverty (Harrison and Schipani, 2007).

To moderate the unrealistic expectations that could result from depending on CBT as a panacea for poverty alleviation, both the benefits and potential pitfalls should be effectively communicated to ensure that the local community are well-informed on the multiple facets of

CBT. Therefore, it is essential that the roles of tourism are properly communicated to the local communities especially the different ways that tourism can function (Figure 8.1).

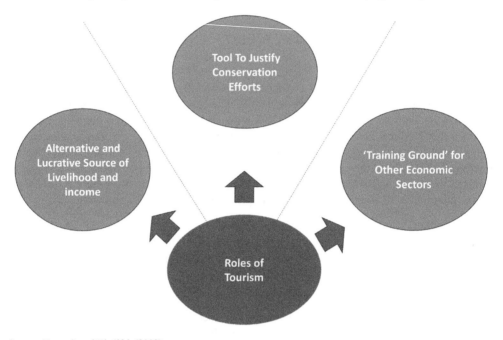

Source: Hamzah and Khalifah (2009).

Figure 8.1   Roles of tourism

Role 1: Tourism as a Potentially Lucrative Source of Livelihood and Income

This particular role is appropriate for communities whose traditional source of livelihood is under serious threat, which may lead to high levels of unemployment and high incidences of poverty, which in turn, may cause social problems especially among the youth. This scenario is exemplified by the transformation of a Maori fishing community at Kaikoura, New Zealand, into one of the most successful whale watching tourism products in the world. In essence the local champion who started Kaikoura Whale Watch took the bold step of starting a non-consumptive wildlife tourism industry in anticipation of the collapse of the traditional fishing industry and railway service that used to provide the main source of employment for the local Maori community (Hamzah and Khalifah, 2009). Not only was Kaikoura Whale Watch able to create an alternative source of livelihood through the co-creation of tourism between the local Maori community and the tourism industry, it was achieved through their shared values after initial apprehensions.

Role 2: Tourism as a Tool to Justify Conservation Efforts

CBT projects initiated by NGOs have been criticized for allegedly giving priority to the conservation agenda over local economic empowerment (Butcher, 2007; Ghasemi and Hamzah, 2010). Furthermore, NGOs have been accused by local communities of being concerned more about securing the next project funding rather than improving the local livelihood (Huxford, 2010). Synergy between tourism and conservation is central to the planning and management of protected areas, and there are numerous success stories of former poachers and loggers being transformed into committed joint custodians of the natural environment. At Miso Walai Homestay in Sabah, Malaysia, the Department of Forestry allocated funding for the local community to be involved in reforestation programmes to support the creation of ecological corridors (Hamzah, 2020). Such collaboration with the related government agencies with the support of donors has created more than 200 jobs for the housewives who could individually earn at least USD 250 per month. In addition, the former loggers and poachers were re-trained and certified as guides and are now reversing their role as proud conservationists. It should be stressed that the new commitment to environmental conservation could only be achieved through the economic viability of the CBT project. This also paved the way for Miso Walai Homestay to develop its Unique Selling Proposition (USP) based on responsible tourism in synergy with the community reforestation programmes – which has empowered the formerly delinquent youth and local housewives.

In the case of Saung Angklung Udjo (SAU), Indonesia, tourism has created significant employment opportunities for the locals, but more importantly, it has also managed to preserve the unique Sundanese/Indonesian cultural heritage, the Angklung musical instrument (Hamzah and Khalifah, 2009). When the late Pak Udjo decided to set up the Angklung Academy way back in 1966, the Angklung was a dying cultural heritage. By creating revenue streams that include entrance fees, scholarships for the young performers, merchandise sales and income from the guest houses and food and beverage services, SAU was able to attain economic viability which indirectly revived local pride in the Angklung as part of the national heritage. As a testimony to the revitalization of the Angklung, SAU's cultural troupes are regularly invited to perform within Indonesia, the ASEAN region and even in Europe, while Angklung clubs have been set up as far as Korea, Australia and Europe. More importantly SAU has created more than 1,200 jobs for women and youth in 11 surrounding villages to produce at least 20,000 Angklung instruments per month to be sold to Angklung clubs in the country and abroad. These villagers are not involved in the cultural performances and thus have little contact with tourists – and yet they are significantly benefiting from the economic opportunities created by SAU along the value chain. The commercial success of SAU as a quintessentially Indonesian tourism experience has allowed the Udjo family to solely focus on the Angklung Academy and the legacy that the late Pak Udjo had envisioned more than 50 years ago.

Role 3: Tourism as a 'Training Ground' for Future Participation in Other Economic Sectors

All too often a successful CBT is seen as an end in itself. While this is commendable, the challenge for CBT is how to gradually grow it from a niche to a mainstream tourism product. By doing so, CBT can be upscaled to become a main source of income instead of being limited to an income supplement. In the same light, CBT should be regarded as a means to an end by empowering and upskilling the local community as rural entrepreneurs. Towards this end the new skills sets, business acumen and connections that the CBT community have acquired could also be applied in other rural economic sectors.

For instance, through their successful CBT project in tandem with community reforestation, the community at Miso Walai Homestay have developed the competency and confidence to bid for government contracts related to large reforestation projects and ancillaries such as the setting up of plant nurseries. In addition, Miso Walai Homestay has begun to embark on biomass production, aquaculture and capacity building and training services. This proves that the skills acquired by the once impoverished community to manage and operate their CBT project are being put to use in venturing into other sectors of the rural economy. By not limiting their involvement in tourism to generating supplementary income, Miso Walai Homestay has shown that CBT should not be regarded as an end in itself but as a 'training ground' in the creation of entrepreneurs in the various sectors of the rural economy (Hamzah, 2020).

The screening process highlighted above and its accompanying questions are critical in deciding whether a particular community is willing to embrace tourism bearing in mind that not every community wants to – and there could be more appropriate alternatives. Having screened and selected the potential villagers, a Situational Analysis should be conducted to assess the community's attitude, aspirations and concerns. The Situational Analysis should cover the following:

What does the community expect to gain from tourism?
It is folly to assume that the community's expectations from being involved in tourism are solely confined to economic benefits such as more jobs and better income. In a nationwide study on the performance of the Malaysian Homestay Experience, it was revealed that while communities that do not suffer from poverty appreciated the extra income from tourism, non-monetary gains such as the increase in social cohesion, pride in local community, increase in self-esteem and forging friendship with people from all over the world were also highly valued by the community (MOTAC, 2016). Therefore, it is critical that the Situational Analysis does not impose on the local community solely materialistic values given that non-monetary gains are considered equally important to the local community.

Determine community values, attitudes, aspirations and concerns
In most communities, the elders command respect and the best way of eliciting views and feedback from the community as part of the Situational Analysis is to seek their assistance as 'gatekeepers'. Furthermore, it is critical that the CBT project does not jeopardize the existing community structure and values that are built around respect for elders and filial piety. In this light the Situational Analysis should include an assessment of the community values, attitude towards tourism, aspirations and concerns. It has to be stressed that concerns about tourism and its impacts are usually underplayed and do not take into consideration the community's lack of exposure to alien cultures and the stereotypical images of tourists as well as their inherent conservatism. During the fieldwork at Sapa, Vietnam and Lijiang, China the Red Dao and Naxi ethnic communities respectively revealed that they were uncomfortable being the subject of the tourist gaze (Hamzah and Khalifah, 2009). Now that both sites have grown from niche to mainstream tourism destinations it would be interesting to revisit their views on how tourism has affected their initial concerns.

Identify the labour force needs for tourism

In identifying the human capital requirement to operate a CBT project, there are three categories that should be considered. First is the pool of local champions from within the community who might lack the skills but are otherwise motivated and committed to improving the community's well-being. The local champions could be sponsored to attend training and internship placements to acquire new skills such as bookkeeping, guiding and human resource management, etc. This category could include the former loggers and poachers who could use their traditional ecological knowledge about the fauna and flora to good effect once they are trained and certified as guides, as evidenced at Miso Walai Homestay (Hamzah and Khalifah, 2009).

The second category are local youth who have left to find work in the nearby cities and towns. Most of them have acquired new skills, established connections and broadened their worldview – ideally, they could be enticed to return to their village and serve the community. The third and final category is the children of the local champions who are pursuing tertiary education in the county's universities. At Miso Walai Homestay at least five of the recent graduates have been coaxed by their parents to return to their village upon completing their studies to take up jobs related to the management and operation of the CBT. This initiative has managed to upscale and upskill the professionalism of the human capital at Miso Walai Homestay (Hamzah, 2020).

STEP 2: BUILDING THE CAPACITY OF THE COMMUNITY FOR TOURISM

Once a community decides to embrace tourism, the next step is to jointly build the local capacity for the opportunities and challenges ahead. While most rural communities are by nature hospitable, tourism as a business presents challenges that have never been confronted before, thus acquiring tourism core skills is imperative. As in the case of Kaikoura Whale Watch, the lack of local capacity during its inception resulted in the marginalization of the local Maori community to the extent that the industry players in the nearby city of Christchurch were monopolizing the tourism business. This led to resentment among the Maori community and the subsequent burning of a tourist coach during an infamous incident dubbed as the 'Crazy Season' (Hamzah and Khalifah, 2009). The 'Crazy Season' marked the turning point for Kaikoura Whale Watch after which the community elders decided to empower the Maori community through capacity building to equip them with tourism core skills as well as ensuring a more equitable partnership with the industry players at Christchurch.

Essentially the many facets of tourism should be communicated to the local community prior to the construction of any form of physical tourism development. Preparing the community for tourism should take a longer time at relatively remote destinations that have little contact with outsiders. The Guisi experience in the Philippines revealed that the government had to spend five years on capacity building before physical development was introduced to transform a traditional fishing community that was practising destructive dynamite fishing as their main source of livelihood. The length of time that needs to be spent on capacity building requires a delicate balancing act. The five years taken by the government to prepare the community at Guisi was considered justified not only to develop the community's skills sets but also to instil a sense of pride and social cohesion, especially among the youth and children – to make them proud of their role as custodians of the outstanding but threatened marine resources surrounding them (Figure 8.2).

Source: Hamzah and Khalifah (2009).

Figure 8.2   The various workshops conducted at Guisi

In contrast Miso Walai Homestay spent only three years on capacity building but sections of the local community were becoming restless and impatient to the extent that the local champions became the target of a hail of abuse. The lesson to be learned is that while spending adequate time preparing the community through capacity building is crucial, the introduction of 'quick wins' along a lengthy process could pacify discontentment and frustrations among the more impatient sections of the community. However the 'quick wins' should not distract the community from the more substantive medium- and long-term recommendations. Preparing the community could be through a series of community workshops with the following objectives:

- **To identify potential tourism products resources and activities**: The community workshops should bring together the entire community to discuss and identify the resources and activities within the village that have the potential of being developed into attractive tourism products. The workshops should initially give the opportunity for everyone in the community to voice their suggestions. Subsequently the workshops should be focused on reaching a consensus on the 'Top 10 Attractions/Activities' from a long list.

- **To determine the CBT's Unique Selling Proposition (USP)**: The nationwide study on the performance of the Malaysian Homestay Experience revealed that only 5 per cent were certain about their Unique Selling Proposition (USP) (MOTAC, 2016). In addition, almost all the homestays were only promoting the attractions in their own village despite the presence of other attractions in the surrounding areas. In many instances, a particular village will not have the strength to stand on its own as a tourism destination. Therefore, follow-up workshops should be held to determine how the village/CBT could be positioned and packaged as part of an attractive tourism corridor or cluster. This will also facilitate the upscaling of the CBT to become part of the mainstream tourism circuit instead of remaining as a niche.
- **To identify the specific roles for different sections of the community**: Having identified the USP and potential tourism clusters and corridors, follow-up workshops should be conducted to determine the role of different sections of the community. For instance, the local youth could be trained to become guides and cultural performers while the artisans within the community could be tasked to be in charge of designing and producing handicrafts. It is also crucial that the workshops identify not only those who could be involved, for instance, in the production of handicrafts but also the individuals who have the marketing and management skills to run a handicraft centre. The Miso Walai Homestay experience revealed that despite the presence of skilled artisans, the homestay committee could not find a local with the necessary skills to operate the handicraft centre as an important income stream (Hamzah, 2020).
- **To identify training and needs**: In the last of the series of community workshops, the community should identify the gaps in their knowledge and skills to be able to operate CBT in a commercial manner. A simple Training Needs Analysis could be conducted by the CBT management to include the following steps: (i) Decide on skills sets; (ii) Evaluate the skills of locals; and (iii) Highlight the skills gap. The findings from the Training Needs Analysis will provide the basis for developing appropriate training modules to bridge these gaps. However, donor-initiated CBT projects mostly prefer to bypass this process in favour of implementing a standard training template, as evident in the Ta Phin Village (Vietnam) case study (Hamzah and Khalifah, 2009). While this approach could be equally effective, it might ignore the existing skills sets of the community, for instance, in story telling based on their traditional ecological knowledge.

As opposed to classroom style learning, hands-on learning, role playing and study trips to established CBT projects are more effective in exposing the community to real-life situations. During the initial capacity building phase, Miso Walai Homestay designed and implemented a study trip for members of the community in a novel and effective manner. Instead of following a regimented programme, the study trip to the main tourism attractions within the state of Sabah was informal, during which the group were pampered while staying in quality hotels as they were 'playing tourists' (Hamzah, 2020). Upon returning from the study trip the participants were asked to recall and list the factors that made their trip enjoyable and memorable which included nice food, fun activities, good service, comfort and safety and security, etc. Subsequently they were reminded to extend the same level of hospitality and service quality that they had experienced from their study trip to their guests in the future. Unfortunately, most of the training modules for CBT are in the form of pedagogical classroom style teaching instead of the more effective hands-on learning and andragogical approaches (Palal and Hamzah, 2019).

In addition to study trips, 'community to community' training is equally effective given the spirit of camaraderie between similar communities and the lack of cultural barriers. Furthermore, a mentor/mentee approach could easily be integrated into a 'community to community' training approach. In this respect Miso Walai Homestay has grown to become a training centre for CBT and other aspects of rural empowerment, in which the local champions are playing the role of mentors to other CBT communities in Malaysia and abroad (Hamzah, 2020).

Capacity building programmes for CBT take many forms that include both formal and informal training. Training should be carried out on a regular basis. Interestingly the training programme for nature and adventure guides at Mulu National Park (and World Heritage Site) in Sarawak, Malaysia is unique given that every Tuesday of the week is allocated as a compulsory training day (for intermediate and advanced training) (pers. comm. Mulu National Park Manager, 2016). Equally important is the documentation of the training materials into a training manual which should be regularly updated preferably in digital form. This is essential to ensure the sustainability of CBT projects from the perspective of human resource development. With the documentation of the training modules and instructions in the form of a training manual, the training structure and system will remain intact although the management committee and trainers may change in the future.

STEP 3: IDENTIFY AND RECOGNIZE THE ROLE OF LOCAL CHAMPIONS

The success of CBT projects is fundamentally dependent on strong leadership, good organization and a market demand for the product and service. Although CBT projects are mostly initiated by government agencies or NGOs, their sustainability depends on a sense of ownership and 'buy in' from the local community. Central to the continuous support from the community is the presence of a strong leader(s) who commands respect.

The leader could be a government-appointed project manager, a technical adviser hired by an NGO, a political leader or a committed and passionate local person. In this light, the job title or designation of the leader is not important compared to his/her commitment, dedication and passion for the job. In the context of CBT, the leader could be more appropriately termed as a local champion due to the ambiguous nature of his/her designation. The local champion need not be officially elected and can also be from outside, albeit having stayed in the area for a considerable length of time.

As presented in the APEC case studies, the local champion has many positive qualities but the most essential prerequisite is the ability to galvanize and transform the community. Though the literature on local champions is sparse, Hatton (1999) was among the first to recognize the role and contributions of such agents, regarding them as a 'spark' to the community. A champion normally utilizes power to influence and initiate change, with transformative motivations, not manipulative or transactional (Crawford et al., 2003). Individuals who are regarded as local champions have the underlying drive to create social value, rather than personal and shareholder wealth (Zadek and Thake, 1997), and they act as change agents in the social sector because they adopt a mission to maintain the social value, recognize and pursue new opportunities to serve that mission and engage in initiatives of continuous innovation (Darabi et al., 2012). During the initial phase of CBT, which is regarded as the 'make or break' period (Mbaiwa, 2004), the role of the local champion is critical.

Notwithstanding the crucial role of local champions in the formative years of CBT, the presence and role of local elites should also be recognized. In contrast to the local champion, the local elite carries a more derogatory connotation. Local elites are defined as individuals or a group of individuals in the community who are considered superior because of their power, talent, privileges (Hornby et al., 1983), with above average skills, abilities and qualities. As opposed to the positive qualities of the local champion, local elites are often negatively regarded as being manipulative with the ability to exploit inequitable power relations within the community for personal economic gains (Scheyvens, 2002; Bramwell, 2014). Despite the noble aim of CBT in involving the local community in the decision-making process and maximizing local control, the inequitable power relations that exist in any heterogeneous rural community have often been cited as the main reason for the ineffectiveness of CBT as a rural empowerment tool (Tosun, 2000; Bramwell, 2014).

However, a dissenting and more sympathetic perspective of local elites has also emerged, which argues that without access to capital, knowledge and business skills, albeit in the hands of a select few, rural communities would not be able to take advantage of the opportunities created by CBT (Varughese and Ostrom, 2001). Critically, it should be recognized that a homogeneous rural community would be severely deficient without the capacity and acumen possessed by a select group of elites with the necessary capital, skills and exposure. Such elites, through their business networks with outsiders and industry players, are able to embrace and benefit from CBT (Zapata and Hall, 2012). It would be unrealistic to expect marginalized communities to be able to bridge their knowledge and skills gaps without the crucial role of agents of change, be it local champion or elite. In this light, it is contended that past critiques of the role of local elites in CBT have been rather simplistic, and more significantly, the distinction between a local champion and local elite is indeed fuzzy.

STEP 4: PREPARE AND DEVELOP A COMMUNITY ORGANIZATION

At this juncture the local champion should attempt to establish an informal community organization that is capable of planning, operating and promoting CBT projects. Given that 'buy-in' from the community is essential, the community organization should represent every section of the community especially the women and youth. It is common for a local champion to initially depend on the local champions to form a core team of committed and passionate individuals. As the CBT matures the management organization will also need to evolve accordingly:

Stage 1: Community Organization in the Initial Phase of CBT – Drawing Solely from Talents within the Local Community

In most of the APEC case studies, the community organization was initially made up of talented and committed individuals from within the community (Hamzah and Khalifah, 2009). Given the voluntary nature of their involvement, having a passion for the CBT ideal and the desire to serve were the two most important qualities that the local champions should possess. As most of the local champions were not experts in the field of tourism, their professionalism and core skills required to operate a successful tourism business were lacking but these short-comings were often compensated by their drive and dedication. Moreover, the nature of the CBT business in the initial stage was small scale, slow paced and relatively less challenging.

Stage 2: Community Organization as CBT Project Matures – Seeking Professional Help Without Sacrificing Community Structure

As CBT projects mature and gradually become integrated into mainstream tourism, the business dimensions and relationship with other stakeholders in the industry also become more complex. Furthermore, the CBT would inevitably attract a more diverse market segment, each with different needs. Consequently, volunteer-based organizations might not be able to cope with the increasing expectations, which could affect the quality of the tourist experience and result in decreasing tourist arrivals.

The above scenario occurred at Saung Angklung Udjo, which forced the family operator to take the radical step of seeking professional help, in the form of hiring a Director of Operations who managed to turn around the business operation without sacrificing its family/community-based structure. Most CBT projects are likely to go through the same life cycle and their long-term viability will be affected if the role of professionals is not recognized as an essential part of the organization (Figure 8.3).

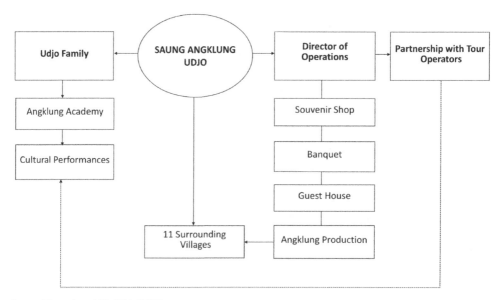

Source: Hamzah and Khalifah (2009).

Figure 8.3   New organization chart for Saung Angklung Udjo

More importantly the initial organization built around the local champion as the change agent needs to be transformed into a broader-based organization such as a local tourism cooperative. In doing so, better transparency and accountability will be ensured through a more diversified management model (Moeurn et al., 2008).

Main Roles of the CBT Organization

Ensuring inclusiveness and transparency

The community organization that manages the CBT project should be able to empower the local women and youth by appointing them to lead specific bureaus. Having a formal tourism cooperative should facilitate the election of bureau heads in an inclusive and transparent manner as well as ensuring that they are given financial remuneration. However, it requires a delicate balancing act to ensure that the pioneering pool of local champions is still recognized while giving the opportunity for the recent university graduates to be absorbed into the management so as to inject new blood with fresh ideas. Petty jealousy might occur if the recent graduates are given a higher financial remuneration than the pioneers, as in the case of Miso Walai Homestay (Hamzah, 2020).

Formulating a common vision with realistic targets

Once the committee organization is in place, it should be able to provide a governance framework to steer the implementation of the CBT in a sustainable manner. Central to the development of the CBT is the formulation of a common vision that encapsulates what form of tourism is desirable and what the community wants to achieve by embracing tourism. The lack of a common vision was the main contributing factor towards the discontent felt by the Maori community when Kaikoura Whale Watch was in its infancy, which triggered the burning of the tourist coach (Hamzah and Khalifah, 2009).

Having formulated a common vision, the organization should then set realistic targets, taking into consideration factors such as the community's level of education, skills and training gaps. Local expectations are often unrealistically high as a result of the initial euphoria triggered by the advent of tourism; therefore, it is crucial that the targets set are modest, incremental in nature and measurable. In addition, the targets should not only include monetary benefits but also non-monetary gains, such as the following.

Nurturing an anti-handout mentality

One of the common features among the APEC case studies is the community's financial independence and anti-handout mentality. Specifically, it was the efforts of the CBT organization in fostering a strong sense of ownership among its community that had been responsible for instilling an anti-handout mentality right from the inception of the CBT. For instance, the local champion who started Kaikoura Whale Watch could not secure assistance from the government or private banks to finance the purchase of its first whale watching boat. Instead it was a small group of Maori elders who came together and took the risk of mortgaging their houses for this purpose, which cemented the community's financial independence (Hamzah and Khalifah, 2009). In a similar vein, the management of both Saung Angklung Udjo and Miso Walai Homestay had inculcated an anti-handout mentality among their community right from the inception of their CBT projects.

Establishing a community fund
At the earliest time possible, the organization should set up a community fund to manage the income and expenditure related to the CBT project. This should preferably be in the form of a revolving fund in which the community could also obtain micro credit at low interest to start small businesses. In addition, a small percentage of any income derived from tourism projects and activities should be channelled to the community fund. At Saung Angklung Udjo the community fund is utilized to provide scholarships for its young performers, in which 80 per cent of the income from the cultural performances is given to the parents and the remaining 20 per cent retained by the community organization to help pay for the children's future education. Likewise a community fund should allow the community to choose and fund programmes that could preserve their threatened cultural assets and strengthen their pride in the local identity and values.

STEP 5: DEVELOP PARTNERSHIPS

As the CBT project evolves into a sophisticated business enterprise, expanding the target market segments is imperative. At this juncture, the CBT project would have reached a crossroads which requires a consensus among the community whether to remain as a niche or to become part of mainstream tourism. The latter would require the CBT to strengthen its competitiveness through establishing strong partnerships with key stakeholders.

The partnerships can take the following four forms.

Partnership with NGOs

Partnership with international and local NGOs will increase the community's capacity in planning and implementing conservation projects which in turn will open up access to new markets such as 'voluntourists'. Many of the APEC case studies were initiated and funded by international donors but the challenge remains how to optimize the 'philanthropic revenue' (Mitchell and Reid, 2001) channelled to the CBT projects to build local capacity through knowledge transfer. The Canadian International Development Authority (CIDA) provided funding for the CBT project in Ta Phin Village, Vietnam with the aim of preserving the unique but threatened culture of the Red Dao ethnic community. Located in a remote and picturesque mountainous region of Sapa, CIDA had focused on preparing the once shy Red Dao ethnic community for a low density and slow-paced form of tourism through a comprehensive training programme (Hamzah and Khalifah, 2009) (Figure 8.4).

More than ten years later, Sapa has grown into a major international tourism destination which is now highly accessible by air, road, rail and even cable car. Against this background it would be interesting to return to Ta Phin Village to assess whether the Red Dao ethnic minority has been able to maintain its community cohesiveness and preserve its soul against the onslaught of mass tourism.

In contrast, Lashihai Homestay in Yunnan, China took a slightly different path in terms of its partnership with NGOs. Located in Nanyao Village, in north-west Yunnan, the CBT project is managed by the Lijiang Xintuo Ecotourism Company which is 100 per cent owned by the local community. In essence the Lijiang Xintuo Ecotourism Company is a social enterprise that started a partnership with an international NGO, the Nature Conservancy in 2000

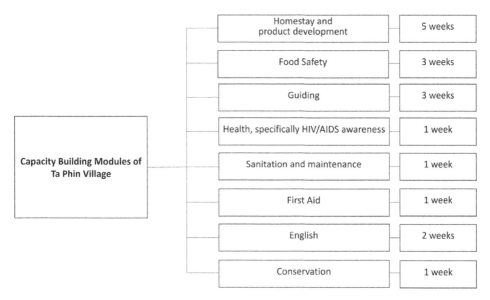

Source: Hamzah and Khalifah (2009).

Figure 8.4   Capacity building modules for Ta Phin Village

to protect the rich natural biodiversity and Naxi ethnic community. The success of the CBT project at Lashihai Homestay is largely attributed to the agility of the local social enterprise in establishing subsequent partnerships with NGOs and specialist tour operators while not compromising its community-based business model.

Partnership with Universities

Partnership with universities could enhance knowledge sharing by leveraging research grants to fund applied research as well as set up research stations at the CBT projects. During the planning stage for the CBT project at Ta Phin Village, CIDA collaborated with Canadian and Vietnamese universities to conduct the baseline studies and assist in the training programme. At Saung Angklung Udjo, local universities were commissioned by the CBT organization to conduct research on the quality of bamboo to produce exquisite sounds from the Angklung instrument (Hamzah and Khalifah, 2009).

Partnership with Government Agencies

Partnership with government agencies may fall into the 'dependency trap' if the focus is misplaced on producing results and not empowerment. For such partnerships to be effective, the related government agencies should take a hands-on approach by having field officers stationed on site to provide mentoring and 'hand holding' to the local community throughout the capacity building process. The success of the Guisi CBT is a testimony to the effective partnership with government agencies – in which the key to its success was the patience and perseverance on the part of the government officials in realizing the realistic targets set for the once impoverished fishing community. Since most CBT projects are located in rural and sometimes remote areas, the setting up of a mobile advisory unit to provide consultancy service to the CBT community is imperative (MOTAC, 2016).

Partnership with the Tourism Industry

Partnership with the tourism industry is important in promoting value chains, enhancing linkages to the tourism market, capacity building and marketing and promotion. In terms of timing, partnership with the tourism industry should commence as early as possible so as to develop mutual trust and raise the bar in terms of the tourist experience expected from the CBT projects. In this light, CBT organizations should form partnerships with tour operators and ground handlers that have established networks with specialist tour operators at the international level. Miso Walai Homestay's early decision to establish partnerships with specialist tour operators that were focusing on 'voluntourism' benefited them in terms of enjoying the continuous arrivals of volunteer tourists who were attracted to the systematic community reforestation programme as the USP. More importantly, by having to adhere to the high safety and hygiene standards required by the international tour operators, the community had no choice but to complete the training modules that were designed to enhance their core skills accordingly. Ultimately the community were rewarded for their diligence and commitment by the strong performance of Miso Walai Homestay in attracting international tourists who valued and were willing to pay a premium for a unique and high-quality tourist experience (Hamzah, 2020).

STEP 6: ADOPT AN INTEGRATED APPROACH

Once the CBT community is comfortable with the many facets of tourism and its highs and lows, they should have the confidence to explore the systemic relationship between tourism and the other economic sectors of the rural economy. As highlighted earlier, tourism should not be seen as an end by itself but a means for rural empowerment and wealth creation.

There are two forms of integration, namely:

Integration with Conservation and Sustainable Development Projects

For CBT projects initiated by NGOs, synergy between tourism and conservation is central to the bigger picture. Sustainable tourism is often the by-product of conservation projects especially in the context of protected area management. As highlighted earlier, many of the NGO initiated CBT projects are essentially conservation or sustainable development projects in which tourism is used to compensate for the loss of income once logging, hunting and other forms of resource exploitation are prohibited. If the potential revenue streams from tourism are optimized, a proportion of the income should be ploughed back into conservation efforts, otherwise the synergistic relationship between tourism and conservation will not be fully realized. Through donor funding, the 'philanthropic revenue' (Mitchell and Reid, 2001) that many CBT projects enjoy should be used not only to finance conservation projects but also to enhance the skills sets of the community in aspects such as project planning, financial management and marketing. By doing so the community will be equipped with new skills sets for them to venture into other rural economic sectors beyond tourism. The success of Miso Walai Homestay epitomizes the ability of the community to financially gain from 'philanthropic revenue' in the short term (jobs and wages for housewives through the reforestation programme) and more importantly, in the medium term and long term, through the creation of rural entrepreneurs (biomass production, aquaculture and seedling nurseries, etc.).

Integration with Other Economic Sectors

As highlighted above, the confidence, organizational skills and networking that the local community are likely to acquire through CBT projects will prepare them to undertake non-tourism projects that also require similar skills sets. In Toronto, Canada the success of the retail business in St. Jacobs County was triggered by the 'magnetic pull' of the Old Order Mennonite Community. St. Jacobs County receives about 1.5 million tourists annually, who are drawn to its idyllic and pastoral landscape and lifestyle. Tourists are also intrigued by the Old Order Mennonite Community who still come to town on horse and buggy, and still live in the traditional way. St. Jacobs County is able to leverage on the appeal factor generated by the Mennonite community to develop a thriving tourist destination in which there are more than 100 shopping, lodging, dining and theatrical cultural attractions (Hamzah and Khalifah, 2009). The tourism industry has created significant employment opportunities especially in the retail and service sector. Most of the locals who are working in this business are women and young adults, not only as employees but also as owners and operators of small businesses. In addition the Mennonite community are able to enjoy the economic spinoff of the thriving tourism industry by supplying hotels and accommodation with their farm produce. While the Mennonite community still resents the attitude of a small minority of tourists who treat them like 'exhibits', they are now at ease and enjoy the economic possibilities in the other sectors, created by tourism.

On the other hand, the Shui-Li Snake Kiln project in Chinese Taipei is a success story in the revitalization of a sunset industry through tourism. Established in 1927, the Shui-Li Snake Kiln is the oldest and most traditional pottery kiln in Chinese Taipei. By the 1970s the pottery industry went into a decline but the owner managed to revitalize the iconic kiln by carrying out restoration works, establishing an exhibition hall and museum and improving guiding and interpretation. As a result, the kiln now attracts more than 200,000 visitors annually besides playing a major role in revitalizing a dying industry (Hamzah and Khalifah, 2009).

STEP 7: PLAN AND DESIGN QUALITY PRODUCTS

In essence Steps 1 to 6 are aimed at preparing the community for an active participation in tourism to be led initially by a pool of local champions and subsequently by an inclusive governance structure. It is also essential that partnerships with other key stakeholders are established at an early stage. With a common vision formulated, the community should be able to progress well in attracting the appropriate segments of tourists to match the USP of their CBT project. As the CBT matures, systematic planning is required to upscale the products, service quality and overall tourist experience.

Planning and designing quality products in Step 7 requires the formulation of a CBT Master Plan or Action Plan. The former is strategic in nature and might or might not be necessary. If there is already a tourism master plan prepared by the national or provincial government that covers the CBT site, there is no need to reinvent the wheel given that the strategic direction for tourism development at the destination is already in place. As such, a CBT Action Plan would be more effective in cascading the strategic direction and thrusts formulated at the national and provincial levels into specific actions at the destination level, together with the proposed milestones, estimated costing and implementation agencies/entities. The CBT Action Plan will first entail a detailed inventory of the tourism resources and activities within the area and along the surrounding tourism corridors. Appropriate techniques such as the Product Inventory Matrix and/or Product Competitiveness Index could be used to assist the inventory. Many of the attractions and activities should have been identified during the community workshops in Step 2.

The aim of the product inventory is to evaluate the quality of the tourism resources, and subsequently, to identify iconic attractions and activities that could be developed and promoted as the core tourism products that portray the USP of the CBT. Consequently, resources and activities of moderate quality and appeal will be categorized as supporting products.

Second the CBT Action Plan should be presented in a user-friendly manner using attractive infographics with minimal text. Cultural mapping should be carried out by involving the community to plot out the locations of cultural and natural resources as well as the possible locations for facilities such as interpretive centre, performance stage, jetty, parking, toilets, etc. Increasingly, however, the use of GIS in combination with drones is gradually replacing cultural mapping using site survey. To save costs, the CBT organization should approach universities, NGOs and volunteer organizations to seek their expertise in the preparation of the CBT Action Plan.

Among others, the Action Plan should cover the following key components:

Product Development

Product development should focus on developing and showcasing the core products to differentiate the village and community from other tourism destinations. However, the village or community by itself might not have the market appeal or iconic value to be developed as a core product, hence the importance of leveraging the other attractions in the surrounding tourism corridors. An iconic feature such as a National Park or World Heritage Site along the tourism corridor should be packaged and promoted as part of a larger tourism cluster or corridor. For instance, Miso Walai Homestay's USP is its systematic community reforestation but its strategic location within a biodiversity hotspot, the Lower Kinabatangan in Sabah is also a major pull factor, where sightings of pygmy elephants, Orangutan, proboscis monkeys, crocodile, and hornbills, etc. have become the highlight of a memorable tourist experience. The development of tourism micro clusters are especially helpful to expand the economies of scope for CBT through collaboration, cost sharing and joint promotion (Michael, 2007). In practice the micro cluster approach has been applied in tourism master plans for Tasmania in Australia, India and specifically in the National Ecotourism Plan for Malaysia (MOTAC, 2016).

Destination Management

Destination management should include the provision of adequate tourist infrastructure and facilities, good interpretation and high-level service quality with the aim of facilitating seamless and enjoyable travel. Good destination management will ensure that the following conditions are created for the comfort and safety of tourists:

1. Ease of making enquiries, booking tours, guides and making forward reservations.
2. Seamless travel with minimal delays at public transportation terminals, check-in counters and during excursions and tours, etc.
3. High level of comfort and safety at public transportation terminals, transportation vehicles, accommodation facilities and at tourism attractions.
4. High service quality offered at the front desk, housekeeping, room service and by tourist guides.
5. Warm hospitality and 'going the extra mile' attitude among the front liners.
6. Clear wayfinding.

Destination management requires close collaboration between key stakeholders and the micro cluster approach facilitates the creation of networks within the clusters to integrate initiatives that support destination management (Michael, 2007). Towards this end the CBT Action Plan should specify the detailed actions required to improve destination management and assign the specific activity and responsibility to the appropriate stakeholder.

STEP 8: DEVELOP TARGETED MARKETING AND PROMOTION

Marketing and promotion have often been incorrectly used interchangeably. In the context of CBT, especially those that were initiated by government agencies, promotional materials such as brochures and pamphlets are regularly printed and freely distributed without initially identifying the target market (MOTAC, 2016). Ideally marketing strategies should be formulated during the inception of the CBT project, especially the identification of the potential market segments. However, most CBT projects are challenged by their lack of clarity in communicating their USP and this hinders their ability to identify their target market. As a consequence, too much emphasis is given to promotion at the expense of targeted marketing.

The marketing strategy for CBT should be formulated based on the following principles: Based on its USP, the CBT organization should determine who will be attracted to its product. A CBT that is rich in educational content should appeal to students while a CBT that offers eco-adventure should attract 'hard ecotourists'. In the case of CBT projects initiated by NGOs, the conservation and sustainable development elements of the project could attract volunteer tourists. Critically the ability to identify and cater for the needs of their target market is one of the critical success factors for the success of the APEC case studies (Hamzah and Khalifah, 2009).

In the early days of CBT in Malaysia, the local champions used to print and distribute brochures at bus terminals and gateways to tourism islands which was relatively effective in targeting international tourists along the tourist flows (Hamzah, 1997). These days the printing and distribution of brochures will only benefit the printing company. Increasingly the use of websites, portals, Facebook, travel blogs and the other variants of social media are becoming more effective as promotion tools for CBT projects. Despite this, word of mouth, and in particular electronic word of mouth (eWOM), has been the most effective tool in promoting CBT (Hamzah, 2020). Lately CBT projects in Malaysia have partnered with booking engines such as Agoda and TripAdvisor to promote their product. However, CBT organizations need to pay up to 15 per cent commission for each successful booking through these platforms. Furthermore, the booking engines are mostly selling accommodation instead of tourism experiences hence often resulting in a mismatch. In view of this, CBT organizations should invest in e-marketing and promotion by purchasing the appropriate hardware and training the local youth to handle e-bookings as well as regularly uploading and posting videos and updates. Ultimately embracing ICT as a promotion tool will also shorten the supply chain through the removal of intermediaries. For CBT that are located in remote areas the lack of internet connectivity will remain a major challenge but this shortcoming could be mitigated through start-ups that are operated by local youth who are now residing in the nearest town.

As a CBT project matures and begins to attract a steady stream of visitors, tour operators and ground handlers are bound to approach the CBT management to set up partnerships. This is an opportunity that should not be missed given that the tour operators and ground handlers are well connected with their international counterparts. By doing so, the CBT organization can then focus its attention on the overall management and product development knowing that its partners will take care of the marketing and promotion. Saung Angklung Udjo practises this business model to great effect by setting up a sophisticated network of tour operators throughout Indonesia that are selling its unique CBT product to various market segments (Hamzah and Khalifah, 2009). The only impediment is that the distribution of profits might not be equitable, which in turn, might lead to accusations of exploitation and friction which will be detrimental to the spirit of the partnership. In the past, there were tour operators who even resorted to unethical practices such as signing a memorandum of understanding (MOU) with a CBT organization for the exclusive right to be the sole promoter of its product. This unfair practice could be avoided by assisting CBT projects in reaching out to a 'pool of partners' to prevent monopoly and to create healthy competition.

Awards and certifications are excellent 'free' promotion which have not been fully optimized by CBT projects. Sustainability certification and ecolabels by Green Globe, the Ecotourism Society and GSTC, etc. will communicate the positive values of the CBT projects to tourists such as their commitment to environmental protection and preservation of cultural heritage. Likewise, awards won by the community such as the Responsible Tourism Award will differentiate the product from the run of the mill competitors. In turn, these positive messages will help shape the branding visibility, credibility and branding of the CBT project which are more effective compared to the countless but repetitive taglines created by advertising firms. Kaikoura Whale Watch is regarded as one of the world's best whale watching products not only because of its unique tourist experience but also because Kaikoura is the first town in the world to be certified as a Green Globe Community (Hamzah and Khalifah, 2009).

STEP 9: MONITORING THE PERFORMANCE OF THE CBT PROJECT

Although monitoring is the final step in the CBT development process, the monitoring activities should actually be carried out throughout the entire process. All too often monitoring is seldom carried out thus making it difficult for the organization to take remedial actions to improve the quality of the CBT products. To ensure the sustainability of CBT projects, monitoring should be integrated into the entire planning and implementation process. There are at least four types of monitoring that could be put in place as an essential component of the CBT development process.

First, the monitoring of guest satisfaction should be carried out by distributing a simple questionnaire form to guests upon checking in. The guests would then be requested to return the completed questionnaire during check out for analysis purposes, and the main findings disseminated among the CBT community at least three times a year to identify gaps in the quality of the tourist experience that require interventions. In addition the findings should be shared with partners from the tourism industry to mutually identify gaps and areas for improvements.

Second is the monitoring of the economic impact of the CBT project. This covers not only the number of jobs created and the income generated but also the distribution of income, economic empowerment of women and youth and the creation of rural entrepreneurs.

Third is the monitoring of the non-monetary impact of the CBT project which should complement the monetary impact. Although subjective in nature, it is nonetheless important to ascertain the social health of the CBT projects in terms of pride in the community, sense of ownership, self-esteem and social cohesion, etc. In most of the APEC case studies, it is the non-monetary gains that were valued more by the local community than the financial benefits (Hamzah and Khalifah, 2009).

Finally monitoring should be carried out as part of a risk management protocol that CBT projects seldom implement. Incorporating a risk management protocol enhances the professionalism and reputation of the CBT and tourists will not mind paying a premium for the assurance. Additionally having a risk management protocol in place will require regular monitoring of the safety and security features of the CBT.

CONCLUSION

As highlighted in the Introduction, the simplistic notion that tourism displaces and marginalizes local communities has been rebutted and replaced by the proposition that local communities are seldom bystanders or passive beneficiaries. Instead they often have a fluid social exchange with tourism that will influence the extent of their support for it. Nonetheless power inequalities have often impeded the optimization of local involvement, and therefore a community-based approach is deemed more appropriate to ensure local control and benefits. Central to the community-based approach is a participatory process that involves the co-creation of unique tourist experiences based on shared values. Against this background this chapter has recommended a practical step by step approach in planning and promoting CBT as a guide for the co-creation of tourism by the local community in partnership with other key stakeholders.

However, it should be stressed that the nine steps are not cast in stone. What is more important is to prepare the community through a systematic process as they embrace tourism. Finally, it should be surmised that like any tourism product, CBT projects need careful planning and management, which should include innovation, targeted marketing and regular monitoring to ensure success. Above all, CBT should be viewed as a means to an end that could nurture thriving rural entrepreneurship in all economic sectors through the continuous process of co-creation.

REFERENCES

Andereck, K., Bricker, K., Kerstetter, D. and Nickerson, N. (2006) Connecting experiences to quality: Understanding the meanings behind visitors' experiences. In G. Jennings and N. Nickerson (eds.), *Quality Tourism Experiences*. Oxford: Elsevier, 81–98.

Ap, J. (1992) Residents' perceptions on tourism impacts. *Annals of Tourism Research*, 19(4), 665–690.

Bramwell, B. (2014) Local participation in community tourism: A critical and relational assessment. In A. A. Lew, M. Hall and A. M. Williams (eds.), *The Wiley Blackwell Companion to Tourism*. Hoboken, NJ: Wiley Blackwell, 554–566.

Briedenhann, J. and Wickens, E. (2004) Rural tourism: Meeting the challenges of the new South Africa. *International Journal of Tourism Research*, 6(3), 189–203.

Britton, S. G. (1982) The political economy of tourism in the third world. *Annals of Tourism Research*, 9(3), 331–358.

Butcher, J. (2007) *Ecotourism, NGOs and Development: A Critical Analysis*. London: Routledge.

Choi, H.-S. and Sirakaya-Turk, E. (2005) Measuring residents' attitude toward sustainable tourism: Development of Sustainable Tourism Attitude Scale. *Journal of Travel Research*, 43, 380–394.

Cohen, E. (1982) *The Pacific Islands from Utopian Myth to Consumer Product: The Disenchantment of Paradise*. Aix-en-Provence: Centre des Hautes Etudes Touristiques.

Crawford, C., Gould, L. and Scott, R. (2003) Transformational leader as champion and techie. *Journal of Leadership Education*, 2, 57–73.

Darabi, R., Rad, S. and Ghadiri, M. (2012) The relationship between intellectual capital and earnings quality. *Research Journal of Applied Sciences, Engineering and Technology*, 4, 4192–4199.

Ghasemi, M. and Hamzah, A. (2010) An evaluation of the role and performance of NGOs in community-based ecotourism at Ulu Geroh, Gopeng, Malaysia. Paper presented at 4th Tourism Outlook and 3rd ITSA Conference.

Goodwin, H. and Santilli, R. (2009) *Community-Based Tourism: A Success?* ICRT Occasional Paper 11.

Hamzah, A. (1997) The sustainability of small-scale tourism in Malaysia. University of East Anglia.

Hamzah, A. (2020) Conversations with the local champions of Miso Walai Homestay: Responsible tourism in practice. In V. Nair, A. Hamzah and G. Musa (eds.), *Responsible Rural Tourism in Asia*. Bristol: Channel View Publications.

Hamzah, A. and Khalifah, Z. (2009) *Handbook on Community Based Tourism: How to Develop and Sustain CBT*. Project Study, Asia Pacific Economic Cooperation Tourism Working Group (APEC TWG). Singapore: Asia-Pacific Economic Cooperation Secretariat, 141–161.

Harrison, D. and Schipani, S. (2007) Lao tourism and poverty alleviation: Community-based tourism and the private sector. *Current Issues in Tourism*, 10(2–3), 194–230.

Hatton, M. J. (1999) *Community-Based Tourism in the Asia-Pacific*. Toronto: School of Media Studies at Humber College.

Hjalager, A.-M. (1996) Tourism and the environment: The innovation connection. *Journal of Sustainable Tourism*, 4(4), 201–218.

Hornby, A. S., Cowie, A. P. and Gimson, A. C. (eds.) (1983) *Oxford Advanced Learner's Dictionary of Current English*. Oxford: Oxford University Press.

Huxford, K. M. L. (2010) Tracing tourism translations: Opening the black box of development assistance in community-based tourism in Viet Nam. Master of Arts thesis, University of Canterbury, Christchurch, New Zealand.

Lee, T. H., Jan, F. H., Tseng, C. H. and Lin, Y. F. (2018) Segmentation by recreation experience in island-based tourism: A case study of Taiwan's Liuqiu island. *Journal of Sustainable Tourism*, 26(3), 362–378.

Lemelin, R. H., Koster, R. and Youroukos, N. (2015) Tangible and intangible indicators of successful aboriginal tourism initiatives: A case study of two successful aboriginal tourism lodges in Northern Canada. *Tourism Management*, 47, 318–328.

MacDonald, R. and Jolliffe, L. (2003) Cultural rural tourism: Evidence from Canada. *Annals of Tourism Research*, 30(2), 307–322.

Mbaiwa, J. E. (2004) The success and sustainability of community-based natural resource management in the Okavango Delta, Botswana. *South African Geographical Journal*, 86(1), 44–53.

Michael, E. J. (ed.) (2007) *Micro-Clusters and Networks: The Growth of Tourism*. Oxford: Elsevier.

Mitchell, J. and Ashley, C. (2010) *Tourism and Poverty Reduction: Pathways to Prosperity*. London: Earthscan.

Mitchell, J. and Muckosy, P. (2008) A misguided quest: Community-based tourism in Latin America. Overseas Development Institute, *Opinion* (May). Accessed 1 May 2020 at https://assets.publishing .service.gov.uk/media/57a08bd2e5274a27b2000d9d/tourism-OpPaper.pdf.

Mitchell, R. and Reid, D. (2001) Community integration: Island tourism in Peru. *Annals of Tourism Research*, 28, 113–139.

Moeurn, V., Khim, L. and Sovanny, C. (2008) Good practice in the Chambok community-based ecotourism project in Cambodia. In P. Steele, N. Fernando and M. Weddikkara (eds.), *Poverty Reduction That Works: Experience of Scaling up Development Success*. London: Earthscan, 3–19.

Ministry of Tourism Art and Culture Malaysia (MOTAC) (2016) *Business Strategies for Upscaling the Malaysia Homestay Experience*. Putrajaya.

Murphy, P. E. (1988) Community driven tourism planning. *Tourism Management*, 9(2), 96–104.

Nunkoo, R. (2016) Toward a more comprehensive use of social exchange theory to study residents' attitudes to tourism. *Procedia Economics and Finance*, 39, 588–596.

Palal, N. H. and Hamzah, A. (2019) Effectiveness of an andragogical approach for upscaling homestay operators. *Sains Humanika*, 11(2). Universiti Teknologi Malaysia (UTM).

Scheyvens, R. (2002) *Tourism for Development: Empowering Communities*. Harlow: Prentice Hall.

Sharpley, R. (2002) The challenges of economic diversification through tourism: The case of Abu Dhabi. *International Journal of Tourism Research*, 4(3), 221–235.

Smith, V. L. (ed.) (1977) *Hosts and Guests: The Anthropology of Tourism*. Philadelphia: University of Pennsylvania Press.

Swarbrooke, J. (1999) *Sustainable Tourism Management*. Wallingford: CABI.

Telfer, D. J. and Sharpley, R. (2008) *Tourism and Development in the Developing World*. London: Routledge.

Timothy, D. J. (2002) Tourism and community development issues. In R. Sharpley and D. J. Telfer (eds.), *Tourism and Development: Concepts and Issues*. Clevedon: Channel View Publications, 149–164.

Tooman, L. A. (1997) Tourism and development. *Journal of Travel Research*, 35(3), 33–40.

Tosun, C. (2000) Limits to community participation in the tourism development process in developing countries. *Tourism Management*, 21(6), 613–633.

Varughese, G. and Ostrom, E. (2001) The contested role of heterogeneity in collective action: Some evidence from community forestry in Nepal. *World Development*, 29, 747–765.

Ward, C. and Berno, T. (2011) Beyond social exchange theory: Attitudes toward tourists. *Annals of Tourism Research*, 38(4), 1556–1569.

Zadek, S. and Thake, S. (1997) Send in the social entrepreneurs. *New Statesman*, 20 June.

Zapata, M. J. and Hall, C. M. (2012) Public–private collaboration in the tourism sector: Balancing legitimacy and effectiveness in local tourism partnerships – the Spanish case. *Journal of Policy Research in Tourism, Leisure and Events*, 4(1), 61–83.

9. Touching the earth, touching people: approaches to sustainability design

Nicholas Coetzer

INTRODUCTION

All architecture, all development, hits the ground.[1] Eventually. The impact is unavoidable; Richard Long's artwork *A line made by walking* tells us that even the most minor human acts can alter the land significantly even if for a limited time. But is it clear what this impact is and what it 'costs'? Or, more importantly, can it be mitigated, or even turned into an overall net gain for the people and land involved in its coming to be? The architecture of sustainable tourism, or more significantly ecotourism and its flagship ecolodges, is arguably caught in a double-bind of wanting to attract visitors whilst somehow wishing they weren't there. How can we work through this contradiction to arrive at least at a workable compromise that 'touches the earth lightly' in all respects, that has minimal impact, that seeks to disappear as did Richard Long's line over the course of a summer? As a contrasting or complementary approach, the challenge might be flipped on its head and more clumsily phrased as 'touch the earth heavily'. This suggests a greater challenge for sustainability architecture in general and the architecture of sustainable tourism in particular; to not hold back in deference but to get stuck into remedial work that can make a big difference and impact on the landscape, the environment, the people, and the Earth.[2] Architecture here might be conscripted to do work that is restorative and counteractive of the devastation wrought on the planet over the past 250 years and the increasing impact of buildings and the built environment in this.

It is obvious that not all sustainable tourism works in the wilderness. Indeed, it can have its greatest impact in urban areas where sustainable development goals can dramatically change an impoverished and struggling area. However, this chapter will mostly focus more on the nature-based or ecotourism sector, as opposed to urban tourism, largely because this is arguably where sustainable tourism building projects might be different or have added dimensions compared to a typical sustainable or 'green' building in an urban context; all buildings should be developed through sustainability principles but those done in sensitive rural or wilderness areas with demands pertinent to tourism might arguably require approaches outside of the norm. And, working in reverse, if it is possible to approach development in this way in highly sensitive areas then it should be more easily achieved in urban areas where infrastructure already exists.

Ecotourism is driven largely by individuals who work more as custodians and stewards of tracts of land that have vestiges of 'the wilderness' before the ravages of the Anthropocene took hold. Or they identify tracts of land as sick portions of the earth that can be sectioned off, stabilized and then returned to their (almost) pristine self – despite a few scars and stents that work as proud open-heart-surgery war wounds, evidence that things can be made better, that a former cattle farm can be turned into a flagship rewilding project. As commissioners of a kind of restorative development – a developmental agenda in reverse – the custodians and stewards spend large sums of money, time and resources in getting the best teams on board from botanists to hydrologists to anthropologists in order to appraise and direct the remediation of 'the wilderness' and associated conservation efforts. Their passion for the land, its animals and other creatures known as humans is inspiring. However, in this focus on the land and the drive to secure it for the future, the 'ecolodge' – the architectural project – is often, quite simply, ring-fenced. This is both literal and metaphorical, but both indicating a separation of the architectural project from the project of the land, and the apparent lack of awareness that the building project itself can be a flagship restorative work that speaks the same language of inspiration as the overall conservation project – from ecolodge to 'ecolodgical', if you will. Just as conservation practitioners are aware that nature knows no man-made boundaries or property – elephants meet fences and the fences lose – so too can we begin to question where the boundary of the sustainable tourism project lies. Any development will activate, engage and redirect a flow of energies and resources into and across the site that perhaps have origins thousands of kilometres away and perhaps have impacts far beyond the boundaries of the sustainable tourism site or the 'ecolodge'. This chapter must problematize the idea of fences and boundaries (literal and metaphorical) that provide a make-believe setting that the site is a magical land apart. Custodians need to pay as much attention to what goes on inside the fenced enclosure housing the 'ecolodge' as they do to what is outside – where the wild things are. And then again, they need to understand both in relation to the land, and people and environments immediately adjacent to their tract of wilderness, and even beyond – where exactly are those building materials coming from? What is their embodied energy? What is the trail of destruction they leave across the world that lands at your front door – even if it is made out of Out of Africa canvas.

So, having made this claim, of requiring the same amount of attention be placed on the building and the architecture of ecotourism as is generally meted out for the tract of wilderness, what is a custodian to do?

STEP 1: DO NOTHING

If you are willing to drive the more than 400 hairpin bends, you can ascend one of the ancient blown-out volcano tops on Reunion Island and find some solace in Cilaos which is a quaint village in the extreme south of France. From Cilaos you can begin one of many daylong treks across some of the most spectacular mountain trails in the world. With some planning you could find yourself in the adjacent caldera of Mafate which is only accessible on foot or by helicopter as part of the daily delivery runs. Here, the small village of La Nouvelle, provides some *gites*, or basic accommodation for weary hikers who might proceed on these routes of the *Grande Randonné*. A return to Cilaos also provides an ample number of *gites* where a good break can be had before returning to the lagoons of the tropical island down below.

The *gites* of Cilaos and Mafate provide an important example where sustainable tourism might aim to do nothing (see Box 9.1). Or rather aim to build nothing. They question whether any building on the land or conservation site that is the destination of tourists is desirable and even necessary. In these cases, there are enough buildings nearby to support travellers who pass through the area and more importantly they support local villagers who have limited sources of income. In such a context the only architectural intervention that might be needed is one of linking the disparate units in some kind of urban design or, possibly at the most, an intelligible marketing initiative that ties them together through a more coherent visual identity and puts them on the map, so to speak. This necessarily requires the buy-in of local communities and highlights the need for community participation in the process.

BOX 9.1 DO NOTHING

- Identify existing infrastructure and accommodation resources in the area
- If appropriate, help make these into an identifiable coherent whole even if just through marketing of the architecture as a precinct
- If appropriate, institute an urban design that links dispersed accommodation through route marking or provides a missing institutional or infrastructural piece that ties them all together
- Gain local support and input through community consultation and/or participation
- Identify existing buildings that can be repurposed for 'adaptive reuse'

Such a strategy is employed in a vastly different context of iKhaya le Langa[3] – located in the Langa Quarter of Cape Town's oldest segregated black township. Thanks to the mentoring and guidance of Tony Elvin – a local social entrepreneur who hosts workshops on entrepreneurship and tourism in Langa – a number of houses have formed an Airbnb network marketed under the 'Langa Quarter' banner that bring tourists directly into township space. The experience is obviously much richer for the tourist who can spend some time with locals in a township rather than going on a drive-by 'township safari' – all the while having the defunct school that iKhaya le Langa operates out of as a secure space to get a cup of coffee at the Sun Diner or take lessons in 'township art'. And there are obvious financial benefits for the local residents who might not be hosts but act as guides or run restaurants and cafés. Similarly, the whole community starts to change as it gears up around the ethos of 'clean, green and safe' that drives the development of the precinct.

The two examples cited above illustrate that one of the first key moves, particularly in urban areas, is to identify resources (both human and infrastructural) that might be supported and invested in to bring tourists closer to local residents. The potential for a more 'authentic' experience and also in supporting local economies can be increased by simply 'doing nothing'. The same logic could be applied to areas surrounding conservation tracts or reserved land that could perhaps be visited from adjacent villages on day tours rather than as places to inhabit. The question remains, does the world really need another building project? Can existing buildings on the site or nearby be repurposed as 'adaptive reuse' projects? And if a new build is needed, then there are ways explored below to mitigate its negative effects, and in some instances, maximize its positive potential.

STEP 2: KNOW YOUR VERNACULAR … AND USE IT WISELY

Before globalization and the commodification of architectural building materials – before online catalogues and travelling sales reps telling unsuspecting architects half-truths about their 'green' products – everyday buildings such as dwellings tended to be similar in an area, used the same easily accessible building materials and had the same overall form and features. This is generally known as vernacular architecture and is widely understood to be a place-bound and place-based traditional architecture – although we can also speak of a contemporary vernacular architecture that is perhaps best called 'the architecture of the everyday'. Vernacular architecture presents a long lead time of hundreds of years of R&D as to what is the most effective, efficient and sensible way to build in a particular area with limited resources[4] and which will in turn provide the most effective climatic and environmental response – although it should be kept in mind that climate change might be undermining the efficacy of vernacular architecture to mitigate hostile environmental factors. Similarly, vernacular architecture presents general patterns in a climatic and geographic region but localized changes and peculiarities should not be overlooked. Neither should localized cultural practices that might bring changes to form, space and material that would otherwise be expected to be consistent across a climatic and geographical region. Nevertheless, there are general responses to overall climatic regions that are useful to understand even before proceeding with any building design project, for example, hot-humid climates near the coast generally do well with lightweight timber buildings that encourage cross ventilation to cool inhabitants, whilst hot-dry climates with high diurnal ranges do well with solid and massive walls with limited window openings and with little ventilation. In this latter context – inland deserts with cloudless night-time skies – the solid mass walls work as a heat sink absorbing the indoor latent energy as the outside walls start to cool down late in the night thereby making the interior cooler than the exterior the next day.

Again, these are general rules of thumb that should be adjusted for localized conditions that might be as simple as a mountain overshadowing the area of concern and creating a micro-climate that contradicts the general climatic regional response. Consequently, should a well-formed vernacular architecture tradition exist in the area it should be appraised, documented and its specific functioning understood as a first step in planning any inhabitation on the site – indeed, some vernacular traditions might be problematic or unnecessarily compromised and should not be applied without first passing through the sceptical lens of science.[5] This appraisal of the vernacular is important even if the future built work on the site does not take the form or characteristics of the traditional vernacular. In other words, there are lessons to be gained from the vernacular response that far exceed what it looks like or how it functions as an overall system – there might simply be real insight as to how low-tech construction methods can work in the area. Similarly, traditional vernacular architecture may be appropriate for dwellings (the sleeping units or apartments of an 'ecolodge') but might become incongruous when confronted by larger scale building requirements such as restaurants or conference facilities; the vernacular tradition can break down and become problematic at a bigger scale that contemporary inhabitation requires. Often this is largely a matter of simple physics[6] whereby building materials of a particular length and form fail when stressed beyond tried and tested capacities, but there is also a potential failure when scaling these elements beyond a particular aesthetic grain; the best vernacular architecture can become monstrous, crude and ungainly when it is demanded to perform beyond its capacities or as a bombastic version of a regular dwelling. Vernacular architecture needs to be studied rigorously and applied judiciously (see Box 9.2).

BOX 9.2   KNOW YOUR VERNACULAR

- Understand the 'types' of vernacular and their general response to broad climatic zones
- Identify and scientifically appraise any existing vernacular architecture in the area and how it might mitigate climatic and weather stresses – but check this against potential climate change shifts
- Understand its use of local building materials and technologies and their immediate availability
- Understand building location and settlement patterns as potential clues to environmental stresses
- Be aware that vernacular architecture might be determined by socio-cultural patterns that might mistakenly appear to be driven through climatic and environmental responses
- Engage an anthropologist to understand the socio-cultural dimensions of the vernacular
- Be aware that vernacular architecture might have some highly localized contingencies that might not translate to your specific site
- Be aware that vernacular technologies and built forms might fail when applied to larger scaled or different use patterns of the new facility
- Be aware that vernacular architecture might perpetuate harmful building and environmental practices
- Be aware of the 'brown-washing' or the veneer application of vernacular architecture for photogenic or marketing purposes
- Ensure that the back-of-house areas, such as staff quarters and mechanical workshops, are treated with the same care and concern as the front-of-house
- Consider upcycling the vernacular through a modern idiom ('critical regionalism') and avoid colonial exploitation
- Be wary of biomimicry which jumps species and scale and hence potentially fails in its functioning

The lessons of vernacular architecture do not begin and end at the perimeter of the built form and how it is made and which building materials are effective. The form, layout and disposition of a group of built units – the settlement pattern – can be instructive of how to arrange buildings in relation to seasonal changes or to dominant winds – or these may have come about for socio-cultural reasons, which an outsider might horribly misunderstand or misread as being relevant for environmental design responses. This points to the importance of having an anthropologist as part of the team to decode these patterns. Vernacular architecture not only manages to create pleasant living environments from meagre means but also manages the dynamic or unpleasant and potentially dangerous effects of weather events. The most obvious in this regard is the potential devastation caused by flash-floods and how far away dwellings and settlements are placed from water courses. The local vernacular architecture might even be suggestive of potential hazards that could exist on the site and how to mitigate them. For example, distinctive architectural features such as Iranian wind-towers or windcatchers work in conjunction with passive water-cooling systems and internal spatial arrangements and yet avoid funnelling sandstorms into the building – important lessons that go far beyond the expressive and iconic power of the architecture. A clear understanding of the relationship of the built form, its materials and its overall spatial arrangements as well as these elements' relationship to the environment and localized weather events are vital lessons to be taken from the local vernacular architecture.

The Iranian wind-towers mentioned above are an example of one of the biggest challenges to projects that have a strong visible and striking vernacular architecture in the area. This is the potential for facile mimicry that copies the styles of vernacular architecture but not the systems, intelligence and symbiotic filters that make the vernacular tradition work so well in its particular context. This is a stylistic appropriation and simplification that tries to make everyone feel good about the project – a local and traditional *looking* building is surely more respectful of the culture in which it is located?! – except that it does not necessarily add up to making guests and employees feel better in the everyday inhabitation of the spaces, and this failure might be indicated with tell-tale banks of air-conditioning units. More cynically, these visual tropes can be used to justify exploitative situations where the stylistic appropriation of vernacular architecture should be labelled as 'brown washing' – literally a mud veneer applied to a 'business as usual' architecture to hide the ugly truth from unsuspecting ecotourists; if it looks like a leopard, it doesn't mean it really is a leopard, it might just be a cardboard cut-out placed for the photoshoot. Indeed, in the sub-Saharan context this appropriation of an unmoored and cynically used 'vernacular' has bred its own self-referring and ubiquitous 'bush-lodge style' of gum-poles, thatch, canvas, and timber decks which seems to be environmentally responsive and sustainably oriented but often is really backed up by massive sliding aluminium doors and air-conditioning units on full blast. Similarly, the back-of-house activities such as staff living quarters, kitchens, waste processing areas and mechanical workshops are also in danger of being the 'out of sight, out of mind' ugly contradiction to the sanitized eco front and deserve as much care and attention as the parts that tourists typically engage with.[7]

The use of vernacular architecture can be a tempting approach largely because the original vernacular response seems to *belong* seamlessly with the landscape, and thus give succour for anxieties about the correctness of the built aspect of the conservation or remediation efforts. Moreover, vernacular traditions can be visually distinctive, powerful and 'other' worldly – hence signifying a real displacement potential for the traveller. The visual distinctiveness of vernacular architecture should be approached with caution and possibly through the lens of 'critical regionalism' which reinvents vernacular architecture through modern requirements whilst trying to avoid colonialist appropriation.

A similar approach of inventive appropriation and upcycling can be found in a related aspect of vernacular architecture which generally goes by the name of biomimicry. Biomimicry can fall into the same trap as vernacular appropriation in that it can provide a compelling narrative about how the architecture is a version of an endemic animal or plant and hence by association the building is secured as endemic in its own right – although this is often a long shot in that, unlike vernacular architecture, biomimicry literally jumps species.[8] Certainly, biomimicry is a fantastic tool at the disposal of an architect, especially when used in harsh climatic conditions; survival can be made easier when the building becomes a machine-organism that can deal with hostile conditions. However, again around issues of scale, caution must be applied – can the same systems evident in flora and fauna be scaled up to a building or do the laws of physics preclude the apparent ease with which this might be made to work? The answer is often 'no' and the buildings can become an indictment and an unintended monument to human misuse of the planet and its flora and fauna as the building becomes a prop for a misguided and poorly functioning gimmick.

STEP 3: TOUCH THE EARTH LIGHTLY ... TOUCH THE EARTH WELL

Glenn Murcutt, one of Australia's earliest proponents of sustainable architecture or 'green' design, popularized – if not invented – the idea of 'touching the earth lightly'. His thinking nevertheless goes beyond the level of slogans:

> Touching the land lightly is not about a building with just four columns ... It's about: where did that material come from? What damage has been done to the land in the excavation of that material? How will it be returned to the Earth eventually, or can it be reused, can it be recycled, can it be put together in a way that can be pulled apart and changed and reused?[9]

Some of Murcutt's ideas might be a bit dated, for example, nowadays we would say that *everything* is recyclable, but at what cost (to the environment, energy use, people, etc.); today it is more important to speak of upcycling. Nevertheless, it still has currency and forms part of this chapter's title because it is an overarching principle that suggests architecture's role in sustainable tourism is to largely minimize its own destructive impact (maximizing its own positive or transformative potential is a question handled more in the next section). This ethos is true even of the use and upcycling of vernacular architecture which might in itself carry some practices that are out of keeping with contemporary ideas of landscape or environmental conservation. But touching the earth lightly doesn't necessarily mean touching the earth well. In fact, without a clear pre-existing vernacular it does mean that there are fewer obvious forms and materials to limit the design and hence the architecture can suffer by being left out in the wilderness – made to find its own way, so to speak – which can have disastrous consequences where 'anything goes' or there is a reversion to stylistic tropes. On top of this, even if the design proceeds with the intention of touching the earth lightly it does not necessarily follow that it will touch the earth well (see Box 9.3).

BOX 9.3   TOUCH THE EARTH LIGHTLY

Without vernacular architecture nearby ...

- Learn to 'read' the landscape for clues as to how and where to build
- Try and build on the most impacted or damaged part of the site and use the building project as a way to remediate or rehabilitate the area
- Recycle existing buildings that are near lifecycle end or are a blight on the landscape
- Minimize disturbing the earth and allow natural systems to continue unimpinged as much as possible
- Consider how the building process will impact the earth and the environment
- Don't use 'decks' as a default approach – engage the ground as part of the project
- Use sustainably sourced building materials and be mindful how they arrive or leave the site
- Consider the project as a future ruin or abandoned structure and how it might return to the earth without poisoning or blighting it
- Consider how passive heating and cooling through correct building orientation can help it be warm in winter and cool in summer

- Minimize energy requirements and use high-tech 'green' technologies like PV panels sparingly
- Use and care for water frugally and wisely, and manage waste carefully
- Consider scaling the accommodation down to a minimum
- Be mindful of the visual impact of the project from afar – rather maximize the experience of being inside the space
- Consider using LEED or BREEAM sustainability evaluation systems, especially in urban areas, but be wary of reducing the complexity of 'touching the earth lightly' to a checkbox list

Even without vernacular architectural models, however, there are still ways to make the buildings 'belong' in the landscape as if a natural extension of its particularities; even in the wilderness there are still clues as to how to survive and where to go and which places to avoid. In such contexts the architect must become intensely attuned to the natural systems of a place – where the dominant winds are, where water is, where threats might lie – and literally 'read' the landscape even if through small things like lichen on rocks or subtle shifts in vegetation where the terrain makes a distinctive place or signals subterranean shifts or water courses.[10] Good architecture – skilled architects – will necessarily engage with both scientific analysis and poetic uncovering in the design process whereby they eventually find a resonance and symbiosis. If these ideas seem too abstract it is probably helpful to introduce a case study that demonstrates the complexities involved and useful strategies in designing buildings in pristine environments and how to touch the earth lightly, and yet to touch the *two* earths well at the same time – this earth being dug up for the project and our Earth that feels the impact of that digging no matter how small.

Architecture Co-op's small camp 'Oudebosch' in the Kogelberg reserve of South Africa's Cape Floral Kingdom shifts the focus away from vernacular architecture to 'minimizing impact' (Figure 9.1). The obvious and most important move for this state-managed project was to identify the key impacted or compromised place in the reserve – this was easy given that there were six existing 'mountain hut' wood cabins on the site that were nearing the end of their lifecycle and whose lack of engagement with the exterior meant they ignored the astounding landscape of this UNESCO World Heritage Site. The old cabins were also placed around a parking circle planted with invasive kikuyu grass at the centre; the site spoke of a hiking world of macho bravura where nature was an immersive blur that you conquered and cabins were places to fall asleep in rather than be enjoyed as part of a convivial setting for families. Bricks were recycled from the old cabins' foundation walls and used for paved surfaces in the new project whilst the kikuyu grass was removed and a new ecological or natural pool and indigenous grass were used to form a new social space at the heart of the scheme – a place-making strategy that gives the site not only amenities but a hierarchy of spaces from public to private whilst securing water as a precious resource in this water-scarce, fire-prone area. The new cabins were deliberately designed as timber framed using locally sourced and sustainably grown pine which allowed them to be built on pad foundations thereby minimizing the impact on the earth. Gabions packed with stone gleaned from the site were used to form small level areas in and around the cabins whilst still allowing natural systems, and their individuated components, to seep, creep and crawl their way through; the architects felt it was important that visitors had some areas of stable ground beneath their feet and that not every surface needed to be made of timber deck which can counter-intuitively provide an uneasy feeling of a whole range of 'wildlife' going on directly beneath your feet.

Source: Rupert Jordi.

Figure 9.1   Architecture co-op. Oudebosch Eco Camp, Western Cape, South Africa

The timber framed units allowed extensive glazing to orientate to the north for solar gain in winter – although the big aluminium sliding doors unfortunately count against reducing carbon emissions while the glazing also allows ambient heat transfer inside in summer. This is one of the few compromises on the project – chosen because they are easy to move and do not warp over time, but more importantly, unlike the previous cabins, create seamless transitions between indoor and outdoor space to maximize family interaction at the threshold between safety and wilderness; arguably, smaller sections of glazing might have achieved the same effect. The timber-framed structures allowed infill panelling to be used as it is easily transported and produces limited waste in a modular construction system. More importantly, it allows sufficient insulation in the hot summer but also allows quick heating of the units from stoves in winter and hence a well-tempered environment can be quickly attained as each new set of inhabitants arrive and without the long lag-time a stone building has in heating a space. Locally sourced timber sapling screens provide privacy on vertical planes and solar protection as horizontal overhangs. Other sustainability strategies are important to note even if they are almost ubiquitous and non-negotiable in contemporary ecological architecture[11] – these range from carefully positioned foul and grey water soakaways that do not contaminate water sources to the use of solar photovoltaic panels that offer a small distinctive triangle element to the roofscape as they twist to the north. The sheet-metal roofs are overlaid with recycled timber pallet boxes filled with soil sacks to allow sedges and succulents to take hold and help provide insulation to the roof. All of these elements can easily be disassembled and reused at lifecycle end, and most of them could simply become part of an elegant ruin returning to the earth should the project suffer calamity and be abandoned in the future. They also add up to useful points scored if the building gets evaluated through the LEED / SITES and BREEAM 'green' building or sustainability appraisal systems – operating mostly in the USA and the UK respectively.[12]

The planted roof speaks to a deliberate and obvious strategy in this example which is to make the development disappear into the landscape and especially when approached from afar on a hiking trail. This was also partially achieved through the extensive use of timber screens. Moreover, the ethos to politely step back and let the landscape do the talking was also carried through in the scale and form of the buildings which were made low and without particularly distinctive vertical forms. Similarly, the disaggregation of the development into five separate cabins allowed the project to never define itself as a big single and distinctive element within the landscape; the way a leopard's spots blend it into the surrounding bush and yet does not negate it as a distinctive single being. After these carefully constructed polite deferences, the joy of the architecture is then found in the inhabitation of the units looking out at the landscape, rather than as a set of distinctive forms viewed from afar. The intimacy and yet generosity of the spaces that manage privacy whilst creating distinctive place becomes the point at which the architecture contributes a memorable part of the experience rather than a stage-set for Instagram posts – although the project manages just fine in that regard too. It is arguably this moment, where visitors are at rest and enjoying a place in comfort, that memories are made in a way that is far more powerful than the fleeting views of distinctive architecture seen from afar.

STEP 4: TOUCH THE EARTH HEAVILY … BUT MAP BEFORE YOU DO IT

After having travelled up close to a 'green' building set in a fairly pristine environment, we are going to zoom out a bit and look at the big picture again by getting ourselves into some maps. Maps don't just tell you where you are, they also tell you where to go. As hinted at in the section above, architects have become far more attuned to a process of mapping to guide and define a design rather than simply providing some incongruous 'signature' building or preferred style. This is especially true when projects find themselves set within a larger urban or landscape context; you have to know where you are and what is going on around you if you don't want to stick out like an idiot, or worse, behave like an idiot. This final section shows not only the importance of mapping and analysis in the development of a design strategy but also how a holistic approach to the design of the built infrastructure can radically change and improve a tourist resource and those who are impacted by it. Rather than sticking out like an idiot, the project can become valued by everyone who is engaged with its becoming and being

– as well as the tourists who are transient guests in its space. This is to understand the design process and the building process as part of an 'ecology' that, if engaged with intelligently and creatively, can be positive, life-affirming and enduring, as opposed to poisonous, life-negating and depleting (see Box 9.4).

BOX 9.4　TOUCH THE EARTH HEAVILY

- Understand the potential for the project to shift from an extractive and exploitative model to a locally oriented sustainable transformation
- Understand that architecture is best when done through an emergent and evolutionary process and not prescribed as a stylistic product
- Assemble a team of transdisciplinary experts led by an architect to help define the brief
- Require the experts to map their fields of interest across the site and translate their findings into a visual language so it remains 'on the table' by being pinned on the wall
- Conduct resource mapping (skills, building materials) as expanding concentric circles from the building site but be sceptical of the usefulness of what you find
- Let scientific analysis appraise whether building materials and practices are safe, suitable and sustainable
- Consider using the project to upskill local communities but be realistic about the potential uptake of 'foreign' practices in the area
- Consider providing legacy infrastructure such as mobile sawmills that can continue to support local economies and manufacturing when given ongoing support
- Be willing to have your sustainability edicts upended by real situations in difficult contexts
- Employ an architect who is reflective, creative and yet systems oriented who is willing to work with experts from other disciplines in defining the brief
- Finally, be sceptical of all checkbox lists and reductive approaches such as this 'step-by-step' guide – responsive and emergent design is always complex, totally specific / unique and, when headed by the right architect, completely surprising

To be clear, this final approach does not negate the preceding sections but underpins them. In fact, it can be applied to *any* building design project in *any* context – which is why it has the anachronous 'Step 4' title; it really should be the step that comes before everything else, before the building site or programme is even defined. It really is about defining the brief for the project as a consultative process – a step which is rarely undertaken and yet is arguably *the* most important step in the entire process that ends up with a sustainable tourism facility. Mapping[13] aims to discover the different systems or potentials at work within a region or landscape and then analyse them as separate concerns. This disaggregation allows each affective system to be identified and studied and then put together to produce a layered reading of a place – design then works to mediate these often contradictory layers and finds a way to synthesize them with the least compromise – or at least by knowingly elevating particular concerns through a clear value system once all the forces and dynamics are present on the table. This disaggregation also allows experts such as anthropologists or botanists or geologists or landscape architects to bring depth to the analysis rather than an architect working through a gut response – not necessarily to be negated mind you – or worse, through a signature building cut from a glossy architecture magazine and pasted with total disregard into its new context. Experts allow the elements that will become important for the design to 'speak' even *before* the design begins, helping set the template for cost-effective and sensible design responses. For example, a geologist might translate what the soil and rocks are saying – might speak for the rocks – so that the architect might understand them and their potential or potential problems. In this 'Stage 0' process – defining the brief – the architect is given the greatest gift by the client of being the facilitator of input from transdisciplinary experts who help formulate the brief from first principles and from direct analysis. It is perhaps the most important step in the whole enterprise; it gets experts and inputs up front and puts their concerns on the table – rather than them being appointed later to try and make sense of the design and mitigate its incorrect moves. This is the gift of an emergent or evolutionary architecture, as opposed to a prescriptive, *a priori* or stylistic architecture.

The work of Collis and Associates provide good examples of how 'touching the earth heavily' and 'mapping before you do it' might be transformative for the architectural project and the sustainable tourism venture as a whole. Although their work is not directly in the ecotourism area, their engagement with sustainability in some extremely challenging contexts – for example, the Koidu diamond mine in Sierra Leone – exists as a good model to think ecotourism projects through. They demonstrate that architecture, or rather the architectural project which involves a variety of stages (from defining the brief to a feasibility study to analyses to the building process and beyond) can be a change agent if the potential of its multiple intersections and interactions with the world can be recognized and optimized; the architectural project can – and must – be a catalyst for change far beyond the 'simple' delivery of habitable rooms and amenities. Counterintuitively, the architectural project is precisely where throughput or linear economic metabolisms which create economic dependencies can be challenged to become regenerative metabolisms that connect to a range of ecologies from the social to the environmental whilst engendering an autonomous local economy (Figure 9.2). By mapping dependencies or how resources and opportunities 'flow' through a site and its surrounds, the project can be located within the dynamics of global systems through a range of perspectives (economic, social, environmental, etc.). This strategy is captured in diagrams that describe a 'business as usual' or colonialist approach where expertise, resources and capital 'lands', are deployed for extractive purposes and then leaves with extracted wealth and a depleted environment, and how this can be changed into a localized or circular and sustainability oriented economy supported by the architectural project – by turning 'red' (solid arrows) to 'green' (outlined arrows). This is a holistic understanding of sustainability that incorporates sustainable building practices and sustainable socio-economic strategies through a highly localized lens – can everything be found and made locally, if appropriate? – whilst also engaging local communities more directly in this.

Apart from conceptualizing the project's potential impact through diagrams, the practice works hard at resource mapping as led and championed by experts in unrelated fields. They also map a range of more architectural concerns, namely, from mapping building materials to mapping local skills and construction methods to local architectural strategies that deal with climate or potentially maximize local labour input as opposed to importing specialist contractors. These resource mappings can be understood to radiate from the centre of the proposed project in expanding circles of availability – the circle immediately encompassing the future building being the most valuable for potential use on account of its probable efficiency and efficacy and limited carbon output, of literally building the building from what is there

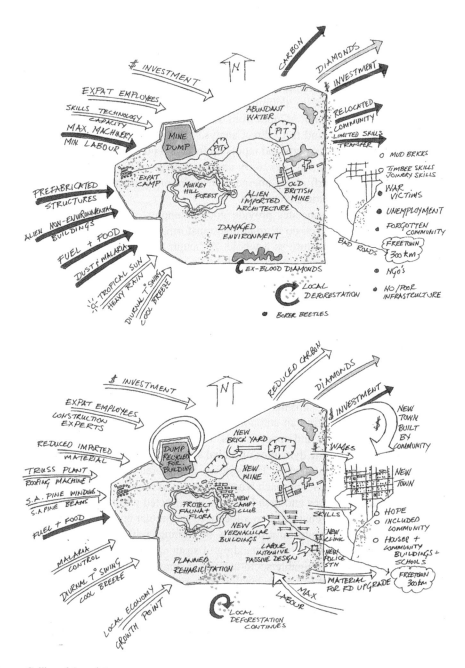

Source: Collis and Associates.

Figure 9.2   *Collis and Associates. Koidu diamond mine, Sierra Leone – from extractive to sustainable development*

(Figure 9.3). For example, this could be where the earth that is going to be dug and removed for foundations can be used for making the walls of the structure or where reeds on the site can be harvested for thatched roofs or even where the topsoil can be carefully set aside for gardening projects to support the food cycle of the building project and its subsequent service of the facility.

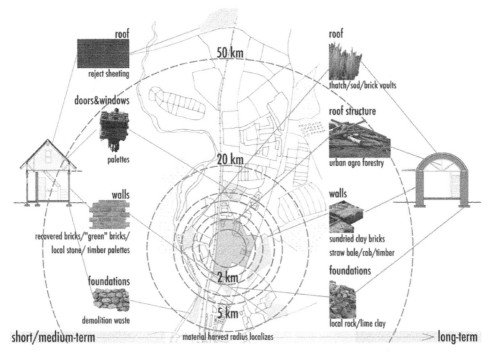

Source: Collis and Associates.

Figure 9.3   Collis and Associates. Site resource mapping

Even these simple initial moves of an immediate circle of resources around the future building generate a complex set of actions and possibly contradictory demands that can spin out from this. For example, soil and stone from the site can be an excellent resource in making the walls and floors of the future building, but it needs serious analysis and appraisal by soil and structural engineers who might not be ready at hand; good intentions might literally make a future uninhabitable building further down the line. Even if these items can be made to work – sometimes with a creative reimaging of 'standard' constituents being substituted for more readily available local materials – there could literally be no one in nearby communities who can build with these items. Hence skills mapping in ever expanding circles from the site needs to be undertaken when the first soil samples are made to ascertain who might be able to build the facility and by using which technologies and with what ease. A strategic decision needs to be taken (for example, if the soil is good but the skills don't exist) as to whether or not a train-ing regime should be undertaken to skill potential workers in the area in a building process that might, due to its perceived or real application of 'foreign' technology, never be adopted as a sustainable local practice once the project is built. On the other hand, when pursued with a well thought out training programme, the architectural project might seed subtle shifts in entrenched building and labour practices that might not be optimal or in alignment with sustainability precepts and hence provide a legacy that moves from the architectural project into the building work of the surrounding areas. Through this, the architectural project can become a catalyst for the transformation of destructive or unsustainable building practices far beyond the gates of the 'lodge'.

Counter to the idea of working with the soil of the site to make the walls and floors, there might be, a few kilometres away, a grove of alien invasive trees – not a tropical hardwood forest, mind you, whose individual trees are crucial parts of a complex ecosystem – blighting the landscape and which can be readily harvested. This resource could provide a timber-frame tourism facility simply by deploying a mobile sawmill and a solar powered kiln that can be left as a legacy from the project; a building of earth might not be wanted or helpful at all. Similarly, if there are no skilled reed thatchers in the area then the harvesting of reeds might be a pointless exercise and designing a roof around this resource might require a specialist team getting flown in every ten years to maintain the building – and to maintain the 'neat' image of sustainability coming from endless updated posts from visitors. On the other hand, making use of local building practices, especially vernacular ones, can mean a constant source of work for, and engagement with, local communities – which might be far more important than the windfall of useful but unusable building matter on the site.

Finally, in what could seem deeply unsettling to sustainability sensibilities, there might be excellent sheet-metal and metalworking skills in the area and easy access to those materials – a truly emergent vernacular or the architecture of the everyday that might bring an extraordinary architecture to the project that does not impact a sustainability equation in any significant way.[14] This kind of resource should not be dismissed out of hand because it does not match some predetermined models or prejudices of what is 'correct' in sustainability terms or the stylistic tropes of 'ecolodge' architecture; the goalposts of sustainability shift as the prioritizing of ecological or social or material concerns takes hold. The design is indeed emergent rather than prescriptive, but the fidelity of this emergence is dependent on the depth and breadth of the mapping. This nuanced approach is perhaps not happening because clients, and even architects, still understand architecture as holding the certainty of a product – things they like and have seen in magazines – as opposed to architecture as an uncertain revelatory process – things that they didn't know they wanted or needed but now realize they could never have had in any other way.

This small example above illustrates that a holistic approach is never a clear, simple or linear process and is beset with value judgements that must be clearly identified and understood so that they are in line with the vision of the sustainable tourism project as a whole. Is it a strident ethical claim about the ecology of an area and a carbon neutral or carbon negative building and the project will be built that way no matter what the impact on surrounding communities and their practices? Or is there appetite to engage with much more complexity that requires much more intelligence, agility and stamina and avoids surface slogans and soundbites in favour of a new soundbite, touching the earth deeply? What is clear is that a strong team is needed – of creative, reflective and lateral-thinking professionals from the architect to engineers to other disciplines willing to work outside of standard details and norms, as well as anthropologists who can unlock human value and meaning in the area. To make a real impact, business as usual thinking has to be challenged and critical and creative engagement with complex issues from first principles needs to drive the project from inception to completion.

TOUCHING PEOPLE

All of the above misses out on one crucial concern from which everything else flows: where is the built project to be sited? Previous sections have suggested that there can be clear cases where there is no need for a built project and that it might already exist in a disaggregated, dispersed and rhizomatic form in adjacent villages or towns. Alternatively, if a project is sited far from local facilities there is a need for a greater understanding of the landscape and its systems of potentials (both positive and negative or destructive like flood plains) to inform some ideal locations of a building site. Similarly, the idea of building only on the impacted parts of the land and using the building as a part of a rehabilitation strategy has been noted; the greatest legacy of the architectural project might be to fix a portion of land that has severe consequences for a greater region in time if its melting erosion is left unattended. These are valid concerns that can be added to any helpful guide as to how to proceed when faced with the extremely challenging task of, what one might facilely note as, 'accommodating tourists'. On top of that the most difficult challenge is to provide the building that transforms the tourist into a 'woke' individual more attuned with the issues and challenges of sustainability by representing and remaking the ethos of the greater conservation or sustainability project in the building itself, by helping them *feel* it as much as they feel the transformative power of an immersion in 'wilderness'.[15] Here it is paramount to work with an architect who is creative as well as systems oriented, who is intelligent and sensitive and can make bold moves and add value to the tourist site or tourist facility at the same time. This sounds unscientific and difficult to operationalize – which it is. As our reality shifts to a world that is simultaneously scientistic and reductive (remembering that scientists hold fundamentally important insight as described above) and yet surface deep driven through attention deficit 'swefties' and their 'swipe-left' images, there is extraordinary value that the right architect can bring to a project. This might be summarized as 'reading' a site, and identifying and maximizing its underlying power, its specificity, its peculiarity and particularity. Mapping can hold all of the concerns enumerated in the sections above and yet also ask: is the land about fissures and big sky? Is it about shelter and thresholds for fear of an overpowering mountain-scape? Is it simply to hear the trickle of water and feel and smell the coolness of mossy ground in-between rocks that speak of the fragility of life? A good architectural response will always be more than the fulfilment of a check-box approach but will mobilize all the concerns noted in the sections above into a coherent approach and outcome that touches and moves people even if they cannot understand how or why. A good architectural project will 'feel' right, will be right and will seem as if it has always been there, always part of the landscape. It is impossible to reduce this to scientific appraisal or an Instagram image – which is why architecture occupies the space between the science and the arts and pulls those together in a synthesis that transcends what either approach can deliver by themselves. Finding and appointing the right architect – someone who can work with experts from many disciplines and who is a creative and reflective practitioner who has an eye on the science – might be the biggest and most important first step to a project that transcends all expectations, that feeds and emboldens and changes the world and yet is still a wonder and delight to return to again and again.

NOTES

1. As noted by Vernon Collis, all things come into the world either by being mined or by being farmed.
2. See Arısoy (2013) for an introduction to 'eco-revelatory design', where the landscape design and remediation becomes part of didactic engagement with visitors, or in this case, tourists.
3. See Dyantyi (2018) for an introduction to iKhaya le Langa.
4. See Watson (2020) for examples as to how close to nature architecture can come.
5. An admirably thorough example of this is to be found in Taner Okan and colleagues' assessment of traditional timber houses in north-eastern Turkey for ecotourism potential and the problem presented by wood borer (Okan et al., 2016).
6. D'Arcy Thompson's *On Growth and Form* (1992) is an exploration of how physics and mechanisms have a determining impact on the form and change in organisms.
7. This was a key factor in David Bristow and Colin Bell's (2013) evaluation of *Africa's Finest* sustainable ecolodges.
8. See Stott (2017) for a description of Vincent Callebaut's biomimicry ecolodge design in the Philippines.
9. As quoted by Wahlquist (2016).
10. Theoretical texts in architecture that deal with this concern can range from the phenomenology of place through a poetic and experiential reading of landscape – the writing of Christian Norberg-Schulz (e.g. Norberg-Schulz, 1980) – to a scientific analysis aimed at designing *with* nature – initiated through Ian McHarg in the 1960s (see McHarg, 1971).
11. Peder Anker (2006) presents a great study of how ecological architecture aims to become almost like a space-pod in its circular self-sufficiency, and hence ironically, deliberately set apart from the ecology it reveres.
12. LEED (Leadership in Energy and Environmental Design) is formulated through the US Green Building Council (www.usgbc.org) and has synergies with the SITES Rating System (www .sustainablesites.org). The Building Research Establishment Environmental Assessment is found at www.breeam.com.
13. Mapping as a design strategy can be said to have emerged with Ian McHarg's *Design with Nature* (1971) and expounded on in a creative way by the landscape architect James Corner (1999).
14. This point is admirably made in the work of Francis Kéré (2016) and his school at Gando, Burkina Faso.
15. Andersen (1993) noted the importance of the ecolodge as a didactic window on nature.

REFERENCES

Andersen, D. L. (1993) A window to the natural world: The design of ecotourism facilities. In K. Lindberg and D. Hawkins (eds.), *Ecotourism: A Guide for Planners and Managers*. North Bennington, VT: The Ecotourism Society, 125–131.

Anker, P. (2006) The closed world of ecological architecture. *Journal of Architecture*, 10(5), 527–552.

Arısoy, N. K. (2013) Eco-revelatory design. In N. Kemal (ed.), *Advances in Landscape Architecture*. London: IntechOpen, 209–226.

Bristow, D. and Bell, C. (2013) *Africa's Finest: The Most Sustainable Responsible Safari Destinations in Sub-Saharan Africa and the Indian Ocean Islands*. Cape Town: I Am Eco Pub.

Corner, J. (1999) *Recovering Landscape: Essays in Contemporary Landscape Architecture*. Princeton, NJ: Princeton Architectural Press.

Dyantyi, H. (2018) 'Ikhaya Le Langa' brings a world of visitors to a vibrant slice of a rejuvenated apartheid township. Accessed 4 April 2020 at http://www.dailymaverick.co.za/article/2018-04-26-ikhaya -le-langa-brings-a-world-of-visitors-to-a-vibrant-slice-of-a-rejuvenated-apartheid-township/.

Kéré, F. (2016) *Francis Kéré: Radically Simple*. Berlin: Hatje Cantz Publishers.

McHarg, I. (1971) *Design with Nature*. New York: Doubleday.

Norberg-Schulz, C. (1980) *Genius Loci: Towards a Phenomenology of Architecture*. New York: Rizzoli.

Okan, T., Köse, N., Arifoğlu, E. and Köse, C. (2016) Assessing ecotourism potential of traditional wooden architecture in rural areas: The case of Papart Valley. *Sustainability*, 8, 974.

Stott, R. (2017) Vincent Callebaut envisions shell-inspired eco-tourism resort in the Philippines. Accessed 4 April 2020 at http://www.archdaily.com/879939/vincent-callebaut-envisions-shell -inspired-eco-tourism-resort-in-the-philippines.

Thompson, D. W. (1992) *On Growth and Form*. Cambridge: Cambridge University Press.

Wahlquist, C. (2016) Glenn Murcutt: Touch the Earth lightly with your housing footprint. Accessed 4 April 2020 at http://www.theguardian.com/artanddesign/2016/aug/11/glenn-murcutt-touch-the-earth -lightly-with-your-housing-footprint.

Watson, J. (2020) *Lo-Tek: Design by Radical Indigenism*. Cologne: Taschen.

10. UN Indicators Programme: informing sustainable development for tourism destinations

Edward W. (Ted) Manning

ORIGINS OF THE UNWTO INDICATORS PROGRAMME

Beginning in 1992, the environmental committee at the World Tourism Organization (WTO, now UNWTO) initiated work to inform improved decision-making by the sector. In response to concern regarding degraded ecosystems, declining attractions, as well as incidents of social problems in tourism communities it became clear that better planning and management was needed. Often degradation of attractions or the decline of tourism came as a surprise as no one had been monitoring the factors which were leading to these problems. Concern was expressed about the industry as a whole, about specific subsectors and destinations and about the performance of enterprises.

Why Indicators?

The basis for indicators is to provide the capacity to see and understand what is happening to the tourism industry and the places it uses. Without the right knowledge there is no capacity to plan or to set specific goals or targets. Without information it is also not possible to discern trends or to identify problems or set directions to solutions. But not all information is useful, and not all can be used to support real decisions.

Indicators are essentially information for risk management. In the work initiated in the early 1990s to develop the information suitable for tourism management it was clear that tourism, because of its complexity, would need to include information on a broad range of factors; economic, socio-cultural, environmental, and institutional, as well as the ability to monitor external changes or potential threats to a destination or its tourism. Tourism is at the top of the food chain, its success based on other sectors and how they are managed. The impetus for the programme came from discussions at the 1992 WTO Environment committee meetings in Madrid. The committee agreed that there was a need to help destinations understand the relationship between environmental and social conditions and the well-being of the tourism industry, particularly at the destination level. The range of possible information can be overwhelming. The challenge is to focus on that information which is likely to be most useful and will be used.

In initial discussions, some argued for a single index of sustainability – a quantitative index derived from manipulating a long list of measurable attributes to create a single number which could characterize the state of tourism. The idea was that all conditions could be quantified, and some form of mathematical model could be contrived to give a numeric value to overall sustainability for a destination based on all relevant factors. (This approach was set aside because no agreement could be obtained on the list of factors and their weighting, particularly across many different types of destinations.) Others present noted that it could take more than 50 indicators just to measure water quality, demographic change or species diversity. The challenge was to capture key information without overload. The programme which evolved from the experts and workshops organized by the sustainable tourism committee is basically issue- and risk-driven. It is designed to help destinations find out what issues are most central to their sustainability. The result is ideally a practical set of meaningful indicators to permit better understanding of the issues facing their specific tourism and effective management of them.

Destinations were selected as the focus for the WTO programme because they are the principal scale of most tourism management and planning organizations. A destination was defined as a location where tourism occurs, and where visitors would spend at least one night. The spatial extent of a destination was considered to contain the support services, attractions, and resources for tourism. Ideally a destination is also congruent with the boundaries of an authority or organization with some planning or coordination authority including responsibility for tourism. Destinations also are the scale where most issues are perceived, where many stakeholders reside and where tourism has direct contact with, and dependence upon, social, economic, environmental and governance conditions. Also, destinations usually can be defined at a scale where problems may be manageable as part of tourism and community plans and where issues interact, and solutions need to be multifaceted.

Initial work was done in three test destinations in Canada (Prince Edward Island), Mexico (Los Tuxtlas), and the USA (Florida Keys) through case studies on the specific destinations and to determine whether key risks and concerns could be captured in a limited number of measures, and actually measured. The Netherlands took a different approach seeking indicators which could be derived from existing regional data integrated at a national level. Expert meetings in Madrid (1992) and Winnipeg (1993) helped to further define the overall programme and its focus on key indicators, and a participatory process to choose them. The central idea was to define the information which is useful, and which is necessary and sufficient to support better decisions on sustainability and which could in practice be available.

Table 10.1 summarizes the linkages between the overall destination planning process and the indicators programme. It is derived from the table contained in the WTO Guidebook (2004). It illustrates the development and use of indicators as part of a larger destination planning process which supports planning and management of a more sustainable destination.

DEFINING A UNWTO INDICATORS APPROACH

The initial Guide *What Do Tourism Managers Need to Know?* (WTO, 1996) (available in several languages) was produced to help destinations to develop indicators. This led to expert workshops and test applications in several destinations with emphasis on key issues and risks. Overall, the objective was to create a programme which was most useful to the destinations themselves, would provide information which would be used, and to provide training for tourism managers from several destinations in each region in the use of indicators. It is important to note that the creation of indicators was not considered to be an objective in itself. It was viewed rather as input to solutions to be applied at a destination, or at parts of a destination, as part of a broader planning and management process. A related objective was to try to create measures and procedures which could be replicated and compared across destinations. The

Table 10.1   *Indicators and destination planning: key links*

Destination planning process	Steps in indicators work	Role of indicators
A. Definition/delineation of the destination /development area.	**Research and organization** 1. Definition/delineation of the destination (to identify scope of information needs for indicators).	The definition of destination reflects data boundaries (management or political units for access and utility).
B. Establishment of participatory planning process.	2. Use of participatory processes for indicators development.	Indicators are part of participatory planning process and catalyst to stimulate it.
C. Formulation of vision and/or mission statement. D. Initial assessment and analysis of assets, risks, impacts (situation analysis).	3. Identification of tourism assets and risks. 4. Long-term vision for a destination – clearly defined.	Key step in indicators work is to identify existing vision, and clearly define key elements.
E. Choice of indicators and their prioritization relative to destination issues and broader context.	**Indicators development** 5. Selection of priority issues and policy questions. 6. Identification of desired indicators. 7. Inventory of data sources. 8. Selection of indicators. **Indicators implementation** 9. Evaluation of indicator feasibility and implementation procedures. 10. Data collection and analysis.	Indicators are essential to clarify key issues, assets, risks and provide accurate information on them. Indicators are used to report on the results of the initial assessment to the stakeholders involved. The UNWTO indicators Guidebook and the UNWTO / UNEP 12 Aims (2018) can serve to suggest areas which may be of importance – a menu of potential goals, issues and risks.
F. Setting up development objectives (for the short, medium and long term according to priority needs). G. Formulation and evaluation of strategies targeting development objectives.	11. Ideally indicators are built into the action phases of planning and implementation. 12. Data gathering, and analysis occur on an ongoing basis. 13. Policy objectives can also target development of data sources and processing capacities that supports indicator application.	Indicators help to provide clarity to development objectives – can be used to set targets and performance measures. Essential for definition of clear targets and timeframes and communicate them to stakeholders.
H. Formulation of action plans and specific projects based on the optimal strategy.		Indicators become performance measures for projects and activities and assist in definition of specific targets and understanding of their achievement.
I. Implementation of action plans and projects.	14. Accountability, reporting and communication. 15. Monitoring and evaluation of implementation should be conducted on an ongoing basis, with periodic reporting of results, using indicators.	Indicators are what is monitored and evaluated including management processes, direct programme and project outputs.
J. Monitoring and evaluation of plan and project implementation.	16. Monitoring of indicators application, priority issues, information sources and processing capacities can change, so it is also necessary to verify the appropriateness of indicators periodically.	Progress in achieving defined objectives. Changes in environmental and socio-economic conditions as a result of actions. Indicators form key part of public accountability for implementation and results. Indicators which are common to many destinations provide benchmarking.

approach to development and use of indicators recommended in the Guidebook is based on both expert input and the experience of application in many destinations. Each destination is unique, but all have some common issues where it is possible to use the same indicators and measures which have proven useful in similar situations in other destinations.

Destination Workshops

Work was undertaken to expand the destination level work on indicators via a series of workshops in many regions. Beginning in 1999 hands-on regional workshops were held in most world regions to make managers aware of the programme and its potential. Each workshop was held in a specific destination and by design involved the local stakeholders, national and international experts and tourism and community officials. Each was done as an example to both produce a case study and to show participants how to do the same in their own destination(s). The programme used this methodology in the following destinations with representatives present in most cases from other countries in the region:

- Keszthely Balaton Hungary, 1999 for Central and Eastern Europe
- Cozumel Mexico, 1999 for Central America and the Caribbean
- Villa Gesell Argentina, 2000 for South America
- Beruwala Sri Lanka, 2000 for Sri Lanka
- Kukljika Croatia, 2001 for the Mediterranean
- Chagauramas Trinidad, 2004 for the Caribbean jointly with Association of Caribbean States
- Phuket Thailand, 2005 for Thailand with a focus on tsunami recovery
- Rurrenabaque Bolivia, 2005 for Andean nations
- Yangshuo China, 2005 for China (see Figure 10.1)
- Jeddah Saudi Arabia, 2006 for Middle East and North Africa
- Lombok Indonesia, 2007 for Southeast Asia
- Kolas Montenegro, 2007 for Balkans
- Bohol Philippines, 2008 for Philippines
- Muscat Oman, 2015 for Oman

The objectives of the destination focused workshops for each destination have been:

- To provide each destination with a set of indicators which will actually be supported and used in planning and management
- To ensure that the indicators cover a range of economic, environmental, social and management issues
- To make sure that concerns central to the success of the destination are not missed
- To make sure that the indicators are evaluated relative to:
  - *Relevance – do they respond to an important issue and really measure it?*
  - *Feasibility – can they be measured (with reasonable effort or price)?*
  - *Credibility – will they be believed (are they based on good scientific information and methods)?*
  - *Clarity – is the result clear and understandable to the managers or stakeholders?*
  - *Comparability – is it similar to the measures used in other destinations? (This last objective has in later workshops been added to assess potential indicators to encourage the use where possible of indicators which are also used in other destinations and can be used as possible benchmarks.)*

Figure 10.1   Yangshuo China

In each destination where a workshop was organized, the process normally would involve the widest range of stakeholders in defining the goals, obstacles, risks and opportunities in their destination and in helping to define what kind of tourism they desire and wish to sustain. One of the challenges for the programme has been outreach after the workshops. While participants have normally been able to take the information and integrate it into their planning management or education work, in several of the destinations there has been limited formal follow-up. The Guidebook produced in 2005 contains the key findings from most of the workshops undertaken to that date along with reviews of indicators used by tourism around the world in support of sustainability. The Guidebook drew on 62 experts from 22 nations to help develop the concept, write the sections and provide case examples. The Guidebook was designed to provide clarity to the indicator development process and define the elements which constitute sustainability for a destination. The recommended approach to creation of indicators for a destination would be through a participatory process and case studies to further validate and test procedures in specific sites. These were outlined in detail in the 2004 Guidebook and accompanying Field Guide. The recommended approach is more an agreed process to help destinations define what is important and measure it than a prescriptive tool as each destination is unique and the goal is to support informed decisions. The feedback from subsequent applications was input into the later development of the Observatories programme. The informal target for indicator selection for practical use in a destination has normally been about 25 to 30 indicators: it has been difficult in most destinations to reduce the list to this level at the workshops although in practice a more limited number have been made operational.

In addition to the UN sponsored workshops, conferences and related destination specific applications which have advanced the understanding and use of the WTO indicators, applications of the approach have also been done in a number of destinations such as Cape Breton Canada, Peninsula Valdez Argentina, Kangaroo Island Australia, Malta, Portugal, Kazakhstan, Cyprus, several destinations in Cuba and in many members of the Association of Caribbean States. Reports from each of these are available from UNWTO in Madrid and from Tourisk Inc. via inquiry at the website www.tourisk.com. The indicators programme was succeeded by the International Network of Sustainable Tourism Observatories (INSTO) programme covered later.

Reasons for a Participatory Approach

When the work to develop indicators began, it became clear that no two destinations were the same. While many of the destinations shared some common issues and similar challenges, each had its own ecological, social and economic conditions and systems of governance. It was clear that full participation of stakeholders would be the only practical means to define these issues and to obtain information about them.

A participatory procedure was developed and modified through several applications. It is defined in the Guidebook (WTO, 2004) and in the Field Guide produced to aid those empirically developing indicators for destinations (Manning and Manning, 2005). While a short list of baseline issues with suggested indicators is provided to destinations wishing to use indicators (as these issues have been found to be important in nearly all destinations), a much larger list and an indicator development procedure are both provided to support other issues which may be important to a destination. The challenge has always been to scope the eventual list down to a practical set. Participation by all stakeholders helps both to scope the entire range of issues and to gain support for implementation.

Findings from the Initial Indicators Workshops

The series of practical workshops was important to the evolution of the UNWTO programme and to its sharing among many participating countries. Several observations are key and provide some direction which may guide future applications:

- Beginning the workshop with an initial focus on long-term goals and common objectives was successful and helped identify key values and issues for the discussions. This is a vital step to mobilize participants and create shared direction.
- It has been important to have workshops in an actual destination and to spend at least some time visiting key sites and understanding perceived issues – as a group (incorporation of a field trip is very positive and also allows local and more distant stakeholders to see and discuss common issues and to hear others' perspectives). This step also facilitated shared experiences and opportunities to discuss common issues.
- Many participants found that they shared long-term goals with other stakeholders who they initially may have considered as adversaries (e.g. Balaton, Beruwala (see Figure 10.2), Cape Breton, Jeddah (see Figure 10.3)). The workshop should provide time to share such experiences.

- The use of indicators helped to clarify what was wanted and how to achieve it (how much, where, who participates, who wins), by urging participants to be specific (e.g. not just more tourists but how many and when and doing what?).
- Indicators once initially chosen and supported can become performance measures: once the information is regularly monitored and shared it can serve as a measure of change relative to agreed goals for specific activities or sectors and can support management decisions on key elements of tourism in the destination. This is a vital element if actual implementation is to occur.
- It has been important to have representation from all stakeholders (even when some do not wish to meet with perceived adversaries).
- It is vital to have some form of destination management authority directly involved and ideally interested or committed to follow with actions designed to achieve the agreed goals or objectives. Where no destination management organization exists, the indicators can help establish support for creating one, or at best become information used by some of the stakeholders in their activities or as a basis for a study or public discussion.
- Without an action plan (and adequate resourcing) indicators development and or workshops become a learning opportunity but may have little lasting impact.
- Where indicators are understood to be an integral step in destination planning and programme or project development, they can be a critical building block – helping to define what it is desired to sustain and helping to design means to get there.

Along with the WTO Guidebook, a shorter Field Guide (Manning and Manning, 2005) was devised to help those who wish to organize workshops on indicators use and implementation. This can be downloaded online from www.tourisk.com/.

ADVANCING DESTINATION KNOWLEDGE-BASED MANAGEMENT

The indicators programme was designed to foster destination knowledge and to support other forms of improved destination management. Many more recent initiatives have drawn on the UNWTO indicators to develop specific indicator sets and related applications appropriate to particular destinations and their issues.

Applications of this methodology have included the Carpathian Indicators, the Sustainable Tourism Zone for the Caribbean, specific indicators sets for Europe and more recent initiatives to create observatories, criteria defining sustainability (GSTC: https://www.gstcouncil.org/for -destinations/) and INSTO's Observatories of Sustainable Tourism where on site application and data sharing are now done.

From the outset, the key objective of the programme was to create something which would be used in practice, and for that reason workshops were done in specific destinations to show utility, test application and train destination managers. Initially there was interest in creating an 'indicators programme' but in retrospect the overall intent was to create an ongoing network of sustainable tourism destinations which supported the use of indicators in their planning and management and shared the information. The UNWTO INSTO programme has now become a network sharing approaches and results. To date, most use of the UNWTO indicators programme has been via specific projects – destination planning and management, park plans, integrated reporting systems, and in other programmes where indicators have been seen as important as planning, management or evaluation tools. In places like Jasper Alberta (Parks Canada, 2011) where ongoing monitoring of many tourism indicators based on the UNWTO approach have been integrated into the municipal planning and reporting process or in the UNIDO Collaborative Actions for Sustainable Tourism (COAST) project in Africa where indicators based on UNWTO are part of the planning and evaluation process, there have been applications derived from the UNWTO approach.

Building Tourism Observatories on the Indicators Programme

UNWTO convened meetings in 2012–2013 of several nations interested in advancing the use of indicators and decisions were taken to proceed towards establishment of observatories of sustainable tourism. The INSTO programme was begun to establish destinations more formally as observatories gathering and sharing information on sustainability.

An early use of the term 'Observatory' was in the Canary Islands as part of efforts to create a Biosphere Reserve Observatory with a strong component of measures relating to tourism (San Blas, 2008). The concept of an observatory is to establish a locale where there is regular monitoring and reporting of changes in key conditions and issues. Indicators are normally a central component but ideally become part of a broader implementation and information sharing programme through international bodies. UNWTO (via INSTO) has worked to make this occur relative to the concept of sustainable destinations.

Initial work to advance the concept of observatories involved bringing together many of the participants in the earlier indicator programme of UNWTO and others who had been working on the monitoring of key changes in tourism worldwide. Work was commenced to establish formal procedures to create and recognize observatories and to begin to establish them in different destinations.

The objective of the UNWTO observatories programme has been to establish a form of laboratory to better understand what sustainable tourism really means in practice. An observatory is locally managed via a tourism authority, university or similar and receives recognition from UNWTO. A methodology was developed based on the work done in development of an indicators programme during the 1990s and early part of the twenty-first century and also on experience in measuring and monitoring the sustainability of tourism in many regions. The programme has been designed to be a network of destinations who gather and share selected information on the state of tourism at the destination level. (See INSTO for specific membership and information sharing.) The methods used are based on those from the 2005 Guidebook but have built on the implementation process and collection and sharing of key indicators.

The UNWTO approach was expanded in the light of considerable field applications and testing, much of which occurred in several Chinese destinations. China was the first to take up the initiative and has established sites (including observatories in Yangshuo and Huangshan – both linked to destination studies from the earlier indicators work). Other sites, such as islands in the Aegean and sites in Argentina, Mexico and Spain began to participate. This has resulted in the UNWTO International Network of Sustainable Tourism Observatories (INSTO). By 2020 development of observatories of sustainable tourism had resulted in nearly 30 sites established and operating around the world.

There are many destinations which have begun to measure trends which relate to their sustainability but are neither part of any formal observatory nor actively exchanging information. Perhaps a clearing house and support or mentoring system would be of benefit to them to incorporate these or support them in their tourism monitoring. Projects such as that in Europe (European Tourism Indicators System) and projects including those by Sustainable Travel International and the World Wildlife Fund have tested the use of information gathering analysis and portrayal and allowed us to better understand what makes tourism sustainable in particular destinations. These are compatible with the UNWTO programme. One of the most advanced applications now in place is that of the state of Guanajuato in Mexico where indicators are gathered and analysed and published annually. The extensive set of information collected refers not only to the entire state but to each sub-region, municipality and organized area within the state. A common methodology is used across the municipalities and it is based on that developed with UNWTO and with indicators used at the national level. Information produced and analysed by the Guanajuato Observatory was critical to the ability to produce a case study of tourism capacity and system sensitivity of the city of San Miguel de Allende (Manning, 2018).

Figure 10.2   Field visit Beruwala Sri Lanka beach erosion

Links between Information and Certification: Criteria for Sustainability

While the UNWTO Indicators Programme was focused on the generation of information which could be used in the planning and management of destinations, later programmes try

Table 10.2   *Comparison of information approaches*

Information	Classification	Validation	Certification	Regulation
UNWTO Indicators	GSTC Destination Criteria (and indicators)	Third party audits re criteria and indicators	Green Globe Green Leaf Blue Flag etc.	Establish and monitor specific standards (e.g. wages, waste) to qualify or to operate
Focus is on objective information	Focus is on what it means to claim sustainability	Focus is on being able to show that you meet standard	Focus is on proving you meet a specific set of standards	Focus is on making site comply to set of rules

to build ability to identify destinations which have achieved standards relative to important criteria and use indicators to measure levels of success or state of achievement relative to these standards. A further step has been to provide certification for those destinations who have satisfied key criteria. Table 10.2 shows what can be characterized as a spectrum of influence, from provision of information through to regulation and compulsory compliance based on measures or indicators. All are being explored in different destinations as means to effect more sustainable forms of tourism.

The remainder of this chapter focuses on assessing the current range of uses and impacts which have occurred related to the extension of indicators to implementation.

What Is a Sustainable Destination?

A destination can have a programme to develop and use indicators for information and to support its planning and management. As well, for the public, a destination can use selected indicators to show that it is satisfying the criteria allowing it to claim to be sustainable or to meet certain key standards. A destination may also have a third-party review of its compliance to prove that its information is real or become certified under a programme to achieve recognition. In addition, a government can require compliance to certain standards – both at an enterprise level or more broadly for a destination.

Some of the UNWTO programme initiatives have led to implementation in different forms. One of the first workshops was held in Cozumel, Mexico. It is possible to trace the origins of programmes such as Mexico's programme measuring comparative indicators for most destinations and reporting nationally back to that event. Antecedents for this programme also can be traced to the initiative by Caribbean States to create a Sustainable Tourism Zone for the Caribbean. The Mexican programme some years later became a full reporting system used at the national level. The UNWTO programme has become an incubator for many other initiatives and is widely used as a key point of reference in measurement and evaluation of the sustainability of tourism.

Defining Sustainable Destinations

The use of shared criteria and indicators can clarify what is really meant by the concept of sustainability – what is important to sustain. The GSTC work to clarify what is meant by a 'sustainable destination', establishing criteria and indicators, was heavily based on UNWTO indicators and destination work: the consulting team to GSTC who compiled and developed the first edition of the criteria and indicators included Sustainable Travel International and

Tourisk Inc. and two of the three consultants who did the analysis and preparation for GSTC were participants in the design and writing of the original UNWTO Guidebook.

GSTC destination criteria (from GSTC, 2019)
The GSTC Destination Criteria and indicators reflect the UNWTO approach and structure. The GSTC work on destinations is a logical step in building on the indicators and can become a catalyst for destinations to adopt holistic approaches to becoming more sustainable in many dimensions.

The GSTC programme has produced a list of criteria which, if achieved, can permit a destination to call itself sustainable (also see Chapter 13 in this volume). The criteria are based on destination level criteria which can be put in place by a destination manager relating to all tourism in a destination. This can become the basis for destination level certification but often the specific actions or activities are outside the control of the destination manager. Often the span of control over social, economic or environmental characteristics (e.g. water quality, social equality, respect for quality or environmental standards) lie with individual parts of a destination and/or outside a general capacity of destination planners and managers to control. As a consequence, most destination level criteria are seen primarily as points of reference or are aspirational targets to be met with the assistance of the planners and managers of any given destination. Many of the criteria measure whether or not a programme or policy has been established in the destination relative to the achievement of more substantive economic, cultural, environmental or governance objectives.

> The GSTC Criteria for Destinations and the related Performance Indicators were developed based on already recognized criteria and approaches including, for example, the UNWTO destination level indicators, GSTC Criteria for Hotels and Tour Operators, and nearly 40 other widely accepted principles and guidelines, certification criteria and indicators. They reflect certification standards, indicators, criteria, and best practices from different cultural and geopolitical contexts around the world in tourism and other sectors where applicable. Potential indicators were screened for relevance and practicality, as well as their applicability to a broad range of destination types. They were field-tested around the world. (GSTC website)

The GSTC Destination Criteria are now (2019/2020) going through a revision (https://www .gstcouncil.org/). Some of the expected uses of the criteria by tourism management organizations include the following (see also Box 10.1):

- Serve as basic guidelines for destinations that wish to become more sustainable
- Help consumers identify sound sustainable tourism destinations
- Serve as a common denominator for information media to recognize destinations and inform the public regarding their sustainability
- Help certification and other voluntary destination level programmes ensure that their standards meet a broadly accepted baseline
- Offer governmental, non-governmental, and private sector programmes a starting point for developing sustainable tourism requirements
- Serve as basic guidelines for education and training bodies, such as hotel schools and universities.

BOX 10.1 GSTC CRITERIA FOR ENTERPRISES

The GSTC has also helped to clarify what is really meant by sustainability when it is applied to tourism enterprises. Through international consultations, GSTC has produced criteria and indicators to clearly identify what is meant by sustainability in many different dimensions and to suggest to destinations how they can measure their status relative to these criteria.

At the level of the enterprise (hotel, resort) many criteria are identified covering the economic, social, environmental and other criteria which logically define an enterprise which can call itself sustainable. Work continues to try and develop certification programmes based on these definitions and measurements. Enterprise level certifications are emerging as the control of most of the criteria lies within the capability of the owner or operator, and an enterprise can be accountable for measurable achievements.

The key GSTC Criteria for Hotels and Tour Operators fall into four categories:

- A: Demonstrate effective sustainable management (14 criteria addressing aspects of management internal to the enterprise and its operations).
- B: Maximize social and economic benefits to the local community and minimize negative impacts (9 criteria relating to relations with employees and the community).
- C: Maximize benefits to cultural heritage and minimize negative impacts (4 criteria relating to the contribution of the enterprise to the conservation and preservation of the heritage of the community).
- D: Maximize benefits to the environment and minimize negative impacts (9 criteria relating to internal environmental management and contribution to the conservation and preservation of the local biosphere and resources).

The full set of criteria and indicators can be found at https://www.gstcouncil.org/gstc-criteria/gstc-industry-criteria-for-hotels/. A revision of these criteria was carried out in 2019 involving those who have used and assessed the practicality of the process and its utility.

Also see Chapter 13 for more information on the GSTC criteria.

Global Applications

The work associated with the UN 10 Year Framework of Programmes on Sustainable Consumption and Production Patterns (10YFP) process, also called the One Planet Network, has identified many projects which can assist in making destinations more sustainable. The GSTC criteria have been explicitly part of site-specific applications in the Grand Tetons (US) and in St Kitts. Through, for example, Earthcheck, certain destinations have received certification as green, based on GSTC criteria (Earthcheck and the Green Collection are examples of GSTC sanctioned certifiers). Vail Colorado, and Huatulco Mexico have been certified.

The UNWTO approach has informed the UNIDO COAST project in Africa which has incorporated indicators based on the UNWTO work, as has the work on UNEP Project screening criteria and the European Commission Indicators Project. The teams working on these used members of the UNWTO Indicators group and contributors to the Guidebook as resources. Many of the 62 experts who were mobilized to work on the 2004 Guidebook have been active in applications in their countries and others in planning programmes involving tourism, evaluation methods for tourism projects, university training courses and curriculum, and the definition of performance indicators for development plans which involve tourism and for community-based reporting systems.

Some Common Observations on Application

Indicators seldom stand alone: they need to feed into other programmes and ideally are part of a more comprehensive planning and reporting process – for destinations, not just for tourism. While there is merit in using common measures, there is also a need to consider specific additional criteria unique to individual destinations which may be central to destination sustainability. The unique combination of environmental, socio-cultural, institutional and economic circumstances of each place needs to be recognized so that the suite of issues/criteria and indicators is most useful to those who make the decisions which affect the sustainability of each destination.

Indicators are one component of destination management which can inform further action to clarify whether destinations or key aspects of them do indeed satisfy the criteria to justify their consideration as sustainable. Measures need to be clearly defined in terms of methodology. If specific standards or criteria must be met, there remains a debate on what those standards should be. To be 'sustainable' or recognized as an observatory or as a certified destination there needs to be a debate on which indicators are to be used, which standards need to be met, and which are compulsory. Can a basic expectation be defined? The work to establish the GSTC standard (see Chapter 13 for more information) helps to determine what can be used as a minimum standard and a point of reference.

Good information using clear methodologies is critical to be able to do this and flexibility will be needed to accommodate unique conditions for application. If a destination bases most of its tourism on seeing wildlife, measures of the health of key watched species and impacts on them may be critical. For others, benchmarking may be more important than establishing required thresholds for many indicators as circumstances vary greatly among destinations. It may not be realistic to require destinations to meet substantive standards which have been developed elsewhere, but shared methodologies and common indicators are important to facilitate exchange and understanding. Lists of required or recommended criteria and indicators become a roadmap, whether or not certification or some form of qualification is sought. A range of regional recognitions and trade certifications like Green Globe, Green Key or Blue Flag can help, and most correspond well to many of the GSTC criteria.

CHALLENGES

Many initiatives have been put in place to help understand and support actions to assist destinations to become more sustainable. While many positive steps can be documented, many challenges remain at all levels to create more sustainable tourism at all scales. For those wishing to initiate a programme of indicators or monitoring for tourism sustainability at the

Figure 10.3   Field visit Jeddah Saudi Arabia workshop

destination level, the following is a list of questions which will need to be answered at the national or destination level:

1. Can we identify and support champions at all scales to keep the momentum and maintain a programme of data gathering and reporting? At the destination level full integration into the planning and management process of the destination is critical.
2. Can we accommodate unique situations and factors which may be central to the existence of the destination as a draw for tourism? Do we have the tools which will allow identification of these for designation or certification? Some may be critical cut-offs (e.g. the state of the endangered species or key asset everyone comes to see).
3. Can we provide practical guidance to destinations in their choice of measures? Some measures, such as establishment of comprehensive monitoring of specific wildlife species, may be nice to have – but will raise costs, particularly if not supported by other programmes. The UNWTO evaluation procedure is designed to cull those measures which are not central to the sustainability of a destination and/or which are not practical or feasible to support. This philosophy was also used to help GSTC deliberations regarding its choice of criteria and indicators for destinations.

4. Is it useful to make any criteria or indicators compulsory? Not all indicators are likely to be equal in importance, so how do we choose which are used?
5. Can we provide a means of guidance for destinations regarding measurement and if we choose to go there, standards? If the measures are used to evaluate compliance are there agreed thresholds for the measures and is valid data available to judge? How will we use the information?
6. Can places which are using indicators now, but are not part of a formal programme be brought into the dialogue and obtain benefit from participation in a national or international network?
7. Can we expand the Observatory programme to encompass and/or recognize sustainability of key sites such as UNESCO World Heritage sites, Man and Biosphere (MAB) sites, or similar and use this to facilitate larger consideration of key destination issues and solutions globally?
8. Is there a role for involvement as, for example, 'Associate Observatories', in places which are now part of other indicators or monitoring programmes such as GSTC, European programmes, and other national planning and reporting programmes)?
9. Can rapid assessment procedures such as GSTC's work on early adopters, Sustainable Travel International's destination evaluation programme, rapid tourism assessment programmes from George Washington University, Bournemouth, and others, be used to help destinations begin the process to achieve sustainability and/or observatory status – and to help them understand how to get there?
10. Can international agencies, companies and NGOs help provide continuing training programmes and workshops for those who wish to learn and possibly participate?

Indicators and evaluation tools are not an end in themselves – they are only tools. These indicators and indicator-based programmes foster debate at global, regional, national, destination and site scales regarding what is most important to sustain and how best to make that happen.

COMPREHENSIVE PLANNING OF TOURIST DESTINATIONS: NEXT STEPS

You cannot plan just tourism. Some of the most effective approaches are based on integrated planning of entire destinations. Many consultants worldwide provide what they call strategic planning for the tourism sector and the community. This is most commonly focused on the destination scale. Some international organizations have played an important role in this approach.

Within the framework of the One Planet Network, the World Tourism Organization (UNWTO) in partnership with the United Nations Environment Programme (UNEP), has recently embarked on the preparation of Guidelines to Integrate Sustainable Consumption and Production (SCP) into Tourism Planning (2018) as part of the implementation of the Sustainable Development Goals, in particular goal 12 on 'Ensuring sustainable consumption and production'.

For the first time the tourism sector has been made a very central part of delivery of the United Nations agenda for the future decades. The UNWTO has also been important as a source of planning methods and is fully backing the integration of tourism into national economic planning (Inskeep, 1994; see also UNWTO, 2013, which mainly focuses on European cases). It is through initiatives such as these that the power of good information on the sustainability of tourism can be fully realized. Many national and regional applications have followed, and the current activity related to implementation of the UN10FYP initiative follows this path.[1]

NOTE

1.   This chapter is partly based on presentations to UNWTO, Madrid, 2013, Kanas China 2015, Guilin China 2017 and University of Manabi, Portoviejo Ecuador 2018 on Sustainable Destinations: Indicators and Observatories – Informing Sustainable Development of Tourism Destinations.

REFERENCES

Blue Flag. https://www.blueflag.global/, accessed 20 July 2020.
Carpathian Indicators. http://www.carpathianconvention.org/tl_files/carpathiancon/Downloads/03%20 Meetings%20and%20Events/Working%20Groups/Sustainable%20Tourism/Brasov%202017/Car pathian%20Indicators_9th%20CC%20WG%20Tourism.pdf, accessed 20 July 2020.
Collaborative Actions for Sustainable Tourism (COAST) Project. http://coast.iwlearn.org/en, accessed 20 March 2020.
Earthcheck. https://earthcheck.org/, accessed 20 March 2020.
European Tourism Indicators System. https://ec.europa.eu/growth/sectors/tourism/offer/sustainable/ indicators_en, accessed 20 July 2020.
Green Globe. https://www.greenglobe.org/, accessed 20 July 2020.
Green Key. https://www.greenkey.nl/, accessed 20 July 2020.
GSTC Destination criteria. https://www.gstcouncil.org/gstc-criteria/gstc-destination-criteria/, accessed 20 March 2020.
GSTC Industry criteria. https://www.gstcouncil.org/gstc-criteria/gstc-industry-criteria-for-hotels/, accessed 20 March 2020.
Inskeep, E. (1994) *National and Regional Tourism Planning: Methodologies and Case Studies*. Madrid: World Tourism Organization/International Thomson Business Press.
Manning, E. (2018) *Carrying capacity for tourism in San Miguel de Allende*. San Miguel de Allende Guanajuato, Mexico / Consejo Turístico de San Miguel de Allende (published in Spanish as *Capacidad de carga turística en San Miguel de Allende*).
Manning, M. and Manning, T. (2005, revised 2019) *A Field Guide for Indicators Development for Tourism Destinations*. Ottawa. http://www.tourisk.com, accessed 20 March 2020.
Parks Canada (2011) Jasper Community Sustainability Plan, 2011, Jasper Alberta. https://www.pc.gc.ca/ en/pn-np/ab/jasper/info/plan/collectiviteJasper-sustainabilityplan, accessed 20 March 2020.
San Blas, A. (2008) La Palma: A biosphere reserve in evolution. *International Journal of Environment and Sustainable Development*, 7(2), 216–228.
Sustainable Tourism Zone for the Caribbean. http://www.acs-aec.org/index.php?q=sustainable-tourism/ programmes/the-sustainable-touism-zone-of-the-caribbean, accessed 20 March 2020.
UNWTO International Network of Sustainable Tourism Observatories (INSTO). https://www.unwto.org/ insto-observatories-advancing-tourism-impact-monitoring-destination-level, accessed 20 March 2020.
UNWTO (2013) *National and Regional Tourism Planning: Methodologies and Case Studies*. Madrid: United Nations World Tourism Organization.
UNWTO Sustainable Development of Tourism Department in collaboration with UN Environment (2018) *Integration of Sustainable Consumption and Production Patterns into Tourism Policies*. https://www.e-unwto.org/doi/pdf/10.18111/9789284420605, accessed 20 March 2020.
World Tourism Organization (1996) *What Do Tourism Managers Need to Know?* Madrid: World Tourism Organization.

World Tourism Organization (2004) *Indicators of Sustainable Development for Tourism Destinations*. Madrid: United Nations World Tourism Organization.

PART II

ENHANCING THE SUSTAINABILITY OF EXISTING TOURISM

11. Sustainable supply chains in travel and tourism: towards a circular approach

Jos van der Sterren

TRAVEL AND TOURISM SUPPLY CHAIN CHALLENGES

What Is Supply Chain Management?

The concept of supply chains was originally used in manufacturing. According to Zhang et al. (2009, pp. 345–347) a supply chain is: "a network of enterprises which are engaged in different functions ranging from the supply of the raw materials through the production and delivery of the end-product to the target customers".

Cooper et al. (1997) mention that a supply chain is comprised of six main business processes that should be managed within an individual business or group of businesses:

- Customer relationship management
- Customer service management
- Demand management
- Supply management
  - *Order fulfilment*
  - *Manufacturing flow management*
  - *Procurement*
- Product development
- Commercialization

A supply chain in industry is always characterized by two flows: a *forward* flow of goods or services and a *backward* flow of information. In a simple supply chain process this can be visualized shown in Figure 11.1.

The goal of supply chain management is to assure that this flow of goods and information is organized in the most efficient and effective way.

Unique Features of a Tourism Supply Chain

The linear visual expression of the supply chain as demonstrated before is not accurate when we speak about travel and tourism. This supply chain is composed of a complex set of relations between suppliers, as we regularly observe in industrial production processes.

According to Zhang et al. (2009, pp. 345–347), tourism supply chain management can be defined as "a network of tourism organizations engaged in different activities ranging from the supply of different components of tourism products/services, such as accommodation and flights, to the distribution and marketing of the final tourism product at a specific destination. It involves a wide range of participants in both private and public sectors."

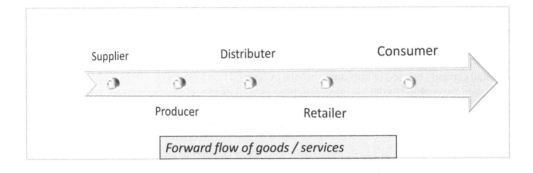

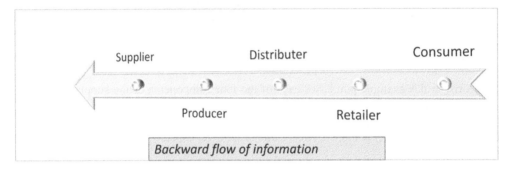

Figure 11.1   Supply chain: flow of goods and information

While following this definition, for the purpose of this chapter we have simplified the supply chain into four categories of services that travellers (consumers) consume:

- Travel services (air/rail/road/sea)
- Accommodation services
- Food & beverage services
- Leisure & business services (e.g. events, attractions, museums, meetings and conferences)

Jointly, these categories compose the travel and tourism (T&T) supply chain. At the same time, each service individually can be seen as a 'second tier chain', operating under a different business logic, different market conditions and thus composed of unique supply chain business processes. Most businesses operating in these second tier chains are small-scaled (micro-, small-, medium-sized enterprises). They sometimes collaborate, but mostly compete. All of them look to maximize returns of their initial investments.

The tourism product cannot be 'stored'. Next to that, distribution channels in the tourism supply chain have changed enormously over the last two decades and therefore, the four sub-chains should be treated separately more and more. Information and communication technology (ICT) has enabled travellers to purchase products and services online. As a consequence, tourism products (the whole set of the four services) are not assembled anymore by a producer (tour operator or travel agent) but by the consumer. Tourists can decide to purchase each of the services from the four second tier chains separately *and* instantly; they are flexible in deciding when and where they purchase a service component. This shifting of power towards consumers has disrupted the tourism supply chain and many businesses feel they have lost control over information and service delivery in their supply chain.

This freedom of consumer choice brings a risk for producers/business owners: it could increase the level of *spillovers* and waste in each of the four chains. Planning of fixed and seasonal capacity needed in airplanes, hotels, buses and other assets becomes a challenge since customers are enabled to decide upon purchase as well as cancel their purchases (e.g. Booking. com) at a very late stage. There is thus a tendency towards overcapacity at second tier level. The following example demonstrates how difficult it is to manage a tourism supply chain:

> *Let us assume a business tourist from Paris, who needs to travel to an industry fair in another city in Europe at a distance of 300 km. He made a hotel reservation through Booking.com and decides to book a one-way train ticket. However, three days before leaving, his friend announces to him that he is also in the city. The tourist cancels the hotel booking and they jointly reserve an apartment at Airbnb, in a different area in the city. Since his friend invites him to go to a concert the first evening, he cancels the dinner that he had reserved in a restaurant where he would go with a business relation. He tells this relation that they will have a cup of coffee at the fair. He decides to stay one night longer, and instead of taking the train back home, he books a low cost flight for the next day.*

The tourist in this example purchases each of the four components of the supply chain, but changes his decisions during the travel experience. For businesses operating at second tier level, planning of asset capacity needed to attend the guests that may or may not make use of the services, is extremely complex. This results in spillover capacity down the supply chain at many levels.

Supply chain management of a tourism product thus is very complex. At the same time, tourism and travel businesses are pushed to develop effective answers to decrease the above mentioned capacity spillovers and at the same time mitigate negative (social, environmental and economic) impacts of tourism on society.

This multiple challenge can be addressed effectively by using a circular economy approach, as we will explain later, making use of smart technologies that are already available. The current state of circular product innovation and information technology makes it possible to improve the management of supply chain processes. Technology enables businesses to be informed at a very early stage about customers' desires (intention to purchase) or actions (real purchase), because decisions are booked, communicated and consumed through mobile phones and can thus be followed and traced.

Unfortunately, at present, most businesses operating in tourism are not sharing relevant information that could enhance customer satisfaction with other stakeholders. Therefore, the backward flow of available information and forward flow of product development are managed inefficiently. Each company designs its own customer relationship management platform, client complaints survey, etc.

The relationship between the second tier supply chains and their key processes can be visualized shown in Figure 11.2.

There are process capacity spillovers in each of the four categories. Whereas travel agencies and tour operators have traditionally been the key distribution channels and business-to-business communication points between the second tier chains, this is now changing. Communication more and more is channelled through business-to-consumer channels. Therefore, for an individual business operating at second tier level, managing the key supply

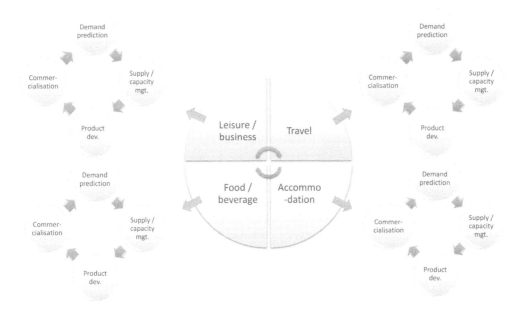

Figure 11.2   Tourism supply chain and key processes

chain processes becomes very complex, without having information flowing in from businesses in the other chains at the same level.

In order to get a grip on capacity issues and manage the *forward* flow of tourist services efficiently and effectively, the key word is *stakeholder collaboration and trust.* If the hotel receives a cancellation through Booking.com, it is relevant to know why this cancellation took place. The owner of the hotel does not know that the tourist is still coming to his city, but sleeps in another place. In addition, the restaurant owner does not know if the tourist will consume a meal in the city or not. If all these businesses would collaborate and have access to these customer data, they could plan their seat capacity in a better way and even assure that the tourist might be receiving a better offer for sleeping, dining or a cup of coffee at the fair. For each of the second tier chains, there are thus options for efficiency gains in the key management processes *demand prediction/customer relationship management, supply and capacity management, product development and commercialization.* We will explore the options of stakeholder collaboration in the following paragraphs.

USING DATA TO SOLVE EFFICIENCY GAPS IN T&T SUPPLY CHAINS

Development of technology has allowed us to work in more efficient and effective ways in process design. The availability of data and tools to analyse them are opening new pathways to improved efficiency gaps. However, still only 65 per cent of travel organizations have a dedicated data, analysis or insight team (Eye for Travel, 2017). These teams are still small and use data through diagnostic, descriptive, and predictive analytics. Many of these teams are not yet able to "use their data to build prescriptive analytics, the most sophisticated form of analytics, which can give travel businesses a complete outlook and strategy" (Eye for Travel, 2017).

Nevertheless, it is clear that supply chain spillovers can be better measured and minimized by modern monitoring systems, making use of analytical tools to analyse big data sets. In this chapter, we will present an overview of tools that could be used in tourism supply chains for solving efficiency gaps in resource planning and use in tourism, for each of the four components in the supply chain mentioned in the previous paragraph.

Demand Prediction and Customer Relationship Management

The first key process in the supply chain that we will explore is the process where most current innovations take place. It relates to demand prediction and customer relations. Information about travel and tourism demand, especially *intended* purchase decisions, can be traced online as well as offline. Mobile phone data are a valuable source of information for these big data analyses. By analysing big data sets on customer behaviour, using artificial intelligence applications, businesses are better informed about potential volumes of future purchases of customers on their tourism products. They can monitor visitor movements in a certain geographical area, and thus calculate the volume of potential buyers. Businesses can study how long customers are waiting in lines, or the time they watch certain entertainment acts. All these data provide a very valuable resource for suppliers further down the supply chain, to accommodate or modify their business processes. Therefore, data (information) that businesses need for planning purchases are available. These should allow companies to make better decisions on capacity planning (seats, purchases), procurement planning and product development.

As opposed to the classical supply chain notion, the speed of analysis of available customer purchase information is such that we can predict changes in tourist consumption up to three months ahead. So some components of the tourism supply chain (in this case the travel services) may base decision-making on a *forward* flow of **demand** information. This knowledge may lead to adjustments in the supply chain, inventory management, as well as product development. There are several examples of demand forecasting:

> **Amadeus** The global reservation company has developed a tool where it uses big data to predict travel movements and patterns, related to big events such as the Olympic Games etc.[1]
> **Forward Keys** analyses travel booking data, cancellations, re-routings or re-bookings, of all flights. If a serious incident is predicted (for example a tropical storm), the company can see how this affects the flight bookings. These data are sold to suppliers and retail companies in airports, for example. These companies can then change their inventory and product offering, according to expected arrivals at major airports.[2]

Demand prediction solutions are becoming more and more accurate. Most applications indicate they can predict traveller movements up to 3–6 months ahead. This knowledge should enable suppliers of tourism services at the destination level to adjust their supply and capacity levels of beds, rooms, tables, etc.

Supply and Management of Asset Capacity

The second process in the T&T supply chain relates to the supply and management of asset capacity. Historically, the travel and tourism industry has been a so-called *asset-intensive* business. Business operators that owned assets where visitors could sleep, eat or travel controlled the supply chains. However, rapidly growing visitor numbers during the last decades and expected future growth in sight, have triggered new providers to offer services; whereas they do not own these typical assets, sharing platforms (e.g. Uber, Airbnb) are enabling private operators to offer their rooms, beds, taxi-seats, etc. which increases supply of these assets mainly in urban areas. Most of these suppliers are offering their assets part-time at second tier chain level. For full-time and specialized restaurants, hotels, taxis and other businesses to remain competitive, they must find ways to optimize their returns by including innovations that enable them to manage key industry assets: rooms, fleets and seats.

A key to profit optimization for a business is effective capacity and price or revenue management. Here is where the challenge comes in to analyse an ever-changing and rapidly increasing amount of data. This includes information that can be collected from customer behaviour together with business data on their purchases of complementary products or services as well as data on capacity optimization.

Optimized capacity planning based on forecasted demands may improve asset utilization. With help from data analytics, T&T businesses in the supply chain may increase their operational excellence, improve the accuracy of their forecasted use of assets, increase their returns and improve the yield on assets.

A hotel wants to achieve the highest occupancy rates of its rooms. But these rooms must be clean and beds comfortable and this requires maintenance. Big data and analytics can help a hotel operator determine optimal capacity as it might not necessarily be 100 per cent at all times. In addition, analytic solutions can help a company determine the right mix of competitive pricing to optimize capacity without sacrificing profitability. Using big data and analytics solutions may help business owners to gain insights from data by detecting patterns, correlations, facilitating predictions, etc. in real time. They can help travel and tourism businesses to improve capacity planning.

For example, by making use of machine learning it is possible to detect patterns in the online behaviour of customers, prior to their cancellation of hotel bookings. These patterns allow business owners to predict with more precision if a booking will be cancelled or not and thus adjust staff and purchase planning accordingly. Several suppliers are offering powerful data analytics tools to predict future revenues for hotels, bus-seats etc.[3]

We learned earlier that travel behaviour and mobility movements by plane, car and train could be predicted through big data analysis, a period of 3–6 months ahead. If this information were always available to suppliers of travel solutions, accommodations, restaurants and bars, and event organizers, this would allow better capacity planning to these companies. Unfortunately, this is not currently happening. Usually, what happens is that a limited number of (large corporate) business owners may have insights into these predicted demands. Smaller business owners, local suppliers of accommodations, food and beverages, or other tourism services, have to guess/estimate future demand in a different way. They may not have the resources to purchase demand forecast reports that are usually expensive. Or the type of demand predicted does not match with their current market positioning. So management of capacity of seats, beds, rooms, and local transport units is a complex issue to solve at a tourism destination. The paradox here is that, if stakeholders would share their market knowledge and exchange their market insights data, they could solve this issue to a large extent. However, instead of sharing predictive market information, business owners tend to keep these data for themselves, because they want to be better prepared than their competitors for a certain opportunity. The old motto 'Information is power' is preventing the suppliers of tourism services from reaching the optimal level of capacity planning of their assets.

There are, however, initiatives that try to break through these market dynamics. Some destinations present open source business data to their local businesses, serving them with market data to predict their purchase and investments. Usually, these require a strong local destination management organization that is created with support of the business associations and chambers of commerce of local business owners. In some areas these initiatives are very successful. A nice example is the Dutch Data and Development Lab developed by the Centre of Expertise Leisure Tourism and Hospitality (CELTH), together with the Dutch destination management organization NBTC.[4]

Product Development: Developing a Sustainable Destination Perspective

The third process in the T&T supply chain relates to the development of products. A tourism destination can be seen as a complex interaction of different stakeholders delivering a set of products and services that are deeply interconnected. The competitiveness of a destination is determined by the way the actors collaborate in creating and sharing knowledge; this can be supported by technological platforms and knowledge-intensive services. A *smart* destination is a place where all stakeholders, residents and tourists, based on dynamic platforms, share and learn from intensive communication flows and decision support systems.

The development of smart destinations usually focuses on ICT applications that are supportive in managing visitor streams and improving the visitor experience. Through monitoring of visitor movements, they can be informed about places that are crowded, traffic congestion, waiting lines, etc. Also, smart destinations know the profiles of their visitors and may inform them of yet unknown alternatives available in the destination. These could be a museum, galleries where a certain art style may be shown, music concerts of the specific artist that a visitor likes, new restaurants of a preferred cuisine, etc.

However, a smart destination also offers potential effects in terms of sustainable development and promoting circular economy principles. ICT applications can be used to monitor energy and water use, as well as recycling opportunities. These features of ICT applications are more geared towards the optimal use of available natural resources.

This use of ICT in destinations requires a joint vision, shared by public and private stakeholders, on how to best develop a geographical area, while making sure that scarce resources are used in an optimal way. A smart destination would then include maximum capacity limits to vulnerable areas such as national parks and protected bio reserves, water areas (beaches). GPS applications may indicate when these limits have been reached and visitors could be informed about how they should behave to improve local supply chains (promotion of locally produced goods and services). Users could also be informed about the most sustainable transport modes within the destination area.

Unfortunately, most ICT applications developed for destinations target the commercial success of businesses and are not promoting the joint development of a sustainable tourism strategy. Their main focus is on increasing visitor numbers and visitor revenues.

From recent studies on overtourism we know that there are tipping points, where negative impacts of visitor crowds not only make the visitor experience less pleasant, but also lead to resistance from local populations (Peeters et al., 2018).

Applications using big data for decision-making should thus take into account the maximum capacity of people (visitors and residents) that a certain area may sustain at a certain moment of time. More and more cities use so-called crowd intensity apps, where visitors can observe in real time how busy certain areas are at any moment, so they may decide to visit other areas. A nice example is the regional destination management organization Visitbrabant in The Netherlands, which has developed a real-time visitor pressure map.[5]

These applications may help to promote a more sustainable development of destinations. For example: visitors are not allowed to go to certain lakes when it is a breeding season for birds and may be warned. Smart ICT could promote localized supply chains for hotels and restaurants that benefit small-scale local producers of agricultural products. This could minimize international transport of these products (grains, meat, juices etc.).

In successful destinations, public and private actors collaborate and jointly develop these solutions. This to assure that, when visitor numbers are restricted or limited in certain areas or during certain times, benefits of tourism are redistributed to all actors in a fair and transparent way. In addition, stakeholders may jointly think of new tourism products that could be offered outside crowded areas, or making use of the locally available knowledge, natural and cultural resources. The future of the tourism product may be based on parameters of sustainable development, attracting fewer, but more loyal future visitors. Eventually, this could potentially lead to a more stable competitive destination product, less vulnerable to trends and shocks.

Commercialization: Enabling Effective Online Presence

The fourth process in the T&T supply chain relates to commercialization of products and services. In T&T services, especially the development of online sales channels is key to a successful commercialization process. Euromonitor predicted that lodging and accommodation online sales growth would be annually more than 8 per cent as opposed to 1.2 per cent offline (phone and other) bookings (Peltier, 2016). In Europe, almost 40 per cent of hotel bookings in 2017 were made through online platforms (Möhring et al., 2019). Travellers increasingly use mobile smartphone devices to not only research, but also book and pay for tickets and hotels (Salecycle, 2018).

For T&T business operators this means that they should develop a fully responsive website that operates on all devices and allows potential visitors to not only research options. Also, visitors should be enabled to complete booking and payments online. Such a responsive website design is not only relevant for increasing revenues; it also allows the business owner to monitor the online behaviour of potential clients. Insights in *abandonment* of website pages, time spent on a page, *click through* behaviour, etc. are crucial to understand how to better persuade a potential visitor to purchase a T&T product.

Data about the online travel purchase funnel, suggest that out of 100% visits of a website page, "46% of users view a travel product, which means they have searched and viewed a hotel room or flight, for example. After this, 17.6% actually begin the booking process. In travel, a greater number of visitors are beginning the booking process, but fewer are completing bookings, only 3.1%" (Salecycle, 2018).

Website search engines such as Google provide key free statistics on search behaviour. These data are key to adjust websites and ensure that search processes and booking processes run smoothly. In addition, information about cross-selling, or insights into referrals from other parties to a company's website, are crucial to understand how a potential visitor can be approached and commercialization of products can be enhanced.

T&T business owners may use the data on client behaviour to adjust their prices to market dynamics. This strategy of *dynamic pricing* is used more and more for booking online hotel rooms, airline and train tickets. Online components that can be added to dynamic pricing strategies relate for example to booking channels used (mobile device, desktop, laptop); locations (physical place from where the online booking takes place); number of components requested in a booking (only airline ticket, or also car rental for example). All these elements can be included in pricing calculations and thus may lead to different revenue streams (Möhring et al., 2019).

Also through online customer reviews, business owners may get a better insight into how customers have perceived the quality of a service delivered. Unfortunately, a contingent risk with customer reviews is that they may be fake and require specialized staff for online monitoring and moderation.

Unfortunately, T&T businesses only use their online commercialization strategies to stimulate or promote their own sales or profits. The potential of online 'traffic' towards a specific corporate or business website is not used to gauge travellers' interest in buying other local products or services. This is a missed opportunity when it comes to fostering sustainable development or stimulating circular economy principles. Online commercialization strategies of T&T businesses should also focus on presenting best practices of local sustainable development, or promoting re-commerce or recycling of products and services. A nice example is the application Stuffstr, which allows clients to recirculate unused garments at a local level.[6]

A CIRCULAR ECONOMY APPROACH TO T&T SUPPLY CHAIN MANAGEMENT

What Is a Circular Economy Approach?

The concept of circularity was introduced by The Ellen MacArthur Foundation.[7] The basic idea of this concept is that an economic system should be aiming at the full elimination of waste and full recycling and reuse of all resources that are involved in the process of design, production, storage, delivery and consumption of services and goods.

A circular economy is based on reuse, sharing, refurbishment, remanufacturing and recycling. Through these techniques, a closed-loop system can be created in which resource inputs are minimized and low levels of waste are created. The idea is that waste becomes food for the next cycle of production and consumption. A circular economy is the opposite of the classical linear economy models, based on 'take, make, dispose'.[8]

A good example of a circular economy toolkit was developed by University of Cambridge.[9] It allows businesses to assess the level of circularity of their business, for products as well as for their consumers. In addition, it offers options and examples to improve circularity in business processes.

Circular Economy Approaches in Travel and Tourism

The principles of a circular economy can well be applied to the design and introduction of sustainable T&T services. There are many opportunities to convert the linear economy models to circular approaches throughout each of the four key processes of the supply chain. T&T stakeholders could agree on application of circular principles of design, monitoring excess use of scarce (water and energy) resources. In addition, they could agree on establishing systems to reduce waste, and reuse and recycle inputs and supplies used for delivery of T&T products. Some good examples of policies have been developed in some destination areas (Manniche et al., 2017).

Key to a circular economy approach is the development of a joint vision and the pooling of private and public resources to translate this into economic and social policies that develop a destination. The City of Amsterdam has embraced a joint vision by designing a circular economy strategy for the city based on the so-called 'doughnut economy'.[10]

Also the country of Slovenia is looking to develop concerted and joint visions as well as implementation plans. The association of towns and municipalities of Slovenia have developed a joint action plan on the circular economy.[11]

At the level of commercial solutions, more recently we observe innovations that are contributing to circular economy principles:

- **Breeze** is the world's first fully energy neutral hotel, in Amsterdam. The design of its airflow and heating and cooling system is based on the natural hot and cool airflows in termite hills.[12]
- The company **Zeromasswater** designed roof solar panels that produce drinking water.[13]

To a certain extent, application of circular economy principles could be seen as a further specialization of more generic approaches to sustainable tourism supply chain management. Whereas earlier research stated that it would be easier to apply principles of sustainable development in accommodations than in air travel (Font et al., 2008), this may now be different because of the rapid growth of the discipline of applied data sciences to travel and tourism.

One example of an integrated circular economy approach to green supply chains was developed by Schrödl and Simkin (2014). In this model, named a circular economy supply chain, the basic stages of any supply chain – *Source, Make, Deliver, Return* – are integrated with principles of circularity in a systematic way. This may be useful for tourism destinations.

HOW TO CONDUCT A CIRCULAR SUPPLY CHAIN ANALYSIS

As we have described before, T&T stakeholders operating in a supply chain of a destination are all struggling with similar challenges to maintain a profitable business operation and at the same time, respond in a dynamic and flexible way to individualized visitor demands.

Many customer and other data are usually accessible for free and thus available to improve decision-making in each of the four components of the supply chain. However, in order to come to a good selection and judgement of these data sets, considerable investments are needed in data analytics. These include trained staff to explore data and find patterns that are relevant for decisions on capacity planning, product development, and commercialization. The roadblock that destination stakeholders face is that neither local governments nor the private sector (mostly small businesses) invest in these areas: they lack knowledge and financial capacity.

The need for T&T operators to respond to visitor and society demands becomes even more urgent because of the impacts of climate change on travel and tourism. To tackle these impacts, stakeholder collaboration is one of the fundamental keys to assure a future sustainable development of the T&T supply chain at destination level. However, in many places, companies as well as public stakeholders are inclined to keep data for themselves and not share them with others, for fear of the loss of potential revenues or in search of competitive advantage. The paradox of this individual attitude of one player is that in the long term it may seriously damage the success and potential positive results of the T&T supply chain as a whole.

In order to analyse the current status of stakeholder collaboration in the T&T supply chain, the current availability and use of data as well as willingness to share for future decision-making, researchers and policy makers can use a survey and scoring tool that we have included here. A qualitative measuring tool allows users to get an insight in the level of data collection and data sharing, as well as the tendency towards a more circular approach in designing the supply chain. The tool is composed of 40 questions in seven categories. The survey should be collected from a representative sample from T&T businesses, as well as all relevant local tourism public stakeholders, such as government departments, a subsidized museum, national parks, etc. It is better if at all levels, differentiated stakeholders are included

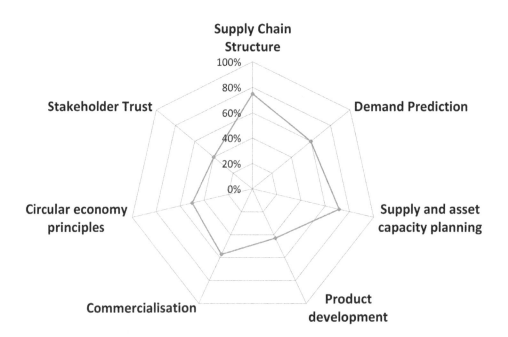

Figure 11.3   Visualizing a circular tourism and travel supply chain

Table 11.1   *T&T circular supply chain scan*

T&T business / Stakeholder name: XXXX	Performance	
	Response	Score
	Yes/No/ NA	1/0/ NA
A *Supply Chain Structure*		
1 We register # visitors	Yes	1
2 We measure how much visitors spend/day and on what items	No	0
3 We have insight in visitor segments/profiles	NA	NA
4 We know our monthly revenues and ROI	Yes	1
5 We measure direct employment	Yes	1
6 We know the number of T&T businesses	NA	NA
B *Demand Prediction*		
1 We analyse future booking patterns and cancellation data	Yes	1
2 We monitor short-term future flight and transport mobility patterns from and to our destination	No	0
3 We monitor website visits and search behaviour	Yes	1
4 We monitor online consumption behaviour of our visitors	Yes	1
5 We nurture online consumption of potential visitors	No	0
C *Supply and Asset Capacity Planning*		
1 We have a data analysis insight team to plan for capacity planning and price determination	No	0
2 We collect third party transactional and geospatial data for capacity planning	Yes	1
3 We use prescriptive analytics to plan capacity and determine prices	Yes	1
4 We use real-time data to adjust capacity and prices	Yes	1
5 We inform visitors through nudging about traffic congestion during their stay	Yes	1
D *Product Development*		
1 We use data analytics to develop and test (pretotype) new tourism products at destination level	No	0
2 We use data to inform our visitors about local supply chains	Yes	1
3 We monitor visitors of protected areas and warn them if capacity limits have been reached	No	0
4 We have a joint public/private platform where we define maximum limits of visitor numbers	Yes	1
5 We monitor visitor waste production, water use and energy use during their stay	No	0
6 We develop and promote electric mobility in our destination through smart applications	Yes	1
E *Commercialization*		
1 We offer all our products online	Yes	1
2 We are connected to secure online payment facilities	Yes	1
3 We make use of online chatbots (AI)	No	0
4 We have online 24/7 assistance to clients in more languages	Yes	1
5 We use social media data in online marketing campaigns	No	0
6 We request and monitor customer feedback	Yes	1
7 We monitor customer satisfaction online	No	0
F *Circular Economy Principles*		
1 We use sustainable construction techniques	No	0
2 We have taken measures to continuously reduce the use of water and energy and the production of waste by our visitors	Yes	1
3 We monitor water and energy consumed by our clients that use our products	Yes	1
4 We have taken measures to continuously reduce water and energy required for the use of our products	Yes	1
5 We have taken measures to encourage sustainable forms of transportation (public transport/video conferencing) in business travel	No	0
6 We offer sustainable forms of transportation to our visitors	No	0
G *Stakeholder Trust*		
1 We share (data) analysis within public–private collaboration	No	0
2 We take decisions on future development of tourism collaboratively	Yes	1
3 We inform our clients about the (potentially) negative environmental or social impacts of the abuse of our products/services	No	0
4 We know how T&T tax income is spent	Yes	1
5 We are informed about T&T investments in our destination	No	0

in the survey. It is important that the survey be filled out together with the researcher, since some questions may be unknown.

The collective data of the survey gives a good scan of the status of knowledge of circular thinking and data-insights at destination level. If aggregated per chain at second tier level, one can analyse differences between travel service providers, accommodation providers, etc.

The scan also allows researchers and planners to understand the general level of data aware-ness at the destination, define scenarios, and discuss future intervention strategies to improve the supply chain towards a more circular approach. A sample is shown in Table 11.1. The scoring table may further be converted into spider diagrams, an example of which is shown in Figure 11.3.

CONCLUSION

In this chapter, we elaborated on the dynamics of travel and tourism supply chains. We have presented a simplified structure of the T&T supply chain, using four main categories of ser-vices and four main supply chain processes.

For each of the processes we have presented options to innovate the supply chains, while making use of visitor and other data to improve the efficiency of business operations and public policies. We have made the case for stakeholders to use these data and define strategies towards a more circular approach to supply chain management. The key bottleneck to success of these tourism strategies is the level of stakeholder trust. This can be built up by designing and implementing true circular economy policies, as developed by the city of Amsterdam.

In order to provide insights into the current level of data insights for each of the supply chain processes as well as level of stakeholder collaboration, researchers often apply qualitative research techniques that are expensive and time-consuming. We included an easy-to-use scan that could overcome this and could be used as a first step for stakeholders that embark on a joint path towards a smart destination based on circular economy principles.

NOTES

1. See https://www.predicthq.com/. Retrieved 17 April 2020.
2. See https://www.forwardkeys.com. Retrieved 19 April 2020.
3. See https://www.techjockey.com/blog/big-data-analytics-tools. Retrieved 19 April 2020.
4. See https://www.nbtc.nl/en/home/activities/intell-insights.htm. Retrieved 22 July 2020.
5. See https://www.visitbrabant.com/nl/routes/routes-in-brabant-nieuwsoverzicht/veilig-recreeren-in -brabant. Retrieved 22 July 2020.
6. See https://www.stuffstr.com. Retrieved 22 July 2020.
7. 'Circularity Indicators'. https://www.ellenmacarthurfoundation.org. Retrieved 19 April 2020.
8. Towards the Circular Economy: An Economic and Business Rationale for an Accelerated Transition. Ellen MacArthur Foundation. 2012. https://www.ellenmacarthurfoundation.org/assets/ downloads/publications/Ellen-MacArthur-Foundation-Towards-the-Circular-Economy-vol.1.pdf. Retrieved 20 April 2020.
9. See https://www.circulareconomyclub.com/listings/tools/. Retrieved 24 July 2020.
10. See https://www.amsterdam.nl/en/policy/sustainability/circular-economy/. Retrieved 24 July 2020.
11. See https://www.interregeurope.eu/fileadmin/user_upload/tx_tevprojects/library/file_1581328309 .pdf. Retrieved 24 July 2020.
12. See https://www.ing.com/Newsroom/News/Breeze-in-breeze-out.htm. Retrieved 22 July 2020.

13. See https://www.zeromasswater.com. Retrieved 22 July 2020.

REFERENCES

Circular Economy Toolkit. Accessed at: http://circulareconomytoolkit.org.

Cooper, M. C., Lambert, D. M. and Pagh, J. D. (1997) Supply chain management: More than a new name for logistics. *International Journal of Logistics Management*, 8(1), 1–13.

Eye for Travel (2017) The State of Data and analytics in travel. Accessed at: https://www.eyefortravel.com.

Font, X., Tapper, R., Schwartz, K. and Kornilaki, M. (2008) Sustainable supply chain management in tourism. *Business Strategy and the Environment*, 17, 260–271.

Manniche, J., Topsø Larsen, K., Brandt Broegaard, R. and Holland, E. (2017) *Destination: A Circular Tourism Economy. A Handbook for Transitioning toward a Circular Economy within the Tourism and Hospitality Sectors in the South Baltic Region.* Accessed at: https://circulareconomy.europa.eu/platform/sites/default/files/cirtoinno-handbook_eng-rev.-4.pdf.

Möhring, M., Keller, B. and Schmidt, R. (2019) Insights into advanced dynamic pricing systems at hotel booking platforms. In J. Pesonen and J. Neidhardt (eds.), *Information and Communication Technologies in Tourism 2019*. Cham: Springer, 265–277.

Peeters, P., Gössling, S., Klijs, J., Milano, C., Novelli, M., Dijkmans, C., Eijgelaar, E., Hartman, S., Heslinga, J., Isaac, R., Mitas, O., Moretti, S., Nawijn, J., Papp, B. and Postma, A. (2018) *Research for TRAN Committee – Overtourism: Impact and Possible Policy Responses*. Brussels: European Parliament, Policy Department for Structural and Cohesion Policies.

Peltier, D. (2016) Four charts showing growth of online and mobile travel bookings by 2020. Accessed at: https://skift.com/2016/06/30/4-charts-showing-growth-of-online-and-mobile-travel-bookings-by-2020.

Salecycle (2018) *Understanding Airline & Travel Booking Trends: Leveraging Past Trends to Increase Future Online Bookings*. A Salecycle data report. Accessed at: https://d34w0339mx0ifp.cloudfront.net/content/Understanding%20Airline%20%26%20Travel%20Booking%20Trends.pdf.

Schrödl, H. and Simkin, P. (2014) Bridging economy and ecology: A circular economy approach to sustainable supply chain management. Paper presented at International Conference on Information Systems, Auckland.

Zhang, H., Song, H. and Huang, G. Q. (2009) Tourism supply chain management: A new research agenda. *Tourism Management*, 30, 345–347.

12. Using mainstream development economics to improve sustainability: a value chain approach
Jonathan Mitchell

INTRODUCTION

Why Are We Interested in the Economic Impacts of Tourism at Destination Level?

Before COVID-19 restrictions grounded the global tourism industry in early 2020, every year over half a billion tourists crossed an international border and visited a developing country (World Bank, 2019). The question this chapter seeks to answer is whether this huge movement of some of the most affluent people visiting some of the most economically fragile countries does, or could, have a positive impact on the lives of low-income people living there?

This is such an obvious question that our team, working in the Overseas Development Institute – a London-based development policy 'think tank' – from 2005, could not believe that it had not already been adequately answered. There was plenty of evidence from tourism trade bodies indicating that tourism is a large and important sector of the economy.

The contribution of academic 'tourism and development' researchers struck us as disappointing. This literature, with some exceptions, was generally wedded to the dependency school of development thinking – a conception of the world where Western 'core' countries used exploitative neo-colonial economic relations to lock low-income 'periphery' countries in a permanent cycle of underdevelopment and poverty. From this perspective, it was so obvious that international tourism damaged developing country destinations economically and culturally that there seemed little point in assessing the empirical evidence, beyond a few anecdotal case studies of exploitation.

With the benefit of hindsight, the reason that our straightforward question of 'how does tourism impact low-income people' remained unanswered was that different groups of people were using different models of development – all of which presupposed the answer to this question.

To illustrate the point, Telfer and Sharpley's sequencing of the seven broad categories in the evolution of development thinking is helpful. Development debates since the 1960s have progressed through the following broad categories: modernization, dependency, economic neoliberalism, alternative development, post-development, human development and global development (Telfer and Sharpley, 2014). Many in the tourist industry implicitly followed the 1960s 'modernization' school of development thinking, some with an update to the 1980s 'economic neoliberalism' (more tourism = development). By contrast, prominent academics in the 'tourism and development' field were both implicit and, in some cases, explicit, advocates of the 1970s 'dependency' approach (more tourism = underdevelopment).

What was striking in 2005 was that the tourism industry and 'tourism and development' academics used entirely different theories of development, both drawn from the previous century and it was this choice of development model which contributed to the dearth of empirical knowledge about the contribution of tourism to poverty reduction (Mitchell, 2019).

Rather than entering a protracted conceptual discussion about development models on issues which had been resolved decades earlier in mainstream development economics, the author saw a more promising route forward being to side-step the conceptual minefield and instead take an empirical focus to address the question, 'can tourism benefit low-income people?'

How Can We Conceptualize the Linkages between Tourism and Low-Income People?

An important starting point is to clearly outline the different pathways through which tourism activity could impact upon low-income people (see Figure 12.1). The source of many disagreements between researchers regarding the scale of benefit flows to vulnerable groups was often caused by different researchers not focusing on the same 'pathway' in their analyses.

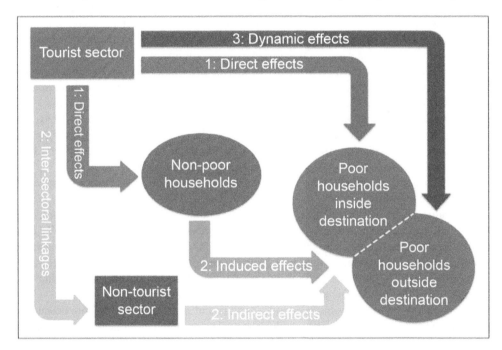

Source: Mitchell and Ashley (2010).

Figure 12.1   Three pathways how tourism impacts on low-income people

What this exercise revealed was that some of the pathways by which tourism can benefit vulnerable people are obvious and direct – a previously low-income person gets a job in a hotel. But many of the ways tourism impacts on the lives of people are indirect (e.g. tourist demand in restaurants increases purchases of food which benefits farmers) or induced (e.g. a well-off excursion owner hires a domestic worker). Dynamic effects are often even less tangible and geographically defined and relate to the longer-term impacts of tourism, such as improving the tax base of the destination which can benefit the vulnerable through social spending by public agencies.

Identifying the pathways through which tourism could benefit low-income groups, helped us choose value chain analysis as a methodological approach to quantify the scale of these flows (Mitchell, 2012).

What Is Value Chain Analysis and What Can It Tell Us (and Not Tell Us)?

Conceptually, value chains do not exist in the sense of having a tangible reality, they are simply a framework for understanding how the world works. A value chain describes the full range of activities required to bring a product or service (e.g. a holiday package) from conception, through the different phases of production and delivery to final consumers (e.g. a tourist) and final disposal after use (Kaplinsky and Morris, 2001). Value chains are a way of understanding the interaction of people and firms with markets and are particularly helpful to understand the complicated supply chains for activities like international tourism. A supply chain represents all the steps required to get a product to market. A value chain details the financial values and describes the transaction at each of these different steps – or nodes – in the chain.

Value chains are, paradoxically, relatively value-free as a framework and have been applied in a range of non-developmental contexts, initially by francophone colonists to extract tropical commodities from Africa more efficiently and later by management scientists from the 1970s during the globalization of production (Altenburg, 2007). It was not until the mid-1990s that development economists coined the term 'global value chains' (Gereffi, 1994) – realizing that this tool, previously used to maximize commercial returns in the North, could be subverted and used to inform the maximization of development returns in the South.

Value chain analysis can make an important contribution to pro-poor economic development for six key reasons.

First, value chains are particularly well-suited to understanding how poor people can engage, or engage more beneficially, with domestic, regional or international trade. The contribution of the global value chain thinkers was a recognition of something very important to the resource poor in rural areas – their lack of power compared with the lead firms setting the 'rules of the game' in the value chain. Trade is about productivity and factor costs, but also about the use of brute economic power to extract value from the chain.

Second, value chain analysis has economic viability and sustainability at its core because of its focus on markets and commercial viability (as well as development concerns). Value chain analysis provides a framework for engagement with both business and beneficiary groups. Successful value chain development projects, therefore, aim for win–win outcomes for all participants. This implies that there is nothing antithetical about generating incentives for the already rich to get richer, providing it is done in a way that includes, and benefits, groups of vulnerable people.

Third, value chains are a strong qualitative diagnostic tool, capable, if employed with skill, of identifying critical issues and blockages for specific target groups and then generating robust and effective policies and development strategies. The key point is that a sound value chain analysis does not simply provide a robust explanation for why the resource poor are vulnerable. It also provides a logical framework to formulate concrete intervention strategies to change their circumstances. In this sense, value chains are a normative, as well as a diagnostic, tool to understand what reality currently is – and how it can be changed for the better.

Fourth, value chain analysis generates solutions which are inherently scalable. This is important because, in the context of the UN Agenda 2030 and following the logic of the Sustainable Development Goals (and particularly SDG1), external donors are increasingly concerned with reducing poverty at scale. Developing value chains which, if successful, benefit only a few beneficiaries is – quite rightly – difficult to justify. Even if the initial focus of a value chain development exercise is on a single producer group or firm, there is no reason why the same logic cannot be scaled up and applied to a cluster of firms or a region or country.

Fifth, value chain analysis is evidence-based and action-oriented. This form of analysis provides tangible recommendations for what specific firms in a specific value chain – and their governments – can do to increase their competitiveness and development impact. A tangible and practical benefit of value chain analysis is that large private sector operators are often familiar with this tool and in many cases – for instance Western outbound tour operators – already view their world through the lens of supply chains.

Finally, value chains provide a clear way forward as a policy and restructuring tool. International evidence shows that achieving systemic competitiveness requires cooperation along the chain, as well as within links in the chain. After all, a chain is only as strong as its weakest link. So the establishment of a collation of interested parties involved in promoting participation by the poor, or the restructuring of value chains, is often a necessary process to ensure that appropriate global competitiveness is realized. Ideally, this includes both private and public sector participants because the analysis typically finds evidence of both market and state failure. From this perspective, realizing global competitiveness involves a joint journey of discovery.

It is for these reasons that value chain analysis has had a profound impact on development studies in recent years and, we believe, has much promise for both measuring and improving the impact of tourism in developing country destinations.

Applying value chain analysis to the tourist sector we developed an approach which 'follows the tourist dollar' through the tourist value chain and associated supply chains. We understand that this approach is partial. It has a focus on economic transfers and on direct, indirect and induced impacts. The treatment of non-economic issues and longer-term dynamic effects is less systematic and, in an ideal world, a pro-poor value chain analysis can be complemented with other, additional, analyses. In essence, we examine the total expenditure of tourists (spending on the package as well as discretionary spending) and follow this expenditure flow to understand who benefits and how. 'Pro-poor income' (PPI) – the wages and profits earned by resource-poor households from tourist spending – can then be compared with total tourism expenditure to assess how pro-poor tourism is at the destination.

Figure 12.2 illustrates a package tourism supply chain for a single hotel and demonstrates the scope of analysis required to 'trace the tourism dollar' effectively. It is immediately apparent that this kind of analysis requires researchers to work with a wide range of stakeholders within the value chain (tour operators; hotel managers; hotel staff; suppliers such as shop owners, guides, farmers, food wholesalers; as well as tourists themselves). The nature of supply chains has a significant impact on their economic footprint – is the fish supplied by the wholesaler imported frozen from Europe or caught locally by artisanal fishermen, for instance? It is important to follow these supply chains as far as possible because this is often where the pro-poor impact – or the opportunity to improve it – is located.

There are also important decision-makers outside the value chain. These include the local tourist association, government tourist department, small business association, tourist training college and others in the external enabling environment – which often have a significant impact on how the tourist value chain operates. It is useful to locate potential participants in the value chain who are currently excluded, in order to understand the barriers to entry to the chain.

Where, by Whom and at What Scale Can It Be Applied?

One of the benefits of tourism value chain analysis is that, although the approach is specific, its application is anything but. Value chains can be applied (see Mitchell, 2019):

- At any scale – from a single firm (e.g. one hotel) to a specific destination to the tourist sector of an entire country;
- In any geography – reflecting the funding from development organizations, our early work was in Anglophone Africa and Southeast Asia before moving into the periphery of Europe with our private sector funded work. However, Truong's (2014) recent analysis has shown this approach has been applied much more broadly – including Latin America, China and even Glasgow;
- By anyone – whilst this approach was conceived by British economists, the approach has been adopted by a very diverse range of researchers across the globe, well beyond the Anglosphere; and
- For a range of different purposes: for an individual hotel operator to improve their social licence to operate; for a destination to increase the positive impact of tourism and mitigate negative impacts; for a country to develop a coherent tourism strategy; or for a donor to understand the most effective point of intervention in their development project.

DESCRIBE THE STEP-BY-STEP APPROACH

This section is structured around three different phases (see Ashley et al., 2009). These phases may be undertaken concurrently but in some situations will be more easily done separately allowing some time for reflection in between:

- **Phase 1. Diagnosis of current situation and context**: This phase includes tools to map the tourism value chain (or economy of the destination), and the participation of low-income people within it. The purpose here is to understand financial flows and how the tourism sector currently works. This phase also helps to understand the policy and regulatory context and the existing tourism market.
- **Phase 2. Project opportunities, prioritization and feasibility**: This phase includes a systematic approach to develop a 'long list' of project options. It then guides the move towards a 'short list' of high priority interventions that should be implemented, by applying specific criteria that include the likely impact of the intervention on poverty.
- **Phase 3. Project planning**: This phase is used to package proposed interventions into bankable projects that can be assessed by potential financiers. This phase provides a structure for reports, and tools to assist in developing institutional arrangements, targets and indicators for monitoring, and also project budgets.

Table 12.1   A step-by-step approach to pro-poor value chain analysis

Phase	Step	What to do?	Why?
Phase 1: Diagnosis	Step 1	Preparation	To define the destination, target group of poor, and the project team
	Step 2	Map the big picture: enterprises and other actors in the tourism sector, links between them, demand and supply data, and the pertinent context	To organize a chaotic reality, understand the overall value chain
	Step 3	Map where the poor do and do not participate	To avoid erroneous assumptions about poor actors and take account of the less visible suppliers
	Step 4	Conduct fieldwork interviews in each node of the chain, with tourists and service providers including current and potential participants	To provide data and insights for Steps 5 to 8
	Step 5	Track revenue flows and pro-poor income and estimate how expenditure flows through the chain and how much accrues to the poor Consider their returns and factors that enable or inhibit earnings	To follow the dollar through the chain down to the poor, and assess how returns can be increased
Phase 2: Identify and appraise opportunities	Step 6	Identify where in the tourism value chain to seek change: which node or nodes?	To use Steps 1 to 5 to select areas ripe for change to ensure Steps 6 to 9 are focused on priority areas
	Step 7	Analysis of strategies: undertake a SWOT analysis to analyse internal and external factors influencing project outcomes	To think rationally about what has to be done, as well as opportunities and risks
	Step 8	Analyse blockages, options, and partners in the nodes selected, to generate a long list of possible interventions	To think laterally and rationally in generating the range of possible projects
	Step 9	Prioritize projects on the basis of their impact and feasibility	To generate a project short list, comprising projects most likely to deliver impact
Phase 3: Programming	Step 10	Project idea: to give a clear and logical statement of the project set-up including a tentative budget and time frame	To structure the presented facts
	Step 11	Project programming	How to package selected projects for funders

Note: These steps have to be iterative and cannot be entirely sequential. For example, some initial thinking from Step 6 (where to focus) will probably inform where you go into most detail in Step 5. Some thinking on partners' activity will inform Step 6, but be more detailed in Step 8.
Source: Ashley et al. (2009).

The basic elements of 'what to do' in a pro-poor value chain assessment, and 'why', are outlined in Table 12.1, with a series of component steps.

Diagnosis

Step 1: Preparation
The scope of the analysis may be included already in your terms of reference, but ensure clarity on:

- The definition of the 'destination' or the geographic/functional target area;
- The target groups (e.g. low-income people, women, people with disabilities, etc.);
- The composition of the study team and its skills;
- How far the study will go in terms of proposing options or detailing their feasibility and plan (phases 2 and 3);
- The precise nature of the project output (e.g. policy options brief for decision-makers or fully-costed project proposal).

The scope of the destination to be assessed may be defined in purely geographic terms, such as a specific destination, the region 100 km from a resort, or a whole country. Often though, there is also a particular type of tourism that is the focus: leisure tourism as opposed to business tourism in a city, safari tourism in a wilderness area, or all-inclusive hotels in a resort area.

Defining the 'destination' is important, because 'big picture' data for the whole destination will be needed. At the least, arrival trends, tourist spending, market segments, and key stakeholders need to be mapped for the whole destination. The scope of the destination has implications for the activities you can do in the available time, and also the size of your study team (see Box 12.1).

BOX 12.1 A TYPICAL ITINERARY: COLLECTING INFORMATION IN THE FIELD (FOR A TWO PERSON TEAM)

Day 1: Arrive at destination, mobilization meetings with sponsor, agree logistics and brief or train local team (finish Step 1 and continue Step 2).

Day 2: Stakeholder analysis: Tourist Department, Hotel Association, Mayor, Department of Trade & Industry, Tourism and Guiding Associations (Step 2 and into Step 3).

Day 3: Local communities: Representatives of producer organizations, community representatives, and NGOs (refine Step 2, expand Step 3).

Interim output: Value chain map with low-income participants identified.

The following 10 days: Step 4 (interviews) by day, with first attempts at Step 5 in the evening and between interviews:

Day 4: Undertake tourist surveys, guide surveys and craft surveys.

Day 5: 4× hotel interviews.

Day 6: 4× hotel interviews.

Day 7: 4× hotel interviews.

Day 8: Tour operators (offices of international operators and local ground-handlers).

Day 9 and 10: Restaurant interviews, food markets, agriculture departments.

Day 11: Craft markets and shops.

Day 12: Excursions and attractions (including entertainment and cultural performances).

Day 13: Support institutions (e.g. hospitality training college, police, immigration department, financial institutions, NGOs, etc.).

Day 14: Analysis (Step 5) and creation of value chain maps.

Day 15: Study team workshop and further analysis (Step 5 and possibly start Step 6).

Day 16: Preliminary findings workshop (confirm Steps up to 5, discuss Step 6).

Day 16–18: A mixture of consultant work and team/stakeholder work. Generate the long list and initial prioritization (Step 7 and Step 8) and discuss the long list and prioritization with stakeholders.

After Day 18: Write up findings, report, summary of diagnostic and recommendations. Discuss further and amend further. Arrange a second round of meetings to confirm selection and start intervention planning.

Perhaps the most challenging and important step in a rigorous project screening procedure is defining the potential target group. The value chain approach starts with an assessment of the tourism economy, working out where the target group already operates and where their participation can be increased. This is by contrast to conventional community-based tourism approaches that tend to start with a target community, and then help them develop tourism products. The complexities of defining the poverty threshold are outlined later.

Agreeing the skills required and team composition of an analysis upfront is critical. Diagnostic studies can be done with many different types of teams. Studies have been done by small teams with two specialist researchers to much larger teams with up to 20 local participants. All team configurations have their own benefits and drawbacks. The only unshakeable rule is that there should always be a local counterpart in all teams. Generally the team leader has solid knowledge of value chain analysis, gender expertise and sustainable tourism experience. This researcher would ideally be supported by a relevant sector specialist (e.g. in food, culture, etc.) and complemented by at least one national consultant to ensure local knowledge transfer. Diagnostics can be done in a participatory way, where the role of the external consultant becomes one of trainer and coordinator, synthesizer and quality control – rather than primary researcher. There is less control over final outputs and more need for quality control and management, but there should also be considerably more buy-in and additional insights that the outsider lacks.

Step 2: Mapping the value chain and context
Analysing existing information is an important precursor to mapping the value chain and context. Developing country destinations vary enormously in the amount and quality of sta-

tistical information on tourism. But if data is there, assimilate it, before starting the fieldwork. Key information to look out for is:

- Tourism supply – the number, type, scale and turnover of enterprises that supply tourists;
- Tourism demand – arrival numbers, length of stay, source markets, and expenditure; and
- Trends – particularly trends that affect the viability of the overall sector, or demand for products provided by the poor.

Although tourism statistics are generally much better than statistics on other service sectors, this basic information is often surprisingly difficult to obtain. Tourism supply and demand information may be available at both local and national level, though there is likely to be more at the national level. Undertaking a value chain analysis in a destination where there has been a recent and thorough tourism master plan can be a benefit. Master planning often involves significant surveys, which collect good quality data which is very useful as an input to a value chain exercise. In the Gambia, for example, the value chain exercise could draw on two robust 2,000 tourist surveys (one in hotels and the other at the airport) which had been undertaken the previous year. This yielded data about tourist behaviour, expenditure and attitudes at a level of statistical significance that would not be possible in an action research survey of 50 tourists.

When using official tourism statistics in developing countries it is vital to never accept data uncritically. This is because data is sometimes wrong, occasionally dramatically so.

The best way to identify incorrect data is to look very carefully at how, and by whom, data is collected and to always try and validate information from more than one source. For instance, hotel interviews in Addis made it quite clear that the official statistics on international arrivals were dramatically overstated and accommodation revenue figures were significantly understated (see Box 12.2).

BOX 12.2 TWO EXAMPLES OF WAYWARD OFFICIAL TOURIST STATISTICS

Vietnam has amongst the richest primary tourism statistics in the world. Hotel owners have to report to the police all foreign nationals staying in their accommodation every night. However, the political culture has two blind spots that can lead to distortions of this excellent primary data. First, Vietnam is highly target-driven and the local tourism department may be under considerable pressure to achieve the arrival statistics targeted in the annual plan. Second, low-end domestic accommodation providers are often accused of promoting 'social evils' (i.e. prostitution) with the result that these types of activity and establishment may disappear from the official statistics.

Ethiopian tourism statistics are often extraordinarily inaccurate. For instance, the statistical bulletin for Addis indicated that hotel revenue for the city was USD 11.1m a year in 2008. Hotel interviews found USD 11.1m is less than half the revenue generated from just one of the top-end hotels in Addis. Both the hotels in Addis with a revenue stream larger than the official figure for the whole destination are government-owned.

Sources: Mitchell and Chi (2007); Mitchell and Coles (2009).

Table 12.2   *Supply and demand information*

Assessment	Information to gather
Tourism demand	Basic tourism statistics demand (i.e. over a 10 year period):
	Numbers of tourists; annual growth; seasonality variations (e.g. high and low seasons during the year); domestic and international; source countries of origin; average length of stay
	More detailed information about tourism demand:
	Reason for travel, such as visiting friends and relatives (VFR), business (professional), holiday, shopping, conferences, religious, etc.; accommodation preferences (i.e. relating to the number of bed nights sold in different types of accommodation); activities undertaken such as culture, business, beach, protected areas, wildlife, adventure, scenic beauty, shopping etc.; type of traveller, for example, backpackers, independent travellers, organized groups, etc.
Tourism supply	Location of tourism operations – what are the tourism clusters (areas of intense tourism activity including accommodation, tourism operators, and other tourism service providers)?; facilities and amenities – which lodging, restaurants, shops, tour operators etc. are being used by tourists?; rates charged – what are the current price levels (inexpensive, moderate and expensive)?; occupancy rates – which properties are successful, how many visitors do they receive per year or season and what is the trend in occupancies?; turnover and profit – what revenues are the enterprises generating and are they profitable or at least commercially viable?; market segments served – who is currently visiting these operations and where do they originate, what brands are being promoted, how are they marketed?; employment – how have the employees changed over the years and are there projected growths or declines in the industry?; sustainability – what measures are in place to minimize negative socio-cultural and environmental impacts and are there current issues with these?
Support services and infrastructure	Accessibility of the locations: Distance from the main country arrival city and the location by various means of transportation, e.g. by car, bus, boat, plane, train (in both time and kilometres/miles); condition of the roads; structure of the roads (i.e. connections between community residences, tourism facilities and potential sites); quality and availability of food, drinking water and sanitation; availability of electricity network; means of communication; availability of telephone, fax, post office, internet, cell phone; forms of health care available; availability and quality of medical services; availability and quality of medicines at or close by the location

Use the guidance in Table 12.2 to collect information on supply and demand, and report your findings under the headers given.

Mapping of stakeholders: You need to know 'who is who' in the tourism sector. Value chains are a useful way of organizing a chaotic reality. Key tourism stakeholders are usually mapped as a participatory exercise at the start of a study. Participants are asked to identify important tourism stakeholder groups on cards in a workshop format. These stakeholders are then grouped into categories and the interactions described, as illustrated below for an exercise undertaken in Vietnam. At the centre of the map are tourists and the radial categories include, for instance, the accommodation sector, restaurants, transportation and a wide variety of supporting institutions. Even after extensive tidying up, the visual impression is often rather daunting.

Figure 12.2 illustrates the key components of a tourism value chain, these include:

- **The main 'nodes' of the value chain**: including accommodation, food and drink, transport and excursions, and craft and curios. These nodes will be represented differently in contrasting destinations, which have different tourist products and patterns of expenditure;

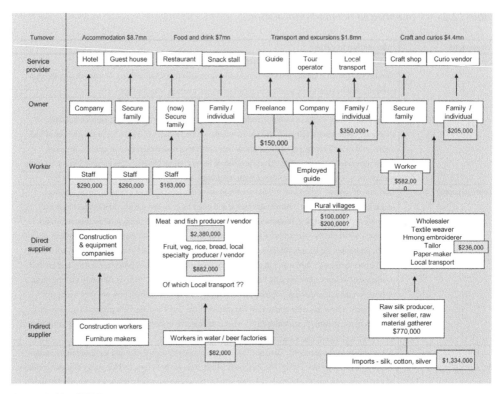

Source: Ashley (2006).

Figure 12.2   Using a value chain format to illustrate tourism stakeholders in a destination

- **Direct service providers**: establishing an inventory of who are the direct service providers in a destination is one of the most critical first actions in a value chain analysis. It is important to avoid missing out a whole category of tourism service providers, like tourist guides;
- **Non-tourism sectors**: tourism demand normally has impacts on the local economy well beyond the hotels, restaurants and transportation services – that constitute the 'tourist sector' in the National Accounts. Craft and agriculture spending by tourists often has very strong pro-poor linkages in a tourist destination.

Government policy inevitably provides the framework for the industry and for the implementation of any project. It is important to consider political stability, strategies, legislation, and plans in relation to their effect on a tourism value chain (e.g. in relation to poverty reduction, environmental management, business development strategy, and regulation of tourism activities).

Step 3: Mapping where the poor participate
Many value chain maps stop at the level of the formal sector enterprise, and do not show the micro entrepreneurs, sole traders, informal sector workers, and staff of businesses. However,

it is at the 'bottom' parts of the chain that the poor are likely to be concentrated, so must be mapped (see Box 12.3).

In the Laos example (see Figure 12.3) several levels were added to the basic map, going below the level of the formal sector hotel, restaurant or shop. By mapping workers, direct suppliers (1st tier) and indirect suppliers (2nd tier), the map could then be annotated to show where the poor participate. It was then annotated differently to show where women participate (one colour for majority, another colour for significant but less than 50 per cent participation), and finally annotated again to show where ethnic minorities participate. Where possible, the estimated number of poor people involved should be added, though it may not be possible to do this for all points in the chain, particularly those that are more remote from the destination.

BOX 12.3 HOW TO? TIPS ON MAPPING LOW-INCOME PARTICIPANTS

- When key informants create a stakeholder map or first value chain, they are unlikely to mention all participants. Craft producers or small transport operators may appear but not all workers and suppliers will.
- After the initial mapping is done, focus on the part that involves enterprises (not the support institutions). Prompt participants to add the workers and suppliers in each node. Then use another colour, or stickers, to illustrate the many points in the whole map where low-income people are engaged.
- If appropriate, you can use colour coding for different target groups (income-poor, rural, women, etc.) or to show whether they are majority or minority participants.
- Your knowledge of where the target group engages will develop further during the work. The final diagnostic report should include a value chain illustrating participation of the vulnerable, based on all inputs received.

Step 4: Conduct fieldwork with tourists, enterprises and support institutions to gather data and perspectives

In the past, many diagnostics have been done based on interviews with government, NGOs and some communities. The emphasis here is on interviewing entrepreneurs (large and small) and workers in the tourism value chain, in addition to interviews with public sector and community interest groups. This section provides guidance on interviews to conduct in each node (accommodation, restaurants, etc.). But, do not embark on this until you are entirely clear on how you will use the information generated.

Hotels are generally the most important part of the tourism value chain for several reasons. Accommodation is usually the largest item of in-country expenditure for tourists and, hence, the largest node – financially speaking – in the value chain. Hotel managers spend their careers with tourists, so have a very useful perspective on how the destination is working outside the hotel (e.g. whether airline services are unreliable or tourists enjoy particular excursions or restaurants). All tourists use some form of accommodation – hotel surveys can provide good data on tourist numbers, source markets, lengths of stay, demand trends, etc.).

The size and complexity of the destination will affect the methodology to survey hotel representatives, because tourist destinations vary hugely. Many tourist destinations in developing countries may only have ten hotels and one or two attractions. However, in larger destinations

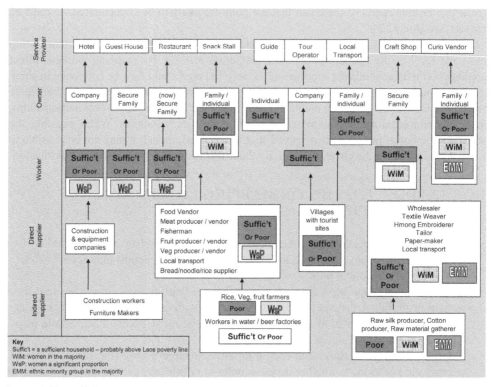

Source: Ashley (2006).

Figure 12.3   *Mapping low-income participants as workers and suppliers in nodes in the value chain in Luang Prabang, Laos*

– where it is not possible to visit all hotels, guest houses, restaurants, markets, shops, tour operators, etc. – it will be necessary to sample a smaller selection of service providers. The key goal of sampling is to ensure the sample is representative of the broader population from which it is drawn.

For hotels we suggest stratifying the inventory of all accommodation providers into top, middle and low-end establishments, drawing a sample from each category (e.g. if possible at least ten enterprises in each category, randomly selected from the population) and weighting the findings by the relative size (i.e. number of hotel rooms) of each type of establishment in the population.

Interviews with tourism managers can be used to understand the financial and operational performance of the hotel, the supply and demand of tourism in the destination, as well as direct flows to poor participants via their enterprise.

The information required in the hotel survey is sensitive, and managers will only disclose it if they have credible reassurances that the information will not be relayed to local authorities or to their competitors and that the study can generate changes that are in the interests of the hotel. This is one part of the study process, which sometimes does not benefit from the presence of local stakeholders – it is sometimes actually a benefit to be an external researcher.

The questionnaire contains a number of internal checks to validate the responses given. For instance, the room revenue should equal the number of rooms multiplied by occupancy levels and room rates. Staff costs should equal staff numbers multiplied by the average wage rates. It is essential to avoid using data in the analysis that you think may be incorrect. When working in a new destination, it is important to try and get one or two cooperative hotels at the start of the study process. Demonstrating that you already have some understanding of the operations of the local market can help encourage other hoteliers to share sensitive data (e.g. asking 'presumably you also find you have to discount room rates to the larger tour operators by as much as 30 per cent during the low season?'). The most cooperative hotels are generally the ones owned by the head of the Hotel Association – often the most supportive private sector operator in the destination and often a dynamic and thoughtful actor.

Sometimes hotel managers of large, chain hotels cannot provide the information required, for a variety of reasons. Some hotel chains have corporate policies about what information can be released. In addition, some hotel managers simply do not have access to the information. For example, most of the hotels around the rim of the Ngorongoro Crater Conservation Area in Tanzania have offices in Arusha that handle all accommodation bookings and manage the supply logistics and finances – so managers may simply not be aware of hotel revenue and food costs (this information should be chased up at the relevant office). Similarly, ACCOR hotels in Dakar, Senegal, do not maintain a central database of operational goods and services that they purchase.

The food supply chain can be an important mechanism for transmitting tourist expenditure to large numbers of some of the poorest rural households. However, it is quite possible for large amounts of food to be purchased by hotels in developing countries with very little impact on poor local communities. Food may be imported or procured from prosperous commercial farmers. Even when food is sourced from smallholders, producers may not benefit if they capture only a small proportion of the wholesale or retail price paid by the hotels.

It is therefore important, not only to establish how much money hotels and restaurants are spending on food, but also who are their suppliers. On the safari route in Tanzania, for instance, some hotels employed intermediaries to go into local markets and 'bulk up' orders by purchasing from several different farmer-run stalls. Other hotels purchased food inputs from the Shoprite wholesaler in Arusha whose supplies were largely imported from South African commercial farmers.

Buying crafts can have an important pro-poor impact in a tourist destination. In Luang Prabang in Laos, for instance, each tourist spends over USD 30 during a three-day visit on crafts and the handicraft sector is dominated by local, ethnic minority women – traditionally one of the poorest sectors of society. Although some silk, cotton and silver is imported, a significant proportion is produced locally and almost all fabrication is local. In the night market, the Hmong women have also upgraded their position from producers to acting also as retailers of crafts directly to tourists. This functional upgrading has allowed the women to capture value at several different nodes of this value chain with an estimated retail value of USD 4.5m per year (Ashley, 2006).

It is important to look beyond the retail transaction between a tourist and craft seller, and as far as possible, to the producers of goods sold for the tourist market. So the craft retail questionnaire is simply the starting point for an investigation into the craft supply chain – not the final word. Without information from the production node of the supply chain and also from wholesalers, it is not possible to understand how to intervene effectively to increase the participation of poor people in the craft supply chain.

A thorough overview of the craft node would need to cover: different types of craft outlets (e.g. textile sellers, silver/jewellery shops, handicraft markets, etc.) and the actual producers of the products. The gatherers or producers of raw materials (e.g. silk, wood, metal, etc.) and others involved in transport, wholesaling, finishing, are also important to include. These actors may be geographically dispersed. If it is not possible to interview each, at least find key informants that can provide information about each level in the chain.

Expenditure on excursions varies greatly in different destinations. In some all-inclusive resorts, few tourists leave the confines of the resort. Elsewhere, excursions may be so integral to the tourist experience that tourist entrance numbers can be a useful proxy for tourist arrival numbers. For instance, a combination of game park entrance figures and hotel occupancy statistics can provide useful statistics to verify official statistics on game park usage.

Entertainment may be provided during these excursions, such as singing, traditional dancing, music, skills demonstrations, and storytelling. These forms of entertainment may also be provided within the hotel where guests are staying. By improving the quality and diversity of the entertainment provided, interventions can help to conserve local culture, and also improve the income people generate from it.

As with all other supply chains, it is important to look beyond the transaction with the tourist to understand the developmental impact of the expenditure. In the Gambia, tourist spending on conventional excursions sold by tour representatives had a relatively limited impact on the local community (see Figure 12.4). This is because the retail margins for these excursions are very large with the local suppliers of excursion services sometimes receiving only 20 per cent of the retail price of the excursion. However, in parallel with these conventional excursions were much more pro-poor products, using locally trained guides, local transport and other service providers. For these excursions, almost all tourist expenditure translates into pro-poor income (Mitchell and Faal, 2007).

It is important to look at the different types of excursions offered by tour operators. This includes those offered in brochures in originating countries, and also those available at the destinations. Avoid just focusing on those that are obviously pro-poor, as the future intervention may in fact be to work on adapting those that are not currently pro-poor.

Depending on the activity of local tourism offices, it can be difficult to obtain reliable information from tourists in the target destination, particularly in developing countries. Even if tourism surveys are done, they may not contain the specific expenditure data that you need. So you may need to collect data from tourists yourself.

A tourist survey should cover the basics that enable you to define the tourist segment and basic parameters (nationality, length of stay, purpose of travel) and some information on expenditure while in the destination (for integrating with PPI estimates). Beyond that, the focus is highly dependent on the type of issues and options you want to explore, whether in relation to upgrading of the overall destination, development of specific excursions, engagement with tour operators or hoteliers. Thus, it is not necessarily ideal to start the analysis with the tourist survey, but to finalize it part way through the fieldwork.

A tourist questionnaire can be adapted for the needs of the specific study. Analysis of these results can provide you with an understanding of tourism demand for different tourism-related services and facilities that can be developed or enhanced in the project.

Step 5: Tracking revenue flows, pro-poor income and barriers facing the target group

This step aims to track how revenue flows through the value chain, and in particular how much is captured by the target group. It also highlights the key factors that determine or inhibit their earnings. This is probably the most demanding part of the diagnostic. Hundreds of pieces of data need to be put together, compared, divided and aggregated to generate the results. However, once the figures emerge, they are an invaluable basis for understanding the financial pro-poor impacts of the tourism economy.

Estimating flows of income to the poor (pro-poor income, or PPI) is a considerable task. Questions need to be asked carefully, and often informed estimates are needed to fill in the gaps. The objective is to collate all the information you have collected from surveys of hotels, restaurants, out of pocket expenditure, tourists, craft stalls to calculate two critical numbers.

First, how much do tourists spend in each node of the value chain (e.g. accommodation, excursions, etc.) in total each year and, second, what proportion of this spending accrues to low-income people.

The first figure is calculated as you would moving from any stratified survey to an estimate of the population. Knowing how many hotels, guest houses and lodges are in the destination in distinct quality and cost categories, you have stratified hotel surveys within each category – so have an estimate of the average turnover per hotel or lodge in each category. Multiplying this average turnover per hotel in each category by the number of hotels will yield a first estimate of total hotel spend in the category and adding up all categories will generate an estimate of total hotel spend in the destination.

These total expenditure figures should then be triangulated with other information you have collected. In some destinations you will have access to a tourist survey which provides robust estimates of expenditure on different expenditure items. In others you will find a well-informed source in the local government or tourist association or tour operator who contracts hotel rooms in the destination, who has this information. If your tourist 'destination' is the tourist sector of a whole country, it is often possible to get reasonably accurate national figures for different items of expenditure from the national accounts or tax authority.

Two key points should be made upfront. First, many private sector operators have an incentive to falsify their income or profit earnings (for instance, to minimize their tax liability). As a consequence, the researcher should not take any responses from entrepreneurs at face value, without probing, testing, validating and ground testing the responses. The second point is that every transaction (e.g. a room rate) has two sides – a hotel manager may understate his or her actual selling room rates, but these figures can be triangulated with the tour operator or tourist buying the accommodation.

Expenditure on other nodes of the value chain (excursions, restaurants outside hotels, crafts, etc.) is calculated in the same way as hotels. So, if a destination has 200 similar craft stalls and 10 craft shops, interview a sample of each to establish average metrics per stall and shop, and then multiply the average figures by the number of outlets in the destination to estimate total craft spend.

In reality, the researcher will generate estimates based upon explicit assumptions and a large spreadsheet model and this requires several iterations, triangulations and validation before settling on a best estimate.

Calculating the share of accommodation, which is pro-poor, can be done in a number of ways:

First, the most straightforward approach is to assume that all non-management wages paid by hotels to accommodation workers (restaurant and kitchen staff are part of the food supply chain) are pro-poor income (PPI). This approach is relatively crude because it assumes all non-management staff are paid wages below the poverty threshold.

A more refined approach is to examine hotel wages against local and internationally defined poverty lines and assess what proportion of non-management wages would fail to raise an average household above the poverty line. More recently, a dynamic assessment of poverty has been used in a number of analyses. With this, hotel managers are asked to estimate the proportion of non-management hotel staff that are from poor backgrounds and this proportion is applied to the non-management payroll. The merit of this latter approach is that it avoids the difficulties inherent in assessing whether an average wage is a poverty wage and rather assesses the ability of the tourist sector to absorb people from poor backgrounds and enhance their livelihoods.

In all cases, a critical and challenging part of the hotel questionnaire is obtaining estimates of salary levels for different types of workers. Knowing how many staff count in your definition of poverty, and the average wage they earn (including tips) is essential. A single typical monthly wage for unskilled and semi-skilled staff may lead to an erroneous aggregate figure if there is wide and uneven variation among them.

Whichever method is used, pro-poor income (PPI) in the accommodation sector tends to be a low proportion of hotel accommodation turnover – 5–15 per cent of room turnover being typical. The PPI share is usually lower for high-end establishments than for more modest accommodation, despite relatively high staff wages and labour-intensive staffing levels in high-end establishments. This is because five star room rates in developing countries are often at international levels with very much lower staff wages than would be the case in New York or Tokyo.

Spending on food is often a major financial flow in the tourism value chain, and one with potential to be a large source of PPI. So, working out the share of food spending that reaches poor people is important (it may be a high share of a high number so it has a big impact on your overall picture).

It is necessary to disaggregate total hotel food consumption into broad categories (i.e. meat, fish, vegetables, fruit, cereals, dairy goods and dry goods). This is important for two reasons. First, different types of hotel have strongly contrasting baskets of food inputs. For instance, basic starch staples often make up a high proportion of total food inputs for domestic tourist hotels with fruit and fish being important costs for top-end hotels. Second, the pro-poor share of the value chain contrasts markedly from one type of commodity to another. For instance, in Ethiopia, poor fishermen receive about one-third of the price paid by hotels for their output. By contrast, for staple cereals a very high proportion of the final retail price is captured by the overwhelmingly poor smallholder sector – with market intermediaries between producers and the hotels receiving very limited margins (Mitchell and Coles, 2009).

Establishing the pro-poor profile of these supply chains does, however, require detailed analysis by an agricultural specialist from the point of production to final consumption.

It is as important in the craft sector as it is in the food sector to track all the way down to primary producers and input suppliers when assessing PPI. Craft cannot be assumed to be proportionately very pro-poor, but assessing PPI can indicate whether it is and whether it can be changed.

The same principles apply to assessing PPI from excursions and transport. But given the diversity of excursions, there are few hard and fast rules. PPI from a two hour paddle boat trip downriver is just a matter of boat fees to the (poor) boatmen minus some immediate

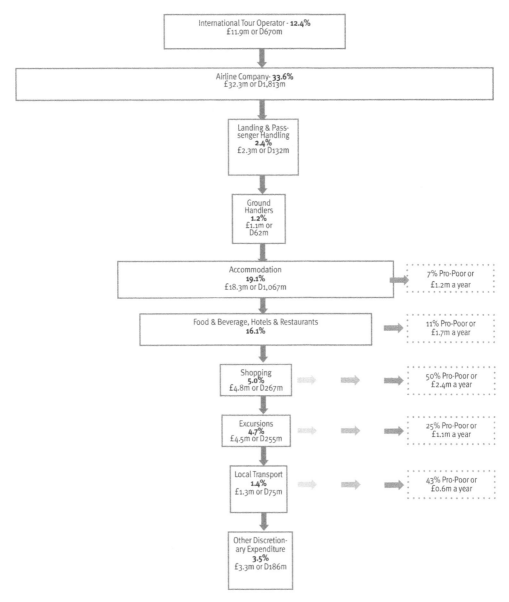

Source: Mitchell and Faal (2007).

Figure 12.4   Use of a value chain to map flows of expenditure and shares reaching low-income groups in The Gambia

expenditures times the numbers of passengers (or numbers of trips, depending on whether fee is per person or per boat). Whereas PPI from a three day up-country 4×4 excursion is complex, involving its own sub-analysis of food, accommodation, etc. Tourists can be charged per-person for entertainment and cultural performances.

Once the jigsaw has been completed, the figures can be aggregated in the value chain map (see Figure 12.4). There are different ways of doing this but essentially they depict the scale of flows to the target group, compared with total economic activity, at each node of the value chain.

Tracking PPI has two main purposes. The first is to provide aggregate figures per year to show the 'big picture' of flows to the poor: broadly where are they earning revenue from tourism. Which nodes are most important for PPI? Which nodes are large financially but poor performers for the poor?

The second purpose is to provide more detailed analysis at key points in the chain on how exactly poor participants are earning their returns and shares. This enables analysis of options and factors that enable or inhibit participation and earnings.

Assessing how much, in total, flows to poor people is useful but too blunt an instrument for project planning. In those areas of the chain of particular interest, more detailed investigation is needed of what, how, why, etc. as shown for food and craft chains above. If income is very small, is this because of unfavourable terms that could be changed, or does it simply reflect the low value of the product? What are the perceptions of the poor concerning the obstacles they face? What are the perceptions of other stakeholders? What barriers can be tackled or new trends exploited?

Project Opportunities, Prioritization and Feasibility

This phase includes a systematic approach to developing a 'long list' of project options, and then to move from there to a 'short list' of high priority interventions that should be implemented. Using the information you collected during Phase 1 you should be able to make some judgements about the likely impact, relevance, sustainability, and the risk and ease of action of the proposed projects.

One of the greatest dangers for tourism value chain research is that practitioners invest time in describing the value chain and then leap to proposing exactly the same kind of intervention as they would have done before. However, it is not always easy to jump from the descriptive analysis of the tourism sector to the prescriptive set of recommendations. Knowing which parts of the tourism value chain are currently pro-poor or not does not, on its own, tell you where to intervene to generate greater benefits for the poor. This step requires assessment of where increases are feasible and where blockages can be removed. In fact, the most critical part of the diagnostic and planning process is judicious use of the information gathered so far to identify first a long list, and later a short list, of possible interventions.

A common mistake in many diagnostic studies is to allocate too many resources to the initial mapping, leaving insufficient time and attention for working through the implications. Another mistake is to jump to assumptions: because something is pro-poor already, it is the best option for expansion.

Step 6: Identifying where in the value chain to seek change
The diagnostic assessment provides the basis for deciding where in tourism to intervene, and how, to enhance benefits to the poor. The mapping should show where the poor participate, where value is created, and why. The next step is to identify where there is scope for greater value creation by the poor and what blockages need to be removed.

By the end of Steps 1 to 5, you should have a map – or several maps – of the tourism value chain. One that shows all the various stakeholders. A version that shows where the poor participate. And a map, probably simplified into key nodes, showing flows of PPI to low-income participants. The next step is to identify key nodes or strands in the chain where you could seek pro-poor change. This will be the basis for scoping possible interventions. While diagnostic value chain assessments vary widely in their approach and recommendations, there are usually five or so areas to focus on:

1. Parts of the value chain that are already fairly pro-poor (in percentage terms). Can production be expanded or producers' role upgraded? What are the blockages?
2. Parts of the chain that are big, high in value creation, but may be low in the share of the poor. Can the share accruing to the poor be increased? Even if only at the margin, a 1 per cent shift of mainstream industry production to a pattern that benefits the poor can generate pro-poor income at volume.
3. Parts of the chain where the share reaching the poor is low compared to international norms. Why is it low? Are these factors fairly fixed or amenable to influence?
4. Parts of the chain where poor people are concentrated. Can they be helped to upgrade their production or function in the chain?
5. Parts of the chain where change is currently occurring. If volumes are going up, it may be easier to boost the share of the poor. If structures are already fluid it is a good time to make pro-poor adaptations.

Action research suggests that the areas chosen as priorities for action are hugely diverse. The key point is to have a framework to encourage an appreciation of the diverse range of pro-poor opportunities and assess them rigorously. At this point, identifying where in the value chain you seek change and pro-poor impact is not the same as identifying where you should intervene. The diagnostic may conclude that a key area for change is the returns to the target group from crafts. In Phase 2, you may nevertheless plan an intervention that works directly with tour operators to help achieve that.

Step 7: Analysis of strategies
The problem analysis comes first, because the activities and objectives of an intervention should not be derived from the donor's perception of problems, but rather relate to specific, real-world problems. The analysis phase should always start with a closer look at the problems. The guiding question is what are the most important problems to be solved by the project and how do these problems interact with each other? This may be done through a participatory exercise with the project's major stakeholders.

Defining the correct problem is often the most difficult part of the exercise because often the most obvious problems expressed by participants in a value chain are symptomatic of deeper underlying problems elsewhere in the system. This is where taking a systems approach is extremely useful.

For instance, in a project in Central Vietnam, the superficial problem was that local people felt that they were not deriving enough benefit from the tourist sector. Analysis indicated a high proportion of the tourism activity taking place was benefiting local people and the local economy – the central challenge was that the size of the tourism sector itself was well below potential. In particular, the leisure segment was being held back by the failure of the local government to effectively exploit the beach which was the greatest tourist asset in the area.

The beach was not being developed because local government had allowed speculators to buy development options on sites and was not enforcing deadlines for the start of development. As a result, the binding constraint was overcome by supporting local government to enforce the restrictions on their beach development options, which resulted in the speculative holders of development options to on-sell them to genuine hotel investors. This has resulted in a very significant expansion of the tourist sector which has generated many tens of thousands of jobs and driven the development of Da Nang City over the past 14 years (Mitchell, 2019).

A SWOT (Strengths, Weaknesses, Opportunities and Threats) analysis is a brainstorming method to analyse internal and external factors influencing project outcomes. The process implies to quickly scan, sort and prioritize potential drivers and risks of the project in order to develop a viable and impactful portfolio of intervention proposals to underlie the strategy (Ashley, 2006).

When analysing different strategies, it is important to differentiate between internal factors (which can be influenced by the project) and external factors (which cannot). The consideration of external factors – the framework of the project – is especially important when assessing preconditions for success and managing risks.

Step 8: Developing a long list of intervention options
Once you have chosen a pressure point (or a strand or supply chain within the value chain), think laterally to generate the long list of possible interventions. The value chain map is an invaluable description of the current situation, but on its own is not sufficient for generating a long list of future intervention options. Nor are the opinions of the consultant undertaking the diagnostic study sufficient basis for picking the long list. It is essential to draw on a range of inputs and analytical techniques:

- Opinions of stakeholders gathered during the mapping process about blockages and opportunities that they perceive and actions they would like to see;
- Information gathered as to why the value chain operates as it does in this destination;
- Consideration of the full-range of options to ensure lateral thinking rather than a focus on the obvious;
- Assessment of existing drivers for change;
- Norms derived from other studies that suggest where this destination is under-performing in pro-poor impact, and why;
- Rough 'what-if' assessments of the scale of possible impact – the numbers of low-income people, or the scale of additional income to the poor;
- Mapping of trade-offs between objectives for comparing options; and
- What others are doing to influence the operation of the value chain and the distribution of the benefits for the vulnerable.

The participation of low-income groups in value chains can be enhanced in many different ways. Current participants may increase the amount they work or sell, and thus their income, or they may find ways to capture a bigger slice of tourism expenditure by changing what or how they work. Or wider pro-poor impact may be achieved not by working with existing producers, but by helping new participants enter the tourism value chain. The options differ in terms of who benefits, how many benefit, and how they affect pro-poor income per person, in aggregate, or as a share of total benefit.

Table 12.3 presents a typology that is intended to help separate and analyse the different options. Use the table to: decide where to focus: a pressure point, an upgrading strategy, a target group, a strand of the chain and impact analysis to prioritize the top one or two as your selected pressure point. Use your understanding of the value chain to assess the problems to be tackled and a long list of possible interventions for the chosen pressure point. Map the blockages facing low-income groups and consider a range of intervention types and points within that strand of the chain.

It can be seen that many value chain improvements will benefit both existing and new entrants, but on the whole they will favour one or the other. There can be a tendency to focus on helping existing participants to upgrade because they are an obvious target group. But helping new people to enter the market can be an equally effective pro-poor strategy sometimes reaching more, or more vulnerable, people.

Doing 'what-if' estimates of increased pro-poor income: One of the advantages of mapping flows through the value chain is that it enables some very rough 'what if?' calculations to be done, to see where there is potentially large financial impact on the poor. If 'x' could be doubled, what would it mean for pro-poor income (PPI)?

On what grounds should interventions be considered for inclusion in the long list? Of course boosting total PPI per year is important, but not the only one. Even at this stage, it is important to identify the key variables and consider trade-offs. This approach will then be pursued in more detail later, when prioritizing the long list and the short list. There are likely to be trade-offs between helping existing participants increase their returns, or bringing in new participants. The former might be easier. The latter might benefit more of the most vulnerable.

Some interventions may generate impressive boosts in PPI per person and significantly alter the share of value captured by the poor, while others only fractionally influence PPI per person, while influencing thousands of the poor. Equally, there may be a trade-off between the number of poor people reached and the extent of involvement of women, minorities, or poorer poor. Intervention options will range from the very local level to the international. At the local level, the link between intervention and impact is quite direct, even if impact is small. Intervening at the national level, in market functions, or internationally is more risky, but potentially creates more impact. Most long lists will contain a variety of possibilities that combine these factors, and should combine some short term 'quick wins' with longer term high impact projects.

To achieve change at any identified area of the value chain, several different interventions should be considered. There are many different ways of influencing value chain development, whether working on supply-side issues (production), demand-side issues (consumers, procurement) or on market-functioning (information exchange, contracts) and the market environment (regulation, market norms).

Step 9: Developing the short list
The short list can be developed from the long list you have devised. For each intervention option, apply the key criteria:

- Eligibility criteria – criteria which must be met for a project to be included for consideration (i.e. that it benefits the vulnerable); and
- Selection criteria – used for comparing and ranking between possible alternatives. These are grouped into two categories – overall scale of impact on low-income people and the feasibility of achieving impact.

Table 12.3   How to conceptualize pro-poor options

Type of pro-poor value chain development	Example	Increases income of current participants	Brings more poor into tourism
1. Expansion of demand for products and services of low-income groups. Through a 'volume upgrade' for current participants and/or 'entering the chain' for new participants	Overall tourism growth in Vietnam and Rwanda leads to more income for existing participants; seasonal hotel workers, craft sellers, food sellers. And new opportunities for more people to enter the chain (see Mitchell and Chi, 2007)	✓	✓
2. Product/process upgrade by poor participants	In The Gambia, training enabled guides to offer a better product and earn more. Juicers improved their product and turnover by establishing small booths on the beach (Mitchell and Faal, 2007)	✓	
3. Functional upgrade by poor participants	In Tanzania, most of the new small ground handler businesses have been established by those previously working as guides	✓	Possible
4. Contractualization to enhance the terms of engagement either horizontally (among producers) or vertically (e.g. with a hotel)	In Tanzania, porters around Kilimanjaro have formed an association to promote their interests (horizontal contractualization). In Jamaica, farmers have been assisted to set up regular contracts with Sandals resorts, giving greater security (vertical contractualization) – see Mitchell et al. (2009)	✓	
5. Entry of new poor participants into the chain due to reduced barriers to entry and/or investment in human capacity of the poor to meet requirements	New small and micro enterprises entered the Spier hotel supply chain when procurement terms were changed (e.g. offering smaller contracts with mentoring support). Training of local residents meant that they were able to occupy 40% of jobs in the Costa Sauipe resort, Brazil – see Mitchell and Ashley (2010)	Possible	✓
6. Exit or diversification from tourism activity	Crafters become exporters, as in Hoi An (Vietnam) where textiles are not only sold to tourists but exported, thus reducing dependence on tourism	✓	
7. Enhanced links between the value chain and host society Better access to infrastructure and services Investment in human capital Collaboration on resource management Stronger local institutions	In Namibia, local conservancies apply skills and strengths gained in tourism to other rural development issues Roads around *Parc National des Volcans* in Rwanda benefit farmers In Cape Verde, tourism encourages return of diaspora, less out-migration and cultural renaissance In Namibia, rural residents benefiting from tourism take responsibility for managing wild resources The Namibian conservancies also apply skills and strengths gained in tourism to other rural development issues	Beneficiaries go beyond those who are economically active in tourism to include a wide range of local residents	

Notes for each strategy:
1. Increased demand: this may be from the whole sector (more arrivals), or a specific part that is fairly pro-poor (e.g. handicraft expansion).
2. Product/process upgrade: It may be the product sold or the production process that improves, often the two go together. Products that use skills and information more intensively reap higher prices (e.g. informatively labelled coffees or soaps, well informed guides).
3. Functional upgrade: moving to higher functions in the chain is a way of capturing more value. Often the poor do not switch to a different function in the chain, but add a new function (e.g. a craft producer starts also employing others, transporting others' products or retailing direct).

4. Forming a collective association among producers (horizontal) is often an important way to change the terms of the relationship with those further up the chain, such as hotel buyers (vertical contractualization).
5. Reducing barriers to entry (e.g. requirements relating to trade, access to capital, volumes), is the other side of the coin of increasing the capacity of poor producers to meet requirements.
6. Exiting the value chain completely can be a pro-poor strategy when, for example, sex-workers find alternative livelihoods.
7. Operation of the tourism sector has many knock-on and dynamic effects on the host community and economy. So interventions might not target roles within the tourism chain, but target how the chain impacts, positively and negatively, those outside.
Source: Ashley et al. (2009).

The objective is to end up with a short list of interventions that are most likely to work and, when they do, will have the biggest impact. In selecting the short list of interventions with local stakeholders, be they local farmers or a national Cabinet or the senior executives of a large tourism business, it is critical to be clear about the choices available and what are the implications of each of these.

Given that these choices often involve juggling several different and conflicting criteria and are often being made in a non-mother tongue language, visual images are often a more effective way to convey choices than a table of numbers and pages of text. For example, after a detailed analysis of the tourism value chain in Cape Verde, it became clear that the widely-held view by public policy makers – that the large All-Inclusive (AI) resorts on Sal and Boa Vista islands were not benefiting Cape Verdeans as much as locally-owned hotels on other islands – was not supported by evidence (Mitchell and Li, 2017). It was found that the most effective way to communicate this important message to policy-makers was with the infographic shown in Figure 12.5. The key message that, notwithstanding foreign ownership and relatively high 'leakages' from the large AI resorts, their ability to retain buoyant room rates and occupancy rates allowed them to pay predominantly local staff competitive rates and absorb high taxes on imported supplies generated significant benefits for Cape Verde. Whilst there are opportunities for growing a more indigenous tourism product on the other islands, this should be conceived as leveraging off the tourism flows and infrastructure created by and for the large AIs, rather than as a substitute for them.

Step 10 and 11: Developing a project idea and programming

Taking a project concept and developing this into a budgeted and implementable intervention is a critical stage in the process of increasing the inclusivity of tourism in developing country destinations. However, this is beyond the scope of this chapter.

CHALLENGES AND LIMITATIONS OF THIS APPROACH

There are two serious limitations of this approach, one inherent and inevitable and the other somewhat easier to mitigate.

The inherent difficulty in any pro-poor analysis and action is defining, precisely, the low-income target group itself. The most seemingly straightforward approach is to adopt the 'dollar a day' (per person at 1995 purchasing power parity level) measure of extreme poverty, more recently amended to USD 1.90 by the World Bank (World Bank, 2018). This definition of poverty threshold has the advantage that it is universal and facilitates comparisons between destinations in different countries. However, in many of the contexts in which development practitioners work, 'dollar a day' poverty lines are of limited relevance because almost

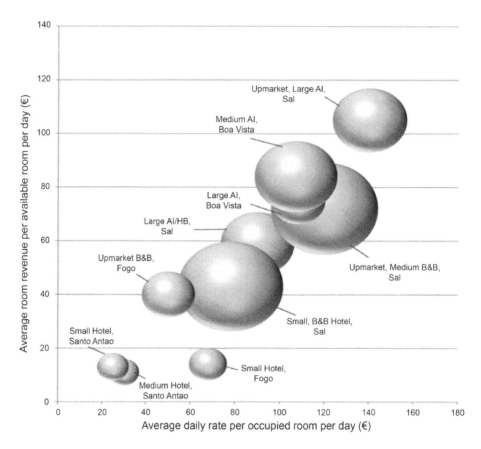

Note: The size of the bubble represents the local benefit (defined as the sum of local staff salaries, procurement of local food and taxes) per hotel room per day.
Source: Mitchell and Martins (2012).

Figure 12.5   Using infographics to support decision making

everyone falls below this poverty threshold. International poverty thresholds obscure the real differences in well-being between households existing significantly below the poverty line and much better-off households that are on, or near, the international poverty line – who would often not be regarded by others, or see themselves, as being resource 'poor'. For this reason, nationally defined poverty levels – which more closely reflect how people perceive poverty – are often very much lower than 'dollar a day' poverty thresholds. So nationally defined poverty thresholds are often more meaningful in the local context and so may be required by the organizations financing a tourism value chain analysis in a particular destination, but this can become a barrier to international comparison.

Linked to the issue of defining 'poverty' there is also a lack of consensus about the meaning of the term 'pro-poor'. Private sector development practitioners tend to adopt the 'broad' definition – growth is pro-poor, as long as the poor benefit in an absolute sense – so the number of people in poverty falls (Ravallion, 2004). The narrow definition of pro-poor growth (expounded by Kakwani and Son, 2003) requires that the poor benefit proportionately more than others, so that inequality is reduced along with poverty. In other words, tourism is only pro-poor if it reduces inequality as well as directing resources to poor people.

Although the authors have found some examples of supply chains into the tourism value chain that may meet this restrictive definition of 'pro-poor', they are few and far between. Tourism is a private sector-driven activity and needs to generate returns to the owners of businesses in order to be sustainable. A pragmatic approach is advocated by Osmani (2005, p. 9) who argues that "pro-poor growth demands a break with the past that makes growth more conducive to poverty reduction … from the point of view of the poor; there must be an improvement over business as usual". So, by this definition, 'pro-poor' growth is simply growth that benefits the poor more than previously.

The faddish 'development industry' has now largely moved beyond the term pro-poor growth and is using terms such as 'inclusive' or 'shared' growth. These terms are compatible with Osmani's pragmatic definition of a pattern of growth which creates more opportunities for low-income households than what preceded it.

An important critique of this approach is that it is anthropocentric and overlooks negative environmental impact and climate change (Peeters, 2009; Sharpley and Naidoo, 2010; Butler et al., 2013). Peeters (2009) suggests that the environmental effects of North–South tourism are sufficiently serious to make this form of tourism incompatible with sustainable development. As a critique, the charge of anthropocentricism is valid. The aim of tourism value chain analysis was to address the gap that emerged in the assessment of the economic impact of tourism, particularly on low-income groups, and so environmental impacts were considered beyond the scope of the analysis.

This was a plausible position when this approach was initially developed from 2005, but has become increasingly tenuous with advances in environmental economics (Stern, 2006). Unpublished research, examining the viability of long-haul tourism at various carbon costs, has found that the benefits of international tourism still far outweighed the costs. However, it was not until 2016 that Scott et al. published an analysis of the costs of tourism engaging with the decarbonization agenda. Their findings showed that a "climate compatible transformation of the tourist sector could be financed through a partial reallocation of cumulate fees and taxes already imposed on travellers by companies and governments" (Scott et al., 2016, p. 68). The tourist sector is indeed responsible for an increasing share of global carbon emissions but, as a high value international service and one that is already heavily taxed, the sector is well-placed to align with the decarbonization agenda. With advances in environmental economics – and particularly in the shadow pricing of carbon – it is now relatively straightforward to price in the cost of climate change into this form of value chain analyses.

FINAL CONSIDERATIONS

The results of applying this approach are, first, that it is practically implementable. The approach was developed during action research projects in very many different contexts. It is practical and generates useful results. The approach is 'field tested' and works. The exponential growth in research studies using this approach is testament to this (Truong, 2014).

Second, the results indicate that international tourism can, sometimes, be an effective way to transfer funds from rich tourists to resource-poor people (Figure 12.6). There are destinations

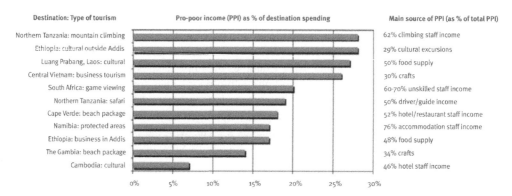

Source: Mitchell and Ashley (2010).

Figure 12.6   Flows of tourist spending accruing to low-income people in various destinations

where for every USD 4 spent by a tourist in-country, USD 1 reaches poor people. This is a highly progressive rate of conversion from aggregate trade receipts to pro-poor benefits and compares favourably with many agricultural value chains. In the 'better practice' examples, where over 20 per cent of tourists' expenditure at the destination accrues to low-income participants in the value chain, a pro-poor impact is generally the result of strong indirect (like hotel construction or agricultural supply chains to tourists) and dynamic linkages (like the taxation of tourists providing a large share of government redistributive spending). In middle-income countries, direct linkages (such as the wages paid to hotel workers) are often a major source of the benefit flow from tourists to low-income communities.

However, just because tourism can benefit the local community does not mean that this effect is inevitable. For example, in cases such as cultural tourism in Cambodia and business tourism in Ghana, less than one-tenth of tourist in-country spending reaches the resource-poor (Mitchell and Ashley, 2010). In these instances, the enabling environment for tourism is poor, which allows for significant 'elite capture' (both legal and informal) of the benefits from tourism. We find little evidence to support widely-held assumptions that particular types of tourism are – or are not – inclusive. Business tourism can benefit the local community and ecotourism can bypass them.

Third, whatever is the pro-poor effect of tourism currently, all our studies have found practical interventions which can be implemented that will increase the flow of resources to low-income people. In some cases the effects have been dramatic and transformative. In others, interventions informed by our analysis have been more incremental (Mitchell et al., 2015) – but in all cases they have been practical and implementable and sustainable.

The implications of this approach are numerous. We have learned to be sceptical of much received wisdom and many widely-held assumptions in 'tourism and development' do not survive empirical scrutiny. We have also learned not to have preconceptions about the commitment of different development partners to inclusive tourism. Some of our research findings, financed by development donors on behalf of governments, who have a policy commitment to poverty reduction, have not been implemented (Mitchell and Font, 2016). And some findings, financed by large corporates, have been implemented fully and successfully. This approach demands that researchers can engage effectively with private sector actors – from smallholder farmers to corporate boardrooms. This often requires skills and a mind-set which is not ubiquitous in tourism researchers. And finally, we have learned that tourism is just another sector of the economy – tourism exceptionalism has done the sector a disservice. Tourism is different from agriculture and manufacturing but the standard research tools in the development economists' toolbox that are relevant for these other sectors can be successfully adapted and applied to the tourist sector. If the contribution tourism can make to inclusive economic development is to be taken seriously by governments, donors and the private sector, the rigorous use of the standard tools of mainstream development economics is not a bad place to start.

REFERENCES

Altenburg, T. (2007) *Donor Approaches to Supporting Pro-Poor Value Chains.* Report prepared for the Donor Committee for Enterprise Development (DCED) Working Group on linkages and value chains, German Development Institute and OECD.

Ashley, C. (2006) *Participation and the Poor in Luang Prabang Tourism Economy: Current Earnings and Opportunities for Expansion.* Overseas Development Institute Working Paper 273. https://www .odi.org/sites/odi.org.uk/files/odi-assets/publications-opinion-files/82.pdf.

Ashley, C., Mitchell, J. and Spenceley, A. (2009) *Opportunity Study Guidelines.* International Trade Centre Publication. http://www.intracen.org/uploadedFiles/intracenorg/Content/Exporters/Sectoral _Information/Service_Exports/Tourism/Opportunity%20Studies%20Guidelines%20TPRP.pdf.

Butler, R., Curran, R. and O'Gorman, K. D. (2013) Pro-poor tourism in a first world urban setting: Case study of Glasgow Govan. *International Journal of Tourism Research,* 15, 443–457.

Gereffi, G. (1994) The organization of buyer-drive global commodity chains: How US retailers shape overseas production networks. In G. Gereffi and M. Korzeniewicz (eds.), *Commodity Chains and Global Capitalism.* London: Praeger, 95–122.

Kakwani, N. and Son, H. H. (2003) Pro-poor growth: Concepts and measurement with country case studies. *The Pakistan Development Review,* 42(4), 417–444.

Kaplinsky, R. and Morris, M. (2001) *A Handbook for Value Chain Analysis.* Ottawa: International Development Research Centre.

Mitchell, J. (2012) Value chain approaches to assessing the impact of tourism on low-income households in developing countries. *Journal of Sustainable Tourism,* 20(3), 457–475.

Mitchell, J. (2019) Value chain analysis in pro-poor tourism: Towards a critical understanding of the contribution of tourism to poverty reduction. Thesis submitted in partial fulfilment of the requirements of the University of Brighton for the degree of Doctor of Philosophy.

Mitchell, J. and Ashley, C. (2010) *Tourism and Poverty Reduction: Pathways to Prosperity.* London: Earthscan.

Mitchell, J. and Chi, L. (2007) *Participatory Tourism Value Chain Analysis in Da Nang.* Central Vietnam Overseas Development Institute report. https://www.odi.org/publications/611-participatory -tourism-value-chain-analysis-da-nang-central-vietnam.

Mitchell, J. and Coles, C. (2009) *Enhancing Private Sector and Community Engagement in Tourism Services in Ethiopia.* Overseas Development Institute report. https://www.odi.org/publications/4770 -enhancing-private-sector-and-community-engagement-tourism-services-ethiopia.

Mitchell, J. and Faal, J. (2007) Holiday package tourism and the poor in the Gambia. *Development Southern Africa,* 24(3), 445–464.

Mitchell, J. and Font, X. (2016) Evidence-based policy in Ethiopia: A diagnosis of failure. *Development Southern Africa,* 34(1), 121–136.

Mitchell, J., Font, X. and Li, S. (2015) What is the impact of hotels on local economic development? Applying value chain analysis to individual businesses. *Anatolia,* 26(3), 347–358.

Mitchell, J., Keane, J. and Laidlaw, J. (2009) *Making Success Work for the Poor: Package Tourism in Northern Tanzania.* ODI Report. https://tnrf.org/files/E-INFO-SNV_Package_tourism_in_Northern _Tanzania_2009.pdf.

Mitchell, J. and Li, S. (2017) Autonomy found: Estimating the local benefit from tourism in SIDS: The case of Cape Verde. *Journal of Policy Research in Tourism, Leisure and Events*, 19(2), 182–200.

Mitchell, J. and Martins, P. (2012) Pro-poor tourism linkages in Cape Verde. Unpublished Overseas Development Institute report for the World Bank.

Osmani, S. (2005) Defining pro-poor growth. International Policy Centre for Inclusive Growth One Pager #9. https://ipcig.org/pub/IPCOnePager9.pdf.

Peeters, P. (2009) Pro-poor tourism, climate change and sustainable development. *Tourism Recreation Research*, 34(2), 203–205.

Ravallion, M. (2004) *Pro-Poor Growth: A Primer*. World Bank Policy Research Working Paper 3242. Washington, DC: World Bank.

Scott, D., Gossling, S., Hall, M. and Peeters, P. (2016) Can tourism be part of the decarbonised global economy? The costs and risks of alternate carbon reduction policy pathways. *Journal of Sustainable Tourism*, 24(1), 52–72.

Sharpley, R. and Naidoo, P. (2010) Tourism and poverty reduction: The case of Mauritius. *Tourism and Hospitality Planning & Development*, 7(2), 145–162.

Stern, N. (2006) *The Economics of Climate Change: The Stern Review*. London: HM Treasury.

Telfer, D. J. and Sharpley, R. (2014) *Tourism and Development in the Developing World*, 2nd edition. London: Routledge.

Truong, V. D. (2014) Pro-poor tourism: Looking backwards as we move forwards. *Tourism Planning and Development*, 11(2), 228–242.

World Bank (2018) *Piecing Together the Poverty Puzzle*. Washington, DC: World Bank.

World Bank (2019) *World Development Indicators*. Washington, DC: World Bank.

13. Establishing sustainability standards in tourism
Randy Durband

INTRODUCTION

What is the value of establishing and applying standards for sustainable tourism? What types of standards are useful? How should standards be created? How many sets of standards does the world need? What about the role of certification? How can one distinguish the quality of the various standards and certification schemes from others?

These are among the myriad questions we are frequently asked at GSTC, the UN-created Global Sustainable Tourism Council. And these are questions we will endeavour to answer in this chapter.

Standards are important and often essential in many organizations, especially for producers of products and services. Tourism involves an extremely complex and varied web of services, products, and service providers, most of which relate to intangible elements of client satisfaction, perceptions, and service levels. Is tourism a single sector comprised of many subsectors, or is it an umbrella term for many sectors? That view of tourism – highly diverse, complex, and service- and experience-oriented – points to tremendous complexity when considering sustainability in tourism. Then consider also the multiple dimensions of sustainability itself – it includes not only environmental aspects, but also social, economic, and cultural aspects. Standards are needed to sort all that out, but also simply to define sustainability in a holistic way. This chapter is an attempt to provide overviews of these considerations.

RESEARCH APPROACHES

Much research is needed relating to the effective application of standards for more sustainable tourism in its many subsectors. There are many layers of complexity – the myriad issues relating to standards generally for the service-driven, experience-based tourism sector, plus the varied conditions within the many subsectors. Another layer is that the private sector operates most of the functions of tourism, but the public sector plays a leadership role in destination management and promotion. Tourism engages an enormous array of players.

The duality of important roles by both the private sector and public sectors led the GSTC to create two sets of standards, the GSTC Destination Criteria as guidance for the public sector in managing tourism generally and destinations specifically, and the GSTC Industry Criteria as guidance for the private sector players. GSTC was formed in 2007 by a union of two UN agencies – UNEP and UNWTO – with conservation organizations and private sector players; initially in order to provide baseline standards for sustainable hotels and tour operators. Later, in 2010, a collection of sustainable tourism experts supporting the development of public sector sustainable tourism standards agreed that GSTC would be the keeper of those standards as well. What later came to be known as the GSTC Industry Criteria were formally launched in 2008 and the GSTC Destination Criteria in 2013.

As varied in application as the Destination Criteria are, based on differences relating to economic development, political forms, cultural norms, types of destinations (cultural, natural, urban, rural, etc.), and more, applications of the Industry Criteria are at least equally varied if not more so. Aviation, accommodation, attractions, tourist shops and restaurants, rental cars, cruise lines, all-inclusive resorts – these are the subsectors of leisure travel, so diverse that they do not even form inclusive trade associations, remaining rather separate.[1] Then we consider business travel – the realm of convention centres, trade fairs, sales calls, business meetings of all sorts. Then too there are festivals of all sorts. And national holidays – day-long or even weeks-long. Another dimension is compression by time period; for example the emptying of many European offices for most of the month of August, or East Asians travelling for the two weeks wrapped around the Lunar New Year. Complexity reigns in this multi-faceted 'sector' or collection of sectors. A common challenge for all situations nested in this complexity for the application of standards is the question of the scope of the standard applied to each subsector.

One important element of scope is to consider the value of the single set of globally recognized sustainability standards for tourism – the GSTC Criteria – being applied alone versus applying larger sets of standards that include some of the GSTC Criteria.

Further, there is much research to be done on the application of standards in the realms of:

1. Measurement and monitoring based on standards. Examples of research opportunities include the nature of existing measurement, whether it is standardized, transparent, audited.
2. Certification – quality of certification; compliance with ISO series 17000 standards.
3. Certification impacts – requiring the research to overcome the challenge that businesses gaining certification were inherently operating more sustainably than average prior to gaining the certification.
4. Communicating certification: (a) in language that impacts market behaviour; (b) that distinguishes true certification from popular misconceptions of the many schemes incorrectly perceived as certification.
5. Awards and other forms of verification and assurance in comparison to certification. These are distinct approaches, but the lines are often blurred in how they are presented, resulting in confusion on what they are and the degree of impartiality applied. In addition to confusion over the differences in these types, there are wide differences of approach within these types; that is to say, the rigour and impartiality of various types of awards, certification, and other verification approaches vary widely.
6. Awareness raising of the holistic sets of issues inherent in a set of standards.

THE CASE FOR STANDARDS

Standards have proven their value in many types of production. For example, electrical appliances must be safe to use; therefore most national governments require the application of safety standards for them. Similarly, hygiene standards with external audits help keep food preparation cleaner and safer for restaurant clients.

In general, one could say standards perform many roles, as tools for:

- Training and education of practitioners and awareness-raising of consumers. This is true of standards in general but is especially important in sustainable tourism. Reason: the breadth and depth of what is meant by the term 'sustainable tourism' is not widely understood by key stakeholders. In fact, tourism consists of many subsectors that interact but do not communicate and collaborate well, meaning that the breadth of tourism as an entity is not well understood and therefore sustainability is not well understood. Standards are necessary to fill these enormous gaps.
- Measurement and evaluation. There is much to measure and evaluate for sustainable tourism, and use of standards provides a checklist and a means for placing organizational weighting and prioritization of certain components.
- Guidelines for legal and regulatory codes. Regulators and law-makers draw from the testing and proven effectiveness of standards in practice. Much more should be done in tourism. WWF sustainable food expert Jason Clay, a prominent thought-leader in the ISEAL Alliance community, has said this: "Today's standards should be adopted legally by governments. Then create higher-aspiration voluntary standards."[2]
- Basis for certification. The processes of certification and auditing require a set of standards to guide the entire process to certify for safety, health and hygiene, quality, and indeed sustainability.
- Market access for certified products and services via eco-labelling. Providing an eco-label without an objective basis is not credible; eco-labelling requires a high level of assurance, with third-party certification at the highest level of assurance, and certification requires standards.

Each is an important function. All of them are better served with very few or even a single standard. Too many standards, especially if they're not similar, make implementation more challenging for each of the above.

WHO USES SUSTAINABLE TOURISM STANDARDS?

Standards provide value to many types of tourism players. All stakeholders benefit from standards as a holistic definition of sustainable tourism. Certification bodies require standards as a basis for certification of tourism businesses or destinations.

National governments use sustainable tourism standards for policy development, awareness-raising and training for stakeholders, and awards schemes and certification schemes as incentives for high achievers. Examples of the latter include tax incentives and discounted promotional fees such as Costa Rica's CST programme in which businesses enjoy a 20 per cent discount for counter/table space at trade fairs for each of five tiers of certification.[3]

In the case of Vanuatu, a Pacific Island nation, the Department of Tourism of Vanuatu employs two parallel schemes – national guidelines are set for minimum requirements of all businesses, plus a more rigorous standard applied to certification for stronger performers. The latter encourages and rewards higher levels of sustainability.

In the case of large multi-location businesses, the businesses' centralized management system can play the role of a set of standards. Prominent examples in tourism include several major hotel groups including Accor's 'Planet 21', IHG's 'Green Engage', and Hilton's

'Lightstay'. Intercruises is a Destination Management Company (DMC) within the TUI Group with approximately 150 port locations servicing cruise ship arrivals; their internal sustainability programme complies with the GSTC Industry Criteria and provides guidance to all satellite locations.

DEVELOPING AND MAINTAINING STANDARDS

Many sectors now have standards for sustainable production. The first prominent international standard became a model for others; in 1993 the Forest Stewardship Council (FSC) was created to establish standards for sustainable production of wood and paper, and for eco-labelling of products from certified producers. Three years later the Marine Stewardship Council (MSC) was created to do the same for fish and seafood. Many other types of commodities followed – RSPO for Palm Oil, ASC for aquaculture, Rainforest Alliance expanded along with many others for various agricultural products – with much guidance from WWF and other international conservation organizations, leading to the formation of the ISEAL Alliance.[4]

That organization provides these codes of good practice for assurance systems of all types – awards, eco-ratings, certification – for any type of sustainable production:

1. ISEAL Standards-Setting Code
2. ISEAL Assurance Code
3. ISEAL Impacts Code

First to consider is the Standards-Setting Code, which provides guidance on how to develop credible standards. This includes highly inclusive processes to develop and occasionally revise the standards. This code complements relevant ISO guidelines for the creation and maintenance of standards. Taken together, these are the leading form of guidance for sustainable production standards.

Inclusiveness is a core requirement of the Standards-Setting Code. This means that standards should consider the perspectives of any and all stakeholders involved in and/or impacted by the production forms in question. Neutral parties need to gather, compile, analyse, and synthesize all the input. The entire process must be transparent. GSTC ensures inclusiveness and transparency by publicizing a timetable in advance of two rounds of public consultation in the development and revisions of its standards.

Field-testing is important. Mature drafts of standards should be tested in a variety of contexts. For three years leading up to the November 2013 release of the GSTC Destination Criteria, 14 disparate touristic destination types – identified as Early Adopters – field-tested a draft version, informing adjustments to the final version. That first version was so well accepted that a review by key stakeholders in 2018 indicated only a modest feeling of need for revision, and when the first revision was released in December 2019, the net result was more about re-organizing the Criteria for the sake of ease of application and very little about content revision.

Another benefit of inclusiveness in creating standards is that it provides high levels of acceptance from various types of potential users and of credibility. Closed-door development can call into question the motives and prejudices of the writers of the standards.

The GSTC Criteria are rare in being made available free of charge in the public domain for all to use. (GSTC reserves the right to charge for the commercial use of the Criteria, but places no limits on their non-commercial usage.) This open access has led to replication of the Criteria in many forms (see below). Standards for sustainable tourism are abundant and widespread. This creates ease of access to the information, but also leads to confusion with many labels and programmes, such that users and potential users of sustainable tourism standards may choose to throw their hands in the air in confusion rather than settling on a consistent approach.

GSTC is regularly informed by entities without formal ties to GSTC that their standards or their operations have been strongly influenced by the GSTC Criteria. Examples of the GSTC Criteria used as the basis of other standards without direct organizational linkage include:

- The Sustainable Tourism Criteria of India (STCI) were developed by an NGO ecotourism society shortly after the formal launch of the GSTC Criteria in 2008, without any formal connection to the GSTC. This had been made known to GSTC through several sources over several years, and was stated verbally August 2015 as fact by members of the STCI leadership to GSTC officials. In December of that year, the Ministry of Tourism 'released' the STCI as national standards.[5] As of this writing, no formal acknowledgement has been made of the genesis of the standards and no formal arrangement exists between the Ministry and the GSTC.
- Thailand's Sustainable Destination standards became formally 'GSTC-Recognized' in 2018. During the course of that process, GSTC learned that the standards had originally been created shortly after the 2008 initial release of the GSTC Criteria and were based largely on them.[6]

An important consideration in the development of standards is to give careful thought to scope and to attaining the appropriate level of detail. There is a tendency to add, add, add in order to satisfy the requests of the myriad stakeholders who should be engaged in the development process. However, the larger the set of standards, and the more detailed, the more difficult it will be to apply the standards in the field. Issues that are not considered critical by users may unnecessarily contribute to some degree of resistance to applying the full set of standards arising from scepticism about relevance of effort for some of the components.

The issue of scope is of particular concern in tourism for the certification of tour operators due to the richness of their supply chains. Certification of tour operators is complex. What happens in the operations of offices of tour operators has minuscule impacts on the environment relative to the impacts of their choices in contracting with transport providers, attractions, accommodations, and more. Certification of actual tours is not feasible and has likely not been done on any significant scale. Tour itineraries change frequently, are increasingly customized, and even for 'set' packages the components and suppliers change frequently. Therefore the certification/audit process of tour operators – as opposed to certification of tours – must review protocols for product development and supplier contracting decisions. The criteria within a set of standards relating to sustainable management are therefore very important, because the management system needs to include guidance to product development staff, and buyers/ contractors on internal protocols for contracting and product development.

Standards must be made according to one of two essential approaches:

- Process-based, meaning the application of the standard must involve some degree of benchmarking to ensure continuous improvement.
- Performance-based, meaning the standard identifies specific levels of acceptable performance in quantifiable measures.

The GSTC Criteria are necessarily process-based in order to be applied broadly. A tourism business or destination in a remote area of a developing economy with limited infrastructure for sewage treatment, waste management, and so forth cannot be held to the same measures as an urban centre of a developed economy. Process-based systems such as the GSTC require and reward continuous improvement.

As such, the GSTC Criteria can be applied broadly. They are suitable for all levels of socio-economic development, for large and small businesses, for urban, rural, and natural areas.

Are there too many standards for sustainable tourism? There are voices that say yes, there are too many standards, but no prominent voices seem to be saying the opposite. The list of types of sustainable standards provides evidence that a significant number of standards is worthwhile, especially to cover various niches within tourism. However, too many standards applied to the same subsectors of tourism clearly create confusion in the marketplace. Society wants clarity, and too many choices promote confusion rather than clarity. Consider this: the author was in the audience during an ISEAL Alliance annual meeting when two of the world's largest certifiers of agricultural products – Rainforest Alliance and Utz – announced their merger. The audience of practitioners, normally a rather staid group, broke into spontaneous, enthusiastic, and sustained applause. During conference networking opportunities they were unanimous in my informal survey that the fewer the standards applied to the same issue the better, and that a single standard is preferable to even a few.[7]

Consider this also: many of the largest sectors of human economic activity function with a small number of standards for quality, safety, sustainability, and other aspects. In many of those, there are fewer than ten standards in use, yet the practitioners who use the standards prefer to have even smaller numbers, and they applaud consolidation and contraction. But in tourism, there are enormous numbers of standards.

Most of the tourism standards are found in the realm of hospitality, of hotels/accommodations. The counts of standards for other subsectors of tourism are much lower. The number of standards for sustainable hotels is probably in the range currently of 250–300. The GSTC makes note in an internal directory of any schemes it is made aware of. The full list is approximately 300, but several have been known to cease operations. It is likely that the current count of functioning standards is approximately 250, but a systematic inventory is needed to validate that estimate.

Yet, multiple standards are necessary to cover subsectors and niches of tourism, and to support national regulations for public sector guidance and regulatory schemes. Here are some examples of types of standards currently in play in global tourism:

- National standards for businesses or destinations. The Ministry of Tourism of Indonesia developed national destination standards, drawn heavily from the GSTC Destination Criteria, as a component of a major policy initiative to capacitate managers at approximately 20 local emerging destinations from 2015.
- Regional international standards, such as ASEAN Tourism Standards by the Association of Southeast Asian Nations.
- Civil society standards relating to the missions of various NGOs, such as the IUCN Green List.
- Hotel chains' internal sustainability programmes, such as Hilton Lightstay, Accor Planet 21, IHG Green Engage, and many more.
- MICE – Meetings, Incentives, Conventions/Conferences, Events.

- Ecotourism standards, such as Kenya Ecotourism, Korea Ecotourism, and many more relating to 'ecotourism' which is highly sustainable tourism to nature-based destinations.
- Specialized standards, such as elephant camp standards, tour boat standards, and countless more (Thailand alone has more than 30 standards for various components of tourism).[8]
- ISO has recently been developing tourism standards.

To summarize: various standards are needed for specific subsectors and niches within tourism, but duplication should be avoided.

STANDARDS: ESSENTIAL FOR CERTIFICATION

Although standards are applied in a variety of ways, much of the discussion and analysis of them surround certification because of the prevalence of certification in all its forms – including misconceptions about what constitutes certification as will be discussed later. Further, certification is complex, raising many questions and necessitating much discussion.

Before commenting on sustainable tourism certification, let us first consider the role of, and case for, certification in any realm. The case for certification includes these outcomes that are typically sought via certification:

- Provide discipline for improvement
- Verify claims
- In the case of sustainable certification, oppose 'greenwashing'
- Risk management
- Market access function; the basis of eco-labelling

Tiers of Certification

Most certification bodies offer multiple tiers or levels of certification, such as:

- Bronze, Silver, Gold, Platinum
- 1 leaf, 2 leaves, 3 leaves, etc. – or keys, stars, etc.

Tiers are typically applied on the basis of merit, meaning to get more stars, leaves, keys, etc. or moving from bronze up to platinum require performance improvement. These are generally preferred to a technique applied by a small number of certification bodies which apply higher levels based upon the number of years the business is engaged in – and paying for – the certification body's services.

For more information on the varied approaches to certification and the audit process, see Chapter 25 of this volume relating to certification audits.

Is a large enterprise's internal sustainability scheme a form of certification? The large international hotel groups with internal schemes such as Accor's Planet 21, Hilton's Lightstay, IHG's Green Engage, among others – are they certification schemes? Using ISO and ISEAL Alliance definitions, these are neither certification bodies nor certification schemes. ISO puts forth definitions and descriptions of certification that exclude internal programmes. In short, you cannot certify yourself; it must be conducted by impartial external parties. Inviting auditors to verify movement up the level of internal schemes is not certification if it does not

Levels of assurance

3rd-Party Certification
by an Accredited
Certification Body

3rd-Party Certification
(impartial)

2nd-Party verification
(impartiality is not certain)

1st-Party Assessment
(NOT impartial)

Source: Diagram created by the author; all rights are granted without permission.

Figure 13.1   Levels of assurance

include comprehensive reviews of performance and does not include occasional on-site audits by qualified auditors. All that is possible, but those schemes themselves should be open to external verification of their certification and audit systems. In general, those programmes are considered 1st-party levels of verification or assurance. They may qualify as 2nd-party or 3rd-party depending on the factors referenced above, albeit in an overly simplified manner (see Figure 13.1).

Interestingly, regardless of policy from the central management system of those hotel groups, many franchise owners and/or property-level general managers decide to gain 3rd-party certification on their own, providing much weight to the argument that those internal programmes are not credible certification schemes. This phenomenon adds to the marketplace confusion. How would a customer interpret an individual hotel property's messaging about two programmes? For example, the Crowne Plaza Amsterdam South marks some of their sustainability actions as Green Engage (the global IHG scheme) but also displays information about Green Globe certification. Consider also this: there are some certification bodies that were created as new brands and entities by long-time auditors working for one or more certification bodies. These auditors developed personal relationships with hotel management and sold some of them on the idea of moving their business to the new entity. This adds to the number of brands in the marketplace. Is that helpful to the hotel community? Perhaps, or perhaps not.

How can we define 'certification'? Is it simply the issuance of a certificate, or must the use of the term be confined to completion of processes that attain a certain level of rigour and quality? Most people would agree, when asked and when giving thought to the matter, that credibility of certification schemes is based on impartiality and rigour. Yet, society tends to accept claims of 'certification' without thought and analysis, thereby remaining open to all sorts of claims. The ISEAL Alliance and its members and subscribers, such as GSTC, believe strongly in 'assurance systems' that adhere to the ISEAL Alliance's Assurance Code which provides guidance on the development and operation of verification schemes including certification and accreditation that follow international norms for impartiality, rigour, and competence.

Few certification schemes adhere to the ISEAL Alliance Assurance Code or to relevant ISO standards (such as ISO 17065, 17021, and 17011). In fact, based on both formal and informal interactions with hundreds of certification schemes and bodies, GSTC personnel have gathered much evidence that few adhere to those prominent guidelines and standards, and indeed many have not even researched and learned of their existence. The result is that many known 'certification bodies' do not follow international norms for impartiality, rigour, and competence, and would not qualify for self-labelling as either a 'certification scheme' or a 'certification body.'

Part of the problem may be linguistics. In English, for example, society accepts that a 'certificate' is sometimes issued for simply attending a training session without even taking an exam. Yet, with the term 'certification' society expects a higher level of evidence of competence.

Assurance and Continuous Improvement

The concepts of assurance and continuous improvement are inherent in certification. 'Assurance' in the community of standards relates to various forms of providing external verification and assurance of organizational claims; these forms range from points systems and awards to certification. Continuous improvement is embedded in sound assurance schemes. Virtually any type of certification scheme includes timely renewals that ensure at minimum the status quo and much more typically some degree of improvement over past practice. The most credible certification systems are those with transparent systems and especially those that open themselves to external review.

A system with a tiered structure of external review is in place for sustainable tourism. Development and coordination of this system is facilitated by the GSTC, and GSTC is not aware of any other impartial and independent external review systems for certification bodies. The system is structured as follows:

Certification bodies
The many organizations in the world referred to in this way range tremendously from very small to medium-sized (none can be considered large), from very poorly structured to very rigorous and impartial, from subnational to international, from environment-only to include also social-economic-cultural elements, from inexpensive to costly, from non-ISO compliant (the vast majority) to ISO-adherent (a very small minority). Many do not qualify for the label based on their lack of key attributes such as transparency of systems, impartiality in general, impartiality in terms of separation of consulting roles from certification decisions, audit processes that adhere to international norms of the meaning of the term, or unqualified certification committees and auditors.

Most lack external review. GSTC is unaware of any external review of certification bodies for sustainable tourism other than the accreditation provided by the GSTC. Fewer than ten are currently accredited or near-accredited at the time of this writing. Governance and scheme ownership are varied: private ownership, non-profit organizations, programmes owned by trade associations (those parents are usually non-profit organizations but some are privately owned), government agencies, and cooperatives.

Some certification bodies may not be interested in the level of rigour required to be accredited by GSTC or to fit the definition of 'certification body' as spelled out in ISO standards. Consider a certification body that conducts infrequent audits and makes certification decisions by unqualified staff, or worse, without careful mechanisms in place to ensure impartiality; but lacks incentive to reduce or remove profits by adding the costs needed to ensure rigour and impartiality.

Standards bodies
Most standards owners are also certification bodies. Most exceptions to that rule are public authorities at the national, provincial, or municipal level.

Accreditation bodies
There are few choices for accreditation services relating to certification of sustainable tourism. Some national certification programmes are likely accredited by national authorities, but this writer is unaware of any specifics. GSTC and its partner Assurance Services International (ASI) are the only known accreditation schemes in place internationally for sustainable tourism; GSTC accredits the certification of sustainable destinations and ASI is under contract with GSTC to accredit certification bodies that wish to certify hotels and/or tour operators using the GSTC Criteria or a GSTC-Recognized standard. ASI performs this function for prominent standards in other sectors, including FSC/Forest Stewardship Council, RSPO/Responsible Palm Oil, and MSC/Marine Stewardship Council. ASI is a full member of the ISEAL Alliance.

GSTC accreditation requirements
These are publicly available from the GSTC website in the form of the 'GSTC Accreditation Manual' (likely to be converted in 2020 from one document to three component documents). Those requirements use the following in some form of normative reference or guidance:

- ISO 17065, ISO 17021, ISO 17011
- ISEAL Alliance Assurance Code, Standards-Setting Code, and Impacts Code
- Frequent consultations with Certification Bodies and other stakeholders
- Internal technical expertise

The first time a hotel or tour operation becomes certified, a benchline is established for current performance on the various elements of the standard. At time of renewal of the certification, evidence must be made of maintaining or improving prior levels of compliance. At the next tier, the certification body gets accredited, which has similar requirements to show evidence of improvement at renewal. GSTC and its partner accreditation body strive to comply with the codes of good practice for assurance, impacts, and standards setting set by the ISEAL Alliance, the global body that sets the codes for sustainability in all sectors.

There is often an additional layer, where a consulting body or a 'Certification Scheme' guides the business towards certification and a particular certification body. Note on terminology: a 'Certification Scheme' is an entity that promotes and prepares for certification, but does not conduct the actual certification/audit process, sending their members/clients to a true, ISO-compliant or GSTC-accredited 'Certification Body' to conduct the actual certification/audit process.

Impacts: Hotels and Tour Operators

One of the motivations for organizations to seek certification is to provide a framework for a disciplined and holistic approach to improvement. However, for most, the stronger motivation is the credibility and brand-enhancement gained by securing external verification of the organization's efforts.

Measuring the impacts of gaining certification in terms of specific performance is very challenging because typically only those qualified for certification tend to apply for it. A proper impact assessment would be to look at organizations that set a multi-year goal of moving from an admittedly low level of sustainable performance to attaining certification. Most organizations do not begin considering certification until after campaigns for improvement are well underway.

Managers of hotels and tour operators regularly state that the certification process creates the needed structure and discipline to motivate and organize for improvement. This means that one impact is an organized, holistic, and disciplined approach to improvement.

Tour operators report an increase in business based on certification, but this is based on anecdotal information and the situation begs for research.

One worthwhile source of data on this subject comes from a study conducted by TUI Group in 2018. TUI has been committed since 2007 to certifying the hotels they own and operate. Box 13.1 presents summary information from that report.[9]

BOX 13.1 CERTIFICATION IMPACTS TUI STUDY 2018

Background

Data analysis of approx. 330 hotels to evaluate the benefits of sustainability certifications for hotels. Data looked at 2017 financial year performance on numerous environmental and socio-economic metrics for hotels with sustainability certifications vs. non-certified hotels (three quarters held sustainability certifications, mostly Travelife but also some other GSTC-Recognized certifications)

Findings

Hotels with sustainability certifications vs. non-certified hotels achieved:

- 10% lower CO_2 emissions per guest night
- 24% lower waste volume per guest night
- 19% less fresh water use per guest night
- 15% less total water use per guest night
- 23% higher use of green energy
- 9% higher employment rate of national employees
- Higher customer satisfaction scores for accommodation overall

Impacts: Destinations

Empirical data is limited on impacts to destination management from the application of standards because there have been very few known cases. The leading players in this regard are clearly GSTC followed by Green Destinations. The quantity of destinations applying their standards is not high, but greater than the other organizations such as development agencies and certification bodies acting in this space.

GSTC maintains a 'Destination Stewardship Working Group' consisting of recognized thought-leaders and practitioners of sustainable destination management. That group has long held the view that adherence to the GSTC Destination Criteria v2.0 Criterion A1 (formerly A2 in the GSTC-D v1.0) is a key driver of success.

> A1 Destination management responsibility: The destination has an effective organization, department, group, or committee responsible for a coordinated approach to sustainable tourism, with involvement by the private sector, public sector and civil society. This group has defined responsibilities, oversight, and implementation capability for the management of socio-economic, cultural and environmental issues. The group is adequately funded, works with a range of bodies in delivering destination management, has access to sufficient staffing (including personnel with experience in sustainability) and follows principles of sustainability and transparency in its operations and transactions.

Evidence to support that view can be considered by analysing the winners for three consecutive years of the WTTC Tourism for Tomorrow Award for Destination Stewardship. These awards are considered by many to be the most rigorous global awards for sustainable tourism, based on three levels of judging including in-depth site inspections of finalists for each category. (Disclosure: the author served as a judge on these awards for several years but disclosed any perceived conflicts of interest to the Lead Judge and recused from meaningful discussions and all decisions relating to any organization with any affiliation.) Regrettably, WTTC chose to cease operating these awards as of 2020.

Two of the three most recent winners were part of GSTC's 'Early Adopter' scheme in which 14 diverse destinations engaged in field-testing and commenting on late drafts of the GSTC Destination Criteria. The other has applied the GSTC Destination Criteria formally as well, via use of a 'GSTC-Recognized' standard. In all cases, management structures based on whole-government approach, inclusive public participation and private sector participation – key aspects of Criterion A1 – and other elements of standards have been identified by the destination management authority and the awards judges as drivers of success.

As an 'Early Adopter' of the draft GSTC Destination Criteria in 2012, the St. Kitts & Nevis Ministry of Tourism formally created a council of diverse stakeholders in compliance with GSTC-D v1.0's criterion A2 (now criterion A1 in GSTC-D v2.0). The Ministry maintained some consistency of internal staff who maintained and gradually strengthened the council. By 2019, the council had proven its effectiveness to the degree that the jury of the WTTC award for destination stewardship specifically referred to it in awarding their top award to the Ministry.

Additionally, another 2018 finalist for the award presents an interesting case study. Destination management is of course generally led by the public sector, because what we normally call 'destinations' consist of municipalities (or districts within them), protected natural areas, and cultural monuments. However, the Riverwind Foundation was created as an NGO when city leaders of Jackson, Wyoming, USA recognized the enormous challenge of coordination of awareness-raising and influencing policy for the myriad jurisdictions involved. Their municipality is physically a small part of an ecosystem that includes a large number of distinct units of protected areas administered by the National Park Service, National Forest Service, Bureau of Land Management, and other state and national entities. The NGO interacts with all relevant agencies with the goal of influencing more sustainable and more coordinated management. This type of approach is worthy of consideration elsewhere in the world, and therefore worthy of research.

MARKET ACCESS FOR PROVIDERS OF 'SUSTAINABLE' PRODUCTS AND SERVICES

Claims of being completely sustainable would be frivolous given the great challenges, but the most valid claims by businesses to be considered somewhat sustainable or striving for sustainability are those verified by independent and neutral third-party entities through a comprehensive certification process. GSTC strongly believes that the most credible labels for sustainability are based on that type of certification, and that *businesses attaining credible certification deserve market access benefits*.

Therefore, market access based on good standards and verified by rigorous certification processes is an essential element of driving tourism to higher levels of sustainability.

The prominent conservation organization WWF believes this. They have developed and refined a market access scheme in many sectors.[10] They began applying their effective strategies commencing February 2016 with their formal partnership with Royal Caribbean Cruiselines (RCL), whereby RCL has adopted WWF's recommendations to show preferred procurement for fish and seafood that is certified to the MSC (Marine Stewardship Council) standard and preferred contracting to land tour operators/transport providers that are certified to the GSTC Criteria framework.[11]

In November 2019 MSC Cruises announced the launch of their sustainable product line 'Protectours', selected shore excursions adhering to certain sustainability guidelines including being operated by tour operators certified by GSTC-accredited certification bodies.[12] Other cruise lines are considering following suit. This is having major impacts: GSTC has seen the number of tour operators certified by accredited certification bodies increase since the 2016 launch of the RCL/WWF scheme, followed by further interest based on the MSC Cruises requirement. Alaska's 'Adventure Green Alaska Standards' gained formal GSTC Recognition in 2018 specifically to align their destination development approaches to fit this impactful supply chain development scheme by the cruise lines.

The takeaway for other industry players is to recognize that becoming certified sustainable from a certification body that is accredited by the GSTC provides a clear message of their level of commitment to Sustainable Consumption and Production (SCP) by selecting verified providers of the certification. The large number of certification schemes create confusion, and the confusion is removed by choosing a certification body that proves its worth by becoming GSTC Accredited.

Another industry leader that is implementing this approach is TUI Group, in which they set a target of providing 'sustainable holidays' to 10 million clients annually, and the measure they use to determine that number is based on the count of clients staying in hotels that are certified to the GSTC framework.[13]

Spain's Iberostar hotel group has established targets for sustainable seafood in 120 hotels and restaurants based on MSC/Marine Stewardship Council and ASC/Aquaculture Stewardship Council labelling.[14] Canadian tour operator Transat features hotels certified as sustainable and beaches labelled as Blue Flag.[15]

MEASUREMENT VIA STANDARDS

Gaining certification for sustainable practices has many benefits. Certification tells the world that a business opened itself to neutral external analysis that verified that the enterprise is doing what it says it's doing. It provides greater market access to those buyers seeking an easily-verifiable way to develop a sustainable supply chain. It provides the discipline to cover all the bases for the broad scope of what is considered 'sustainable' or 'responsible'.

As the hospitality industry develops more and better systems of measurement for the various elements included in these broad areas of clean energy and proper waste management, certification schemes can apply those measurement schemes directly into the certification process. This includes the initial certification, the renewal or maintenance of the certification status, and the audits that support them. This harmonization of certification with the application of the growing body of systems of measurement make both more productive.

Duplication and overlap must be avoided as efforts proceed to develop practical and affordable methods to improve the performance of hotels/accommodation in terms of truly sustainable and responsible practices. The GSTC offers accreditation to certification bodies whether they conduct their certification using the GSTC Criteria directly, or by using their own set of standards if it complies with the GSTC Criteria. That flexibility is allowing GSTC to build a global network of Certification Bodies (CBs) and on-site field auditors that have undergone the GSTC intensive review of their impartiality and effectiveness. That means for hotels seeking certification, by choosing one of GSTC's accredited CBs, they can be assured of a high standard of certification.

That also means that the approach taken by GSTC to incorporate reliable measurement approaches to certification schemes that it can accredit, ensures duplication and overlap of measurement schemes is reduced for individual hotel properties and for the global community of hospitality providers.

The GSTC scheme is globalized and relevant to all types of hospitality providers because it is process-based rather than performance-based, which is to say it is based on continuous improvement rather than expecting properties of various types in various locations to achieve the same precise targets.

Properties need to be benchmarked at the start of the certification process. Utilizing the measurement schemes developed by the experts in each type of endeavour allows GSTC to set baselines and to set targets for continuous improvement based on real numbers and objective measures.

Many of the social and cultural components of sustainability standards can be less easily data-driven than environmental components, but will increasingly rely on the reporting schemes developed in the Corporate Social Responsibility (CSR) community for businesses relating to fair hiring practices, child-safe protections in the travel and hospitality sectors, and the like.

Choosing certification as opposed to building capacity for measuring key indicators is not necessary. The two are not mutually exclusive. Hotel managers can set their own priorities on how deeply they go into the measurement of specific elements of sustainable management, and pursue certification to verify that they take a holistic approach to reach minimal levels of sustainable practices.

CONCLUSIONS

Standards exist to create order, comprehensive approaches, and consistency. Many subsectors of tourism lack adequate standards; these empty spaces should be filled, especially for cruise-ship operations, attractions, and rental cars. Aviation would also benefit from a clearer guidance system.

A strong case can be made that too many standards and certification schemes exist for hotels/accommodations. There is little evidence that anyone finds this situation to be advantageous. Making meaningful impacts to sort this out will likely require at least one of the five largest global hotel groups to take a lead in identifying and implementing a strategy to clarify and consolidate the plethora of approaches.

NOTES

1. The World Travel & Tourism Council (WTTC) is a global association including all those subsectors, but trade associations as broad as that in membership and scope do not exist at the national, regional or local level. Generally speaking, tourism trade associations include only one or a very few subsectors as members.
2. Jason Clay, WWF USA Chapter – from notes taken by the author during the ISEAL Alliance annual conference, Berlin, Germany, 21 May 2015.
3. According to multiple informal GSTC discussions with CST leadership and certified businesses.
4. ISEAL Alliance's three codes of good practices are available for download at https://www .isealalliance.org.
5. See for example https://www.traveldailymedia.com/india-establishes-sustainable-tourism-criteria/.
6. Tourism consultant Mr Peter Richards informed the author in person of the original creation of the standards and his account of the subsequent assignments of ownership of the standard was confirmed to GSTC in 2018 by senior officials of DASTA, the public agency Designated Areas for Sustainable Tourism Administration.
7. Per notes taken by the author during the June 2017 annual conference of the ISEAL Alliance, Zurich, Switzerland.
8. See the list here: https://www.dot.go.th/storage/Services/hxQqMjrn1sJ50JBrzJNYpCT7vbfS6Gk 1ImYOCqxO.pdf
   or access five of the standards in English here: https://secretary.mots.go.th/ewtadmin/ewt/strategy/ download/article/article_20170509103058.pdf.
9. 'Encouraging sustainable procurement practices through the use of third-party certification schemes', provided by TUI Travel for the UN One Planet Network. https://www.oneplanetnetwork .org/sites/default/files/encouraging_sustainable_procurement_through_the_use_of_third-party _certification_schemes.pdf.
10. See this TED Talk by WWF's Jason Clay, describing the value and the approach of providing consumers sustainably produced products, entitled 'How Big Brands Can Help Save Biodiversity', July 2010. https://www.ted.com/talks/jason_clay_how_big_brands_can_help_save_biodiversity.
11. 'How to influence supply chains to effect change at scale: interview with WWF's Jim Sano', 7 December 2016 by Anula Galewski, published on Travindy. https://www.travindy.com/?s=sano.

12. See for example: https://www.travelpulse.com/news/cruise/msc-cruises-announces-new-protect ours-program.html.
13. This programme is tracked in TUI's annual 'Better Holidays Better World' report issued each June relating to the previous calendar year.
14. See for example: https://www.fastcompany.com/90421348/this-international-hotel-groups-attempt -to-move-to-sustainable-fish-is-a-lesson-in-the-hard-path-to-sustainability.
15. As described on Transat's website: https://www.transat.com/en-CA/corporate-responsibility/op erations/more-sustainable-offering.

RESOURCES

Bien, A. (2005) International Accreditation System and Consolidation of National Systems for Sustainable Tourism Certification to Facilitate Small and Medium Enterprises (SMEs). Competitiveness and Market Access. Activity 3.1.4.4: Field tests of marketing 'lessons learned'.

Bien, A. (2007) *Simple User's Guide to Certification for Sustainable Tourism and Ecotourism*, 3rd edition. The International Ecotourism Society and Rainforest Alliance.

Bien, A. (2009) *Una guía básica sobre la acreditación de programas de certificación de turismo sosteni-ble*. Rainforest Alliance. Available on request from abien@gstcouncil.org.

Denman, R. (2010) *Tourism Sustainability Council Accreditation Manual: A Guide to the Accreditation of Sustainable Tourism Certification Programs*. Report to the Global Sustainable Tourism Council. Draft version 1, 29 March.

Dodds, R. and Joppe, M. (2005) CSR in the tourism industry? The status of and potential for certification, codes of conduct and guidelines. Study prepared for the CSR Practice Foreign Investment Advisory Service Investment Climate Department, June.

GSTC Criteria. Available free of charge for their non-commercial use on the GSTC website: https://www.gstcouncil.org. [From the 'criteria' section, two sets of Criteria, the GSTC Destination Criteria and the GSTC Industry Criteria. The latter are available in isolation and in separate versions including Performance Indicators for Hotels/Accommodations and for Tour Operators/Transport Providers.]

Honey, M. and Rome, A. (2001) *Protecting Paradise: Certification Programs for Sustainable Tourism and Ecotourism*. October. Washington, DC: Institute for Policy Studies.

International Ecotourism Society and Rainforest Alliance. http://www.responsibletravel.org/projects/documents/certification_reports/ Marketing_field_testing.pdf (accessed 1 April 2013).

Mohonk Agreement (2000) Prepared by Guy Chester et al. and adopted 19 November 2000 by partici-pants to the Sustainable Tourism and Ecotourism Certification Workshop, Mohonk Mountain House, New Paltz, New York.

Spenceley, A. (2018) Sustainable tourism certification in the African hotel sector, Tourism Review, https://doi.org/10.1108/TR-09-2017-0145.

14. Designing and delivering wildlife viewing protocols that enhance sustainability

Jeff R. Muntifering and Wayne L. Linklater

INTRODUCTION

Global tourism, a multi-trillion dollar industry, presents both challenges to, and opportunities for, biodiversity conservation (Buckley, 2011). Wildlife tourism, particularly, is growing rapidly (Balmford et al., 2015) as demand to view and interact with wildlife increases (Higham et al., 2008). While tourism provides significant direct and indirect benefits to wildlife conservation (Buckley et al., 2012; Morrison et al., 2012; Naidoo et al., 2016; Muntifering et al., 2017) negative impacts and costs to wildlife also occur (reviewed in Buckley, 2011, e.g.: penguins (Trathan et al., 2008), Olympic marmots *Marmota olympus* (Griffin et al., 2007), Rocky Mountain elk *Cervus elaphus* (Preisler et al., 2005), cetaceans (Higham et al., 2008), Arctic fox (Larm et al., 2018), brown bears in North America (Penteriani et al., 2017), and gorillas (Shutt et al., 2014)). In this context, evidential or precautionary approaches to eliminate or minimize tourism-induced wildlife disturbance is warranted.

Some practitioners claim to make wildlife tourism sustainable by embracing wildlife habituation to reduce disturbance and improve tourists' viewing experience (e.g. gorillas). Others have expressed concern that wildlife habituation puts tourists and wildlife at greater risk (e.g. elephant aggression (Ranaweerage et al., 2015)) and elevating their vulnerability to hunters (Knight, 2009) and disease transmission (Hanes et al., 2018).

Memorable tourist–wildlife encounters and wildlife welfare and protection would appear, at first, to be a zero-sum trade-off. In other words, benefits that tourism may provide to wildlife protection (e.g. increased monitoring or financial gain) are equally offset by the costs (e.g. potential disturbance effects on animal welfare). Nonetheless, strategies might be designed that reduce the trade-off, at least mitigate its worst consequences or, at best, produce net positive outcomes for both. Those strategies should be designed, implemented and evaluated evidentially (Sutherland et al., 2004; Stewart et al., 2005). Although there is an abundance of studies demonstrating negative tourism-induced impacts on wildlife (see above), much less effort has been invested in operationalizing this knowledge into 'on-the-ground' action or measuring for improved conservation and tourism outcomes. Closing this research–implementation gap may dramatically improve tourism's contribution to conservation and the industry's collective progress towards sustainability.

In this chapter, we share our experience applying a policy-development and adaptive-management approach to design, implement and evaluate a wildlife viewing protocol that minimized, if not eliminated, the tourism–conservation trade-off by identifying and optimizing shared wildlife values and decision-making. In so doing, we also consider what suite of quantitative and qualitative tools and techniques (other than habituation) exist to assist researchers and practitioners in developing more sustainable wildlife viewing policies and practices. We have structured the chapter according to the seven functions of the Decision

Process Framework (Clark, 2002) including a primer on effective decision-making from the policy sciences to introduce the subject matter. Throughout, we offer real-world examples from over 25 years of direct experience in southern Africa monitoring, researching, designing and delivering rhinoceros-viewing protocols to demonstrate its application.

The case study utilizes a prototype developed at Desert Rhino Camp (DRC), a private commercial tourism lodge within the 5,800 km² government-administered Palmwag Tourism Concession (13° 56'13"E, 19° 53'12"S) in north-western Namibia. DRC operates as a joint venture between a private tourism company (Wilderness Safaris-WS), local NGO (Save the Rhino Trust-SRT) and three adjacent Community Conservancies (Anabeb, Sesfontein and Torra) where 3,666 people reside (Muntifering et al., 2020). DRC specializes in black rhinoceros-based tourism, supports rhino monitoring and research (Buckley, 2010), and has exclusive commercial tourism access to approximately 1,365 km² to conduct their trademark black rhinoceros tracking safaris (Muntifering et al., 2019; Muntifering et al., 2020).

APPROACH: THE DECISION PROCESS

For evidence-based wildlife viewing protocols to have conservation impact (i.e. be implemented), research(ers) contributing knowledge towards their development must appreciate and anticipate that their work is not only based upon sound science but will also be integrated within the decision process that establishes policy for the tourism operation. Fundamental to that integration is an understanding of how that process functions and, particularly, where research inquiry is embedded in it. Decision-making processes from a diverse range of disciplines are applicable, such as behavior change (Michie et al., 2011), systems thinking (Gunderson et al., 2008) including scenario planning (Carpenter et al., 2006) and the policy sciences (Lasswell, 1963; Clark, 2002). Here, we will focus on the policy sciences, a well-respected discipline now having had 50 years of development (Lasswell, 1963; Clark, 2002). The policy sciences approach is underpinned by the foundational assumptions that (1) all decision-making seeks to secure a common good and is achieved by (2) the ongoing, iterative interaction of people in their efforts to obtain what they value (Clark, 2002). The policy sciences provide both a theoretical underpinning and practical framework for effective problem solving, notably of complex problems. This includes a systematic, analytical integration of biophysical information with a rational theory for societal decision-making. This makes the policy sciences particularly useful for addressing conservation challenges that are characteristically embedded within a complex social-ecological system (SES) where humans and nature interact (Berkes and Folke, 1998). Wildlife-based tourism, especially when multiple stakeholders are involved (i.e. conservation organization, local community institutions, government, resource users), constitutes an SES.

The policy sciences characterize the decision process in terms of seven functions or activities: intelligence, promotion, prescription, invocation, application, termination and appraisal (Clark, 2002). During the design and development of wildlife viewing protocols within a tourism operation, researcher(s) aim to identify the stages of the decision process for their study system. The stages where intelligence is appropriate, and where there are potential failures in the uptake of provided intelligence should be considered. Malfunctions can be evaluated against a set of well-established criteria (Clark, 2002).

Data on decision process functions can be gathered using multiple means including reading and analyzing reports, interviews, publications, and newspapers, or collecting personal observation data through conversations, interviews, focus groups and meetings attended (Clark, 2002). In Table 14.1 we outline the seven decision functions and some key questions to consider when identifying successes and possible pitfalls particularly with respect to establishing wildlife viewing policy. It is also possible (and recommended) to take this a step further by drilling deeper into the context by describing how each relevant decision function is performed in reference to the problem (i.e. wildlife disturbance) by employing **feature analysis**. Feature analysis requires the following questions to be addressed for each relevant decision function: who participated, with what perspectives, in which arenas, using what values, in what strategic ways to generate what outcomes in reference to each of the decision functions (Clark and Willard, 2000). The method provides a more nuanced, comprehensive understanding of any decision-making context to help identify faults and where potential inadequacies may occur.

Table 14.1   *Summary of key questions to inform and document (i.e. quantitatively map) the decision process for designing and implementing wildlife viewing protocols*

DECISION PROCESS FUNCTION	Activity Description	Key Questions	Criteria of Success
1. INTELLIGENCE	Gather information at the study site to clarify program goals, define the problem, and measure outcomes	Is data being collected for all components of the wildlife viewing problem and from all affected people (stakeholders)? To whom is this data being communicated and when?	Factual, complete, appropriate, and inclusive
2. DEBATE / PROMOTION	Present and discuss protocol alternatives	What groups are urging which sources of information and courses of action? What values are being promoted or dismissed by each alternative and what groups are served by each?	Rational, holistic and comprehensive
3. PRESCRIPTION	Set rules, guidelines, and policies for action	How will the new viewing protocol(s) harmonize or conflict with existing rules? What rules do the operators (managers, guides) set for themselves and which are binding?	Rational, inclusive, prospective
4. INVOCATION	Characterize compliance and consequences of rule-breaking	Is implementation consistent with prescription? Who should be held accountable for following the rules? Who will enforce the rules? What sanctions will be applied in which situations? Are resources available to carry out the rules?	Timely, dependable, non-provocative, implementable
5. APPLICATION	The actual implementation of the event(s) in terms of the prescription	Will an authority resolve disputes? How do participants interact during a dispute?	Meets rules, contextual, works in practice, and constructive
6. APPRAISAL	Evaluate outcomes with respect to goals	Who was served by the protocol and who was not? Is the protocol evaluated fully and routinely? Who is responsible for identifying success and failure? Who appraises the appraisers?	Unbiased, dependable, ongoing and practical
7. TERMINATION	Previous, unsustainable practices are ended	Who should stop or change the rules? Who is served or harmed by ending a program?	Timely, factual and supportive

Source: Adapted from Clark (2002).

This systematic process integrates learning to management actions similarly to the adaptive environmental assessment and management model (Gunderson et al., 2008). It can also be illustrated as an iterative cycle to emphasize how the decision process is embedded with research inquiry (e.g. measuring human–wildlife interactions: Figure 14.1) to ensure that research informs wildlife viewing policies. For example, in reference to Figure 14.1, the resource issue we explored was tourism and rhinoceros conservation coexistence with one problem identified by participants as minimizing rhinoceros disturbance caused during tourist–rhinoceros encounters. We then used research and modeling of these encounters to build evidence in support of the (1) intelligence function in the decision process framework. This set the stage for the rest of the process to ensue, running from (2) Debate through to (6) Appraisal before splitting back into a new problem definition and/or (7) Adaptation/ Termination of previous behavior.

This chapter uses policy science's decision process framework to demonstrate how integrated social and ecological research guides more effective and sustainable policy and management. Researchers primarily operate within the intelligence function of the decision process but informing other functions requires that these are understood. Moreover, other functions will inform adaptive iterations of intelligence gathering: timing and type of data collection, analysis and presentation. Thus, we provide a detailed focus on tasks in the intelligence function followed by brief descriptions and examples for the subsequent six functions of the decision framework.

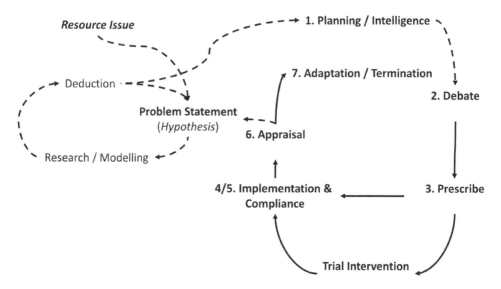

Note: Dashed lines represent assessment phases while the solid lines represent adaptive management.
Source: Adapted from Muntifering et al. (2020).

Figure 14.1   *Diagram illustrating the convergence of the adaptive environmental assessment and management model (Gunderson et al., 2008) and the policy science's decision process (Clark, 2002) framework (numbered 1–7 as labeled in Table 14.1)*

Intelligence

Equipped with an understanding of the decision process, the research inquiry task (intelligence function) can now begin. The intelligence function involves a stepwise process designing, conducting, analyzing and informing the decision process with research. For wildlife viewing protocols, this chapter presents a statistical modeling technique blending human and animal behavior data to identify and measure what most influences animal responses (e.g. aggression or displacement) and tourists' experience. It also characterizes the viewing protocols that are plausibly sustainable (hypotheses) and prioritizes their consideration and testing. Research transforms anecdote and interesting but vague notions about what human factors or environmental conditions drive wildlife's responses and tourists' experience into testable, alternative protocols.

Context

Unlike the decision process framework, which can be applied in many contexts, employing a statistical modeling approach to characterize and predict wildlife and tourist interaction may not be suited to all situations. In our experience, it is most likely to be best suited where tourist–wildlife encounters:

- Involve animals easily disturbed or where the consequence of, even infrequent, disturbance is severe and/or management goals prefer to minimize;
- Involve dangerous animals; and/or
- Habituate target wildlife and increase their vulnerability.

Define the problem

The literature documenting the adverse impacts of human-induced wildlife disturbance (a handful were listed above) continues to grow. A reasonable, responsible goal of wildlife-based tourism operations should be to minimize their impact on wildlife and seek to make their business sustainable. Nonetheless, the interests of tourists' experience and wildlife are frequently framed, at least to begin, as in conflict. It is critical at this early stage, therefore, to reframe the problem towards finding common values among participants in the decision process. Research (intelligence) is useful for informing a common understanding and appreciation about *why* wildlife disturbance, for example, is a problem. And, the problem should be empirically described and communicated in ways that appeal to tour operators' values. This may seem trivial or irrelevant to some researchers, especially among ecologists, but it is essential for establishing trusting, inclusive and engaged relationships among stakeholders, the foundation upon which the research can influence on-the-ground actions, including wildlife viewing protocols that are adopted and implemented by tour operators.

  For some wildlife species, presenting why human-induced disturbance (HID) is a problem for the tourism operation will be straightforward. It is, for example, comparatively easy to explain why it is undesirable for a bull elephant to charge tourists; because it is dangerous. But for other species that may not pose an immediate danger to people (e.g. some birds or smaller mammals), do not show clear signs of disturbance, or especially where, as is often true, information is scarce, it is less clear. It would be prudent in those circumstances to advocate for a precautionary approach (especially for endangered species) and design and carry out additional research to determine the type and magnitude of any adverse human-disturbance impacts resulting from encounters with tourists. Reasons for targeting (and minimizing) wildlife disturbance will likely vary by species and environment but generally may be due to a number of reasons such as:

1. Tourist safety
2. Preventing a decline in the number of animals available for viewing (due to reduced number, displacement into inaccessible areas, feeding, breeding, disease transmission)
3. Preventing a decline in animal quality (i.e. welfare concerns – see ABTA Animal Welfare Guidelines, Wildlife Viewing Manual)

Whatever the early justifications are, whether focused on wildlife welfare or business sustainability or (ideally) both, what is key here is that the majority (if not all) of the key decision-makers for the tourism operation participate in an open discussion and come to some consensus with other stakeholders about how better wildlife viewing practices may serve their own interests and the greater good. In fact, the tourism operation may already conduct such policy-oriented planning or review meetings for other reasons (e.g. work planning, staff welfare). If so, researchers can take advantage of using the existing arena as an opportunity to facilitate a discussion (or debate) about why wildlife disturbance is not desirable and how a viewing protocol may help mitigate problems. Facilitating this discussion may also usefully serve the researcher's entry into the decision process but also the establishment of an open 'policy arena' which will be a critical communication platform as researchers begin to collect data, produce and share results and ultimately empirically decide among alternative management strategies (i.e. viewing protocols). The absence of this type of inclusive arena is often a root cause of good science producing little to no management action.

Define the target wildlife response
Now that (hopefully most of) the tourism operators are supporting work towards a sustainable wildlife viewing protocol in everyone's best interest, a researcher must define what data should be collected. Again, it is useful to introduce the topic and facilitate a further discussion with stakeholders about specifically what wildlife behaviors should be targeted with the tourism operation participants. Clearly defining the target wildlife species' response is central to understanding what drives it and how to mitigate against it. Here, it is key to know or have some experts engaged in describing and selecting the specific behavioral responses that signify various levels of disturbance for the target species. For example, a study of black rhinoceros responses to encounters with tourists by the authors, found rhinoceros would typically exhibit three stages of behavior: (1) Unaware, defined as the rhinoceros showing no signs of awareness to the tourist group; (2) Disturbed, defined as a change in the behavior of rhinoceros after they demonstrate awareness (alert posture directed at the tourists); and (3) Displacement, defined as any movement following a disturbed state whereby the rhinoceros either walked or ran in excess of 50 meters. The transition from one stage to the next is typically abrupt and unambiguous (although 'habituated' rhinoceros may not readily show awareness of human presence). Other highly sought-after tourism drawcard species, such as elephant and lion, also produce observable responses to human-induced disturbance such as distinctive ear and body posture responses or showing teeth. What is key with this step is that the response is not only observable but also predictable from its context, such as the presence or behavior of tourists (e.g. interaction time and distance, vegetation cover and wind direction). It is also useful, but not entirely necessary if we accept and adopt a precautionary approach, to consider wildlife

responses that have a demonstrated consequence for animal fitness or welfare. All these potential influences must be identified, defined and measured.

Identify and define predictors

Thinking through what factors influence and predict wildlife's behavioral responses is paramount to a sustainable tourist-viewing protocol. The search must be exhaustive to include expert opinion as well as published information. First, a review of the literature regarding the target species behavior, habitat requirements, and movement ecology will be useful. Second, documenting the knowledge and opinions of people who have spent significant time observing the target species in the wild (experts) is important. Fortunately, the wildlife that attract tourists most are also more studied such as elephant, lion, cheetah, and tiger.

When generating a list of hypothetical predictors, it is also useful to begin thinking about how they can be measured. Continuous scale measurements, where possible, are most powerful (e.g. slope in degrees from zero, or distance in meters). However, sometimes those are not possible (because it cannot be measured: e.g. tree density near an animal without disturbing it) or appropriate (because the influential variation is described better by class than scale: e.g. vegetation type) and predictors must be categorical. Nonetheless, the explanatory power of categories can be improved by ordering them by their magnitude. Tree density near an observed animal, for example, might be reliably placed in separate categories from least to most dense. Distance from the animal could be placed in ordered categories too, especially using some easily comparable *yardstick*, for example: <10, 10–20, 20–50, 50–100 and >100 vehicle or animal body lengths. The categories need not be of equal size but chosen to correspond to the hypothetical values thought most influential on animals' behavior.

The measurement method should provide a meaningful characterization of the predictor relative to the response behavior while also reasonably easy to repeat with minimal subjectivity. Reducing subjectivity is especially important if the research data will be collected by several different observers. In this case, it is imperative that the differences in data collection recorded by the different observers (called inter-observer variability) is at best minimized or at least noted and assessed as part of the research findings. If substantial and unavoidable, inter-observer variation should be quantified and its measurement included in subsequent analysis so that relationships between predictors and wildlife responses can be shown to be statistically discernible and independent of observer bias. During this step, it is useful to begin summarizing each factor by providing a brief description or justification for its inclusion (including relevant references), a detailed explanation about how it will be measured in the field and lastly a statement predicting its influence. Table 14.2 is an example from research in Namibia (Muntifering et al., 2019). The table can be expanded horizontally adding new predictor variables and their summary information as additional columns.

The predictors chosen and how they are measured will also be influenced by the statistical analysis and modeling approach decided on. In statistical jargon, predictor variables are called *fixed-effects* if their influence is assumed to be the same (constant) across the sampled population. As an example, for the purpose of testing its influence, vehicle noise is assumed to have the same influence on all wild rhinoceros in a population and variation in responses reliably represented by an average and measure of variability (variance) among the individual values used to calculate it. Sometimes, however, a predictor variable's influence is not the same across the sampled population. Averages and their variance might, for example, be smaller or larger in different habitats. Sampling can also be clustered such that measurements

Table 14.2   *Example table summarizing the identification and definition of selected*
predictor variable(s)

EXAMPLE: Summarizing predictor variables for inclusion in data collection	
1. Predictor Variable	Closest tourist approach (distance)
2. DESCRIPTION / JUSTIFICATION	Reviews on tourist wildlife viewing suggest that physical proximity between humans and the wildlife plays a major role in driving disturbance and displacement (Stankowich, 2008), particularly for Asian rhinoceros (Lott and McCoy, 1995)
3. MEASUREMENT	For each sighting measure how close the group approached the rhinoceros, using laser rangefinders (± 1 meter accuracy)
4. PREDICTION / HYPOTHESIS	Expectation that approach distance would be negatively related to disturbance likelihoods, i.e., the closer a group was to a rhinoceros, the more likely it was to have been disturbed and displaced

of predictors in the same cluster are not independent and might be different between clusters. For example, if a group of rhinoceros are encountered, the responses of one rhinoceros in the group towards the same tourists is likely to be influenced by how other rhinoceros in the group respond. If more than one rhinoceros in the group was sampled and entered the dataset, their data would be a cluster. In other words, each of their responses cannot be attributed only to the 'fixed' predictor variables but also according to the cluster. Or perhaps the same individual rhinoceros was sampled multiple times in the dataset, different rhinoceros encountered more or less frequently. In these cases, a predictor for 'area', 'group' or 'identity' can be added as a variable but called a *random-effect* because averages and variance within and between areas, groups and individuals are expected to be different and those differences are of interest to the study. Random effects can also be layered in a hierarchy such that individuals sampled more than once may also form social groups thus requiring a random effect first for social group and then for individual. A multi-variate model, such as a regression, may contain only fixed effects, only random effects or a combination of the two, which are termed *mixed-effects* models. Which effects are included depends on the hypotheses being tested and how the population, wildlife and tourists, is sampled.

In the case of wildlife viewing protocols random-effect variables are often required for data that may be influenced by social relationships or repeated sampling of the same individual animals. However, it is important to note that models, even mixed-effect models, with random effects require larger amounts of sampling. They are also more challenging to interpret. Thus, if adding random effects does not improve the model then it would be best to remove them and focus on the analysis of fixed effects. Assessing whether including a random effect(s) is warranted can be done by repeatability analysis using and comparing variance contributions by comparing the full mixed-effects model with models without fixed effects to examine whether the inclusion of the random effects added any explanatory power to the model (Nakagawa and Schielzeth, 2013). If the random effects contribution was trivial, then we recommend focusing on fixed-effects only models.

Lastly, once plausible predictor variables have been selected and defined, it is good practice to begin defining a set of multiple **Working Hypotheses**. Two alternate approaches are possible and which is chosen depends on the extent to which the problem has already been investigated. If there is already a well-developed literature describing current knowledge and supported hypotheses, and stakeholders' beliefs and speculations about predictors and their additive and interacting influence on wildlife disturbance are well-formed then those can be described as hypotheses, and represented by combinations of our predictors in models. Those models, collectively, would be described as the 'candidate model set' and each model in it tested against the others in the way described in our '*Data analysis and model selection*' section. This process requires careful thought and will benefit from thoroughly exploring relevant published literature as well as collating expert opinion.

An example, using a short list of predictors, is provided below (X denotes *Predictor Variable* and H denotes a single *Working Hypothesis*):

Predictor Variables (not limited to):

X_1: *Group's closest approach distance to rhinoceros (meters)*
X_2: *Group size including guides and trackers*
X_3: *Time at closest distance (minutes)*
X_4: *Rhinoceros group composition (single male, female, females with calf)*

Working Hypotheses (including the relationship among predators as additive or interactive but not limited to):

H_1: *X_1 and X_2 and X_3 and X_4 – all four predictors have an additional influence*
H_2: *X_1 and X_3 and X_4 – only 3 of the 4 predictors, 1, 3 and 4, are influential*
H_3: *X_1 and X_3 – only two of the predictors, 1 and 3, are influential*
H_4: *$X_1 + X_3$ and $(X_1 \times X_3)$ – only two predictors, 1 and 3, are influential and the influence of each is magnified by the magnitude of the other, i.e., their combined effect is interactive*
H_5: *No fixed-effect variables – none of the predictors are influential*

However, in many cases stakeholders' beliefs are no more elaborate than lists of potential influences (single predictors) and the literature or prior knowledge are insufficient to specify detailed and multiple working hypotheses. In such cases, the working hypotheses are models formed by all possible combinations of the predictors (fixed-effects) with the full complement of random-effects and a process called 'model averaging' (see section '*Measures of evidence and model-based inference*' below) employed to compare the models against each other. In most circumstances where the work is a first attempt at developing an evidence-based tourist wildlife viewing protocol, model averaging will be necessary and preferable. It is the approach we adopted for Namibia rhinoceros and which we elaborate on below. Future, now better informed, improvements on our model averaging work, however, would inevitably advance to more complex candidate model sets and the first approach described.

Whichever of the two approaches is adopted, deciding on working hypotheses is conducted *a priori* to data collection and analysis, forming a critical part of what is termed an **Information-Theoretic (IT)** analysis.

Although IT analysis has been around for decades, its use and application has been subordinate to conventional null hypothesis testing methods and incremental model building techniques (e.g. step-wise regression). Yet, there are numerous reasons why an IT approach is superior and preferable, particularly for establishing evidence-based wildlife viewing protocols. First, more than one hypothesis, representing the diversity of stakeholders' views and beliefs, can be evaluated concurrently providing shared responsibility and ownership of hypothesis formulation, testing and outcomes and, therefore, assisting in collaboration and support for a consensus. Second, an *a priori* set of working hypotheses can represent the totality of current knowledge, as well as speculation, providing the basis for measurable improvements in collective understanding. Questions such as: 'what is the empirical evidence for H_1 relative to H_2 or H_3?' can be answered. In other words, IT analyses allow thinking, collaboration and testing to move beyond conventional 'is there an effect?' to become a repeating iterative journey towards truth. It is better suited to topics about which there can be much disagreement but the great need for cooperation towards consensus and collective ownership and responsibility of outcomes. This chapter will not delve more into the theory here but we refer readers to David Anderson's text on *Model Based Inference in the Life Sciences* (Anderson, 2008) for further information on theoretical underpinnings and additional practical examples. The chapter also refers to this resource later when presenting some modeling and evidence interpretation techniques.

Set up the data collection procedure
With candidate hypotheses described, models to represent them built and the response and predictor variables decided and defined, fieldwork can begin. Data will be collected during actual encounters with the target wildlife with at least one observer recording data during the event. In general, it is easiest to limit the number of different observers to a few individuals 'trained-for-purpose' to reduce inter-observer variation in the dataset. Alternatively, inter-observer variability could be assessed by incorporating observer identity as a random-effect in subsequent models (see above for more details on random-effects).

Data gathering is, often, limited by resources, especially time. Although a larger dataset is generally better, not all observations are equally valuable for testing hypotheses. A single observation (response and predictor measurement) from each wildlife encounter contributes a unique record. Statisticians call such unique records 'independent'. Gathering multiple measurements of the response and predictor variables during the same encounter can more quickly build a large dataset but each measure is not independent, because it will be more like the others than they will be to measurements taken during different encounters. Statisticians call such data auto-correlated. Auto-correlation is a problem because statistical analyses assume independent observations. Where auto-correlation occurs the dataset has less power to discriminate among hypotheses than its size would ordinarily indicate if all observations were independent. To avoid auto-correlation, it is recommended to only take one sample per encounter including one measurement of the response and associated predictor variables. Every encounter will be presented by just one line (row in spreadsheet) in the dataset.

In addition, the measurement of predictors should occur during the encounter when they trigger a measurable response so that a causative relationship between predictor and response variables is tested. Rapid behavioral change during encounters can make recording multiple measurements over a short time period challenging. Advance planning and an efficient data-recording regime and tools will be an advantage. A simple data collection sheet is often sufficient and used to also capture background information on 'Pre- and post-viewing information' (e.g. name of observer(s), date, time, location, purpose of the trip). It helps if predictor and response variables can be measured simply (e.g. response classified as unaware, disturbed, displaced). The units for each measurement should be standardized and clearly indicated on the sheet. A sample data collection form is presented in Appendix A. Although we've found sheets more reliable in field conditions with a diversity of observers, such forms can also be digitized and completed electronically too, albeit adding an additional layer of complexity and training to the research.

The sample collection could be set up to be conducted experimentally or opportunistically during real tourist–wildlife encounters. This will depend upon the situation. In the case where the research must be incorporated within existing tourist–wildlife encounters, it is most appropriate to standardize the data collection point at the 'closest approach distance' as this will typically align with normal operating procedures for the viewing encounter. When data collection can be conducted experimentally, a randomized set of predetermined plausible viewing scenarios could be chosen and replicated for sampling.

The more predictor variables and associated levels in the study, the more independent samples will be required. More complex hypotheses, represented by models with many more predictors, demand more data. Confidence in the results generated through an IT approach is improved if the ratio of sample number (n) is 40 times or larger than the number of model parameters (K, e.g., for a simple linear regression: the count of predictors, interactive terms, an intercept and variance term). Thus, H_4 noted above, represented by a linear regression model and predictors would have a $K = 2 + 1 + 1 + 1$ and so a sample size of 200 observations (K × 40) is advised. Nonetheless, compensations during analyses for smaller samples are available (Anderson, 2008). Another general rule-of-thumb is to plan to attain a minimum of 7–10 independent samples per predictor (Kutner et al., 2004). Thus, if the candidate set of *working hypotheses* includes 6 possible predictor variables, at least 42–60 samples should be collected. Additional techniques to estimate appropriate sample sizes are Monte Carlo simulation studies and power analysis (Muthen and Muthen, 2002) which can be applied after a pilot study or the first data are gathered to estimate how much more data should be gathered for confidence in comparative statistical outcomes.

Data analysis and model selection
A candidate model set specified *a priori*, and describing targeted wildlife disturbance response as a function of different combinations of predictor variables, is a stronger test of hypotheses when possible. However, a model-averaging approach using Generalized Linear Models (GLM) is better suited to maximize the inference and application derived from the data collected where *a priori* knowledge is weak. We describe the model averaging approach here. The analyses, following the collection of field data, will provide empirical estimates of each model's parameters and their associated variance. Model parameters are estimated through various approaches including least squares (which include general linear models, maximum likelihood and Bayesian methods). Each has advantages and disadvantages and numerous texts and references provide detailed descriptions. These computations, which can range from simple to highly sophisticated, can be generated from numerous software packages most notably the open-source R statistical software. Numerous 'packages' in R that will produce model statistics given any dataset have been created and put through stringent peer-review. Their capacity and limitations are known. It is up to the researchers to choose the most appropriate modeling package for their data and question. For example, in the case of Namibia, the research applied the *lme4* package (Bates, 2010) to perform the mixed-effects modeling to obtain model parameters and other important statistical values for each model (Muntifering et al., 2019). As new code is regularly updated, it is useful to always check for the latest version of both R and associated statistical packages.

Once the model parameters have been estimated for each working hypothesis, another value can be derived that is key for moving forward with model selection and interpretation known as the *maximum log likelihood*. It is this value that will link the data analysis to information theory (hence the term 'information-theoretic') to enable a more rigorous evaluation of the strength of evidence for each of our working hypotheses by using it to calculate Akaike's Information Criterion (AIC). It is useful here to conceptualize AIC as providing the link between information theory and mathematical modeling. The AIC, named after the Japanese mathematician Hirotigu Akaike who introduced the approach in the mid-1970s, was a major breakthrough which provides a measure of 'information' lost when approaching full reality (truth) by any one of the candidate models, given how many parameters it uses to describe reality (Anderson, 2008). The objective of multi-model selection and inference is to find the simplest explanation (model), i.e., parsimony. Any model, if it has a large enough number of parameters, can appear to explain wildlife disturbance but have no predictive power. Thus, an AIC for each candidate model is computed, that penalizes larger models with more parameters, and used to rank the models and make inferences. It is the AIC which enables a much broader set of questions to be asked about each model. It can be used to find out which working hypothesis has the most empirical support as being closest to the truth and by how much compared to other hypotheses.

Another useful application of this approach enables inferences to be made from all the hypotheses. This is important especially when a lot of 'information' is explained by many of the working hypotheses or, in other words, no single hypothesis stands out as being clearly 'the best'. In this case, it makes good sense to make use of as much 'information' as possible to estimate model parameters. This is called model averaging and is one of a number of useful techniques generally known as multi-model inference. Like the packages created to estimate model parameters using GLMs, another package called the *MuMIn* package (Barton, 2016) may be used to perform the multi-model inference analysis (model-averaging).

Keeping in mind that these models are not and will never be true reality, it is important to find the model that represents the closest estimation of true reality from all those proposed. Conceptually, information theory posits this estimation can be described as expected 'information lost' or 'distance' from the approximating model to true reality. AIC values are an empirical output that links maximum log likelihoods generated by statistical analysis to this 'information' or 'distance' (known as Kullback-Leibler Information). For those interested, a full derivation of the linkage can be found in Burnham and Anderson (2002). In practice, this simply means given the data, the model in the candidate set of working hypotheses with the lowest AIC (shortest distance from true reality or least amount of information lost) should be used for any subsequent inference. AIC estimates for any given dataset and associated model(s) are now commonly presented in analysis outputs alongside other model parameters within most statistical software packages including the R package mentioned above. One last general note on AIC values is that they are only useful within a single dataset and/or candidate set of working hypotheses as they are a function of sample size. AICs should thus not be compared across datasets.

In addition to these metrics, it is also important to report for each candidate model the (1) model number and description of which predictors are included – this could also be written out in the table caption and numbers or symbols used to denote the predictors (see below example), (2) the number of parameters in the model + 1 for σ^2 (residual variance in the regression) denoted as K, and (3) log likelihood value derived from either least squares or maximum likelihood estimation. Depending upon the number of models in the candidate set, it may also be prudent to restrict the reporting table to include only the top ten models, for example, or at least the convention of all models with Δ AICc ≤ 2 as an *ad hoc* rule-of-thumb (see below in '*Measures of evidence and model-based inference*'). An example summary table is shown in Table 14.3 (Muntifering et al., 2019).

Table 14.3   Best models for disturbance logistic regression with AICc ≤ 2

Model	K	logLik	AICc	Δ AICc	Weight w$_i$
Displacement Model Set					
279	4	55.5905	119.52	0.000	0.1080
2789	5	55.0605	120.63	1.114	0.0620
1279	5	55.1353	120.78	1.263	0.0576
2679	5	55.1976	120.91	1.388	0.0541
2579	5	55.3771	121.27	1.747	0.0452

Note: Variables in the Disturbance Model Sets are numerically denoted as: Composition = 1, Distance from closest location = 2, Habitat = 3, Initial behavior = 4, Cumulative time = 5, Number of people = 6, Individual encounter exposure = 7, Season = 8, Time at closest distance = 9.

Measures of evidence and model-based inference

Once AIC values are estimated they must be interpreted as they provide the basis for a number of inferences that can now be made about the models. Three of the most useful are illustrated below:

1. The most straightforward interpretation is simply ranking the models by AIC value beginning with the lowest numerical value. This is the 'best' model relative to other candidate models in the set of working hypotheses. Often, this information is presented as a change in AIC often denoted as 'Δ AIC'. In this case, the 'best' model would be attributed as a 0 for Δ AIC and the differences in associated AIC values relative to the 'best' model would be reported for the others in the candidate model set. A model with Δ AIC >2 is often described as substantially poorer.
2. The probability of each candidate model being estimated as the 'best' in the set can also be estimated and reported as Akaike weight. This can be easily calculated for each candidate model and then dividing each by the sum of all the calculated numbers. For example, in Excel you can simply enter the formula for each model = exp (–0.5* Δ AIC$_{model\ x}$) with Δ AIC$_{model\ x}$ being indicated in the summary table as presented in Table 14.3.
3. Evidence ratios can also be reported to specify support for/against certain models. Here simply divide the Akaike weights. For example, Model 1's Akaike weight is estimated to be 0.1080 while Model 2 (which includes an additional predictor variable) has an Akaike weight of 0.062. The evidence suggests that Model 1 is 1.74 times (0.1080 divided by 0.0620) times more likely than Model 2 to be the 'best' model.

The above example (Table 14.3) also illustrates another important consideration for inference when there is very little difference among the best models. The 'best' model (Δ AIC = 0) is represented by including 3 predictor variables but has a model probability of only 0.1080. In fact, as stated, it is only 1.74 (0.1080 divided by 0.0620) times more likely to be chosen than the second 'best' model and only 1.87 (0.1080 divided by 0.0576) times more likely than the third. Here, the evidence strongly suggests that there is relevant 'information' in models ranked below the estimated best model. Thus, much information could be 'lost' by only making inferences from the estimated best model. This is where multimodel inference can be particularly useful.

While many techniques exist to perform **multimodel inference**, two are particularly useful in wildlife viewing protocol context and both are easy to compute: (1) estimating the relative importance of each predictor variable and (2) utilizing the 'information' in the full set of models for inference through a procedure called model averaging. First, in addition to interpreting the evidence for or against each candidate model, it is also interesting to examine the relative importance of each predictor variable in the dataset. This can be particularly useful during even exploratory phases of research when investigators are unsure of the type and magnitude of influence that certain predictor variables actually have on a response variable. This is computed simply by summing the weights of each model that included each variable, respectively. Considering all the possible candidate models ensures that each predictor variable is provided an equal chance. The approach is also highly relevant when using GLMs such as linear or logistic regression as it permits inspection into a predictor variable's true influence on the response variable as each predictor will appear on its own in some models as well as with other predictor variables in others. It should be noted, however, that this should only be done when the number of each predictor variable is balanced across the candidate model set and all possible combinations of predictors are presented as models. When the stakeholders produce their own set of models using unique sets of predictor variables, model averaging should not be attempted and the relative importance of each predictor variable cannot be reliably estimated.

Lastly, as noted earlier, model probabilities clearly (especially in the example above) suggest that useful 'information' exists in models ranked below the 'best' in the candidate set. Since even the 'best' model is far from full reality, it only makes sense to make use of this lower-ranking information, particularly when the lower ranking models are only slightly lower than the top 'best' model. Model averaging performs this task and also ensures that 'better' models also have more influence than relatively poor models as it uses the model probabilities in its calculations. They are also fairly simple to compute, and numerous packages exist to compute these given the data and other multimodel statistics in R including the AICcModavg and MuMIn packages. *Here, it may also be useful to engage with a statistician or another researcher more fluent in modeling for assistance.*

Using model predictions to establish plausible wildlife viewing scenarios

With the analysis complete and either the 'best' model or model averaged parameters estimated, it is now possible to transfer these mathematical representations of the tourist–wildlife encounter model into useful and user-friendly management tools. In this case, this last and final step can produce an actual viewing protocol or at least strong evidence-based recommendations on viewing guidelines. This can be accomplished in a number of different ways, but this chapter highlights an integrated (both ecological and social elements) four-step process to get from mathematical models to wildlife viewing protocols. If researchers are comfortable using scripts in R, the multimodel packages mentioned above will run predictions using the model parameters. Alternatively, it is very straightforward to run a series of model predictions in an Excel spreadsheet given the model parameters.

It is likely in most tourist–wildlife encounter contexts, that two viewing predictor variables will be important: closest approach distance and time at closest distance. Not only is this logical and realistic but also convenient as both variables can be directly managed by operators (typically managers/guides) and logically would form part of any viewing protocol. This is also useful as predictions can target producing a matrix of wildlife response probabilities (disturbance measure) as a function of various approach distances and associated viewing times while holding the other predictor variables constant at their averages. If preferred and well warranted, other predictor variables could be varied in the scenario predictions (although this could become complicated and confusing with too many predictions). Advancing on this example, two key steps are briefly outlined below:

1. Produce a wildlife behavior response probability matrix by simply making a series of predictions on the response variable given specified model-averaged (or best model) parameters and possible scenario values for each predictor variable in the model. This approach emphasizes the closest approach distance and viewing time by specifically varying these values in relation to each other while holding the other predictor variables at a fixed mean/median. Figure 14.2 illustrates the approach in an Excel spreadsheet using tourist–rhinoceros encounter data from Namibia.

2. The predictive matrix can be transformed into a figure (line graph) that clearly illustrates how wildlife disturbance probabilities vary as a function of possible approach distances

X_2	VIEWING TIME (minutes)							
X_1	5	10	15	20	25	30	45	60
50	33%	46%	60%	73%	83%	89%	98%	100%
100	11%	18%	28%	41%	55%	68%	92%	98%
150	3%	5%	9%	15%	24%	35%	75%	94%
200	1%	1%	2%	4%	7%	12%	43%	81%
250	0%	0%	1%	1%	2%	3%	16%	52%
300	0%	0%	0%	0%	1%	1%	5%	21%
350	0%	0%	0%	0%	0%	0%	1%	7%
400	0%	0%	0%	0%	0%	0%	0%	2%
450	0%	0%	0%	0%	0%	0%	0%	0%
500	0%	0%	0%	0%	0%	0%	0%	0%

(CLOSEST APPROACH DISTANCE (meters))

$$=1 / (1 + EXP(-(\beta_0 + (\beta_{distance} * X_1) + (\beta_{time} * X_2) + ...(\beta_r * X_r))))$$

Note: Where the equation in the bottom box indicates the typed formula structure for Excel to calculate probabilities based on the model parameters (β_0 = intercept, $\beta_{distance}$ = coefficient for distance, X_1 = the distance scenario in meters the formula should reference, β_{time} = coefficient for time, X_2 = the time scenario in minutes the formula should reference, and ($\beta_r * X_r$) being the addition predictor variable coefficients and associated fixed (mean or median) values for the scenario). Thus the calculated % in the table (e.g. 33% indicated in the bottom box) is the probability of a rhinoceros becoming disturbed given the associated distances (X_1 = 50m) and times (X_2 = 5 minutes).

Figure 14.2   *Matrix of rhinoceros disturbance probabilities calculated as a function of specific varying distances and times using fitted model parameters*

and viewing time given mean/median values for the other predictor variable. This is simply completed by graphically illustrating the relationships between wildlife disturbance response (calculated in Step 1 above) given associated times and distances in the scenarios (also presented in the above example). The graph (Figure 14.3) provides an example of one possible model illustrating how rhinoceros disturbance probabilities (y-axis) vary by closest approach distance (x-axis) under a fixed 5 minute viewing time. This is simply the first column of probabilities calculated in Step 1. If desired, multiple models can be illustrated together simply by adding more columns (fixed time values, for example 10 minutes, 15 minutes, etc.) to the graph.

Once at this stage, the decision process can now shift from the intelligence to the debate function of the decision-process.

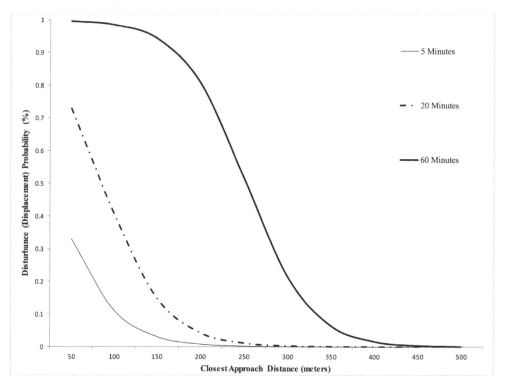

Figure 14.3   *Example of graphic illustration of model-based rhinoceros viewing scenarios showing rhinoceros disturbance as a function of closest approach distance for 3 fixed viewing time values (5 minutes, 20 minutes and 60 minutes)*

Debate

Moving along the decision process, once adequate attention has been given to the gathering of intelligence on the problem, the data collected, analyzed and interpreted should be openly debated. The debating should take place in an open arena with as many participants present and engaged in the debate as appropriate.

For the researcher, now it is time to present the findings making sure to emphasize and channel discussion on the final scenario-based graph or other illustrations with the predictive viewing models. Several possible and modeled viewing scenarios and their associated predicted disturbance probabilities could be evaluated and presented to inform the discussion. This is useful as it immediately places 'ownership' back into the hands of the managers and individuals responsible for implementation. Presenting a set of scenarios avoids imposing one single 'solution' developed by the researcher(s) in lieu of multiple alternative possible 'proposals' that can be openly challenged and discussed. For instance, in the above example, one possible viewing protocol could set the desired disturbance probability to 10%. Under this scenario, given the models presented, encounters could take place at ~100 meters for 5 minutes, ~150 meters for 20 or ~350 meters for 60 minutes. Additional model probabilities (20%, 50%, etc.) and associated viewing conditions can be proposed and discussed alongside each other. Ultimately, a choice will need to be reached as to where to set the desired (accepted) disturbance probability for a viewing protocol to be designed and adopted. Unless additional research or knowledge is available upon which to base this decision, it will likely be arbitrary at the onset. In this case, what 'risk' management is willing to accept, that a rhinoceros–human encounter will result in the rhinoceros becoming (in this case) displaced by the event, becomes important to the decision. Debate might focus again on issues mentioned earlier such as safety and/or concern over the rhinoceros' well-being. Whatever the initial justification, the policy can always be adjusted following implementation and evaluation (appraisal) produces new insights that suggest otherwise. In the context of tourism, it is also important to consider the appeal and practical appropriateness for the guest experience. The experience, certainly influenced by the viewing protocol(s), needs to meet or exceed expectations of the guests. In other words, if the accepted risk model predictions render an experience that is likely to produce very low satisfaction feedback from guests (and this certainly could be tested), the entire experience should be reconsidered. Thus, it is prudent that at least informal, but preferably formal, surveys with paying guests are conducted as part of the intelligence function to ascertain guest expectations for the proposed experience. This could, and should, also be performed as part of the model validation or appraisal function, with guests who participated in the experience. This information is even more useful as research questionnaires can go beyond asking hypothetical questions about the viewing experience and rather evaluate how well expectations were met given a known viewing experience.

Prescription

Once a decision has been reached during the debate, an actual viewing protocol may be prescribed. The new prescription can now be referred to as the 'Wildlife Viewing Protocol'. Tools can be developed that help illustrate and make the protocol more user-friendly to managers and implementers than graphs and models. For example, in Namibia *Rhino Viewing Cards* were created from the accepted model scenarios that provide simple guidance on the viewing protocol. These cards would be used by the individuals delivering the viewing encounter in several ways. Most notably, they would be presented and explained to the tourists prior to the wildlife encounter as the camp's wildlife viewing policy (e.g. see real examples of Rhino Viewing Card: Viewing Policy (front) and Speaking Points (back) in Figures 14.4 and 14.5).

RHINO VIEWING CARD

Closest **DISTANCE**	Maximum **TIME**
100 *meters*	**5** *minutes*
150 *meters*	**15** *minutes*
200 *meters*	**25** *minutes*
250 *meters*	**45** *minutes*

Figure 14.4   Rhino viewing card: viewing policy (front)

Invoking and Implementing the Prescribed Protocol

Once the prescription for an actual viewing protocol and tools for explicitly describing and communicating the 'rules' have been established, the decision process is ready to move towards implementation. Prior to actual implementation, however, it is essential that the prescription is in some way invoked. In other words, decisions must be made regarding how the implementation will be conducted. Specifically, who will be held accountable to follow the rules and how will 'enforcement' occur to ensure compliance. One conventional example would entail camp managers choosing to establish dis-incentives or formal consequences for rule-breaking. Importantly, these should be discussed, debated and agreed upon openly in the policy arena. Compliance measures could then be inserted into a mini-contract that each implementing individual (i.e. guide) could sign as acknowledgement of the rules and consequences of rule-breaking.

Less coercive strategies should also be considered. One strategy employed in Namibia, for example, broadened the use of the Rhino Viewing Cards to assist with guide compliance. The approach mandated that guides present the viewing protocol (using the Rhino Viewing Cards to illustrate) to the tourists the night before the rhinoceros tracking experience. The tourists may ask questions and discuss the policy with the camp manager and/guides directly engaging the guides in explaining more about why the policy exists and how it is enforced (largely by the guides and trackers). The guides may again present the cards to the tourists just before approaching the animal as a reminder. In this manner, the approach has two benefits. First, it provides a basis for re-aligning guest expectations. Often, tourism camp staff are unaware of precisely what experience the guests expect. Ensuring guests clearly understand what

Using the Rhino Viewing Card

What is the Rhino Viewing Card?
✓ The Rhino Viewing Card is Desert Rhino Camp's (DRC) rhino viewing policy.
✓ It provides rhino viewing guidelines under different conditions that minimize the chances of a rhino viewing event resulting in a disturbed rhino.
✓ This card is based upon research jointly conducted at DRC since 2003.

Why do we need a Rhino Viewing Card?
✓ Research has also confirmed that our rhino are very sensitive to human disturbance and will move into areas that are less safe (higher risk of being poached), lower quality habitat, and more difficult for tourists to see.
✓ Our ideal rhino sighting is achieved when we observe our rhinos completely unaware of our presence – providing guests with an authentic experience with wild rhino and Save the Rhino Trust with the ability to monitor them.
✓ The Rhino Viewing Card is thus a means to both illustrate our genuine intent to *practice responsible rhino tourism* to our guests while providing our guides with a *simple tool* for attaining a respectable number of ideal rhino sightings.

Where did the numbers come from?
✓ Our rhino viewing policy is the result of research designed specifically to help understand how to approach our wild rhino without disturbing them.
✓ Based upon detailed information collected during hundreds of rhino viewing events over many years, we now understand:

1. *The main factors that drive rhino disturbance*: wind direction, whether the rhino is sleeping or active, the approach distance, and the viewing time;
2. *Associated viewing times and approach distances that result in only a small number of rhino disturbance events*

✓ The research findings were then translated into a set of 'rhino viewing scenarios' displayed on this card to help guide each rhino viewing event.

Desert Rhino Camp is the only place on earth where guests may go on foot with Save the Rhino Trust trackers to observe the last population of truly wild black rhino living in their natural environment. You can help us sustain our responsible tourism business and rhino conservation project by respecting these simple guidelines so our success may endure for generations to come.

Figure 14.5   Rhino viewing card: viewing policy: speaking points (back)

their experience will likely entail, especially rules and regulations, is vital to avoid future disappointment and displeasure. Handled well, it can add value to the guests' experience: provoking their participation and emphasizing the sustainability credentials of the operation. Second, it provides a basis for holding the guides accountable to also respect and comply with the viewing policy – a problem encountered in other places (Sandbrook and Semple, 2006) by creating a 'self-policing' situation whereby any rule-breaking would directly contradict their own word(s). Further, any rule-breaking behavior often would emerge at the evening campfire following the experience as tourists enjoy 're-living' their encounter and sharing it with everyone. Ensuring each guide recognizes and understands this reality also places constructive peer-pressure upon them to avoid one group receiving unfair advantages. While this has not yet been tested empirically, very few incidences of rule-breaking have occurred. It might be useful to also consider providing specific incentives for guides which could include performance bonuses or rewards for positive tourist feedback that clearly demonstrates that the protocol was properly presented and adhered to. After at least one invocation strategy is chosen and applied, the protocol may now be implemented. Initially, this might take the shape of a trial or test run (see Figure 14.1). This is a useful approach since participants will recognize that there may be considerable adjustments following appraisal, the next function in our decision process cycle. For more description on the basis for, and application of, these strategies, see Muntifering et al.'s (2020) case study example.

Appraisal and Termination

During implementation, particularly any trial interventions, it is essential that the activity is evaluated against original desired goals and objectives. This is the appraisal function and the most critical step in adaptively managing (i.e. learning) the system. In the case of wildlife viewing protocols, this can be straightforward and may essentially be a more focused extension of the initial data collection (intelligence) period. At this stage, the focus may still be upon the viewing protocol whereby a separate, independent dataset must be collected using the key drivers (predictor variables) upon the response variable to assess (validate) the protocol's (model) predictive accuracy. For example, if the pre-scripted viewing policy set the disturbance response probability at 10%, then the appraisal investigation following successful (i.e., full compliance) implementation should yield no more than 1 out of 10 wildlife disturbance events. The same data collection protocol may be utilized. It is also worth mentioning that this particular action may also form part of the intelligence function, especially if management may require additional supporting evidence on the model's predictive power *prior to* implementation.

In addition to validation, several other indicators may be assessed during the appraisal function. For example, it would be useful to analyze and interpret any possible negative effects upon the target wildlife species as a function of tourism activity particularly movement (i.e., displacement effects) and/or breeding performance (biological effects). Monitoring systems to record data on these basic indicators should be ongoing and could then be compared to a baseline collected from either information on the same population before the tourism activity or from a 'control' population persisting under similar conditions in the absence of tourism. In addition to providing insights on any adaptive management, this type of information is often of interest to tourists who generally appreciate knowing their activity did not negatively impact the animal. Importantly, as mentioned previously, feedback from tourists should also feature in the appraisal. If the experience is not meeting visiting tourist expectations then either the expectations need to be further adjusted or the viewing protocol needs to be revisited. This information could be actively collected by customizing camp evaluation forms to include specific questions about the wildlife encounter or more passively by examining online resources such as TripAdvisor (see Muntifering et al., 2019). However, tourist satisfaction is heavily influenced by whether or not expectations are met. This re-emphasizes the importance of communicating not just the rules of the prescribed wildlife viewing protocol to the tourists but also the rationale focusing on authenticity and sustainability. Properly communicating the viewing protocol, especially well before the actual experience occurs, will ensure that expectations for the vast majority of visiting tourists matches the local context. Lastly, once the viewing protocol has been sufficiently appraised and adjusted accordingly, any previous viewing practices or policies should be terminated.

CONCLUDING REMARKS

The rise in demand from tourists for wildlife encounters in the wild provides opportunities and challenges for both business and conservation. Central to managing these trade-offs is the search for strategies that seek to enhance sustainability that will provide net positive returns for both business and conservation. Here, we presented a suite of techniques and tools that guide both the design and delivery of wildlife viewing protocols that improve sustainability by reducing tourism-induced disturbance while maintaining satisfaction.

The practical application is demonstrated by numerous examples given at each step from our own experience in Namibia where the approach has helped advance rhinoceros-based tourism over the past 18 years. For instance, following the full implementation of the Rhino Viewing Cards and associated strategic messaging, rhinoceros displacement events at DRC were reduced by 80% while maintaining a 95% positive feedback rating from guests (Muntifering et al., 2019). Furthermore, revenue generated from the lodge has continued to sustain the vital routine monitoring and surveillance efforts by SRT ensuring nearly every individual rhinoceros in the camp's vast operational area is observed at least once per month. Despite numerous poaching cases in nearby areas and even greater poaching frequencies throughout Namibia between 2012 and 2018, not a single rhinoceros has been poached in DRC's area of operation (Muntifering, 2019). The subsequent expansion of rhinoceros-based tourism in the region from initially just a single enterprise (DRC) to currently six community-based joint-venture enterprises generated more than USD 250,000 in 2017 and over USD 1,000,000 between 2012 and 2017 in direct cash payments to local communities. This is testament to the success and replicability of the operational model beyond a single luxury camp and may extend across other camps that cater to different segments of the tourism market (Muntifering, 2019). We speculate that sustainable tourism and its benefits to the local community and rhinoceros surveillance have contributed to this success.

In summary, from our experience described above we emphasize three vital elements to negotiating the complex social-ecological system that are wildlife tourism cooperatives. We call this the ACE approach: (1) establish an *Arena* for inclusive, open debate; (2) identify and use *Conservation-oriented messaging*; (3) adopt participatory *Evidence-based management* for action, feedback, and learning (Muntifering et al., 2020). These lessons may help advance the practice of conservation tourism for the benefit of both wildlife and humans alike.

REFERENCES

Anderson, D. (2008) *Model Based Inference in the Life Sciences*. New York: Springer Publishing.
Balmford, A., J. M. H. Green, M. Anderson, J. Beresford, C. Huang, R. Naidoo, M. Walpole and A. Manica (2015) Walk on the wild side: Estimating the global magnitude of visits to protected areas. *PLOS Biology*, 13(2). https://doi.org/10.1371/journal.pbio.1002074.
Barton, K. (2016) Mu-MIn: Multi-Model Inference. R Package Version 0.12.2/R18. http://R-Forge.R -project.org/projects/mumin/.

Bates, D. (2010) *Lme4: Mixed-Effects Modeling with R.* New York: Springer.

Berkes, F. and C. Folke (1998) *Linking Social and Ecological Systems: Management Practices and Social Mechanisms for Building Resilience.* New York: Cambridge University Press.

Buckley, R. (2010) *Conservation Tourism.* Wallingford: CABI.

Buckley, R. (2011) Tourism and environment. *Annual Review of Environment and Resources*, 36, 397–416.

Buckley, R. C., J. G. Castley, F. de Vasconcellos Pegas, A. C. Mossaz and R. Steven (2012) A population accounting approach to assess tourism contributions to conservation of IUCN-Redlisted mammal species. *PLoS ONE*, 7(9). https://doi.org/10.1371/journal.pone.0044134.

Burnham, K. and D. Anderson (2002) *Model Selection and Multimodal Interference: A Practical Information-Theoretic Approach.* New York: Springer.

Carpenter, S. R., E. M. Bennett and G. D. Peterson (2006) Scenarios for ecosystem services: An overview. *Ecology and Society*, 11(1). https://doi.org/10.5751/ES-01610-110129.

Clark, S. G. (2002) *The Policy Process.* New Haven, CT: Yale University Press.

Clark, S. G. and A. R. Willard (2000) Analyzing natural resource policy and management. In S. G. Clark, A. R. Willard and M. Cromley (eds.), *Foundations of Natural Resources Policy and Management.* New Haven, CT: Yale University Press, 32–44.

Griffin, S., T. Valois, M. L. Taper and L. S. Mills (2007) Effects of tourists on behavior and demography of Olympic Marmots. *Conservation Biology*, 21(4), 1070–1081.

Gunderson, L., G. D. Peterson and C. S. Holling (2008) Practicing adaptive management in complex social-ecological systems. In J. Norberg and G. S. Cumming (eds.), *Complexity Theory for a Sustainable Future.* New York: Columbia University Press, 223–240.

Hanes, A. C., G. Kalema-Zikusoka, M. S. Svensson and C. M. Hill (2018) Assessment of health risks posed by tourists visiting mountain gorillas in Bwindi Impenetrable National Park, Uganda. *Primate Conservation*, 32, 123–132.

Higham, J. E. S., L. Bejder and D. Lusseau (2008) An integrated and adaptive management model to address the long-term sustainability of tourist interactions with cetaceans. *Environmental Conservation*, 35(4), 294–302.

Knight, J. (2009) Making wildlife viewable: Habituation and attraction. *Society & Animals*, 17(2), 167–184.

Kutner, M. H., C. J. Nachtsheim, J. Netter and W. Li (2004) *Applied Linear Statistical Models*, 4th edition. Chicago, IL: McGraw-Hill.

Larm, M., B. Elmhagen, S. M. Granquist, E. Brundin and A. Angerbjörn (2018) The role of wildlife tourism in conservation of endangered species: Implications of safari tourism for conservation of the Arctic Fox in Sweden. *Human Dimensions of Wildlife*, 23(3), 257–272.

Lasswell, H. D. (1963) *The Future of Political Science.* New York: Prentice Hall.

Lott, D. and M. McCoy (1995) Asian rhinos *Rhinoceros Unicornis* on the run? Impact of tourist visits on one population. *Biological Conservation*, 73(1), 23–26.

Michie, S., M. M. van Stralen and R. West (2011) The behaviour change wheel: A new method for characterising and designing behaviour change interventions. *Implementation Science*, 6(1), 42. https://doi.org/10.1186/1748-5908-6-42.

Morrison, C., C. Simpkins, J. G. Castley and R. C. Buckley (2012) Tourism and the conservation of critically endangered frogs. *PLoS ONE*, 7(9), e43757. https://doi.org/10.1371/journal.pone.0043757.

Muntifering, J. R. (ed.) (2019) *Large-Scale Black Rhino Conservation in North-West Namibia.* Windhoek, Namibia: Venture Publication.

Muntifering, J. R., S. Clark, W. L. Linklater, S. !Uri-≠Khob, E. Hebach, J. Cloete, S. Jacobs and A. T. Knight (2020) Lessons from a wildlife tourism cooperative: The Namibian black rhinoceros case. *Annals of Tourism Research*, 82, 102918. https://doi.org/10.1016/j.annals.2020.102918.

Muntifering, J. R., W. L. Linklater, S. G. Clark, S. !Uri-≠Khob, J. K. Kasaona, K. /Uiseb, P. Du Preez, K. Kasaona, P. Beytell, J. Ketji, B. Hambo, M. A. Brown, C. Thouless, S. Jacobs and A. T. Knight (2017) Harnessing values to save the rhinoceros: Insights from Namibia. *Oryx*, 51(1), 98–105.

Muntifering, J. R., W. L. Linklater, R. Naidoo, S. !Uri-≠Khob, P. D. Preez, P. Beytell, S. Jacobs and A. T. Knight (2019) Sustainable close encounters: Integrating tourist and animal behaviour to improve rhinoceros viewing protocols. *Animal Conservation*, 22(2), 189–197.

Muthen, L. K. and B. O. Muthen (2002) How to use a Monte Carlo study to decide on sample size and power. *Structural Equation Modeling*, 9, 599–620.

Naidoo, R., L. C. Weaver, R. W. Diggle, G. Matongo, G. Stuart-Hill and C. Thouless (2016) Complementary benefits of tourism and hunting to communal conservancies in Namibia. *Conservation Biology*, 30(3), 628–638.

Nakagawa, S. and H. Schielzeth (2013) A general and simple method for obtaining R^2 from generalized linear mixed-effects models. *Methods in Ecology and Evolution*, 4(2), 133–142.

Penteriani, V., J. López-Bao, C. Bettega, F. Dalerum, M. del Mar Delgado, K. Jerina, I. Kojola, M. Krofel and A. Ordiz (2017) Consequences of brown bear viewing tourism: A review. *Biological Conservation*, 206, 169–180.

Preisler, H. K., A. A. Ager and M. J. Wisdom (2005) Statistical methods for analysing responses of wildlife to human disturbance. *Journal of Applied Ecology*, 43(1), 164–172.

Ranaweerage, E., D. Ashoka, G. Ranjeewa and K. Sugimoto (2015) Tourism-induced disturbance of wildlife in protected areas: A case study of free ranging elephants in Sri Lanka. *Global Ecology and Conservation*, 4, 625–631.

Sandbrook, C. and S. Semple (2006) The rules and the reality of mountain gorilla *Gorilla beringei beringei* tracking: How close do tourists get? *Oryx*, 40(4), 428–433.

Shutt, K., M. Heistermann, A. Kasim, A. Todd, B. Kalousova, I. Profosouva, K. Petrzelkova et al. (2014) Effects of habituation, research and ecotourism on faecal glucocorticoid metabolites in wild western lowland gorillas: Implications for conservation management. *Biological Conservation*, 172, 72–79.

Stankowich, T. (2008) Ungulate flight responses to human disturbance: A review and meta-analysis. *Biological Conservation*, 141(9), 2159–2173.

Stewart, G. B., C. Coles and A. Pullin (2005) Applying evidence-based practice in conservation management: Lessons from the first systematic review and dissemination projects. *Biological Conservation*, 126(2), 270–278.

Sutherland, W., A. Pullin, P. Dolman and T. Knight (2004) The Need for Evidence-Based Conservation. *Trends in Ecology & Evolution*, 19(6), 305–308.

Trathan, P. N., J. Forcada, R. Atkinson, R. H. Downie and J. R. Shears (2008) Population assessments of Gentoo penguins (*Pygoscelis Papua*) breeding at an important Antarctic tourist site, Goudier Island, Port Lockroy, Palmer Archipelago, Antarctica. *Biological Conservation*, 141(12), 3019–3028.

APPENDIX A

Rhino HID Form

PRE-VIEWING CHARACTERISTICS							
Name:			**Date:**		**Location:**		
Zone:	1	2	3	4	**Purpose:**	Tourism	Patrol
Number of Observers:	Total	**Number of cars?**		**Wind?**	Strong	Breezy	Calm

When you first spot the rhino....						
Type of sighting:	Vehicle	Foot	**Other animals present?**			
Time of sighting:		**Habitat:**	Riverbed	Plain	Steep slope	Gentle slope	Hill Top
Initial Behaviour:	Lying	Standing	Walking	Browsing	Running	**Rhino Group Size:**
Wind Direction (Observers were....from Rhino):		Upwind	Downwind	Crosswind	Swirling	
GPS Datum/coordinates: WGS84 / decimal degrees		**GPS:**			

When you arrive at the closest distance to rhino....	
Use your watch	***Use your binoculars***
	Disturbance level at arrival: Unaware Aware
What time did you stop approaching?	Displaced
What time did the rhino become aware?	**Rhino's name:**
What time was the rhino displaced?	**Rhino's condition:**
Total time spent at closest distance:	**Final Disturbance level:** Unaware Aware Displaced
Use your rangefinder	**Why was the rhino displaced?**
The closest distance to rhino was:	Wind change noise airplane other animals unknown
Distance the rhino ran: out of sight	Other reason for displacement?

Figure 14A.1   Rhino HID form

15. Consultation approaches in sustainable tourism
Carolin Lusby

INTRODUCTION

Consultation is often needed during studies of sustainability. Consultation approaches, just like the situations a researcher might be asked to consult, can be extremely diverse. Just consider the following examples:

- Juan is the owner and manager of a beautiful ecolodge in Southeast Asia. After growing his lodge for two decades, he is looking into getting his property certified so future guests can easily see the authenticity of his sustainable efforts.
- Indian Rock is a small village with 400 residents in Central America. The community boasts ancient Mayan ruins, a nature preserve and culture. It wants to attract tourists to stay in the community and participate in a niche market of sustainable tourism called community-based tourism. This way, they hope to support local livelihoods and conserve their culture and way of life, as well as the environment around them.
- A region in Southern Europe is looking into becoming a sustainable destination. Tourism leaders and local politicians are eager to know what the steps are to make a destination sustainable and market these efforts to future travelers.

In each of these scenarios, sustainable tourism research is needed. The approaches of the researcher of course, are highly different in each of the circumstances to include local realities, and yet there are steps that are universally valid. In this chapter we examine the approach to consultation, levels of participation of the various stakeholders in the consultation, and tips on how to consult with them. The researcher could be a paid consultant, a student or another practitioner.

STAKEHOLDER ANALYSIS

One of the first and most vital steps a researcher would take, regardless of the type of client, is identifying, analyzing and evaluating which stakeholders have an interest, influence and say in the project. Anyone who is directly or indirectly influenced by the project (positively or negatively) is a stakeholder. A stakeholder is also anyone who can influence the outcome. This means stakeholders can come from various backgrounds, including individuals, private or nonprofit organizations, communities, politicians, religious or conservation influencers and the like.

A primary stakeholder is anyone that is *directly* or *immediately* impacted by the action, be that in a positive or negative way. A secondary stakeholder is *indirectly* or *gradually* impacted by the action. A key stakeholder is someone with significant influence on the organization (Byrd, 2007).

To identify stakeholders, first think of anyone that has an *interest or influence* in the project. After you brainstorm that list, ask the identified stakeholders and anyone else who is active in the community in this area of interest for other contacts. We will also identify some tools to create a list of stakeholders.

STAKEHOLDER ENGAGEMENT HISTORY 101

- It is said that discussion of legal issues in regards to the duties corporations have to their stakeholders formed the beginning of stakeholder awareness in the 1930s.
- Over the next years other constituents including health and safety were added.
- In the 1980s a book by Edward Freeman (Freeman, 1984) joined the idea with management.
- Corporate Social Responsibility (CSR) became widely accepted in the 1990s and reshaped the way stakeholder thinking is viewed.

According to the International Finance Corporation (IFC, 2020), stakeholder engagement involves various steps including:

- Stakeholder Identification and Analysis
- Information Disclosure
- Stakeholder Consultation
- Negotiation and Partnerships
- Grievance Management
- Stakeholder Involvement in Project Monitoring
- Reporting to Stakeholders
- Management Functions

For a project to be successful, it is imperative that stakeholders are identified and involved as appropriate. Why is stakeholder analysis important? A failure to engage and consult key players at the early stages of a sustainable tourism project could lead to catastrophic outcomes and failure of the project. Main stakeholders can be brainstormed through a tool called *impact zoning* (IFC, 1998) which requires four steps, as listed by IFC:

1. Draw a sketch map of the key design components of the project, both on and off site, that may give rise to local environmental or social impacts (e.g. the project site; ancillary infrastructure such as roads, power lines, and canals; sources of air, water, and land pollution).
2. Identify the broad impact zones for each of these components (e.g. the area of land, air and water pollution receptors, etc.).
3. After identifying and mapping broad stakeholder groups, overlay those groups over the impact zones.
4. Through consultation with relevant stakeholder representatives, verify which groups are potentially affected by which impacts. This exercise may be performed more efficiently by using aerial photographs.

STAKEHOLDER MAPPING

Once the main stakeholders are identified, it is important to analyze which are important to involve or manage. One of the techniques for stakeholder analysis is stakeholder mapping, in which stakeholders are plotted on a diagram featuring two variables: interest and influence. The diagram then has two axes, one horizontal and one vertical. In this matrix main stakeholders not only become easily visible, but also are rated according to their influence and interest. Stakeholder mapping should be used at the beginning of a new project, to get an overview for new initiatives, or when business environments or situations change.

Stakeholder mapping further allows you to understand relationships between your stakeholders. It helps to determine groups of stakeholders with the same interest. And lastly it allows you to evaluate the strength of each stakeholder relationship.

The process of stakeholder mapping should be done by a diverse group of people from various industries and backgrounds and can be achieved within one to two hours. Groupmap (2020) suggests six main steps to take in stakeholder mapping:

1. Scope of the project
2. Brainstorm an inclusive list of stakeholders
3. Position the stakeholders on the map in regards to both influence and interest
4. Rate the level of support (adversary to advocate) of each stakeholder
5. Action Plan by assigning responsibilities and deciding actions and timeframes
6. Share the outcomes.

The resulting stakeholder matrix then has four quadrants, showing what type of action is appropriate based on perceived level of interest and influence, as can be seen in Table 15.1.

Table 15.1   Stakeholder mapping matrix based on interest and influence

Satisfy/Communicate (High Influence, Low Interest)	**Manage/Engage** (High Influence, High Interest)
Monitor (Low Influence, Low Interest)	**Keep Informed** (Low Influence, High Interest)

This table makes it visually very easy to see in what way to engage and include the various stakeholders. Other models also include variable salience, which assesses the degree to which an issue is important to the stakeholder. Yet others include variables such as urgency, legitimacy and perceived power to classify stakeholders (Mitchell et al., 1997). Community profiles help establish current and future conditions in a situation. They include amenities, population demographics and economic history.

Interests and issues should be identified with each stakeholder. This could be as easy as asking the following questions: What is important to you? Why? Professor Neely from the Cranfield School of Management in the UK developed a SWANS (Stakeholder Wants and Needs) and OWANS (Organizations Wants and Needs) approach to examine the wants and needs of the organization versus its stakeholders. This may be useful to include in your analysis. This model then helps to identify what processes and strategies to put in place to engage with these stakeholders.

STAKEHOLDER ENGAGEMENT

Stakeholder engagement encompasses understanding stakeholder views, consulting them, and being accountable to them. It also means incorporating the information gained from them in your decisions. In that sense, stakeholder engagement is about building long-term collaborative relationships with your stakeholders, and the ways in which you keep in contact with them.

Stakeholder engagement can best be understood on a continuum from least to most engaged. Based on the needs of your stakeholders, the type of project, and impacts of the project, stakeholder engagement could be as simple and unengaged as informing your stakeholders of what you are doing, or consulting them for information about a project. It could also mean involving or engaging your stakeholders, which would be a middle of the road approach. And on the more engaging end of the spectrum would be to allow a stakeholder to make final decisions regarding your project (see Box 15.1).

BOX 15.1 INFORM, CONSULT, INVOLVE, COLLABORATE, EMPOWER

Inform: Stakeholders are given clear information about the aim, solutions and problems of the project. It is one-way communication without the opportunity for input.

Consult: This allows stakeholders to give input or feedback on the information presented. This could be ongoing or a one-time activity through for example online surveys.

Involve: While not involved in final decision making, stakeholder concerns and desired outcomes are taken into consideration by working directly with stakeholders throughout the process.

Collaborate: You achieve consensus on what needs to be done at each step of the process by collaborating with stakeholders in decision-making.

Empower: This level of engagement is very rarely used. You allow stakeholders to make final decisions. This could be done through voting ballots or a referendum.

Looking again at Table 15.1, stakeholders that place in the 'satisfy' column would then be at the lower engagement side of the spectrum, and informing or consulting might be a sufficient level of involvement.

Table 15.2   Stakeholder consultation techniques based on level of engagement

Inform	Consult	Empower/Involve
Newsletter	Surveys	Advisory Board
Briefing	Focus Groups	Committees
Meetings	Interviews	Voting
Hotline	Public Workshops	Polling
Factsheet	Comment forms (suggestion box)	Focus Group
Website		
Presentation		

What exactly can you do to keep your stakeholders engaged and informed? Table 15.2 gives some example ideas for each level of engagement.

HIERARCHY OF STAKEHOLDER INVOLVEMENT

Sustainable tourism, by definition, has various social, economic and environmental objectives. As such, the process is multidisciplinary and social. Stakeholders hence come from various backgrounds and perspectives and participation of vital stakeholders is key to a successful project. Pretty (1995) developed a hierarchy to explain stakeholder participation.

Levels of participation range from *passive* (only being told what has been decided) to *self-mobilization* (participating independently and keeping control). In between are *participation by consultation*, in which stakeholders are consulted by answering questions, but do not share in decision-making; and *functional* (participation in groups to meet established objectives) and *interactive* participation (analyzing and developing action plans). Stakeholder engagement is highly situational and depends on the outcomes of the stakeholder mapping process (Pretty, 1995). Besides these considerations, there are also various local and international standards that dictate stakeholder engagement and need to be considered. Table 15.3 summarizes some of these international standards.

Table 15.3   Knowledge box: international standards for stakeholder engagement

UN Global COMPACT	Commits signatory companies to support and respect the protection of internationally recognized human rights, labor and environmental standards
FTSE4 Good Index Series	Benchmark indices for socially responsible behavior
Global Reporting Initiative	A comprehensive set of social, economic, environmental, and governance indicators, including a sub-set on stakeholder engagement
Dow Jones Sustainability Index	Sets standards for corporate governance and stakeholder engagement, including corporate codes of conduct and public reporting

CONSULTATION TECHNIQUES

There are a plethora of consultation techniques available for you as a researcher, including but not limited to: workshops, focus groups, panels, surveys, interviews, town hall meetings and other participatory tools. Table 15.4 summarizes the main tools, when to use them and the advantages and disadvantages of each approach.

Town Hall Meetings

Town hall meetings are a great tool to get input from a community of people. Find a space and time that is natural and comfortable for the community. Many traditional or indigenous communities might already have a set time and space for daily meetings. If so, it makes sense to align with those.

Table 15.4   *Summary of consultation techniques with advantages and disadvantages*

Technique	Use when you want to	Advantages/Disadvantages
Town Hall Meeting	Reach a large audience simultaneously Provide information and get feedback	Advantages: Cheap and quick, shows your willingness to be open, allows you to reach large number of people at one time Disadvantages: Some people might not feel comfortable speaking (see section on gender), some groups or individuals might be very vocal and hijack the meeting
Focus Groups	Gather baseline data Pilot test or gain feedback on an output Monitor social performance of an operation Identify stakeholder views	Advantages: Give detailed information on feelings and perceptions of groups, more time and cost effective than individual interviews, can provide broad information due to group interaction Disadvantages: Small number of informants, participants might not be representative
Workshops	Rank/prioritize issues Involve stakeholders in thinking through a problem or issue Form relationships with stakeholders	Advantages: Increases sense of ownership by participants Builds relationships Disadvantages: Can be costly to organize Some relevant stakeholders may not be able to attend
Surveys	Monitor impacts Get an objective overview Gather data Identify stakeholder issues and needs of community	Advantages: Detailed data on an issue Anonymous feedback for maybe sensitive topics Widely accepted Disadvantages: Can be leading Takes time and resources to prepare Response rate can be low
Interviews	Allow stakeholders to speak confidentially Build relationships with specific stakeholders Identify issues of specific stakeholders	Advantages: Builds relationships Detailed info due to interpersonal communication Disadvantages: Not necessarily representative as it relies on self-report Time and resource intensive

Post flyers and spread the word inviting community members. Be sure the invitation also reaches members of the community that might be overlooked in some way. Town hall meetings are fantastic to get a pulse of what the needs and current situations of the community are, and where they want to go. Use clear and easy language. If you do not speak the language of the stakeholders, pick an interpreter you trust that the community accepts (preferably a known member of the community or someone that has credibility with them). Give space for members to express their opinions, but facilitate the discussion. It is a good idea to come up with a structured way to ask your questions and follow up on questions beforehand. In your facilitation, be aware of people who steal time and take over the talk, and also include members that might be shy to share. Town hall meetings are a good way to share your ideas, as well as seek input from all. Take good notes of the conversations. Before the town hall meeting is adjourned, make sure to communicate clearly what was decided on and what the timelines, responsibilities and next steps would be for each stakeholder. Then be sure to follow up with these commitments to build further trust with the community.

Things to consider when working with minority or indigenous groups are issues of gender and power. Who generally makes decisions regarding the community? How do women and/ or youth communicate their needs and ideas, if at all? How are meetings usually structured? Are there individuals who have credibility or generally lead meetings of the community? If so, it might be good to involve them to ensure people show up. Once your participants show up, work with the ones who are there. They are interested enough to carve time out of their lives, so engage them, instead of being preoccupied to reach a majority of the population.

Surveys

The idea of a survey is in essence to gather information and data about a group or groups of people. This group of people in research is called your *population*. The instrument is the tool that is developed to gather this information, which could be attitudes, characteristics, opinions, previous experiences and the like. Most often, questions are asked in a *closed-ended* fashion via a *written questionnaire*. This means that answer choices are predetermined and limited (such as Yes/No; disagree, agree, agree very much). That way, data can be quantified, input into a statistical software and analyzed.

In order to avoid having to ask everyone in your population, surveys are usually passed out to a carefully selected *sample* that is representative of the population. If your sample is not representative, it inhibits you from *generalizing* results to the bigger population. As such, great care needs to be taken when selecting your sample, or the people that will participate in your survey. Your *sample size* depends on the size of your population and how accurately your data will represent the population. Once you identify how many people to include in your sample, it is important to determine how you will select these individuals, to ensure that they are representative of the population as a whole. This process is called *probability sampling*, which means each member of the population has an equal chance (or probability – hence the name) of being selected. It includes four types: *simple random sampling, cluster sampling, systematic sampling* and *stratified sampling*. Using systematic sampling to sample 100 individuals out of a population of 1,000, you could create a random list of the 1,000 individuals by name and select each tenth person. Applying simple random sampling would mean you give every one of the 1,000 individuals a number and then use a random number generator (think: bingo or similar lotteries) to randomly select 100 numbers which will then make up your sample. *Nonprobability sampling* by comparison is conducted in a way in which not every individual has an equal chance of being selected, which means data are not generalizable to the entire population. This type of sampling is convenience based and could include individuals that are accessible at the time the research is done.

One of the big advantages of survey research is that it can easily be made anonymous, meaning responses cannot be traced back to a specific individual. In order to achieve that, any identifiers should be taken out of the survey (this also includes web links for online surveys, tracing back to a specific computer, etc.). This gives individuals the opportunity to freely voice their opinion without fear of repercussion. Data is markedly self-reported and as such might be subject to false memories or how the individual currently feels, at a specific point in time, which might be different in an hour.

Scales: When developing your instrument, it is important to think about what the purpose of the data is. This determines what kind of data to collect and in what way. There are four basic forms of measurement, called scales: nominal, ordinal, interval and ratio. In what way we measure, or in other words, what type of scale is applied, influences what kinds of statistical tests can be run. A *nominal scale* is the most restrictive and only allows us to use limited statistics, such as mode or percentages. Asking about hair color or gender are good examples of a nominal scale. An *ordinal scale* allows the researcher to expand the range of tests available, it helps determine more or less, but does not allow us to see by how much. An example of an ordinal type question would be: How was your flight with X Airlines? Better than expected, worse than expected or as expected? An *interval scale* is widely used in questionnaire research. It is defined by equal intervals between the degrees of attitudes. The most common is a Likert type scale, which measures attitudes in increments of equal distance to get an understanding of degrees of opinion. This allows the researcher to draw conclusions of how much individuals or groups differ in their attitudes and opinions. A ratio scale has an equal interval of measures and a true zero point, which allows us to calculate ratios. Height and weight are good examples of ratio scales, which allow the most comprehensive set of statistical analyses.

When developing your instrument, you need to consider that the instrument really measures what it intends to measure. This is called *validity*. This question has to do with what are valid measures for the construct that you are trying to measure. Validity is easily detectable, for example, on a scale that shows a 10 kilogram weight as measuring 20 kilograms. Anyone can see this is not a valid measure. But in social sciences this is harder to prove. If you want to measure self-esteem for example, what is a valid measure? If you think self-esteem is linked to assertiveness in speaking, and you only measure how assertive a person is, are your results valid? If you want to examine life satisfaction of a person, and you only ask about where they live, how much money they make, if they have insurance or work, are you really measuring their life satisfaction, or maybe just a similar related construct such as quality of life? Reporting on a person's socio-economic status without asking about income in some form would also be an invalid measure.

Reliability of your instrument refers to the fact that it can measure the same construct over and over and give the same result. A thermometer that shows different temperatures when held in boiling water three different times is not a reliable instrument. To test reliability a researcher can report test-retest statistics which show how reliable the questionnaire is. If you want to collect more detailed information with a richer or open-ended content, then interviews might be a better option and are discussed in more detail in the following section.

Interviews

If you want to collect more in-depth and complete information from a smaller group of stakeholders, an interview is preferred. As opposed to most surveys, interview questions can be *open-ended*, allowing for richer descriptions and data. Interviews can be either *structured* or *semi-structured*, depending on the flexibility in asking additional questions. Interviews are most commonly done one-on-one, either in-person or over the phone. In order to ensure that you answer all your research questions with your interview, an *interview guide* is usually developed beforehand to aid in the interviewing process. It is helpful to write down research questions and specific interview questions and follow-up questions you will ask for each of your research questions so you can make sure you have sufficient data. In order to assure credibility and trustworthiness of your data, it is recommended that you record your answers verbatim. Usually this is done by *tape recording* and later *transcribing* word by word the entire interview. Once you have all interviews on paper you can look for keywords, themes and compare answers. When writing up your results, use the terms your interviewees used. It is useful to build a rapport with the participant beforehand and get written consent to record and collect data. It should also be made clear how data will be used and in what ways privacy will be ensured. How will you keep data *confidential*? Where will you store it and how can you assure that participants stay *anonymous*?

Other things to consider are interview location, to minimize outside noise and make the interviewee and yourself comfortable. Most commonly a neutral location is chosen. Your study subjects should be representative, and sampling techniques should reflect that. In some cases, getting opposing or extreme points of view might be an advantage, and as such a form of purposive sampling could be applied. An important aspect of interviews to consider is that you as the researcher are a part of the research process. Your observations, way of speaking and listening all influence the information collected far more than in a written questionnaire that is passed out for example. As such, be cognizant of your own views and presumptions and stay as open as possible. Be aware of your subjects' culture. Is the culture permitted to speak freely of a certain topic? Are there beliefs or values that might hinder the collection of relevant data? Interviews can also be done in groups in rare circumstances. In the following section a special type of group interview is discussed.

Focus Groups

Focus groups are in essence interviews done with several people at the same time. However, focus groups differ from merely being a group interview, in that the interaction between participants is an integral part of the process. As such, focus groups consist of purposefully selected participants who are asked certain questions in a facilitated discussion within a group setting, and hence can influence each other. The role of a skillful facilitator becomes vitally more important to capture all viewpoints and voices, avoid conflict, and synthesize data. Using visual aids, sticky notes and other tools to keep participants engaged is helpful. The facilitator, just like the interviewer, should be neutral and preferably a third party. Focus groups can also be held online, which is more cost effective and allows participation by individuals who might be physically far apart. It is also more anonymous, which could mean participants feel more comfortable to genuinely speak. The evaluator of the focus group ensures participants that anonymity is preserved. This person is also tasked with asking the questions and follow-up questions, keeping the discussion on topic, making sure all are involved and the focus group is recorded. As such, it is recommended that two people facilitate the focus group. One researcher will moderate the group and the other researcher will record the focus group, also observing body language, themes, mood and other details that might help to get a deeper understanding.

First determine what information you want to collect. What is it that you want to know? Then determine the number of focus groups and the number of participants in a focus group. You want enough participants to encourage a richness of data, and yet keep the number small enough to allow for meaningful conversation; this means usually between 6 and 13 participants. Based on what you want to know, your participants might be selected because of opposing or diverse viewpoints or backgrounds (this sometimes is called maximum variation sampling), or they can be purposefully homogeneous. When you recruit participants, make sure to mention the length and purpose of the focus group, what is expected of them and if participation will have any rewards associated with it. When drafting your questions consider their applicability to all participants. Your questions should be open-ended to encourage rich responses.

Focus groups collect qualitative data and, just like interviews, are an interpersonal method of data collection. This method is preferred when information about perceptions, attitudes and subjective understandings are collected. Data should be tape recorded, transcribed and then analyzed. Ethical considerations for this method include collecting informed consent from participants before engaging in data collection.

Workshops

Workshops are a great way to engage stakeholders and can be used for a variety of purposes including to: ensure buy-in, analyze results, prioritize audiences or steps, validate findings, or to better understand the problem. Workshops are similar to focus groups in that the idea is that of group interaction. As such, the number of participants should be carefully selected to ensure enough diversity to receive the richness and depth of data needed. However, a maximum number of 60 participants should be considered, to allow all to participate in a meaningful way.

Before running the workshop, you should run a situation analysis, program and audience analysis. Planning for your workshop can take several weeks, while the actual workshop might only be one or two days. Based on this information, you set your goals and objectives of the workshop, assign tasks and responsibilities, and identify stakeholders to invite, based on what perspective or information they can provide. The next step is setting your budget, as this influences the venue and amount of people to invite among others. Then choose your duration (one to three days usually), dates and locate an appropriate venue. Draft the agenda for the workshop by keeping in mind who should speak, open or close the event; when people will eat and arrive; and any religious or food preferences or other obligations. When conducting the workshop, draft discussions and activities to gather the information needed. Activities depend on the purpose and can range from small group tasks, mapping, flow diagrams, ranking, sorting, brainstorming, partner discussions, stories, case studies, harvesting, and many more. It is important to try and include a number of these different activities to ensure active participation of all the participants. Once your data is collected, your next step will be to analyze your data. The following section discusses this process in more depth.

ANALYZING DATA

Interviews, focus groups and workshops most often result in qualitative data. After transcribing your interview, you can look for themes by comparing each interview transcript to the others in response to each question. This process allows you to code the spoken, by ascribing themes to each answer, and then organizing the themes in order, with suitable sub-themes. Then data are triangulated by going back to the literature or finding other points of data to validate findings, such as research reports, expert opinions, etc.

Surveys and closed-ended interviews result in *quantitative data*. These need to be input into a statistical software program and can be analyzed. While inputting you code the specific answer, turning words into numbers in essence (as in 1-Yes, 2-No). Several statistical tests can be run including t tests to compare two groups, ANOVA to compare multiple groups, and regressions to test relationships between a dependent and one or more independent variables. One issue to consider when running your tests, is where to set your confidence level. Most studies choose a P value of 0.5 (or 5%), meaning that they are willing to accept a 5% chance of being wrong about the hypothesis, or in other words that the null hypothesis is correct. Another way to interpret the p value is the point at which your results are statistically significant. So any relationship observed that has a p value of greater than 0.05 would be dismissed as insignificant. When reporting, data are usually presented in an aggregated form, ensuring the confidentiality of individual data and the anonymity of respondents, though including anonymous quotes/statements from participants can add qualitatively to your analysis. The next section will cover these and other ethical considerations in more detail.

ETHICAL CONSIDERATIONS

There are a variety of state and federal laws that might apply to your specific research. One of the first and most important steps is to understand these laws and what they mean for your research. One of the primary ethical concerns in collecting data from human subjects is the privacy and protection of personal data of the research participants (confidentiality). Privacy refers to measures to protect the person, such as how they will be selected and contacted and what information will be asked. Confidentiality refers to how the data is handled, who has access to it, and how it is protected to ensure identifiable data is not revealed. As such, the European Union in 2018 implemented the General Data Protection Regulation (GDPR). This law applied to any company or enterprise that collects and processes data of European Union citizens and non-compliance could result in heavy fines. Under this regulation, data processers need to ensure that collected data is private, that data is collected only based on consent, that it remains anonymous and that pseudonyms are used when needed. These principles highlight some general ethical issues and considerations when collecting data. Some of these have been briefly addressed in the prior sections describing methods. One of the first considerations is the importance of the research. In other words, your research questions should be important enough to justify the time and inconvenience your research participants will commit themselves to. Risks and benefits need to be clearly explained to the participants. Participation is voluntary, no one can be forced. Participants need to be informed about the purpose, duration and processes of the study. All of this is usually done through an informed consent form, which is collected directly from the participants before data collection. It is also common that an independent review panel approve the study for its ethical considerations, ensuring that participants are not subjected to physical or emotional risks, and that all is done to minimize risks in general. In the United States this is often done through the Institutional Review Board (IRB). Participants need to be respected, which also means the right to withdraw from the study or to not participate. Special considerations also need to be made for especially vulnerable groups such as children, ethnic minorities or tribal communities which often haven special protective laws in place.

GENDER/YOUTH AND STAKEHOLDER CONSULTATION

In a world where social responsibility is an important business concept, hearing the voices of all becomes vitally important, so that the needs and interests of diverse groups can be addressed. As such, hearing from groups that might not be the most powerful, loudest or most aggressive to voice their opinions is important in stakeholder analysis. Often assumptions regarding the research process might make the research inadvertently exploitative rather than inclusive. Assuming that communities are homogeneous might be one of those dangerous assumptions. For example, women play different roles than men in most societies and your project might impact them differently than men. They also have different access to financial and other resources such as education. Sometimes opportunities and control or power are limited for women.

Including these groups can pose certain challenges. In some cultures, women might not feel comfortable speaking their opinion in a mixed group of men and women. In these cases, organizing women-only focus groups or workshops might be an important step. Care should be taken that the results of these workshops/focus groups get communicated and considered equally when writing up final results. This could be done by reporting data by gender as well. When administering a survey, a systematic or stratified sampling method could be used to assure you select equal numbers of female and male participants. In one traditional community I worked with in Brazil, only men met daily to decide on important issues facing the community. Women stayed at home. Men also were the ones to reach out and communicate with outside agents such as consultant researchers to aid the community. Women, especially older ones, did not learn Portuguese, but rather spoke only their native language. By virtue of that, getting direct input from these women proved to be difficult, as translators were mainly men of the community, perpetuating the traditional power structures. Women were playing different roles than men. This demonstrates differences in access to education, resources and power. Women especially might need to be assured that their responses are confidential and anonymous so as to allow more confidence in speaking freely. Also, methods used might have to be adjusted, such as using a facilitator that women feel open and comfortable with, and asking questions in a way that allows women to apply their skills and ideas. A facilitator could ask specific questions about how the project would impact women and men. The workshop could also be structured so that after a plenary session with all, smaller group discussions could be organized for specific groups such as youth, men, women and elderly. In that sense, especially when working in an international context, it is important to have a deep understanding of the culture. Are women free to attend a workshop outside of their home? If so, at what times are they freer of obligations? What are cultural norms for how women behave and speak? Are there locations that are naturally comfortable for them? Will there be repercussions if it is thought that they spoke to someone perceived as coming from the outside?

Youth have generally been overlooked as important stakeholders as well. Engaging youth might take many shapes and, as is the case with women, could also be done through separate meetings and workshops. One way to assure adequate representation of age groups could be through stratification of your participation on the basis of generation.

In conclusion, stakeholder engagement is vital for the success of sustainable tourism projects. Stakeholders should be clearly identified and the extent of their involvement outlined based on the principles covered earlier in this chapter. A stakeholder matrix will inform how and to what extent stakeholders will be involved. Once your key stakeholders have been identified, a suitable technique to gather information from them needs to be selected. Research methods such as focus groups, interviews, surveys and workshops are all vital techniques to consult and involve stakeholders. Special attention needs to be given to ethical considerations such as adhering to local and state laws; ensuring privacy and confidentiality; informing participants about the purpose, scope and length of the study; and the risks and benefits associated with participation. The study should be reviewed by an independent third party for ethical issues. The collection of informed consent is another vital step in ethical research practices. Researchers also need to consider vulnerable or historically underrepresented groups carefully to avoid implicit bias. Lastly, once data has been collected and analyzed, it needs to be presented to the appropriate channels so that the results are indeed used in decision-making. These channels might include local policy makers, politicians, special interest groups or tourism organizations.

REFERENCES

Byrd, E. T. (2007) Stakeholders in sustainable tourism development and their roles: Applying stake-holder theory to sustainable tourism development. *Tourism Review*, 62(2), 6–13.

Freeman, E. (1984) *Strategic Management: A Stakeholder Approach*. Cambridge: Cambridge University Press.

Groupmap (2020) Stakeholder Analysis. Accessed March 20, 2020 at: https://www.groupmap.com/map-templates/stakeholder-analysis/.

IFC (1998) *Doing Better Business Through Effective Consultation and Disclosure*. Washington, DC: IFC.

IFC (2020) Stakeholder Engagement IFC. Accessed March 18, 2020 at: https://www.ifc.org/wps/wcm/connect/affbc005-2569-4e58-9962-280c483baa12/IFC_StakeholderEngagement.pdf?MOD=AJPERES&CVID=jkD13-p.

Mitchell, R., Agle, B. and Wood, D. (1997) Toward a theory of stakeholder identification and salience: Defining the principle of who and what really counts. *Academy of Management Review*, 22(4), 853–886.

Pretty, J. (1995) Participatory learning for sustainable agriculture. *World Development*, 23(8), 1247–1263.

PART III

BALANCING OVERTOURISM AND UNDERTOURISM: VISITOR MANAGEMENT IN PRACTICE

16. A research strategy to understand what biophysical and social conditions are appropriate and acceptable in tourism destinations

Stephen F. McCool

INTRODUCTION

High visitor use levels have become the curse of many, but not all, tourism destinations in the world. One is only a click away, it seems, from rueful stories of how destinations, whether the great cities of Europe, the remote destinations of the Americas or Asia, or the unique landscapes of northern Europe have become over-run it seems by those who have come to visit. Whether it is historical cityscapes, culturally important monuments, diverse wildlife habitat, or uninhabited areas, tourists (and many of them) are already there. And while the sheer number of these tourists may be both overwhelming and surprising, it's their behavior and impacts that may be the most difficult aspect of their presence.

The effects of tourists have long been well known in the academic literature (e.g., see Allen et al., 1988; Ap, 1990; Mathieson and Wall, 1982; Pizam, 1978 for frequently cited early examples). Citations of research and commentary concerning impacts appear with relative frequency in that literature. This literature has included negative effects on the environment, society and economics and has been examined at a variety of scales. The effects of high use have been recently, for example, examined by the European Union's Policy Department for Structural and Cohesion Policies (European Union, 2018) and other scientists (for example, Hadinejad et al., 2019). These negative effects include impacts to resident quality of life, the environment, and impacts on economies. These impacts occur worldwide in cities like Amsterdam, Barcelona, and Venice but also in or near protected areas such as Yellowstone, Iguacu, Plitvice Lakes, Kruger, and the Great Barrier Reef, where visitation has risen to not only high levels, but rapidly.

Not all managers of destination sites and protected areas are faced with the challenge of dealing with tourism visitation, but those in charge of the most popular, and the most politically important ones are. Often, the relatively unknown sites have low or stable visitation rates, but still need to prepare for that one event, such as an Instagram photo, that may propel them to fame. For example, pop singer Justin Bieber's setting of Fjaðrárgljúfur, a canyon in Iceland, for a video caused such an instant dramatic rise in visitation to the canyon that it was closed to protect the ecosystem there.[1]

And then there are small rural communities the world over that by choice or accident, either have lost their primary industry or don't have any, and have turned to tourism for jobs, income or cultural preservation. For these communities, tourism development poses a special problem because they are particularly vulnerable to socio-cultural impacts. For them, the question of appropriate social and biophysical conditions is both important and thorny. Tourism, based on the cultural ecosystem services that are available in a natural protected area (Roux et al., 2020) may employ many people in lodging, guiding and other service industries, but may have many negative impacts to the same local culture and environment, because tourism may result in negative impact to them such as prostitution, drugs, and commodification of culture, congestion or competition for social or recreational sites.

Such challenges stem from a wide variety of sources – shifts in demand, popular social media, the flightiness of human populations – but others are functions of the unpreparedness of managers of destinations, whether cities or protected areas: an almost total focus on gaining foreign exchange, lack of a vision, strategy, or management plan, lack of transfer of knowledge or poor or no technical capacity to manage tourists, lack of funding, the type of problem and so on. And while these are important, and often immediate issues the current day managers face, they almost surely arise from earlier decisions, whether explicit or implicit, on how tourism was defined as an economic activity.

The COVID-19 crisis of 2020 served to highlight these challenges. The coronavirus served to accentuate the connected nature of our economies, cultures, tourism behavior, and lack of knowledge. It underscored not only how interdependent our tourism challenges have become but also the change, uncertainty, and complexity we in the tourism field face. Researchers are particularly challenged to come up with responses that are relevant to real world needs, that will help people, and that has implications for policy and management. Finally, these two trends – increasing tourism and the COVID-19 crisis – emphasized the complexity and uncertainty we face in the world today. We will need to better understand the complex nature of the challenge in the post COVID-19 world as we recover and rebuild our economies.

In this chapter, I propose a research strategy to deal with appropriate conditions, whether biological or social by first defining this problem, and taking some time to do so, because understanding the problem, which we rarely do, is the key to developing a research strategy and tactics to its resolution. I focus mostly on the strategic component of research, the *why* and the *what*, and less about the *how*, the specific research methodologies, because, (1) that is my strength, academically, and (2) there are other chapters in this book that deal with the *how*. One is not better than the other, but we, as a profession have emphasized, like many other arenas of economic endeavor, the *how* first.

For example, one of the most important decisions we must make, whether urban or rural, concerns the appropriate or acceptable conditions on site. These are decisions that deal with such essential items as the amount and type of impacts on the biophysical conditions of the area – the impacts on soil, vegetation, wildlife, water, etc. There are decisions that impact the community itself, such as what vision it has for the next 20 years, or how its economy is structured or what role its specific culture may play in its vision. Or decisions that ultimately impact the tourists themselves, such as the number and behavior of other tourists present, or the impact of tourists on residents and what infrastructure the community builds to accommodate tourists. Or they may include even the perception of visitors on how responses to these questions affect the community or biophysical conditions. These topics have been well studied in various regions of the world, but the lessons learned have not necessarily been translated to other regions. *Importantly, these are decisions that are separate, in time and space, from how we manage tourists.*

After we have a better understanding of the problem, I then turn to a research strategy which I feel will lead to better tactics that will provide us with the quantitative and qualitative responses that will help managers of destinations deal with tourism.

This chapter is primarily written for researchers.[2] However, destination managers, whether those stewarding national parks or those marketing urban destinations should find the strategy useful in changing or establishing a new complementary research program to go along with marketing and management. Destination management cannot competently proceed without a research program tailored to the size, complexity and type of area nor the context in which it is situated. It simply cannot. Managing tourism is too complex and changing to forgo the important values at stake.

TOURISM MANAGEMENT PROBLEMS HAVE CHANGED FROM THE TAME TO THE WICKED

Our research has not been very helpful in changing policy and management (Weaver, 2013). Sure, we often know who our markets are, their size, where tourists live and socio-demographic characteristics; we know what messages seem to appeal to them, we understand (sometimes) how much they spend, the economic impacts on local economies, and where tourists go if they are on a tour. We know how long their trips are, and where they enter and leave the country. But do we really understand the product of tourism? (I was once told that the product of bus tours was the tour, not the important destinations tourists visited, the lessons they learned or the inspiration they stimulated.) Do we understand, or even ask the question, what does tourism sustain? (Making the connection between tourist spending and local high school graduation rates is exceedingly difficult for those in the tourism industry.) Do we ever ask the question why isn't all tourism sustainable or why this is a specialty market? (Don't we want big hotels to adopt environmentally sensitive practices?) Do we understand what the social and cultural impacts of tourism may be? Do we have a vision of what is to be produced by tourism marketing? (Is it the hike or the increased health from hiking?) Do we even know what marketing is? (Is it promotional literature or web pages or is it making connections between destinations and visitors?) And can we connect the social, economic, and environmental conditions on the ground with the experiences that visitors have?

We do a great job through our international tourism shows of connecting wholesalers with retailers. That is what we do well. But as researchers do *we* do our job well? (Do we study parts of a system or do we study the system as a whole?)

This chapter is about how we can make our science better and more relevant and resolve tourism management problems, particularly those that deal with appropriate conditions. It is about how we frame our challenges and how that affects our research strategies to resolve the questions above.

To examine this, we begin with how we look at tourism management challenges; in other words how our deep paradigms of research, even the way we scientists look at the world, affect how we frame strategies, and that by changing our paradigm we can make our research more relevant to the needs of tourism managers.

Tourism was initially framed as a tame problem. These are the kind of problems through which much of our conventional research has been framed. Tame problems are deeply underlain by assumptions that the world is Predictable, it is Linear, it is ultimately Understandable, and it is Stable (Kohl and McCool, 2016); this world can be termed PLUS. These assumptions are based on a Cartesian or Euclidean view of the world (Friedmann, 1993), that problems can be reduced to those that are measurable and solvable. They assume that we agree on objectives of tourism and cause–effect relationships. Such a view also assumed, for example, that tourism is a benign form of development; thus, everyone would want tourists to visit their community. A definition of tourism as a tame problem assumed that the more advertising or promotion that is invested, the more visitors will come to destinations. And thus, tourism research focused on such questions as: Does a brochure work? Does television advertising get us a sizable market? Can we get a good return on our investment? What would be useful sustainable tourism indicators? These questions focused primarily on 'how' tourism would be promoted and managed; but they did not emphasize 'why' tourism is being promoted.

But then, we began seeing people express concerns about or even rebel against tourism development. Research began finding people with reservations about tourism's social and environmental consequences. A field of literature developed around resident perceptions of tourism and the congestion and other negative impacts it may bring with it (Hadinejad et al., 2019 as a recent example).

This research led to recognizing that there were more difficult and complex questions related to tourism than originally thought but frequently asked: How do we provide opportunities for high quality visitor experiences and not negatively impact the heritage that tourism is based upon? Can we boost the tourism economy and yet ensure that there is little or no congestion? How do we promote our destination while maintaining residents' quality of life? Can increased tourism promote more equal income distribution while being sustainable? And more recently, how does the tourism industry recover and rebuild safely after the COVID-19 pandemic? How do we integrate tourism development with livelihoods and health and safety?

Rittel and Webber (1973) recognized that the type of these latter questions was not tame but *wicked*, where goals may be in dispute and cause–effect relationships may be unknown or in disagreement. Wicked problems, they suggested, have other characteristics, among them no conclusive answer, are connected with other problems, are ill-defined and have no definitive 'stopping rule' such that we know when we have solved them. Wicked problems are complex ones and the approaches to them are different from tame problems: there are no right or wrong answers just more or less useful ones, and wicked problems cannot be transformed into tame problems. *And these types of questions are not resolved through conventional planning and research tactics.* This has been realized for a long time *"To every complex question, there is a clear, simple solution ... and it is wrong"* (attributed to H. L. Mencken) but not formulated until the 1970s. The presence of wicked problems was certainly not recognized in tourism until the early 2000s (the earliest uses in a tourism context I can find are Hall, 1998 and McCool, 1996).

Rittel and Webber (1973) argued that applying tame problem solutions to the wicked social problems we have today leads to failure and public discord:

> One reason the publics have been attacking the social professions, we believe, is that the cognitive and occupational styles of the professions—mimicking the cognitive style of science and the occupational style of engineering—have just not been successful on a wide array of social problems. The lay customers are complaining because planners and other professionals have not succeeded in solving the problems they claimed they could solve. (Rittel and Webber, 1973, p. 160)

Rittel and Webber and Allen and Gould (1986) argue that contemporary planning was designed to address tame problems but fails when confronted with wicked problems. I believe that tourism research is faced with the same conclusion: that the approach to doing research needs to consider strategy as well as the tactics we have conventionally used in our work.

A different set of assumptions underlie wicked problems than tame ones. These are that the world is Dynamic, Impossible to completely understand, Complex (for example a little bit of change in one variable may cause a lot of change in another, and connections between cause and effect may be loose) and Ever-changing (see Kohl and McCool, 2016). In short, wicked problems occur in a DICE world. Simplistic solutions don't work for wicked problems (Head and Alford, 2015).

Thus, a tourism manager functions in an era and place of incredible complexity, an immense uncertainty and enormous wickedness. While we seem to be sure that the more the promotion reaches our potential market, the more the market responds positively, we may be surprised by the antagonism generated locally by those for whose benefit we thought we were doing the promotion. We have a lot of parts to this system, but now we are unsure what the outcomes will be. Surprises happen. We have a wicked problem on our hands.

One of the worst things we can do is approach a wicked problem with the methodologies that are appropriate only for tame problems. Those methodologies work well for tame problems, which are easy problems to address because they are well defined and most likely have homogeneous constituencies. But the resolution to wicked problems requires people with different interests to settle on an agreement which may be difficult to build.

So, how do we move forward?

There are four parts to the response to this question: (1) we understand the research question, and we do that by (2) appreciating that tourism development is a wicked problem, (3) using systems thinking to help us resolve wicked problems, and (4) holding or constructing a vision for a tourism destination.

We face wicked problems and complex challenges every day, in both our personal life, such as a surprise traffic jam on our way to work, and in our professional life, such as being late to our meeting at work for how to reduce congestion at the city center!

The response to complexity is to act on three fronts: (1) recognize that tourism management challenges, and therefore research, deal with wicked problems, (2) engage this complexity by recognizing that thinking in systems ways can help provide more useful research, and (3) work with tourism managers, scientists and the public in developing a vision for the site, whether urban destinations or remote protected areas. These three areas help form the context for the problem statement, and as Morris and Martin (2009, p. 157) note, in the context of sustainability:

> these approaches are as much about 'problem finding' and 'problem exploring' as they are about problem solving. Our contention is that learners cannot deal with the wicked problems of sustainability without learning to think and act systemically.

Ultimately, this is why, in a book that is a research handbook, we spend time, in this chapter, discussing the nature of the problem, because if we do not, we will frame the problem inappropriately as a tame problem when it is really a wicked problem.

USING SYSTEMS THINKING

Systems thinking, Senge (1990) tells us, is a way of thinking about the 'Whole'. The whole is the purpose or function of a system. A system is composed of (a) parts, (b) relationships among parts, and (c) delays in those relationships. Each system is a self-organizing entity that is embedded in other systems and itself is the context for other systems. The entity has a purpose. A collection of items is not necessarily a system if the items are not related to each other. The purpose is an emergent property, a property that does not exist at smaller scales. An automobile for example is a complex system whose emergent property is transportation; that emergent property does not exist in a collection of items that may make up the system, such as wheels, seats, and engines when they are collected and are lying on the garage floor.

BOX 16.1 HOW A RESEARCH STRATEGY IS LIKE A NEW YORK CITY BROADWAY OR A LONDON WEST END MUSICAL

There can be much in common between research strategy and musicals. Just think about it. To be successful, like the popular and powerful musical *Hamilton* (Alexander Hamilton was a founding father of the USA), the writer had to have some kind of vision of what the story would be and how that story would impact audiences. He would have to think about how that story would be expressed, in words and then with music to go along with those words. He would have to have a set suitable to the story and to the limitations of theater. He would then have to recruit, audition and select actors, who would then have to be able to sing and dance. A theater would have to be found that could present the play. And finally, the musical must have the logistics designed and implemented, everything from the set and lighting to stage hands to selling tickets.

All these steps are designed to work together to enhance the story that is being told by the actors as they implement the musical. Everything is a function of a vision. That vision may come from anywhere, as simple as reading a book, but all oriented toward presenting the vision. Like a musical, there is a lot of creativity that goes into a research strategy.

So, what is the vision for your research?

When we think about the whole, we think about it first and about its function, and then only do we think about the parts. Research helps us determine the relationship between the part and the whole (see Box 16.1 for an example from the arts). Research is not focused on analyzing the part, but rather on synthesizing how the part relates to the whole. So, in tourism research we ask for example, how a promotional program will contribute to a more satisfying visitor experience or higher incomes for local people. We move to understanding how our research helps solve a complex problem. In the words of Gharajedaghi (2011, p. 335) systems thinking is about simplification:

> Systems thinking is the art of simplifying complexity. It is about seeing through chaos. We see the world as increasingly more complex and chaotic because we use inadequate concepts to explain it. When we understand something, we no longer see it as chaotic.

In this process we need to differentiate between a complicated problem and a complex system. Complicated systems are not necessarily complex systems. Complicated systems do have a lot of parts, but putting them together in the right way, say with algorithms and processes to produce something can be done. And the outcomes can be relatively predictable. Complex systems use parts too, but solutions in complex systems put parts together to build a product that is emergent. It is not possible to use the same algorithm in a complicated problem to apply to complex systems. Complicated problems are difficult to solve (sending a person to the moon requires a lot of parts), but the outcome is relatively predictable, but complex problems require a much higher order of thinking and the result is unpredictable (raising a child).

Reed (2006) indicates that a system approach involves three activities:

1. **Identify a System.** After all, not all things are systems. Some systems are simple and predictable, while others are complex and dynamic. Most human social systems are the latter.
2. **Explain the Behavior or Properties of the Whole System.** This focus on the whole is the process of synthesis. Ackoff says that analysis looks into things while synthesis looks out of things.
3. **Explain the Behavior or Properties** of the thing to be explained in terms of the role(s) or function(s) of the whole.

So, when we go to determine the appropriate biophysical and social conditions of a site, we first determine what the system components are, then we determine how the system as a whole works and then we look at the importance or relevance of the biophysical and social properties. We look at how those properties are affected by visitors and how visitors are affected by those properties.

Using systems thinking is one way to address complex systems and the wickedness of the problems presented by them. For example, a tourism destination is a complex system, in that it contains attractions, food, lodging, transportation (to the site and within the site at different scales), local people, guides, tour operators and other components as necessary. Each component of this system works together to produce a good visitor experience (an emergent property). When one or more components are not functioning well with other components (such as an unexpected delay in transportation, a botched lodging reservation, the closure of an attraction) the experience falters. The extent to which it falters may fall into a property of the tourism system termed resilience.

Complex problems are displayed graphically differently than complicated problem solving (Figure 16.1). In conventional problem solving we display these problems through a graphic that shows principally a one-way type of thinking, but complex problems show the effects of feedback, either positive or negative, and thus are circular in nature. Thus, in the example above, conventional thinking may be shown as the graph ((A) in Figure 16.1), but systems thinking shows possible feedback and side effects, which are shown on the graph at the bottom (B). The whole is represented by the function of the whole graph at the bottom, which is to produce more visitors to the tourism system.

But too often, we have not studied the *system as a whole* (in Figure 16.1 (B) how all the parts labeled in the system are shown). We have done, most likely, a great job of studying the attraction (how it is preserved or managed), the transportation (e.g. number of people on trails or streets), lodging (satisfaction with rooms), promotion (whether the advertising gets to the market) and so on *individually*. We have not asked why the system exists, what need it fulfills, or what the system's purpose is. We have not asked how the part (lodging, food, transportation, etc.) relates to other parts or the purpose of the system. This, I believe, is one of the greatest failures in research in general, and tourism research specifically.

A systems approach helps us understand the complexity of the system, the feedback that occurs, how an action may have effects other than those intended. By studying the whole, we

(A)

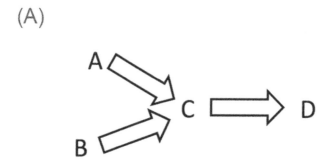

(B)

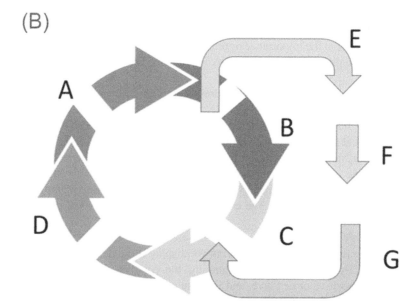

Note: In (A), event oriented thinking is linear, searches for a cause and does not search for feedback loops. (B) demonstrates the use of causal loops in systems thinking. The figure shows that A does cause eventually D, but D is a feedback that changes A. Systems thinking also recognizes that surprises occur, through the loop shown in light color (Did anyone expect that A would cause E, F, and G? And the presence of delays is also shown by the break in the arrows).

Figure 16.1   *Graphic on difference between conventional event oriented and systems thinking*

find out the purpose of the system, the *why* if you will. By knowing the why, we can intervene at a systems level the leverage points to most effectively act on a system to move it in the direction we want it to go (McCool et al., forthcoming). For example, we may have a tourism system that arose to enhance the quality of life of residents. If that system is not achieving that goal, then a systems analysis lets us uncover what we can do most effectively to move that system in the right direction.

Vision

We may not even know the purpose of the system. Wicked problems usually involve disagreement as to what its actual purpose might be: Does a tourism system exist to provide jobs? Does it exist to protect a local community's culture? Does it provide the increased income needed to protect an attraction? Does it exist to provide personal income? Does it make a community more resilient? Or does it have some other objective or objectives, such as the vitality of the community or even the reduction of spousal abuse?

We often don't ask the question of *why*, as McCool and colleagues note. The *why* can be looked at as the purpose of the tourism system, and it is probably the most important question that tourism destination managers and scientists can ask. We often ask *what* we will do, or *how* we will do it, to advance the effectiveness of tourism and such questions are often the first questions we ask. But these questions may be the wrong questions to ask until we understand the *vision* for what tourism in that place and time is designed to achieve.

Developing a vision for a tourism destination is also one of the hardest things to do. For two reasons: (1) we have little experience in building visions for destinations, and (2) there are multiple interests in any complex problem, and when confronted with the task of vision building, those interests are made explicit, and there may be significant differences among those interests about a vision for tourism.

There are many ways to write a vision. I like a vision that is written collaboratively among managers, scientists and constituencies, which is the most difficult situation I admit. But those difficulties exist anyway, so a scientist may argue that we are all better off if we tackle a difficult problem together. A scientist could have several roles in this process. One is to present what a vision statement is and is not. This is an important role (described below) that influences the remaining process. A scientist could act as one of the constituencies in the process, contributing to the development process. And the scientist could also serve as measuring the effectiveness of a vision statement in organizing social action to achieve this vision.

I think there are three important characteristics of a vision statement. First, a vision statement is written about a condition or set of conditions, not actions. A good vision statement may be: "a vibrant community serving guests" or "a visitor experience producing amateur historians" or even "increased cardiovascular health of residents or visitors". These examples may or may not be useful, but they point to visions based on conditions. These vision statements are also short but are not slogans for an agency. And they do not include actions or strategies to achieve those visions as actions that are a way to achieve an end state. Constructing an integrated set of actions is a different task altogether.

Second, they are short, and ideally would be motivational for guests and staff. Staff would see their work has a larger purpose than managing tourists, and visitors would see themselves as part of something important. Certainly, a vision statement can be longer, and that is not a problem except that the longer the statement is, the less likely it will be visionary and the more likely it will contain strategies and actions.

And third, the vision is shared (Senge, 1990). It is developed out of individual visions, but not the sum of those individual visions. It is constructed from those individual visions in such a way that an organizational vision that is shared among managers, employees and the public is derived from them. It is an emergent property that is very real.

Visions are important components of management, and if a researcher understands that, then there will be appreciation for the role of research in contributing to achieving that vision. There will be more appreciation for how a vision functions in management as Senge (1990, p. 192) argued:

> Few, if any, forces in human affairs are as powerful as a shared vision ... A shared vision is not an idea ... It is not even an important idea ... It is palpable ... People see it as if it exists as an actual entity, as if it is something alive.

Section Conclusion

And so, we have these three very real components of complexity of the finding and setting the appropriate social and biophysical conditions by tourism scientists and managers: the wickedness of the problems are created by complexity of the situation; use of systems thinking to build a picture of the system that is involved; and holding a vision of the future as to what the problem is all about. And there are other contextualizing factors that make planning more complex: the type of public involvement, the character of the communities in and around the area, politics and governance systems, public sentiment and so on. But of course, planners already know this but often they ignore this reality and exclude it from planning, seeing their role as merely making recommendations and letting those in policy positions deal with them. This extensive discussion was needed to describe the nature of the problem for developing strategic research of desired social and biophysical conditions at a tourism destination.

WHAT DO WE DO FOR RESEARCH ON TOURISM CONDITIONS IN THE TWENTY-FIRST CENTURY?

As mentioned in the previous section, there are a great many approaches to the issue of establishing what is socially and biologically acceptable and what needs to be done. The focus in this chapter is *why* something needs to be done and *what* needs to be done, but not *how*, which is the specific research techniques. The actual research procedures, whether qualitative or quantitative, are established in the literature of social and biological sciences, some of which is mentioned or exemplified in the chapters in this book. Readers are recommended to inspect these chapters for ideas on research methodology.

This section presents a strategy to provide the information needed to address this question in complex, wicked situations. It is built upon an understanding that tourism is a system and incorporates systems thinking by including a vision and feedback loops in the research questions to address desired questions.

The strategy is defined by two major sets of questions (Figures 16.2 and 16.3) that all planners ask, but often just implicitly. This research strategy makes these questions explicit but implicitly defines this kind of research as applied research, that is research that has immediate benefits to destination managers, whether those destinations are communities or protected areas. I will briefly describe each set of questions in the sections below.

Defining Questions

These three questions underlie applied research and management of destinations. And they somewhat overlap the Working Questions discussed below. They are similar to Sinek's 'Golden Circle' (2017) but ordered differently to account for the way in which researchers approach science and they focus on the principal way we think in systems terms.

The questions are: Why do we want to describe acceptable and appropriate conditions? What are we going to do to define these conditions? And, how are we going to do this? These questions are shown in Figure 16.2 in a graphic that shows their relationships. The questions relate to each other, are not independent and they provide great direction to those who use them in the order we are discussing here.

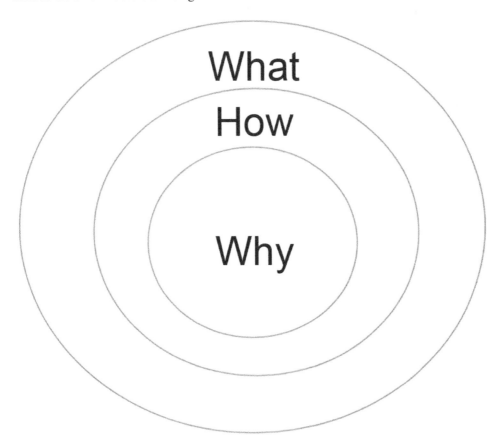

Source: Inspired by Sinek (2017).

Figure 16.2   *What Sinek terms the 'Golden Circles'*

The first question consists of "Why must we describe appropriate biophysical and social conditions?" Generally, the response to this question is that currently conditions are not appropriate or acceptable to the current vision (or the current populations of visitors/residences). Or the response may also be that a rationale, such as legislation/rule/administrative mandate requires a review of current and appropriate conditions (planners often plan because they are told to do so in these legal documents). Regardless, the research has a normative foundation for its conduct and is thus linked to a specific course of action.

The second question is "What are we going to do to define these conditions?" This is a role for tourism and recreation research and this set of questions deal principally with the "What?": What are we going to do about it? Generally, we will bring in scientists to assess the current conditions and the acceptability or appropriateness of some set of future conditions. This tends to be a major component of research, but perhaps not in the conventional methodology. We may do an inventory of the relevant set of conditions, such as the number of current tourists, their location, their temporal use patterns, visitor perceptions and attitudes toward conditions. These are the questions of *what*. These questions are influenced by the *why*.

The final question is the "How": "How are we going to do this?", which for the most part is a tactical question of research methodology and knowledge sharing, whether produced only by the scientist or jointly produced by the scientists and client of the research. The question of how we inventory visitor-use patterns, for example, may be conducted by some available secondary data, visitor diaries, questionnaire or observation. The question of how we do this is not described in this chapter because there are many sources available on research methodology, including this book.

These three questions are related, the *Why* influences the *What*, which then in turn influences the *How*. The results of the research may influence the *Why*. So, this apparently small system contains feedback which may lead to important consequences.

Working Questions

Once the Guiding Questions have acceptable responses, then researchers can turn to the Working Questions that detail how the research will proceed. These questions are depicted, as a system itself, in Figure 16.3. The Guiding Questions begin with Why; this is done to ensure that the following set of questions are directly related to the purpose of the research; in this case, describing the set of appropriate and/or acceptable conditions.

But then the research gets into more detailed questions, beginning with the question of "*What is?*" This is the question of what conditions exist on site, or in the system now, currently. This question may deal with the social, biological, or both. This question is important, because usually the reason for the research is to change the situation: tourist use appears to be high, or too low, leads to consequences that are socially or politically unacceptable or inappropriate, or maybe tourism appears to be needed as an economic or social development tool, or maybe the question is not explicitly specified. For example, the *What is* question may focus on the conditions themselves or focus on the secondary or even tertiary effects: What is the level of tourist use? What conditions does it lead to (e.g. 'congestion')? What is the resulting water consumption or energy use? What is the reaction of local residents to tourism use or conditions?

These questions may lead to a journey that wasn't anticipated when the tourism research was originally conceived, and indicate that systems thinking has more benefits than conventional "let's do a carrying capacity study" or "find the 'magic number'" style thinking. For example, I once facilitated a three-day discussion about the use of a Limits of Acceptable Change

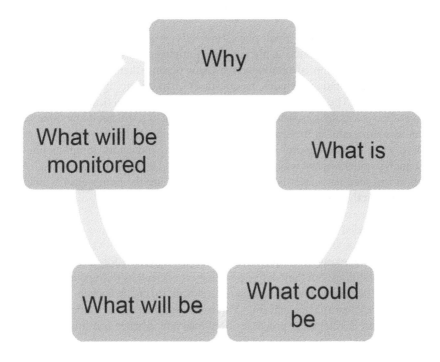

Figure 16.3   Important questions asked during planning that relate to research

approach (a popular US created approach to defining social and biophysical conditions, see Borrie and Bigart, Chapter 17 in this volume, or McCool et al., 2007, or Stankey et al., 1985 for discussion of this) for a community in southwestern Oregon, USA. A community member stated about half way through the workshop, that (paraphrased) "she was involved because she saw that tourism development might help the spouse abuse problem in that community, but if it did not, she would participate in something else". So, a workshop on tourism development turned into a workshop about how tourism development could help address an important social development problem.

The next working question is *"What could be?"* In this question, destination managers, constituencies and scientists explore what alternative futures could lead, realistically, from the existing conditions to the future, given the vision that was identified earlier. There is often more than one route to the desired future, and this step identifies what seems to be possible. Science plays an important role in describing the negative and positive aspects of the different pathways to the described future. This helps destination managers and local constituencies in defining the possibilities and understanding the different pathways that are available without judging those possibilities.

The next question is *"What will be?"*, which is the chosen pathway. Whether it is creating jobs, increasing labor income, protecting local culture, scientists can help make this selection. They can lead discussions, do research on what the costs and benefits of selecting the chosen pathway to the future, helping people understand what the chosen alternative is. It should be noted that this is an inherently political decision, but the scientist can play the roles identified above.

Following this question is the 'final' one: "*How will we implement and monitor the chosen alternative?*" This question connects planning with implementation, an often-neglected planning phase, and connects implementation to the vision because there is directly noted feedback to the vision. Implementation includes the questions of who is going to do what, when, how and with what costs. The decision includes both strategic and tactical implementation and monitoring of those and their impacts. Without monitoring, we will not know if the decision to implement was successful in the sense of achieving a vision. Scientists can play a major role here in developing monitoring protocols (such as selecting indicators, sampling intervals and locations, analysis methods and ways to display data so that it is easy to understand). And then, this question will feed back into the *why*: Are we achieving the purpose for which we have engaged to conduct the research?

Section Conclusion

These defining and working questions describe not just a process for developing appropriate and acceptable conditions, but they define a strategy for scientists to engage tourism development processes. They show how science can be relevant to, and influence, tourism planning, they form a strategy that science can follow to make itself salient to tourism and not just an 'add-on' to tourism development processes. It shows how science can inform each stage of tourism planning.

CONCLUSION

Tourism development is a complex process, especially in the twenty-first century world of wicked problems that will be resolved by systems thinking and directed by a vision of the future for tourism destinations. Visions of the tourism destination are difficult to construct because of the multiple interests that are involved in development decisions – an essentially political process. However, scientists can play a role in facilitating that discussion because they are supposed to be neutral in their interests, although many are not. It's time we practice that value.

And, since many of the challenges tourism development faces are wicked rather than tame, they will be difficult to resolve, but still require the use of scientifically developed information. Wicked problems always have differences in goals and science does not all the time agree on cause–effect relationships which impact how we go about resolving problems (think of coronavirus and how the tourism industry will recover as an easy example). We can move forward in selecting those resolutions by using systems thinking to understand how feedback and system delays always affect our decisions. A strategic research process focused on identifying acceptable and appropriate conditions is needed to address many of the challenges faced in the near run future. There are several significant questions to be asked (such as *why* and *what*) before we ask *how*.

The question of "How we do our research?" was not addressed in this chapter because understanding and deciding social and biophysical conditions is such an important question and there are few such papers that look at the strategic implications of this research. The tourism literature that recognizes that this question is wicked and that a systems approach is required to approach it is just at its beginning stage. Thus, there are tools here to look at tourism research more strategically than the past; it is up to the reader to employ them.

NOTES

1. See: https://www.usatoday.com/story/travel/2019/03/24/justin-bieber-blamed-too-many-tourists-ic eland-closes-canyon/3264731002/.
2. I have written primarily in the first person as this is a result of my experience as a tourism researcher, working with researchers, and assisting managers to enhance capacity to provide managers with the capability to provide opportunities for quality visitor experiences. This chapter is also designed to be provocative.

REFERENCES

Allen, G. M. and Gould, E. M., Jr. (1986) Complexity, wickedness, and public forests. *Journal of Forestry*, 84(4), 20–23.

Allen, L., Long, P., Perdue, R. and Kieselbach, S. (1988) The impacts of tourism development on residents' perceptions of community life. *Journal of Travel Research*, 27, 16–21.

Ap, J. (1990) Residents' perceptions research on the social impacts of tourism. *Annals of Tourism Research*, 17, 610–616.

European Union (2018) Research for TRAN Committee – Overtourism: Impact and possible policy responses. Policy Department for Structural and Cohesion Policies, Policy Department for Structural and Cohesion Policies. Directorate-General for Internal Policies. PE 629.184 – October. Brussels.

Friedmann, J. (1993) Toward a non-Euclidian mode of planning. *Journal of the American Planning Association*, 59(4), 482–485.

Gharajedaghi, J. (2011) *Systems Thinking: Managing Chaos and Complexity – A Platform for Designing Business Architecture* (3rd edition). Amsterdam: Elsevier.

Hadinejad, A., Moyle, B. D., Scott, N., Kralj, A. and Nunkoo, R. (2019) Residents' attitudes to tourism: A review. *Tourism Review*, 74(2), 157–172 .

Hall, C. M. (1998) The institutional setting: Tourism and the state. In D. Ioannides and K. G. Debbage (eds.), *The Economic Geography of the Tourist Industry: A Supply-Side Analysis*. London: Routledge, 199–219.

Head, B. and Alford, J. (2015) Wicked problems: Implications for public policy and management. *Administration and Society*, 47(6), 711–739.

Kohl, J. and McCool, S. F. (2016) *The Future Has Other Plans: Planning Holistically to Conserve Natural and Cultural Heritage*. Golden, CO: Fulcrum Publishing.

Mathieson, A. and Wall, G. (1982) *Tourism: Economic, Physical and Social Impacts*. London: Edward Arnold.

McCool, S. F. (1996) Searching for sustainability: A difficult course; an uncertain outcome. In M. L. Miller and J. Auyong (eds.), *Proceedings of the 1996 Global Congress on Coastal and Marine Tourism*. Washington Sea Grant Program and School of Marine Affairs, University of Washington, 19–22.

McCool, S. F., Clark, R. N. and Stankey, G. (2007) *An Assessment of Frameworks Useful for Public Land Recreation Planning*. Gen. Tech. Rep. PNW-GTR-705. Portland, OR: US Department of Agriculture, Forest Service, Pacific Northwest Research Station.

McCool, S. F., Freimund, W. and Besancon, C. (forthcoming) Complex contexts and uncertain futures: An essay on finding our way to more effective visitor management.

Morris, D. and Martin, S. (2009) Complexity, systems thinking and practice. In A. Stibbe (ed.), *The Handbook of Sustainability Literacy*. Totnes, UK: Green Books, 156–164.

Pizam, A. (1978) Tourist impacts: The social costs to the destination community as perceived by its residents. *Journal of Travel Research*, 16, 8–12.

Reed, G. (2006) Both the parts and the whole: Leadership and systems thinking. *Defense AT&L*. https://thesystemsthinker.com/both-the-parts-and-whole-leadership-and-systems-thinking/.

Rittel, H. W. J. and Webber, M. M. (1973) Dilemmas in a general theory of planning. *Policy Sciences*, 4, 155–169.

Roux, D. J., Smith, M. K. S., Smit, I. P., Freitag, S., Slabbert, L., Mokhatla, M. M., Hayes, J. and Mpapane, N. P. (2020) Cultural ecosystem services as complex outcomes of people–nature interactions in protected areas. *Ecosystem Services*, 43, 101111.

Senge, P. M. (1990) *The Fifth Discipline: The Art and Practice of the Learning Organization*. New York: Doubleday.

Sinek, S. (2017) *Find Your Why: A Practical Guide for Discovering Purpose for You and Your Team*. New York: Penguin.

Stankey, G. H., Cole, D. N., Lucas, R. C., Peterson, M. E. and Frissell, S. S. (1985) *The Limits of Acceptable Change (LAC) System for Wilderness Planning*. U.S. Forest Service, General Technical Report INT-176. Ogden, UT: USDA Forest Service Intermountain Research Station.

Weaver, D. (2013) Wither sustainable tourism? But first a good hard look in the mirror. *Tourism Recreation Research*, 38(2), 231–234.

17. Visitor use management framework

William T. Borrie and Elena A. Bigart

SUSTAINABLE VISITOR USE

There are estimated to be over 238,000 natural protected areas worldwide and many more culturally significant protected areas (McCool, 2019). These areas play important roles in our society including the provision of outstanding opportunities for recreation experiences and for sustainable tourism development. As a result, the world's terrestrial protected areas receive approximately 8 billion visits per year and it is expected this will increase in the future (Balmford et al., 2015). Given this, there is a fundamental need to know what's going on and to protect the qualities of the resource and the experience that these areas were established for. The Visitor Use Management Framework provides a planning process designed to maximize the benefits for visitors while proactively preserving the environmental, social, and managerial conditions that are so valued.

Protected areas are of vital importance to our society. In an increasingly urbanized world, they provide sanctuary and relief and can be sources of inspiration, delight, and respite. Protected areas are a shared heritage and a chance for citizens and tourists to learn the story of the land and its people. They help us know who we are as a people and the places that we live in. Parks and protected areas are a commitment to honor the past and protect the future. As McCool (2019, p. 1) suggests:

> societies flourish when their members connect with and bond to their heritage, both cultural and natural. … This heritage and the connections it provides may be recreational (as when we seek outcomes such as adventure, challenge, escape, solitude and stress release), educational (such as learning about natural processes), cultural (such as appreciating how our societies have developed and understanding notable events of the past), spiritual, or utilitarian (such as harvesting resources for sustenance and shelter).

Parks and protected areas are places for healthy and social activities, as well as the chance to enjoy, wonder, and learn about the natural beauty around us. These areas inspire and move us. They contribute not just to human satisfaction and well-being but also to non-material aspects of our quality of life and values that exist independent of humankind.

Quality visitor experiences are at the heart of sustainable tourism and are "an essential component of protected area stewardship" (Priskin and McCool, 2006, p. 1). Not only do quality experiences develop an appreciation and respect for the natural and cultural values of the area but they also underpin much of the financial and political support for the area's protection. High quality and memorable visitor experiences can also lead to return visitors, recommendations to friends and family, sustained employment and resilient rural economies (Miller et al., 2019).

Outdoor recreation experiences can be restorative, rejuvenating, stress-reducing, and relaxing. As Bratman et al. (2012) review, nature experiences have profound effects on human cognitive capacity, psychological functioning, and mental health. Kellert (1995) suggested that humans have an almost universal affinity and bond with the natural world. Studies in international tourism have documented many visitors continuing to seek opportunities for getting away from daily routines for self-reflection and for learning about themselves and their place in the world. Significant documentation of the personal, social/cultural, and economic benefits of recreation have been provided in Moore and Driver (2005) and Driver et al. (1991). Table 17.1, taken from Shultis (2003), provides a comprehensive list of the many documented benefits. Combined, these benefits are clearly more than just 'fun and games', representing fundamental aspects of human health and of well-functioning societies. A direct link has been documented between visits to protected areas and individual well-being. These mental health benefits have been estimated globally to be around USD 6 trillion per annum (Buckley et al., 2019). There is also good evidence that protected areas have positive effects on human well-being in neighboring communities (Naidoo et al., 2019).

However, if parks and protected areas are

> the foundation for a vibrant nature-based tourism industry, their managers are then confronted with the challenge of providing diverse, sustainable opportunities for high quality, rewarding visitor and recreation opportunities. Such opportunities simply do not happen. They are deliberately constructed with careful attention to the capabilities of the area, the heritage values protected within it, the conservation objectives established for it, the capacity of local business and communities to implement tourism and the expectations held by potential visitor. (McCool, 2006, p. 3)

VISITOR USE MANAGEMENT

Effective visitor management is a crucial task for protected area managers. The preservation of desired experiences and the conditions that visitors seek is best achieved through a rigorous and scientific approach. Various visitor management frameworks have been developed to guide the process of formulating management objectives along with indicators and standards of quality. All these frameworks have a common goal of "an institutionalized system for learning that provides a basis for science-based decision making for managers of sustainable tourism" (Miller et al., 2019, p. 59). A fundamental requirement is descriptive data of existing conditions, of who the visitors are, what the visitors are doing and experiencing, where the visitors are, and the fundamental visitor behavior patterns. The overall aim is to identify and protect what is most important about protected areas and proactively manage visitor use. It is tempting for managers to jump to solving a perceived problem without first knowing what is going on (Miller et al., 2017). A systematic accounting of visitor use is first required for effective visitor use management.

The management of visitors to parks and protected areas is a complex task and seemingly simple solutions rarely succeed in the longer term. The preservation of the ecological and experiential conditions of the area requires a shared commitment between land managers, tourism industry representatives, scientists, environmental concerns, local and indigenous communities, and visitors themselves. Planning for sustainable nature-based tourism development requires a systematic process well informed about visitation, clearly focused on outcomes or conditions to be achieved, and a transparent and accountable statement of how these outcomes are monitored and preserved (McCool, 1994).

Table 17.1   *Personal, social/cultural, economic, and environmental benefits of recreation*

Personal Benefits

1.   Psychological (mental health)
- Holistic sense of wellness
- Stress management (prevention, mediation, and restoration)
- Catharsis

- Prevention and reduction of depression, anxiety, and anger
- Positive changes in mood and emotion

2.   Personal development and growth
- Prevention of problems with at-risk youth
- Value clarification
- Improved academic/cognitive performance
- Independence and autonomy
- Sense of control over one's life
- Humility
- Leadership
- Aesthetic and creativity enhancement
- Spiritual growth
- Self-confidence, self-reliance, self-competence, self-assurance

- Adaptability
- Cognitive efficiency
- Improved problem-solving ability
- Nature learning
- Cultural and historical awareness, learning, and appreciation
- Environmental awareness and understanding
- Tolerance
- Balanced competitiveness
- Balanced living
- Acceptance of responsibility

3.   Psychophysiological
- Cardiovascular benefits
- Reduction and prevention of hypertension
- Reduced serum cholesterol/triglycerides
- Improved control or prevention of diabetes
- Prevention of colon cancer
- Reduced spinal problems
- Decreased body fat and obesity/weight control
- Improved neuropsychological functioning
- Increased bone mass and strength in children

- Increased muscle strength and better connective tissue
- Respiratory benefits
- Reduced incidence of disease
- Improved bladder control for the elderly
- Increased life expectancy
- Management of menstrual cycles
- Management of arthritis
- Improved functioning of immune system
- Reduced consumption of alcohol and use of tobacco

Social and Cultural Benefits

- Community satisfaction
- Community, regional and national pride
- Cultural/historical awareness and appreciation
- Reduced social alienation
- Community and political involvement
- Family bonding
- Reciprocity and sharing
- Social mobility
- Community integration
- Nurturing of others
- Greater community involvement in environmental decision-making

- Understanding and tolerance of others
- Environmental awareness and sensitivity
- Social bonding, cohesion, and cooperation
- Conflict resolution and harmony
- Developmental benefits of children
- Social support
- Support for democratic ideals of freedom
- Enhanced world view
- Socialization and acculturation
- Prevention of social problems by at-risk youth

Economic Benefits

- Reduced health costs
- Increased productivity
- Reduced work absenteeism
- Fewer on-the-job accidents

- Decreased job turnover
- Balance of payments (tourism)
- Local and regional economic growth
- Contribution to net federal economic development

Environmental Benefits

- Maintenance of physical facilities
- Stewardship/preservation of options
- Improved relationships with nature
- Development of environmental ethic
- Public involvement in environmental issues

- Environmental protection
- Ecosystem sustainability
- Preservation of species diversity
- Maintenance of natural scientific laboratories
- Preservation of particular natural and cultural site

Source: Adapted from Driver and Bruns (1999) by Shultis (2003).

Visitor Use Management Frameworks

A variety of planning and management frameworks have been developed for parks and protected areas to address visitor experiences in sustainable tourism settings. Their use is increasing around the world (Leung et al., 2018). McCool et al. (2007), Manning (2011), Newsome et al. (2013), and Nilsen and Tayler (1997) all provide comparisons of the Limits of Acceptable Change (LAC) process (Stankey et al., 1985), Carrying Capacity Assessment (Shelby and Heberlein, 1986), Visitor Impact Management (VIM) (Kuss et al., 1990), Visitor Experience and Resource Protection (VERP) (National Park Service, 1997) and, the focus of this chapter, the Visitor Use Management (VUM) framework (IVUMC, 2016).

In particular, LAC explicitly incorporates the commitment of the Recreation Opportunity Spectrum (Clark and Stankey, 1979) to defining and describing a diversity of visitor opportunity classes. In doing so, most visitor use planning frameworks acknowledge that there is no one ideal set of resources and social conditions. Instead, specific locations have different objectives (including different types of visitor experiences available), different concerns, and different conditions prioritized for protection. In particular, visitor behavior may be managed differently (i.e. more or less regulated) creating different social conditions.

The Interagency Visitor Use Management Council (IVUMC) introduced the first edition of the Visitor Use Management (VUM) framework in 2016. It is described as a "proactive and adaptive process for managing characteristics of visitor use and the natural and managerial setting using a variety of strategies and tools to achieve and maintain desired resource conditions and visitor experiences" (IVUMC, 2016, pp. 1–2). The VUM framework builds on, and is consistent with, previous planning frameworks, particularly LAC and VERP. It aims to avoid some of their constraints and suggests that the amount of effort for a project should be commensurate with its complexity and the consequences of the decision. This approach is called a "sliding scale of analysis" and is intended to match the investment of time and resources with the level of uncertainty and risk associated with the issues being addressed. Further, whereas earlier frameworks were designed and implemented within specific land management agencies (e.g. US Forest Service and the National Park Service, respectively), the VUM framework was proposed for consistency in managing and monitoring visitor use across six federal agencies (Bureau of Land Management, National Park Service, US Fish & Wildlife Service, Forest Service, National Oceanic and Atmospheric Administration, and US Army Corps of Engineers).

As a flexible and scalable process, VUM includes:

- Identifying desired conditions for resources, visitor experiences and opportunities, and facilities and services;
- Gaining an understanding of how visitor use influences achievement of desired conditions; and
- Committing to active/adaptive management and monitoring of visitor use to meet overall goals (Cahill et al., 2018).

A Sliding Scale Approach

A sliding scale of analysis is used to match the required staff time, money, and resources to the complexity and consequences of the visitor use management situation. Smaller projects, such as reducing the size of a campground, might require only several hours of analysis and documentation (including a short description of current and desired conditions, a simple list of appropriate visitor activities and facilities, development of a single indicator and associated threshold based on existing information, and continued monitoring of one or a small number of indicators). Large-scale or park-wide planning might take several years with large teams and research (with potentially multiple zones, each with detailed descriptions of ecological, social and managerial conditions, many indicators, extensive research and public engagement processes for setting triggers and thresholds, detailed rationale for appropriate levels of service, and a detailed, peer-reviewed and scientifically robust monitoring program).

Four criteria are suggested to determine the appropriate level of analysis: (a) Issue uncertainty – the degree to which the project can be clearly delineated, completed on time, with few unanticipated problems and few alternatives to be considered; (b) Impact risk – the degree of risk to natural and cultural resources and to visitor experience; (c) Stakeholder involvement – the degree to which community and interest groups are organized and watching the decision-making process and wish to present diverse, and often conflicting, levels of support; and (d) Level of controversy – the degree to which legal and public opinion battles are likely. A decision support tool is available (IVUMC, 2016). As the number of issues and the level of controversy and risk associated with them goes up, the need for rigorous, well-documented analysis increases. However, it is important not to underestimate the uncertainty, complexity, and controversy of visitor use management. The long-term costs of insufficient analysis and documentation can far outweigh short-term savings.

DIVERSITY OF RECREATION OPPORTUNITIES

In setting objectives for sustainable tourism management, it is important to understand that 'one-size doesn't fit all' and that a diversity of outdoor recreation opportunities will be needed to meet the wide-ranging needs of the public. Any single location is unlikely to be able to provide for the full range of tourists, given they have broad motivations and expectations for their visits. It has been said that attempting to do so is akin to designing conditions for an "average camper who doesn't exist" (Shafer, 1969). Some visitors expect fairly developed, even urban, conditions, while others seek primitive and remote conditions. Averaging preferences and opportunities sought and providing a single, homogenized set of conditions is not responsive to the wants and needs of visitors and is unlikely to satisfy the majority.

The Recreation Opportunity Spectrum (ROS) was developed as a planning framework to ensure diversity in parks and protected areas (Brown et al., 1978; Clark and Stankey, 1979). Driver et al. (1987) describe the fundamental structure of ROS as: "specifying recreational *goals* in terms of broad classes of recreation opportunity, identifying specific *indicators* of these opportunities that permit their operational definition, and defining specific *standards* for each indicator that make distinctions among the opportunities possible" (p. 202, our emphasis).

ROS focuses on three specific setting conditions, each of which has indicators and standards:

I.   Environmental (biophysical and cultural-historic resources)
II. Social (the visitors, their densities, and their behaviors)
III. Managerial (rules, regulations and regimentation, presence of management staff, level of facility development and services provided).

These setting conditions combine into a number of ROS classes, typically five or six, ranging from primitive through to rural and/or urban. Each ROS class, then, determines the type, amount and qualities of the recreation opportunities available to match the conditions. ROS has been the basis of other similar regional zoning approaches such as the Tourism Opportunity Spectrum (Butler and Waldbrook, 1991) and the Ecotourism Opportunity Spectrum (Boyd and Butler, 1996). The provision of a diversity of recreation opportunities has been described as "the key to quality recreation and park-based tourism" (Eagles et al., 2002, p. 103).

THE VUM FRAMEWORK

Planning and management frameworks provide a process and structure for informed decision-making. As McCool et al. (2007) review, these frameworks point out which questions need to be answered by "focusing attention on important elements of the political and social environment ... by gaining the public support that is needed for implementation, and ... by forcing consideration of who wins and who loses" (p. 5). That is, they impel explicit consideration of the issues and consequences. McCool (2016) defines a planning framework as not necessarily leading to the one correct or optimal answer to an issue, but rather "provides the conceptual basis through which thinking is conducted, questions asked, or discussion occurs leading to resolution of the issue" (p. 106). In concluding, McCool suggests that, "sustainable tourism management is as much about the values and preferences of constituencies – including community members, visitors, tour operators, environmentalists, government officials – as it is about technical concerns of biophysical impacts" (p. 113).

Visitor use management frameworks all share more or less the same key steps (Fefer et al., 2016; Miller et al., 2017) including:

1. Examining the legal mandates and stated purposes for the park or protected area, and identifying the issues or points of controversy
2. Establishing management **objectives** and, in particular, **desired conditions**
3. Identifying **indicators** and **standards** for those desired conditions
4. Inventory and assessment of indicators
5. Identifying and implementing management **strategies** and practices to maintain the standards, and
6. **Monitoring** and evaluation of indicators to assess effectiveness of management actions, including needed adjustments based on monitoring results.

Indeed, the need for specific, achievable management objectives for wilderness and protected area conditions has been a constant imperative for visitor use frameworks. These **objectives** should "describe ends rather than means – conditions rather than management actions" (Cole and Stankey, 1997, p. 6). It is the **desired conditions** that represent and produce the outcomes sought. And, as Watson et al. (2007) stress, "identifying the experiences, through research, that people are currently receiving is an important step in setting management objectives" (p. 887).

Indicators are quantifiable proxies of management objectives and should be stated specifically enough to make monitoring easily prescribed (Watson et al., 1998). Indicators should be sensitive to threats to the resource and social environment. **Standards/Thresholds**[1] define the "maximum departure from pristine indicator conditions that are allowed to occur due to the presence of these threats (i.e. the limits of acceptable change)" (Watson et al., 1998, p. 331).

Standards are "absolute limits – not just warnings. Violations of standards shouldn't be tolerated" (Cole and Stankey, 1997, p. 8).

The Visitor Use Management (VUM) framework includes the above steps in four elements (Build the Foundation; Define Visitor Use Management Direction; Identify Management Strategies; Implement, Monitor, Evaluate, and Adjust) as seen in Figure 17.1. It should be noted that this framework is intended to be highly iterative and repeated with continued monitoring and adjustment.

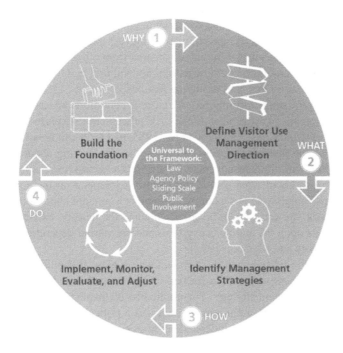

Source: IVUMC (2016).

Figure 17.1   Overview of the Visitor Use Management framework

Element 1: Build the Foundation

The first element focuses on understanding why a project is relevant, how best to approach and organize it, and which resources are needed to complete it. It includes the following four steps (IVUMC, 2016, p. 23):

- Step 1. Clarify the project purpose and need.
- Step 2. Review the area's purpose(s) and applicable legislation, agency policies, and other management direction.
- Step 3. Assess and summarize existing information and current conditions.
- Step 4. Develop a project action plan.

It is suggested to start with determining the project issue and reason for management decisions. Issues can vary from very simple and localized that affect only a limited number of people to more complex involving a high level of controversy and multiple stakeholders. Stankey et al. (1985) suggest that citizens and managers should meet to identify what special features or qualities within the area require attention and which concerns need to be dealt with. The recognition of needs and priorities may also come from visitor input. While analyzing an issue, it is crucial to understand why it is happening, which values are or could potentially be affected, and who exactly can be affected.

The next step begins with a review of legislative mandates, historic documents, current policies, and various land management and conservation plans. Eagles et al. (2002) argue that special values may be specifically recognized in enabling legislation or in government policy statements. Those are the values that differentiate an area from other areas and what makes it important. The values, in particular, could be natural and cultural and include spiritual meanings, historically significant events, and/or unique features.

The extent to which existing information and current conditions are assessed and documented depends on the scope of the project. In the LAC process, this step is to "inventory existing resource and social conditions" (Stankey et al., 1985, p. 11). It can be a time-consuming and expensive part of the planning process, but it is vital for making accurate evaluations and decisions, and knowing the consequences of different alternatives. Eagles et al. (2002) emphasize that decisions about what should be inventoried depend on the context and specific project issues and objectives. For example, if there is a concern about increased level of impact in a marine park, the data should be collected about the density, extent, and degree of human-induced impacts upon the marine ecosystems and the marine-dependent visitor experiences in the area (Stankey and McCool, 1992).

The last step within the first element is a project action plan. It should specify the scope of the project, team members responsible for certain tasks, needed and available resources, timeline, and public involvement strategy. The public involvement strategy would depend on the scope of the project and legal requirements, but it is a critical aspect of natural resource management and provides local and independent sources of information (Krishnaswamy, 2012), and contributes to building trust and sense of ownership (Lachapelle and McCool, 2005; Wang and Wan Wart, 2007).

Element 2: Define Visitor Use Management Direction

The goal of the second element is to describe the desired conditions and explain how those conditions would be tracked over time. It includes three steps (IVUMC, 2016, p. 29):

- Step 5. Define desired conditions for the project area.
- Step 6. Define appropriate visitor activities, facilities, and services.
- Step 7. Select indicators and establish thresholds.

Desired conditions are defined as the biophysical, social, and managerial conditions, outcomes and opportunities prioritized and maintained for the future. They are "statements of aspiration that describe resource conditions, visitor experiences and opportunities, and facilities and services that an agency strives to achieve and maintain in a particular area" (IVUMC, 2016, p. 30). Borrie et al. (1998) argue that clearly stated objectives identify the appropriateness of various management actions and provide criteria by which to judge their success. Large areas may be divided into management zones, each with a separate description of desired conditions. As mentioned above, zoning specifically allows for a diversity of conditions, experiences, and levels of service.

After defining desired conditions for the area, and potentially its zones, the next step is to understand more specifically which visitor activities, facilities, and services are appropriate there. When making a decision, the purpose of the area, applicable legislation, and desired conditions should be taken into consideration. For example, where the area is managed primarily for wilderness values, mountain biking will not be appropriate (as "mechanical transport" is explicitly prohibited in any wilderness area (Wilderness Act of 1964)). As in the previous step, the area may be divided by zones and each will have different regulations about the human-induced change that is permitted and appropriate.

Selecting monitoring indicators and establishing a threshold for each indicator translates desired conditions into measurable attributes. These can be tracked over time, and, thus, define the focus of the monitoring efforts. Indicators usually include both social and resource conditions and should be easy to measure quantitatively (Eagles et al., 2002). Examples of social indicators include the number of encounters with other groups on the trail during the day, or a number of campsites occupied within sight or sound. Examples of resource indicators include the number of damaged trees at one campsite, the number of new informal or visitor-created campsites, or the amount of soil erosion per square mile. (Hennings, 2017 provides a recent review of recreation ecology – the scientific study of resource impacts associated with recreation activities in protected natural areas, as do Marion et al., 2016.) Examples of managerial indicators include the number of educational programs delivered, miles of trail maintained, or number of regulations imposed upon visitors. Appendix A of the IVUMC's *Monitoring Guidebook* provides a longer list of example indicators (IVUMC, 2019).

Thresholds define the minimally acceptable conditions for each indicator and serve to define the limits of change acceptable to the public and managers. They are not ideal or target conditions, but represent a marker of when conditions have been impacted to the extent to which they are unacceptable or out of standard. That is, they are the "guardrails" beyond which conditions should not go and management strategies should "achieve and maintain desired

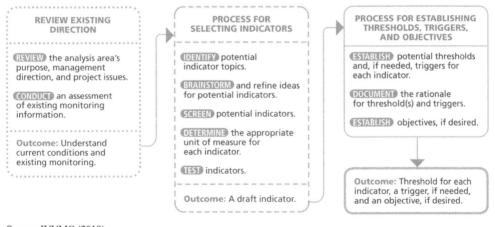

Source: IVUMC (2019).

Figure 17.2   Monitoring steps

conditions *before* reaching thresholds" (IVUMC, 2019, p. 10, our emphasis). There are many ways to set the thresholds such as by exploring visitor perspectives, what has particular visibility and interest for the public, and the acceptability of various ecological and social conditions (Manning et al., 2017). The IVUMC's *Monitoring Guidebook* provides further guidance on setting thresholds (IVUMC, 2019).

In addition to thresholds, IVUMC suggests establishing **triggers** for complex planning projects. A trigger is defined as "a condition of concern for an indicator that is enough to prompt a management response to ensure that desired conditions continue to be maintained *before* the threshold is crossed" (IVUMC, 2016, p. 39, our emphasis). For example, for an indicator of "the number of trees in a backcountry campsite showing damage such as broken or cut limbs, knife or axe scars, or nails", with a threshold of "10 damaged trees per campsite", a trigger may be "4 damaged trees per campsite". Triggers help prevent or reverse decline with less effort and urgency than when conditions reach an unacceptable threshold. Figure 17.2 provides more direction about reviewing existing directions, selecting indicators, and establishing triggers, thresholds, and objectives. Figure 17.3, taken from IVUMC (2016), shows the interrelationship of triggers and threshold and when monitoring of conditions points to a need for management actions.

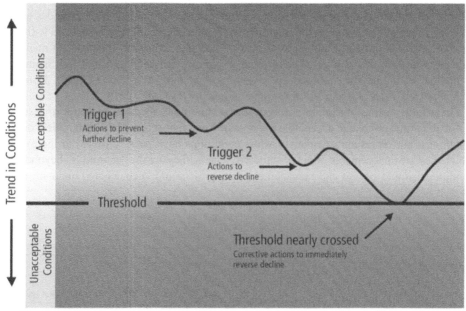

Source: IVUMC (2019).

Figure 17.3   *Trends in conditions in relation to triggers and thresholds*

The selection of indicators is one of the most difficult steps in the monitoring process. Selection forces consideration of what the conditions mean for visitor experiences and should, therefore, be systematic and not arbitrary. While there is less science telling which indicators do well at detecting changes in conditions (Krumpe and McCool, 1997; United States Forest Service, 1987), three characteristics for good indicators are provided by Watson et al. (2007): *significance* (are they related directly to desired conditions?); *efficiency* (do they capture more of the conditions than just themselves?); and *relevance* (are changes in the indicators caused by changes in levels of human activity?). Given that a small number of indicators have to be sufficient to represent complex, adaptive social-ecological systems, these characteristics build on common criteria such as *ease of measurement*, *cost-effectiveness*, and *sensitivity to change*. Indeed, the adoption of indicators must take into account how they will be monitored as they will be used to watch trends in conditions and to judge the effectiveness of management actions (IVUMC, 2019).

Element 3: Identify Management Strategies

The third element is focused on identifying management strategies and actions that will help to achieve and maintain the desired conditions of the project area. It includes the following four steps (IVUMC, 2016, p. 43):

- Step 8. Compare and document the differences between existing and desired conditions, and, for visitor use-related impacts, clarify the specific links to visitor use characteristics.
- Step 9. Identify visitor use management strategies and actions to achieve desired conditions.
- Step 10. When necessary, identify visitor capacities and additional strategies to manage use levels within capacities.
- Step 11. Develop a monitoring strategy.

Understanding the relationship between existing and desired conditions is a problem analysis. Those comparisons aim to reveal if desired conditions are being achieved or could fail to be achieved in the near future. When there is no reason to believe that conditions might change and existing conditions are within the established thresholds, proceed directly to step 11. However, when existing conditions are close to thresholds management action is required.

Manning et al. (2017) suggest four basic strategies that managers can choose from to achieve desirable objectives: (i) increase supply of recreation opportunities, (ii) reduce recreation demand or limit the amount of use, (iii) reduce the impact of use through modifying use patterns or activities, and/or (iv) increase the durability and resistance of the resource/experience. Within each of those, there are several distinct sub-strategies, such as to modify, disperse, or concentrate use; develop facilities or harden sites to increase the ability of sites to handle use; or modify the location or the timing of use. The choice of the strategy depends on many factors and should take into consideration local context, historic trends, and current data. Once a strategy has been selected, then specific actions to implement the strategy are chosen. Actions are defined as tools applied by managers to accomplish the strategies and can be both direct, with an emphasis on regulation of visitor behavior, or indirect, with an emphasis on influencing or modifying behavior (Manning et al., 2017). IVUMC (2016) identifies three categories of possible management actions: engineering (i.e. site design, construction, and maintenance such as strengthening and hardening trails), education (i.e. information such as Leave No Trace outdoor ethics programs, interpretive signs and contact with rangers, all to encourage low-impact visitor behavior and change the location and distribution of use patterns), and enforcement (i.e. rules and regulations to restrict or prohibit visitor behavior such as on length of stay, group size, or location of travel).

Visitor capacity is defined as "the maximum amounts and types of visitor use that an area can accommodate while achieving and maintaining the desired resource conditions and visitor experiences that are consistent with the purposes for which the area was established" (IVUMC, 2016,

p. 50). The limitations of the carrying capacity approach have been emphasized in the literature over the years (e.g. Eagles et al., 2002; Kohl and McCool, 2016), but in some cases establishing visitor capacity is appropriate and/or legally required. Borrie et al. (1998) identify nine requirements for the applications of carrying capacity and subsequent use limits. Many scholars (e.g. Eagles et al., 2002; Manning et al., 2017) argue that limiting use should be considered as a last resort (given its intrusive and heavy-handed approach) and that more indirect practices (including educational and improved visitor management strategies) should be implemented first. The link between limiting use and improved ecological and social conditions must be clearly documented and continually monitored.

Developing a monitoring strategy is the last step of the third element of VUM. Monitoring can be defined as the periodic and systematic measurement of key indicators of biophysical and social conditions (Borrie et al., 1998). Basically, it focuses on the indicators selected in step 7 and compares their condition with those identified in the thresholds. Monitoring is an integral component to any management planning process (Eagles et al., 2002) and should be conducted regularly and systematically. Monitoring is a sustained and consistent documentation of indicators (IVUMC, 2019). Information developed in the monitoring process is used to evaluate the success of management actions and to maintain a formal record of resource and social conditions over time. IVUMC (2016) notes that it is not always implied that a substantial research, staff, and funding investment is required; rather, monitoring efforts should be commensurate with the scope of the project but with a long-term commitment towards the monitoring effort.

Element 4: Implement, Monitor, Evaluate, and Adjust

The last element of the framework provides a process for implementing management actions, monitoring them, evaluating results, and making adjustments when necessary. The process is reflected in the following steps (IVUMC, 2016, p. 58):

- Step 12. Implement management actions.
- Step 13. Conduct and document ongoing monitoring, and evaluate the effectiveness of management actions in achieving desired conditions.
- Step 14. Adjust management actions if needed to achieve desired conditions, and document rationale.

This implementation plan should detail actions, costs, timetables, and responsibilities. Managers need to make sure that resources are available and that relevant staff members are trained on the new actions and desired conditions. When management actions are put into effect, visitors' immediate reactions should be watched closely and necessary support should be provided on the ground to increase the chances of success.

The monitoring strategy that was developed in step 11 is then implemented. The IVUMC defines monitoring as "the process of routinely and systematically gathering information or making observations to assess the status of specific resource conditions and visitor experience" (2019, p. 87). It is an essential part of visitor use management which helps managers to evaluate the effectiveness of the chosen actions in achieving and maintaining desired conditions. As mentioned earlier, both resource and social conditions are usually monitored with the choice of specific indicators depending on the issues, objectives, desired conditions, and other factors. In general, monitoring provides the data and fundamental information for the science-based management, allows transparency in the decision-making process, and can sometimes justify funding proposals. As the monitoring definition suggests, it needs to be done *systematically*, thus avoiding accusations of being arbitrary and capricious (see Table 17.2 for examples of steps in the VUM framework).

Table 17.2   Examples of the VUM framework

Example from Flathead River Wild and Scenic River System in Montana, United States	Example from Glacier National Park (GNP) in Montana, United States
The Flathead River was one of the 27 rivers designated by the United States Congress under the Wild and Scenic Rivers Act of 1968 that established a nationwide system of outstanding free-flowing rivers. Such rivers possess "outstanding remarkable values" within its immediate environment. The Flathead River originates in the Canadian Rockies to the north of Glacier National Park and flows southwest into Flathead Lake, eventually emptying into the Clark Fork River. It provides exceptional recreational opportunities, in particular for fishing, rafting, and scenery and wildlife viewing. *The Flathead National Forest and Glacier National Park currently manage the 219 miles of the three forks of the Flathead River under the Flathead Comprehensive River Management Plan (CRMP). Section 3(d) of the Wild and Scenic River Act requires that river management plans designated prior to 1986 be reviewed (USDA, 2019). Such revision was conducted in 2019, consistent with the guidance provided by the IVUMC (NPS, 2019). The following VUM steps can be recognized.* *Step 1.* The project purpose was (a) to protect and enhance the outstandingly remarkable values identified in the original designation, and (b) to update the existing river management plan as required to maintain compliance with the Wild and Scenic Rivers Act and to reflect changes that have occurred since designation (1976) in forest and park management, special status species, and other laws that affect resources within the Flathead River corridor. *Step 7.* Proposed indicators included the number of sites associated with trails, take-outs, boat ramps, parking lots, campgrounds, roads, etc. that show evidence of erosion; and number of human waste deposits and/or direct conduits from fecal source to surface water body. Thresholds for these indicators were set, for example as "0 sites" and "1 instance of unburied human waste observed per site visit", respectively. *Step 9.* Potential management actions included constructing sustainable facilities, routes, and river access points; designating and directing visitors to sustainable facilities, routes and river access points; closing and rehabilitating unsustainable facilities and constructing sustainable ones; informational signage with education on "pack it out" requirements and defecating away from surface water; fixing the cause of contamination; and providing sanitary facilities where possible. *Step 11.* Frequent monitoring of the proposed indicators related to scenery, wildlife, botany, geology, fisheries, water quality and quantity, history and ethnography is encouraged. It is partly conducted in collaboration between the land management agencies and the University of Montana.	GNP is one of the iconic parks in the United States that protects 1 million acres of the scenic northern Rocky Mountains in Western Montana. It is part of one of the largest, most intact ecosystems in North America called the Crown of the Continent. Named for the glaciers that carved the landscape during the last ice age, GNP is known for its rugged peaks, crystalline turquoise lakes, waterfalls, forests, and biodiversity. Today, the park attracts more than three million visitors a year from all over the world. Many of them drive along its famous Going-to-the-Sun Road to Logan Pass. It also has more than 700 miles of foot and horse trails (NPS, 2016). *In 2019, the National Park Service conducted the Going-to-the-Sun Road Corridor Management Plan Environmental Assessment, consistent with the guidance provided by the IVUMC (NPS, 2019). The following VUM steps can be recognized.* *Step 1.* The project purpose was to address three issues: visitation increases, vehicle congestion, and potential for alternative transportation. *Step 5.* Desired conditions were determined for visitor use and experience (such as managing the corridor to maximize safety for all users); natural resources (such as to maintain and improve clean water and air); cultural resources (such as to preserve historically and culturally significant transportation tours and services); and park operations (such as ensure the ability of the park to have the critical staffing). *Step 7.* Indicators for transportation included: vehicles at one time at key destinations, shuttle wait time for visitors, roadway level of service, and preservation of historic road features. *Step 10.* Visitor capacities were defined for nine most popular locations (such as Avalanche Developed Area, the Loop, Logan Pass, etc.) as POAT increments (People at One Time, the total number of people that are present at a site at any given point in time). *Steps 6 & 9.* Two alternatives were developed (the no-action, and adaptive management alternatives) and specific actions were proposed for different locations for each of them. Examples included adding shuttle stops, improving visitor orientation, adding parking spaces, and others. *Step 11.* Monitoring includes continued monitoring of the proposed indicators to track whether thresholds for trail use levels, closures and traffic slowdowns, crowding at key sites, and natural and cultural resource degradation are being exceeded.

Monitoring

IVUMC (2019) emphasizes that a robust and comprehensive monitoring strategy is one of the keys for success for visitor use management. It is necessary to specify exactly what is going to be monitored and why, where the monitoring will occur, who will collect the data, how often each indicator will be monitored, and how the data will be collected, analyzed, managed and reported. Monitoring requires a commitment to collecting and evaluating data over an extended period of time, as visitor use and visitor behaviors are susceptible to change. Monitoring shows how conditions change over time, including the rate and magnitude of change.

Development and implementation of monitoring should be done before critical decisions are made. A well-planned, holistic, and systematic monitoring effort "provides for transparency, communication, and potential cost savings" (IVUMC, 2019, p. 33), and helps managers recognize trends over time. Griffin et al. (2010) emphasize that consistent visitor data collection can improve efficiencies in resource allocation. In particular, the monitoring data could prevent the misalloca-tion of resources to services and facilities that visitors do not regard as important and which do not contribute to conservation or other agency objectives.

In regards to visitor monitoring, several methods and techniques have been suggested for protected areas with the advantages and disadvantages of different options well discussed in the literature. Visitor monitoring in recreation areas can employ both quantitative and qualitative approaches. The former may include monitoring number of visitors, number of visits, visitor flow, visitor timings, and visitor density. Quantitative methods can include direct observation, video observation, counting devices, and registration books (Cessford and Muhar, 2003; Muhar et al., 2002). Other visitor monitoring methods include visitor surveys and in-depth interviews in order to document visitor and visit characteristics, activities, experiences, expectations, motivations, and behavior (Manning et al., 2017).

Counting the number of visitors in the field can be labor-intensive; therefore, automatic counting devices are becoming more and more popular as they can reduce costs and provide more systematic observations. Several software packages and equipment have been developed for trail and road traffic counting that help to collect, organize, and analyze the big data, such as TRAFx (Simpson, 2018) and JAMAR (www.jamartech.com). Two main challenges when using mechanical devices (in particular infrared trail, road counters, or game cameras) are the site-specific set-up and the accuracy of the data. The manuals for the equipment usually provide details and advice on how to set up the equipment properly and make sure that recording is accurate. However, it is suggested to always examine the data closely for accuracy, as the counters may wrongly record visitors walking in groups and/or record wildlife. Often, calibration using field observations and/or camera data is needed to improve the counts, in which researchers should look at the correlations between the hourly/daily sums of visitors and the corresponding sensor signals. In addition, vandalism of the equipment can become a problem (either the stealing of counting devices or their manipulation so that they report no or wrong results). The application of buried counters (where the direct pressure triggers a sensor) might be a useful alternative or researchers can do their best to hide the counting devices as best as possible. In addition to the different mechanical, pressure, optical, magnetic and other devices, Cessford and Muhar (2003) provide a nice summary and overview of other counting methods that include direct observations and visitor registration cards.

Visitor surveys and interviews are often used to explore visitor expectations, deep experiences, and to better understand visitor satisfaction, motivations, attitudes and behavior. In addition, there are examples of using on-site interviews to better understand visitor patterns and behaviors with case studies in the US and around the world (e.g. Fredman et al., 2007; Nickerson, 2016; Rice et al., 2019). When resources permit, mixed monitoring methods can be used to increase the accuracy of the data and obtain additional information that will help interpret the results. Muhar et al. (2002) argue that a combination of methods should be considered in order to compensate for the disadvan-tages of a single counting technique and to allow for comparisons and correlations.

Despite the many advantages and necessity of the monitoring process, its role has often been overlooked. Monitoring approaches undertaken by land management agencies in different countries are described in numerous contexts (e.g. Cope et al., 2000; McClaran and Cole, 1993; Washburne, 1981). In many cases, it was found that a high proportion of managers were undertaking some sort of visitor monitoring but that the methods used widely varied from place to place, thereby preventing comparability and/or tracking of trends across time. In the US context, Borrie et al. (1998) argued that monitoring generally has been conducted informally and inconsistently, with little systematic planning and implementation. Monitoring often "suffers from perceptions, such as that it detracts from higher priority work, that it is overly expensive, and that it is time consuming" (IVUMC, 2019, p. 7). However, VUM emphasizes that monitoring is "an *essential* component of good visitor use management" (IVUMC, 2016, p. 39).

In the last step of the VUM framework, monitoring results are used as a tool to inform ongoing adjustment of management strategies and actions. If conditions are not improving, the intensity of the management effort might need to be increased or new actions implemented; it is a continual process, and is often depicted as a repeated circle of planning (IVUMC, 2016; Stankey et al., 1985). Adaptive visitor use management is a continuous process of mutual learning and growth.

CONCLUSION

While the preservation of the ecological and heritage conditions and the high-quality experiences enjoyed there are fundamental to the mission of protected area managers, visitor use management continues to be a complex and contentious task. The VUM framework provides a best-practice and step-by-step process for specifically defining the desired environmental, social, and managerial conditions and setting indicators and thresholds that help track those conditions over time. Social science and the systematic and rigorous monitoring of visitors, their behaviors and experiences has been a crucial and important component in the application of VUM.

VUM is applicable across a diversity of sustainable tourism situations and a variety of projects ranging from small-scale local initiatives to large-scale/park-wide planning efforts. It was designed to support and integrate into existing US land management planning policies, regulations, and procedures. As demands for the opportunities and benefits of world-class visitor experiences continue to rise, the need for a science-based, transparent, and defensible approach to managing sustainable tourism on public lands will also increase. VUM provides such a consistent and systematic framework for application across a variety of global jurisdictions and is an important part of the adaptive visitor management concept.

NOTE

1. The Visitor Use Framework (IVUMC, 2016) replaces standards with thresholds, which are defined as "minimally acceptable conditions associated with each indicator" (p. 29). This clearly signals that thresholds aren't desirable or optimal (unless they have been exceeded, in which case they become targets for recovery). *The Monitoring Guidebook* (IVUMC, 2019, p. 10) specifically states that the term "threshold" is synonymous with "standards" or "quality standards".

REFERENCES

Balmford, A., Green, J. M. H., Anderson, M., Beresford, J., Huang, C., Naidoo, R., Walpole, M. and Manica, A. (2015) Walk on the wild side: Estimating the global magnitude of visits to protected areas. *PLoS Biology*, 13(2), e1002074. doi:10.1371/journal.pbio.1002074.

Borrie, W. T., McCool, S. and Stankey, G. H. (1998) Protected area planning principles and strategies. In K. Lindberg, M. E. Wood and D. Engeldrum (eds.), *Ecotourism: A Guide for Planners and Managers* (pp. 133–154). North Bennington, VT: The Ecotourism Society.

Boyd, S. W. and Butler, R. W. (1996) Managing ecotourism: An opportunity spectrum approach. *Tourism Management*, 17, 557–566.

Bratman, G. N., Hamilton, J. P. and Daily, G. C. (2012) The impacts of nature experience on human cognitive function and mental health. *Annals of the New York Academy of Sciences*, 1249, 118–136.

Brown, P. J., Driver, B. and McConnell, C. (1978) *The Opportunity Spectrum Concept and Behavioral Information in Outdoor Recreation Resource Supply Inventories: Background and Application. Proceedings of the Integrated Inventories of Renewable Natural Resources Workshop* (Gen. Tech. Rep. RM-55). US Department of Agriculture, Forest Service, Rocky Mountain Forest and Range Experiment Station.

Buckley, R., Brough, P., Hague, L., Chauvenet, A., Fleming, C., Roche, E., Sofija, E. and Harris, N. (2019) Economic value of protected areas via visitor mental health. *Nature Communications*, 10(1). doi:10.1038/s41467-019-12631-6.

Butler, R. and Waldbrook, L. (1991) A new planning tool: The tourism opportunity spectrum. *Journal of Tourism Studies*, 2(1), 2–14.

Cahill, K., Collins, R., McPartland, S., Pitt, A. and Verbos, R. (2018) Overview of the interagency Visitor Use Management framework and the uses of social science in its implementation in the National Park Service. *The George Wright Forum*, 35(1), 32–41.

Cessford, G. and Muhar, A. (2003) Monitoring options for visitor numbers in national parks and natural areas. *Journal for Nature Conservation*, 11(4), 240–250.

Clark, R. N. and Stankey, G. H. (1979) *The Recreation Opportunity Spectrum: A Framework for Planning, Management, and Research* (Gen. Tech. Rep. PNW-98). US Department of Agriculture, Forest Service, Pacific Northwest Forest and Range Experiment Station.

Cole, D. N. and Stankey, G. H. (1997) Historical development of Limits of Acceptable Change: Conceptual clarifications and possible extensions. In S. F. McCool and D. N. Cole (eds.), *Proceedings – Limits of Acceptable Change and Related Planning Processes: Progress and Future Directions. From a workshop held at the University of Montana's Lubrecht Experimental Forest* (Gen. Tech. Rep. INT-GTR-371, pp. 5–9). US Department of Agriculture, Forest Service, Rocky Mountain Research Station.

Cope, A., Doxford, D. and Probert, C. (2000) Monitoring visitors to UK countryside resources: The approaches of land and recreation resource management organisations to visitor monitoring. *Land Use Policy*, 17(1), 59–66.

Driver, B. L., Brown, P. J. and Peterson, G. L. (1991) *Benefits of Leisure*. State College, PA: Venture Publishing.

Driver, B. L., Brown, P. J., Stankey, G. H. and Gregoire, T. G. (1987) The ROS planning system: Evolution, basic concepts, and research needed. *Leisure Sciences*, 9(3), 201–212.

Driver, B. L. and Bruns, D. H. (1999) Concepts and uses of the benefits approach to leisure. In T. Burton and E. Jackson (eds.), *Leisure Studies at the Millennium* (pp. 349–369). State College, PA: Venture Publishing.

Eagles, P. F., McCool, S. F., Haynes, C. D. and Phillips, A. (2002) *Sustainable Tourism in Protected Areas: Guidelines for Planning and Management* (Vol. 8). Gland, Switzerland: IUCN.

Fefer, J. P., De-Urioste Stone, S., Daigle, J. and Silka, L. (2016) Using the Delphi technique to identify key elements for effective and sustainable visitor use planning frameworks. *SAGE Open*, 6(2), 215824401664314. doi:10.1177/2158244016643141.

Fredman, P., Friberg, L. H. and Emmelin, L. (2007) Increased visitation from national park designation. *Current Issues in Tourism*, 10(1), 87–95.

Griffin, T., Moore, S., Crilley, G., Darcy, S. and Schweinsberg, S. (2010) *Protected Area Management, Collection and Use of Visitor Data: Vol. 1, Summary and Recommendations*. Goldcoast, Queensland: CRC for Sustainable Tourism.

Hennings, L. (2017) *Hiking, Mountain Biking, and Equestrian Use in Natural Areas: A Recreation Ecology Literature Review*. Metropolitan Regional Government. https://www.oregonmetro.gov/sites/default/files/2017/09/28/Metro-Recreation-Ecology-Literature-Review.pdf.

IVUMC (Interagency Visitor Use Management Council) (2016) *Visitor Use Management Framework: A Guide to Providing Sustainable Outdoor Recreation* (Edition One). https://visitorusemanagement.nps.gov/VUM/Framework.

IVUMC (Interagency Visitor Use Management Council) (2019) *Monitoring Guidebook: Evaluating Effectiveness of Visitor Use Management*. https://visitorusemanagement.nps.gov/VUM/Framework.

Kellert, S. R. (1995) *The Biophilia Hypothesis*. Washington, DC: Island Press.

Kohl, J. M. and McCool, S. F. (2016) *The Future Has Other Plans: Planning Holistically to Conserve Natural and Cultural Heritage*. Golden, CO: Fulcrum Publishing.

Krishnaswamy, A. (2012) Strategies and tools for effective public participation in natural resource management. *Journal of Ecosystems and Management*, 13(2), 1–13.

Krumpe, E. and McCool, S. F. (1997) Role of public involvement in the Limits of Acceptable Change wilderness planning system. In S. F. McCool and D. N. Cole (eds.), *Proceedings – Limits of Acceptable Change and Related Planning Processes: Progress and Future Directions. From a workshop held at the University of Montana's Lubrecht Experimental Forest* (Gen. Tech. Rep. INT-GTR-371, pp. 16–20). US Department of Agriculture, Forest Service, Rocky Mountain Research Station.

Kuss, F. R., Graefe, A. and Vaske, J. J. (1990) *Visitor Impact Management: A Review of Research, Vol. 1*. Washington, DC: National Parks and Conservation Association.

Lachapelle, P. R. and McCool, S. F. (2005) Exploring the concept of "ownership" in natural resource planning. *Society and Natural Resources*, 18(3), 279–285.

Leung, Y.-F., Spenceley, A., Hvenegaard, G., Buckley, R. and Groves, C. (2018) *Tourism and Visitor Management in Protected Areas: Guidelines for Sustainability*. Gland, Switzerland: IUCN.

Manning, R. E. (2011) *Studies in Outdoor Recreation: Search and Research for Satisfaction* (3rd ed.). Corvallis, OR: Oregon State University Press.

Manning, R. E., Anderson, L. E. and Pettengill, P. (2017) *Managing Outdoor Recreation: Case Studies in the National Parks* (2nd ed.). Wallingford: CABI.

Marion, J. L., Leung, Y.-F., Eagleston, H. and Burroughs, K. (2016) A review and synthesis of recreation ecology research findings on visitor impacts to wilderness and protected natural areas. *Journal of Forestry*, 114(3), 352–362.

McClaran, M. P. and Cole, D. N. (1993) *Packstock in Wilderness: Use, Impacts, Monitoring, and Management* (Gen. Tech. Rep. INT-GTR-301). US Department of Agriculture, Forest Service, Intermountain Research Station.

McCool, S. F. (1994) Planning for sustainable nature dependent tourism development. *Tourism Recreation Research*, 19(2), 51–55.

McCool, S. F. (2006) Managing for visitor experiences in protected areas: Promising opportunities and fundamental challenges. *Parks*, 16(2), 3–9.

McCool, S. F. (2016) Tourism in protected areas: Frameworks for working through the challenges in an era of change, complexity and uncertainty. In S. F. McCool and K. Bosak (eds.), *Reframing Sustainable Tourism* (pp. 101–117). Dordrecht: Springer.

McCool, S. F. (2019) Information needs for building a foundation for enhancing sustainable tourism as a development goal: An introduction. In S. F. McCool and K. Bosak (eds.), *A Research Agenda for Sustainable Tourism* (pp. 1–13). Cheltenham, UK and Northampton, MA, USA: Edward Elgar Publishing.

McCool, S. F., Clark, R. N. and Stankey, G. H. (2007) *An Assessment of Frameworks Useful for Public Land Recreation Planning* (Gen. Tech. Rep. PNW-GTR-705). US Department of Agriculture, Forest Service, Pacific Northwest Research Station.

Miller, Z. D., Fefer, J. P., Kraja, A., Lash, B. and Freimund, W. (2017) Perspectives on visitor use management in the National Parks. *The George Wright Forum*, 34(1), 37–44.

Miller, Z. D., Rice, W. L., Taff, B. D. and Newman, P. (2019) Concepts for understanding the visitor experience in sustainable tourism. In S. F. McCool and K. Bosak (eds.), *A Research Agenda for Sustainable Tourism* (pp. 53–69). Cheltenham, UK and Northampton, MA, USA: Edward Elgar Publishing.

Moore, R. L. and Driver, B. (2005) *Introduction to Outdoor Recreation: Providing and Managing Natural Resource Based Opportunities*. State College, PA: Venture Publishing.

Muhar, A., Arnberger, A. and Brandenburg, C. (2002) Methods for visitor monitoring in recreational and protected areas: An overview. In A. Arnberger, C. Brandenburg and A. Muhar (eds.), *Monitoring and*

Management of Visitor Flows in Recreational and Protected Areas. Conference Proceedings (pp. 1–6). Institute for Landscape Architecture & Landscape Management, Bodenkultur University.

Naidoo, R., Gerkey, D., Hole, D., Pfaff, A., Ellis, A., Golden, C., Herrera, D., Johnson, K., Mulligan, M. and Ricketts, T. (2019) Evaluating the impacts of protected areas on human well-being across the developing world. *Science Advances*, 5(4), eaav3006.

National Park Service (1997) *VERP. The Visitor Experience and Resource Protection (VERP) Framework: A Handbook for Planners and Managers.* US Department of the Interior, National Park Service, Denver Service Center.

National Park Service (2016) *Glacier National Park: Foundation Document.* https://www.nps.gov/glac/learn/management/upload/GLAC_FD_SP.pdf.

National Park Service (2019) *Going-to-the-Sun Road Corridor Management Plan Environmental Assessment.* United States Department of Interior.

Newsome, D., Moore, S. A. and Dowling, R. K. (2013) *Natural Area Tourism: Ecology, Impacts and Management* (2nd ed.). Bristol: Channel View Publications.

Nickerson, N. P. (2016) *What We Know about Crowding and Visitor Experiences.* Institute for Tourism and Recreation Research Publications, 340, University of Montana.

Nilsen, P. and Tayler, G. (1997) A comparative analysis of protected area planning and management frameworks. In S. F. McCool and D. N. Cole (eds.), *Proceedings – Limits of Acceptable Change and Related Planning Processes: Progress and Future Directions. From a workshop held at the University of Montana's Lubrecht Experimental Forest* (Gen. Tech. Rep. INT-GTR-371, pp. 49–58). US Department of Agriculture, Forest Service, Rocky Mountain Research Station.

Priskin, J. and McCool, S. (2006) The visitor experience challenge. *Parks*, 6(2), 1–2.

Rice, W. L., Taff, B. D., Newman, P., Miller, Z. D., D'Antonio, A. L., Baker, J. T., Monz, C., Newton, J. N. and Zipp, K. Y. (2019) Grand expectations: Understanding visitor motivations and outcome interference in Grand Teton National Park, Wyoming. *Journal of Park and Recreation Administration*, 37(2).

Shafer, E. (1969) *The Average Camper Who Doesn't Exist* (Res. Pap. NE-142). US Department of Agriculture, Forest Service, Northeastern Forest Experiment Station.

Shelby, B. and Heberlein, T. A. (1986) *Carrying Capacity in Recreation Settings.* Corvallis, OR: Oregon State University Press.

Shultis, J. (2003) Recreational values of protected areas. In D. Harmon and A. D. Putney (eds.), *The Full Value of Parks: From Economics to the Intangible* (pp. 59–75). Lanham, MD: Rowman & Littlefield.

Simpson, G. (2018) Use of a public fishing area determined by vehicle counters with verification by trail cameras. *Natural Resources*, 09(05), 188–197.

Stankey, G., Cole, D., Lucas, R., Petersen, M. and Frissell, S. (1985) *The Limits of Acceptable Change (LAC) System for Wilderness Planning* (Gen. Tech. Rep. INT-176). US Department of Agriculture, Forest Service, Intermountain Forest and Range Experiment Station.

Stankey, G. H. and McCool, S. F. (1992) Managing recreation use of marine resources through the limits of acceptable change planning system. Unpublished paper. School of Forestry, University of Montana.

United States Department of Agriculture (USDA) (2019) Flathead Wild and Scenic River. Proposed Action for the Comprehensive River Management Plan. Flathead National Forest. Glacier National Park.

United States Forest Service (1987) The Bob Marshall, Great Bear and Scapegoat Wildernesses. Recreation Management Direction. United States Department of Agriculture. Forest Service Flathead, Lolo, Helena, Lewis & Clark National Forests.

Wang, X. and Wan Wart, M. (2007) When public participation in administration leads to trust: An empirical assessment of managers' perceptions. *Public Administration Review*, 67(2), 265–278.

Washburne, R. F. (1981) Carrying capacity assessment and recreational use in the national wilderness preservation system. *Journal of Soil and Water Conservation*, 36(3), 162–166.

Watson, A. E., Cronn, R. and Christensen, N. A. (1998) *Monitoring Inter-Group Encounters in Wilderness* (Res. Pap. RMRS-RP-14). US Department of Agriculture, Forest Service, Rocky Mountain Research Station.

Watson, A. E., Glaspell, B., Christensen, N., Lachapelle, P., Sahanatien, V. and Gertsch, F. (2007) Giving voice to wildlands visitors: Selecting indicators to protect and sustain experiences in the eastern arctic of Nunavut. *Environmental Management*, 40(6), 880–888.

Wilderness Act of 1964, Pub. L. No. 88-577, § 16 U.S. C. § 1131–1136.

18. Developing targets for visitation in parks

Paul F. J. Eagles, Andjelko Novosel, Ognjen Škunca and Vesna Vukadin

INTRODUCTION

One of the most essential and controversial aspects of sustainable tourism is that of developing targets for visitation. The real issue is not tourist numbers, but desirable levels of tourist impacts. Any plan must aim to gain maximum positive impacts, while limiting negative impacts. Accordingly, the visitor impact goals must be carefully developed and explicitly stated to reach the sweet spot of maximum positive and minimum negative impacts.

There are many visitor impact fields within sustainable tourism, such as: environmental, fiscal, economic, social and cultural. Each of these major fields has subfields of importance. The most important subfields must be identified and chosen for review. It is best if standards can be developed within each field to provide numerical limits that enable monitoring to assess if the limits have been reached.

Mulholland and Eagles' (2002) model of financial and ecological sustainability is modified here into a more general model of tourism sustainability (Figure 18.1). This model uses both minimum and maximum tourism volumes to determine an acceptable range.

Figure 18.1   Model of tourism sustainability

A critically important impact field is that of finance. All successful sustainable tourism venues, similar to any business, have a minimum level of financial income that must be earned for operation. Therefore, the lowest tourism volume target will be set by the minimum financial goals. The much more controversial target is that of maximum target goals. For parks, Mulholland and Eagles (2002) proposed that the maximum volumes will be based on the impacts on ecological values. We propose in this chapter for the broader field of sustainable tourism, that these maximum volumes will be set by a combination of economic, environmental, social and cultural impact goals. These goals are almost always set politically, as the power politics of various influential groups determine the volume allowed.

The private, profit-making sector in tourism has little problem in setting maximum target goals for visitation. Theatres, tour companies, and sport venues develop facilities and programmes that set both minimum and maximum targets, largely on financial goals and service quality outcomes. Sporting events have long created capacity limits, usually determined by physical capacities such as the number of seats in the arena. Golf tournaments have long established methods to set the maximum number of clients that will be allowed onto the golf course and along each hole. The number of seats provides a maximum number of clients allowed in a theatre, with no opposition from clients when the capacity is reached. Tour companies set maximum numbers of clients per tour based on both physical capacities, such as the number of seats in the bus, and social capacities, such as the ability of the guide to manage the group while providing effective interpretation services.

Oddly, the public, outdoor recreation sector has had major problems in creating upper limits. Stankey and Manning (1986) reported that many park managers found the carrying capacity difficult to understand and implement. Importantly, they reported that many managers could not establish capacity limits and implement those limits. Manning (2002) reported that the US National Park Service established the Visitor Experience and Resource Protection (VERP) framework to create visitor use limits through formulation of indicators for impact and standards of quality.

Apparently the situation has not improved, especially in the USA, as Zion National Park is still unable to deal with increasing levels of visitation that appear to cause major crowding and visitor concern (Wadsworth, 2017). Why do so many sustainable tourism destinations operated by governments, such as national parks, have problems in setting visitation targets?

Variations in social values create different goals for outdoor recreation participation. Goal interference occurs when different stakeholders have divergent goals; resulting in conflict. For example, some groups want very high use levels due in order to gain more income, such as tour operators, while others want lower levels in order to maintain recreation values, e.g. quiet or solitude, such as wilderness enthusiasts (Hammitt, 1989).

When the management institutions attempt to satisfy all interest groups, political gridlock may occur with many actors with conflicting demands that are too difficult to manage. However, there are examples of the successful development and implementation of targets for sustainable tourism in national and provincial parks. Three case studies will be discussed in this chapter; providing a basis for future managerial and research efforts.

INTRODUCTION TO PEAK LOAD MANAGEMENT

Much discussion in sustainable tourism revolves around visitor capacity numbers, often expressed as visitors per day, per month, or per year. However, the limits are often met during much briefer periods of time, such as visitors attempting to use a specific place at a specific time, for example visitors arriving at the start of holiday weekend at a park entrance, on roads, at trailheads, or at washrooms. Dealing with this issue may be best thought as an issue of peak load management. Oddly, the literature on visitor use capacities has often dealt with long-term visitor numbers, such as annual levels, rather than the much shorter time period of peak loads in terms of hours.

Peak load management is an important principle in many fields, such as transportation, hospitality, tourism, and retail sales. There are two overall approaches to peak load management: one is varying the supply and the other is varying the demand. Tourism often has a management issue due to strong peaks and troughs in visitor volumes over time; such as daily, weekly, and seasonally. Daily, higher volumes tend to occur at midday and early afternoon, while lower volumes occur in the early morning, later evening, and overnight. Weekly higher volumes occur on weekends and holidays, with lower volumes at other times. Yearly, higher volumes occur in warmer weather, with lower volumes in the coldest and hottest periods. Tourism managers have developed many options to deal with the issue. High volumes can lead to problems of crowding, lowered tourist satisfaction, and the overwhelming of infrastructure. Lower volumes will lead to problems of low income leading to financial issues associated with staffing and capital maintenance.

Baum and Lundtorp (2001) identified issues that arise from seasonal variation in tourism use, including:

- A short operating season associated with a long non-operating season, such as occurs in parks with cold winter periods;
- The need to generate a year of revenue in a short period; such as the warmer summer months;
- Overutilization of capital assets in one period and underutilization in another period, such as occurs during peak loading;
- Problems with attracting capital investment for short season facilities;
- Supply chain problems due to variations in use, such as obtaining high levels of supply for only a few periods over the year;
- High variations in employment levels, with much short-term employment in high load periods;
- Problems with maintaining service and product quality in the absence of permanent, long-term employees.

Many park agencies and individual parks have extensive experience in dealing with seasonal variations in visitor flows. For example, northern countries usually see much higher visitor numbers in the warmer summer months than in the colder months. Each of the issues identified immediately above are dealt with to various degrees of success. This chapter cannot cover all of the management responses used, but a few key ones will be discussed. Societies with experience in tourism seasonality have developed the capability to respond effectively, with park management being able to utilize that capability. For example, suppliers of food and equipment are often themselves designed to ramp up their activities in the high use periods. The heavy use of short-term employment in parks often works well with the needs of university and college student employees whose school terms occur during the colder months and work terms occur during the warmer months. It is critically important that the management agency has the capacity to retain tourism income in high use periods for expenditures in lower use periods. Service and product quality concerns are usually only addressed through consumer complaints, without systematic service quality measurement programmes. This is not ideal; but often the only option that is feasible.

An effectively operated tourism activity must be undertaken within an overall management plan. All decisions should be anchored to the site's goals and objectives, as stated in that plan. Many parks have visitor facilities and programmes that were developed individually over long time periods, without reference to an overall plan. The reconciliation of these older facilities and programmes can be a major issue in new, overall management planning.

The Development of Standards

The initial efforts in any field are devoid of standards. In the case of the establishment of minimum and maximum use levels, standards must be developed and refined over time. However, as experience is gained, standards are developed and refined. Standards are an agreed upon way of operation. They can be specific, such as road standards, or general, such as management practices. A standard provides a reliable basis for people to share the same expectations about a product or service. This helps to:

1. Facilitate trade;
2. Provide a framework for achieving economies, efficiencies and interoperability;
3. Enhance consumer protection and confidence (BSI, 2019).

Tourism operations use hundreds of standards, such as those involved in aircraft construction, operation and maintenance, or those involved in computer equipment, or those involved in food safety.

Tourism organizations can use:

1. A quality management standard to help work more efficiently and reduce product failures;
2. An environmental management standard to help reduce negative environmental impacts, reduce waste, and be more sustainable;
3. A health and safety standard to help reduce accidents in the workplace;
4. An information technology security standard to help keep sensitive information secure;
5. A construction standard for facilities;
6. An energy management standard to minimize energy consumption;
7. A food safety standard to help prevent food from being contaminated;
8. An accessibility standard to help make buildings accessible to disabled users;
9. An interoperability standard to ensure that bank and credit cards fit into ATMs and can be used throughout the world (BSI, 2019).

The consumer benefits from the use of standards, so that travel expectations can be realistically accessed. Standards require the development of monitoring programmes that reveal fulfilment. One of the most important aspects of the development of sustainable tourism targets is the understanding of service quality standards. The most successful tourism operations are those that have service quality standard targets and measurement programmes to ensure that those standards are met.

There is a massive literature on the development and operation of service quality standards. One of the most successful measurement approaches is that of SERVQUAL. This is a multi-item scale developed to assess customer perceptions of service quality in service and retail businesses (Parasuraman et al., 1985, 1988). The scale describes the notion of service quality through five constructs as follows:

1. Tangibles – physical facilities, equipment, staff appearance, etc.;
2. Reliability – ability to perform service dependably and accurately;
3. Responsiveness – willingness to help and respond to customer need;
4. Assurance – ability of staff to inspire confidence and trust;
5. Empathy – the extent to which caring individualized service is given.

SERVQUAL represents service quality as the differences between a customer's expectations for a service offering and the customer's perceptions of the service received, requiring respondents to answer questions about both their expectations and their perceptions (Parasuraman et al., 1988). The use of perceived as opposed to actual service received makes the SERVQUAL measure an attitude measure that is related to, but not the same as, satisfaction (Parasuraman et al., 1988). Parasuraman et al. (1991) presented some revisions to the original SERVQUAL measure to remedy problems with high means and standard deviations found on some questions and to obtain a direct measure of the importance of each construct to the customer (IS Theory, 2019).

Service quality standards can provide a firm basis for the determination of visitor use volumes, both minimum and maximum. The number of people encountered on a trail, in an outdoor programme, or at a special event can be partially determined by the service quality standard target. All sustainable tourism venues should develop service quality standards, and measure the attainment of those standards. Not only must standards be used, the consumer must be told about those standards and their fulfilment.

Nykiforuk and Eagles (1999) proposed that Parks Canada use ISO 9004 standards for service quality measure, a recommendation that was not accepted by the park agency, for unexplained reasons. Accordingly, it is very rare for tourism providers to provide to their customers their service quality standards and the attainment of those standards. This is especially true for national parks and protected areas, where service quality standards are extremely rare. This has left the door open for independent measurement programmes to develop. Programmes without service quality standards are almost guaranteed to have problems.

Tourism often occurs well away from home and it is very difficult for the consumer to develop an understanding of the quality and value of the programme offering before making the purchase decision. The consumer may not trust the information provided by the tourism operator, or in the case of many sustainable tourism operations information is not provided at all. This has led to internet programmes of consumer-led service and facility quality reporting, such as those provided by TripAdvisor (Limberger et al., 2014). These evaluations are a form of standard measurement, where the consumer provides their evaluation of the value of the product compared to the cost of that product. Later in the chapter we describe how a reduction in TripAdvisor rankings in a Plitvice national park was used to identify the need for management change.

Options for Peak Load Management

When demand exceeds supply in peak load periods, rationing recreation and tourism services is necessary (McLean and Johnson, 1997). There are two major issues in rationing. One is to develop capacity limits and the second is the implementation of those limits. Managers can place arbitrary limits on use, without concern about where the excess volume goes. They can deflect some of the use from higher volume times to lower volume times. They can create infrastructure and programmes to allow higher maximum numbers, but this ultimately has limits. Once the limits have been set, there are eight techniques that enable the achievement of the goals of public recreation and tourism, as well as serving the public good: (1) price, (2) queuing, (3) lottery, (4) priority based on need, (5) access to use rules, such as skill levels, (6) time allotment, (7) demarketing, and (8) vouchers. Managerial judgement will determine the technique used.

There are many examples of physical limits determining use levels. For example, theatres have a seat limit, which cannot be exceeded. The seat capacity has been predetermined by the capital monies available for construction, the anticipated demand, and by the applicable safety, health, and fire standards. When a theatre's seats are all sold, potential clients must deflect to a different time. It is not possible to exceed the assigned capacity limit, largely for safety reasons. This is an example of the determination of fixed physical capacity limit, with a deflection strategy when demand exceeds supply.

The use of higher prices to deflect peak load use to times of lower demand is common in private sector tourism management, as evidenced by changing resort and hotel prices over time. However, most park managers have been slow to adopt this policy.

There are many infrastructure changes that can be made to handle peak load, but these can be expensive and ultimately a firm limit will be reached. This limit is largely determined by the financial cost, compared to the benefits of developing infrastructure for peak loads. It is often too expensive to build a site's infrastructure to handle the brief periods of very high use. This results in crowding, line-ups and client dissatisfaction.

Transportation Policy for Peak Load Management

In sustainable tourism, the impacts of high volumes involve more than the people themselves. Since many parks and sites are remote from cities and transit, visitors often travel in their own vehicles. The space needed for vehicles is usually larger than the space needed for people. Some parks and sites have developed policies that limit transportation space and facilities.

Zion National Park in the USA has a very attractive main canyon which attracts high volumes of use in the warmer periods of the year. The peak load parking at Zion is in desig-nated sites outside the national park. The transit system introduced in 2000 moves people from those parking areas into and through the main canyon of the park. The shuttle system, which transports visitors up the 6.5-mile Zion Canyon Scenic Drive during peak visitation times, was designed for 2 million to 2.5 million annual visitors in the year 2000 (Wadsworth, 2017). Since that time, the number of visitors continued to increase, crowding became a major problem due to congestion at the parking area and within the park, and the park has not been able to find an acceptable solution. This example shows that peak load and congestion can pose intractable management problems at some locales.

The Niagara Parks Commission manages the tourism along the Niagara River and Niagara Falls in Ontario, Canada (Figure 18.2). This site has the highest tourism volume of nature-based sites in Canada, with up to 16,000,000 visits per year. Interestingly, the Commission receives no money from government, and all its expenses must be covered by various tourist fees and charges. This site does not charge for the main attraction, viewing Niagara Falls, but does charge for parking, a substitute for an entrance fee. The price for parking varies according to the level of access to the main viewing sites, with higher fees for closer access. Remote access parking at lower prices is provided and a transit system is used to connect that parking to the main viewing areas. This example outlines the importance of both consumer choice and pricing policy in peak load management.

Figure 18.2   Transportation and service facilities at Niagara Falls, Canada

Capacity Limits

Many tourism programmes and facilities have established capacity limits, created by a suite of underlying factors. Facilities typically have load capacities, as defined by the weight of the cargo, the number of seats in the bus, or the number of beds in the hotel. These limits are set by building codes, manufacturing specifications, and insurance coverage. Consumers are accepting of capacity limits that are explained as a combination of safety and service quality.

Managers must realize that there is no magic formula for the creation of tourism capacity limits in a destination. Beyond those set by professional practice and regulation, mentioned above, the others must be set by a managerial decision influenced by stakeholder involvement. The Limits of Acceptable Change Process is a good method to develop those limits. The US

National Park System attempts to use the Visitor Experience and Resource Protection process. However, the organization must have the capability to implement the limits so developed.

CASE STUDIES

We will next outline three case studies of management planning in parks purposively reducing visitor numbers in order to more effectively manage visitation. They occur over a 50 year period, from the early 1970s for Pinery Provincial Park, the 1980s for Point Pelee National Park, and the 2010s for Plitvice National Park. These examples reveal that setting and implementation of maximum visitor use levels in public institutions is feasible.

Point Pelee National Park Case Study

Background
Point Pelee National Park is Canada's smallest national park, at 15.5 km². As 72 per cent of the park is wetland, there is only a small land area for visitor facilities and use (Figure 18.3). The park was established in 1914, largely to protect and manage migratory bird populations. Pelee is one of the top bird watching destinations in Canada with very high avian diversity, with over 390 species recorded, and high levels of visitor use during spring migration in April and May, each year. It also has high use in the warm summer months due to an attractive sandy beach on Lake Erie (Point Pelee National Park, 2010).

The first 50 years of management saw extensive levels of development in the park, including 300 private cottages, two hotels, and as well as farms with asparagus fields and apple orchards. There was a school, life-saving station and commercial fishery. Much of this development was a holdover from before park creation. By the 1950s with lax parking regulation, including parking on the beach, the park would accommodate up to 6,000 vehicles at one time in a very small land area (Boissoneault, 2019). Over time, changing societal attitudes recognized that this level of development was unacceptable in a national park. Starting in the 1950s planners and managers began to deal with the issue of high levels of development and use with several policy changes to create a new physical capacity limit.

Management policies
Park officials started to reduce the human footprint in the 1950s. The park removed more than 350 buildings and two roads (Hill, 2018). Park maintenance facilities were moved outside the park. Annual visitation peaked in 1963 at 781,000, with Point Pelee, the smallest of Canada's national parks, the most heavily used (Point Pelee National Park, 2010). Park managers and planners realized that limits to use involved not only the total numbers of visitors, but also their distribution across the park. In 1971 a shuttle service from the Visitor Centre to the Tip was established to control both visitor numbers and concentrations in this part of the park. This was supposed to be the first step in a three-stage plan to remove all private vehicles from the park, by creating parking areas outside Pelee's boundaries and extending the shuttle system to the entire park. Although endorsed by the 1972 Park Master Plan, the first such management plan for a national park in Canada, the full shuttle system was not implemented as it was unpopular locally and unsupported by municipal zoning to allow park lots outside the park (Boissoneault, 2019). This 1972 plan was the first national park management plan created in Canada, follow-

Figure 18.3   Point Pelee National Park is mostly wetland, with only a small dry area for visitor facilities and use

ing by one year the plan for Pinery Provincial Park which was the first management plan in provincial parks in Canada.

By 1975, park management used a cut-off figure of 1,400 cars at any one time in the park, a capacity number determined by the professional judgement of park management. Once this limit was reached, the park gates were closed to further entry until vehicles left. Ad hoc parking on the beaches was no longer permitted and formal parking areas were established for beach users. The cut-off point was only reached during the peak use periods of smelt fishing season, the birding season, and three or four Sundays in the summer (Boissoneault, 2019). Duck hunting was eliminated in 1989 after vigorous public debate concerning the negative impact of hunting on bird populations in the park.

Ecological integrity became the first priority in park management due to changes in the National Parks Act in 1988. This concept provided a legislative basis for better management of the human pressures in national parks in Canada.

Over the next fifteen years or so, visitor use patterns changed as smelt fishing was eliminated and swimming in Lake Erie decreased due to water pollution from nearby towns and cities. The heaviest visitor use during this period occurred during late May when bird migration was at its peak, and the cut-off limit was used as required. When the Canadian–American border was hardened after 9 September 2011, the birding visitation from the USA dropped considerably. These reductions in smelt fishing and American birding numbers lowered the peak load pressures.

Between 1986 and 1990 the cut-off figure for the number of parking spaces was lowered once more, this time to 1,150 vehicles, again by the professional judgement of park managers. As of 1997 this had apparently been reduced again, as an article in the September *Legion* magazine states there were 1,000 parking spaces in the park. The superintendent is quoted in the same article as saying there was "No assessment of how many total visitors are acceptable" from an ecological standpoint. The reduction in the number of parking spaces may have been due to high water levels and a severe storm that destroyed the infrastructure at East Beach, which was not replaced, rather than a specific concern for visitor numbers or concentrations at this location (Boissoneault, 2019). This level of use has been retained to the present.

This system of using a defined level of parking as the indicator of physical capacity was successfully put into place in the early 1970s and reduced in increments over the next 50 years. Each of the physical carrying capacity limits was set by the professional judgement of park management.

Lessons learned from the Point Pelee visitor capacity policies
There are valuable lessons learned from the Point Pelee management planning for visitor use. These include:

1. The removal of private cottages, farms, roads, and other buildings reduced the human footprint considerably.
2. Visitation peaked in 1963. The subsequent reductions occurred due to the demands of visitors and environmental groups requesting lower levels of tourism impact, and a new peak load strategy that limited daily numbers to a predefined level.
3. Heightened public concerns led to the development of the first management plan for a national park in Canada in 1972.
4. The introduction of the concept of ecological integrity to the National Parks Act in 1988 gave new impetus to better manage the human footprint in the park.
5. Ecological restoration efforts were successful.
6. The birding community was highly supportive of policies to reduce the human footprint.

7. The use of parking spaces was a visible signal of park physical capacity that was easily accepted as a reasonable policy by park visitors.
8. The shuttle system reduced the parking pressure in the southern part of the park.
9. Canadian society generally, and park visitors specifically, accepted well-argued visitor capacity limits as expressed through the number of parking spaces available.
10. Over time, visitor use moved from extractive uses, such as duck hunting and smelt fishing, towards appreciative recreational activities that were supportive of the concept of ecological integrity, such as birding and environmental education.

Pinery Provincial Park Capacity Case Study

Background

Pinery Provincial Park in Ontario, Canada was established in 1957; when the Government of Ontario purchased a large block of land. The park on Lake Huron has many kilometres of attractive beach and the most significant oak pine forests on sand dunes in Canada. These dune systems are easily damaged by visitor use (Figure 18.4). The park is close to major urban populations of Ontario, Canada and Michigan, USA. Soon after purchase, rapid infrastructure development in the early 1960s led to increases in public use. By 1970, use reached a high of 1.2 million visitors per year. The political recognition of problems associated with this very high use, by sectors of civil society, and within the Ontario Parks Branch, led to a major revaluation of park management. New staff members were hired and a new approach to park planning and management was implemented. In 1971 a park master plan was approved

Figure 18.4   Pinery Provincial Park dunes and foreshore on Lake Huron, an area of very high sensitivity to visitor use

for Pinery Provincial Park, the first of its type in Canadian park history. This plan used the concept of carrying capacity, with recreational and ecological components, as the underlying theoretical construct. This was the first time this carrying capacity theory had been used in park planning in Canada, and possibly anywhere. The full issue is addressed by Eagles (2010), and an overview is provided below.

Management plan policies
This 1971 plan introduced major changes into the operation of the park. Prominent new visitor and resource management policies were introduced. There was less emphasis on tourism volume and more on experience quality through a major reduction in tourism volume. Some facilities were removed. A prohibition on all-terrain vehicles, horseback riding, and motorcycles was introduced. A permanent prohibition of organized sport facilities and power boating on the Ausauble River was introduced. A new visitor centre was proposed, and was constructed in 1993. Sand dune restoration programmes were successful. A new zoning system introduced nature reserve zones with no visitor facilities allowed. Commercial logging and waterfowl hunting were prohibited. A policy to encourage scientific research on targeted species, ecosystems and visitor management was implemented. Better training for park rangers as police officers was introduced in order to have strict enforcement of new rules governing visitor behaviour. In the early years of the implementation of this plan, Ontario Provincial Police officers patrolled the park to assist the park rangers. All of the proposed

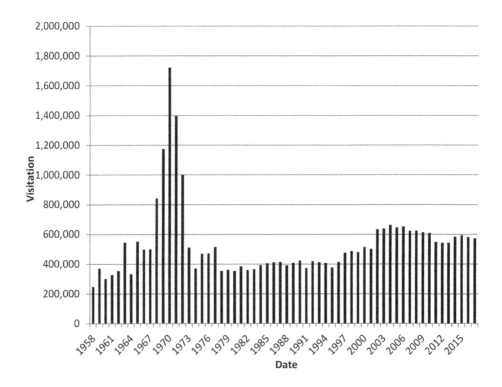

Figure 18.5   Visitor use of Pinery Provincial Park (1958–2018)

policies were implemented, with the exception of a proposed transit system which became unnecessary when lowered visitation volumes were attained.

The volume of use was reduced from 1.72 million visitor days per year in 1970 to 0.37 million visitor days per year by 1975, almost certainly the largest reduction in park use volumes to be planned and implemented in Canadian history and possibly anywhere. This reduction was well received by both the environmental movement and supportive segments of the visiting public. The use then slowly increased under the new management regime and is now stabilized at just less than 600,000 visitor days per year (Figure 18.5). This increase was accepted by the visiting public as it is carefully tied to the physical capacity of the infrastructure and judicious management of visitor impact on the natural resources. The decisions for the 1971 management plan were prepared by one field planner, with the assistance of a small team of planners in the head office of the Parks Branch of the Ministry of Natural Resources, the governing park management body.

Lessons learned from the Pinery management plan
The Pinery Provincial Park planning was successful in reducing visitation to a level that is more socially, culturally and environmentally acceptable to the park managers, and to the environmental and user community. The key to the success of this effort was a supportive political environment in the Ontario Government and in the park agency that demanded the creation and implementation of a sustainable tourism plan for a major tourist facility in public ownership. The Government of the day reacted to public comment about negative social and environment impacts of the visitor use and insisted that the park managers respond accordingly. The head office of Ontario Parks accepted the political imperative for change and introduced new staff and operational procedures to create solutions to the problems. The creation of the Pinery Provincial Park Master Plan was the first overarching management plan done in Canadian parks, at either the provincial or national level. This started the move towards the creation of management plans in provincial parks, with the Bronte Creek Provincial Park Master Plan published in 1973 and the Algonquin Provincial Park Master Plan in 1974 (MacKay, 2019). Later the governing legislation was changed in Ontario to ensure that management plans were created for all complex parks and management statements for parks with less complex management issues.

Many important factors led to the successful development and implementation of the Pinery Management Plan in the early 1970s:

1. The high levels of visitor use led to major negative ecological and social impacts that in turn led to public demands for change.
2. Negative media reports stimulated discussion at all levels, including the Ontario Government.
3. Provincial environmental groups took a position demanding change.
4. The Ontario Parks branch head office became concerned by the public outcry and received political support from government.
5. A new management regime was created that assigned a field planner to tackle the problems supported by a team of head office planners.
6. Conflict on site between the new planner and existing site managers was resolved by the head office staff supporting the new plan process over the older management regime.

7. There was widespread public support for the creation of lower capacity limits, including the many park users who wanted a higher quality visitor experience.
8. The new planners on site and in head office both understood the carrying capacity argument through their university studies in forestry and recreation management.
9. The plan process was long enough, two years, to ensure that all the required studies were done and alternative plans evaluated. It was short enough that political support, within the park agency and the government, was maintained.
10. The carrying capacity limit was a managerial decision that was politically acceptable.
11. Those opposed to change were not politically organized or effective.
12. The resultant plan was published, widely accepted, and praised.
13. The 1971 Pinery Master Plan was the first management plan for a provincial park or national park in Canada, setting a precedent that was extensively followed by later plans.

Plitvice National Park and World Heritage Site Peak Load Management Case Study

Background

Plitvice National Park is the oldest, the largest, and the most visited national park of the Republic of Croatia, designated as such in 1949, with a total area of 296 km² and in 2018 with approximately 1.8 million visitors per year. International value was confirmed in 1979, with UNESCO World Heritage designation. Interaction of water, air, geological foundation and organisms, coupled with specific physical, chemical and biological conditions, enables the formation of tufa barriers that have divided the original river valley and created a cascade of 16 larger and several smaller lakes with a myriad of waterfalls between them (Figure 18.6). The site's Outstanding Universal Value ultimately stems from the totality of these processes and their unique ecology, in combination with the extraordinary beauty of the area. The most attractive and visited lake and canyon zone represents approximately 1 per cent of the park surface.

This area has long attracted nature enthusiasts and has over 150 years of organized visitation. A visitation system within the lake zone was established towards the late 1970s, as a response to the first rapid rise in the number of visitors from around 150,000 per year in 1965 to over 700,000 in the 1980s. A system of narrow trails was constructed to ensure low levels of environmental impact and high levels of visitor safety in the main valley of the park (Figure 18.7).

The number of visitors doubled between 2007 and 2017 (Figure 18.8) resulting in increasingly serious congestion and crowding as the capacities of all parts of the existing visitation system (parking lots, entry reception points, trails, boardwalks, docks and boats, stations and panoramic vehicles) became insufficient for peak loads during summer months. In 2007, the recorded maximum stood at 10,718 visitors in a day; in 2017 the level became 16,125 visitors in a single day. This high level of visitation led to concerns by park managers, some members of the public and eventually UNESCO about the issue of tourism in the park. As a result, a park management plan effort was undertaken from 2014 to 2018 to develop a new park management plan, resulting in a new plan released in 2019 (Plitvice Lakes, 2019).

The management plan (Plitvice, 2019) describes the visitor capacity problem as follows: "The situation that the Park is increasingly facing is the number of visitors exceeding the designed capacity of the existing visitation system in the lake zone ... Inevitable consequences

Figure 18.6   The hundreds of waterfalls in Plitvice National Park are attractive to visitors

*Figure 18.7   Narrow boardwalks in Plitvice Lakes National Park allow access to
waterfalls but are best used through one-way flows*

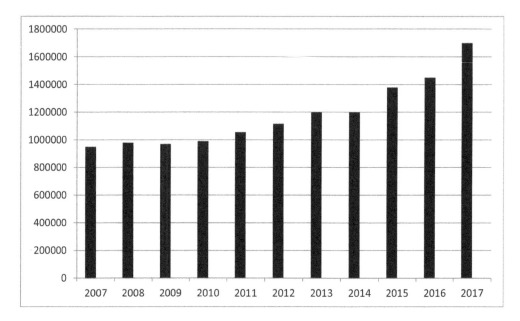

Figure 18.8   Yearly visitor entrances to Plitvice National Park (2007–2017)

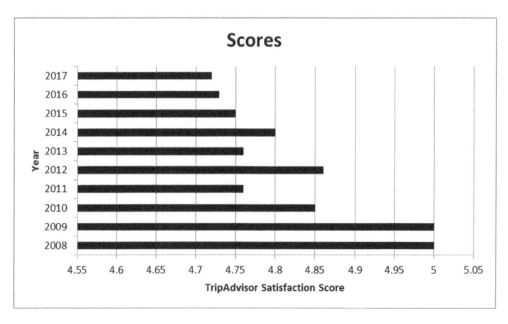

*Figure 18.9   Decreasing rankings of visitor satisfaction reported on TripAdvisor
(2008–2017)*

of letting more visitors enter the Park per hour include crowding, waiting and, in general terms, decreasing quality of visitor experience and quality of presentation of Park values."

The park planners used TripAdvisor rankings over time to reveal the declining level of satisfaction by visitors (Figure 18.9), due to the crowding, congestion, and lengthy wait times. The excessive use levels and the decreasing visitor satisfaction encouraged UNESCO to intercede on behalf of the World Heritage management process to encourage the creation of a new management plan.

Park planners and consultants determined that physical capacity for the trail and boardwalk visitation system in the lake zone is about 1,300 entrants per hour, a figure calculated from the length of the trails and an adopted standard of 3 metres per person as the minimal acceptable distance between two adjacent visitors on the narrow boardwalk.

After analysis and discussion, the planning team concluded that it was not possible to increase the capacity of the existing visitation system through building more boardwalks. The consensual decision was made to introduce an hourly use limit and to attempt to more evenly distribute the visitors in time. Policies were introduced to increase revenues per visitor in order to finance the management of the congestion problems.

Management plan policies
To deal with the problem of congestion in the lake zone, the park management plan introduced new policies. An hourly use limit at entrances was created. A new on-line ticket sale system per hour and per entrance point enabled better flow management. A new pricing policy used high prices in peak periods in an attempt to move visitation to off peak periods. Improved communication to visitors and tour agencies on the new management policies occurred. The lake zone trails were limited to one-way movement. The visitor infrastructure within the lake zone was updated with new appreciation points; and some new boardwalks to improve one-way flow on circular trails. Improved organization of the official parking sites and the prevention of illegal parking within the park assisted with management. Monitoring of the defined bio-physical, social and managerial indicators was started. Policies were introduced to increase the average revenue per visitor in the park and local area. One major problem remained: the jurisdiction of the park authorities over private land inside the park. Development of tourist facilities on some of these private lands occurred during the plan development.

Lessons learned from the Plitvice Lakes management plan
The park authority recognized the tourism problem and initiated the development of a new and revised management plan. The high environmental, cultural and social values of the site created a strong interest from many different concerned stakeholders that created persistent pressure towards all relevant authorities to address the problem. The World Heritage designation added an international dimension which placed pressure on the Government through the threat of designation as a World Heritage Site in Danger.

Complex circumstances involving many interested stakeholders with different interests and perceptions of the problem required a structured, comprehensive and participatory planning process facilitated by use of a methodological conceptual framework for visitor use management planning. Elements of the planning process are listed below.

The plan was developed by the park staff members facilitated and supported by international and national consultants, all of which ensured the park's ownership of the plan. The involvement of both international and domestic planning consultants provided credibility, guidance on best international practice in visitor use management planning, as well as familiarity with local context.

Limits of acceptable change (LAC) and recreation opportunity spectrum (ROS) planning frameworks enabled development of commonly agreed management objectives and standards.

Stakeholders were involved throughout the planning process; their concerns were addressed and a common understanding of issues and solutions that are in the best common interests was developed. Many misconceptions were clarified. Plan review and approval involved the entire range of political stakeholders, from local county officials and national environmental bodies, to the national government and the United Nations agency UNESCO.

The planning process was long enough to ensure that all issues and options were carefully considered and evaluated, while short enough that the political impetus did not abate. The planning process was sufficiently robust to withstand changes in senior management in the park, in the government, and in the cabinet ministry responsible for the park.

Effective planning and management of visitor use required both human and financial capacity of the park authority. The park administration had extensive experience and competencies in tourism management. Park staff members were supportive of the development of new policies and procedures to address overuse problems that were obvious to those who worked in the park. Due to a range of tourism-based income sources, the park had sufficient financial resources to finance the comprehensive participatory planning process and the implementation of the plan. Solid and defensible visitor use statistics were available.

The concept of physical capacity of the boardwalks and valley infrastructure was used to set a use limit within the wider context determined by adopted management objectives and standards. The use limit based on the physical space required per person on a narrow trail was relatively easy and convincingly determined. This relatively simple physical capacity of 3 metres of trail per person is reasonable, easy to understand, and became widely acceptable to most stakeholders.

The first year of visitation under the new policies, 2019, showed that the new management system was effective, as reported by park staff members involved with tourism management.

Summary of the Implications of the Three Case Studies

Any sustainable tourism destination must have sufficient management capability to deal with visitor use targets; a research priority (Eagles, 2013). The case studies discussed in this chapter, Niagara Falls Park Commission, Point Pelee National Park, Pinery Provincial Park, and Plitvice National Park, revealed management bodies with sufficient management capability to deal with existing tourism capacity problems.

Rae and Eagles (2007) developed a set of standards that could direct the level of sophistication needed for effective visitor and tourism management. Let us explore the management capacity issues that are most critical for effective planning and management.

Implementation of new capacity limits
If the capacity limits are below current use level, managerial policies must be developed to bring in new limits over time. It is best to introduce those limits within the context of an overall park management plan review. Many of the use level problems were the result of fragmented decisions made in previous periods.

Communication of the new policies is a critical element. Those institutions heavily involved, such as local hotels, must be given comprehensive information. The private tourism sector usually requires an 18-month advance notice of new prices and new access policies.

Individual potential visitors can be informed through normal web-based information sources, including the booking system. As shown with the Plitvice National Park management plan process, the systematic development and explanation of a new carrying capacity limit that is implemented by a carefully designed visitor management program can be widely acceptable.

Managing a package of services

Sustainable tourism involves a package of services, such as:

- Destination sites (parks, waterfalls, trails, overlooks, etc.);
- Transportation networks bringing people to the park and returning them later;
- Accommodation providers (both inside and outside the destination);
- Food providers (both stores and restaurants);
- Infrastructure (roads, washrooms, sewage systems, water systems, etc.);
- Information providers (guides, books, internet services).

Each of these will have capacity limits. For example, a common limit is the washroom capacity at a site. Therefore, an overall capacity limit must be a sum of each of these individual service capacities. Those involved in some of those services may attempt to maximize their own tourism yield; overtaxing some other service. For example, a transportation service may try to maximize income by transporting a maximum number of passengers, which might be larger than the destination infrastructure can handle. Therefore, the development of an overall capacity target must consider the individual capacity limits and the political interests of those who argue for a certain use level. The complexity of the decisions argues for the use of a comprehensive management planning process.

Political priority

The creation and implementation of visitor capacity limits must be politically acceptable. The planning effort will involve many stakeholder groups, often with conflicting agendas. The political planning process must be capable of dealing with this conflict, to ensure that a limit is identified, and an approach for implementation created. Powerful stakeholder groups may wish to deflect or stop the planning process in order to achieve their own objectives by derailing the process. In the case of public bodies, the politicians must be willing to support the planning effort and to ensure that any resultant policies are fully implemented. In the case of private companies, the board of directors and senior management must be willing to accept and implement the necessary policies. In the case studies outlined in this chapter, the plans developed were controversial; and the controversy created political imperative to develop effective new policies.

Finance

All management is dependent upon sufficient finance. Fortunately, at high volume tourist destinations sufficient finance should be available through higher use fees. But some public park agencies may not be able to fully function as tourism businesses and cannot charge peak load fees. Perversely, in many public park agencies high tourism volumes cause a financial problem when they should provide a financial solution.

The park agency must have the legal and policy authority to retain all income, in order to use that income effectively to manage the tourism loads. This retention must include year-end carry over, so that money earned in one year can be carried over to the next fiscal year. This policy is critically important for prepaid bookings. If a tourism provider pays for a scheduled booking, in one period, for the differential use of the facilities in a later period, the park must be able to use that income earned in one period to deliver the service in another period. All theatres function in this manner.

Policies must be developed to ensure that the tourism management is financed effectively. Unfortunately, some park planning frameworks ignore finance and management capability, such as the major frameworks coming out of the USA such as the Outdoor Recreation Spectrum (ORS) and the Limits of Acceptable Change (LAC). Plans created without concern for the finance needed for implementation and the management capability to implement those plans are prone to failure.

Revenue management in tourism

In travel and tourism, yield management is used to describe the process of managing revenue against demand. It is simply about using price to manage demand and revenue. Many parks do not use efficient yield management, due to weakness in business expertise, inability to vary prices according to demand, and restrictions in pricing policy.

A good yield management system benefits both the destination and the visitors. It helps some travellers to get lower-rated facilities and programmes during times of low occupancy and other travellers to get these during periods of peak demand. Since it is hard to find a destination during periods of peak demand, some travellers are willing to pay full rates at these times. In this way, rather than cutting costs, destinations increase their revenue. In yield management, the following strategies are helpful to achieve higher revenues (Canina and Enz, 2008). It is best to price on value of the product, not just the cost of production. Value pricing is difficult as tourism values are often hard to predetermine. Values are often known after periods of use. It is important to convert customers' non-price outlay into value. A value determination is constantly changing and elusive. Risk to the provider can be mitigated through advance purchase; involving some type of refund for unused booking. Advance booking can be very important in yield management. It is important to lower the time and effort exerted by the customer to purchase or use the service for additional payment. The customer can become an active agent and may pay for some level of control. Segment and price can be assigned through self-selection by the buyer. It is important to identify the benefits obtained by the buyer and what attributes have delivered them. Careful yield management can provide higher financial return to the provider and services that are better tailored to the client, yielding high levels of client satisfaction.

Pricing

A destination needs full powers to set and implement pricing policy and to adapt when needed. This includes the ability to design and implement differential pricing, such as higher prices at peak loads and lower prices in lower load periods, as was done in Plitvice National Park.

Price is used as an allocation device throughout the private sector tourism industry. Virtually every destination, attraction, and transportation utility varies the price according to level of demand. Lower prices and pre-booking of access are both used to deflect use from periods of high demand to periods of lower demand, while attempting to retain the client.

Time-based pricing is the standard method of pricing in the tourist industry. Higher prices are charged during the peak season, or during special-event periods. In the off-season, hotels may charge only the operating costs of the establishment, whereas investments and any profit are gained during the high season. Time-based pricing can involve higher prices during rush hours.

Peak load pricing has several advantages, because it encourages casual users to visit during low load periods. High prices during peak periods encourage visitors who value the experience the most (Loomis and Lindberg, 2006). For pricing to be used effectively in park tourism, the government park agency must be able to function like a business. Many park agencies are government agencies restricted in business operation by policy and law. Such agencies cannot set prices; this is done by political bodies far removed from site management. Some government protected area agencies cannot retain earned income as all income goes to some higher level of management authority or government. Many cannot move income between fiscal years. These policies dictate a management structure unable to use price and income effectively.

Research in pricing policy for park tourism is a priority (Eagles, 2013). Pricing can be used to deflect use from high to lower use periods. Variable prices can be used to also maximize income for management. Peak load management requires substantial financial resources and tourism income is always critically important. It should be possible to earn sufficient income under high levels of use.

Of the three case study parks discussed in this book chapter only the Plitvice plan had explicit policies in regard to pricing and yield management. In the other two parks pricing was an issue, but was determined each year in agency operational plans, not in the management plan.

Advance booking

Theatres, hotels and restaurants maximize their use through advance booking by clients. The advantages to the destination include: (1) ability to prepare in advance for service delivery, (2) movement of access from higher use periods to lower use periods, and (3) more efficient management of staff and service provision. Once capacity limits are established, advance booking has major advantages for tourism volume management. Increasingly, parks and other sustainable tourism destinations use advance booking for accommodation, but less commonly for day visitors or environmental education programmes.

Payment at the time of advance booking has major advantages for tourism operations. It provides income upfront and provides stronger assurance that the programme will be utilized. Booking in the absence of payment can lead to high levels of absenteeism in programmes because the cost to the consumer is very low. Recently, the major internet booking company Expedia started providing a lower hotel booking cost by giving the option to pay upfront for the hotel at a slightly reduced price.

Many travellers prefer advance booking arrangements so that access to programmes and facilities can be assured. Ontario Parks introduced a telephone booking system for campsite reservations in 1990. This later evolved into an internet booking system. The system is highly used, with only 5.45 per cent of campsite registrations made upon arrival at the park, with 94.5 per cent done through advance booking (Eagles, 2014).

In Ontario Provincial Parks, campers pay an extra booking fee at the time of campsite booking; payment for the concessionaire who operates the booking system. This booking system has been very successful in all respects, highly valued by both the campground managers and the campers. Some users complained about paying the booking fee, but the cost does not appear to impact their use of this service. The US National Park Service is considering reservation systems for day use in some parks with high visitor usage at peak periods (Peltier,

2018), but is a laggard in the use of advance booking systems. When tourism destinations do not use advance booking to its fullest extent there can be load problems.

In the case studies discussed in this chapter, only the Plitvice plan explicitly outlined policies for advance booking; a major policy used to assist with visitor flow management. In the other two parks advance booking was introduced for camping in operational plans, and was not mentioned in the management plans.

Tourism staff numbers and expertise
A tourism business must have sufficient numbers of staff members trained in hospitality and tourism. Strangely, many parks and park agencies do not have such staff, even though they are major tourism providers. Many management plans ignore the staffing numbers and competency needs that result from the new management policies. In all three case studies in this chapter, staffing needs are an important component of the management plans. This is most effectively outlined in the newest plan, that for Plitvice National Park and World Heritage Site. The other two plans did not explicitly deal with staff numbers or expertise. These issues were dealt with during yearly operational plans.

Legal framework
For a park to function effectively as a tourism operator, including effective peak load management, it must have a legal basis that allows the development and implementation of tourism policies. These policies include issues such as: pricing policy, revenue retention, peak load management, implementation of use restrictions, allocation of access, staff hiring and retention, and marketing. Unfortunately most management plans do not fully outline the legal framework deficiencies that may exist. In all three case studies, there was little to no explicit mention of the legal frameworks in place, and no mention of legal limitations to full plan implementation.

Marketing
A tourism business must have the capacity to develop and implement tourism programmes. This is much more than advertising. For example, for peak load management it may be decided to offer specialized, guide-led programmes during peak load periods. This would assist with the movement of visitors through the site, allow for effective implementation of capacity loads, and boost income. The development of those programmes would be based on a carefully crafted marketing strategy. Once the strategy is developed, there would be a period of targeting communication to the tourism industry and consumers. Many parks and park agencies are weak in marketing, often with no trained staff in this important field. The newest plan outlined in this book chapter – that for Plitvice National Park and World Heritage Site – has the most fulsome discussion of marketing policies. The other two parks deal with marketing within annual operational plans, not in the management plan.

SUMMARY

When substantial goal conflict occurs and there is a weak management body, targets are difficult to set as political deadlock occurs. The three case studies discussed here are examples of strong management bodies that could effectively tackle complex visitor management issues and establish acceptable maximum levels of visitation for a park. In these case studies, minimum visitation levels are not addressed as each park had developed very high levels of visitation before management planning took place as a professional activity. This chapter reveals that the model of tourism sustainability is useful in the setting of targets for visitation.

Hyslop and Eagles (2007) identified the 31 policy areas which are of most concern in park visitor management. Many important policies, such as pricing and staff qualifications, were dealt with in yearly operational plans and not explicitly mentioned in management plans. These case studies revealed that there is disagreement at which level of planning each of these policy areas must be addressed in park management: system policy, management plans, or yearly operational plans. This is an important area for future research.

This chapter has discussed three successful examples of maximum tourism volumes being set and implemented: Point Pelee National Park in Ontario, Canada (1989); Pinery Provincial Park in Ontario, Canada (1971); and Plitvice National Park and World Heritage Site in Croatia (2019). All three case studies concentrated on the need to set upper limits of visitation to maintain environmental and visitation quality, and revealed that sufficient finance was available. For the effective implementation of those limits, a fully competent management plan and management institution was necessary. All three case studies provide a set of lessons learned that may be applicable in other jurisdictions. These examples reveal that setting and implementation of maximum visitor use levels in public institutions is feasible. The setting of limits was done through the professional judgement of planners; not through a mathematical formula which the carrying capacity argument often seems to imply. These judgements were politically acceptable with most of the major stakeholder groups, including the park managers and the government. All three sites had sufficient management capacity to undertake management planning processes and the ability to implement those plans. It is probably not possible to undertake fully effective visitor management without sufficient management capacity.

REFERENCES

Baum, T. and Lundtorp, S. (2001) Introduction. In T. Baum and S. Lundtorp (eds.), *Seasonality in Tourism* (pp. 1–15). Oxford: Pergamon.

Boissoneault, M. (2019) Limits on visitor use at Point Pelee National Parks. Unpublished personal communication.

BSI (2019) *What Is a Standard?* Accessed 30 July 2019 at https://www.bsigroup.com/en-CA/Standards/Information-about-standards/What-is-a-standard/.

Canina, L. and Enz, C. A. (2008) Pricing for revenue enhancement in Asian and Pacific region hotels: A study of relative pricing policy. *Cornell Hospitality Report* (February).

Eagles, P. F. J. (2010) Changing societal values and carrying capacity in park management: Fifty years at Pinery Provincial Park in Ontario. *Leisure/Loisir*, 34(2), 189–206.

Eagles, P. F. J. (2013) Research priorities in park tourism. *Journal of Sustainable Tourism*, 22(4), 1–22.

Eagles, P. F. J. (2014) Fiscal implications of moving to tourism finance for parks: Ontario Provincial Parks. *Managing Leisure*, 19(1), 1–17.

Hammitt, W. E. (1989) The spectrum of conflict in outdoor recreation. In A. H. Watson (ed.), *Outdoor Recreation Benchmark 1988: Proceedings of the National Outdoor Recreation Forum* (pp. 439–450). Asheville, NC: Southeastern Forest Experiment Station.

Hill, S. (2018) Playground or protection? 100-year-old Point Pelee National Park finds a balance. *Windsor Star*. Accessed 21 August 2019 at https://windsorstar.com/news/local-news/playground-or-protection-100-year-old-point-pelee-national-park-finds-a-balance.

Hyslop, K. E. and Eagles, P. F. J. (2007) Visitor management policy of protected areas in Canada and the United States. *Leisure/Loisir*, 31(2), 475–499.

IS Theory (2019) *SERVQUAL*. Accessed 30 July 2019 at https://is.theorizeit.org/wiki/SERVQUAL.

Limberger, P. F., Anjos, F. A. D., Meira, J. V. D. S., and Anjos, S. J. D. (2014) Satisfaction in hospitality on TripAdvisor.com: An analysis of the correlation between evaluation criteria and overall satisfaction. *Tourism and Management Studies*, 10(1), 59–65.

Loomis, J. and Lindberg, K. (2006) Pricing principles for natural and cultural attractions in tourism. In L. Dwyer and P. Forsyth (eds.), *International Handbook on the Economics of Tourism* (pp. 173–188). Cheltenham, UK and Northampton, MA, USA: Edward Elgar Publishing.

MacKay, R. (2019) *Algonquin Park: A Place Like No Other*. Whitney, ON: Friends of Algonquin Park.

Manning, R. E. (2002) How much is too much? Carrying capacity of national parks and protected areas. In A. Arnberger, C. Brandenburg and A. Mular (eds.), *Monitoring and Management of Visitor Flows in Recreational and Protected Areas. Conference Proceedings* (pp. 306–313). Institute for Landscape Architecture & Landscape Management, Bodenkultur University.

McLean, D. J. and Johnson, R. C. A. (1997) Techniques for rationing public recreation service. *Journal of Park and Recreation Administration*, 15(3), 76–92.

Mulholland, G. and Eagles, P. F. J. (2002) African parks: Combining fiscal and ecological sustainability. *Parks*, 12(1), 42–49.

Nykiforuk, C. and Eagles, P. (1999) Standards for service quality: Is there a place for them in the Parks Canada system? *Proceedings of Ontario Parks Research Conference* (pp. 153–160). Guelph, Ontario.

Parasuraman, A., Berry, L. L., and Zeithaml, V. A. (1985) A conceptual model of service quality and its implications for future research. *Journal of Marketing*, 49(4), 41–50.

Parasuraman, A., Berry, L. L., and Zeithaml, V. A. (1988) SERVQUAL: A multiple-item scale for measuring consumer perceptions of service quality. *Journal of Retailing*, 64(1), 12–40.

Parasuraman, A., Berry, L. L., and Zeithaml, V. A. (1991) Refinement and reassessment of the SERVQUAL scale. *Journal of Retailing*, 67(4), 420–450.

Peltier, D. (2018) With overtourism. *Skift*. Accessed 5 August 2019 at https://skift.com/2018/03/02/u-s-national-parks-arent-sure-how-to-deal-with-overtourism/?utm_campaign=Skift%20Weekly%20Review%20Newsletter&utm_source=hs_email&utm_medium=email&utm_content=61087574&_hsenc=p2ANqtz--6DwzuX6ZBlkj39k5b62Eoipr1fqX-St609g-CkrhsPGSAa1GllP6vUQVc58D8KffRfWe9yxcf_Mp-1HNodbq2xlXyhg&_hsmi=61087574.

Plitvice Lakes (2019) *Plitvice Lakes National Park Management Plan 2019–2028*. Plitvice Lakes National Park Public Institution.

Point Pelee National Park (2010) *Management Plan*. Accessed 21 August 2019 at https://www.pc.gc.ca/en/pn-np/on/pelee/info/plan.

Rae, K. and Eagles, P. F. J. (2007) Management of a river recreation resource: The Lower Kananaskis River – a case study. NERR Conference, Bolton Landing, NY.

Stankey, G. H. and Manning, R. E. (1986) *Capacity of Recreation Settings: A Literature Review*. INT 4901, Publication 166, The President's Commission on Americans Outdoors.

Wadsworth, R. (2017) This is what Zion National Park might do to solve overcrowding issues; how to comment. Accessed 31 July 2019 at https://www.stgeorgeutah.com/news/archive/2017/07/18/raw-this-is-what-zion-national-park-might-do-to-solve-overcrowding-issues-how-to-comment/#.XUH8AOhKiUl.

19. Optimization of tourism development in destinations: an approach used to alleviate the impacts of overtourism in the Mediterranean region

Ante Mandić

INTRODUCTION

Overtourism is not a new concept, but a new term, first used in the *Sydney Morning Herald* in 2001 (Petersen, 2001) which describes phenomena and issues (host–visitor relations, authenticity, over-visitation, overcrowding, carrying capacity, etc.) which have been discussed in the literature over the last four decades. In recent literature, the term relates to hosts or guests feeling that too many tourists visit a place and that this changes its character, causing it to lose authenticity (Capocchi et al., 2020). It is the opposite of responsible tourism which is about using tourism to make better places to live in, and better places to visit, or as UNWTO (2018b) defines it:

> Overtourism happens in destinations where hosts or guests, locals or visitors, feel that there are too many visitors and that the quality of life in the area or the quality of the experience has deteriorated unacceptably.

The relevance of overtourism has been acknowledged at the European Union (EU) level with the publication of 'Overtourism: impact and possible policy responses', research for the TRAN Committee delivered by Peeters et al. (2018). The spurred interest of the research community in this phenomenon is additionally reflected in the publication of a special issue of *Tourism Planning & Development* on 'Overtourism and Tourismphobia' (volume 16, issue 4, 2019), and several books, among others *Overtourism: Issues, Realities and Solutions* by Rachel Dodds and Richard W. Butler (2019), and *Overtourism: Excesses, Discontents and Measures in Travel and Tourism* (2019b) edited by Claudio Milano, Joseph M. Cheer and Marina Novelli. The leading cause of overtourism is tourism growth, while the main symptoms are overcrowding and social unrest. Tourism growth is induced by accessibility and affordability of travel, growth and volume focused policies, new groups of tourists, broader access to media and information, disintermediation and peer-to-peer (P2P) platforms and destinations' lack of control. On the other hand, overcrowding and social unrest relate to seasonality, visitors' concentration and pressures, urbanization pressures, gentrification, the proliferation of tourist accommodation, generic competition for space, the nature of attractions, amenities and services, and imbalance of power among stakeholders.

As a phenomenon, overtourism reflects the desperate addiction of tourism destinations to growth, which is often incompatible with sustainability goals and principles. Higgins-Desbiolles (2018) suggests this growing fetish resulting in *tourism killing tourism* can be reversed only by adapting and integrating tourism into a broader context of sustainability, suggesting the transformation of relevant international organizations as well as employment of diverse approaches to tourism strategies for development and new ways of regulating and managing tourism as solutions. Acknowledging that the tourism growth ideology is not compatible with long-term sustainability, Higgins-Desbiolles (2011) and Hall (2009) call for degrowing[1] tourism. Sustainable degrowth in tourism requires a redefinition of tourism and prioritizing the rights of local communities above the rights of tourists for holidays and the rights of tourism corporates to make profits (Higgins-Desbiolles et al., 2019), which might be challenging for destinations and economies highly dependent on tourism development. According to Milano et al. (2019a), the strategies based on tourism degrowth may not be sufficient to entirely shift from a sector engrained with the "growth for development" paradigm, to a "growth for liveability" one. However, the complementarity of degrowth approach with 5Ds, i.e. deseasonalization, decongestion, decentralization, diversification and deluxe tourism, may provide a context-adaptable and useful tool to deal with overtourism if approached within the more comprehensive urban political agenda. Fletcher et al. (2019) concluded that the transition towards tourism degrowth could comprise both top-down and bottom-up elements, with pushes for systemic structural change at global and societal levels combined with more localized and individual practices contributing to downsizing on the ground.

Most of the overtourism challenges are related to a negative perception of tourism – residents encounter, an excessively high number of tourists at a specific time in certain places, or exceeding of ecological, physical, social, psychological or economic capacities in a destination (Peeters et al., 2018). Considering the complexity of tourist–resident interrelations, Seraphin et al. (2020) identify four archetypes of locals concerning their attitudes towards the tourist in an overtourism-threatened destination, namely, (1) locals who are helpless victims, (2) peaceful activists, (3) vandals, and (4) resilient locals. The authors conclude that local populations are resilient groups which should focus on managing tourism to achieve a balance between tourism degrowth and provision of a quality experience to avoid a potential "Trexit" (tourism exit) as the most radical and destructive strategy. Recently Lalicic (2019) provided an environmental psychology perspective of these interrelations by discussing '*solastalgia*' ("the homesickness you feel when you are still at home"), a relatively new measure of residents' responses to adverse changes in their home environment in a context of excessive tourism development. The analysis suggests that residents are starting to feel distanced and sad about the development of their home environments which is an alert for their governments and urban planners. The latest cases of residents' rebellion in several Mediterranean coastal destinations, e.g. Spain, Italy, Malta, France, suggest that solastalgia is real. The global relevance of this phenomenon, on the other hand, is reflected in a number of case studies, including Venice (Seraphin et al., 2018), Santorini (Sarantakou and Terkenli, 2019), Dubrovnik (Panayiotopoulos and Pisano, 2019), Munich (Namberger et al., 2019), Palermo (Shoval et al., 2020), Budapest (Smith et al., 2019), Norway (Oklevik et al., 2019), China (Cheung and Li 2019) and New Zealand (Otago region) (Insch, 2020).

Scholars have also discussed solutions facilitating the balance within destinations experiencing overtourism, among others, economic taxation (Nepal and Nepal, 2019), enhancement of resilience of local communities (Cheer et al., 2019), sustainable degrowth (Cheung and Li, 2019), shaping of tourist behaviour within destinations (Shoval et al., 2020), demand-side and supply-side interventions (Goodwin, 2019) or more sophisticated technologically-driven approaches such as creating a foundation of collaborative reflections on overtourism through the development of a smart city hospitality framework (Koens et al., 2019). Oklevik et al. (2019) discuss an optimization-based approach to destination management that seeks to increase the value obtained from maintaining or even decreasing visitor numbers, which is contrary to maximization, i.e. pro-growth strategies. This chapter utilizes a case study approach to analyse the responses aiming to optimize tourism development to alleviate existing and prevent the potential impacts of overtourism in Split, a vibrant Mediterranean tourism destination. In the context of this study, optimization refers to public policies, i.e. management and governance responses, which could be proposed or inaugurated on the local scale throughout the participatory planning approach. To deliver our conclusions, we extend the DPSIR (Drivers–Pressure–State–Impact–Response) (Ness et al., 2010) framework by integrating the context description and monitoring (CM), which are core elements of the Tourism Optimization Management Model (TOMM) (Miller and Twining-Ward, 2005). By doing so, we address the causal chain and structural deficiency (Helming et al., 2011) as the fundamental criticisms and drawbacks of this approach. Thus, the primary purpose of this chapter is to structure and analyse the causalities in specific tourism destinations facing overtourism and to critically evaluate the usability of the extended CM-DPSIR framework for integrative sustainable tourism planning in complex socio-economic ecosystems.

THE STUDY APPROACH

According to the DPSIR framework, this chain of causal links starts with driving forces, through pressures to state, and impacts on ecosystems, human health and functions, eventually leading to political responses (Kristensen, 2004) (Figure 19.1). It is developed as a system-based approach to capture key relationships between society and the environment (Atkins et al., 2011), which implies the need for demarcation of a particular system of interest with explicit or implicit boundaries (Wätzold et al., 2007). The challenge of defining the boundaries, of impacts, driving forces and responses relates to the complexity of the phenomenon itself, e.g. in a context of excessive tourism development, the driving force could be global (tourism growth), the impacts local (overcrowding), and the required response national (public policies).

In the general model proposed by Kristensen (2004), a "driving force" is a *need*, while recent studies discussing the sustainability of the complex socio-economic systems, emphasize *social and economic development* as key drivers of change (Atkins et al., 2011; Ness et al., 2010). Drivers, as well as other elements of this framework, adjust to the phenomenon which is being addressed, e.g. management of marine environments (Atkins et al., 2011), sustainable tourism development (Mandić, 2020), the sustainability of coastal areas (Bidone and Lacerda, 2004), pollination loss (Kuldna et al., 2009), but also to the approach (e.g. system approach, stakeholder approach) and scope (e.g. local, regional, national) of the analysis. Drivers pose pressure on ecosystems, which results in the change of its state. These changes reflect impacts, which in a context of sustainability of socio-economic ecosystems should be addressed from an economic, social and environmental perspective and traced throughout appropriate indices (Mandić, 2020). When the threshold levels are passed (e.g. overtourism), social responses in the form of public policies are needed to restore and maintain the balance of the system. These interventions should be ecologically sustainable, technologically feasible, economically

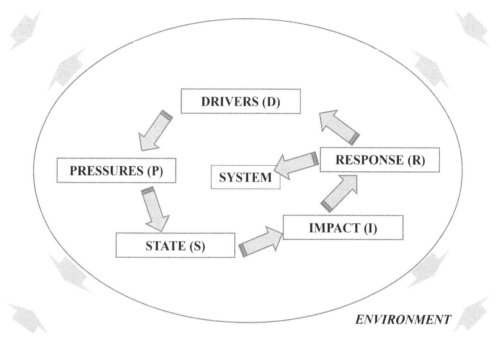

Figure 19.1   A generic DPSIR framework in the tourism subsystem and environment

viable, socially desirable, legally permissible and administratively achievable (Atkins et al., 2011).

The main criticism of this approach refers to the structural deficiency (i.e. exclusive focus on one-to-one causal relations and single and unidirectional causalities between indicators), and oversimplification of complex relationships (Carr et al., 2007; Helming et al., 2011; Niemeijer and De Groot, 2008). Thus, the framework would benefit from the focus on interconnections between indicators, as well as from integration and discussion of different levels of drivers and responses, considering it would enhance its usability by providing a holistic perspective and empowering policymakers and managers to determine the starting points to act. This is particularly important for complex systems such as tourism destinations where numerous stakeholders continuously interact to deliver visitors' experience. Furthermore, tourism development provokes direct, indirect and induced impacts on the local economy, community and environment, leading to conclusions that the analysis of one aspect of sustainability of tourism development would yield an incomplete outlook of what is going on in particular destinations. Thus the individual elements of the DPSIR framework applied in specific tourism destinations must discuss the multiple interactions and diverse (scale and type) impacts.

In its generic form, the framework seems to be insufficient to address such complexity of interrelations within vibrant tourism destinations. However, an integrated[2] approach might turn the framework into a valuable, sustainable tourism planning tool, primarily by enabling tourism managers to structure thinking processes to deliver timely responses to address the excess of ecological, physical, social, psychological, or economic capacities in a destination.

Thus, this study couples generic DPSIR with context description and monitoring (CM), the core elements of TOMM, and suggests the triple-bottom-line approach to the analysis of change in the state and European tourism indicator system (ETIS) based indicators of impact for the case study area Split, Croatia to discuss the optimization of tourism development aiming to alleviate the effects of overtourism. The data on tourism development in Split was drawn from multiple sources, including the strategic marketing plan for Split,[3] the carrying capacity study for the Split-Dalmatia county,[4] official statistics on a county level[5] and the official statistics on a national level.[6] Additionally, while writing this study, the author was involved in the development of *Strategic Development Plan Split 2030*, where he co-authored the analysis of tourism as one of the strategic industries.

FINDINGS

Context Analysis

The context analysis is the initial stage in TOMM which provides the outlook of tourism activities within the destination, including trends, tourism growth, tourism product, market opportunities and community values (Miller and Twining-Ward, 2005). The analysis also discusses the alternative tourism development scenarios, aiming to identify optimal conditions that tourism should aim to build, and which are the basis for defining tourism indicators. A genuine DPSIR framework starts with the identification of driving forces, and to some extent ignores the context analysis. However, to structure the thinking process concerning complex problems such as overtourism is, in complex ecosystems which tourism destinations are, the framework should integrate context analysis. At this stage of the investigation, there is no need to discuss the alternative scenarios, to identify optimal conditions and indicators. This is mostly because the state variables within the DPSIR framework reflect the status of observable changes in the system and thus aim to broaden the understanding of what is going on in tourism destinations, which indicators of change should be considered, and which thresholds followed.

Split is a leading Croatian tourism destination, facing continuous growth of both arrivals and overnights (Figure 19.2). Like many other Mediterranean destinations highly dependent on sun-sea-sand (3S) tourism, Split faces extremely high seasonality with 30 times the number of tourists in the most visited in comparison to least visited month.[7] The continuous growth, as well as seasonality, reflects national, regional, and international tourism industry trends (UNWTO, 2018a). The seasonality in Split is a consequence of 3S-focused tourism development, additionally enhanced with uncontrolled growth of peer-to-peer accommodation (70% of total accommodation in 2017[8]). Thus, over the last five years, the highest growth of demand is recorded for peer-to-peer accommodation, with the highest numbers recorded in 2016 (i.e. 193% of growth considering arrivals and 431% of growth considering overnights). Visitors staying in peer-to-peer accommodation arrive mainly during the summer and thus create an incentive for seasonality.[9] Recently, cruising tourism development gained a lot of attention. However, currently, Split does not have a strategic tourism development plan, nor cruising tourism development plan or impact assessment.

Visitors from ten leading emissive markets accounted for 59% of all arrivals in 2017.[10] The top four markets were the UK, Netherlands, USA, and Croatia. The strategic marketing plan for Split additionally points to France, Italy and Germany as priority markets.[11] The structural

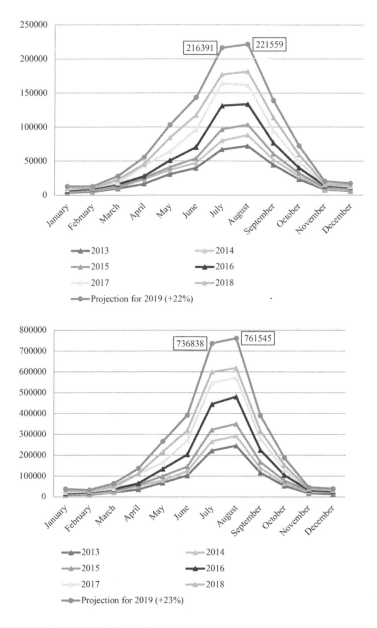

Source: Official statistics of Split-Dalmatia county.

Figure 19.2   The tourist arrivals (above) and overnights (below), monthly, 2013–2018, and projection for 2019 (average growth rate)

change ongoing in destination suggests there is a transition from traditional to new emerging markets and that the list of ten leading outbound markets in Split will be significantly different in ten years from now. This is particularly evident when focusing on seasons (spring – summer – autumn) rather than the annual average. For example, the visitors from Scandinavian countries (only Sweden in the top ten), as well as those from South Korea, for the last two years record massive growth of arrivals in the shoulder season. Thus, to fight seasonality and overcrowding Split might benefit from placing focus on new markets and destimulating the traditional ones.

Driving Forces

In the DPSIR terminology, the driving forces arise from the fulfilment of human needs; thus they are described as social, demographic, and economic development in societies that can originate and act globally, regionally or locally (EPA, 2015). The primary 'need' of the tourism sector, for a long time, is (responsible) **growth**.

Tourism growth is driven, among other things by the affordability of travel, the emergence of new groups of tourists, the influence of technologies, destinations' lack of control (Dodds and Butler, 2019), policies promoting volume (Peeters et al., 2018), and disintermediation and peer-to-peer platforms (World Bank Group, 2018). In 2018, international tourist arrivals grew 5% and reached the 1.4 billion mark, almost two years ahead of the UNWTO forecast (World Travel Organization, 2019). Europe accounts for half of the world's international arrivals and nearly 40% of global tourism receipts. Within Europe, the most visited region is Southern and Mediterranean Europe. Within this region, Croatia recorded 6.7% growth in 2018 in comparison to the year before and holds 2.3% of market share. In 2018, Split recorded 14% growth in arrivals and 17% in overnights (Figure 19.2). When considering the five years, the average growth rates are 23% for visitors and 22% for overnights. This trend reflects local tourism growth-focused policies and mindset. The latter leads to the second driving force, which is **governance and destination management**.

Growth is not an enemy if we know how to manage it; however, given global growth of tourism reaching its limits, the question that emerges is whether mature or rapidly growing destinations should continue to pursue volume growth strategies (Oklevik et al., 2019). Questioning growth itself as the basis of sustainable tourism has now become part of sustainable tourism discourse (Fletcher et al., 2019). Thus, current discussion of overtourism should be understood as a product of structural dynamics within the global capitalist system as a whole. The key questions "How many is to many", "What management strategies can be used to balance supply and demand", remain the fundamental challenges regardless of the trajectory that tourism takes (Wall, 2020). Joppe (2018) points out that governments at all levels value tourism's economic contributions, so they focus on increasing visitor numbers and maximizing revenues derived from them. Thus, the idea of integrated development that is responsive to community desires and needs in many cases gets suppressed by the profit-driven decisions of a small but powerful share of the stakeholders, which creates an enabling environment for overtourism. One might conclude, overtourism is mainly a result of weak governance and inadequate planning and management strategies on all levels which fail to address tourism growth. However, the reality seems to be more complicated than that. It seems that we all (all stakeholders, not just public authorities or tourism businesses) have our share in both, good stories about destination growth, and those unfortunate about its decline. Although Split does not have a strategic tourism development plan, local public authorities have contracted the development of a carrying capacity study for the county. This praiseworthy project makes Split one of the rare Mediterranean destinations with potential to make a turn before it is too late, and to develop sustainably. The critical challenge that remains is the fact that plans and strategies are rarely implemented (Jamieson and Jamieson, 2019).

Pressures

Drivers exert pressures which are defined as human activities derived from the functioning of driving forces that induce a change in the environment, or social behaviours that can influence human health (EPA, 2015) divided into three main types, namely, (1) excessive use of environmental resources, (2) changes in land use, and (3) emissions to air, water and soil (Kristensen, 2004). EPA (2015) highlights pressures are not stressors, which are components of the state that are changed by pressures. However, this definition reflects mainly the environmental pressures; thus, it has to be modified to address the complexity of influences that overtourism-related drivers might induce in a tourism destination. Within the tourism industry, pressures can be addressed comprehensively by employing a triple-bottom-line approach.

The pressures in the tourism destination Split, induced by *growth* and spurred by (inadequate) *governance and destination management* could be structured as:

1. *Economic pressures:* **Tourism revenue dependency** resulting from the reliance of the local economy almost exclusively on tourism development, and the local community on tourism as a source of revenue. The most pronounced pressures associated with overtourism in the Split context include:
   (a) The proliferation of peer-to-peer tourist accommodation
   (b) Gentrification
   (c) Increasing prices in the city.
2. *Social pressures:* **The attitudes, consent and behaviour of the local community** are highly related to the scale of tourism development and the perception of impacts and distribution of benefits of tourism in the destination. Thus the social pressures associated with overtourism in Split include:
   (a) Overcrowding
   (b) Competition for services and amenities
   (c) Imbalance of power among stakeholders.
3. *Environmental pressures:* **Land use and treatment of space and resources** are related to the scale of tourism development and reflect the alterations of local resources associated with tourism development. The environmental pressures related to tourism development in Split include:
   (a) Excessive use of destination resources and coastal development
   (b) Competition for space and resources
   (c) Discharges and pollution.

Tourism accounts for approximately 20% of Croatian GDP (Ministarstvo turizma, 2018). Thus, both the economy and society have developed a dependency on tourism revenue, fostering, among others, the proliferation of (un)regulated peer-to-peer tourism accommodation as an "easy way to make money". The growth of tourism enabled the gentrification, and increase of prices in the city centres and coastal region, leading to over-urbanization and loss of authenticity. In many cases, villas and holiday homes are built before communal infrastructure (e.g. sewerage), resulting in illegal discharges and sea pollution. The pronounced seasonality and growing popularity of this vibrant destination spurred overcrowding and, during summer, traffic jams. The competition for resources and amenities, as well as imbalance of power among stakeholders, started creating a critical mass within the local community which is ready to accept trade-offs only if tourism is developed for the benefit of society and the city and not for the benefit of tourism businesses solely.

State

The state describes the condition or observable changes in the natural and built environment and human system induced by the pressure (Ness et al., 2010). The state analysis should follow the logic of the triple-bottom-line approach and be based on available data. The subsequent analysis utilizes the data presented in a carrying capacity assessment for Split, and official statistical reports for Split-Dalmatia county.

State of the local economy
Split is the centre of the Split-Dalamatia county, often discussed as a driver of its development. The county accounts for 8.2% of Croatian GDP. The service sector, of which a large share constitutes tourism and hospitality, yields 25% of its GDP.[12] Within the county, at the same time, tourism is considered to be a significant driver of economic development and a source of pressure on the local community. The latter is mainly due to a lack of investments in public infrastructure, poor regional spatial planning, and lack of strategic planning.[13] The research conducted for the benefit of the strategic marketing plan in Split[14] has shown that tourism is recognized for its multiplicative effects, and positive impacts on employment, local community revenues, and the development of cultural and sports services and amenities. On the other hand, its adverse effects are mainly related to the seasonality, gentrification, traffic congestion, competition for public and beach space, overcrowding, uncontrolled urbanization, increase of prices and living expenses, pollution and overuse of resources, and negative impacts on the local community and its identity.

State of the local community
Twenty-nine per cent of the local population in Split embrace tourism development.[15] The index of irritation suggests that the local community is in the initial stage, with 16% of them tolerating tourists and 5% of them avoiding tourists by leaving the city in the primary season. The negative attitudes of the local community towards tourism development are mostly driven by lack of parking spaces (54%), trash (46%) and overcrowding: beach (46%), traffic (54%). The majority of the local community consider that in the primary season tourism should be sustained as it is (49%), while 12% felt that the numbers should be lower by up to 50%. Thirty-six per cent of locals believe the number of tourists should be increased in main seasons, while it is a unanimous opinion that the numbers should grow in the shoulder season.

The diversity of attitudes towards tourism development question the usability of the carrying capacity approach to address the complexity of overtourism. When defining and setting mechanisms to monitor and manage excessive tourism, the use of Limits of Acceptable Change (LAC) might ensure a more comprehensive vision, and that the community values and culture are linked to the amount and type of visitor use (Fai et al., 2018; UNWTO, 2018b).

State of the local environment

With 29% of the coastal line classified as construction land, Split has the most prominent plot ratio in Split-Dalmatia county. With less than 3 square metres per person, beach capacity is unsatisfactory. The quality of the bathing water is rated as excellent on 18 measurement points, and satisfactory on one. The town has reliable electricity and water supply; however, the problems are drainage and waste management. The traffic infrastructure is a severe constraint to further tourism development due to traffic congestion, lack of parking places as well as lack of capacities for nautical tourism.

The indicator of tourism density rate in Split (251.60 in August 2018) is high above the average value for both historical and urban destinations[16] (Gössling et al., 2018), suggesting that the city has reached its infrastructural limits in the primary season. Although Split has not reached the average value for historic destinations, the tourism penetration rate (11.21 in August 2018) suggests the relatively high intensity of tourism development (i.e. relatively high number of visitors with regard to the local community). Split has reached its physical capacities and is threatening to cross its environmental and social capacities thresholds in the primary season. Thus, at this point, tourism policies seeking to optimize tourism development by limiting growth in the primary season should be inaugurated.

The analysis ends with holistic expert assessment (Figure 19.3) evaluating the state of the critical elements of the local economy, environment and community. In this case study, we assess whether the observable change is satisfactory, unsatisfactory or neutral. The assessment could be conducted using the Delphi method approach.[17]

Figure 19.3   *Assessment of the state of the local economy, community and environment in Split*

Impact

The changes in the state induced by excessive tourism development may have diverse implications for the functioning of the destination's ecosystem. Impacts are often stated as measurable damages to the environment or human health (Ness et al., 2010). The system approach to the state change–impact analysis provides an opportunity to evaluate these implications in a context of a tourism destination comprehensively, to identify the scale of the impacts, stakeholders involved and the shift away from the desired optimal condition. We first define the optimal conditions within a destination, and then suggest the indicators to trace the impacts (i.e. shift away from the optimal state).

The optimal conditions (Table 19.1) are driven from the context and state analysis and reflect the desired future state of the tourism destination. The indicators of change are derived from the ETIS for sustainable destination management.[18] In this analysis, we rely on existing,

Table 19.1   *Optimal conditions and indicators of change*

	Optimal condition	Indicators of change*
Economy	The number of visitors and overnights is sustained in the primary season, and increases in the shoulder season. The visitors' satisfaction with the tourism offer as well as with beach facilities and cleanliness and public spaces is maintained or enhanced. The level of growth of peer-to-peer accommodation is sustained and the quality of the accommodation offer improved. Seasonal fluctuations in the number of visitors are decreasing. Small scale traditional businesses are encouraged to operate within the centre of the old town.	Number of tourist nights per month Number of same-day visitors per month Visitor satisfaction with different elements of destination's offer including facilities and infrastructure The occupancy rate in commercial accommodation per month and average for the year % of peer-to-peer accommodation % of locally produced food, drinks, goods and services sourced by the destination's tourism enterprises Number of tourism-related SMMEs operating in the destination
Environment	The ecological processes are improved in the areas where tourism activity occurs. The public, communal and transportation infrastructure within the tourism destination is improved. The share of the coastal land designated to construction is sustained. The system of waste management is established.	% of tourism accommodation and attraction infrastructure located in 'vulnerable zones' Funding of public and private finance spent in the improvement of the physical urban environment The land occupied by artificial surfaces within the first 500m of the coast (in %) % of total waste recycled per tourist compared to total waste recycled per resident per year
Society	The share of the local population feeling irritation regarding tourism and tourists is decreasing. Majority of residents consider they can influence tourism-related decisions. Public spaces, amenities and recreational facilities are accessible to residents. The local community is retained within the centre of the old town.	% of residents who are satisfied with tourism in the destination (per month/season) % of residents that are satisfied with the impacts of tourism on the destination's identity Degree of stakeholder participation in the planning process and in the process of implementing plans (Low/medium/high) Accessibility of public spaces, amenities and recreational facilities to residents (Yes, No) The number of permanent inhabitants in the old city centre

Note: * ETIS based.

participatory based strategic documents and available statistical data. If these documents were not available, to set the optimal conditions, workshops with relevant stakeholders would have to be conducted to discuss the current state and the plans for tourism development.

Optimal conditions reflect the restored and maintained balance within the tourism destination. Thus, interventions, i.e. public policy responses, are expected to improve or sustain the state of the ecosystem. The overtourism induces local-scale impact; however, its roots are in national, often ambitious growth-focused development plans lacking the courage to limit the visitor number or to address the seasonality with feasible policies. Consequently, in some cases, indicators will point out the change of the local ecosystem; however, the responses to address them might be inaugurated only by the central government.

Responses

Responses are seen as actions by relevant stakeholders to prevent, compensate, or adapt to changes in the state of the environment (EPA, 2015), that may feed back to the drivers, pressures, state or impacts (Helming et al., 2011). In this context, societal responses reflect the different level government, i.e. public sector inaugurated, often participatory based, policies.

Table 19.2 summarizes the responses on all levels that seek to establish and maintain the balance within the tourism destination. The reactions in a context of driving forces, pressures and state aim to address the causes and to create an appropriate environment within a destination to develop tourism sustainably. On the other hand, the impact-related responses are focused on mitigating the consequences of unsustainable growth and seasonality; therefore, they are more focused and should be followed with an exact period of completion, measures and control. In reality, these responses together are the reply of a tourism destination and policymakers to overtourism-related challenges, which emphasizes the importance of considering them integratively. This case study focuses on one destination (city) within a more extensive destination system (country); thus, central government, i.e. Ministry of Tourism and Croatian tourism board, hold the responsibility to address the impact of drivers, i.e. to 'manage' growth and seasonality and to improve the efficiency of destination management. The duty to address pressures and change in the state is shared between local and regional authorities, i.e. cities and counties. The latter is mainly because of legislation, shared responsibility as well as the fact that Split is the centre of the county, and their tourism development paths intervene. The impacts happen on a local scale, and the city holds the responsibility to mitigate them.

Monitoring

The CM-DPSIR framework considers monitoring to be a circular, i.e. continuous process integrating implementation, result and effectiveness monitoring, and policy adjustment. Once the optimal conditions and adequate range of indicators are defined, the DMOs hold the responsibility to collect the information, to analyse the data and to transform the knowledge into intelligence. If necessary, based on data retrieved throughout visitor and resident surveys, and relevant public data analysis, DMOs can propose to adjust responses, or even to inaugurate new indicators to trace the shift from optimal conditions. This process should happen annually and should remain related to destinations' long-term goals. Generally, the framework allows DMOs to define new optimal conditions or new responses, as long as they are data supported and participatory driven.

IMPLICATIONS AND CONCLUSIONS

As an alternative to the maximization of tourist numbers, this study discusses and advocates the optimization and system approach to tourism development and planning. The optimization facilitates reconciliation of environmental and socio-cultural goals within the tourism destination system (Gössling et al., 2018) while seeking to increase financial returns by maintaining or even decreasing international arrival numbers (Dolnicar, 2014). While most of the approaches to optimization are essentially market segmentation exercises (Dolnicar, 2014), this study advocates the integration of optimization principles into the tourism management

Table 19.2   *Driving forces, pressures, state and impact based responses with indicated decision-making level*

Elements	Responses	Decision-making level
Driving forces	1. Develop long-term strategic national tourism development plan concerning sustainable growth and seasonality as two most pronounced challenges. 2. Improve and further develop the destination marketing and management system (DMO).	1. National 2. National
Pressures	1. Set up the limits for tourism growth in the destination. 2. Decrease funds for the promotion of tourism toward a destination in the primary season (de-marketing) and increase funds to stimulate tourism in shoulder season. 3. Develop a strategic plan of subsidies of public funds to the tourism industry private sector. 4. Implement more restrictive urban planning policies for tourism accommodation. 5. Revise the current spatial plan concerning land use. 6. Increase the participation of the local community in decision-making processes. 7. Initiate the empowerment and education of the local community about potentials and impacts of tourism development for the local community. 8. Increase the accessibility of public spaces and services. 9. Establish a waste management system.	1. Regional/Local 2. Regional/Local 3. Local 4. Local 5. National/Regional/Local 6. Local 7. Local 8. Local 9. Regional/Local
State	1. Revise the spatial and urban planning. 2. Implement community-based (tourism) development. 3. Establish visitor management and impact monitoring.	1. Regional/Local 2. Local 3. Local
Impacts	1. Increase the subsidies to the tourism industry private sector for programmes aiming to attract tourists in the shoulder season. 2. Increase the public funds for the development of tourism products in the shoulder season. 3. Set up an annual visitor satisfaction survey. 4. Limit the categorization of peer-to-peer tourist accommodation. 5. Establish the subsidies for small scale traditional businesses operating in the centre of the old town. 6. Increase the funds for maintenance and improvement of public infrastructure. 7. Implement more restrictive and environmentally conscious urban planning. 8. Increase the funds for waste management. 9. Further, develop a wastewater system and ensure all households are connected. 10. Empower the local community and foster their participation in development planning. 11. Educate the local community about the impacts of tourism development and the way they can benefit from it. 12. Improve the accessibility of public spaces and facilities. 13. Develop a strategic plan for retaining and stimulating the local community to stay in the centre of the old town.	1 to 13: Local

and planning by using the CM-DPSIR framework to structure thinking processes within destinations facing overtourism and to contemplate the responses (Table 19.2). The advocated system thinking facilitates the identification and mitigation of both causes and consequences of overtourism within a destination, with the potential to induce long-lasting transformative impacts. The core of this framework is vertical cooperation, i.e. the distribution of responsibilities between the local, regional and national level public institutions involved in tourism planning and development. The approach acknowledges the structural differences between tourism destinations, as well as the fact that there are no unanimous solutions that might be applied for all. The challenges associated with overtourism vary and depend on the type of destination, the characteristics of destination space, as well as primary tourism product, characteristics of dominant visitor groups and most importantly efficiency and nature of governance and destination management. The most 'threatened' are those destinations lacking control over tourism development, which are primary growth-focused, profit-driven, and experience the imbalance of power between different stakeholder groups and often, but not in all cases, pronounced seasonality. Although governance requires collaboration between different stakeholder groups voluntarily, local communities have little meaningful input into policymaking deliberations (Joppe, 2018). Community-based governance often gets substituted by hierarchies, or a market approach (Hall, 2011) focused on growth, job creation, increasing tourism volume and spending, all of which facilitate the development of overtourism. Finally, due to existing adverse impacts of tourism on different aspects of ecosystems, Mediterranean destinations should not strive only for the sustainability of resilience, but to the paradigm shift towards regenerative tourism[19] which would contribute to repairing the harm already done in the destination.

The adaptation of this approach for structuring thinking processes when planning for tourism development requires bearing in mind the following:

- *Context analysis* – It has to be comprehensive, relevant and objective. The conclusions drawn from context analysis are a prerequisite for defining the optimal conditions, choosing indicators of change as well as setting up policy responses. The context analysis should discuss the destination, which is a subject of the sustainable tourism planning within the broader geographical and tourism system context. That means that the report has to consider the regional, national and worldwide tourism development, as well as demand trends.[20]
- *Data* – The analysis depends on the available data. The planners should identify which, and how to collect them. The data might be obtained from official statistics, reports, surveys, studies or even some novel approaches of data collection could be used, e.g. scraping social media data as in the ShapeTourism project (http://www.shapetourism.eu/main-output/shapetourism-observatory/).
- *Participation and cooperation* – Participation can be achieved via traditional approaches, e.g. establishment of a forum of stakeholders, or more advanced and sophisticated technology-driven approaches, e.g. development of living labs (Mandić and Garbin Praničević, 2019). Participation should be fostered through education, especially in a context of benefit sharing, and the potentials of tourism for community development. Training might facilitate the establishment of networks and involvement in decision-making.

- *Monitoring* – This study discusses monitoring as a continuous process aimed to collect data on results induced by responses employed. The data obtained by monitoring should be used to improve the existing or propose new interventions.
- *The complexity of the planning approach* – The DMOs require more efficient tools which might be used to mitigate pressures and to address the local-scale overtourism-related impacts. The CM-DPSIR framework allows DMOs and decision-makers to logically structure thinking processes to monitor what is going on in tourism destinations regularly, holistically, and to provide timely responses. The framework depends on the assumptions of the active participation of all relevant stakeholders and proactivity of DMOs.

Finally, tourism destinations behave as dynamic, evolving and complex adaptive systems, encompassing numerous factors and activities that are interdependent and whose relationships might be highly nonlinear (Baggio, 2008). The capacity of destinations to adapt is crucial to survive and thrive in the context of continually changing circumstances, related to among others, recent phenomena such as overtourism, COVID-19, climate change and many more. Unfortunately, the concept of destination as an adaptive system is not yet widely embraced in the field of tourism development and planning (Hartman, 2020). Thus, this study discussing the CM-DPSIR framework, to some extent, integrates the critical principles of the adaptive management approach (Islam et al., 2018) to tourism destination management and demonstrates that the positive change might occur at destination level by embracing a holistic approach, learning-by-doing philosophy, and by considering all stakeholders involved in the tourism value chain.

NOTES

1. Degrowth analysis considers ways to create economies that eschew a growth imperative while still supporting human thriving (Kallis, 2011).
2. For example, Atkins et al. (2011) and Hou et al. (2014) couple ecological integrity, ecosystem services and well-being within the DPSIR framework.
3. Retrieved from https://visitsplit.com/hr/3136/strateski-marketing-plan, December 2019.
4. Retrieved from https://www.dalmatia.hr/hr/priopcenja/studija-prihvatnih-kapaciteta-na-podrucju -splitsko-dalmatinske-zupanije-10z, December 2019.
5. Retrieved from https://www.dalmatia.hr/hr/statistike, December 2019.
6. Retrieved from https://mint.gov.hr/pristup-informacijama/dokumenti-80/statistike/11514, December 2019.
7. Own calculation based on official statistical data for 2016, retrieved from https://www.dalmatia.hr/ hr/statistike, December 2019.
8. Retrieved from https://www.dalmatia.hr/hr/statistike, December 2019.
9. Own calculation based on official statistical data for 2018, retrieved from https://www.dalmatia.hr/ hr/statistike, December 2019.
10. Retrieved from https://www.dalmatia.hr/hr/statistike, December 2019.
11. Retrieved from https://visitsplit.com/hr/3136/strateski-marketing-plan, December 2019.
12. Retrieved from https://www.dalmatia.hr/hr/priopcenja/glavni-plan-razvoja-turizma-splitsko-dalm atinske-zupanije-40, January 2020.
13. Retrieved from https://www.dalmatia.hr/hr/priopcenja/studija-prihvatnih-kapaciteta-na-podrucju -splitsko-dalmatinske-zupanije-10z, January 2019.
14. Retrieved from https://visitsplit.com/hr/3136/strateski-marketing-plan, January 2020.
15. Retrieved from https://www.dalmatia.hr/hr/priopcenja/studija-prihvatnih-kapaciteta-na-podrucju -splitsko-dalmatinske-zupanije-10z, January 2019.

16. Tourism density rates for selected historic destinations: Venice 158.4; Prague 99.4; Salzburg 396.6. Tourism density rate for selected urban destinations: Copenhagen 315.8; Dublin 228.2; Lisbon 306.8.
17. More information at https://www.sciencedirect.com/topics/neuroscience/delphi-method, March 2020.
18. Retrieved from https://ec.europa.eu/growth/sectors/tourism/offer/sustainable/indicators_en, January 2020.
19. The term regenerative tourism is becoming increasingly popular in the media. It reflects tourism that creates solutions for tourism-induced challenges and by doing so, contributes to repairing the damage already done within the destination.
20. While local, national and regional trends and tourism development can be discussed considering national statistics, strategic documents and reports, the valuable sources of data for macro regional, and worldwide trends are, among others, the reports from OECD (OECD Tourism Trends and Policies 2020), UNWTO (UNWTO Tourism highlights; UNWTO Tourism Barometer), and the EU (European Union Tourism Trends, EU Tourism Statistics).

REFERENCES

Atkins, J. P., Burdon, D., Elliott, M. and Gregory, A. J. (2011) Management of the marine environment: Integrating ecosystem services and societal benefits with the DPSIR framework in a systems approach. *Marine Pollution Bulletin*, 62(2), 215–226.

Baggio, R. (2008) Symptoms of complexity in a tourism system. *Tourism Analysis*, 13(1), 1–20.

Bidone, E. D. and Lacerda, L. D. (2004) The use of DPSIR framework to evaluate sustainability in coastal areas. Case study: Guanabara Bay basin, Rio de Janeiro, Brazil. *Regional Environmental Change*, 4(1), 5–16.

Capocchi, A., Vallone, C., Amaduzzi, A. and Pierotti, M. (2020) Is 'overtourism' a new issue in tourism development or just a new term for an already known phenomenon? *Current Issues in Tourism*, 23(18), 2235–2239.

Carr, E. R., Wingard, P. M., Yorty, S. C., Thompson, M. C., Jensen, N. K. and Roberson, J. (2007) Applying DPSIR to sustainable development. *International Journal of Sustainable Development and World Ecology*, 14(6), 543–555.

Cheer, J. M., Milano, C. and Novelli, M. (2019) Tourism and community resilience in the Anthropocene: Accentuating temporal overtourism. *Journal of Sustainable Tourism*, 27(4), 554–572.

Cheung, K. S. and Li, L. H. (2019) Understanding visitor–resident relations in overtourism: Developing resilience for sustainable tourism. *Journal of Sustainable Tourism*, 27(8), 1197–1216.

Dodds, R. and Butler, R. W. (eds.) (2019) *Overtourism: Issues, Realities and Solutions*. Berlin: Walter de Gruyter.

Dolnicar, S. (2014) Market segmentation approaches in tourism. In S. McCabe (ed.), *The Routledge Handbook of Tourism Marketing* (pp. 197–208). London: Routledge.

EPA (2015) *Using the DPSIR Framework to Develop a Conceptual Model: Technical Support Document*. EPA/600/R-15/154 (August). Retrieved from http://nepis.epa.gov/Exe/ZyPURL.cgi ?Dockey=P100O10D.TXT.

Fai, Y., Spenceley, A., Hvenegaard, G. and Buckley, R. (2018) *Tourism and Visitor Management in Protected Areas: Guidelines for Sustainability*. Gland, Switzerland: IUCN.

Fletcher, R., Murray Mas, I., Blanco-Romero, A. and Blázquez-Salom, M. (2019) Tourism and degrowth: An emerging agenda for research and praxis. *Journal of Sustainable Tourism*, 27(12), 1745–1763.

Goodwin, H. (2019) Overtourism: Causes, symptoms and treatment. *Tourismus Wissen* (April), 110–114.

Gössling, S., Scott, D. and Hall, C. M. (2018) Global trends in length of stay: Implications for destination management and climate change. *Journal of Sustainable Tourism*, 26(12), 2087–2101.

Hall, C. M. (2009) Degrowing tourism: Décroissance, sustainable consumption and steady-state tourism. *Anatolia*, 20(1), 46–61.

Hall, C. M. (2011) A typology of governance and its implications for tourism policy analysis. *Journal of Sustainable Tourism*, 19(4–5), 437–457.

Hartman, S. (2020) Adaptive tourism areas in times of change. *Annals of Tourism Research*, June, 102987. https://doi.org/10.1016/j.annals.2020.102987.

Helming, K., Krippner, B., Tscherning, K., Paloma, S. G. and Sieber, S. (2011) Does research applying the DPSIR framework support decision making? *Land Use Policy*, 29(1), 102–110.

Higgins-Desbiolles, F. (2011) Death by a thousand cuts: Governance and environmental trade-offs in ecotourism development at Kangaroo Island, South Australia. *Journal of Sustainable Tourism*, 19(4–5), 553–570.

Higgins-Desbiolles, F. (2018) Sustainable tourism: Sustaining tourism or something more? *Tourism Management Perspectives*, 25, 157–160.

Higgins-Desbiolles, F., Carnicelli, S., Krolikowski, C., Wijesinghe, G. and Boluk, K. (2019) Degrowing tourism: Rethinking tourism. *Journal of Sustainable Tourism*, 27(12), 1926–1944.

Hou, Y., Zhou, S., Burkhard, B. and Müller, F. (2014) Socioeconomic influences on biodiversity, ecosystem services and human well-being: A quantitative application of the DPSIR model in Jiangsu, China. *Science of the Total Environment*, 490, 1012–1028.

Insch, A. (2020) The challenges of over-tourism facing New Zealand: Risks and responses. *Journal of Destination Marketing and Management*, 15, 100378. https://doi.org/10.1016/j.jdmm.2019.100378.

Islam, M. W., Ruhanen, L. and Ritchie, B. W. (2018) Adaptive co-management: A novel approach to tourism destination governance? *Journal of Hospitality and Tourism Management*, 37, 97–106.

Jamieson, W. and Jamieson, M. (2019) Overtourism management competencies in Asian urban heritage areas. *International Journal of Tourism Cities*, 5(4), 581–597.

Joppe, M. (2018) Tourism policy and governance: Quo vadis? *Tourism Management Perspectives*, 25, 201–204.

Kallis, G. (2011) In defence of degrowth. *Ecological Economics*, 70(5), 873–880.

Koens, K., Melissen, F., Mayer, I. and Aall, C. (2019) The Smart City Hospitality Framework: Creating a foundation for collaborative reflections on overtourism that support destination design. *Journal of Destination Marketing and Management*, March, 100376. https://doi.org/10.1016/j.jdmm.2019.100376.

Kristensen, P. (2004) The DPSIR framework. Workshop on a Comprehensive/Detailed Assessment of the Vulnerability of Water Resources to Environmental Change in Africa Using River Basin Approach. UNEP Headquarters, Nairobi, Kenya. https://doi.org/10.1007/978-3-642-20736-5.

Kuldna, P., Peterson, K., Poltimäe, H. and Luig, J. (2009) An application of DPSIR framework to identify issues of pollinator loss. *Ecological Economics*, 69(1), 32–42.

Lalicic, L. (2019) Solastalgia: An application in the overtourism context. *Annals of Tourism Research*, April. https://doi.org/10.1016/j.annals.2019.102766.

Mandić, A. (2020) Structuring challenges of sustainable tourism development in protected natural areas with driving force – pressure – state – impact – response (DPSIR) framework. *Environment Systems and Decisions*. https://doi.org/10.1007/s10669-020-09759-y.

Mandić, A. and Garbin Praničević, D. (2019) Progress on the role of ICTs in establishing destination appeal: Implications for smart tourism destination development. *Journal of Hospitality and Tourism Technology*. https://doi.org/10.1108/JHTT-06-2018-0047.

Milano, C., Novelli, M. and Cheer, J. M. (2019a) Overtourism and degrowth: A social movements perspective. *Journal of Sustainable Tourism*, 27(12), 1857–1875.

Milano, C., Cheer, J., Novelli, M. (eds) (2019b) *Excesses, Discontents and Measures in Travel and Tourism*. CABI.

Miller, G. and Twining-Ward, L. (2005) *Monitoring for a Sustainable Tourism Transition: The Challenge of Developing and Using Indicators*. Wallingford: CABI.

Ministarstvo turizma (2018) *Turizam u brojkama 2018*. http://www.mint.hr/UserDocsImages/150701 _Turizam014.pdf.

Namberger, P., Jackisch, S., Schmude, J. and Karl, M. (2019) Overcrowding, overtourism and local level disturbance: How much can Munich handle? *Tourism Planning & Development*, 14(4), 452–472.

Nepal, R. and Nepal, S. K. (2019) Managing overtourism through economic taxation: Policy lessons from five countries. *Tourism Geographies*. https://doi.org/10.1080/14616688.2019.1669070.

Ness, B., Anderberg, S. and Olsson, L. (2010) Structuring problems in sustainability science: The multi-level DPSIR framework. *Geoforum*, 41(3), 479–488.

Niemeijer, D. and De Groot, R. S. (2008) Framing environmental indicators: Moving from causal chains to causal networks. *Environment, Development and Sustainability*, 10(1), 89–106.

Oklevik, O., Gössling, S., Hall, C. M., Steen Jacobsen, J. K., Grøtte, I. P. and McCabe, S. (2019) Overtourism, optimisation, and destination performance indicators: A case study of activities in Fjord Norway. *Journal of Sustainable Tourism*, 27(12), 1804–1824.

Panayiotopoulos, A. and Pisano, C. (2019) Overtourism dystopias and socialist utopias: Towards an urban armature for Dubrovnik. *Tourism Planning and Development*, 16(4), 393–410.

Peeters, P., Gössling, S., Klijs, J., Milano, C., Novelli, M., Dijkmans, C., … Postma, A. (2018) Research for TRAN Committee – Overtourism: Impact and possible policy responses, October. http://www.europarl.europa.eu/RegData/etudes/STUD/2018/629184/IPOL_STU(2018)629184_EN.pdf.

Petersen, F. (2001) Blast from the past. *The Sydney Morning Herald* (July). https://www.smh.com.au/national/blast-from-the-past-20011215-gdf4yo.html?fbclid=IwAR19NzmyUepcDz5AZtWFtn1T6hDCuxiUTd6PQa-BY5JNbMkE2Kar-nEf21g.

Sarantakou, E. and Terkenli, T. S. (2019) Non-institutionalised forms of tourism accommodation and overtourism impacts on the landscape: The case of Santorini, Greece. *Tourism Planning and Development*, 16(4), 411–433.

Seraphin, H., Ivanov, S., Dosquet, F. and Bourliataux-Lajoinie, S. (2020) Archetypes of locals in destinations victim of overtourism. *Journal of Hospitality and Tourism Management*, 43, 283–288.

Seraphin, H., Sheeran, P. and Pilato, M. (2018) Over-tourism and the fall of Venice as a destination. *Journal of Destination Marketing and Management*, 9, 374–376.

Shoval, N., Kahani, A., De Cantis, S. and Ferrante, M. (2020) Impact of incentives on tourist activity in space-time. *Annals of Tourism Research*, 80, 102846. https://doi.org/10.1016/j.annals.2019.102846.

Smith, M. K., Sziva, I. P. and Olt, G. (2019) Overtourism and resident resistance in Budapest. *Tourism Planning and Development*, 16(4), 376–392.

UNWTO (2018a) *UNWTO Tourism Highlights 2018*. https://doi.org/10.18111/9789284419876.

UNWTO (2018b) *'Overtourism'? – Understanding and Managing Urban Tourism Growth beyond Perceptions, Executive Summary*. World Tourism Organization (UNWTO); Centre of Expertise Leisure, Tourism & Hospitality; NHTV Breda University of Applied Sciences; and NHL Stenden University of Applied Sciences. https://doi.org/10.18111/9789284420070.

Wall, G. (2020) From carrying capacity to overtourism: A perspective article. *Tourism Review*, 75(1), 212–215.

Wätzold, F., Rothman, D., Siepel, H., Svarstad, H. and Petersen, L. K. (2007) Discursive biases of the environmental research framework DPSIR. *Land Use Policy*, 25(1), 116–125.

World Bank Group (2018) *Tourism and the Sharing Economy: Policy & Potential of Sustainable Peer-to-Peer Accommodation*. Washington, DC: World Bank Group.

World Travel Organization (2019) International Tourism Highlights: International tourism continues to outpace the global economy. https://doi.org/https://www.e-unwto.org/doi/pdf/10.18111/9789284421152?download=true.

PART IV

MONITORING AND
EVALUATION

20. Visitor counting and surveys
Joel Erkkonen and Liisa Kajala

THE IMPORTANCE OF VISITOR MONITORING

Protected and recreational areas are increasingly important visitor attractions, and information on visitors is a necessity for the successful management of these areas. Visitor information is essential in ensuring the protection of nature and cultural heritage, quality recreation experiences, sustainable tourism development, promotion of public health and well-being, and showcasing the multiple benefits of protected areas. The visitor monitoring data provides critical indicators of sustainable tourism, including natural, socio-cultural and economic aspects.

When visitor data is gathered in a uniform and systematic manner, it provides possibilities for diverse analyses, reporting and comparisons, both across areas and across time, and at different levels from local to regional, national and international (Hornback and Eagles, 1999; Kajala et al., 2007; Kajala and Karoles-Viia, 2016). On the other hand, ad hoc information gathering can yield non-comparable or inaccurate results and conclusions.

Visitor data is essential for local land managers and for local tourism development, as well as for regional, national and international policy, planning, reporting, research and comparisons. Moreover, visitors themselves are often interested in such information and as citizens they have a right to know about visitation to the areas. Reliable visitor data is essential not only for planning and management, but also for well-informed policy making (Kajala, 2012).

A good visitor monitoring programme consists of visitor surveys and visitor counting (Hornback and Eagles, 1999). With visitor counting one obtains estimates on the amount of use, whereas with visitor surveys one can obtain more descriptive information, e.g. on the types of visitors, their recreational behaviour, motives, needs, opinions, expenditures, and perceived health benefits. By combining these two types of information, one can draw a much more diverse picture of protected area visitation than with either one type of information alone (Kajala and Erkkonen, 2018).

A successful visitor monitoring programme requires administrative procedures in the following areas: agency policy, monitoring objectives, level of programme development, staff resources, financial commitments, measurement technologies, data storage, and communication technologies (Eagles and Kajala, 2014). The choice of methods and resources in any particular visitor monitoring programme depends not only on the resources available, but also on the aim of data collection and ambition on the level of reporting. All in all, a visitor monitoring programme requires long-term commitment from the administrative organization or agency.

This chapter gives an overview of the entire visitor monitoring process from data collection and storage to using the data in reporting, management, communication and decision making. The main focus of the chapter is on practical matters: how to carry out visitor counting and visitor surveys, how to report the results and how to make use of the information obtained. (This chapter has made extensive use of the Nordic-Baltic visitor monitoring guidelines given in Kajala et al., 2007.)

HOW TO IMPLEMENT VISITOR MONITORING IN PRACTICE

Visitor Counting

Visitor counting produces data on the amount of recreational and tourism use, and on the temporal and geographical distribution of those visits. Information can be produced on an hourly, daily, weekly, monthly, seasonal or yearly basis, depending on how detailed the information needs to be.

Visitor numbers can be gathered using various methods, including indirect, direct and automatic methods. Indirect methods include signs of use such as tracks, wear and tear of vegetation and terrain, guest books in cabins, trail logs, and other self-registration methods, fishing and hunting licences, permits, parking and entrance fees, statistics and information from other agencies or companies. Direct methods include manual observation by personnel at ground level and observations from the air (e.g. with drones, ultra light air vehicles). Automatic methods include electronic counters counting either vehicles, bicycles or people, mechanical counters as well as digital or video cameras. Each of these methods has its strengths and weaknesses.

In selecting suitable visitor counting methods, one should take into account the goals of the counting, type of area, seasons to be covered and the resources available. Well-chosen methods yield accurate and detailed enough results in relation to the costs. It is important that counting is done systematically, while recognizing the sources of error. The staff of the protected or recreational area are central to the functionality of the counting system. Their task is to observe that the counters work and solve any error situations promptly.

The available amount of staff and other resources affects the design of the counting system. For example, if the resources are scarce, one can estimate the baseline visitation data by implementing one year of intensive counting, aiming at covering all the main entrance points. This can be followed by less intensive years of visitor counting using just a few counters to extrapolate the results to the rest of the entrances, assuming that the visitor flow patterns remain the same.

The sites for installing visitor counters should be chosen so that they give the most representative picture of the movements of visitors in the area. In other words, it is advisable to install the counters where the main visitor flows occur. If there is no prior data on visitor flows, one can get started using the best available local knowledge of personnel.

The choice of counter model and type is influenced by the characteristics of the site, and the amount and quality of the information needed, as well as the resources and staff capacity available. The features of the installation site to be considered include the width of the passage, the possibilities for reading, monitoring and installing the counter, and the electricity supply available. Another consideration in selecting the counter model is whether the information is needed all year round or not.

Compared to electronic counters, camera or video monitoring provides more information on visitation. It allows studying visitor profiles to find out activities, e.g. walkers, cyclists, dog walkers, gender or number of children. Utilizing cameras to count visitors has proven to be accurate, traceable and rich in features (Arnberger et al., 2005). However, extracting data from the imagery manually consumes large resources, limiting the utilization of camera observations to short-term monitoring projects. The approach of applying computer vision seems to be capable of quantifying visitors to protected areas. However, it is important to know the legal framework of each country when using cameras (Staab et al., 2018). Moreover, technical development and new innovations may open unforeseen possibilities for visitor counting.

This chapter describes the widely used methodology related to automatic registration methods, especially electronic counters, and how to calibrate and calculate the results with the aid of manual observations. The other methods have their justifications, and they may be the optimal solution in certain situations. Currently, in most cases the automatic registration methods allow for the most systematic procedures which can produce reliable, accurate and consistent estimates of the number of visits. Moreover, modern electronic counters, especially remote reading counters, are cost-efficient in the long run and require little maintenance on-site.

Visitor counting with electronic counters

Visitor counting includes several successive and in part overlapping phases (Figure 20.1). The phases generally pertain to all visitor counts regardless of what kinds of counters are being used. The stages follow each other more or less chronologically.

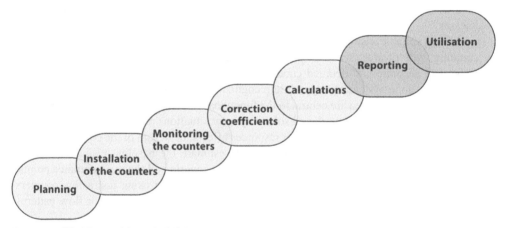

Source: Modified from Kajala et al. (2007).

Figure 20.1   The stages of visitor counting when using counters

The **planning stage** is crucial to the success of visitor counting. Often, there is a desire to know the total number of visits to an area. In this case, it is a good idea to start planning with a map analysis of main entrance points, using the local knowledge of park staff and other people familiar with the area. When planning the locations for the counters, the aim should be for the counters to cover most of the visits to the area. In some cases, there is only a need for knowing visitation at a certain point (trailhead, bird watching tower, etc.). In both cases, one needs to get started with single counters, which reach the proportion of the visitors who go past counting points.

It is important to make the choices based on the specific conditions prevailing in the area, such as climate and expected weather conditions, terrain, accessibility of the measuring points, maintenance and service routines, purpose of measurement, type of object to be measured, level of accuracy needed, etc. When considering the amount and types of counters needed and their installation sites, these aspects may be helpful:

- What is the purpose of the counting? Is there a need for single location visitation numbers, area specific numbers, or both?
- What should the counter be measuring? Persons travelling on foot, on horseback, by snow-mobile, bicycle, car, etc.
- The amount and quality of the information needed, e.g. is there a need for distinguishing direction of visitor flow (in and out), or need for hourly information?
- Is there electricity available, or should the counter operate on batteries?

The careful **installation of counters**, combined with well thought out servicing and reading procedures, is the cornerstone of visitor counting. With all counters it is best to install the counter at a place where the visitors do not usually make a stop and where they are not able to walk side by side. Narrow passages such as stairs or duckboards are often the best installation sites. With gates one should be extra cautious. They can be either good or bad locations, if people move back and forth when closing the gate. Another important consideration when selecting the installation site, is to aim at minimizing the potential error effects caused by animals or branches waving in a storm, etc.

The counters should be located so that visitors do not pay attention to them to avoid both manipulation of the readings and vandalism. Vandalism directed at counters or intentional manipulation of the statistics can at worst render the count useless and cause considerable financial loss. Other more technical requirements for the installation site depend on the type of counter to be used. One should therefore refer to the manufacturer's instructions in each individual case.

Monitoring the counters is relevant. The accuracy of readings is significantly influenced by equipment selection. By selecting equipment that allows for remote reading, the reading process becomes easier and the reading accuracy is significantly improved compared to counters that require reading on-site. Moreover, remote reading counters can send alerts to personnel in charge of the counters, so error situations are noticed immediately.

In connection with reading the counters on-site, the functioning of the counters, the direction and camouflaging of the sensors are checked, and batteries are changed where necessary. During servicing, possible sources of error are also checked. There should be no branches, grass or brushwood in the line of optic sensors, for instance.

In order to ensure quality and comparability of the results, the personnel in charge of visitor counting should be trained to deal with the basic elements and aims of counting, as well as counter technology and installation techniques.

At **correction coefficients stage** calibration is needed because each counter calculates visitors somewhat differently, depending on the installation of the counter, its placement and the technical qualities of the counter. Also, different weather conditions may affect the counters. For these reasons, each counter must be calibrated independently, after which each counter has its own coefficient. After calibration one can calculate the counter's final result, which is a prerequisite for calculating the estimated total number of visitors to a specific area.

Calibration is based on comparing counter readings with actual observations on-site. The correction coefficient is defined for each counter on the principle that, as far as possible, only real visitors are registered and preferably only once. Visits of servicing and other personnel, or animals, etc., should be excluded from the final estimates of the number of visits. The correction coefficients help to eliminate sources of error.

There are two types of error sources. Technical errors are caused by characteristics of the counter and the installation site. Such errors are caused, for example, when visitors are side by side or too close to each other, especially when the passage is wide. In addition, weather conditions (misting or ice) may cause technical problems. Qualitative errors are caused by movements that do not represent real customers or visitors. These include movements of servicing and other personnel and animals. Different calibration procedures are described in more detail, e.g. in Kajala et al. (2007, pp. 59–61 and appendices 2 and 3).

Calculation of the number of visits for any given location is obtained by multiplying the counter reading for counting period by the correction coefficient. Hourly, daily, weekly, monthly, seasonal or annual numbers of visits are available, depending on the type and technical qualities of the counter installed on the site. If the counter has not functioned for a certain period, estimates can be calculated using best available local knowledge, or previous counter readings from a similar kind of period.

Estimating the number of visits to an area

With single counters, one reaches only that proportion of the visitors who go past those counting points. If there is a need for information on the area's total number of visits, as is often the case, this requires knowledge or at least estimates on the share of the counting points compared to the total visitation of the area. There are numerous ways of producing the area level visitation numbers, many of which are described in detail in Kajala et al. (2007, pp. 61–76).

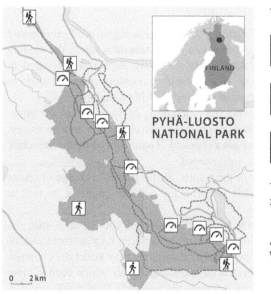

PYHÄ-LUOSTO
NATIONAL PARK

0   2 km

The coverage percentage

 Visitor flows at main entrances are covered by visitor counters (**b**) **99 740 visits**

 Estimated number of visits outside the counters (**c**) **34 700 visits**

 Estimated number of visits outside the recreational infrastructure (**a**) **1%**

The calculation formula for coverage percentage (**x**)

$$x = b/(b+c)*(100-a)$$
$$= 73,4\%$$

Annual total number of visits (**V**)

$$V = b/(x/100)$$
$$= 99\ 740/(73,4/100)$$
$$= 135\ 886$$

Source: Case example from Pyhä-Luosto National Park.

Figure 20.2   Parks & Wildlife Finland extrapolates the point specific visitation entrance counts obtained by electronic counters into area level visitation numbers using estimated area coverage percentage as illustrated in this figure

One practical approach has been developed and used for more than ten years by Parks & Wildlife Finland (P&WF). It has proven to be fairly easy to apply in practice by park managers. It is illustrated here by the case of Pyhä-Luosto National Park (Figure 20.2). First, all the designated entrance points to the park were identified (12 entrances), and entrances with major visitor flows (8 entrances) were covered by modern electronic counters, which record visits in and out on an hourly basis. For the other entrance points, the amount of entering visits was estimated based on the best available local knowledge. In addition, the share of scattered use outside trails was estimated. The counting period's number of visits for the whole area is obtained by dividing the sum of visits for each entrance point by the coverage percentage of counters in the area. Once the coverage percentage is calculated, it can be used for extrapolating visitation figures for different periods of time, from daily visitation numbers to annual ones.

The logic of the P&WF system is that while the absolute number of visits to an area is at its best an estimate, keeping the counting logic the same from year to year gives the possibility to analyse trends in visitation. If more counters become available, they are installed at the next busiest entrances according to the analysis. Additional resources increase reliability of counting thus increasing also the coverage percentage of counters in the area.

Visitor Surveys

Visitor surveys aim at collecting detailed information on visitors. Usually the goal is to do a survey representing all the visitors during a certain time period. Surveys use questionnaires to obtain information on the characteristics of the visitors and their visits. Surveys can be implemented with potential visitors before their visits, with actual visitors during their visit,

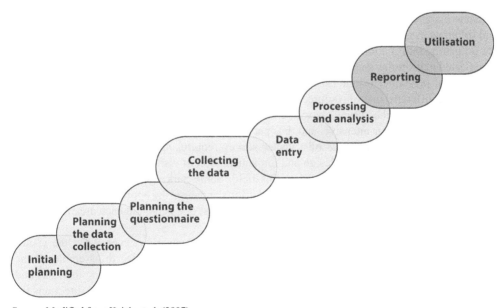

Source: Modified from Kajala et al. (2007).

Figure 20.3   *The stages of a visitor survey in more or less chronological order*

or with past visitors once they leave the area. The methods described here focus on obtaining information on the actual visitors towards the end of their visit.

A visitor survey process consists of several successive and partly overlapping stages (Figure 20.3). All in all, a visitor survey process can take from a few months up to a year or more, depending on the area's characteristics, the amount of visitation, etc.

The following advice is at a general level. For detailed information on any of the planning stages, we recommend reading the respective chapters in Kajala et al. (2007, pp. 81–118).

Initial planning

Survey objectives need to be identified and kept in mind at all times. It is important to consider what sort of visitor information is relevant at a local, regional, national or international level. Figure 20.4 illustrates key issues that most managers to parks and protected areas are interested in. These include visitor profile, activities in the area, the geographical distribution of visits, the duration and repetition of visits, expenditure and economic impacts of visitation, visitor satisfaction, motives of the visitors and health and well-being impacts of the visit as perceived by the visitors. Moreover, there may be some additional issues that the managers wish to clarify in the area through a visitor survey. The clear survey objectives help significantly in keeping the survey to the point, thus avoiding the gathering of too much either irrelevant or 'nice to know' data.

The experience has shown that, if one is to study actual visitors to parks and protected areas, the on-site guided survey works well. Therefore, this chapter focuses on how to carry out on-site guided visitor surveys. However, there are many other methods to find out more detailed visitor information, such as internet surveys, in-depth interviews, observation, group discussions, examination of existing data, and social media. (See more detailed description of other methods available in Kajala et al., 2007, pp. 83–84.) These other methods can provide valuable insights into visitors' values, desires, activities etc., as well as provide information and solutions to practical management problems. Nevertheless, they are usually not that suitable for getting information on changes, which requires long-term monitoring methods that can be repeated in a similar manner across time and areas.

Sufficient personnel resources, time and money must always be reserved for the visitor survey. The different sorts of resources needed for performing a visitor survey vary depending on the objectives of the survey, as well as the location, size and other characteristics of the area. Surveys are labour intensive, and thus personnel costs represent the greatest expense.

Implementing different stages of a visitor survey requires special knowledge and skills. Experience has shown that the design and implementation of visitor surveys should be supervised by a person who is specialized in this field. Some park agencies have a specialized visitor monitoring group coordinating national efforts and ensuring appropriate and consistent field methods. In addition, it is recommended that at least one person in each area is assigned responsibility for carrying out the visitor survey.

Some sort of documentation is advisable for every visitor survey, even when the visitor survey has no 'scientific' goals. As a matter of fact, it is a good idea to assemble all the essential matters pertaining to the visitor survey in a planning folder, recording the tasks and responsibilities of different individuals, schedules, sampling arrangements, and directions for data collectors. The folder has been found to be a very handy document, from which one can easily check details related to a specific visitor survey.

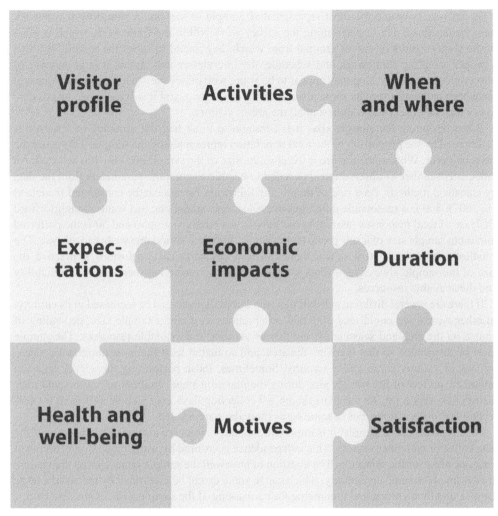

Source: Modified from Erkkonen and Sievänen (2001).

Figure 20.4   Key issues to be clarified by a visitor survey, with the variables describing them

Planning the data collection

The number and structure of visitors are generally not known well enough to allow for defining the size of the sample to ensure that it represents all the visitors within a certain margin of error. Many parks and protected areas receive tens of thousands of visits yearly, and interviewing or assessing the opinions of every visitor is completely impossible in practice. Usually one wants to evaluate parameters and draw conclusions that can be generalized to apply to all visitors during a given period of time. In order to do this, one needs to obtain a **representative sample of visitors** to an area at a given time period.

In order to assemble the most representative sample of visitors, a **sampling framework** must be designed. Those performing the survey work within the framework, which is a list of the units (visitors or visitor groups) from which they intend to select the sample. Without a proper sampling framework and schedule, the interviewer may gather a large number of observations and everything may appear to be going well otherwise – but the observations will have been gathered from the same place within a day or two, and it will no longer be possible to say that the observations represent all the area's visitors.

When designing the **sample size**, it is common to think that the accuracy of a survey is determined by the proportion of the total population represented by the sample. This is not the case, however. What matters more is the absolute size of the sample and how it is selected. An 'adequate' number of observations is needed to be able to compute parameters from the data by statistical methods. As a rule of thumb, the following figures can be considered (Kajala et al., 2007): 300 is a reasonable minimum overall sample size if one just wants straightforward analyses of total responses (assuming the sample is a random sample) and 50 is the preferred minimum sample size of a sub-group (for example, female visitors) one wishes to analyse. The smallest sample size is 30, with which one can draw any statistical conclusions. In practice, the size of the sample always represents some sort of compromise between statistical reliability and the available resources.

If there are several different sub-samples, the sample's size must be increased in its entirety. In other words, we could take 300–500 observations as a target sample size, depending of course on the area and seasonality, number of visitors, and available resources. The sample must be distributed so that it covers the area, and so that at least the most important concentrations of visitors come under scrutiny. Sometimes, those performing the survey take too optimistic a view of the sample size during the planning stage. Number of visitors and their distribution vary a lot. As a rule of thumb, 40 collecting days may well be sufficient for collecting 500 observations, but in some cases more days are needed.

For a representative sample, it is important that the visitors are chosen independently of the data collector and other visitors. This independence is ensured by using random selection in at least one phase of the sampling. The question of how well the sample represents all the visitors always involves some uncertainty, which can to some extent be controlled by means of a large sample, and by planning and organizing the canvassing of the sample with all possible care.

Sampling methods for on-site guided surveys

A number of alternative sampling methods exist for the actual collection of visitor data. Below we present three different alternatives. Naturally, many factors will influence which of those alternatives one chooses. Their adaptability will vary from case to case. Generally, only persons 15 years and older are picked for the sample, since the visitors should understand all the questions on the form. Sometimes it may be justifiable to select younger people for the sample as well. Random sampling can be recommended as a universal sampling method, if some other reason does not argue more for other sampling methods.

In **random sampling**, all individuals who come past the survey point are selected as they arrive; that is, as the data collector finishes with the preceding respondent. Some visitors may pass the survey point without being picked for the sample – that is, while the data collector is dealing with other visitors (during an interview, for example).

In **systematic sampling**, every third visitor, for instance, is picked for the sample at a given point on a given collection day. In principle, the first person picked for the sample is selected randomly. Systematic sampling can be applied well when a lot of people visit the area. If visitors are few, the data collection will proceed slowly and laboriously.

In **stratified sampling**, a decision has been reached during the sample definition phase to divide the sample, on the basis of prior information, into various strata. Stratified sampling can be applied when the area's visitor profile (gender and age group) is known in advance or is clarified by observation as data are being collected. In this case visitors can be picked for the sample so that it corresponds roughly to the known visitor profile. Observation forms can be used as an aid.

Planning the questionnaire

Surveys use questionnaires to produce sets of data that accurately describe the visitors and their visits. Surveys can yield information, e.g. on the visitor profile, activities, mode of travel, the geographical distribution of visits, the duration and repetition of visits, expenditure, visitor satisfaction, motives of the visitors and arrival at the area. In addition, there may be some special issues that the managers wish to clarify through a visitor survey in a particular area.

Careful questionnaire design is essential to quality answers. Questionnaires need to be short, especially if they are answered on-site. The planning and design of the questionnaire should be accomplished very carefully. If at this phase mistakes are made, the impacts on the processing of the data, on the interpretation of the results, and on reliability may be tremendous. If one asks well-designed questions that are easy to understand and to reply to, one obtains high quality answers and fewer refusals. On the other hand, poor question wording can at worst render the responses useless. In other words, the importance of this stage of the work must not be underestimated.

If those involved begin the survey form's design from a blank piece of paper, without prior experience, several weeks will be easily consumed. Those involved must decide what questions are essential, how they will be presented so as to be understood clearly, and how they will be measured and coded. In addition, the personnel implementing the study must decide what the natural order is for presenting the questions, and how to fit all the questions into a couple of pages. Planning a questionnaire requires many experiments, compromises, decisions, and pre-testing with real visitors.

The model questions presented in Kajala et al. (2007, appendix 4) have been planned carefully and tested in practice in several areas. It must be remembered, however, that it is impossible to create a perfect questionnaire. There will always be someone who understands a question differently from what was intended.

Phrasing of the questions must be precise, since not all visitors will necessarily understand a question as intended. The questions should be posed so that they are easy to understand and can be answered clearly. The questions should be presented in the same form to all visitors. It is best to use ordinary language in the questions and to avoid expressions that are foreign or otherwise difficult to interpret.

The questionnaire must be clear and easy to understand and fill in. The form's cover page has to make it evident that a visitor survey for a specific area is involved. It is also a good thing for the cover page to offer clear directions in respect of answering, returning the form, and further information, as well as the name and contact information of the survey's author or commissioner.

For information on planning the questionnaire, with detailed examples on questions that have been widely tested to be useful in field circumstances, we recommend reading the detailed instructions in Kajala et al. (2007, pp. 101–108, including appendices).

Collecting the data

Of all the phases in the process, collecting the visitor survey's data involves the most work. If the sampling and schedule plans, pre-testing and other initial preparations have been completed carefully, the data collection generally proceeds without worries or major problems.

In the case of on-site surveys, on data collection days, the data collectors should preferably be released from other tasks. It is also important for the person in charge of the visitor survey to be readily available on the first few collection days in case problems arise. The collection plan can still be changed if it is noted, for example, that a certain survey point is not going to work in the way envisaged at the start. Unpredictable weather conditions or a lower-than-expected number of visitors can lead to changes in the plan. During the first stage of collection, it is also best to be certain that most of the visitors are able to fill in the forms properly. At the end of the first day, the collectors will do well to get together and discuss possible problems or successes before these are forgotten.

Well-prepared interviewers are necessary for the collection of high-quality data. Experience, motivation, social and language skills are very important characteristics for the person collecting the data. He or she must be easily recognizable as a representative of the organization performing the visitor survey.

It is useful for the data collector to maintain a separate survey diary for each day of data collection and each site. One can use it to note factors bearing on the data collection, such as the weather, the duration of the collection, large groups, the direction of travel along trails, the number of visitors at the collection site, the number of questionnaires collected, the number and reasons for refusal, and the collector's own feelings and observations regarding factors affecting the collection. One can also record things in the diary that emerge in free-form discussions with visitors.

Data entry, processing and analysis

For basic data entry a spreadsheet such as Microsoft Excel is often sufficient. Before data entry takes place, every form has to be numbered consecutively, for example in a place reserved for that purpose on the cover page. Data entry and coding of the questions has been planned already when designing the questionnaire, but adjustments may be required when the data entry begins in practice. Each variable and response requires its own place. Data entry can be made more efficient by specific database programs, where one can create a user-friendly data entry form. Moreover, in a database program, one can define, e.g. acceptable entry values, which can help in controlling both logical and typing errors in data.

Once the data have been entered, it is time to check the material. The checking must be done with care and patience. It is annoying if mistakes are left in the data at this stage, since a lot of time and trouble has gone into the data collection. Material that is completely free of mistakes will scarcely be obtained: one hopes, however, that the mistakes will cancel each other out, and that no systematic error will remain in the data. Generally, checking the data takes a few days.

Sometimes the visitors' responses are not logical and consistent. It is worthwhile at first examining the results' distributions in the database, in order to detect extraordinary or divergent observations there. These observations need to be checked against the questionnaires and, where necessary, corrections have to be made in the database. It has to be remembered, however, that some of the extraordinary observations, too, may be absolutely correct, and that sometimes there is no reason to change them.

Reporting of Visitor Monitoring Data

Reporting of visitor monitoring should take into account different target groups. For example, high-level government decision-makers would potentially prefer short two-page policy briefs, whereas local citizens are more likely to engage with information shared through the media, including social media.

It is a good idea to harmonize reporting across areas and time when feasible, especially when monitoring with a uniform methodology. Cooperation between agencies is useful both in monitoring and reporting. This way visitor information from different areas will adhere to the same format and make the comparison of results easier. The results of visitor monitoring are typically needed quickly, and standardization can also help speed up the reporting process. Examples on different kinds of reporting are provided in a case example below, as well as in Spenceley et al.'s forthcoming publication *Visitors Count! Guidance for Protected Areas on the Economic Analysis of Visitation.*

Case Example of a Visitor Monitoring System from Parks & Wildlife Finland

Parks & Wildlife Finland (P&WF) is a unit within Metsähallitus, managing Finland's national parks and other state-owned protected and recreational areas. P&WF established a national visitor monitoring system of parks and protected areas in the late 1990s (Erkkonen and Sievänen, 2001; Horne et al., 1998). There are 61 protected areas in the monitoring system across Finland. This includes 40 national parks, 5 national hiking areas, 8 historical sites and 8 other recreationally important nature protection areas.

For **visitor counting**, P&WF uses mostly data storing electronic people counters located at main entry points. In some areas, where roads capture the visitor flows well, data storing electronic traffic counters are used. Nowadays, all the new counters purchased by P&WF include a remote reading feature. Each area is counted with several electronic counters permanently located at main entrance points. Electronic counters provide continuous hourly counting data all year round. Summer and winter counter locations vary, depending on trails in use. The point specific visitation counts obtained by electronic counters are extrapolated into area level visitation numbers by area coverage percentage.

Visitor surveys are implemented by P&WF as standardized on-site guided surveys (Kajala et al., 2007). The sampling aims to be as close to a random sample as possible, yet taking into account the limitations brought by resources and demanding circumstances out in the field. The visitors are asked to fill in the questionnaire towards the end of their visit, ideally when they are exiting the site. The interviewer is available for questions and further information, but typically respondents fill out questionnaires independently. The respondents answer the questionnaire nowadays mostly on a weather-proof tablet, on which the questionnaire is available in Finnish and several other languages. Paper questionnaires are also available as a back-up and for those people who prefer not to use modern technology. Each protected area with significant recreational use is surveyed with the same methodology on average every five to ten years, which means annually close to ten surveys to be administered across Finland.

Visitor monitoring data allows for calculating the local economic impacts of protected area visitation. The impacts are calculated by means of a method developed by Parks & Wildlife Finland and the Natural Resources Institute Finland. This method is based on the Money Generation Model 2 (MGM2) developed in the United States for the National Park Service by Michigan State University. The method uses visitation numbers, visitor spending figures and multipliers describing the flow of money in the local economy. The multipliers used in the model were last updated in 2019 (Vatanen and Kajala, 2020). The total income and job effects to the local economy consist of direct and indirect impacts of visitor spending per year. The method studies the impacts of all visitors, but also of those visitors that choose the study area as the main motive for the visit in the visitor survey.

For data entry, storage, management and reporting, P&WF uses the ASTA visitor information database system, which has been in use since 2006.

Results are reported for each area, but also as national statistics. The reports on visitor counting, visitor spending effects and health and well-being effects perceived by visitors are published annually in January separately for each protected area and as cumulative national figures (Metsähallitus, 2020a, 2020b, 2020c).

Visitation to Finnish national parks shows a significant increase over the period of the last 17 years (Figure 20.5; Metsähallitus, 2020a). Parallel to the increase in national park visitation, the visitor spending effects have increased even more rapidly. In 2010 the local economic impacts of visitors' spending to 35 national parks were 108.9 million euros and in 2019 with 40 national parks, they had doubled to €219.3 million. According to the P&WF assessment €1 investment in national parks and other key protected areas results, on average, in €10 return to local economies (Metsähallitus, 2020b).

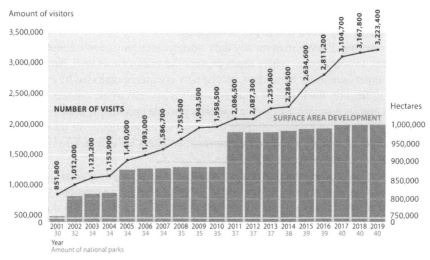

Note: In addition to the apparent increase in the popularity of national parks, the number of visits has increased due to enlargement of existing national parks as well as establishment of new national parks.
Source: Metsähallitus (2020a).

Figure 20.5   *The development of the number of visits to Finland's national parks, the number of parks, and the surface area of the parks during years 2001–2019*

P&WF also monitors the health and well-being effects perceived by visitors. Visitors to Finland's national parks estimate their health and well-being benefits to be around €100 (median) per visit. With 3.2 million visits to Finnish national parks in 2019, the total health and well-being value as perceived by visitors is roughly €322 million (Metsähallitus, 2020c).

CONCLUSIONS

Challenges and Limitations

Developing visitor monitoring methodology is not without challenges. When establishing a long-term visitor monitoring programme, one should carefully think through all the stages of visitor counting and surveys and ensure sufficient resources are available (Hornback and Eagles, 1999). Each stage needs to be implemented in order to obtain accurate and useful results.

Technological development may provide new possibilities for visitor monitoring. For example, mobile phone data can become accurate enough and affordable for use in visitor monitoring. The potential of social media in providing complementary visitor information has also been studied (Heikinheimo et al., 2017; Tenkanen et al., 2017; Staab et al., 2018). However, in the term monitoring there is embedded the idea of consistency. No changes should be implemented into the methodology without a careful analysis of how methodology might influence the data, if one is not to lose the comparability of the data. Comparable information is essential, if one is to track trends in visitation over time or to compare across areas.

It is possible to improve the accuracy of the results without losing comparability, as long as the core elements of a visitor monitoring programme are not changed. For example, one can take into use or add more remote reading electronic counters as long as the counting logic remains the same. Similarly, one can add new questions to visitor surveys, as long as the core questions remain the same.

One limitation related to the methodology described in this chapter is that one obtains information only on the actual users of the area. In other words, one does not obtain information on non-visitors, e.g. potential visitors, which is important as well. This kind of information requires a different approach, such as population surveys.

It should also be noted that, by definition, monitoring means inflexibility. Establishing a visitor monitoring programme requires adopting a defined methodology, which reduces flexibility compared to case studies. With case studies one can test and use e.g. the newest technical solutions or ask questions on current management issues. Consequently, no matter how good a visitor monitoring system, it can never solve all the information needs related to visitor use and management in protected areas. Thus, in addition to a visitor monitoring programme, other ways of gathering visitor data should also be considered. For example, for management planning information needs, GIS-based internet surveys allowing visitors to give feedback and ideas in connection to a particular location are becoming a very useful tool. When developing specified services related to parks and protected areas, a service design approach can provide valuable insight into visitors' needs and perceptions.

Benefits of Systematic Visitor Monitoring

When visitor data is gathered in a uniform and systematic manner for several years, it provides possibilities for versatile analyses, reporting and comparisons, both across areas and across time, and at different levels from local to regional, national and international. This kind of information is vital not only for planning and management, but also for well-informed policy making (Kajala, 2012).

The amount of recreational use of protected areas is a fundamental basic information for any protected area. If one was to select only one single indicator of visitor use in protected areas, it would be most likely the amount of use. Number of visits is a useful indicator alone, but also a necessity for any additional calculations on management effectiveness, such as visitor spending effects or effects on health and well-being. Moreover, the amount of use is a key starting point when estimating sustainability of recreational use and tourism in protected areas.

Visitor monitoring is a strategic decision, which requires positive attitude and long-term commitment at every level of the organization. Even though establishing and maintaining a comprehensive visitor monitoring system requires significant investment in both time and resources, P&WF managers think that this investment is not only useful but a necessity for successful management as well as for showcasing the benefits of the protected areas. Moreover, a systematic, well documented visitor monitoring programme increases the credibility of the agency's statistics. Systematic visitor monitoring data thus provides enhanced cooperation possibilities with partners and stakeholders, including research institutes.

REFERENCES

Arnberger, A., Haider, W. and Brandenburg, C. (2005) Evaluating visitor-monitoring techniques: A comparison of counting and video observation data. *Environmental Management*, 36, 317–327.

Eagles, P. F. J. and Kajala, L. (2014) Administrative procedures for operation of a national visitor use monitoring program in protected areas. Proceedings of the 7th International Conference on Monitoring and Management of Visitors in Recreational and Protected Areas (MMV), 20–23 August, Tallinn, Estonia, pp. 171–172.

Erkkonen, J. and Sievänen, T. (2001) *Kävijätutkimusopas* [In Finnish, title means Manual on visitor surveys]. Metsähallituksen luonnonsuojelujulkaisuja, B, 62. 73 pp.

Heikinheimo, V., Di Minin, E., Tenkanen, H., Hausmann, A., Erkkonen, J. and Toivonen, T. (2017). User-generated geographic information for visitor monitoring in a national park: A comparison of social media data and visitor survey. *ISPRS International Journal of Geo-Information*, 6(3), 85.

Hornback, K. E. and Eagles, P. F. J. (1999) *Guidelines for Public Use Measurement and Reporting at Parks and Protected Areas*. Cambridge, UK and Gland, Switzerland: IUCN, Parks Canada, Cooperative Research Center for Sustainable Tourism for Australia and World Commission on Protected Areas.

Horne, P., Sievänen, T., Alenius, V., Iisalo, H. and Friman, T. (1998) *Kävijälaskentaopas* (In Finnish, title means Manual on visitor counting). Metsähallituksen luonnonsuojelujulkaisuja, B, 45. 68 pp.

Kajala, L. (2012) Estimating economic benefits of protected areas in Finland. In M. Kettunen, P. Vihervaara, S. Kinnunen, D. D'Amato, T. Badura, M. Argimon and P. Ten Brink (eds.), *Socio-Economic Importance of Ecosystem Services in the Nordic Countries: Synthesis in the Context of the Economics of Ecosystems and Biodiversity (TEEB)* (pp. 255–259). Copenhagen: TemaNord.

Kajala, L., Almik, A., Dahl, R., Dikšaitė, L., Erkkonen, J., Fredman, P., Jensen, F., Søndergaard, K., Sievänen, T., Skov-Petersen, H., Vistad, O. I. and Wallsten, P. (2007) *Visitor Monitoring in Nature Areas: A Manual Based on Experiences from the Nordic and Baltic Countries*. Stockholm: Swedish Environmental Protection Agency.

Kajala, L. and Erkkonen, J. (2018) Why count visitors? Twenty years of experiences on visitor monitoring in Finland's protected areas. The 9th International Conference on Monitoring and Management of Visitors in Recreational and Protected Areas (MMV9), 28–31 August, Bordeaux, France. Abstract, pp. 50–52.

Kajala, L. and Karoles-Viia, K. (2016) Long term visitor monitoring in protected and recreational areas: Results from Finland and Estonia. Monitoring and Management of Visitors in Recreational and Protected Areas, 26–30 September, Novi Sad, Serbia. Abstract, pp. 134–136.

Metsähallitus (2020a) https://www.metsa.fi/en/outdoors/visitor-monitoring-and-impacts/visitation-numbers-and-visitor-profiles/, accessed 19 January 2021.

Metsähallitus (2020b) https://www.metsa.fi/en/economic-benefits-of-national-parks/, accessed 19 January 2021.

Metsähallitus (2020c) https://www.metsa.fi/en/outdoors/nature-and-health/health-benefits-from-national-parks/, accessed 19 January 2021.

Spenceley, A., Schägner, J. P., Engels, B., Engelbauer, M., Erkkonen, J., Job, H., Kajala, L., Majewski, L., Metzler, D., Mayer, M., Rylance, A., Scheder, N., Smith-Christensen, C., Souza, T. B., Cullinane Thomas, C. and Woltering, M. (In prep) *Visitors Count! Guidance for Protected Areas on the Economic Analysis of Visitation*. BfN.

Staab, J., Taubenböck, H. and Job, H. (2018) Monitoring visitor numbers with computer vision. The 9th International Conference on Monitoring and Management of Visitors in Recreational and Protected Areas (MMV9), 28–31 August, Bordeaux, France. Abstract, pp. 127–129.

Tenkanen, H., Di Minin, E., Heikinheimo, V., Hausmann, A., Herbst, M., Kajala, L. and Toivonen, T. (2017) Instagram, Flickr or Twitter: Assessing the usability of social media data for visitor monitoring in protected areas. *Scientific Reports*, 7. Article number 17615.

Vatanen, E. and Kajala, L. (2020). Kansallispuistojen, retkeilyalueiden ja muiden luontomatkailullisesti arvokkaiden suojelualueiden paikallistaloudellisten vaikutusten arviointimenetelmän kertoimien päivitys 2019 [Update of multipliers used by the method assessing the local economic impacts of national parks, hiking areas and other protected areas valuable as nature tourism destinations, 2019, in Finnish, abstract in English]. *Nature Protection Publications of Metsähallitus*. Series A 232. https://julkaisut.metsa.fi/julkaisut/show/2413.

21. Economic effects assessment approaches: US National Parks approach

Cathy Cullinane Thomas and Lynne Koontz

INTRODUCTION

The US National Park Service (NPS) manages 419 of America's most treasured places, including iconic national parks, battlefields, historic sites, recreation areas, seashores, and scenic rivers and trails. On vacations or on day trips, more than 300 million visitors spend time and money in the communities surrounding NPS sites across the United States each year. Spending by NPS visitors generates and supports vital economic activity within local gateway regions throughout the nation. In 2018, NPS visitors spent USD 20.2 billion in park gateway regions, and this spending contributed 329,000 jobs and USD 40.1 billion in economic output to the national economy (Cullinane Thomas et al., 2019a). The objective of this chapter is to describe the data and processes used by the NPS to assess and showcase the significance of visitor spending contributions to local regions and the nation. The chapter provides a step-by-step example of the methods for estimating park-level visitor spending and economic effects for Yosemite National Park, and describes how park-level data are combined to produce state- and national-level estimates.

OVERVIEW OF ECONOMIC EFFECTS ANALYSES

The NPS has been measuring and reporting visitor spending and economic effects for individual parks and the park system as a whole for more than 30 years. The Money Generation Model (MGM), developed in 1990, was the first tool used to estimate economic contributions of NPS visitor spending (National Park Service, 1995). In 2001, an updated version of the Money Generation Model (version 2; MGM2) was used to produce the first NPS system-wide economic effects estimates (Stynes et al., 2000; Stynes and Sun, 2003). In 2012, the NPS transitioned to the Visitor Spending Effects (VSE) model for estimating annual system-wide economic effects. Methods for the VSE analysis are based on the framework developed by Stynes et al. (2000) for the MGM2. Similar methods have been adopted by other US Federal agencies as well as researchers in other countries including Germany (Mayer et al., 2010), Finland (Huhtala et al., 2010), and Brazil (Souza, 2016). The Stynes framework is also the foundation for the Tourism Economic Model for Protected Areas (TEMPA) tool described in Chapter 22 in this volume.

Economic effects analyses measure the economic activity stemming from tourism spending. This includes three categories of activity: (1) the direct economic activity resulting from visitors purchasing goods and services from local businesses, (2) the indirect effects of local businesses purchasing inputs from local suppliers, and (3) the induced effects of employees of directly and indirectly affected businesses spending their incomes on goods and services

380

within the local economy. The indirect and induced effects of spending are called secondary effects and describe how an injection of money into a regional economy (direct effects) 'ripples' or 'multiplies' to create additional economic activity (secondary effects). Secondary effects include multiple rounds of spending backwards through supply chains and only include goods and services purchased from businesses located within a defined local region. Purchases made from businesses located outside of the local region are 'leaked' from the economy and are not included in the multiplier effect.

The NPS uses an economic input–output modeling framework to estimate the multiplier effects of visitor spending. Economic input–output models capture the interactions between producers and consumers within a defined regional economy and describe the secondary effects of visitor spending through regional economic multipliers (Archer, 1977). The NPS defines regional economies at the park-level (park gateway regions including the set of counties located in each park's nearby area), the state-level, and the national-level.

Four economic effects metrics are reported: jobs, labor income (LI), value added (VA), and economic output. Jobs are a measure of the annualized full and part time employment supported by NPS visitor spending; labor income is a measure of the employee and proprietor wages, salaries and benefits earned through supported jobs; value added is a measure of the contribution of visitor spending to the Gross Domestic Product (GDP) of a regional economy; and economic output is a measure of the total estimated value of production of goods and services supported in a region by visitor spending.

There are two types of economic effects analyses: contribution analyses and impact analyses (Watson et al., 2007). Economic contribution analyses describe the gross economic activity associated with NPS visitor spending in a regional economy. Results can be interpreted as the relative magnitude and significance of the economic activity generated through NPS visitor spending in a regional economy. Economic contributions are estimated by multiplying *total visitor spending* by regional economic multipliers. Total visitor spending includes spending by both local (resident) visitors who live in gateway regions and non-local (non-resident) visitors who travel to NPS sites from outside of gateway regions. The visitor spending effects report released by the NPS annually is an example of a contribution analysis describing the importance of park tourism to the economic vitality of local regions and the nation (Cullinane Thomas et al., 2019a).

Economic impact analyses estimate the net changes to the economic base of a regional economy that can be attributed to the inflow of new money to the economy solely from non-local visitors. Economic impact analyses are most often used to estimate how a change in visitation or visitor spending might affect local economies. For example, effects on local jobs and business activity of decreased visitation resulting from a new park policy to limit certain types of recreation, or effects of increased visitation resulting from a new visitor center or increased access.

NPS VISITOR SPENDING EFFECTS: ANNUAL CONTRIBUTION ANALYSIS METHODS

The NPS produces annual estimates of the economic contributions of NPS visitor spending to local communities, states, and the nation using the Visitor Spending Effects (VSE) model (Cullinane Thomas et al., 2019a). This section details the data and methods used in the VSE model to estimate park-level visitor spending and economic contributions, and the methods used to roll these estimates up to state and national-level contributions. Steps for visitor spending estimation include: segmenting visitors into distinct lodging-based segments that describe differences in spending patterns; transforming visitor count data and spending data into compatible units of measure; and determining the portion of time and trip expenditures spent in local gateway regions that can be attributed to national park visitation. Economic contributions are estimated by combining visitor spending estimates with region-specific economic multipliers.

Required Data

Three pieces of data are required to estimate the economic effects of NPS visitor spending: park visitation data, spending patterns and trip characteristics derived from visitor survey data (VSE profiles), and regional economic multipliers.

Visitation data

The NPS Visitor Use Statistics Office reports annual estimates of NPS recreation visits for most NPS units (Koontz et al., 2017; Ziesler, 2019). Recreation visitation data available from the NPS are measured in terms of *visits*, which are defined as the annual number of individuals who enter NPS sites for recreation purposes. One entrance per individual per day is countable under the NPS counting procedures. This measure of visitation is problematic for visitor spending estimation because a single visitor can count as multiple visits. For example, a family of 4 taking a week-long vacation to Yosemite National Park and staying at a lodge outside of the park could be counted as 28 visits (4 individuals who enter the park on 7 different days); while a different family of 4, also taking a week-long vacation to Yosemite National Park but lodging within the park, could be counted as 4 visits (4 individuals who enter the park on a single day and then stay within the park for the remainder of their trip). To remedy this counting issue, park visits are converted to visitor trips by dividing visits by average park entry rates for each visitor segment. Data required for this conversion come from visitor surveys, described in the visitor survey data section below.

Visitor survey data

The NPS conducts in-park visitor intercept surveys to collect visitor spending and trip characteristic data required for the VSE analyses (see RSG, 2019). Visitor survey data are used to derive VSE profiles that describe visitor spending patterns and trip characteristics for specific parks or sets of parks (an example VSE profile is included in the Yosemite National Park example below; see Cullinane Thomas et al., 2019b for details about how VSE profiles are derived from survey data).

For each VSE profile, sub-profiles are developed for visitor segments to separate visitors into groups with distinct spending patterns (Stynes and White, 2006). The NPS uses lodging-based visitor segments that include day trip segments (Local Day Trip and Non-Local Day Trip), and overnight segments split into camping in and out of the park, back-country camping, lodging in and out of the park, and other overnight stays in the nearby area (NPS Back-country, NPS Camp, Camp Outside Park, NPS Lodge, Lodge Outside Park, and Other).

Visitor spending patterns describe average expenditures made by national park visitors within local gateway regions surrounding parks. NPS surveys ask respondents to report total trip expenditures for their party (defined as themselves and their personal group) during their time in the park and the nearby area. Eliciting party expenditures, as opposed to individual expenditures, is a common practice in visitor spending surveys because couples and families may have difficulty separating out individual expenditures (Stynes and White, 2006). Spending patterns are estimated for each visitor segment and are converted to spending per party per day for day trip segments and spending per party per night for overnight segments by dividing average per party per trip expenditures by average lengths of stay in the nearby area (Sun and Stynes, 2006; Cullinane Thomas et al., 2019b). Spending profiles describe average spending by category to enable expenditures to be bridged to economic sectors for contribution analyses. NPS spending categories include lodging, camping fees, restaurants, groceries, gas, transportation, recreation industries, and retail purchases. Only spending made within the gateway region surrounding the park is included in the survey data and economic model. Expenditures on durable goods (such as vehicles and boats) are excluded because these expenditures represent goods that are used for more than a single visit to a protected area. Travel costs incurred outside of the local gateway region (such as airfares) are excluded because these expenditures do not contribute to local-area economic activity.

In addition to spending patterns, VSE profiles describe several trip characteristic variables including: segment splits, which describe the percentage of visits in each visitor segment; average entry rates, which measure the number of days a visitor enters or re-enters the park over the course of a trip; average party size, which measures the number of people in a personal group that are traveling together and sharing expenses; and average attributed length of stay, which measures the length of stay in the nearby area attributed to the NPS visit (attributed length of stay is described in terms of days for day trip segments and nights for overnight segments; for more information on park attribution see Cullinane Thomas et al., 2019b). Trip characteristic variables are used to convert NPS visitation data and VSE spending patterns into compatible units of measure. NPS visitation data are measured as visits, but visitor spending profiles are in terms of spending per party per day/night. To bring these data into compatible units of measure, visit data are converted to party days and party nights. Party days/nights are the combined annual number of days (for day trip segments) and nights (for overnight segments) that parties spend in the nearby area that can be attributed to the park. The conversion process, from visits to visitor trips to party trips to party days/nights, is described in detail in the Yosemite National Park example below.

Regional economic multipliers
The NPS uses regional economic multipliers derived from the IMPLAN software and data system (IMPLAN Group LLC)[1] to calculate the direct and secondary effects of visitor spending, expressed in terms of jobs, income, value added, and output. IMPLAN is an input–output modeling system and social accounting matrix (SAM) that describes the US economy at national and sub-national levels. The SAM framework describes inter-industry transactions and transfers within an economy and extends input–output accounts to internalize institutions (households and governments). In addition to inter-industry transactions, the SAM also captures information on market transactions between households and businesses, payments of taxes by households and businesses, transfers of government funds to households and businesses, and transfers of funds from households to households (IMPLAN Group LLC). The NPS uses IMPLAN data aggregated to defined regional economies at the park-level, the

state-level, and the national-level. Details about study area and multiplier data used for the VSE analysis are included in the Yosemite National Park example below.

Example Park Analysis: Yosemite National Park

This example is designed to provide readers with a step-by-step walkthrough of the data and analyses used to estimate park-level visitor spending and economic contributions. Data and results are for Yosemite National Park, in California, USA for the year 2018. Yosemite is located in the Sierra Nevada Mountains of central California and is an iconic park known for its majestic granite dome formations, waterfalls, and wildlife. All data required to reproduce the Yosemite contribution results presented in Table 21.5 are included in this chapter.

Visitor spending effects profile
VSE profile data for Yosemite were derived from a visitor survey conducted in the park in June of 2015 and include trip characteristics (Table 21.1) and spending patterns (Table 21.2) for eight visitor segments. Survey respondents were asked to report only spending that occurred within the park and the nearby area surrounding the park (i.e. spending within the park's gateway region). The Yosemite gateway region was identified through conversations with park staff who were asked to identify the nearby towns and cities where visitors typically stop and make purchases or spend the night while visiting the park. The local gateway region was then defined as the set of counties that include the park and the identified towns and cities visited by park visitors. For Yosemite National Park this includes Fresno, Inyo, Madera, Mariposa, Merced, Mono, and Tuolumne Counties in California.

Table 21.1   Trip characteristic data for Yosemite National Park, 2018

Variable	Local day trip	Non-local day trip	NPS back-country	NPS camp	Camp outside park	NPS lodge	Lodge outside park	Other
Segment split	5.25%	11.16%	1.10%	6.73%	8.60%	8.32%	55.60%	3.24%
Entry rate	1.00	1.00	1.24	1.54	1.98	1.58	2.02	1.31
Party size	2.75	3.28	2.47	3.00	3.29	3.62	3.09	3.24
Length of stay (attributed to NPS)*	1.0	0.7	3.5	3.6	2.1	3.1	2.3	2.2

Note: * Length of stay is described in terms of days for day trip segments and nights for overnight segments.

Visitation data
Yosemite National Park received 4,009,436 recreation visits in 2018 (Ziesler, 2019). Figure 21.1 steps through the conversion from total recreation visits to party days/nights by visitor segment. First, visits are split into visits by segment using segment split data. Next, visits are converted to visitor trips by dividing by average entry rates, then visitor trips are converted to party trips by dividing by average party size. Finally, party trips are multiplied by attributed lengths of stay to estimate party days/nights by visitor segment.

Table 21.2   *Spending patterns for Yosemite National Park (USD 2018)*

Spending category	Local day trip	Non-local day trip	NPS back-country	NPS camp	Camp outside park	NPS lodge	Lodge outside park	Other
Camping fees	0.00	0.00	3.42	23.52	27.28	0.78	0.91	0.00
Equipment rental	0.00	2.26	2.37	2.21	3.95	2.83	1.87	0.00
Gas	22.01	31.41	14.07	26.55	26.66	24.80	26.13	15.70
Groceries	11.25	10.98	10.14	19.12	21.84	27.34	21.58	23.06
Guides and tour fees	0.12	1.25	1.25	8.20	10.92	11.12	30.08	15.67
Hotels	0.00	0.00	3.59	8.88	4.34	290.90	193.04	0.00
Public transportation	0.00	0.00	0.16	0.20	0.46	0.50	1.03	0.00
Recreation and entertainment	1.20	0.00	0.00	0.09	2.15	2.24	4.11	2.90
Rental cars	0.00	13.44	2.85	12.69	11.54	30.23	35.48	8.99
Restaurants	14.72	18.78	7.53	17.18	18.21	75.03	60.46	10.49
Souvenirs and other retail	24.08	34.21	4.62	15.56	15.73	32.44	34.61	12.03
Total spending per party per day/night	**73.38**	**112.33**	**50.00**	**134.20**	**143.08**	**498.21**	**409.30**	**88.84**

Note: Spending is expressed in terms of spending per party per day for day trip segments and spending per party per night for overnight segments.

Visitor spending estimation

Total visitor spending (Table 21.3) is calculated by multiplying spending per party per day/night (Table 21.2) by total party days/nights (Figure 21.1).

Estimating party days/nights : Yosemite National Park

    Recreation visits (from NPS visitor statistics)
    Trip characteristics (from Table 26.1)
    Intermediate results
    Party day/night estimates by visitor segment

Total Recreation
Visits: 4,009,436

		Local Day Trip	Non-Local Day Trip	NPS Backcountry	NPS Campground	Camp Outside Park	NPS Lodge	Lodge Outside Park	Other
×	Segment Split	5.25%	11.16%	1.10%	6.73%	8.60%	8.32%	55.60%	3.24%
=	Visits	210,495	447,453	44,104	269,835	344,811	333,585	2,229,246	129,906
÷	Entry Rate	1.00	1.00	1.24	1.54	1.98	1.58	2.02	1.31
=	Visitor Trips	210,495	447,453	35,568	175,218	174,147	211,130	1,103,587	99,165
÷	Party Size	2.75	3.28	2.47	3.00	3.29	3.62	3.09	3.24
=	Party Trips	76,544	136,419	14,400	58,406	52,932	58,323	357,148	30,606
×	Length of Stay	1	0.7	3.5	3.6	2.1	3.1	2.3	2.2
=	Party Days/Nights	76,544	95,493	50,400	210,261	111,158	180,802	821,440	67,334

Figure 21.1   *Estimating party days/nights: Yosemite National Park, 2018*

Economic contribution estimation

Yosemite National Park economic data were derived from the IMPLAN Pro v3.0 2017 dataset for the study area comprised of the seven counties in the park's gateway region (Table 21.4).

Table 21.3　　*Total visitor spending by spending category and visitor segment for Yosemite National Park (USD 1000s, USD 2018)*

Spending category	Local day trip	Non-local day trip	NPS back-country	NPS camp	Camp outside park	NPS lodge	Lodge outside park	Other	Total spending (USD 1000s)
Camping fees	0	0	172	4,945	3,032	141	748	0	9,038
Equipment rental	0	216	119	465	439	512	1,536	0	3,287
Gas	1,685	2,999	709	5,582	2,963	4,484	21,464	1,057	40,943
Groceries	861	1,049	511	4,020	2,428	4,943	17,727	1,553	33,092
Guides and tour fees	9	119	63	1,724	1,214	2,011	24,709	1,055	30,904
Hotels	0	0	181	1,867	482	52,595	158,571	0	213,696
Public transportation	0	0	8	42	51	90	846	0	1,037
Recreation and entertainment	92	0	0	19	239	405	3,376	195	4,326
Rental cars	0	1,283	144	2,668	1,283	5,466	29,145	605	40,594
Restaurants	1,127	1,793	380	3,612	2,024	13,566	49,664	706	72,872
Souvenirs and other retail	1,843	3,267	233	3,272	1,749	5,865	28,430	810	45,469
Total (USD 1000s)	**5,617**	**10,726**	**2,520**	**28,216**	**15,904**	**90,078**	**336,216**	**5,981**	**495,258**

Table 21.4　　*Capture rates, direct effects ratios, and multipliers by spending category for the Yosemite National Park 2018 visitor spending effects model*

Spending category	Capture rate %	Direct effects ratios			Multipliers			
		Jobs per output	Labor income per output	Value added per output	Jobs	Labor income	Value added	Output
Camping fees	100.0	0.000019	0.631	0.684	1.242	1.338	1.543	1.630
Equipment rental	100.0	0.000014	0.438	0.598	1.291	1.429	1.622	1.617
Gas	16.4	0.000008	0.586	0.746	1.513	1.324	1.466	1.587
Groceries	27.9	0.000012	0.493	0.699	1.331	1.373	1.473	1.557
Guides and tour fees	100.0	0.000016	0.403	0.534	1.255	1.462	1.648	1.585
Hotels	100.0	0.000009	0.341	0.628	1.404	1.497	1.443	1.484
Public transportation	100.0	0.000021	0.422	0.554	1.219	1.526	1.666	1.659
Recreation and entertainment	100.0	0.000016	0.403	0.534	1.255	1.462	1.648	1.585
Rental cars	100.0	0.000005	0.185	0.585	1.66	1.808	1.457	1.452
Restaurants	100.0	0.000015	0.363	0.566	1.217	1.429	1.494	1.486
Souvenirs and other retail	50.7	0.000019	0.559	0.700	1.223	1.354	1.515	1.610

Source: Data are derived from the IMPLAN Pro v3.0 2017 dataset for the study area comprised of Fresno, Inyo, Madera, Mariposa, Merced, Mono, and Tuolumne Counties, California, USA.

The calculation of economic contributions is based on three types of economic data: capture rates, direct effects ratios, and economic multipliers.[2]

The capture rate is the portion of visitor spending that stays in the local gateway region. NPS visitor spending patterns only include expenditures made within the park's gateway region; for this reason, capture rates for spending categories associated with service sectors are equal to 100%. Capture rates for retail sectors are equal to the retail margin for the associated sector (retail margins are the markup rates applied by retail sellers to the price of a good). The cost the retailer paid for a good purchased for resale is assumed to be leaked from the local area (this makes the conservative assumption that goods sold at retail stores are not produced locally). Direct output is calculated by multiplying total spending by the capture rate. Hence, direct output can be interpreted as the direct sales that stay in the gateway region economy.

The other direct effects of Yosemite visitor spending (i.e. direct jobs, labor income, and value added) are calculated by using direct effect ratios. The ratios are estimated from study area data and describe for each sector of the economy the ratio of the sector's total output to total jobs, total output to total labor income, and total output to total value added. Direct output estimates are multiplied by jobs per output, labor income (LI) per output, and value added (VA) per output to estimate direct jobs, direct labor income, and direct value added, respectively.

Multipliers describe the ripple effects (i.e. indirect and induced effects) of visitor spending. The multipliers used in the NPS analysis are 'Type SAM' multipliers which include indirect effects (resulting from inter-industry spending) and induced effects (resulting from household spending of income earned by employees and proprietors of directly and indirectly affected industries). Secondary effects are equal to the sum of indirect and induced effects. Total economic effects are equal to the sum of direct effects and secondary effects and are calculated by multiplying direct effects by multipliers.

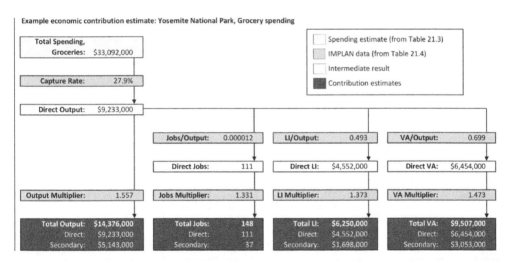

Figure 21.2   *Example economic contribution estimate: Yosemite National Park, grocery spending*

Figure 21.2 steps through how economic contribution estimates are derived from spending estimates, using the example of grocery spending in Yosemite. In 2018, visitors spent an estimated total of USD 33,092,000 on groceries in the local gateway region while visiting Yosemite. Because groceries are a retail good, only the retail margin (27.9%) is captured and counted as direct output, resulting in a direct output estimate of USD 9,233,000. For the 2018 Yosemite analysis, the output multiplier for groceries was 1.557; multiplying the direct output estimate of USD 9,233,000 by the output multiplier gives the total output estimate of USD 14,376,000. The difference between total output and direct output gives the secondary output estimate of USD 5,143,000. Direct effects ratios are used to estimate direct jobs, labor income, and value added; for Yosemite groceries, there is an estimated 0.000012 jobs per dollar of direct output (this translates to 12 jobs per million dollars in direct output), 0.493 in labor income per dollar of direct output, and 0.699 in value added per dollar of direct output; these ratios result in estimates of 111 direct jobs, USD 4,552,000 in direct labor income, and USD 6,454,000 in direct value added in the local gateway economy supported by Yosemite visitor spending on groceries. Multipliers are used to estimate total jobs, labor income, and value added. There are separate multipliers for each economic metric; for Yosemite groceries, the jobs multiplier is 1.331, the labor income multiplier is 1.373, and the value added multiplier is 1.473.

Capture rates, direct effects ratios, and multipliers for all spending categories for the Yosemite example (Table 21.4) can be combined with park spending estimates (Table 21.3) to estimate park economic contributions (Table 21.5).

Table 21.5   *Visitor spending and economic contribution estimates for Yosemite National Park, 2018*

Spending category	Total visitor spending (USD 1000s)	Jobs		Labor income (USD 1000s)		Value added (USD 1000s)		Output (USD 1000s)	
		Direct	Total	Direct	Total	Direct	Total	Direct	Total
Camping fees	9,038	172	214	5,703	7,631	6,182	9,539	9,038	14,732
Equipment rental	3,287	46	59	1,440	2,058	1,966	3,189	3,287	5,315
Gas	40,943	54	82	3,935	5,210	5,009	7,343	6,715	10,657
Groceries	33,092	111	148	4,552	6,250	6,454	9,507	9,233	14,376
Guides and tour fees	30,904	494	620	12,454	18,208	16,503	27,197	30,904	48,983
Hotels	213,696	1,923	2,700	72,870	109,086	134,201	193,652	213,696	317,125
Public transportation	1,037	22	27	438	668	574	956	1,037	1,720
Recreation and entertainment	4,326	69	87	1,743	2,548	2,310	3,807	4,326	6,857
Rental cars	40,594	203	337	7,510	13,578	23,747	34,599	40,594	58,942
Restaurants	72,872	1,093	1,330	26,453	37,801	41,246	61,622	72,872	108,288
Souvenirs and other retail	45,469	438	536	12,887	17,449	16,137	24,448	23,053	37,115
Total	**495,258**	**4,625**	**6,140**	**149,985**	**220,487**	**254,329**	**375,859**	**414,755**	**624,110**

Note: These results can be reproduced from data published in this chapter. Results in this table differ slightly from those published in Cullinane Thomas et al. (2019a) due to rounding differences.

State and national level contribution estimation

In addition to park-level analyses, the NPS also reports economic contributions at the state and national levels. To estimate state-level visitor spending, park-level visitor spending estimates are summed for all parks within each state. As with the park-level analyses, only spending made within park gateway regions is counted; this means that some visitor spending made within a state (such as intrastate travel expenditures) are not included in state-level analyses. In 2018, NPS visitor spending in California was estimated to be USD 2.67 billion, which is the sum of park-level visitor spending for the 26 NPS units in the state (Table 21.6). Similarly, the national-level visitor spending estimate is equal to the sum of visitor spending for all NPS units included in the VSE analysis.[3]

State and national level economic contribution estimates use study area and multiplier data from state and national IMPLAN models, respectively. The size of the region included in a contribution analysis influences the magnitude of the economic multiplier effects. This is because as the economic region expands, the amount of secondary spending that stays within that region increases (i.e. less money is 'leaked' from larger regional economies) which results

Table 21.6   Visitor spending estimates for California NPS units, 2018

California national park units	Total visitor spending (USD 2018)
Golden Gate National Recreation Area	1,038,370,000
Yosemite National Park	495,258,000
Joshua Tree National Park	146,480,000
Death Valley National Park	141,260,000
Muir Woods National Monument	108,380,000
Point Reyes National Seashore	107,440,000
San Francisco Maritime National Historical Park	106,000,000
Sequoia National Park	94,430,000
Fort Point National Historic Site	82,700,000
Kings Canyon National Park	61,150,000
Cabrillo National Monument	49,730,000
Mojave National Preserve	46,480,000
Santa Monica Mountains National Recreation Area	38,490,000
Redwood National & State Parks	31,070,000
Lassen Volcanic National Park	30,330,000
Whiskeytown National Recreation Area	25,810,000
Channel Islands National Park	22,910,000
Pinnacles National Park	13,120,000
Manzanar National Historic Site	11,030,000
Devils Postpile National Monument	9,070,000
Lava Beds National Monument	5,480,000
Rosie the Riveter WWII Home Front National Historical Park	3,420,000
John Muir National Historic Site	2,770,000
Cesar E. Chavez National Monument	750,000
Eugene O'Neill National Historic Site	200,000
Port Chicago Naval Magazine National Memorial	40,000
Total	**2,672,168,000**

Table 21.7   Park-level, state-level, and national-level visitor spending and economic contributions for Yosemite National Park local area economy, the California economy, and the US national economy, 2018

Analysis level	Total visitor spending ($1,000,000s)	Jobs		Labor income (USD 1,000,000s)		Value added (USD 1,000,000s)		Output (USD 1,000,000s)	
		Direct	Total	Direct	Total	Direct	Total	Direct	Total
Yosemite National Park	495	4,625	6,140	150	220	254	376	415	624
State of California	2,672	24,714	35,720	893	1,598	1,442	2,654	2,248	4,221
National	20,234	197,400	329,000	6,055	13,616	10,321	23,443	16,585	40,212

in larger economic multipliers. Thus, multipliers for the national level are larger than those for the state level which are larger than those for the park level. Table 21.7 shows park (Yosemite National Park), state (California), and national-level VSE estimates for 2018. Implied multipliers can be derived by dividing total effects by direct effects; for output this gives output multipliers of: 1.5 (Yosemite National Park), 1.9 (California), and 2.4 (National). Implied job, labor income, and value added multipliers can be derived in the same manner.

DISCUSSION

The recognition and quality of the VSE program is due to several factors including the ongoing collection and availability of quality data and an effective communication strategy.

The foundation of the VSE program is park-level visitor count data, which the NPS has been continuously collecting for most park units since the early 1900s (Koontz et al., 2017; Ziesler,

Figure 21.3   National Park Service, social media infographic

2019). Trip characteristic and spending pattern profiles are derived from visitor surveys which have been conducted periodically for a subset of parks. Data gaps in park-level survey data have required the use of generic VSE profiles for parks without primary surveys, and some parks are not well represented by the generic profiles (Cullinane Thomas et al., 2019a, 2019b). The NPS recognizes the importance of continuing to improve the quality and quantity of survey data that is representative of the variety of visitor uses and demographics from across the park system. To address this need, a formal socioeconomic monitoring program is being established to systematically survey park visitors across all NPS units. This program will supply the VSE analysis with new survey data from 24 park units each year which will greatly increase the availability of park-specific VSE profiles and reduce and eventually eliminate the VSE reliance on generic profiles.

The NPS has an effective communication strategy to release VSE results to the American public. Communication is typically initiated with a national media briefing and news release. In the days following the national media release, individual parks send out local press releases on the park-level VSE results for their local economy. These press releases generate substantial media coverage; for example, in the first week following the VSE release in 2018, there were more than 552 media publications with a one-day peak of 377 publications about the economic benefits of NPS tourism in newspapers across the country. The total monetary value of media coverage within the first week of the VSE release in 2018 was USD 1,883,000 with a one-day peak of USD 1,357,000. In addition to traditional media outlets, the NPS reached new audiences in 2018 with the release of an infographic on social media outlets (Figure 21.3). To increase the visibility and use of the VSE annual report results, the NPS collaborates with the US Geological Survey to produce a web-based interactive data visualization tool.[4] This tool allows users to visually view year-by-year trend data and explore current year visitor spending, jobs, labor income, value added, and economic output effects by sector for national, state, and local economies (Cullinane Thomas et al., 2019a). Many media publications utilize graphics from the web tool to visualize park results.

CONCLUSIONS

Over the past 30 years, the annual NPS visitor spending contributions report has become a well-recognized and respected indicator of the economic significance of national parks. The estimates provide park staff with a better understanding of the economic relationship with their gateway communities for planning, management, and local public outreach needs. The national estimates and press release highlight the tremendous benefit parks have on the nation's economy and underscore the need to adequately maintain parks and fund the NPS.

The ability of the NPS to produce visitor spending and economic contribution estimates relies on foundational data collection efforts to monitor visitor count data and to collect visitor trip characteristic and spending data. These data are key inputs to the visitor spending effects analysis, and similar monitoring efforts at other parks and protected areas could be used to make these types of estimates. Not all parks and protected areas will have the resources required to collect all required data; Chapter 22 in this volume on the TEMPA tool describes potential secondary sources of data for researchers interested in producing similar effects estimates for protected areas with primary data gaps.

NOTES

1. Any use of trade, firm, or product names is for descriptive purposes only and does not imply endorsement by the US Government.
2. Note that the IMPLAN software combines all of these data for users; users of IMPLAN need only enter spending data into appropriate sectors and the software will estimate direct and secondary effects. The bridge used to match VSE spending categories to IMPLAN sectors is included in Cullinane Thomas et al. (2019a).
3. The visitor spending effects analysis estimates visitor spending and associated economic effects for NPS units that collect visitation data; in 2018 this included 382 of 419 National Park units.
4. Available at https://www.nps.gov/subjects/socialscience/vse.htm.

REFERENCES

Archer, B. (1977) *Tourism multipliers: The state of the art*. Bangor Occasional Papers in Economics. Bangor: University of Wales Press.

Cullinane Thomas, C., L. Koontz and E. Cornachione (2019a) *2018 National Park Visitor Spending Effects: Economic Contributions to Local Communities, States, and the Nation*. Natural Resource Report NPS/NRSS/EQD/NRR—2019/1922. National Park Service, Fort Collins, Colorado.

Cullinane Thomas, C., E. Cornachione, L. Koontz and C. Keyes (2019b) *National Park Service Socioeconomic Pilot Survey: Visitor Spending Analysis*. Natural Resource Report NPS/NRSS/EQD/NRR—2019/1924. National Park Service, Fort Collins, Colorado.

Huhtala, M., L. Kajala and E. Vatanen (2010) *Local Economic Impacts of National Park Visitors' Spending in Finland: The Development Process of an Estimation Method*. Working Paper, Finnish Forest Research Institute.

IMPLAN Group LLC, IMPLAN System (data and software). Available from 16740 Birkdale Commons Parkway Suite 206, Huntersville, NC 28078 (https://www.implan.com).

Koontz, L., C. Cullinane Thomas, P. Ziesler, J. Olson and B. Meldrum (2017) Visitor spending effects: Assessing and showcasing America's investment in national parks. *Journal of Sustainable Tourism*, 25(12), 1865–1876.

Mayer, M., M. Müller, M. Woltering, J. Arnegger and H. Job (2010) The economic impact of tourism in six German national parks. *Landscape and Urban Planning*, 97(2), 73–82.

National Park Service (1995). *The Money Generation Model*. Denver, CO: National Park Service.

Resource Systems Group (RSG) (2019) *Implementation Plan for a Socioeconomic Monitoring Program in the National Park System*. Natural Resource Report NPS/NRSS/EQD/NRR—2019/1891. National Park Service, Fort Collins, Colorado.

Souza, T. V. S. B. (2016) Recreation classification, tourism demand and economic impact analyses of the federal protected areas of Brazil. DPhil dissertation, University of Florida, Gainesville, FL.

Stynes, D. J., D. B. Propst and Y.-Y. Sun (2000) *Estimating National Park Visitor Spending and Economic Impacts: The MGM2 Model*. Report to the National Park Service. East Lansing, MI: Department of Park, Recreation and Tourism Resources, Michigan State University.

Stynes, D. J. and Y.-Y. Sun (2003) *Economic Impacts of National Park Visitor Spending on Gateway Communities: Systemwide Estimates for 2001*. East Lansing, MI: Michigan State University.

Stynes, D. J. and E. M. White (2006) Reflections on measuring recreation and travel spending. *Journal of Travel Research*, 45(1), 8–16.

Sun, Y.-Y. and D. J. Stynes (2006) A note on estimating visitor spending on a per-day/night basis. *Tourism Management*, 27(4), 721–725.

Watson, P. S., J. Wilson, D. Thilmany and S. Winter (2007) Determining economic contribution and impacts: What is the difference and why do we care? *Journal of Regional Analysis and Policy*, 37(2), 1–15.

Ziesler, P. S. (2019) *Statistical Abstract: 2018*. Natural Resource Data Series NPS/NRSS/EQD/NRDS—2019/1219. National Park Service, Fort Collins, Colorado.

22. Economic effects assessment approaches: Tourism Economic Model for Protected Areas (TEMPA) for developing countries

Thiago do Val Simardi Beraldo Souza, Alex Chidakel, Brian Child, Wen-Huei Chang and Virginia Gorsevski

INTRODUCTION

The economic impact and financial sustainability of protected areas (PAs) is a concept that is poorly understood in theory and in practice. We suggest that most PAs generate a positive economic effect, especially when we use a total economic value framework (Krutilla, 1967), an ecosystem services framework (Millennium Ecosystem Assessment, 2005) or, in PAs with significant tourism, measure the total economy of it, not just revenues originated from PA fees. In this usage, the term 'economics' refers to the full value of the PA to society including monetized values and other societal effects. However, few PAs are supported by business models that reflect these values. Despite positive economic impacts, many PAs are financially non-viable and cannot cover the costs of basic functions – resource protection and monitoring, equipment and infrastructure, tourism management, essential community or public outreach and administration. This applies even to North American PAs, which are increasingly over-crowded and underfunded (Koontz et al., 2017; Simmonds et al., 2018).

Resolving this challenge requires improvements in governance including simple fixes such as revenue retention at PA level coupled with improved financial effectiveness (Reed, 2002), more complex fixes like payments for ecosystem services and political choices like replacing subsidized access with user-pay strategies. Therefore, it is crucial to first understand the economics and finances of PAs.

This chapter focuses on the measurement and distribution of the economic benefits associated with PA-based tourism. Results from three case studies highlight the fact that reasonable public investment in PAs can result in substantial financial and societal benefits. In some cases, PAs can serve as an engine for sustained rural development (Child, 2004).

BACKGROUND

The Tourism Economic Model for Protected Areas Framework for Estimating National, Provincial and City Level Effects

The objective of the Tourism Economic Model for Protected Areas (TEMPA) framework is to guide users in estimating the economic effects of PA-based tourism in developing countries and working with stakeholders to understand the value of PAs in serving not just conservation purposes, but as engines for relatively low-impact, high added-value economic growth.

Like the Visitor Spending Effects model used by the US National Park Service described by Thomas and Koontz (Chapter 21, this volume; see also Cullinane Thomas et al., 2019), TEMPA is based on the Money Generation Model (MGM2) developed in 1995 (Stynes et al., 2000). The TEMPA framework can be used with different levels of information depending on budget, time and capacity constraints that PA managers from developing countries may face. TEMPA can help managers and consultants design a study, gather the appropriate information and present the results.

Economic effects analysis is based on the interrelationships between changes in final demand and economic sectors and yield estimates of the possible changes in an economy due to actual or potential scenarios. Economic effects analysis of PA-based tourism can be used for different objectives, each of which may call for different approaches.

Common objectives in the economic analysis of PA-based tourism include increasing support for raising PA budgets, for building partnerships and for influencing local policies and planning decisions. For this type of advocacy, lower levels of accuracy may be required to demonstrate the importance of the activity compared with studies focused on evaluating the economic outcomes of management alternatives, such as decisions about new investments or new facilities and services that will economically impact government or concessionaires. The framework may also be applied for the purpose of adaptive management and/or to integrate an economic effects analysis with a livelihoods or social analysis of a PA, revealing non-monetary costs and benefits. In such cases, a more rigorous, bottom-up approach may be called for, drawing on primary data from surveys. Our case studies illustrate several of these approaches. Guidance is also provided to assist in the interpretation and reporting of results to policy makers whose typical and narrow focus on gate fees greatly under-values many PAs.

The Framework

As outlined by Thomas and Koontz (Chapter 21, this volume), the economic effects of tourism spending can be estimated using the combination of three sets of variables:

*Economic Effects = Number of Visitors * Average spending per visitor * Economic multipliers*

Depending on available resources and the desired accuracy these three variables can be estimated at three levels of rigor, as outlined below and in Table 22.1.

Table 22.1   Decision box for selecting the appropriate level of information and rigor

	Number of visitors	**Visitor spending**	**Economic multipliers**	
Level 1 (expert judgment)	Estimate from expert judgment	'Engineer' a visitor-spending profile	Use an aggregate multiplier from expert judgment	
Level 2 (secondary data)	Total count (e.g. using gate records)	Borrow profile from similar area or market (total or segmented)	Use sector-specific multipliers borrowed from similar area or previous study	
Level 3 (primary data)	Segmented count (e.g. air vs. ground arrivals, foreign vs. domestic, etc.)	Survey of visitor spending and/ or inventory of lodges	Survey-based approach to measure indirect and induced effects	Use input-output matrices or SAM to calculate regional multipliers

Source: Adapted from Stynes et al. (2000).

Level 1 approaches (expert judgment)

Expert judgment may substitute for survey data or official records, particularly for estimating the amount spent by the average visitor. The 'engineering' method of generating a visitor-spending profile involves making an itemized list of the typical expenses of an individual or party (e.g. on transportation, lodging, activities, food, etc.), averaged by the typical length of stay (in nights). Visitor volumes and spending are the most important variables but will be less precise when estimated in this manner. For this reason, the use of sector-specific multipliers (i.e. for different categories of spending) at this level would introduce needless complexity. Aggregate multipliers (i.e. those applied to an overall spending total) are more appropriate.

In the absence of multipliers for a specific region of interest, multipliers based on economic studies of similar regions can be used as a substitute. Important factors for comparison when determining the suitability of borrowed multipliers include the geographic region, total population, population density and specific type of activity the multipliers were generated for (e.g. PA tourism or general tourism).

Level 2 approaches (secondary data)

If visitor volumes and spending are estimated with a greater degree of precision using available gate records and secondary data from other studies, the use of sector-specific multipliers may be justified. Again, these multipliers may be borrowed from a study of a similar region, if available. To simplify the calculations converting visitor volumes, spending across multiple categories, and multipliers into economic effects, we developed a spreadsheet tool that automatically performs these calculations (PANORAMA, 2020).

Level 3 approaches (primary data)

This level is differentiated by the use of primary data from surveys and/or economic models known as input–output tables and social accounting matrices (SAMs). Appropriate sector-specific multipliers that match PA tourism spending categories can be extracted from these models. The expertise for working with these models, however, cannot be expected of PA managers. For this reason, we have begun to consolidate multipliers from a growing set of countries in the spreadsheet tool.

At local scales in developing countries (e.g. between 30 and 50 km from a PA boundary), particularly in rural areas, economic models will almost certainly be unavailable and generic multipliers, which are intended for more economically defined regions (e.g. cities, provinces, nations), are thus inappropriate. In these settings there is no substitute for collection of original data pertaining to effects. While there are multiple ways of obtaining the relevant data in theory, we outline an approach informed by lessons from real-world experience. Specifically, we offer guidance on integrating data from surveys of tourists, tourism business proprietors, tourism workers, local business owners and households to put the economic effects of a PA in the context of the local economy.

Conducting a Tourism Economic Study

The first and most important part of an economic effects assessment of tourism in PAs is to define the nature of the problem being evaluated and intended purpose of the results. There are seven factors that should be noted when defining the economic assessment (Stynes, 1997):

1. **Define what will be evaluated:** This may include government investment, changes in policies or marketing, or changes in the quantity or quality of tourist facilities. If the study is just evaluating effects of existing visitation activity (i.e. no change), be sure to define who is your visitor. For example, if the study will evaluate impacts instead of contributions, local residents should be removed from the analysis.
2. **Identify the variation in the kind and amount of visitation/tourism activity likely to be caused by the action being studied (if applicable):** If change resulting from a management action is being evaluated, this action must be defined precisely enough in order to estimate the variation in the types and number of visitors and/or expenditures likely to result. Analysis should look at 'with vs. without' the action instead of simply 'before vs. after'. For example, if visitation has been increasing by 10% per year and a new marketing program increases it to 20% next year, only half of the 20% growth should be attributed to the action. Identifying the net changes can be complex in situations of uncertainty, so it is recommended to make several estimates under different assumptions.
3. **Identify what types of expenditures will be included:** Visitation may impact the local economy through trip expenditure, government spending or investment, or purchases of durable goods, among others. The definition of the problem will define what to include in the analysis.
4. **Identify the study region:** An important part of the tourism economic assessment is the definition of the study region. The region defines where effects will be evaluated, as well as types of spending that are relevant. An economic assessment analyzes the impacts on households, businesses and organizations within the defined region. For example, local economic analyses do not include expenditures made at home or en route to the destination. Another aspect is to define the size of the economic region depending on the objective of the analysis (e.g. the local, state or national level). When defining local effects, the size of the region should be noted since it influences the multipliers. A good indicator is population. The size of the population is correlated with the size of the local economy (Chang, 2001).
5. **Define key economic segments and desired segment details:** The study should define which economic sectors will be included in the analysis based on the results desired. Visitation and tourism expenditures typically affect hospitality, food, retail, transportation and government sectors most directly. The consideration of impacted sectors will help determine the expenditure categories used for surveys and multipliers. The desired segment details define the presentation of results. For example, in some cases just an aggregate measurement may be desired, while in other cases interest in which particular sectors are mostly affected may be important, as well as jobs broken down by sector.
6. **Define measurements of economic activity:** Tourism effects may be presented in terms of visitor spending, business sales, proprietor's income and profits, wage and salary income, employment and value added (i.e. contribution to GDP).

7. **Define what levels of error are tolerable:** Requirements to gather more precise local data on visitation, expenditure and economic activity are related to the level of accuracy demanded. For example, annual economic contribution reports require less accuracy than studies that will drive investments decisions. Better data allows for the fine tuning of the number of visitors, expenditures estimates or multipliers, however, such fine tuning will demand time, funds and knowledge that must be weighed against the benefits of the improved estimates. It is wise to balance errors across the three estimate components.

OVERVIEW OF CASE STUDIES

The methods described above were tested in three settings (Figure 22.1): (1) on a National PA System (Brazil), (2) in a landscape with a complexity of public, private and community conservation areas (the Greater Kruger National Park [GKNP]), and (3) at a discrete national park (South Luangwa National Park [SLNP], in Zambia).

Brazil manages a system of 334 federal PAs comprising 170 m hectares through the Chico Mendes Institute for Biodiversity Conservation (ICMBio). The motivation for analyzing the economic contributions of tourism was to advocate for greater funding of PAs and to develop an understanding of where investment in the system could generate the greatest economic returns. With this objective for the Brazil case study, a spreadsheet version of the TEMPA model was developed to estimate jobs, income, value added, spending, captured sales (i.e. portion of spending that does not immediately leak from the region) and other economic effects to the economy from visitor spending at PAs. The spreadsheet uses a set of country-specific multipliers for 12 tourism-related economic sectors. These multipliers are derived from the National Input–Output Matrix of the Brazilian Economy. Multipliers from economic sectors (e.g. food production, retail, etc.) were mapped to the respective visitor-spending categories (e.g. groceries, restaurants, etc.) such that the only inputs required for estimating effects are visitor volumes and daily spending per visitor. The top-down model allows for estimates of effects at sub-national scales (i.e. province or city level) (Souza, 2016).

The motivation for an economic study of the GKNP (22,686 km²) was the inclusion, for the first time, of the contributions of the highly commercialized private reserves neighboring Kruger National Park, which benefit from their proximity to the national park and its wildlife. The system also includes provincial reserves and a contractual park owned by a local community. This diversity of management authority and tenure configurations and the varying economic and financial performance of different reserves was a ripe subject for academic inquiry (Chidakel et al., 2020) but the lesson we highlight here relates, more simply, to the importance of defining the system of study from a tourism perspective – which often transcends property boundaries. Many PA systems across Africa, and in developed countries, consist of multiple property owners and managerial authorities which may share a common brand and resource and have exposure to the same risks/benefits of policy or investment decisions. These qualities justify economic impact studies of tourism at scales that combine data from multiple different stakeholders and institutions, presenting a unique challenge where there is little or no centralized coordination or keeping of appropriate records. The scale and complexity of the GKNP dictated a high-level approach that mainly depended on the development of an inventory of tourist lodges across multiple reserves and a survey of lodge managers. We include this case study to illustrate its use of the lodge inventory method of spending estimation and to emphasize the importance of including the impacts of tourism in neighboring PAs.

For South Luangwa National Park in Zambia (9,050 km²), there was interest by stakeholders in assessing economic impacts both locally and nationally. In the absence of economic research, only anecdotal evidence supported the observations that local residents were highly dependent on the park for jobs and that the park spurred growth of the local business economy. Nationally, the park's significance stems from the fact that it is among the premier tourism destinations in the country, catering mostly to the foreign luxury tourism market.

Because 100% of park fees are retained by the park authority's local office, the park also serves as a potential model for successfully funding PA management in Zambia. However, large areas of the park are underutilized for tourism, under-patrolled, and have low wildlife concentrations while the park faces the ongoing threat that the US$3 m income from user-fees will be centralized to the national coffer. Reliable data on economic impacts justify greater investment in infrastructure and management operations to expand the tourism base at SLNP and other PAs in the country. To generate this data we applied several approaches, including one involving rapid surveys of the local business economy and households. The relatively small scale of the local community and of tourism at SLNP allowed for a bottom-up analysis of tourism's downstream effects across an area spanning 30 km from the park's southeastern boundary that is home to roughly 62,000 people (16.3/km²). At the national level, we modeled tourist spending using multipliers extracted from a social accounting matrix (SAM).

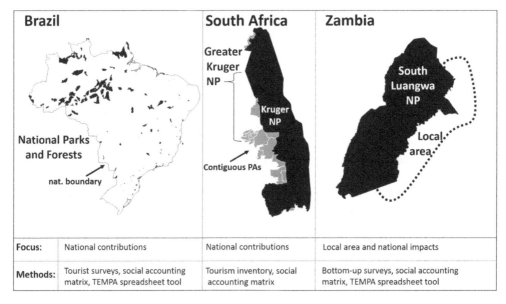

Figure 22.1   Maps of case study locations, indicating unique features, focal measures and methods used

CASE STUDIES

System of PAs in Brazil

The Chico Mendes Institute for Biodiversity Conservation (ICMBio) is the federal agency responsible for the management of the Federal Protected Areas in Brazil. ICMBio manages a system of 334 federal protected areas comprising 170 m hectares (ICMBio, 2020). In 2019, an economic effect analysis of tourism assessed 120 PAs of Brazil.

Methods

Visitor volume
In 2018, from the 334 protected areas of the country, 120 counted or estimated visitor-days using different direct (e.g. personal count or camera recording), indirect (e.g. fees and permits) and automatic methods (e.g. mechanical and optical counters). Only the data of these 120 PAs was considered in the study and together they reported 12.4 m visits.

Visitor spending
For management purposes, PAs in Brazil are grouped on Classes of Recreational Use: Extensive, Intensive and Highly Intensive (Souza and Thapa, 2018):

- **Extensive Use** (10,001 to 100,000 visits) Regional tourist destinations. Management focuses on conservation but also recreation opportunities. Basic infrastructure is offered at designated sites, such as rustic visitor centers, campgrounds, restrooms, etc.
- **Intensive Use** (100,001 to 1,000,000 visits) National destination or nearby a large city. Recreation is one important mission of the PAs and more attention is given to the quality of the experience, safety of visitors and management of sensitive areas. There is a good variety of activities and services offered.
- **High Intensive Use** (> 1,000,000 visits) Region is a consolidated international destination, usually located in the most developed and high-density areas of the country. Recreation is one management priority with more attention to the quality of the experience, safety of visitors and management of sensitive areas. A good variety of activities and services are offered.

Due to resource constraints, only one PA of each recreational class was selected to develop a visitor profile. Those profiles were used to calculate visitor spending data for all the PAs of that recreational class. Visitor spending data was collected from 2016 to 2018 from three protected areas (i.e. Canastra National Park, Chapada dos Guimarães National Park and Tijuca National Park) through on-site interviews and e-mails. Right now, ICMBio is working to increase the number of PAs surveyed.

Multipliers
Multipliers and ratios were developed for the Brazilian economy from the Input–Output (I-O) Matrix of Brazil 2013 – 68 sectors (Souza et al., 2019). The data were formulated from National Accounts based on the methodologies described in Guilhoto and Sesso Filho (2005) and Guilhoto and Sesso Filho (2010). Sector-specific multipliers and ratios were developed for five different generic regions based on population size. (As a reference Table 22.2 presents

Table 22.2   *National multipliers and ratios developed from the Input–Output (I-O) table*
for Brazil (2013) – 68 sectors

Sector	Direct effects			Indirect effects	Total effects (direct + indirect + induced)			
	Jobs	Income	Value added	Output I	Output II	Jobs II	Income II	Value added II
Accommodation	14.69	0.45	0.58	1.62	4.50	34.77	1.21	1.70
Eating & drinking	18.32	0.41	0.50	1.79	4.63	39.50	1.20	1.64
Creative arts and entertainment activities	22.5	0.50	0.57	1.59	4.71	42.66	1.31	1.78
Terrestrial Transport	9.58	0.35	0.45	1.97	4.58	27.94	1.10	1.52
Wholesale trade and retail trade, except motor vehicles	14.49	0.46	0.64	1.53	4.36	33.03	1.20	1.71

Note: 'I' refers to type I multipliers (including direct and indirect effects). 'II' refers to type II multipliers (including direct, indirect and induced effects). All multipliers are ratios of direct output or per US$ 1m in direct output in the case of jobs multipliers.

Table 22.3   *Comparison between aggregated different area size multipliers used in*
TEMPA for Brazil

	Rural	Small Metro	Larger Metro	State	National
Total sales	2.17	2.41	2.73	3.52	4.29
Capture rate	52.8%	62.9%	72.3%	84.3%	96.3%
Total output multiplier	1.14	1.52	1.98	3.52	4.13
Total income	1.35	1.54	1.79	2.31	2.82
Total value added	1.75	1.87	2.11	2.62	3.16
Total jobs	1.13	1.27	1.42	1.77	2.17

Note: 'Capture rate' is the percentage of spending that does not immediately leak from a region.

sector-specific multipliers at national level and Table 22.3 presents aggregated multipliers for the different five generic regions.) Rates for sales captured from the Brazilian economy were applied and impacts and contributions were calculated to local, state and national level.

Results

Table 22.4 summarizes PA tourism's national economic contributions in 2018. Visitor expenditure generated total direct sales of US$ 596 m, but this expanded to US$ 2.6 bn including indirect and induced economic effects. Likewise, the 41,049 entrepreneurs and people employed directly in PA-based tourism earned US$ 235 m, but this about doubled once multiplier effects were considered to 89,250 jobs and US$ 666 m in income. Protected area visitation added US$ 294 m in direct value and US$ 935 m in total value added to the GDP.

The analysis revealed the economic magnitude of tourism and outdoor recreation, an important ecosystem service provided by PAs. The initiative reinforced the fact that economic contributions of tourism directly influence the PAs, as well as indirectly other businesses and the local communities, generating greater economic benefits for local communities that have a higher household dependency on the surrounding natural resources. Figure 22.2 shows that Brazil's PAs operate at a financial loss, with direct income of US$ 19 m (mainly in PA fees) compared to a budget of US$ 166 m. However, from a broader economic perspective, Brazil's

Table 22.4   *Direct and total effects of visitor spending in Brazil – 2018 / US$ (million)*

Spending category	Sales captured	Jobs	Personal income	Value added
Accommodation	181	10,882	80	105
Meals	130	11,967	53	65
Gas & oil	61	4,041	2	2
Local transportation	53	3,411	17	23
Activities and guided tours	101	6,615	50	57
Retail stores	11	773	4	4
Other expenses	11	652	4	4
Total Direct Effects	**596**	**41,049**	**235**	**294**
Secondary Effects	1,632	42,995	355	529
Total Effects	**2,560**	**89,250**	**666**	**935**

PAs operate profitably by generating direct economic contributions of US$ 596 m in sales captured (US$ 294 m in GDP) and total economic contributions of US$ 2,560 m in sales captured (US$ 935 m in GDP). Thus, each US$ 1 invested as budget in PA management generates US$ 15 for the economy, even before the value of biodiversity conservation and ecosystem services are considered. Moreover, many PAs are located in remote areas, generating alternative livelihoods and economic benefits for local communities that have a higher household dependency on the surrounding natural resources.

PA managers are realizing the importance of this type of data and the fact that economic analysis is an important tool to demonstrate PA values for the general public that may be less interested in conservation. TEMPA economic analysis of tourism provides an opportunity to engage with stakeholders and inform them of the value of PAs in serving not just conservation purposes, but as engines for relatively low-impact, high added-value economic growth, presenting how many jobs, income and GDP are generated. Overall these results highlight the importance of tourism in PAs and the adjacent regions for the Brazilian economy and provide a persuasive argument to increase the budget allocation for PAs to stimulate the local and national economy. The statement that each dollar invested in the PA system produced US$ 15 in economic benefits in 2018 became a mantra for the agency staff.

The Greater Kruger National Park, South Africa

Though South African National Parks (SANParks) keeps detailed records of jobs, visitation to, and receipts of spending at the national park, the dozen neighboring private and provincial reserve management authorities had comparatively little relevant information to offer for an economic study because, unlike SANParks, their direct responsibilities do not include tourism – in concessioned PAs and in multi-property conservancies, commercial responsibilities lie mainly with individual tourism operators. In the absence of reliable, consolidated records of visitation at these reserves, and given luxury tourists' poor knowledge of itemized prices within packaged trips, visitation and spending had to be estimated indirectly. First, a complete inventory of tourism lodges and campgrounds was key in establishing accommodation capacity. These sites totaled 144 in the neighboring private and provincial reserves. The number of beds and room rates for each lodge were recorded as well as the type of service offered (self-catered vs. full-service) and the predominant clientele marketed to (foreign vs. domestic). Almost all lodge operators had websites on which these details could be found and interviews

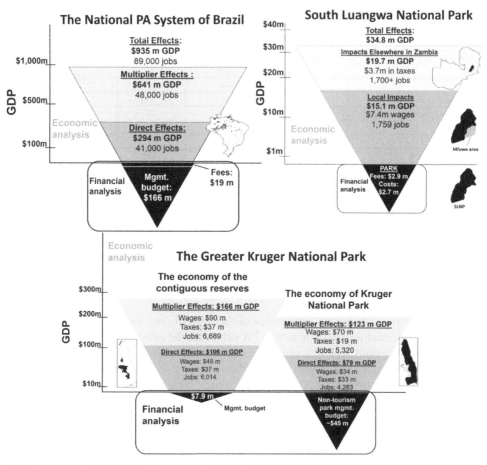

Note: The mode of disaggregation (direct vs. multiplier effects and local vs. non-local effects) vary in each case.

Figure 22.2   Depicted as inverted pyramids, the PA economies from the three case studies are clearly seen as disproportionate to their financial bases, indicating strong returns on investment

with commercial peers and PA managers were useful in filling in or corroborating information (e.g. active/inactive status of lodges).

Second, profiles of visitor spending and of lodge businesses were constructed from surveys and expert judgment. This step was necessary for several reasons: a significant part of trip-related spending can include transportation to the PA and other purchases not related to lodge services; lodges are often booked at well below capacity; publicly listed rates will not reveal the commission paid to non-local travel agents; and interviews with proprietors are useful for estimating jobs, local procurement and social investment. For example, in the contiguous reserves of the GKNP, visitors to higher end lodges spent substantially more on domestic transportation to the park than lower-end lodges (via air as opposed to ground); occupancies averaged around 65% but varied by lodge segment; between VAT and commissions-paid, tourism operators could receive as little as 55% of listed prices; and higher end lodges employed more staff per bed. But once these parameters are estimated, an inventory of accommodation can form the basis of extrapolation of visitation and spending to the entire PA system.

Headline results from the combined GKNP system are captured in Figure 22.2, including a PA economy contributing R$ 6.6 bn (US$ 468 m) in GDP through multiplier effects (calculated using a SAM of the South African economy) as compared to management costs of R$ 740 m (US$ 52 m). The major finding of the study was that although the (mostly) private reserves neighboring the national park cover only 12% of the land, tourist spending in these reserves constituted nearly 60% of job, wage and GDP contributions from the whole system (Figure 22.2). As our case study was conducted at a time when collective governance of the GKNP was being formalized through cooperative agreements between member reserves, one outcome of this research has been a commitment by SANParks to regularize socio-economic monitoring of the entire system. For PAs embedded in larger conservation landscapes it is thus important to evaluate the system as a whole. Efforts to do so may even contribute to strengthening institutional partnerships which may then facilitate data collection and data sharing in the future.

South Luangwa National Park, Zambia

Our study of SLNP's economic impacts began with a review of available data, guided by the questions in Box 22.1.

BOX 22.1 SLNP RESEARCH QUESTIONS

Visitation data

- Are accurate, up to date records kept of park visitation and are they easily accessible (e.g. centralized and digitized)?
- Are visitor records meaningfully disaggregated by criteria affecting spending (e.g. type of visitor, time of year, etc.)?

Visitor spending and supply-side data

- Are up to date records of park authority revenues available?
- Is an itemized park-authority budget available (for showing wages and other direct impacts)?
- Is an inventory of park-related tourism businesses, their prices, and the number of jobs they provide available?

Economic data

- Does an input–output model for the specific local area or for a similar area exist?
- Does a national input–output model exist and is it current? Does the model have an appropriate sector into which park-tourism spending can be allocated?

Our initial assessment revealed that the park authority aggregates visitation records in an electronic spreadsheet not only by the month and residency status of visitors, but also by the name of the lodge at which visitors stayed. All of these factors are important because they determine prices that visitors pay. The park authority also made available financial records of income and spending for PA management, as well as a record of all tourism lodges operating in the area and the number of employees working at each. As expected, however, no input/output model existed of the local economy.

Given that the non-direct and more diffuse impacts of tourism on the local area were of primary interest, and in the absence of an economic model, we used five short surveys to profile the local tourism value chain (i.e. the set of business activities that add value to the park) and trace the flow of tourism money from when it first enters the area near the park until it leaves this region. The five surveys are described below, though it should be noted that expert judgment may substitute for any survey – provided that all assumptions are made explicit – but a survey increases confidence in results.

Survey of tourists

Though tourists are responsible for the most important, initial round of spending, surveys of tourists can be challenging and may not yield good information. Two problems are common to tourist surveys at luxury tourism destinations. First, it may be difficult to encounter guests of lodges or PA visitors at a place and time convenient for conducting interviews. Second, tourists themselves are often ignorant of spending arrangements. Many tourists book trips through travel agencies that bundle together multiple destinations and services, which means that details of the spending done on their behalf must be sought elsewhere. For these reasons our survey of tourists at SLNP yielded useful information only about local out-of-pocket spending on minor goods and services that were not included in tour packages, as well as the spending by tourists in the budget travel segments.

Survey of tourism-business managers

The bulk of local expenditures are usually received by tourist lodges and therefore, if details of tourist spending are difficult to gather through surveys of tourists, a survey of lodge managers or owners can be a critical source of data. However, revenue and business expenses are obviously sensitive subjects. Without the trust of local proprietors, meaningful cooperation with the research effort is unlikely. We attempted to maximize cooperation by raising awareness of our study through the local association of safari tourism providers before commencing with interviews. Additionally, all interviews were conducted in person (emails are easy to ignore) and assurances made as to the confidentiality of all shared data and the aggregation of results across all businesses before reporting.

The most important information that managers can provide is annual revenue, wages, other expenditures, the number of annual bed-nights sold and the portion of each related to PA tourism. It is unlikely, though, that all requested information will be divulged, which means that alternative ways of obtaining it will often be necessary. For example, if revenue is not disclosed, a rough estimate can be calculated from knowing the average occupancy percentage of a lodge and the published nightly rate – though adjustments to calculations may be necessary on account of the inclusion of taxes and commission paid to travel agencies in the published rate. The amount spent on local procurement and/or charitable causes are also key pieces of data, as are the names of the major local suppliers that a lodge depends on. This information will help to guide the survey of general businesses in the local area (discussed below).

Survey of tourism workers

The benefit of obtaining wage information directly from employees is that more accurate profiles can then be created for workers of each skill type (i.e. unskilled/semiskilled, skilled and management level positions). Employee interviews are also necessary to understand the importance of tourism income to local households and how wages feed back into the local economy through household consumption.

Survey of local businesses

The local value chain may extend beyond direct providers of tourism goods and services and include suppliers of inputs. Proprietors of tourism businesses can help (through the above survey) to identify the major retailers/wholesalers or producers. A list of each tourism operator's five main local suppliers of goods and services will give an idea of what is available in the local area and of the scale and location of the supply chain (i.e. businesses or individuals that sell products or services to tourism lodges). This information may be used to follow up with a sample of the supplying businesses and obtain values for the average price markup, the proportion of goods that are produced locally and the number of employees or producers supported by these indirect effects of tourism.

In addition to characterizing and quantifying the local supply chain, business surveys can also place the effects of tourism into the context of the local economy in order to gauge its dependence on the PA. A more generalized survey that includes not just links in the supply chain, but all local businesses can be used to estimate the scale of the local business economy and workforce. Key questions include annual sales, number of staff, wages and the respondent's own estimated dependence on tourism. Because these interviews are very basic, such surveys can be implemented rapidly to cover hundreds of businesses. As with the other surveys described, extrapolation of data is necessary in order to estimate aggregates for the entire study area and this means that segmenting the sample by business type (large/small, goods/services, type of merchandise, etc.) is important. This information should also be recorded for businesses not responding to the survey. At SLNP we counted almost 300 shops and vendor stalls and, employing local enumerators, obtained information from almost 200 proprietors in a week of surveying. This survey allowed us to estimate the total sales turnover of local businesses to be approximately US$ 4.9 m, of which indirect effects through the tourism supply chain were responsible for about 18%. As noted below, the induced effects of tourist spending on local businesses were much larger.

Survey of households

A survey of local households can help to place tourism impacts in a meaningful context. Knowing that wages from tourism constitute 40% of overall local income, for instance, may be just as, if not more important than knowing the specific value of wages from tourism. The distribution of tourism benefits by distance from a PA can also inform PA management strategies. Questions regarding income, income sources and consumption spending can be added to a survey of attitudes/perceptions or livelihoods around a PA, or asked as a standalone survey. Methods for conducting household surveys, including details of sampling strategies, are described by Franks and Small (2016). At SLNP, a survey of 419 households was completed in two weeks by 15 local enumerators. The results underscored the importance of PA tourism, showing that the park was responsible for half of formal employment and half of income among the local population.

Bringing it all together
Analyzing data across multiple sampling tiers involves several steps. Averaged values of individual units from each tier need to be extrapolated to arrive at estimates of aggregated totals (e.g. extrapolating average tourist spend on a visitor-night basis to total tourist spend). Estimates made on the basis of one survey tier can then be cross-checked against, or substituted by estimates made by other means (e.g. tourist spend at lodges against lodge-reported or inventory-estimated lodge income). We suggest several means of extrapolation, substitution and cross-checking in Table 22.5. Local effects estimates may then be calculated as sums of values within (e.g. direct income) or across tiers (e.g. total income).

Table 22.5   Important survey values and means of extrapolation, substitution and cross-checking

Units or 'tiers'	Important values	Means of extrapolation	Substitutable sources of data and/or means of cross-checking extrapolated survey data
Tourists	Spending	# of visit-days by tourist segment	gate records; inventory of beds & prices with estimates of occupancy; published air/bus fares
Tourism businesses	Income/spending (local, non-local)/jobs	# of beds per tourist segment	inventory of beds & prices with estimates of occupancy
Employees	Wages/local-spending	# of jobs per skill level	manager-reported wage-bills; employee-reported wages
General businesses	Turnover/jobs	# of businesses per size class (small/micro/medium/large) and type (goods/services; retail/wholesaler/producer)	employee or household-reported spending at local businesses
Households	Income/income sources	# of households	manager or employee-reported wages

National effects calculations were comparatively much simpler because national level multipliers could be extracted from a SAM for the Zambian economy. Thus, the procedure reduced to multiplying these ratios by visitor spending only. Effects calculations were simplified further by designing a spreadsheet tool that mapped visitor spending categories to the appropriate multipliers, automating all steps of the process once segment-specific visitor volumes and spending were entered. Figure 22.2 combines the local economic contributions through multiplier effects with the national contributions through multiplier effects, placing the emphasis on their geographic distribution.

The key message
It is important that the key message is not lost in an abundance of data. At SLNP, we used Figure 22.2 to illustrate financial and economic impacts (local and national), as well as to provide details on wages, jobs and taxes. Annual GDP contributions through multiplier effects of tourism spending were shown to be greater than ten times the operational budget for man-

agement and wages from tourism were responsible for half of all income to the 62,000 people living within 30 km of the park. Further, approximately 70% of local business activity depends either on the spending of these wages or on tourism supply chain effects (Figure 22.3). These results demonstrate that SLNP is not only an engine for local economic growth, but also that reduced financial support would risk significant economic consequences and that an expansion of infrastructure that increased visitation could easily be justified on an economic basis.

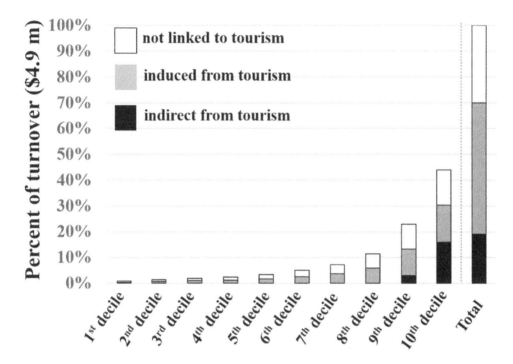

Figure 22.3   The impact of the park on the local business economy, where as much as 70% of all turnover is linked to tourism

Protected areas are a critical strategy for conserving biodiversity and for connecting people with nature. Many PAs – especially national parks – attract tourists who spend money to experience nature and wildlife at close range. Some countries such as the United States regularly quantify the benefits of these PAs on the local and national economy, highlighting the important role that they play in sustaining incomes and providing jobs. This type of analysis is less common in developing countries, causing policy-makers to overlook or to underestimate the vital economic contributions of PAs with tourism potential. With fewer staff, data and analytical resources at the disposal of PA agencies, it is necessary to adapt simplified methods of economic tracking for the developing country context.

    This chapter has highlighted several such approaches. When visitor volumes and prices are recorded or estimated, a simple aggregate multiplier, sector-specific multipliers, or multipliers from the TEMPA spreadsheet tool can be used to convert this information into direct effects and multiplier effects on larger regions. At smaller scales, such as those typical of many rural communities neighboring wildlife PAs in Africa, information of much higher detail may be both desired and feasible to obtain through the bottom-up sampling approach described in this chapter. In either case, the framing of results may be just as, if not more important in influencing policy as their precision – our case studies have highlighted economic returns from PAs that are vastly disproportionate with management costs and past infrastructure investment. We hope that the lessons from our experience and the tools we outline will serve as a useful starting point for documenting more of these outcomes and for articulating the connection between economic value and financial sustainability.

REFERENCES

Chang, W. H. (2001) Variations in multipliers and related economic ratios for recreation and tourism impact analysis. Dissertation, Michigan State University, East Lansing, Michigan.

Chidakel, A., Eb, C. and Child, B. (2020) The comparative financial and economic performance of protected areas in the Greater Kruger National Park, South Africa: Functional diversity and resilience in the socio-economics of a landscape-scale reserve network. *Journal of Sustainable Tourism*, 28(8), 1100–1119.

Child, B. (2004) *Parks in Transition: Biodiversity, Rural Development and the Bottom Line*. London: Earthscan.

Cullinane Thomas, C., Cornachione, E., Koontz, L. and Keyes, C. (2019) *National Park Service Socioeconomic Pilot Survey: Visitor Spending Analysis*. Natural Resource Report NPS/NRSS/EQD/NRR—2019/1924. National Park Service, Fort Collins, Colorado.

Franks, P. and Small, R. (2016) *Social Assessment for Protected Areas (SAPA). Methodology Manual for SAPA Facilitators*. London: IIED.

Guilhoto, J. J. M. and Sesso Filho, U. A. (2005) Estimação da matriz insumo–produto a partir de dados preliminares das contas nacionais [Estimating the input–output matrix from preliminary data of national accounts]. *Economia Aplicada*, 9(2), 277–299.

Guilhoto, J. J. M. and Sesso Filho, U. A. (2010) Estimação da matriz insumo–produto utilizando dados preliminares das contas nacionais: Aplicação e análise de indicadores econômicos para o Brasil em 2005 [Estimating the input–output matrix from preliminary data of national accounts: Application and analysis of economic indicators for Brazil in 2005]. *Economia & Tecnologia*, UFPR/TECPAR. Ano 6, Vol. 23.

ICMBio (2020) Visitors numbers in protected areas. General coordination of public use and business. CGEUP, Brasilia (internal document).

Koontz, L., Cullinane Thomas, C., Ziesler, P., Olson, J. and Meldrum, B. (2017) Visitor spending effects: Assessing and showcasing America's investment in national parks. *Journal of Sustainable Tourism*, 25(12), 1865–1876.

Krutilla, J. V. (1967) Conservation reconsidered. *The American Economic Review*, 57(4), 777–786.

Millennium Ecosystem Assessment (2005) *Ecosystems & Human Well-being: Synthesis*. Washington, DC: Island Press.

PANORAMA (2020) *Assessing Economic Impacts of Visitor Spending in Protected Areas – IUCN*. PANORAMA Solutions. https://panorama.solutions/en/solution/assessing-economic-impacts-visitor-spending-protected-areas-brazil.

Reed, T. (2002) *The Function and Structure of Protected Area Authorities: Considerations for Financial and Organizational Management*. Washington, DC: World Bank.

Simmonds, C., Annette, M., Reilly, P., Maffly, B., Wilkinson, T., Canon, G., … Whaley, M. (2018) Crisis in our national parks: How tourists are loving nature to death. https://www.theguardian.com/environment/2018/nov/20/national-parks-america-overcrowding-crisis-tourism-visitation-solutions.

Souza, T. V. S. B. (2016) Recreation classification, tourism demand and economic impact analyses of the federal protected areas of Brazil. DPhil dissertation, University of Florida, Gainesville, FL.

Souza, T. V. S. B. and Thapa, B. (2018) Tourism demand analysis of federal protected areas of Brazil. *Journal of Park and Recreation Administration*, 36(3), 1–21.

Souza, T. V. S. B., Thapa, B., Rodrigues, C. G. O. and Imori, D. (2019) Economic impacts of tourism in protected areas of Brazil. *Journal of Sustainable Tourism*, 27(6), 735–749.

Stynes, D. J (1997) *Economic Impacts of Tourism: A Handbook for Tourism Professionals*. Illinois Bureau of Tourism, Tourism Research Laboratory, Michigan State University.

Stynes, D. J., Propst, D. B. and Sun, Y.-Y. (2000) *Estimating National Park Visitor Spending and Economic Impacts: The MGM2 Model*. Report to the National Park Service. East Lansing, MI: Department of Park, Recreation and Tourism Resources, Michigan State University.

23. Biodiversity and stressors rapid assessment

Shane Feyers, Gretchen Stokes and Vanessa Hull

INTRODUCTION

Nature-based tourism (including ecotourism) is a 120-billion-dollar industry occurring in every country on earth (World Travel & Tourism Council, 2019). Rapid growth of nature-based tourism operations and demand (hereafter referred to as 'tourism') has affected humans and the natural environment in complex ways (Moorhouse et al., 2017). Sustainability of tourism operations has become a rising priority, as evidenced by over 100 different certification programs worldwide. Yet, to date, none of these programs measure the impacts of tourism on biodiversity, defined as the variety of life in a given area. Given that biodiversity is often the focal point and a requisite for successful tourism operations, an improved understanding of baseline biodiversity, as well as the impact of tourism on biodiversity is essential for optimizing tourism business.

Assessing impacts of humans on biodiversity requires the use of indicators and benchmarks from which changes over time can be determined (Buckley, 2003). Of the environmental impacts caused by tourism, physical impacts from tourist activities are most often targeted for monitoring. These primarily include evaluations of trail conditions and damage to the environment from waste production (Buckley, 2003; Newsome et al., 2012). Evaluating the impacts of tourism on biodiversity remains more complex to assess because they are interdependent and less commonly measured (Wardle et al., 2018).

Growing evidence indicates that a wide variety of tourism activities, including non-motorized transportation and passive viewing, can have detrimental impacts on biodiversity (Larson et al., 2016). For example, the creation of new trails in Vail, Colorado (USA) has led to a decline in elk from over 1,000 individuals in 2009 to only 53 today (Peterson, 2019). In another example, when viewing endangered mountain gorillas in East Africa, 25% of visitors admitted they would join gorilla treks while sick (Hanes et al., 2018) and safe-distance restrictions were violated in 98% of tours (Weber et al., 2020). The compounding effects of tourism can fundamentally alter wildlife and natural habitat and damage tourism products (Shannon et al., 2017).

It is important to address these effects because nature-based tourism acts as a 'human shield', helping to protect a variety of threatened and endangered species (Buckley et al., 2016; Fitzgerald and Stronza, 2016). This industry offers many wide-ranging benefits to conservation funding, in addition to being a source of growth for local economies, improved community welfare and livelihoods, and increased cultural awareness (Twining-Ward et al., 2018).

To reap these positive benefits, active monitoring and better control of anthropogenic impacts is needed (Green and Giese, 2004). This may require more regulation, habitat protection, tourism activity shifts, and less development of hardscape (Williams and Ponsford, 2009). Knowing how and where to undertake these efforts relies on detailed information about local biodiversity. Such data are routinely collected by scientists in natural resource management fields but are underutilized in the tourism industry.

To address this gap in knowledge and practice, in this chapter we aim to provide a set of tools for assessing biodiversity and identifying stressors within tourism operations. The process is designed to be performed and accomplished by non-experts and citizen scientists. Once baseline data are obtained, a tourism manager can aid in identifying issues and opportunities.

TOOLS

Nature-based tourism can result in many direct and indirect impacts on biodiversity in the short and long-term, from temporary changes in animal behavior to increased mortality (Blumstein et al., 2017; Geffroy et al., 2015). Yet, central to any conservation matter is the core question: *Are animal (or plant) populations increasing, decreasing, or remaining stable?* (Buckley et al., 2016; Gill et al., 2001). Accordingly, here we present two primary tools and associated driving questions:

Tool #1: Survey baseline biological conditions for (a). Habitat (where habitat is defined as the natural features needed for species of interest) and (b). Species variety and counts

- *What is the quality, structure, size, and connectedness of habitat?*
- *Where, how many, and what kinds of plants and animals exist?*

Tool #2: Identify the presence and severity of stressors and consider potential impacts over time

- *What stressors are present and how might these relate to, or negatively affect the findings of Tool #1 over time?*

Therein, this chapter focuses on baseline observations of tourist activities and local ecological conditions, which will aid developers, managers, and other industry stakeholders in identifying the biological heritage around them and establishing a general understanding of how they are affecting local plant and animal species, including those used and needed for tourism business.

Given that the work conducted for natural heritage programs often does not require quantitative sampling, the process we present here is descriptive and qualitative. While less statistically rigorous and intensive, these methods are a sufficient starting point for identifying the general impact of tourism activities on biodiversity at one's operational site.

We also see data collection as an asset to any nature-based tourism operation. Tourists can be afforded the opportunity to collect data that will be useful both to the operation and to the larger scientific community. Data collection activities and participatory monitoring can be incorporated into daily programming for tourists and promoted as citizen science (i.e., scientific research conducted by non-professionals) (Gura, 2013). Intensive citizen-science-based species recording events (e.g., 'bioblitzes') can be an effective way to engage visitors and draw attention to biodiversity conservation (Pollock et al., 2015). Useful citizen science platforms (e.g., citisci.org) aid in creating projects, building custom datasheets and visualizing results. Likewise, mobile applications provide a user-friendly interface for visitors to record findings, identify species, and contribute to the broader science community.

In the following sections, we introduce the two tools that practitioners can use to assess habitat, species variety and count as well as to gauge the potential impact of stressors on biodiversity.

TOOL #1. RAPID BIOLOGICAL ASSESSMENT – SURVEYING HABITAT AND SPECIES

- **Questions**: Which habitats are of interest? Which species are present and how many are there? How do I measure the current and ongoing condition of biodiversity assets?
- **Who this is for**: Stakeholders who have property rights or leases within areas of operation, or others who have permission to engage in scientific data collection for environmental impact assessment, citizen science, research, or restoration.
- **Why it is important**: Rapid biological assessments are a way to obtain ecological data quickly and effectively and track changes over time. Current conditions can be adopted as the best available baseline even though some anthropogenic impacts may have already occurred. Alternatively, a surrogate baseline survey could be created using nearby habitats in a similar area to predict the biological profile before tourism operations began.

Conducting a biodiversity inventory generally includes the following steps (Figure 23.1):

1. Delineate the boundaries of the overall area
2. Compile information on species and habitats in this area using scientific data
3. Identify species of interest and their protection status under national or international law
4. Choose sites and metrics and design a data collection protocol that corresponds to priorities
5. Complete a field assessment by:
   (a) Habitat surveying
   (b) Wildlife surveying (species variety, species counts)

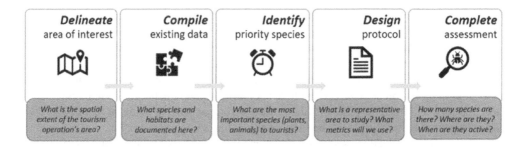

Figure 23.1   Biodiversity baseline rapid assessment

Distilled from Good Practices for Biodiversity Baselines (Gullison et al., 2015), Nature Serve's Biodiversity Inventory of Natural Lands for Foresters and Biologists (Cutko, 2009), and Conservation International's Core Standardized Methods for Rapid Biological Assessment (Larsen, 2016), which are all themselves established from a consensus of experts across taxonomic groups, this section relays simplified, reliable, and systematic methods for carrying out these steps.

An important consideration in the steps listed below is the co-production of knowledge and inclusion of local communities and experts, where appropriate. Particular attention should be given to the contributions of traditional, indigenous, or local knowledge (i.e., traditional ecological knowledge, local ecological knowledge), as these perspectives may offer insight to the process and conditions that would otherwise be unavailable (Danielsen et al., 2014). Stakeholder consultation is a crucial contribution to understanding biodiversity values of those within the project area of influence, and those potentially impacted beyond project sites (Grodzińska-Jurczak and Cent, 2011).

Process

Step 1. Delineate area of interest
The first step is to identify the overall baseline study area, or 'assessment area'. This includes the **tourism location** (where direct impacts of tourism occur), and its **area of influence** (where indirect impacts of tourism activities occur). The tourism location is where the primary footprint from infrastructure and visitor use occurs (e.g., roads, trails, swimming, and boating areas). The area of influence is the space affected by facilities and activities that would not happen in the absence of the tourism venture. Depending on tourism activities, selecting the assessment area may require expanding the study area to a landscape or watershed level. The spatial scale of the assessment can be determined by considering where tourism activities take place and the related habitat and species affected. **Timescale** should also be considered to determine the need for historic data or projection into the future. For migratory species, it is appropriate to consider non-adjacent sites used in migration.

Step 2. Compile existing data
The next step is to overlay the assessment area with **species and range data** to generate a list of animals (and possibly plants) present. If data are available, natural processes, species trends, and environmental influences already affecting the space can be documented. Preparing a cat-alogued map is helpful in the design of field surveys and for identifying biodiversity resources and areas of interest for tourism. This information can be obtained through geographic infor-mation systems, landowner history, local knowledge, and biological databases.

Before conducting the rapid assessment, it is important to collate already available data. Table 23.1 lists digital databases widely used for understanding the variety of species in a loca-tion, their distribution, protection status, and threats (Ball-Damerow et al., 2019). For some platforms, tourism operators are encouraged to contribute data to the catalogue.

Step 3. Identify priority species and habitats
Data should be collected to identify key ecological attributes (KEA) that may be impacted by tourism activities. Key ecological attributes are natural variables (species and habitats) that are critical to a given tourism activity and any potential disturbances. Changes to KEA – such as impacts to population size, food resources, breeding populations, characteristic species, or species relationships – can lead to degradation or loss of biodiversity. The choice of KEA is important for defining the scope and range of the rapid assessment and the consideration of effects on biodiversity from tourism.

To maximize conservation of tourism assets, KEA should be selected and prioritized based on irreplaceability and vulnerability. Irreplaceability is a value determined by the geographic extent of the biodiversity asset and its commonness; vulnerability refers to the impact of tourism and the likelihood of future threats (Cutko, 2009). If a habitat or species is rare, meaning that they are only found in a small area (i.e., limited species distribution range),

Table 23.1   *Digital databases for plant, animal and habitat information**

	Primary focus	Coverage	Features and advantages
GBIF (Global Biodiversity Information Facility)	Open access biodiversity (occurrences) database	Global	> 1.6 billion records, >55,000 datasets; search by species, location, or timeframe
Nature Serve Explorer	Search distributions, images, conservation status maps	USA, Canada	In-depth coverage for rare and endangered species; 95,000 plants and animals; >10,000 ecosystems and vegetation communities
Protected Planet (World Database on Protected Areas)	Online database and maps of global protected areas	Global	Downloadable dataset on protected areas, updated monthly; marine and terrestrial
BioTIME	Open source database of biodiversity time series data	Global	>12 million records; 50,000 species; 600,000 locations; marine, freshwater, terrestrial
FishBase	Global information system on marine and freshwater fishes	Global	>34,500 fish species; ~3 million records; life history, taxonomy, biology and historical data
World Database on Key Biodiversity Areas	Hotspot ecosystem profiles and priority ecosystems	Global	Led by BirdLife International and IUCN; includes areas important for birds
Integrated Biodiversity Assessment Tool	Customized profiles for individually-delineated areas	Global	Rapid visual screening of critical areas, free version or pay for additional services
IUCN Red List of Threatened Species	Search for species and their conservation status	Global	128,500 species assessed; species description, range, life history, concerns and status
WORMS (World Register of Marine Species)	Comprehensive taxonomic database for marine species	Global	Search by geounit or species, see taxon trees and relationships; view photo galleries
Avibase World Bird Database	Online database of bird distributions and species	Global	>37 million records; 10,000 species, 20,000 regions; species names in >175 languages
PREDICTS (Predicting Responses to Ecological Diversity in Changing Terrestrial Systems)	Portal of modeled biodiversity responses to human impacts	Global	>2.5 million biodiversity records; 21,000 sites; 38,000 species; terrestrial
VertNet	Searchable database for vertebrate occurrences	Global	Search by region, species; see recorder, date, maps and media

Note: * Information and estimates as of January 2021, subject to change over time.

species only found in certain habitats, or habitats are restricted to small areas, it is highly irreplaceable. It is important to note that "rare" does not mean rarely observed; some elusive species are difficult to see but may have a wide geographic distribution. If the species is endangered, has experienced rapid loss, or is at risk of local decline, it is vulnerable. Referring to the IUCN Red List of Threatened Species, examples of wildlife with high vulnerability and irreplaceability include the proboscis monkey, Chinese alligator, vaquita dolphin and Javan rhino.

KEA could also be species with important ecological or cultural value. Some species can serve as an indicator of environmental changes or exposure to stress and degradation. KEA may include keystone species which serve a critical role in local ecosystems. For tourism, KEA may include charismatic and iconic species (i.e., species important to cultural identity or with popular appeal) such as lions, pandas, polar bears, whales, and sea turtles. Similarly, KEA may include habitats that are essential to monitor because of their commercial or public appeal. Examples include rainforests, savannahs, coral reefs, and glacial fields. Priorities should be placed on species and habitat affected by tourism or central to tourism enterprises.

Step 4. Design a field protocol, choose measurement criteria

The next step is to select metrics. Metrics are measures needed to assess current conditions of biodiversity. For this rapid assessment, metrics have been preselected to focus on **habitat quality**, **species variety**, and **species counts**, as data for these metrics are straightforward to collect and are responsive to stressors discussed in Tool #2 of this chapter. These metrics can act as indicators of the integrity of the natural system. These data can also be applied to promotion and marketing of tourism activities (e.g., we have this habitat, these species, and this many plants or animals of interest).

Reference sites and **monitoring sites** should be established for comparison. Reference sites (or 'control sites') represent areas which are intact or have minimal human disturbance and resemble the natural range of variation of the habitat. These may be areas measured prior to tourism activity, or similar nearby sites. Least-disturbed condition or best-attainable condition may be used in the absence of intact areas. Reference sites should be established in areas where tourism impacts are not anticipated. By contrast, monitoring sites include the aforementioned assessment area (comprised of tourism locations receiving direct impacts and areas of influence receiving indirect impacts). For both sites, areas should accommodate multiple species. This will reduce cost while increasing the ability to predict broader trends. These data will also be valuable for further research should the need for intervention arise.

Step 5. Complete a biological assessment / collect observation data

The final step of the rapid assessment is to collect field data at reference and monitoring sites. The collection of field data provides real-time information that can later be used to make judgments in a systematic and repeatable manner. The objective is to assess changes in species and habitat(s) in response to tourism activity and stressors.

The minimum data required for a rapid assessment includes (a) information about habitat condition (i.e., quality, habitat connectedness, size) and (b) variation and counts of plant or animal species. Since biodiversity will vary based on day, month, and year, the timing of surveys should be standardized and occur at least once per year. By using non-random sampling methods (i.e., choosing what to measure and where), it is possible to target and document occurrences of KEA of interest associated with tourism.

When collecting data, a greater number of points covering the greatest variety of areas will result in a more complete assessment. Data collection should be consistent and comparable internally and across sites.

Sampling procedures

This rapid assessment will consist of (a) habitat surveying, and (b) wildlife surveying (variety and counts).

A. Habitat surveying

Habitat makes up the underlying elements that provide food, shelter, and services needed to support biodiversity. Habitat consists of physical and biological features. It usually encompasses terrestrial or aquatic vegetation, plus substrate and abiotic characteristics (e.g., depth, flow, turbidity) in the case of aquatic areas. Habitats can range from micro-habitat (e.g., a log) to macro-habitat (e.g., a river system). The ecological health of habitat is determined by an assessment of structure, function, and connectivity of vegetation, and compared between monitoring and reference sites.

Composition

Habitat composition is the variety of plant species sharing a physical space. Measuring composition requires establishing a field plot and documenting those species. At a sampling point, create a 15-meter radius (0.1 acre) plot. Using a plant guide, record the presence-absence of key species and similarity to reference conditions determined in step three.

Density

Plant density is the concentration and distribution of specied across an area. Density can be measured by counting the number of each plant species. Within the sample plot, document the number of individual key plant species present and their spacing (highly concentrated, moderately concentrated, low concentration) and similarly to reference conditions.

Structure

Habitat structure is the arrangement and growth stage of plant species. Structure can be measured by observing the height and thickness of trees and shrubs. Within the sample plot, document the major layers: what is the appearance of canopy and understory–homogenous (same shapes and sizes) or heterogeneous (different shapes and sizes)?

Cover

Cover can be the thickness of the tree canopy overhead and the amount and type of low growing plant species on the ground. Measure out from the center of the sample plot 50 meters. Walking along the line, each 10 meters look up and record percentage of vegetation versus sky; look down and record percentage and type of plants (or ground cover) versus bare earth.

Cultural Land Uses

Cultural land uses are structures or vegetative composition that are human-generated or introduced. Within the plot and along the 50 meter transect, record the percentage of vegetation or growing crops that is man-made.

Size

Size is the amount of area that the sampled habitat expands to across the assessment area. Through ground truthing or using aerial photography and/or remote sensing imagery, estimate the contiguous amount of space that this specific community of key plant species covers.

Occurrence

Occurence is the number of times that a specific habitat type exists across the assessment area. Each habitat must be discrete and separate from other groupings of similar habitat by different habitat or human land uses. Using ground truthing, aerial photography, or remote sensing, estimate the number of times this habitat type is repeated in the assessment area.

Connectivity

Connectivity is the presence of natural features (i.e., buffer zones or linear corridors) that link individual occurrences of habitat to other habitats (which can be the same or different). Using ground truthing, aerial photography, or remote sensing, estimate distance between habitats and amount of buffer or corridor between.

Figure 23.2   Habitat surveying components, descriptions, and instructions

A number of rating systems exist for classifying habitat conditions. Similarly, there are a variety of methods to assess the composition of species. For this assessment, habitat condition and composition will be estimated qualitatively using personal judgment and field data, guided by conditions adapted from NatureServe's "Ecological Integrity Assessment Model" (Faber-Langendoen et al., 2016) and *Monitoring Animal Populations and Their Habitats: A Practitioner's Guide* (McComb et al., 2010).

Habitat is species specific, so unless there are key species desired for monitoring, this assessment should focus on evaluating general habitat types across the assessment area. Monitoring changes in habitat requires repeatable sampling protocols at the same location over time. The process begins by locating plots to identify species and appearance of vegetation. Figure 23.2 provides basic sampling instructions. The Habitat Assessment Worksheet and Key in Appendix A can then be used to rate and document individual survey site conditions for monitoring over time.

To complete these measurements, aerial photography, GIS information, and data from the preliminary assessment should be used to locate sample points randomly in the reference and monitoring sites. GPS data for these points should be recorded and used permanently, if feasible. Multiple random plots (four or more) should be chosen per habitat type and measurements should be taken over multiple field seasons to sample the full variation.

B. Wildlife surveying

The second part of this rapid assessment is to survey wildlife species of interest. In the case of tourism, public preferences lean towards charismatic wildlife species that attract viewers, contribute greater human benefits, or are more sensitive to changes in abundance (Colléony et al., 2017; McGinlay et al., 2017). Iconic and charismatic species also have greater fundraising potential (Senzaki et al., 2017). Often these include large, terrestrial vertebrates. Additionally, select bird and fish species can be flagship species for tourism (Ebner et al., 2016; Veríssimo et al., 2009) and can be used as indicators of environmental health, anthropogenic disturbances, and habitat changes (Hocutt, 1981; Smits and Fernie, 2013). Therein, this assessment will focus on survey methods for birds, fish, and terrestrial vertebrates.

Ideally, population sizes and distributions (i.e., relative abundance) would be measured. However, for the purposes of a rapid assessment, species counts can be achieved by estimating where focal species are found and where they are not found (i.e., presence–absence). Similarly, comprehensively sampling for species variety would be challenging in many tourism destinations. For this reason, key species to be surveyed can be selected based on the needs of the tourism operator (e.g., species that serve important functions or have high tourist value). These selections come from step 3 above.

For this assessment, surveying techniques will focus on camera traps (i.e., camera automatically triggered by motion or other change in activity within its field of view, such as animal movement) and audio/video recording devices. These techniques rely on point-based sampling methods that estimate species occurrence and reveal species–habitat associations (Sollmann, 2018). Camera traps and remote devices are used for species inventories, species discovery, activity studies, and population dynamics (Rowcliffe and Carbone, 2008). Recording devices are shown to be sensitive to changes in population and, in some cases, can estimate abundance of common species without tracking individuals (Moeller et al., 2018). Camera trapping and remote recording are popular ways to establish the presence or absence (or, more accurately, detection or non-detection) of species (Herzog et al., 2016).

Using remote recording devices offers a fast and affordable method for monitoring. The goal of this survey technique is to confirm or disconfirm a species occupying habitats within a study area, their distribution, and changes in either (Joseph et al., 2006). For species that have a low detection rate, presence and absence can be used for population monitoring by comparing the percentage of sites that have changed from locations where species were found, to ones where focal species are no longer detected (Joseph et al., 2006). Repeat point counts minimize detection errors and bias in estimates and can provide benefits over other types of sampling (Royle and Nichols, 2003). Boxes 23.1–23.3 describe example instructions for collecting presence and non-presence data from remote recording devices.

BOX 23.1 TERRESTRIAL VERTEBRATES VIA CAMERA TRAPS

- **Number of sites**: Using more than one camera improves detection probability by up to 80%; ten cameras or more will increase this even higher (O'Connor et al., 2017). The use of two to three cameras placed in 10 to 20 sampling points is sufficient to estimate 50–75% of species variety.
- **Timing**: Points should be sampled sequentially across multiple sites for two to three weeks at each site. For species with low detection rates, cameras should be deployed for a minimum of 30 days.
- **Location**: Sampling units must be spatially independent of each other and spaced at least one home-range diameter of the target species apart. For undefined species, a general distance of $2km^2$ separation can be used. Unless the study is dependent on specific habitat type or areas (e.g., riparian), cameras should be distributed systematically across the assessment area.
- **Positioning**: Cameras should be placed on a stable post or tree 30–50 cm off the ground in order to detect a range of species, positioned so animals must pass into the field of view.
- **Settings**: Time-lapse, flash, infrared (or motion) sensitivity, and other settings should be determined based on the anticipated behavior of the species and the desired data analysis methods.
- **Analysis and recording**: Location, size of assessment area, and size of surveying site should be recorded. The number of stations, spacing between stations, and number of days sampling (trap effort) should also be documented. Technical details such as direction of the camera and size of trapping area (the length and width of space the camera can record) will be helpful in the analysis. When reviewing footage, all instances of species captured should be tallied and species type, time, and number of individuals should be documented. Species *not* detected should also be noted.

Source: Larsen et al. (2016).

BOX 23.2 BIRDS VIA ACOUSTIC RECORDING DEVICES

- **Number of sites**: Every habitat type should be surveyed and analyzed separately. The use of one to two recording devices in 10–30 sampling points per habitat type will capture the presence or absence of most species. Sites should be georeferenced using GPS.
- **Timing**: Conducting two to three, 15-minute stationary dawn chorus recordings each morning for 8 to 10 days of surveying should be sufficient to record 80% of resident species. Opportunistic sound recordings are appropriate where dawn chorus surveying may not capture certain species (such as nocturnal or daytime active birds).

Detectability of certain species will vary seasonally, so surveys should be carried out at different times of the year, especially at peak migration season.

- **Location**: Location will depend highly on habitat, micro-habitats, and elevation. Recording devices should be stationed in each visibly distinct location throughout the course of surveying. Minimum distance between stations should be 200–400 meters when separating by habitat or elevation.
- **Positioning**: The microphone should be positioned at an angle of 20 degrees above the horizontal or ground level in forest habitats and 0–10 degrees in low-growth habitats such as grass and scrubland. If the recording device is hand-held, the microphone should be rotated 90 degrees every minute until two full circles are completed then directed in any manner for a subsequent seven minutes.
- **Analysis and recording**: Rapid analysis of bird species only requires identifying habitat type, location, time, and species. Species that are absent from the recording should also be documented. Computer software of other experts (e.g. xeno-canto) can then be used for identification.

Source: Herzog et al. (2016).

BOX 23.3 MARINE MEGAFAUNA VIA UNMANNED AERIAL VEHICLES (UAVS)

- **Number of sites**: Each direct habitat type used in ecotourism operations should be surveyed, if possible, as well as a surrounding habitat to account for daily animal movements. Multiple UAVs (or drones) may be used concurrently to survey a larger area.
- **Timing**: Flights should be conducted in clear weather and calm conditions for increased detectability. The time of day should be considered and appropriately adjusted for, to reduce glare and reflectance issues.
- **Location**: Areas of at least 3 km^2 should be surveyed using 5 to 10 transects. GPS should be used to track the UAV location and path, and later identify the location where animals are detected.
- **Positioning**: UAVs should be flown 30–60 meters above the surface for optimal detection while minimizing disturbance to animals. Flights should overlap by approximately 10% if possible, in the case that an animal is found on a flight line.
- **Settings**: High resolution cameras with still image or video capability are preferred (e.g., SLR camera, Go-Pros). Cameras should be installed facing downward and UAVs should be flown as laterally as possible.
- **Analysis and recording**: Visual examination of images should be used to identify individual animals. Total counts should be made based on expert identification of species within all images of a site. Size of the animal can be estimated based on flight height and angle.

Source: Hensel et al. (2018).

TOOL #2. OPERATOR AND VISITOR IMPACT EVALUATION – IDENTIFYING STRESSORS

- **Questions**: How is wildlife responding to tourists at my site? What are the potential stressors to wildlife that exist as a result of our operations? Is there evidence of wildlife responding negatively to my tourism services and customers (and thus potentially impacting the future of my business operations)?
- **Who this is for**: Tourism operators, managers or stakeholders who visit, guide, or oversee visitation and guiding in areas where they encounter wild flora and fauna.
  - *NOTE: If your tourism operations occur in a space shared by multiple tour operators, this tool will allow you to assess only stress related to your operations, though potential compounding effects of multiple operators may occur.*

- **Why it is important**: Managers are often overwhelmed with the economic burdens, social responsibility, policy compliances, and environmental standards of management. It is seemingly beyond their scope, or capacity, to also manage individual guests' behaviors towards wildlife. In these cases, responsible tourist–wildlife interaction guidelines should be entrusted to operators.

Stressors are physical, chemical, or biological perturbations to a system that are either foreign to that system, or natural to the system but applied at an excessive or deficient level (Rapport and Whitford, 1999). Stressors cause significant changes in the ecological components, patterns, and processes within natural systems. Here, we provide a simplified tool for better understanding stressors to wildlife from visitor interactions and operations.

Three main effects of tourism stressors on wildlife are: (1) behavioral effects, (2) physiological effects, and (3) habitat and population changes. Behavioral effects include animals spending less time feeding or resting; expending more energy to escape a stressor; or shifting to a more remote or less productive feeding ground, which might increase competition and risk of predation. For example, monkeys exposed to tourists move higher into the canopy, and rhinoceroses show increased vigilance and decreased feeding when tourists are present (Lott and McCoy, 1995; Treves and Brandon, 2005). Physiological effects include increased release of stress hormones, reduced immune function, or decreased reproductive capacity. These effects have led to reduced maternal care in dolphins, increased anxiety in macaque monkeys, and reduced survival in penguin fledglings (Mann and Smuts, 1999; Maréchal et al., 2011; McClung et al., 2004). Examples of habitat and population changes resulting from tourism include broken corals in reef systems, forest clearing and fragmentation for tourism infrastructure, displacement of species, transmission of disease, and declines in reproductive success (Blumstein et al., 2017).

Measuring physiological or behavioral changes in animals is complex and often requires specialized training or equipment and extensive time. As such, this tool focuses on monitoring the third type of disturbance effect (habitat and population changes) by measuring the activities or actions (i.e., stressors) that can create physiological or behavioral effects, rather than the effects themselves. We identify nine types of stressors to wildlife that are linked to the above effects: handling or harassing; overcrowding, pursuing, or encroachment; feeding or baiting; habitat damage; harvesting and removal; disease transmission or introduced species; artificial light; noise pollution; and boat or vehicle collisions (Table 23.2).

Table 23.2   *Tourism stressors to biodiversity*

Disturbance	Examples	Wildlife responses, implications	Possible interventions
Handling, Petting, Riding, Harassing	• Holding/petting a wild animal for a photograph • Coercing an animal to sit/stand/behave abnormally • Riding a dangerous animal	• Defensive reaction to stimulus • Increased unpredictability of animal behavior • Loss of energy expended for defense • Physiological and behavioral stress	• Prohibit touching of wildlife • Educational programs • Encourage tourists to see wild animals as wild (not expected to perform) • Restrict access to high animal areas
Overcrowding, Pursuing Encroaching	• Chasing or corralling animals to see them more closely • Large groups of people surrounding an animal • Boats crowding aquatic species	• Feeling trapped/no escape • Defensive behavior • Area avoidance, relocation to non-preferable area (e.g., less food) • Disruption (e.g., feeding, mating) • Physiological and behavioral stress	• Restrict access with limits to number of visitors, amount of time spent per visit, total time spent, distance allowed between visitor and wildlife • Use staff/rangers to monitor and control crowd behavior
Feeding, Baiting	• Unauthorized baited traps to attract specific species • Intentional feeding animals to gain closer access • Unintentional feeding with scraps or unattended items	• Habituation • Dependency • Reduced fear, aggressive behavior • Culling of animals that respond with aggression	• Education programs about harm of feeding • Proper waste disposal systems for human food • Provide storage containers when necessary
Habitat Damage	• Walking on coral reefs • Trampling burrows, eggs, or nests • Off-trail visitor activity • Human and pet waste • Off-roading vehicles • Boat anchors raking seabed	• Habitat degradation, habitat fragmentation • Soil compaction, vegetation loss • Species decline, increased vulnerability • Reduction of habitat available to wildlife • Cascade declines (e.g., coral bleaching)	• Build raised platforms, boardwalks or trail systems to reduce trampling • Monitor and restrict critical habitat zones and nesting areas • Require 'leave no trace' practices • Permanent moorings • Require flotation devices to restrict diving, sea walking
Harvesting, Removal, Entanglement	• Removal of flowers, shells, or specimens (e.g., bones) • Illegal harvesting • Entanglement from nets or foreign objects (e.g., clothing)	• Death or injury • Area avoidance • Behavioral and physiological stress	• Exit monitoring, bag checks • Prohibit equipment that could be used for removal or harvesting • Education programming
Disease Transmission, Introduced species	• Zoonotic, pathogenic diseases • Introduced/invasive species	• Death or illness • Increased susceptibility to predation • Species decline, species invasions	• Boot scrub stations before/after entering sensitive areas • Proper hygiene, avoided contact
Artificial light, flash photography	• Spotlighting nocturnal animals with unfiltered light • Flashlights on beach, use of flash photography at night or in low light areas	• Disorientation of wildlife (e.g., female turtles nesting on beach, hatchlings) • Area avoidance, move further away with increased predation risk • Physiological and behavioral stress	• Mandatory red filters at night • Restricted access to sensitive habitats, area closures when necessary • Blackout programs for beach tourism activities and hotels
Noise Pollution	• Screaming or yelling • Blowing whistles • Playing loud music or other sound-making devices • Helicopters/planes over herds or sensitive species	• Startling animals while foraging, breeding, resting • Detracting from ability to find prey • Depletion of energy reserves • Disorientation, migratory disruption • Mask important calls (territorial, mating)	• Restricted time of day/number of repetitions for activities that produce loud noises (e.g., helicopters, motors) • Instill sense of respect for wildlife • Restricted access during critical periods (e.g., mating, nesting)
Boat or motor vehicle collisions	• Propeller or boat strikes to marine mammals • Roadkill near high-use areas	• Death or injury • Increased vulnerability from roadkill attractant as food source • Avoidance of certain areas	• Restricted access during high-use • Limits to number of boats, types of engines, types of boats • Reduced speed areas, increased signage and enforcement

As part of the biodiversity assessment toolset, we use a stressor checklist (Appendix B) and scorecard (Box 23.4) that allows users to evaluate the current stressors in a site. The scorecard approach provides a way to assess the presence of stressors, their extent, and possible outcomes.

BOX 23.4 TOURISM STRESSORS SCORECARD

Score 1–2, Good: Rare frequency, low duration, and/or intensity of stressor. Minimal changes likely to biodiversity assets resulting from operation activities.

Score 3–4, Fair: High intensity, low duration and rare frequency; or frequent activity with low duration and intensity. Some negative changes to biodiversity assets possible.

Score >4, Poor: High frequency and duration and/or intensity of stressor. Negative and possibly major changes likely in biodiversity assets resulting from operation activities.

Duration, **intensity**, and **frequency** must be considered for each of these stressors. Using the tourism stressors calculator (Figure 23.3), users score these metrics for each of the nine stressors (Table 23.2). Duration-intensity and frequency should be multiplied together for individual disturbance scores. Then, sub-scores for each disturbance are averaged and multiplied for overall disturbance score. Total scores are generated by adding all sub-category scores into a composite stressor score for the record. The scorecard should be completed twice annually, to account for seasonal changes in tourism activities and animal behaviors. An example of the stressor checklist is provided in Table 23.3.

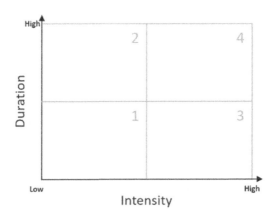

Frequency	1	2	3	4
	Rarely	Sometimes	Frequently	Always
	Stressor created occasionally (less than 20%) in visitor interactions	Stressor created in some (20–50%) visitor interactions	Stressor created in most (>50%) visitor interactions	Stressor created in all (100%) visitor interactions

Figure 23.3   Tourism stressors calculator

Table 23.3   Tourism stressor checklist example

Disturbance category	Disturbance description (specific activity, location, species, time)	Duration-intensity (DI)	Frequency (F)	Disturbance score (DI * F)
(Stressor)	1. Encroaching on space and pursuing manatee in springs at gathering area mid-afternoon	2: High duration, low intensity	2: Stressor created in 20–50% of visitor interactions	4: Fair, negative changes possible
	2. Attempting to take a picture with a bison	1: Low duration, low intensity	3: Stressor created in >50% of interactions	3: Fair, negative changes possible
	3. Visitors went off-trail to track elk during gestation season	4: High intensity, high duration	1: Stressor created in less than 20% of interactions	4: Fair, negative changes possible
Sub-score (Average DI * Average Freq.)		**2.33**	**2**	**4.66:** Poor, negative changes likely

These measurements are important as not all countries control the use and exploitation of wildlife in tourism. Policy, regulations, enforcement, and animal welfare standards vary globally. In many places, enforcement is lacking. However, identification and mediation of stressors needs to be universally addressed, particularly in areas where standards may not exist.

Most of the stressors can be addressed with education and enforcement. Education for guides and visitors is one of the most cost-effective, positive reinforcement mechanisms to improve stress index scores and mitigate effects in the short and long term. In addition, the following may be considered for managers to facilitate improved practices by guides and visitors:

- Regulate against captive wildlife exhibits and activities that are harmful to wildlife welfare.
- Require trained guides for certain activities, encounters, or interactions.
  - *An education and certification program for guides to learn best practices may be valuable*
- Provide constant and consistent messaging regarding appropriate distance and behavior with wildlife to business operators, contractors, and visitors.
- Increase fees for encounters to discourage overcrowding effects on habitat and wildlife.
- Restrict and enforce trail access to wildlife, including:
  - *Areas accessible to visitor use, away from sensitive breeding and foraging habitat*
  - *Time of day and amount of time spent with animals (per day/month/season)*
  - *Number of visitors, number of vehicles, and distance to animals*
- Reinforce fines and penalties for harmful behaviors or non-compliance to regulations, such as trail closures and animal handling.
- Monitor and manage entry of pets and domestic animals.
- Create photo opportunity areas and discourage location information sharing in photographs.

APPLICATIONS AND BENEFITS

To understand the effects of stressors on biodiversity at tourism sites, it is necessary to establish a long-term monitoring program. Monitoring can become passive once **assessment points** are assigned to indicate a range of expected or acceptable conditions. Defining safe operating conditions allows tourism practitioners to discern changes to biodiversity that may impact business or require further evaluation. These assessment points will clarify the trajectory of metrics (i.e., habitat condition improving or degrading; wildlife counts going up or down) and, when compared to the natural range of variation, can signal undesirable transitions.

Data collection by non-experts is critical for the tourism industry. Despite limitations, it is a reliable tool for enhancing scientific data and increasing public engagement with nature (Kallimanis et al., 2017). Non-expert data collection can expand knowledge of species ranges, track changes in the timing of migrations or blooms, and document species in areas where scientific research is limited (Green and Giese, 2004). A growing number of user interfaces aid visitors in rapidly documenting their sightings (e.g., photos and geolocations), generating species lists, contributing to wildlife counts, and communicating with scientists about their findings (Table 23.4). On some of these platforms, expert scientists validate many millions of observations, which further increases the robustness and credibility of data.

Table 23.4   Examples of citizen science and participatory data-collection platforms

Tool, app name	Sponsoring organizations	Target groups	Data inputs	Features	Scientific contribution
iNaturalist	California Academy of Sciences, National Geographic	All	Upload photos, add notes, transmit location, date and time of the observation	Add observations to projects, create your own collections	Global biodiversity database from over 1 million users
BirdLog	Audubon Naturalist Society, Cornell Lab of Ornithology (eBird)	Birds	Enter location, date time of observation, how spotted, number of species	Shared observations; checklist function	Abundance and distribution of species, range shifts over time
Leaf Snap	Columbia University, University of Maryland, Smithsonian Institution	Plants	Upload picture of a leaf, location and species	Electronic field guide to help identify species	Map distributions of flora
Project Noah	New York University, National Geographic	Wildlife & plants	Upload wildlife photos; categorize, geolocate, add tags, habitat, etc.	Create a personal nature journal, mission tool to connect with specific data needs	Database of georeferenced photos; add to global or local projects
BudBurst	National Ecological Observatory, Chicago Botanic Garden, National Science Foundation	Plants	Create a list of plants (leafing, flowering, fruiting) to track, enter data and images on a regular basis	Recommends plants to track, flora-caching game	Document phenological changes, climate effects on leafing

Rapid assessments can also be used for environmental impact statements, restoration planning, fundraising, or strategic business marketing. These types of projects equally serve as internship opportunities or additional tourism products and services. Rapid assessments can function as a direct route to certification and offer evidence of responsible operations that support natural resources and the economy. By incorporating citizen science and biodiversity monitoring into tourism services, providers can build in new ways to increase enjoyment in their operations while expanding knowledge, skills, and conservation values among the countless number of tourists that travel the world to see wildlife today.

LIMITATIONS

If statistical rigor is needed, more extensive analyses must be undertaken in collaboration with scientists and natural resource managers beyond what we propose here. Furthermore, although this assessment does not evaluate more complex biological factors (e.g., population, community level interactions) such can be incorporated as needed with scientific research partnerships and training.

CONCLUSION

In response to emerging evidence of tourism impacts on natural landscapes, this chapter consolidates data collection methods as a tool for evaluating the ecological changes that occur from human use in tourism areas. Paired field assessment of habitat and species provide a baseline for monitoring efforts, and evaluation of stressors informs potential impacts and any necessary management interventions. In summary:

1. Wildlife species and habitat monitoring is essential to the conservation of biodiversity assets important to nature-based tourism.
2. Baseline data collection can be initiated any time with minimal cost (time, financial) and limited training requirements. Efforts should prioritize regular, standardized protocols to maximize efficiency and usefulness of comparisons over time.
3. Ecosystem monitoring can be incorporated in nature-based tourism activities (e.g. citizen science activities, bioblitzes) to further enhance tourism experiences.
4. Data collected from the tools in this chapter can allow any tourism official or manager to identify issues and opportunities, create specific measures and/or individualized standards, and adjust their effects on habitat and wildlife at a site-wide scale.

There is great value in the accumulation of accurate and relevant information gathered by those working in the tourism industry. Careful monitoring of changes in wildlife behavior, populations and habitat quality is essential for any quality wildlife tourism operation to continue without causing undue disturbance, and is also highly valuable as a research tool if results are shared.
Ronda Green and Melissa Giese, 2004.

REFERENCES

Ball-Damerow, J. E., Brenskelle, L., Barve, N., Soltis, P. S., Sierwald, P., Bieler, R., ... Guralnick, R. P. (2019) Research applications of primary biodiversity databases in the digital age. *PloS ONE*, 14(9), e0215794.
Blumstein, D. T., Geffroy, B., Samia, D. S. and Bessa, E. (eds.) (2017) *Ecotourism's Promise and Peril: A Biological Evaluation*. Cham: Springer International.
Buckley, R. (2003) Ecological indicators of tourist impacts in parks. *Journal of Ecotourism*, 2(1), 54–66.

Buckley, R. C., Morrison, C. and Castley, J. G. (2016) Net effects of ecotourism on threatened species survival. *PloS ONE*, 11(2), e0147988.

Colléony, A., Clayton, S., Couvet, D., Saint Jalme, M. and Prévot, A. C. (2017) Human preferences for species conservation: Animal charisma trumps endangered status. *Biological Conservation*, 206, 263–269.

Cutko, A. (2009) *Biodiversity Inventory of Natural Lands: A How-To Manual for Foresters and Biologists*. Arlington, VA: NatureServe.

Danielsen, F., Jensen, P. M., Burgess, N. D., Coronado, I., Holt, S., Poulsen, M. K., … Sørensen, M. (2014) Testing focus groups as a tool for connecting indigenous and local knowledge on abundance of natural resources with science-based land management systems. *Conservation Letters*, 7(4), 380–389.

Ebner, B. C., Morgan, D. L., Kerezsy, A., Hardie, S., Beatty, S. J., Seymour, J. E., … Espinoza, T. (2016) Enhancing conservation of Australian freshwater ecosystems: Identification of freshwater flagship fishes and relevant target audiences. *Fish and Fisheries*, 17(4), 1134–1151.

Faber-Langendoen, D., Nichols, W., Rocchio, J., Walz, K. and Lemly, J. (2016) *An Introduction to NatureServe's Ecological Integrity Assessment Method*. Arlington, VA: NatureServe.

Fitzgerald, L. A. and Stronza, A. L. (2016) In defense of the ecotourism shield: A response to Geffroy et al. *Trends in Ecology & Evolution*, 31(2), 94–95.

Geffroy, B., Samia, D. S., Bessa, E. and Blumstein, D. T. (2015) How nature-based tourism might increase prey vulnerability to predators. *Trends in Ecology & Evolution*, 30(12), 755–765.

Gill, J. A., Norris, K. and Sutherland, W. J. (2001) Why behavioural responses may not reflect the population consequences of human disturbance. *Biological Conservation*, 97(2), 265–268.

Green, R. and Giese, M. (2004) Negative effects of wildlife tourism on wildlife. In K. Higginbottom (ed.), *Wildlife Tourism: Impacts, Management and Planning* (pp. 81–97). Altona, Victoria: Common Ground Publishing.

Grodzińska-Jurczak, M. and Cent, J. (2011) Can public participation increase nature conservation effectiveness? *Innovation: The European Journal of Social Science Research*, 24(3), 371–378.

Gullison, R. E., Hardner, J., Anstee, S. and Meyer, M. (2015) *Good Practices for the Collection of Biodiversity Baseline Data*. Multilateral Financing Institutions Biodiversity Working Group & Cross-Sector Biodiversity Initiative Acknowledgments.

Gura, T. (2013) Citizen science: Amateur experts. *Nature*, 496(7444), 259–261.

Hanes, A. C., Kalema-Zikusoka, G., Svensson, M. S. and Hill, C. M. (2018) Assessment of health risks posed by tourists visiting mountain gorillas in Bwindi Impenetrable National Park, Uganda. *Primate Conservation*, 32, 123–132.

Hensel, E., Wenclawski, S. and Layman, C. A. (2018) Using a small, consumer-grade drone to identify and count marine megafauna in shallow habitats. *Latin American Journal of Aquatic Research*, 46(5), 1025–1033.

Herzog, S. K., O'Shea, B. J. and Pequeño, T. (2016) Toward a standardized protocol for rapid surveys of terrestrial bird communities. In T. H. Larsen (ed.), *Core Standardized Methods for Rapid Biological Field Assessment* (pp. 94–107). Arlington, VA: Conservation International.

Hocutt, C. H. (1981) Fish as indicators of biological integrity [Quality of a water resource]. *Fisheries (USA)*, 6(6), 28–30.

Joseph, L. N., Field, S. A., Wilcox, C. and Possingham, H. P. (2006) Presence–absence versus abundance data for monitoring threatened species. *Conservation Biology*, 20(6), 1679–1687.

Kallimanis, A. S., Panitsa, M. and Dimopoulos, P. (2017) Quality of non-expert citizen science data collected for habitat type conservation status assessment in Natura 2000 protected areas. *Scientific Reports*, 7(1), 1–10.

Larsen, T. H. (ed.) (2016) *Core Standardized Methods for Rapid Biological Field Assessment*. Arlington, VA: Conservation International.

Larsen, T. H., Viana, L., Thyberg, T. and Ahumada, J. (2016) Camera trapping. In T. H. Larsen (ed.), *Core Standardized Methods for Rapid Biological Field Assessment* (pp. 50–57). Arlington, VA: Conservation International.

Larson, C. L., Reed, S. E., Merenlender, A. M. and Crooks, K. R. (2016) Effects of recreation on animals revealed as widespread through a global systematic review. *PloS ONE*, 11(12), e0167259.

Lott, D. F. and McCoy, M. (1995) Asian rhinos *Rhinoceros unicornis* on the run? Impact of tourist visits on one population. *Biological Conservation*, 73(1), 23–26.

Mann, J. and Smuts, B. (1999) Behavioral development in wild bottlenose dolphin newborns (*Tursiops sp.*). *Behaviour*, 136(5), 529–566.

Maréchal, L., Semple, S., Majolo, B., Qarro, M., Heistermann, M., and MacLarnon, A. (2011) Impacts of tourism on anxiety and physiological stress levels in wild male Barbary macaques. *Biological Conservation*, 144(9), 2188–2193.

McClung, M. R., Seddon, P. J., Massaro, M., and Setiawan, A. N. (2004) Nature-based tourism impacts on yellow-eyed penguins *Megadyptes antipodes*: Does unregulated visitor access affect fledging weight and juvenile survival? *Biological Conservation*, 119(2), 279–285.

McComb, B., Zuckerberg, B., Vesely, D. and Jordan, C. (2010) *Monitoring Animal Populations and Their Habitats: A Practitioner's Guide*. London: CRC Press.

McGinlay, J., Parsons, D. J., Morris, J., Hubatova, M., Graves, A., Bradbury, R. B. and Bullock, J. M. (2017) Do charismatic species groups generate more cultural ecosystem service benefits? *Ecosystem Services*, 27, 15–24.

Moeller, A. K., Lukacs, P. M. and Horne, J. S. (2018) Three novel methods to estimate abundance of unmarked animals using remote cameras. *Ecosphere*, 9(8), e02331.

Moorhouse, T., D'Cruze, N. C. and Macdonald, D. W. (2017) Unethical use of wildlife in tourism: What's the problem, who is responsible, and what can be done? *Journal of Sustainable Tourism*, 25(4), 505–516.

Newsome, D., Moore, S. A. and Dowling, R. K. (2012) *Natural Area Tourism: Ecology, Impacts and Management*. Bristol: Channel View Publications.

O'Connor, K. M., Nathan, L. R., Liberati, M. R., Tingley, M. W., Vokoun, J. C., and Rittenhouse, T. A. (2017) Camera trap arrays improve detection probability of wildlife: Investigating study design considerations using an empirical dataset. *PLoS ONE*, 12(4), e0175684.

Peterson, C. (2019) Americans' love of hiking has driven elk to the brink, scientists say. *The Guardian*. https://www.theguardian.com/environment/2019/aug/25/hiking-elk-driven-to-brink-colorado-vail.

Pollock, N. B., Howe, N., Irizarry, I., Lorusso, N., Kruger, A., Himmler, K. and Struwe, L. (2015) Personal BioBlitz: A new way to encourage biodiversity discovery and knowledge in K-9 education and outreach. *BioScience*, 65(12), 1154–1164.

Rapport, D. J. and Whitford, W. G. (1999) How ecosystems respond to stress: Common properties of arid and aquatic systems. *BioScience*, 49(3), 193–203.

Rowcliffe, J. M. and Carbone, C. (2008) Surveys using camera traps: Are we looking to a brighter future? *Animal Conservation*, 11(3), 185–186.

Royle, J. A. and Nichols, J. D. (2003) Estimating abundance from repeated presence–absence data or point counts. *Ecology*, 84(3), 777–790.

Senzaki, M., Yamaura, Y., Shoji, Y., Kubo, T. and Nakamura, F. (2017) Citizens promote the conservation of flagship species more than ecosystem services in wetland restoration. *Biological Conservation*, 214, 1–5.

Shannon, G., Larson, C. L., Reed, S. E., Crooks, K. R. and Angeloni, L. M. (2017) Ecological consequences of ecotourism for wildlife populations and communities. In D. T. Blumstein, B. Geffroy, D. S. Samia and E. Bessa (eds.), *Ecotourism's Promise and Peril: A Biological Evaluation* (pp. 29–46). Cham: Springer International.

Smits, J. E. and Fernie, K. J. (2013) Avian wildlife as sentinels of ecosystem health. *Comparative Immunology, Microbiology and Infectious Diseases*, 36(3), 333–342.

Sollmann, R. (2018) A gentle introduction to camera-trap data analysis. *African Journal of Ecology*, 56(4), 740–749.

Treves, A. and Brandon, K. (2005) Tourist impacts on the behavior of black howling monkeys (*Alouatta pigra*) at Lamanai, Belize. In J. D. Paterson and J. Wallis (eds.), *Commensalism and Conflict: The Human–Primate Interface* (pp. 147–167). Norman, OK: American Society of Primatologists.

Twining-Ward, L., Li, W., Bhammar, H. and Wright, E. (2018) *Supporting Sustainable Livelihoods through Wildlife Tourism*. Washington, DC: World Bank.

Veríssimo, D., Fraser, I., Groombridge, J., Bristol, R. and MacMillan, D. C. (2009) Birds as tourism flagship species: A case study of tropical islands. *Animal Conservation*, 12(6), 549–558.

Wardle, C., Buckley, R., Shakeela, A. and Castley, J. G. (2018) Ecotourism's contributions to conservation: Analysing patterns in published studies. *Journal of Ecotourism* [Online], 1–31.

Weber, A., Kalema-Zikusoka, G. and Stevens, N. J. (2020) Lack of rule-adherence during mountain gorilla tourism encounters in Bwindi Impenetrable National Park, Uganda, places gorillas at risk from human disease. *Frontiers in Public Health*, 8, 1.

Williams, P. W. and Ponsford, I. F. (2009) Confronting tourism's environmental paradox: Transitioning for sustainable tourism. *Futures*, 41(6), 396–404.

World Travel & Tourism Council (2019) *The Economic Impact of Global Wildlife Tourism: Travel & Tourism as an Economic Tool for the Protection of Wildlife*. WTTC.org. https://www.wttc.org/priorities/sustainable-growth/illegal-wildlife-trade.

APPENDIX A

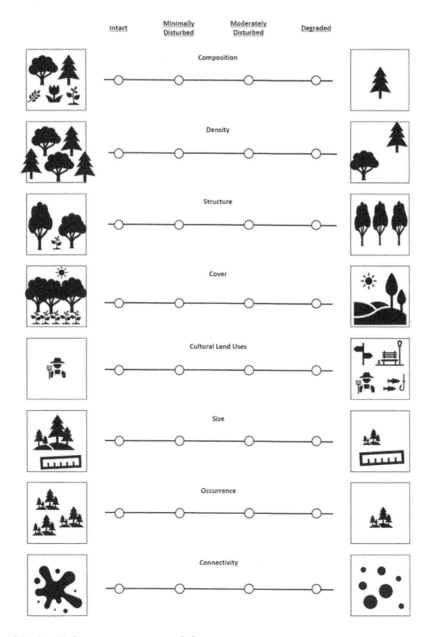

Figure 23A.1   Habitat assessment worksheet

Habitat Conditions Key

Intact

- Composition – Fits natural range of variation. All key plant species are present. Very few or no invasive species are present.
- Density – Fits natural range of variation, meets reference conditions of habitat type.
- Structure – Fits natural range of variation, meets reference conditions of habitat type.
- Cover – Fits natural range of variation, meets reference conditions of habitat type.
- Cultural Land Uses – No cultural land uses, no anthropogenic disturbances.
- Size – Very large contiguous habitat.
- Occurrence – There are many other similar habitats in the area.
- Connectivity – There is ample buffer zone and linear natural corridors that allow dispersal of species to surrounding area. No or very few man-made barriers exist between habitats.

Minimally Disturbed

- Composition – It is functioning within the natural range of variation. Most key plant species are present. Invasive species are only present in minor amounts or have minor impact.
- Density – Functions within natural range of variation, meets most reference conditions of habitat.
- Structure – Functions within natural range of variation, meets most reference conditions of habitat.
- Cover – Functions within natural range of variation, meets most reference conditions of habitat.
- Cultural Land Uses – Few cultural land uses, minor anthropogenic disturbances.
- Size – Large to medium size contiguous habitat.
- Occurrence – There are some other good condition habitats in the area.
- Connectivity – There is some buffer zone and a few natural corridors that allow dispersal of species to other surrounding habitats. Some man-made barriers exist between habitats.

Moderately Disturbed

- Composition – Altered outside of natural range of variation. Some key plant species are absent. Invasive species are present in a large amount but have not overtaken native species.
- Density – Altered outside of natural range of variation, deviates from many reference conditions.
- Structure – Altered outside of natural range of variation, deviates from many reference conditions.
- Cover – Altered outside of natural range of variation, deviates from many reference conditions.
- Cultural Land Uses – Multiple cultural land uses, several anthropogenic disturbances.
- Size – Small, near minimum acceptable limits for functioning habitat.
- Occurrence – There are one or two other surrounding habitats.

- Connectivity – There is no or very little buffer, at least one natural corridor is available for dispersal of species to other surrounding habitats. Multiple man-made barriers exist between habitats.

Severely Degraded

- Composition – Minimal or no similarity to natural range of variation. Few key plant species are present. Invasive species are present in large amount and exert a strong impact on other species.
- Density – Minimal or no similarity to natural range of variation, does not fit reference conditions.
- Structure – Minimal or no similarity to natural range of variation, does not fit reference conditions.
- Cover – Minimal or no similarity to natural range of variation, does not fit reference conditions.
- Cultural Land Uses – Mostly cultural land use, with high amounts of anthropogenic disturbances.
- Size – Habitat is very small and limited in its function for other species.
- Occurrence – There are no other surrounding habitats.
- Connectivity – The habitat is fragmented and disconnected from other natural areas.

APPENDIX B

Table 23B.1   Stressor checklist

Disturbance category	Disturbance description (specific activity, location, species, time)	Duration-intensity score (D.I.)	Frequency score
Handling, Petting, Riding, Pursuing	1.		
	2.		
	3.		
	Sub-score (Average DI * Average Freq.)		
Overcrowding, Encroaching	1.		
	2.		
	3.		
	Sub-score (Average DI * Average Freq.)		
Feeding, Baiting	1.		
	2.		
	3.		
	Sub-score (Average DI * Average Freq.)		
Habitat Damage	1.		
	2.		
	3.		
	Sub-score (Average DI * Average Freq.)		
Harvesting, Removal, Entanglement	1.		
	2.		
	3.		
	Sub-score (Average DI * Average Freq.)		
Disease Transmission, Introduced Species	1.		
	2.		
	3.		
	Sub-score (Average DI * Average Freq.)		
Artificial Light, Flash Photography	1.		
	2.		
	3.		
	Sub-score (Average DI * Average Freq.)		
Noise Disturbance	1.		
	2.		
	3.		
	Sub-score (Average DI * Average Freq.)		
Boat or Motor Vehicle Collisions	1.		
	2.		
	3.		
	Sub-score (Average DI * Average Freq.)		

24. Social and cultural impact assessment of tourism

Jacqueline N. Kariithi

DEFINING CONCEPTS

The impacts of tourism on the host community and culture often emerge slowly, affect each destination and individuals within it in different ways, and are difficult to isolate from other causes (Inkson and Minnaert, 2018). Social impacts usually refer to interpersonal relations, social conduct, crime, safety, religion, language and health. Cultural impacts usually refer to material and non-material forms of culture (e.g. heritage and religious buildings, artefacts, rituals) and processes of cultural change (Wall and Mathieson, 2006). Like all impacts, tourism's social and cultural impacts may be positive or negative. Major claims have been made for tourism as a force for peace and greater understanding between communities, but the experience of tourism in host communities in many destinations shows that tourism can be a force for rapid and undesirable social change (Shafaei and Mohamed, 2015; Bimonte and Punzo, 2016).

In general terms, Social Impact Assessment (SIA) involves analysing, monitoring and managing the social consequences of development. However, there are different levels at which to understand the term 'SIA'. SIA is a field of research and practice, or a paradigm consisting of a body of knowledge, techniques, and values. SIA includes the processes of analysing, monitoring and managing the intended and unintended social consequences, both positive and negative, of planned interventions (policies, programmes, plans, projects) and any social change processes invoked by those interventions (Vanclay, 2003). Its primary purpose is to bring about a more sustainable and equitable biophysical and human environment.

In the same vein, any impact assessment carried out does not happen in isolation and there needs to be a recognition that social, economic and biophysical impacts are inherently and inextricably interconnected. According to Vanclay (2003), a social impact assessment needs to build on local knowledge and utilize participatory processes to analyse the concerns of interested and affected parties. For any planners, policy makers and developers, the development of the social impact assessment revolves around the concept of involving stakeholders. SIA is developed with the view to identify development goals, ensure that positive outcomes are maximized, and can be more important than minimizing harm from negative impacts.

The definition of Cultural Impact Assessment (CIA) is a process of evaluating the likely impacts of a proposed development on the way of life of a particular group or community of people (Partal and Dunphy, 2016), with full involvement of a group or community of people and possibly undertaken by the same group or community of people. Another recognized definition is the CIA is seen as "a method of analysing what impacts a development policy or action may have on the cultural aspects of the environment" (Sagnia, 2004). A CIA will generally address the impacts, both beneficial and adverse, of a proposed development that may affect, for example, the values, belief systems, customary laws, language(s), customs, economy, relationships with the local environment and particular species, social organization and traditions of the affected community. One of the major challenges of CIA is that defining 'culture' and therefore 'cultural impact assessment' is difficult. In this chapter, culture is defined as a set of basic assumptions and values, orientations to life, beliefs, policies, procedures and behavioural conventions that are shared by a group of people, and that influence each member's behaviour and his/her interpretations of the 'meaning' of other people's behaviour (Spencer-Oatey and Franklin, 2012). Culture is divided into seven sub-domains of: identity and engagement; creativity and recreation; memory and projection; beliefs and ideas; gender and generations; enquiry and learning; and health and well-being (Partal and Dunphy, 2016).

In the past the social and cultural impact assessment activities have been carried out with less involvement of other stakeholders, in host and resident communities who are greatly impacted by tourism development. Furthermore, certain demographic groups such as youth, persons with disability and women were excluded during consultations. The possibility of exclusion has further aggravated the situation, with communities becoming antagonistic to tourism expansion and in effect advancing localized conflicts in existence. Recent trends in sustainable tourism development have shown a strong growing need for communities and other stakeholders to be fully involved in conservation matters in their environments. Consequently, private sector investors in tourism plus government tourism initiatives have entrenched the practice of stakeholder engagement in recognition of diverse interests and values in their approaches as a way of gaining communal support.

Additionally, the demands of stakeholder consultation can lead to fatigue in communities and local governments, particularly in situations with multiple developments. These challenges are exacerbated where there is limited engagement, leading participants to question the value of their involvement (Esteves et al., 2017). For this reason, it has necessitated tourism planners to embrace an interactive participatory approach to facilitate community discussions about desired futures, gaining a good understanding (i.e. profiling) of the communities likely to be affected by the policy, programme, plan or project including a thorough stakeholder analysis, scoping the key social issues (the significant negative impacts as well as the opportunities for creating benefits (Esteves et al., 2012)). In addressing social issues and risks associated with tourism development, both SIA and CIA provide an avenue to anticipate the negative aspects of tourism impacting the physical, social, cultural and economic environments.

The identification and standardization of tools for cultural and social impact assessment remains elusive and thus there is a need to simplify the standard methodologies already utilized in social and cultural impact assessments in tourism development. The primary objectives of carrying out both the SIA and CIA are analysing, monitoring and managing the social and cultural consequences of planned interventions (Esteves et al., 2017), and by logical extension the social and cultural dimensions of development strategies. Nevertheless, the emerging challenges and problems associated with the impact assessment associated with interventions, project planning and policy development have been a great hindrance towards attaining the project goals. The objective of this chapter is to provide an overview and guide for the implementation of social and cultural impact assessments before and after tourism operationalization of businesses and destination, with the explicit view of attaining long-term sustainable tourism development. Furthermore, emphasis will be placed on the significance of involving key stakeholders in the assessment process.

DESCRIPTION OF IMPACTS

With an increasing awareness of environmental protection, climate change and other major changes there has been an increase in the discourse and engagement on the adverse effects of tourism on natural resources. Additionally, the cross-sectoral nature of tourism with other industries such as agriculture, transport, education, and energy requires careful planning and development. A clear, structured and straightforward assessment of impacts first requires identification and description which can then be followed by quantification and categorization to enable the development of a systematic framework. According to a recent Environmental & Social Management System report (IUCN, 2016) the identification and assessment of impacts needs to take the following into consideration:

- Direct or indirect impacts occurring at the project site or within the project's wider area of influence. Indirect impacts include inadvertent knock-on effects or side-effects of the project given the complexity of social processes and the human–environment interface.
- Impacts within the project's wider area of influence including transboundary impacts, where relevant.
- Negative impacts triggered immediately as well as longer term impacts.
- Cumulative effects that materialize through interaction with other developments at the project site as well as in the wider area of influence.

Social Impacts of Tourism

Most studies have been based upon the resident/host perception approach. The social and cultural impacts of tourism are dependent on the relationship between tourists and host community. The host community's perceptions and attitudes towards tourism need to be assessed in order to identify the effects of tourism development on local communities.

There are a number of reasons to identify social impacts:

- Enhance understanding of differences in individuals' perceptions regarding the personal and community-wide impacts of tourism.
- Advance understanding of the influences on residents' perception of tourism impacts at the personal and community levels.
- Assess the degree to which tourism activity contributes to the identified social impacts.

Social impact assessment

Social impact, as one of the fundamental pillars of tourism impacts, has been consequently investigated from different perspectives (Shafaei and Mohamed, 2015). The recognition of host communities as key stakeholders and partakers of resources is considered vital if sustainable tourism development is to be attained. Communities and especially those living adjacent to tourism amenities and attractions should be involved in the social impact assessment process in a participatory and inclusive manner. This includes identifying local needs in anticipation of future changes in economic growth and social and cultural identity. The role of the social impact assessment is to mitigate negative social impacts on the community. The core positive and negative social impacts are listed in Table 24.1 (Vanclay, 2003).

Cultural Impacts of Tourism

The admiration of tourists for local culture, arts, traditions or customs can increase the cultural pride of the local community and revive aspects of culture that might have been declining (Inkson and Minnaert, 2018). Certain art forms or traditions, for example, can be mainly kept alive by an older generation: the positive attention of tourists can encourage young people in the host community to become actively involved as well. Additionally, investment by government and private sector in cultural, sport or leisure activities can provide an improved standard of living for the local community as a way of taking a greater interest in a specific culture and further allowing communities to take an interest in their own cultural heritage.

However, with every positive input to the local culture there is the possibility and real chance of a negative outcome particularly if the tourism industry starts to grow exponentially. Furthermore, if there are no adequate mechanisms to protect the host community's needs, sensitivities and environment despite the incentives received from tourism development, negative impacts on host culture will inevitably manifest over time.

Cultural impact assessment

The ultimate success of the CIA lies in the initial crucial phase in actualizing the management actions prescribed. Mapping of cultural activities, field surveys and significance assessment in accordance with specific legislation are a good way to start. In order to strengthen the CIA practice, it is recommended to include establishing agreed definitions of culture and cultural impact, and validated tools, including measurement frameworks and indicators. The lack of clear definition of culture results in a commensurate challenge of understanding impacts on and of culture (Partal and Dunphy, 2016).

APPROACHES OF IMPACT ASSESSMENTS

The process of developing impact assessments has been difficult. In a truly international context, there are many issues to consider. The regulatory context varies, the cultural/religious context varies, and social and economic priorities for development vary (Vanclay, 2003).

The International Association for Impact Assessment (IAIA), founded in 1980, defines Impact Assessment (IA), as "the process of identifying, predicting, evaluating and mitigating the biophysical, social, and others relevant effects of development proposals prior to major decisions being taken and commitments made" (IAIA, 2009, p. 1).

IA has become a well-established practice across a range of sectors, including environment, economics, social services and health (IAIA, 2009). The need to apply IA to strategic levels of decision-making (e.g. policies, legislation, plans, programmes) has led to the development of a more integrated process of strategic environmental assessment. An integrated process has a wider purview, generally considering "environmental, social, economic, and health issues", aiming to "mainstream and ensure the sustainability of strategic decisions" (IAIA, 2009, p. 2).

IAs are used to predict the future, assisting decision-makers to conceptualize what might happen if an intervention, such as a new policy or action, is implemented. They are also used at the opposite end of the decision-making process, to understand what has been affected by a particular course of action. Impact assessments can include both qualitative and quantitative methods. The main aim for SIA and CIA is to be available to practitioners around the world and provide guidelines in consultation with a range of stakeholders; therefore the need to develop a framework for planning considerations enables the successful development and implementation of both assessments. To effectively apply the social and cultural impact assessments to tourism planning, Imperiale and Vanclay (2016) and Vanclay et al. (2015), suggest the following steps:

Phase 1: Understanding the Local Context

Understanding a project's biophysical, social and institutional context helps clarify the specific needs and social development goals for an appropriate intervention and helps decision-makers comprehend the place of the intervention (Slootweg et al., 2001).

Phase 2: Recognizing Local Concerns and Capacities

The 'recognizing' phase involves predicting, analysing and assessing the likely impacts of the proposed intervention and helps development agencies refine their proposals to better address local needs and perceptions and to recognize resilient capacities.

Phase 3: Engaging Local Communities

The main objectives of encouraging local participation include the building of a community vision of shared problems and strategies, and encouraging participation of a diverse representation from a community such as youth, women and persons of disabilities. Additionally, focusing on efforts to increase awareness of local cultural and natural heritage, building local capacities and promoting greater use of local resources, are further aims.

Phase 4: Empowering Socially Sustainable Transformations

The development of community agreements offers an improved approach to sustainable rural development by "balancing the costs of projects with desired community benefits; incorporating local knowledge and concerns; feeding back and responding to information about ongoing impacts; [and] defining the local communities, economic participation in the development" (Nish and Bice, 2011, p. 59).

DEVELOPING A FRAMEWORK FOR PLANNING CONSIDERATIONS

Tourism as an international system of exchange displays tensions around the interface between space and experience that reaches into the conceptual heart of globalization (Robinson and Phipps, 2003). Each nation, no matter what their position in any notional global political league table, promotes tourism as an actual and potential source of external revenue, a marker of political status that draws upon social, natural and cultural capital, and as a means to legitimize itself as a territorial entity. Thus, social practitioners can help decision-makers, development agencies, and local communities to achieve improved social outcomes through enhanced understanding and better management of the social issues associated with development projects (Imperiale and Vanclay, 2016).

Over the years there have not been any consistent or standard frameworks of assessment, including indicators and scales, and insufficient information has been published about any of these concepts to enable observation of any patterns or themes (Partal and Dunphy, 2016). It is important to underline the enormous resource capacity that will be required to implement social and cultural impact assessments within a scheduled timeframe. Monitoring and evaluation needs to be done during the impact assessments of tourism development to inject improvements into the implementation process.

According to McCombes et al. (2015), the impact assessment process is essentially a learning and iterative process comprising four sequential but overlapping phases: (i) understand the issues; (ii) predict, analyse and assess the likely impact pathways; (iii) develop and implement strategies; and (iv) design and implement monitoring. These phases are anchored in stakeholder identification and analysis as well as embedding the social and cultural context of the tourism activity, intervention or project. Additionally, summarizing significant issues in a way that can be easily understood by a non-technical audience, in particular local stakeholders, enables the identification and analysis of potential adverse impacts and ensure that the needs and conditions of people affected are considered in the impact assessment process.

Social and cultural impacts assessments are best understood as an umbrella or overarching framework that embodies the evaluation of all impacts on humans (Vanclay, 2003) and on all the ways in which people and communities interact with their social and cultural surroundings. Vanclay (2003) further explains that due to their crosscutting effect and links with a wide range of specialist sub-fields involved in the assessment of areas such as aesthetic impacts, archaeological and cultural heritage impacts (both tangible and intangible), community impacts, demographic impacts and development impacts; both SIA and CIA should not be undertaken by a single person, but require a multidisciplinary team approach. Stakeholders' analysis should be integrated in the framework that considers costs and benefits for all stakeholder groups (Gravagnuolo and Girard, 2017). The benefits of integration are realized when tourism practitioners together with decision-makers, development agencies, and local communities coalesce efforts to achieve improved social and cultural outcomes through enhanced understanding and better management of the social and cultural issues. The specific characteristics of SIA and CIA and sources for accessing baseline information are detailed in Appendices A and B. It is recommended that as a principle, implementation of social and cultural impact assessments for a specific project should focus on the goals and outcomes according to specific context through the process detailed below.

Scoping of Key Social and Cultural Issues

Discussions about what is important is an essential and detailed first step in the process of social and cultural assessment. These discussions are needed to develop a baseline and context of the issues in order to create a profile of the overarching and implicit issues and can be achieved in the following ways:

- *Profiling of host communities*: categorizing main social groups and their socio-cultural characteristics disaggregated between men and women; emphasis on indigenous peoples and vulnerable groups such as landless persons, the elderly, persons with disabilities, children, ethnic minorities or displaced persons.

- *Assessing historical and cultural events* relevant to the ethnic identity, cultural expressions of the communities involved, interests and developmental aspirations of social groups and their attitudes.
- *Scoping of key economic activities and livelihood patterns*: formal and informal, subsistence and commercial, including dependence on natural resources or on illegal activities such as poaching or illegal trade.
- *Identifying social issues and risks faced by social groups*: including issues related to access to resources and to social services as well as to their capabilities and development opportunities.
- *Profiling of visitors* including domestic and international visitors and trends, origins, demographics and typical segmentation of the visitor market, transportation and typical tourism routes, expenditure, accommodation preferences, and activities.
- *Development and assessment of alternatives* in the context of a community tourism strategy, regional and district tourism plans, local and regional social, environmental and conservation policies, and structure plans.

Stakeholder Identification and Analysis

The purpose of the stakeholder identification and analysis is to clarify who should be involved in the impact assessment process and how. It also provides the avenue to engage all relevant stakeholders who have an interest in or might influence the project, disaggregated between men and women where relevant and feasible. Tourism planners should make use of the SIA process to rigorously conduct a stakeholder analysis done during the design process (IUCN, 2016). Furthermore, an additional layer to the SIA involves elaborating on potential project impacts as identified by stakeholders. Concurrently, the process of analysis might include identifying new stakeholders as well as assessing current stakeholder groups and interest. The process of identification and analysis of stakeholders should be described according to the following aspects:

- Their interests in and expectations from the project
- How they might influence the project (positively or negatively)
- How their livelihoods could be impacted by the project (positively or negatively)
- How they could be involved in the development of tourism.

In real time application, an impact assessment requires an understanding of its core concepts such as culture, community, power, human rights, gender, justice, place, resilience, sustainable livelihoods and human capital, as well as of the theoretical bases for participatory approaches. These concepts need to be integrated in the CIA and SIA process due to the following reasons:

1. Promotes a sense of ownership in the impact assessment plan, the overall output and ensures stakeholders support the implementation process.
2. Promotes and sustains an inventory of their socio-cultural resources for community stakeholders, tourism information centres and tour operators which provides the long-term management of local resources in tourism development.

3. Assists in strengthening social security, protects traditional user rights of natural resources in the tourism sector.
4. Fosters communal risk adjustment strategies, i.e. group based collective decision-making either in utilizing or protecting the resources.
5. Ensures that social, cultural, environmental and economic dimensions are protected in tourism activities and programmes.

Embedding Social and Cultural Impacts in Tourism Planning

The socio-cultural consequences of tourism are the least obvious and hardest to measure (Inkson and Minnaert, 2018). Environmental and socio-cultural resources are often regarded as zero-priced public goods and people rarely can appreciate their vulnerability (Buhalis, 1999). Additionally, whatever is available is biased as it focuses attention upon the detrimental impact of tourism on the host population (Buhalis and Cooper, 1998). Little attention has been paid to assessing social and cultural impacts on the tourist population, which can be either positive or negative. Providing essential information for accommodative and modification strategies in tourism destination planning prevents the unethical use of social and cultural resources utilized by all stakeholders.

Social and cultural impacts tend to contain a mixture of both positive and negative strands and affects both hosts and guests (Mbaiwa, 2005). It has been established that tourism can have a range of positive and negative social and cultural impacts on destinations. Not all these impacts are present in all destinations, and in some the overall balance will be positive whilst in others the balance will be negative. Socio-cultural impacts are dependent on differences between the hosts and the tourists (Inskeep, 1991) in terms of basic value and logic systems, religious beliefs, traditions, customs, lifestyles, behavioural patterns, dress codes and attitudes towards strangers. Management of tourism activities also has a significant social and cultural impact.

Tables 24.1 and 24.2 display the positive impact and potential negative impacts of tourism. Although there are many more impacts that need to be tested, the descriptions in the tables are an indicator of the reasons why carrying out social and cultural impact assessments is essential in the planning and development stages of tourism to mitigate against unanticipated negative impacts due to the nuanced and subtle manner in which they occur.

Table 24.1   A comparison between potential positive and negative social impacts of tourism

Positive impact	Negative impact
Broadening experiences, tourism provides diverse experiences for both hosts and visitors.	Conflict of interests in the use of amenities such as beaches may create conflict between locals and visitors, e.g. locals will use the beach for fishing whilst tourists seek relaxation and leisure.
Social interaction and strengthening relationships within communities and with residents and their visitors.	Resentment of lifestyles, wealth, amenities and opportunities that tourists have access to that locals do not.
Improved infrastructure and amenities improve the overall social well-being of the community.	Crime, prostitution and begging by host communities which are aimed at tourists.

Source: Adapted from Inkson and Minnaert (2018).

Table 24.2   *A comparison between potential positive and corresponding negative cultural impacts of tourism*

Positive impact	Negative impact
Revival of culture	Loss of cultural pride
Improved standard of living for host communities	Pressure on limited resources as result of expansion and construction
A better understanding between cultures of hosts and visitors	Staged authenticity and commodification of host culture

Source: Adapted from Inkson and Minnaert (2018).

Analysis of Alternatives

It has become important to have a holistic approach towards social and cultural issues before undertaking any development activities in any place or ecosystem. Both social and cultural impacts should be assessed throughout the tourism development process with a view to taking some corrective action in the course of any intervention; it is therefore important to identify other options to achieve tourism project objectives and compare their impacts (IUCN, 2016). Identification of alternatives is generally required only if the identified impacts are very significant, for example construction of accommodation and hospitality amenities. Carrying out the analysis systematically compares feasible, less adverse alternatives – including the 'no project' option – to the proposed project site, technology, design, and operation in terms of:

- Effectiveness in achieving the project objectives as well as potential trade-offs
- Potential cultural and social impacts
- The feasibility of mitigating these impacts
- Operational requirements and their suitability under local conditions
- Institutional, training, and monitoring requirements
- Estimated cost-effectiveness
- Conformity to existing policies, plans, laws, regulations.

COMPLEXITIES OF SOCIAL AND CULTURAL DIMENSIONS OF TOURISM

In order to embrace an authentic understanding of both the cultural and social dimensions of tourism, it requires describing the overarching complexities by paying attention to how economy, environment and social issues interact. The win–win consensus of sustainable tourism discourse has led to the different stakeholders' competing for the use of limited resources (Hultman and Säwe, 2018). Unpacking the complexities of social life and cultural dimensions is a necessary manoeuvre as meanings appear to exhibit more value among stakeholders.

Tourism is the only industry in the world where the product is consumed at source thus the consumer travels to the origins of the 'product' referred to as the destination. Thus, in many examples worldwide, the host community become secondary in importance despite the product being consumed in their locality. Additionally, in certain contexts the host community have to sacrifice the quality of their well-being in preference to the tourism industry through unintended consequences and pressure on local resources and infrastructure. Furthermore, tourism activities may cumulatively impact on the social and cultural fabric of the resident community which manifests in ways that may be beyond their control.

Tourists are often encouraged to choose and explore destinations through labels such as 'locality', 'uniqueness' and 'authenticity', insofar as every place can be said to be local, unique and authentic. The objects being commodified in tourism are often traditions, place-specific assets, and landscape features (George et al., 2009; Hultman and Hall, 2012). However, these resources are impossible to frame within a traditional economic valuation paradigm through demand and supply models.

In practice, the private sector in tourism typically adopts a rather limited, ad hoc approach to managing their social impacts through the implementation of their corporate social responsibility (CSR) or other internal sustainability management activities (McCombes et al., 2015). The overriding objective of the private sector in managing their destinations and businesses is to sustain the unique values and resources (Buhalis, 2000). The private sector encompasses a variety of existing sustainability techniques such as industry regulation, codes of conduct, environmental management systems, certification schemes, self-assessment and reporting initiatives, and a range of socio-economic responsibility initiatives and actions for employees and local communities. Streamlining these measures to enable practitioners and policy makers to identify strategies creates a challenge and thus it is suggested to include multi-dimensional, multi-criteria and multi-stakeholder evaluation tools in impact assessment (Gravagnuolo and Girard, 2017). Incorporation of such tools further increases the complexity by requiring more resources, technology, and trained resource persons to address social and cultural dimensions.

CONCLUSIONS

Tourism can be a means of cultural revitalization, revival and rejuvenation of the local arts and cultures (Sharma, 2008). Furthermore, tourism activity not only gives shape to the land, and provides jobs and income to local peoples, but also produces powerful social, cultural meanings and representations (Milne and Ateljevic, 2001). The aim of this chapter was to provide a blueprint for practitioners and planning development and policy in the tourism industry. It does not claim to offer any definitive solutions to the issues that it raises. However, it does seek to locate the processes that constitute social and cultural impact assessment tourism as part of a wider set of contexts that are historically embedded but are changing constantly. According to Imperiale and Vanclay (2016), to ascertain feasibility for new tourism ventures or ascertain what impacts they have had over time, the following actions need to be included as facilitative and cooperative measures in tourism development:

- Identify and mitigate the social risks and vulnerabilities that characterize the social context.
- Address the negative social impacts and human rights issues that may be created by the project at the community level.
- Acknowledge local needs and desires for, and perceptions of, past, present and future development.
- Recognize the local knowledge and local capacities that need to be engaged and strengthened.

Increasing investment and focusing on cultural activity and recognition is of value in the development of social and cultural tourism 'products' as consumed by the tourist (Partal and

Dunphy, 2016). There is a need for a continuous and ongoing process of negotiation between social groupings relating to access to various configurations of places, social and cultural resources, and rights to utilize and express these in particular ways. Social and cultural impacts in the tourism sector are often diffused and cumulative, therefore a community, or wider, perspective is needed to assess them (IUCN, 2016). Additionally, ethnographic and case-based accounts of the way in which the tourism economy is embedded in cultural contexts (Milne and Ateljevic, 2001) allow us to move beyond some of the globalization effects that precipitate the negative impacts generated from tourism interventions, activities and projects. We can witness creative and innovative developments within social and cultural tourism, together with challenges and changes to the very political and social frameworks that shape it.

REFERENCES

Bimonte, S. and Punzo, L. F. (2016) Tourist development and host–guest interaction: An economic exchange theory. *Annals of Tourism Research*, 58, 128–139.

Buhalis, D. (1999) Limits of tourism development in peripheral destinations: Problems and challenges. *Tourism Management*, 20(2), 183–185.

Buhalis, D. (2000) Marketing the competitive destination of the future. *Tourism Management*, 21(1), 97–116.

Buhalis, D. and Cooper, C. (1998) Competition or co-operation? Small and medium sized tourism enterprises at the destination. In E. Laws, B. Faulkner and G. Moscardo (eds.), *Embracing and Managing Change in Tourism* (pp. 45–56). London: Routledge.

Esteves, A. M., Factor, G., Vanclay, F., Götzmann, N. and Moreira, S. (2017) Adapting social impact assessment to address a project's human rights impacts and risks. *Environmental Impact Assessment Review*, 67, 73–87.

Esteves, A. M., Franks, D. and Vanclay, F. (2012) Social impact assessment: The state of the art. *Impact Assessment and Project Appraisal*, 30(1), 34–42.

George, E. W., Mair, H. and Reid, D. G. (2009) *Rural Tourism Development: Localism and Cultural Change*. Bristol: Channel View Publications.

Gravagnuolo, A. and Girard, L. F. (2017) Multicriteria tools for the implementation of historic urban landscape. *Quality Innovation Prosperity*, 21(1), 186–201.

Gutierrez, E., Lamoureux, K., Matus, S. and Sebunya, K. (2005) *Linking Communities, Tourism, & Conservation: A Tourism Assessment Process – Tools and Worksheets*. Conservation International and the George Washington University.

Hultman, J. and Hall, C. M. (2012) Tourism place-making: Governance of locality in Sweden. *Annals of Tourism Research*, 39(2), 547–570.

Hultman, J. and Säwe, F. (2018) A minor matter of great concern: The different sustainability logics of 'societal benefits' and 'socio-economic profit'. In W. Filho (ed.), *Handbook of Sustainability Science and Research* (pp. 57–70). Cham: Springer.

IAIA [International Association of Impact Assessment] (2009) *What Is Impact Assessment?* Fargo, ND: IAIA.

Imperiale, A. J. and Vanclay, F. (2016) Using social impact assessment to strengthen community resilience in sustainable rural development in mountain areas. *Mountain Research and Development*, 36(4), 431–442.

Inkson, C. and Minnaert, L. (2018) *Tourism Management: An Introduction*. London: Sage.

Inskeep, E. (1991) *Tourism Planning: An Integrated and Sustainable Development Approach*. New York: Van Nostrand Reinhold.

IUCN (2016) *Environmental and Social Management System (ESMS), Social Impact Assessment, Guidance Note Manual*. https://www.iucn.org/sites/dev/files/iucn_esms_sia_guidance_note.pdf.

Mbaiwa, J. E. (2005) The socio-cultural impacts of tourism development in the Okavango Delta, Botswana. *Journal of Tourism and Cultural Change*, 2(3), 163–185.

McCombes, L., Vanclay, F. and Evers, Y. (2015) Putting social impact assessment to the test as a method for implementing responsible tourism practice. *Environmental Impact Assessment Review*, 55, 156–168.

Milne, S. and Ateljevic, I. (2001) Tourism, economic development and the global–local nexus: Theory embracing complexity. *Tourism Geographies*, 3(4), 369–393.

Nish, S. and Bice, S. (2011) Community-based agreement making with land-connected peoples. In F. Vanclay and A. M. Esteves (eds.), *New Directions in Social Impact Assessment* (pp. 59–77). Cheltenham, UK and Northampton, MA, USA: Edward Elgar Publishing.

Partal, A. and Dunphy, K. (2016) Cultural impact assessment: A systematic literature review of current methods and practice around the world. *Impact Assessment and Project Appraisal*, 34(1), 1–13.

Robinson, M. and Phipps, A. (2003) Worlds passing by: Journeys of culture and cultural journeys. *Journal of Tourism and Cultural Change*, 1(1), 1–10.

Sagnia, B. K. (2004) *Framework for Cultural Impact Assessment*. International Network for Cultural Diversity (INCD). http://dmeforpeace.org/sites/default/files/FRAMEWORK%20FOR %20CULTURAL%20IMPACT%20ASSESSMENT%20(INCD)_2004.pdf.

Shafaei, F. and Mohamed, B. (2015) A stage-based model development study on tourism social impact assessment. *International Journal of Scientific and Research Publication*, 3(5), 279–284.

Sharma, R. (2008) Tourism and the value system: An impact assessment from socio-cultural perspective. *Himalayan Journal of Sociology and Anthropology*, 3, 106–125.

Slootweg, R., Vanclay, F. and Van Schooten, M. (2001) Function evaluation as a framework for the integration of social and environmental impact assessment. *Impact Assessment and Project Appraisal*, 19(1), 19–28.

Spencer-Oatey, H. and Franklin, P. (2012) What is culture? A compilation of quotations. *GlobalPAD Core Concepts*, 1–21.

Vanclay, F. (2003) International principles for social impact assessment. *Impact Assessment and Project Appraisal*, 21(1), 5–12.

Vanclay, F., Esteves, A. M., Aucamp, I. and Franks, D. M. (2015) *Social Impact Assessment: Guidance for Assessing and Managing the Social Impacts of Projects*. Fargo, ND: IAIA. https://espace.library .uq.edu.au/data/UQ_355365.

Wall, G. and Mathieson, A. (2006) *Tourism: Change, Impacts, and Opportunities*. Harlow: Pearson Education.

APPENDIX A

Table 24A.1   Characteristics of SIA

Goal	Outcome	Sources of information
Create an ecologically, socio-culturally and economically sustainable and equitable environment.	Promotes community development and empowerment, builds capacity, and develops social capital (social networks and trust).	• Field trips at different times of year • Community meetings • Consultation with scientists/naturalists • Local conservation publications and websites
Proactive stance to development.	Assisting communities and other stakeholders to identify development goals, to maximize positive and minimize harm from negative impacts.	• Local and regional tour operators (meetings, consultations, surveys) • Governmental natural resources departments and websites • Tourism boards or administration investment promotion offices
Develop a crosscutting multi-disciplinary tool.	Undertaken on behalf of a wide range of actors, and not just within a regulatory framework.	• Community mapping meetings and focus groups consultations, surveys) • Consultation with scientists/naturalists • Governmental natural resources departments and websites
Contribute to the process of adaptive management of policies, programmes, plans and projects.	Informs the design and operation of the planned intervention.	• Local and regional tour operators (meetings, consultations, surveys)
Involve stakeholders in the assessment of social impacts.	Builds on local knowledge and utilizes participatory processes to analyse the concerns of interested and affected parties.	• Resident surveys and interviews • Consultation with scientists/naturalists • Local conservation publications and websites
Analysis of the social impacts that occurred because of past activities.	Reflexive and evaluative of its theoretical bases and of its practice.	• Community mapping meetings and focus groups • Resident surveys and interviews

Source: Modified from Gutierrez et al. (2005) and Vanclay (2003).

APPENDIX B

Table 24B.1   Characteristics of CIA

Goal	Outcome	Sources of information
Identify attributes and values.	Involve stakeholders and experts in the identification of attributes and values of cultural heritage.	• Field trips at different times of year • Community mapping meetings and focus groups • Resident surveys and interviews
Identify and prioritize actions for conservation and development.	Develop strategies to mitigate cultural impact and enhance cultural resilience.	• Government departments and websites • Consultation with scientists/naturalists, park and wildlife services • Local tourism association websites
Understand vulnerability.	Assess vulnerability of heritage to socio-economic stresses and climate change.	• Government websites • Travel guidebooks • Consultation with scientists/naturalists • Local tourism associations
Planning and design interventions for regeneration.	Identify cultural heritage sensitivity areas and develop regeneration projects.	• Local and regional tour operators (meetings, consultations, surveys) • Consultation with scientists/naturalists • Governmental natural resources departments and websites
Protect cultural resources, values and attributes.	Mapping and survey of cultural and natural resources.	• Community mapping meetings and focus groups • Local conservation publications and websites • International conservation NGOs (e.g. Conservation International, Nature Conservancy)
Create collaborations that contributes to the process of adaptive management.	Establish partnerships and local management frameworks for each project, intervention, and programme.	• Tourist surveys and interviews • Governmental natural resources departments and websites

Source: Modified from Gutierrez et al. (2005) and Gravagnuolo and Girard (2017).

25. Tourism certification audits: reviewing sustainable certification programs
Monica Mic

INTRODUCTION

Theoretical Approaches to Certification Audit Support

In recent decades, a considerable body of research has developed around tourism certification. Practical analysis, however, relevant to the certification audit process and compliance has been in far shorter supply. Paradoxically, even though the notion of certification audits has been present in certification analysis for about 20 years, explicit information on audit processes and compliance has been weakly considered. The most significant organizational efforts are those of the International Social and Environmental Accreditation and Labeling (ISEAL) Alliance, the global membership association for credible sustainability standards, and those of the Global Sustainable Tourism Council (GSTC), the global membership organization for international baseline standards for sustainable tourism. These efforts identify sustainable tourism indicators and standards, the justification for them, and their underlying relations, along with some specification for how to meet sustainable standards in ensuring compliance. These elements are essential for understanding the basic functioning of certification systems and the establishment of standards. The assurance that certification systems are effective must be based on periodic audits of compliance.

The purpose of this chapter is to document the concept of certification audits in a concrete and useful manner to understand their value and the processes around them. We begin by exploring the process of certification in depth, especially audit logistics and compliance. The following two sections examine the components that support the operationalization of certification audits.

Certification Governance in Tourism

GSTC criteria and accreditation program
Certification systems help firms adapt and work with specific social and environmental rules and requirements. In ensuring the productive capacity of a certification system, support for the formulation of sustainability standards and the application of such standards is provided by GSTC, the leading international accreditation body governing certifications of sustainable tourism products. It is essential to acknowledge that accreditations influence the capacity of certification systems to absorb auditing processes and compliance requirements. Thus, accreditation refers to the certification process, whereas a standard is a level of quality, typically quantifiable.

GSTC has been in operation since 2007. GSTC responded to increasing industry pressure for mutually agreed-upon environmental and social standards. The GSTC Criteria and

Accreditation Program adheres to the ISEAL Alliance Good Practice Codes, namely the Standard-Setting Code and the Assurance and Impact Codes. ISEAL Alliance operates to standards from specialized systems for worldwide standardization like the International Organization for Standardization (ISO) and the International Electrotechnical Commission (IEC). Specific to certification are:

● ISO/IEC Guide 23:1982 – Methods of indicating conformity with standards for third-party certification systems;
● ISO/IEC Guide 60:2004 Conformity assessment – Code of good practice;
● ISO/IEC 17065:2012 Conformity assessment – Requirements for certification bodies attesting products, processes, and services (revised and conformed in 2018).

Collectively, these international standards serve as criteria for accreditation and certification bodies, peer assessments, official designations, system owners, etc. This chapter makes use of these standards, especially the ISO/IEC 17065 and the GSTC Accreditation Manual, to enable a better understanding of the global consensus on audit procedures for certification bodies.

ISO/IEC conformity assessment tools
Honey (2003b, p. 10) defines certification as a "procedure that assesses, audits, and gives written assurance that a facility, product, process, or service meets specific standards". As a condition for effective functioning, certification systems must ensure the acceptance of their standards as an obligation. Compliance with certification standards requires periodic evaluations since, without specific steps in certification systems, conflicts over standards would never be solved. The role of an audit is to ensure compliance of a product or service with specific predefined quality requirements. A knowledge of compliance with standards is often used to prove that requirements are met and can be used for setting requirements or as methods for testing (Hunter, 2012).

Conformity assessment tools ensure products and services meet their given requirements. For example, ISO/IEC GUIDE 23 is directed to conform with standards for third-party certification systems. At the same time, ISO/IEC GUIDE 60 "recommends good practices for all elements of conformity assessment, including normative documents, systems, schemes, and results" (ISO, 2004). Further, ISO/IEC 60 targets individuals and bodies who wish to provide, promote, or use ethical and reliable conformity assessment services (ISO, 2004), while ISO/IEC 17065 is the official international standard for certifying bodies and thus ensures certification results – the focus of this chapter. The ISO/IEC 17065 standard (last revised in 2013) identifies, in action analysis, separate categories of requirements such as legal and contractual matters, application review and certification decisions, and preventive actions. The application of 17065 is "shifting towards requiring third-party accreditation of certification bodies" (Buzard, 2015). Third-party accreditation of certification bodies is subject to rigorous and regular evaluations against ISO tools to ensure the performance of viable assessments against their standards. Accreditation bodies like GSTC and other independent organizations offer year-round training to educate certification stakeholders about these ISO/IEC requirements.

STEP-BY-STEP APPROACH TO AUDITING PART I

Introduction

Auditing typically involves the three different stages of strategizing, auditing, and reporting on issues found during the audit. Prepared by the ISO Committee on Conformity Assessment (CASCO), the International Standard ISO/IEC 17065 includes several requirements of different categories, namely legal, contractual, and process requirements, as well as resource management and management systems requirements. The ISO/IEC 17065 classification represents a simplified version of the International Standard document. However, being a member of an ISO/IEC 17065 accreditation body, though, finds much in common with these criteria. Collectively, the above requirements outline a globally adopted framework by certification bodies. The GSTC Accreditation Manual is mainly in agreement with these requirements, with enhancements for specific requirements for certification of sustainable tourism.

The following step-by-step approach to auditing is based on the ISO/IEC conformity assessment tools, primarily the ISO/IEC 17065 tool, and appreciation of the GSTC Accreditation Manual – Requirements for Certification Bodies section. The approach covers fundamentals for auditing, such as how to conduct and assess a certification system and establish whether a tourism facility has met a sustainable standard, as well as GSTC competencies for audit professionals.

GSTC Framework of Support

GSTC aims to support all certification systems to become GSTC-Recognized, GSTC-Approved, or GSTC-Accredited. GSTC-Recognized means that a sustainable tourism standard has met the GSTC criteria. GSTC-Approved indicates acceptance procedures for third-party certifications. GSTC-Accredited represents a reliable and cost-effective way to establish market credibility of sustainable tourism certification. GSTC accreditation for certification bodies includes gaining accreditation from an already accredited body, which conforms to the GSTC-Accredited requirements of accreditation bodies and is endorsed by the GSTC Accreditation Panel. As a well-networked accreditation organization that works to reward best practice tourism certifications worldwide, GSTC criteria are both destination-based (for public policymakers and destination managers) and industry-based (for hotels and tour operators). GSTC criteria include all the elements that a certification system should consider. Hence, although many other tourism certifications and eco-award programs exist to provide guidelines (guidelines that are sometimes created differently and based on various criteria), GSTC is the most widely recognized best practice for tourism certification. It does not certify any products or services, but accredits those that do.

Once GSTC accreditation status is gained, license to use the GSTC accreditation assets is granted to the certification body in question. GSTC accreditation bodies are to manage compliance of GSTC accredited certification bodies through periodic assessments against GSTC-Accredited – Requirements for Certification Bodies of the GSTC Accreditation Manual. Certification bodies can carry out audits against their GSTC-Recognized Standard, as well as the GSTC criteria and their Indicators and Guidance (GSTC Sustainable Enterprises – Hotels and Tour Operators, or GSTC Destinations). (Also see Chapter 13 on the GSTC standards.)

Certification Body Conformity Requirements

Certification body members are required to use the accreditation auditing guidelines of the Accreditation Auditing Practice Group (AAGP), including the AAPG Key Criteria document. Certification body members are assessed against AAGP and the AAPG Key Criteria guidelines for their ability to deliver risk-free auditing results.

Scope, integrity, and normative references

Audits are a combination of assessing expectations and requirements. During the strategizing stage, a clear scope and scale of the auditing task at hand needs to be determined. Collecting relevant information and supporting documentation is an initial step in preparing an audit. For the evaluation to be accurate, it must be objective. Objectivity is understood to mean the absence of conflict of interests or the presence of solutions to conflict of interests "so as not to influence the activities of the body adversely" (ISO, 2012). Certification bodies need to submit to the reason for certification and purpose of audit and prioritize these reasons to their own. The rule of the audit is made public through various conformity assessments and codes of good practice like ISO/IEC Guide 60 on principles of good practice on performing audit activities and results. For certification bodies, clauses regarding management impartiality specify a minimum of two years' break between consulting and auditing the same client.

Additionally, GSTC relies on an Integrity Program with ten different implementation principles. These are integrity, credibility, impartiality, accessibility, comprehensiveness, rigorousness, effectiveness, transparency, diversity, and achievability (GSTC, 2011; see also GSTC, 2020). These principles apply to all aspects of the GSTC programs; including work performed by certification scheme members. Auditing members are encouraged to address anything that might affect their fairness in conducting and completing an audit. There are plenty of online resources available in this regard, although searching for context-based resources relevant to the subject matter of the audit is recommended.

Predominantly cited within specialized conformity assessments are normative references. Normative references are informative references that assist auditors in a subject area. Normative references are necessary for the application of the Standard in which they are mentioned. The following normative references are complementary to the implementation of ISO/IEC 17065:

- ISO/IEC 17000:2004 Conformity assessment – Vocabulary and general principles;
- ISO/IEC 17020:2012 Conformity assessment – Requirements for the operation of various types of bodies performing inspection;
- ISO/IEC 17021:2015 Conformity assessment – Requirements for bodies providing audit and certification of management systems;
- ISO/IEC 17025:2017 General requirements for the competence of testing and calibration laboratories.

Beyond that, the GSTC Accreditation Manual references additional normative documents relevant to certification audits, namely:

- ISO/IEC 17065:2012 Conformity assessment – Requirements for bodies certifying products, processes, and services;

- ISO/IEC 17067:2013 Conformity assessment – Fundamentals of product certification and guidelines for product certification schemes;
- ISO/IEC 19011:2011 – Guidelines for quality and, or environmental management system auditing;
- ISO/IEC Guide 2:2004 Standardization and related activities – General vocabulary.

Accreditation Audit Practice Group (AAPG) Guidance Documents are the following:

- ISO/IAF AAPG Auditing the Certification Bodies Impartiality Committee;
- ISO/IAF AAPG Key Criteria for assessing the competency of CBs and their ability to deliver credible results;
- ISEAL Code of Good Practice for Setting Social and Environmental Standards.

Normative references are considered necessary for an advanced audit inquiry. When audit work is to be performed, the dimensions of the audit need to be considered, and normative references are useful in preparing certification bodies to comply with the legal and operational requirements of the jurisdiction of their client. Reviewing all the above normative references is outside the scope of this chapter, but overlooking them in conducting an audit can lead to a restrictive conceptualization of compliance.

Contractual requirements and classification

While the GSTC Accreditation Manual dedicates considerable space to the legal responsibility of auditing participants, more focus seems to be on accreditation bodies than on certification bodies. The GSTC-Approved Manual used for GSTC-Recognized Standards includes contractual specifications that are devoted to certification programs. Thus, the requirements specific to ISO/IEC 17065 as the basis for contractual structures and responsibilities for auditing participants are discussed next.

Certification bodies cannot operate unless they are legally registered in their jurisdiction of choice. Governmental certification bodies are also held accountable based on governmental status. Local and regional bylaws need to be reviewed for specific legal contexts for both industry and government certification bodies. Typical contractual structures involve certification agreements and use of license, certificates, and marks of conformity.

The certification body is responsible for putting in place an enforceable certification agreement with its clients.

Typical client responsibilities include:

- Conforming with the recognized Standard and relevant certification requirements;
- Communicating the meaning of the certification correctly, avoiding misleading claims and withdrawing reference to certification following any termination;
- Recording, handling, and informing complaints and corrective actions steps;
- Complying with certification requirements;
- Updating the certification body on any changes that may affect compliance with certification requirements within ten days of them occurring;
- Providing all necessary information and arrangements for the certification audit process.

Typical responsibilities for certification bodies include:

- Carrying out a competent and impartial evaluation;

- Communicating any changes in the Standard and requirements to clients;
- Providing information to clients on its certification procedures.

Risk assessment requirements

Certification bodies are encouraged to determine the level of risk of an organization before performing audits:

- High risk: Environmental Management System (EMS) required for being in culturally sensitive or environmentally protected areas;
- Low risk: Risk Assessment and Environmental Action required.

Certification bodies do not determine the risk category of a company based on its size or revenue; instead, they use the conditions mentioned above. Minimum audit frequency consists of a full on-site audit once a year for high-risk companies and every two years for low-risk ones. High-risk companies also get a desk audit on-site, while low-risk ones get surveillance on-site.

Process Requirements: Collecting, Evaluating, and Sampling Evidence

Application review and evaluation

Generally, certification bodies are responsible for obtaining the information needed to complete the certification process per the relevant certification scheme. Process requirements for ISO 17065 offer ISO 19011 guidance. The GSTC Accreditation Manual requires specification of the tourism category assessed, namely, accommodation, tour operators, destinations, and other sectors included in the GSTC criteria and indicators. For a legal process of certification, the certification body reviewing the information obtained should identify any products, documents, or schemes that are new to them. A record of these shall be maintained, and the certification body needs to address any lack of competency or capability for the certification activities they are undertaking. Any documentation deficiencies need to be resolved before on-site evaluations. Third-party stakeholder interviews might be conducted in case certification bodies are not satisfied with the level of the information supplied by the applicant. The applicant needs to be formally informed about any stakeholder consultation undertaken, but the information received during the interview(s) is confidential.

Decision, surveillance, and status changes

At least one person or a group of persons can be involved in certification-related decisions. The condition is that the certification body chooses decision-making people independent from the people involved in the process for evaluation. If decision-making is in favor of the applicant and certification is granted, it shall be valid for no longer than three years from the date on which it was issued and as per the certificate document. The certification body needs to conduct on-site surveillance visits at least every two years and also undertake random unannounced monitoring visits. The process of renewal of certification requires the same steps as applying for one.

Certification bodies are responsible for communicating any change in requirements about certification introduced prior, during, or after the audit. Verification of the implementation of these changes rests with the certification body. Auditors can use Annex E of the ISO/IEC

Guide 20:2004, Standardization and related activities – General vocabulary, to familiarize themselves with aspects related to a notice of changes in requirements. The applicant also has the right to initiate changes if it chooses to, and the certification body needs to consider these changes and decide approaches and courses of action. For more information on the changes affecting certification, refer to section 7.10 of the ISO/IEC 17065.

Termination, complaints, and appeals

The certification process can result in termination, reduction, suspension, or withdrawal of certification (by the applicant), most commonly due to nonconformity with certification requirements. The result depends on how many requirements the client is complying with. If the client requests termination or suspension of certification or simply decides to withdraw its participation, the certification body is responsible for ensuring that all necessary modifications in the official documentation of certification are addressed, to avoid confusion about whether the product remains certified or not. In the case of a reduction in certification, the degree of certification remaining needs to be precise. Communication about these facts needs to be in plain language and made official. The same approach applies to suspension or reinstatement of certification. Certification bodies need to record these changes.

GSTC Competence Requirements for Audit Professionals

The GSTC Accreditation Manual includes competence requirements for audit professionals specific to sustainable tourism certification. We previously pointed out that certification body decision-making people are independent of those involved in the evaluation process. Thus, the first phase involves auditing bodies preparing and conducting assessments. The second phase involves a general analysis of the audit framework and action and a formulation of support on behalf of the decision-making body if certification is to be granted.

Auditor body criteria

Assessing sustainable tourism certification schemes goes beyond the modern version of audit body requirements. In terms of this framework's needs, audit bodies need to be trained to cover the various dimensions and elements of sustainability throughout the functional systems of a business.

Auditor body criteria include auditing techniques, GSTC Criteria, Indicators, and the GSTC-Recognized Standard if applicable, sustainable tourism enterprises, and sustainable tourism destinations. Competency criteria also include sections 10.4, 10.5, and 10.6 of the GSTC Accreditation Manual, namely stakeholder consultation, local knowledge, and language requirements. These criteria are not so much about auditor training or requirements as about auditor education. For this chapter, we focus on auditor training and requirements.

Skill qualification and competency requirements for enterprise-level audits include:

- Approved GSTC auditor training on assessing against GSTC Criteria. Training consists of one-day on-site practice in evaluating/auditing sustainable tourism and a three-day theory course;
- Successful examination of the GSTC Criteria content;
- Successfully passing the evaluation for the GSTC-Recognized Standard if required;
- Successful testing of the GSTC Sustainable Tourism Training (STTP) Program.

Experience requirements include:

- At least two EMS or ISO audits;
- Two audits of GSTC Criteria or GSTC-Recognized Standard or both.

In the event of changes to the GSTC Criteria, its Standards or Certification Requirements, the Certification Bodies must comply with these new modifications. Qualification and skill requirements for sustainable tourism destinations are similar but at a destination scale. There is also a corresponding transition towards a more management-aligned mindset. Certifying tourism destinations involves a much ampler auditing scheme with various stakeholders and audit professionals involved, including destination managers and tourism destination auditors.

Decision-maker requirements
Decision-maker criteria are more robust, covering auditing techniques, international norms for certification, and the GSTC criteria. However, the level of preparation and training for decision-making bodies is far more advanced than in the case of auditor bodies.

Skill qualification and competency requirements for auditing criteria include:

- Pass or register as an EMS or Quality Management System (QMS) auditor with the International Register of Certificated Auditors (IRCA) or Exemplar Global, a Personnel Certification Body; or,
- Equivalent auditor qualification to achieve the competencies.

Skill qualification and competency requirements for international forms of certification include:

- Formal training of ISO 17065:2012 or minimum of five years' experience as a decision-maker with an ISEAL or International Accreditation Forum (IAF), an accredited certification body; or,
- Knowledge of certification principles, procedures, and techniques to enable the auditor to be a better decision-maker.

The qualifications and competency requirements for GSTC criteria for decision-makers are the same as for auditors.

Triple-bottom-line requirements
Companies are often judged by how they approach sustainability. Certification bodies require a genuine understanding of the triple-bottom-line approach to tourism development. As discussed later in this chapter, the triple-bottom-line approach proposed by Brundtland in 1992 draws upon environmental, economic, and social considerations of development. Thus, the distinguishing aspects of sustainability, business management, and indicators and measures of sustainability are used as a frequent basis for making audit comparisons, and ecological and socio-economic considerations are always included.

Certification bodies are judged on their knowledge on sustainability issues and the application of their expertise to auditing through:

- A witnessed audit; or,

- A review of two audit reports.

This verification is usually carried out through a GSTC accreditation body. Awareness of micro- and macroeconomic principles, environmental risk problems and best practice in energy efficiency is required on behalf of the certification body audited. This verification concerns both the decision-makers and the auditors as part of the GSTC Approved Accreditation Manual Auditor for Audit Standards.

STEP-BY-STEP APPROACH TO AUDITING PART II

GSTC Certification Spectrum

Several certification options are available through GSTC, such as single certifications (for organizations operating out of one site), and multi-site certifications (organizations at more than one location). There are also certification programs with multi-level award systems, group certifications (organizations with numerous locations), and large-scale tourism operators' certifications for which a certification scheme is not yet available.

Certification programs with multi-level award systems operate on a 3 to 5 level scheme in which the lowest level must comply with all GSTC Criteria and must hold a valid GSTC status. These programs are widespread for hotels.

Group certification refers to individual businesses coming together to share the financial responsibilities and compliance requirements of an accredited third-party audit with internal inspections. Group certification is, therefore, an agreement amongst several businesses to adhere to a standard through which they are all connected. The process needs to involve group members, a group manager, an internal management system, and a certification body assessment for the performance of the group.

Group requirements
The certification body that audits the party needs to:

- Communicate information on standards and certification requirements for group certification, including any additional scheme-specific requirements;
- Put into place an enforceable certification agreement with the group manager to meet the standards and certification requirements;
- Monitor significant changes in the group production and management system and address any shortcomings in the system;
- Choose adequate personnel to assist with auditing activities and decision-making;
- Support certification body personnel with training to the certification of groups.

More information on group certification can be found in section 19 of the GSTC Accreditation Manual.

SUMMARY APPROACHES TO AUDITING

We have covered the basics of auditing. Auditing involves evaluating the information prepared by someone else and deciding the level of credibility of this information. The chapter's focus has been on certification auditing, which evaluates the correctness of reports prepared by tourism companies, groups, or certification programs presenting their position of sustainability. Certification auditing, like all auditing, requires a continuous transformation of auditors' skills based on rationality and specialized training. The purpose of an audit is to gather evidence and evaluate whether the evidence makes sense and to keep a backup that clients make in certification statements. Based on the auditor's assessment, a report is then issued that includes the auditor's opinion as to the accuracy of the statements. The report is sent to the decision-makers of the certification bodies who decide if certification is granted.

Benefits of ISO /IEC 17065 Managed Certification Systems

Tourism certification systems that are GSTC accredited follow ISO/IEC 17065 accreditation norms. ISO/IEC 17065 accreditation norms include required factors for the process, product, and contract compliance of the certification system, which depend mostly on the intent, method, and the result of the system. Thus, ISO/IEC 17065 norms require and allow the following:

- Required conformity of products and their manufacture;
- Required contractual conformity;
- Required efficiency of systems, particularly by relevant laws;
- Required systematic selection of scope for product groups and processes;
- Allowable assessment of customer requirements;
- Required auditor qualifications specific for product and process;
- Allowable surveillance of standardized rules by the scheme owner;
- Required annual certification cycle – providing valuable assurance of consistency.

The evaluation and assessment of certification programs has led to the calculation of whether the criteria are met and the estimate of when they can be achieved and surpassed. As a result, audit professionals with wide knowledge and experience in certification technology, environmental mechanisms, and sustainable procedures should carry out evaluations. Typically, several steps are taken in advance when evaluating a certification system, using different techniques, which in some cases may be advanced. The assessment itself is a dynamic exchange of data from site inspections, stakeholder data, and stakeholder inquiries between management, social, and environmental activities. Nonetheless, its economic success is a determining factor in assessing a certification program. The decision-making process usually involves compliance with requirements, which is one of the fundamental yet most challenging problems of certification systems.

Certification and Accreditation in Review

To understand the evolution of certification and accreditation as a standardized process, we need to investigate the motivations that drive the allocation of voluntary certification values in the face of improving tourism sustainability. Cassen (1987) and Elkington (1998) have attributed the different theoretical interpretations of sustainability to the triple-bottom-line approach. Many researchers use this as a frequent basis for making comparisons, and often, environmental, and social considerations are included (Bushell and Bricker, 2017; Haaland and Aas, 2010; LePree, 2009; Mahony, 2007; Molina Murillo, 2019; Whitt and Read, 2006). Thus, the fundamental purpose of certification systems is to achieve a greater extent of sustainable development of businesses and activities and to stimulate on-going measurement of the sustainability components of certification.

The absence of a generally accepted definition of sustainable development vastly complicates the measurement of sustainability. Gaps in the definition include the breadth of the indicators, the lack of specific sustainability performance measurements, the complexity and uncertainty of sustainability management practices, and the difficulty in measuring and implementing sustainability at various levels and scales. The lack of a single definition is transferred to all the sectors and disciplines that adopt sustainability. Thus, the ramifications of how to define and measure sustainability are seen in various guises. While each field is striving to reach the same goal, each has its own approach since the starting points and interim goals vary. This absence of consensus has led to a lack of consistency in implementation approaches and strategic directions, conflicting views, and less collaboration. Certification is no stranger to these shortfalls.

Since 2000, considerable effort has been made to realize sustainable tourism at regional, national, and local levels, and the scope is growing. The application of sustainable tourism by governments and industry often results in certification. Enhanced use of certification can result in bottom-up initiatives (Font et al., 2003), environmental performance (Ayuso, 2007), market positioning (Esparon et al., 2014), and community investments (Blackman et al., 2014), to name a few. Businesses are also motivated to join such programs due to the environmental education that accompanies the programs (Bien, 2007). However, such programs are not always within a business's reach. A barrier to certification is each stake-holder's concern with what seems to be its immediate interests, in this case, marketing. The implementation of successful certification programs is largely limited to "only a few individuals with personal interests in enhancing environmental management".

Furthermore, Bowman (2011) and Graci and Dodds (2015) find that effective certification programs need a simple implementation process but also the ability to overcome challenges while maintaining benefits. Many more studies illustrate certifications' restrictive support of business (Bricker and Schultz, 2011; Bucar et al., 2019; Dunk et al., 2016; Hunt and Durham, 2012; Klintman, 2012), although well-known benefits such as marketing and promotion are generally recognized (Font, 2002b; Margaryan and Stensland, 2017; Spenceley, 2017). In practice, however, few certification programs benefit from market reputation and recognition given high program proliferation – despite the low level of consumer interest (Thwaites, 2007) – and the paucity of external auditing assessments and accreditation (Font, 2002a; Haaland and Aas, 2010). A study that assessed compliance with National Ocean and Atmospheric Administration (NOAA) guidelines by dolphin-watching operators in clearwater (Whitt and Read, 2006) found that operators adhered to the guidelines about 60 percent of the time only. This issue extends beyond the tourism industry. A study comparing claims for sustainability with assurance for organic farming practices revealed a lack of record-keeping by farmers and insufficient testing to validate that standards are met. The organic farm industry is vulnerable to consumer backlash as is tourism. Some of the key industry standards are violated, thus diminishing the functional capability of certifications (Ascui et al., 2020). In this way, we need to switch from performance-oriented systems in stable and predictable settings to systems that have a much higher level of adaptability, flexibility and can change to meet new requirements.

EVALUATION OF TOURISM CERTIFICATION AUDITS

Certification Methodology

The approach for certification is process-based and performance-based (Honey, 2002). Things tend to complicate when, for example, interactions or cooperation between two forms of tourism (i.e. conventional and sustainable) or certification methodology (i.e. process and performance) create a so-called 'hybrid' model (Honey, 1999). The Green Globe system is a good example of the former. Until recently, Green Globe awarded corporate and destination level certification rather than a site-specific, individual unit, or product certification (a characteristic of ecotourism certification systems) (Honey, 2002). Businesses or destinations can receive Green Globe certification for the establishment of their process but not for the achievement of standards or benchmarks (Honey, 2002). Following their adaptation to the much-promoted sustainable tourism phenomenon, Green Globe is turning its traditional market profile into a more competitive one by prioritizing an approach to environmental management systems. To date, more than 100 Caribbean hotels and resorts are part of the Green Globe Certification Program (Green Globe, 2016).

Classification, Distribution, and Evaluation of Selective Tourism Certification Systems

More than 250 tourism certificates have been reported worldwide, yet only 34 are currently considered 'credible or workable'. A basic overview of several destination and industry-based certifications is given in Appendix A. These have been selected after a keyword search has been used to identify the most popular tourism certification websites, and the most relevant information for the search query. Apart from the scope and intent of each system, ecotourism indicators, including variations of such symbols, were considered to make categorization of certifications possible. Therefore, 17 of the 34 selected programs were classified as a hybrid, 13 as sustainable, and only 4 as ecotourism. It is nevertheless recommended that the operations and functions of each of these systems be studied in greater detail to strengthen the basis of this classification. Two of the 34 programs specialize in small-scale tourism accommodations such as ecolodges. These are Costa Rica's sustainable travel program (CST), and the Smart Voyageur program from Ecuador. The rest of the programs concentrate on certification for entire tourist destinations with a simultaneous focus on hotel chains, a common trait of certifications. The programs were compared against Honey's (2002) certification classification system, and the criteria of GSTC-Accredited, and GSTC-Recognized indexes were added.

Certification agreements may vary from public to private partnerships. For example, the Australian Eco Certification Program (NEAP) encompasses five different categories of certification from climate action certification to ecotourism guide certification operated by Savannah Guides, a private tour operator. Another example is Green Globe, whose certifications are run entirely by the Asia Pacific subsidiary of Earth Check ECO, and the Rainforest Alliance, whose certifications are provided by NEPCon, an international non-profit organization offering certification services through branches in 25 countries.

Of the 34 credible/workable certifications, 2 are GSTC-Accredited and 18 are GSTC-Recognized, which does not mean that the certification process is effective, but that the set of standards used to certify includes the necessary elements to ensure reliability (GSTC, 2020). Indeed, Australia's NEAP ensures evaluations only every three years (Honey and Rome, 2001). However, NEAP, along with Costa Rica's Certification for Sustainable Tourism (CST), is among the few programs that have gained widespread recognition, leaving a huge gap in most countries. CST is a well-respected certification program explicitly designed for ecotourism, and NEAP is a collaborative effort of the Australian Tour Operators Network and the Ecotourism Group of Australia (EAA). Some countries do not have a certification presence at all. For example, given its rapidly growing tourism sector and demand for sustainable tourism, South East Asia has no established tourism certification systems, nor does it adhere to any of those listed here. The only presence in this region is the Japan Ecolodge Association, which has now merged with the Asian Ecotourism Network (AEN) (Asian Ecotourism Network, 2019).

The next section of this chapter focuses on CST and how it operates. The assessment is focused on the importance and efficacy of CST in ensuring the right level of auditing performance and draws upon online CST resources and regulatory documents such as the CST Regulation Document (Reglamento del Programa de Sostenibilidad Turistica, n.d.).

COSTA RICA SUSTAINABLE TOURISM CERTIFICATION (CST)

Scope and Purpose

Established in the late 1990s by the Costa Rican Tourism Board (ICT), CST is the instrument by which Costa Rica continues to distinguish itself worldwide as a sustainable tourism destination. CST is used as a tool for providing reliable information on accredited tourism companies and organizations and for ensuring economic sustainability in the tourism industry. CST has now expanded beyond hotels to oversee environmental practices in a range of service industries such as food and beverage, transport, environmental conservation, travel agencies, theme parks, and hot springs. CST was initially established for sustainable tourism but now incorporates all facets of tourism, such as mass tourism, environmental tourism, and ecotourism. CST also works closely with the Blue Flag ecological program to certify Costa Rica's beaches.

Ownership

Strengthening CST through government ownership and government funding firmly established CST and has meant it has been commonly used for the last 20 years. For these reasons, Costa Rica's sustainable tourism system is regarded as iconic and is widely considered to be state of the art. However, CST was never introduced outside Costa Rica, despite it initially having been intended to be the official tourist standard of all seven countries in Central America (Honey, 2003a). A possible explanation is the voluntary nature of certification programs and the industry dealing with problems associated with implementation processes.

ICT funding covers CST certification expenses, rendering CST a free and open-source membership. Free membership is an incredibly rare credential, as participation in such services may amount to USD 15,000, e.g. the Green Globe (Rome et al., 2006). CST also benefits from international financial assistance through numerous contributions from the Spanish government, the Inter-American Development Bank, and the USAID-supported initiative PROARCA in Central America (Rome et al., 2006). This structure appears to be a source of criticism (Rome et al., 2006) due to lack of financial flexibility and allegations of greenwashing, but it did not prevent CST from recruiting a large portion of all service industries with almost 400 officially certified companies.

CST's strategic elements are the Costa Rican National Accreditation Board (NSA), which owns and controls intellectual rights in certification requirements, and the Central American Institute of Business Administration (INCAE), which provides adequate technical support to CST. NSA's full members include the Ministry of Tourism, the Ministry of Environment and Energy (MINAE), the National Centre for Biodiversity (INBio), the University of Costa Rica (UCR), and the Regional Chamber for Tourism (CANATUR).

Criteria

CST criteria refer to social, environmental, and economic aspects and are both performance- and process-based. The organizational components of the system are (1) physical-biological, (2) service facilities, (3) guest relations, and (4) socio-economic environment (Instituto Costarricense de Turismo, 2019a). The biological aspect is concerned with the effect on the natural environment. The infrastructure part looks at management policies and operating systems. The socio-economic aspect assesses the level of engagement with local communities, and finally, the external customer side analyzes the company relationships and successful partnership strategies of the firm.

CST criteria are translated into different types of performance indicators: basic standards, compulsory metrics, continuous measures, and external indicators (Instituto Costarricense de Turismo, 2019b). Basic metrics are used as a guide to meet the CST criteria. They must be real, reportable, and feasible. Compulsory requirements are minimum steps to accredit CST. External measures focus on social problems and community support.

The above indicators are used to compile a questionnaire of approximately 160 yes/no questions graded to determine the applicant's degree of impact on the country's natural and socio-economic resources. Each question is weighted on a scale of one to five that represents the level of CST experience, the most significant being five. In some cases, the quality of the experience is expressed in the form of nature services (i.e. parks, tours) and educational services offered (i.e. study or educational facilities, online pre-arrival courses on the local natural environment), the products and consumer goods purchased locally, and the company's appreciation for local culture. The final score of each variable is calculated using a formula. Enterprise productivity rates will vary from 20 to 100. The lowest final score for any of the four groups will be the company's overall sustainability ranking. For example, Level 1 companies meet between 20 and 40 percent of the requirements,

Level 3 companies 60–80 percent, and Level 5 companies meet 90 percent. Furthermore, applicants who comply with the CST requirements are chosen for the following levels: basic level – complete compliance with the required mandatory indicators; and elite level – compliance with 30 percent of the progress and continuity indicators and 70 percent of the external indicators.

This method of scoring is built on areas of operations where sustainability is advancing (Honey, 2003a). It is difficult to achieve. Consequently, unlike many guidelines, including the Green Globe Tourism Standard, the CST implementation process does not fail; instead, it motivates companies to fix shortcomings and develop operations continuously.

Competency Management

The CST Program and the CST Standard are the intellectual property of ICT, responsible for the creation, implementation, and promotion of CST following the rules of the ICT Board of Directors. According to the aims and goals of the ICT, the CST has a three-level functional framework: (1) Certification Department, responsible for the CST Professional Unit, and monitoring all aspects of CST auditing; (2) Department of Promotion and Marketing, responsible for sub-management and ICT advertisements; and (3) Technical Training team responsible for updating seminars, creating training curriculum, and promoting CST awareness.

The ICT Board of Directors of the CST Program supports the CST Standard and its subsequent modifications and updates. It enforces internal regulations needed to implement and operate the CST Program. The ICT General Management of the CST Program recommends to the Board of Directors the approval of the CST Standard corresponding to each tourism activity, including the introduction of new technical sustainability requirements, improvements or adjustments and the organization, management, and oversight of specialized units and institutional settings and access to resources. As Chief ICT Officer, ICT General Management submits recommendations for the organization, implementation, and development of the CST Program to the Board of Directors, where applicable. The ICT general management team also coordinates with the Deputy Management and Marketing Division, the CST technical unit and the administrative units deemed to be feasible and necessary for the needs of the CST, and the planning and management of the CST.

Structure and Functions of the Technical Unit of ICT

The ICT Certification Division oversees the CST technical unit program. The layout of the CST technical unit is as follows:

- Audit Team: a team made up of ICT officials certified as Lead Auditors in Integrated Quality Management Systems ISO 9001:2015 and Environmental Management Systems ISO 14001:2015, approved or revised by the Costa Rican Institute of Technical Standards (INTECO). The lead auditor may be assisted by other auditors, technical experts, or consultants when appointed to audit for CST.

- Training Team: a team of ICT officials assigned to produce content, workshops, and assistance for businesses or organizations interested in participating in the CST process and who will not be able to inspect applicants for the CST Program at the same time.

The CST technical unit has several functions, including evaluation of technologically necessary changes to the CST Standard, execution of formalities and procedures related to the award, extension, suspension, and revocation of the CST Certification, and supervision of the lead auditors. Further functions include compliance with the requirements, implementing the financial and logistical enabling processes for the CST Program objectives and public relations, and privacy in matters of interest to tourism companies or organizations.

Functions of the CST audit team include:

- Perform electronic inspection audits of CST accepted applicants to report compliance and recommendations. CST has an online inspection tool.
- Conduct spot checks and create an internal inspection database.
- Follow up on tourism companies and organizations.
- Maintain confidentiality in matters of the CST tourism companies or organizations.
- Suggest necessary changes or adjustments to the CST criteria requirements and indicators.
- Carry out other functions as delegated by the ICT's general administration.

The CST training team is responsible for training applicants through community workshops and developing analytical instruments to support the implementation of the CST Standard.

CST Technical Verification Commission (CTV-CST)

The CST Technical Verification Commission (CTV-CST) is affiliated with ICT and provides CST with economic, technical, and personnel support. The CTV-CST Commission is composed of a delegate and a replacement for each of the following entities:

- A delegate named by the ICT General Management, chairing the CTV-CST.
- A representative appointed by the Minister of Environment and Energy and one by the Ministry of Culture and Youth (MCJ).
- A delegate named jointly by the National Tourist Boards (CANATUR) and the National Chambers of Ecotourism and Sustainable Tourism (CANAECO).
- A delegate named jointly by INBio's Director General and the International Union for the Conservation of Nature (IUCN) Central Directorate.
- Joint delegate of INCAE and UCR.

Members of the CTV-CST carry out their duties ad hoc and are appointed for two years from the date on which they are sworn in. The vice president is appointed from among the CTV-CST's members. CTV-CST members preside over meetings in the absence of the president. The responsibilities of the CTV-CST Commission include the appointment, suspension, or cancellation of tourism companies or organizations to the CST; suggesting collaborations for the ICT Board of Directors with national and international organizations in support of the CST Program; ensuring correct application of the certification process for the CST; and maintaining strict compliance with the terms of CST regulations.

CTV-CST sessions are held at least once a month and more frequently when necessary. The minimum requirement for quorum is four participants. Agreements are reached by an absolute majority of the participating members, which is ratified at the next meeting as necessary by the General Law of the Public Administration unless two-thirds of the votes of all CTV-CST members are approved by the members present. In the case of a tie, the president has the deciding vote.

CST Audit Procedure

The CST audit procedures can last up to seven months per application. The process is divided into two phases: (1) assessment against the CST Standard through the online platform and procedure of the CST and (2) the general specifications of the registration process for participation in the CST. The answers provided by the applicant need to be reviewed by ICT when registering on the CST online platform. Applicants must register using the online CST platform. The electronic application must be submitted by the legal representative of the company or tourist association. The application serves as a statement and includes an undertaking before ICT to be up to date with the legal aspects applicable to the company. It is, therefore, an absolute requirement for the processing of the request. Companies and organizations must, therefore, comply with the legislation that relates to their service.

CST Audit Process

The CST initial audit process for certification has eight steps:

1. *Applicant registration*: requires a demonstrated tourist organization and an organization representative to manage the process. The deadline to complete this application is immediate.
2. *Self-appraisal*: a minimum of 150 indicators must be addressed one by one and supplemented by proof within three months.
3. *Audit request to the ICT technical unit*: once all questions have been answered and documentation is given in support of their responses, candidates can request the audit through the online portal.
4. *Application review period*: all evidence presented by the applicant is reviewed by the lead auditor assigned to the case, and a first report is made a maximum of 15 business days after application. The report is then forwarded to the applicant.
5. *Review period by the applicant*: applicant(s) have 15 days to review and table an action plan to address the questions raised in the lead auditor's report.
6. *Final review of the lead auditor*: a review of the corrections and the action plan by the lead auditor and the site visit are mandatory in the next 20 business days following the review period of the applicant.
7. *Completion of audit*: drafting and submitting the technical sheet to the CTV-CST Commission for consideration, together with the applicant's dossier within five business days after the previous stage.

8. *The CTV-CST Certification Process*: CTV-CST Commission assessment of the level of performance obtained. The decision goes public in 30 business days following the completion of the audit.

Audit Requirements

Tourism firms or organizations licensed and given CST will be re-audited in the following cases:

- At the end of two calendar years following certification.
- When the interested party registered with the CST demands a new assessment, which can be done six calendar months after they received the CST certificate.

Suspension and Revocation of the CST

CST is suspended or revoked in the following cases:

A. If a registered tourism company or organization fails to comply with the basic requirements of the CST Standard.
B. Use of the CST logo outside of its purpose, or for non-audited organizations or business activities not included in the CST.
C. When a tourism company or organization makes misleading claims about the CST received.
D. When a tourism company or organization fails to maintain its basic CST Standard.
E. Where the tourism company or organization does not provide proof of continued work in its action plan as requested by the auditor.

Suspension of the CST for six months results as a violation of the grounds set out in paragraphs (D) and (E). Suspension starts on the day following the notification of the final decision by the CTV-CST Committee. The corporation or agency involved will be removed from the system during the CST suspension period.

CST revocation is a result of a violation of the grounds set out in paragraphs (A), (B), and (C). Companies cannot reapply to the CST system until a term of two years has passed from the day following the notification of the decision by the CTV-CST Committee. Also, a new application for registration on the CST online platform must be launched by the tourism company or organization with the canceled CST for eventual reintegration into the CST online platform once the two-year duration stated above has expired.

When the CST is suspended or revoked, the interested party may file an appeal for revocation or replacement before the CST Technical Review Commission (CTV-CST) within three business days from the date of the contact of its solution agreement. If the CTV-CST Commission announces the cancellation or re-establishment of CST, the administrative route will have been exhausted.

Review of the CST Certification Process and Audit Method

The CST certification process consists of the CST Standard, an online assessment tool, a guide to the application of the CST Standard, verification processes, and an administrative framework consistent with international requirements. Since its launch in 1998, CST has progressed from initial site visits by ICT workers to technical seminars on the CST Standard, illustrating the CST Program. One dimension of transition is third-party auditors that CST now benefits from.

The auditing process begins with the initial CST Standard technical workshop. The purpose of the workshop is to direct companies and organizations in the implementation of the CST norm. The workshop is organized by the CST Technical Training Team several times each month and across different regions of Costa Rica, with five or more participants needed to hold the event.

First, following online registration and compliance with general standards and procedures, a formal evaluation is made based on guidelines and recommendations. This assessment forms the bulk of the multi-stage auditing process. Once the lead auditors have certified the implementation, a written report is sent to the CTV-CST Board. Electronic self-assessments allow companies to decide where changes are needed, and monitoring audits are expected to be repeated every six months to one year (Honey and Rome, 2001). The lead auditors are, therefore, responsible for collecting information and reviewing reports, proposing amendments, and preparing and submitting a final audit report to the CTV-CST Committee. The CTV-CST Committee reviews the entire audit process, ensures that the procedure is correct and complies with the CST standards and is responsible for awarding the CST.

The CTV-CST Commission has a technical role in the CST Program, and its members do not exceed five with representation from different program stakeholders. The CTV-CST Commission aims to build and protect program credibility. Therefore, the CTV-CST Commission manages the activities of the CST technical unit and is responsible for the effective implementation and application of the CST Standard. The technical unit hires and supervises auditors, assigns auditors to review applications, and prepares auditing schedules. ICT staff serve as auditors, but they could also be NSA employees. They follow international audit standards specifications and are accredited as lead auditors in ISO systems, approved by INTECO, and allowed to undergo CST training.

Unique accreditation solutions are used in different types of certification systems. Some options include major multinational certifiers that are interested in ISO 9001:2015 and 14001:2015 certification schemes. In general, third-party certifiers set their rates and operate anywhere in the world, although they are sometimes licensed by local agencies (Toth, 2000). Certification programs that use these accreditation types must recognize accredited facilities and review their certifiers and their auditors' results and make sure that their schemes are consistent with each other (Toth, 2000). This approach is not always simple, but it is the best way to evaluate certification programs because it delivers better performance results.

Authorization to participate in CST includes several conditions. CST is a free and government-owned system that uses its certification of compliance for the CST Standard due to having a well-developed infrastructure of ICT certified auditors and support for its operations from the NSA. Having a pool of auditors is a function of its governance structure. Private approved certifiers and qualified auditors are not readily available globally due to a lack of compliance tools, although they are a better cost choice than their international certifying counterparts (Toth, 2000). This issue is another challenge for audit participants to ensure the correct level of efficiency and effectiveness of audit activities.

CST is a GSTC-Recognized standard since 2012, expanding its evaluation tools to direct tourism businesses and organizations to continued development support and place communities as sustainable tourist destinations, and adding value in positioning and promotional activities. Inspired by the Sustainable Development Goals (SDGs) developed by both the World Tourism Organization (WTO) and the UN Environment Programme (UNEP), CST has a well-established system of free membership and independent accreditation. However, there have been debates on whether it is autonomous.

CONCLUSION

The tourism industry now has a global certification network in place. It is prolific to develop, implement, assess, and maintain quality in every industry, particularly in the field of tourism. The tourism sector is ready to change, contributing to calls for sustainability and social justice. In comparison, economic, social, and cultural differences create barriers at certification level, such as various limitations and lack of support for both qualification providers and those who want to follow them. It was suggested that the secret to certification is a repeated qualification exam that can help fulfill the criteria. Although there are successful certification templates, some of them fail. What makes a successful certificate authority are third-party examinations. By subscribing to third-party examinations, those seeking to establish a certification system to gain market recognition do so by adhering to international regulations that have nothing to do with them as a company.

This chapter presents observations on certification systems and auditing processes, including the similarities between what certification systems must be and how they are evaluated. When structurally symbiotic, audit and certification are strongly linked and co-dependent. Certification is a system that tracks, checks, and assures that an individual, product, process, or service meets quality. Audit includes evaluating evidence and determining whether the information is credible. This chapter focused on certification audits, which analyze the performance of reports produced by firms, organizations, or certification programs reflecting their sustainability status. Auditing requires ongoing efficiency-based auditing expertise, and specialized training. The purpose of the audit is to gather evidence, agree on the value of the evidence and establish confidence in the agreed statements of the clients. The auditor's analysis would then produce a report on the performance of the audit. The report is submitted to certification decision-makers deciding whether certification is issued.

Certifications started with a relatively simplified and in many respects more insightful and detailed view. As the sector grew, the issue moved to how companies and programs continue to maintain a certain level of standards and how to best comply with industry and market shifts when pursuing certification.

Summary Advantages and Disadvantages of Certification and Accreditation

Through the years and as the sector evolved, various certification and accreditation advantages and disadvantages were recognized, as shown in Table 25.1. Nevertheless, the specific nature and intent of the certification, accreditation and quality concepts are relevant to be noted. As explained above, a certification process is accepted while a standard is typically quantifiable at a level of quality. The certification process is recognized or approved, although standard consistency is usually measured. Accreditation thus refers to the process of qualification. By accepting and in certain cases even accrediting, accreditations will improve the certification programs.

Table 25.1   Advantages and disadvantages of certification and accreditation

Advantages	Disadvantages
Environmental performance	Lack of widespread credibility: Both accreditation agencies and certification programs work for a fixed purpose or a limited distance.
Market positioning	High costs: Accreditation and certification is costly to obtain and retain, and these expenses are often passed on to clients (e.g. certifying bodies) in the form of membership fees.
Environmental education	Complex structures: Hundreds of different certification and accreditation systems are available worldwide, some of which are run by certifying industry bodies, others by separate accreditation bodies, some by governments and some constitute a joint effort of such entities. Most developed countries tend only to formally recognize the degrees awarded by themselves; and do not readily accredit the credentials of even leading bodies in other nations.
Community investments	Limited advantages: Accreditation and registration are costly and complex. The more qualified / licensed a person or an organization is, the more effective the product or service the approved body offers, and the more costly they are but the benefits offered remain the same.

REFERENCES

Ascui, F., A. K. Farmery and F. Gale (2020) Comparing sustainability claims with assurance in organic agriculture standards. *Australasian Journal of Environmental Management*, 27(1), 22–41.

Asian Ecotourism Network (2019) International Board 2020. https://www.asianecotourism.org/aen -international-board2019.

Ayuso, S. (2007) Comparing voluntary policy instruments for sustainable tourism: The experience of the Spanish hotel sector. *Journal of Sustainable Tourism*, 15(2), 144–159.

Bien, A. (2007) *A Simple User's Guide to Certification for Sustainable Tourism and Ecotourism*. Handbook 1. Washington, DC: Center for Ecotourism and Sustainable Development.

Blackman, A., M. A. Naranjo, J. Robalino, F. Alpízar and J. Rivera (2014) Does tourism eco-certification pay? Costa Rica's blue flag program. *World Development*, 58, 41–52.

Bowman, K. S. (2011) Sustainable tourism certification and state capacity: Keep it local, simple, and fuzzy. *International Journal of Culture, Tourism and Hospitality Research*, 5(3), 269–281.

Bricker, K. S. and J. Schultz (2011) Sustainable tourism in the USA: A comparative look at the global sustainable tourism criteria. *Tourism Recreation Research*, 36(3), 215–229.

Bucar, K., D. Van Rheenen and Z. Hendija (2019) Ecolabelling in tourism: The disconnect between theory and practice. *Tourism*, 67(4), 365–374.

Bushell, R. and K. Bricker (2017) Tourism in protected areas: Developing meaningful standards. *Tourism and Hospitality Research*, 17(1), 106–120.

Buzard, M. (2015) ISO/IEC 17065: The standard for certification bodies – A review of the requirements. https://incompliancemag.com/article/isoiec-17065-the-standard-for-certification-bodies-a -review-of-the-key-requirements/.

Cassen, R. H. (1987) Our Common Future: Report of the World Commission on Environment and Development. *International Affairs*, 64(1), 126.

Dunk, R. M., S. A. Gillespie and D. Macleod (2016) Participation and retention in a green tourism certification scheme. *Journal of Sustainable Tourism*, 24(12), 1585–1603.

Elkington, J. (1998) Partnerships from *Cannibals with Forks: The Triple Bottom Line of 21st-Century Business. Environmental Quality Management*, 8(1), 37–51.

Esparon, M., E. Gyuris and N. Stoeckl (2014) Does ECO certification deliver benefits? An empirical investigation of visitors' perceptions of the importance of ECO certification's attributes and of operators' performance. *Journal of Sustainable Tourism*, 22(1), 148–169.

Font, X. (2002a) Critical review of certification and accreditation in sustainable tourism governance. Leeds Metropolitan University.

Font, X. (2002b) Environmental certification in tourism and hospitality: Progress, process and prospects. *Tourism Management*, 23(3), 197–205.

Font, X., R. Sanabria and E. Skinner (2003) Sustainable tourism and ecotourism certification: Raising standards and benefits. *Journal of Ecotourism*, 2(3), 213–218.

Global Ecotourism Network (2019) A basic overview of global certification. https://www.globalecotourismnetwork.org/certifications/.

Global Sustainable Tourism Council (GSTC) (2019) What is the GSTC? https://www.gstcouncil.org/about/about-us/.

Graci, S. and R. Dodds (2015) Certification and labelling. In C. M. Hall, S. Gössling and D. Scott (eds.), *The Routledge Handbook of Tourism and Sustainability* (pp. 200–208). London: Routledge.

Green Globe (2016) Green Globe certifies the greenest hotels & resorts in the Caribbean. https://greenglobe.com/caribbean-2/green-globe-certifies-the-greenest-hotels-resorts-in-the-caribbean.

GSTC (2011) *GSTC Accreditation Manual*. Washington, DC: Global Sustainable Tourism Council. https://www.gstcouncil.org/wp-content/uploads/2012/06/GSTC-Accredited-Manual-v2.2-29-2-2016.pdf.

GSTC (2020) Accreditation / Certification / Recognition. https://www.gstcouncil.org/certification/accreditation-certification-recognition/.

Haaland, H. and Ø. Aas (2010) Eco-tourism certification: Does it make a difference? A comparison of systems from Australia, Costa Rica and Sweden. *Scandinavian Journal of Hospitality and Tourism*, 10(3), 375–385.

Hamele, H. and D. Núñez (2016) Sustainability in tourism: A guide through the label jungle. https://destinet.eu/who-who/civil-society-ngos/ecotrans/publications/guide-through-label-jungle-1/download/en/5/Labelguide%202016%20EN.pdf?action=view.

Honey, M. (1999) Treading lightly? Ecotourism's impact on the environment. *Environment*, 41(5), 4–9.

Honey, M. (2002) *Ecotourism and Certification: Setting Standards in Practice*. Washington, DC: Island Press.

Honey, M. (2003a) Ensuring tourism contributes to conservation. In R. Bushell and P. Eagles (eds.), *Tourism and Protected Areas: Benefits Beyond Boundaries: The Vth IUCN World Parks Congress* (pp. 168–190). Wallingford: CABI.

Honey, M. (2003b) Protecting Eden: Setting green standards for the tourism industry. *Environment*, 45(6), 8–20.

Honey, M. and A. Rome (2001) *Protecting Paradise: Certification Programs for Sustainable Tourism and Ecotourism*. https://www.ips-dc.org.

Hunt, C. A. and W. H. Durham (2012) Shrouded in a fetishistic mist: Commoditisation of sustainability in tourism. *International Journal of Tourism Anthropology*, 2(4), 330–347.

Hunter, R. D. (2012) Conformity assessment. In R. D. Hunter, *Contracts for Engineers: Intellectual Property, Standards, and Ethics* (pp. 173–185). Boca Raton, FL: CRC Press.

Instituto Costarricense de Turismo (2019a) Certificación para la Sostenibilidad Turística (CST). https://www.turismo-sostenible.co.cr/images/PDF/ESTÁNDAR CST.pdf.

Instituto Costarricense de Turismo (2019b) Estandar CST Instructivo de Orientacion para el empresario. https://www.turismo-sostenible.co.cr/proceso-de-certificacion.

ISO (2004) *Guide 60: Conformity Assessment – Code of Good Practice*. Geneva: ISO.

ISO (2012) *ISO/IEC 17065: Requisitos Para Entidades Certificadoras de Produtos, Processos e Serviços*. Geneva: ISO.

Klintman, M. (2012) Issues of scale in the global accreditation of sustainable tourism schemes: Toward harmonized re-embeddedness? *Sustainability: Science, Practice, and Policy*, 8(1), 59–69.

LePree, J. (2009) Certifying sustainability: The efficacy of Costa Rica's certification for sustainable tourism. *Florida Atlantic Comparative Studies Journal*, 11, 57–78.

Mahony, K. (2007) Certification in the South African tourism industry: The case of Fair Trade in Tourism. *Development Southern Africa*, 24(3), 393–408.

Margaryan, L. and S. Stensland (2017) Sustainable by nature? The case of (non)adoption of eco-certification among the nature-based tourism companies in Scandinavia. *Journal of Cleaner Production*, 162, 559–567.

Molina Murillo, S. A. (2019) Certificación turística sostenible y los impactos socioeconómicos percibidos por hoteles en Costa Rica. *PASOS: Revista de Turismo y Patrimonio Cultural*, 17(2), 363–372.

Reglamento del Programa de Sostenibilidad Turistica (n.d.) https://www.ict.go.cr/es/documentos -institucionales/legislación-de-empresas/leyes-y-reglamentos/590-reglamento-para-el-otorgamiento -del-certificado-de-sostenibilidad-turistica/file.html.

Rome, A., A. Crabtree, A. Bien, H. Hamele and A. Spenceley (2006) Financial sustainability of sustainable tourism certification programs. *The International Ecotourism Society* (November).

Spenceley, A. (2017) Tourism certification in African hotels. https://pt.slideshare.net/TAPASGroup/ session3-01-anna-spenceley/1.

Thwaites, R. (2007) The Australian EcoCertification program (NEAP): Blazing a trail for ecotourism certification, but keeping on track? In R. Black and A. Crabtree (eds.), *Quality Assurance and Certification in Ecotourism* (pp. 435–463). Wallingford: CABI.

Toth, R. B. (2000) *Implementing a Worldwide Sustainable Tourism Certification System*. Alexandria, VA: R. B. Toth and Associates.

Whitt, A. D. and A. J. Read (2006) Assessing compliance to guidelines by dolphin-watching operators in Clearwater, Florida, USA. *Tourism in Marine Environments*, 3(2), 117–130.

APPENDIX A

Table 25A.1   Tourism and ecotourism certification programs

#	Name	Scope of certification	Year est.	Country of origin	Ownership	Operator	GSTC	Website
1	**Eco Certification Program (Previously NEAP)**	**Nature-based, ecotourism, and advanced ecotourism operators**	**1996**	**Australia**	**Ecotourism Australia (not-for-profit)**	**TiCSA (not-for-profit, member-based organization)**	**Y**	**https://www.ecotourism.org .au/our-certification-programs/ eco-certification/**
2	*Climate Action Certification*	*Hotels, attractions, tours, transport, restaurants, travel agents, tourism commissions and industry bodies*		*Australia*	*Ecotourism Australia*		Y	*https://www.ecotourism.org.au/ our-certification-programs/eco -certification-3/*
3	*EcoGuide Certification*	*Tour operators, protected area managers, and accredited training deliverers*		*Australia*	*Ecotourism Australia*	*Savannah Guides (not-for-profit)*	Y	*https://www.ecotourism.org.au/ our-certification-programs/eco -certification-5/*
4	**Ecotourism Destination Certification**	**Protected areas**		**Australia**	**Ecotourism Australia**		**Y**	**https://www.ecotourism.org .au/our-certification-programs- ecotourism-destination -certification/**
5	*Certification for Sustainable Tourism*	*Hotels, local tour operators, eco lodges, and car rentals*	*1995*	*Costa Rica*	*Costa Rican Tourism Institute (GOV)*		Y	*https://www.govisitcostarica .com/travelInfo/government -programs/cst-program.asp*
6	*EarthCheck Certified*	*Hotels, activities, attractions, restaurants, transport & mobility services and destinations*	*1987*	*Australia*	*EarthCheck (benchmarking certification and advisory group for travel and tourism; for profit)*		Y	*https://earthcheck.org*

#	Name	Scope of certification	Year est.	Country of origin	Ownership	Operator	GSTC	Website
7	**EarthCheck ECO**	**Ecotourism operators operating in both terrestrial and marine parks**	**1987**	**Australia**	**EarthCheck**		**Y**	**https://earthcheck.org/ products-services/certification/ earthcheck-eco/**
8	Green Globe Certification	Tour operators, travel agents, intermediaries; transport & mobility services; accommodation providers; restaurants & catering services; attractions; activities; shopping	1994	Australia	Green Globe (for profit)	Earthcheck (Asia Pacific)	Y	https://greenglobe.com/about/
9	*Sustainable Tourism Eco-Certification Program (STEP)*		*2002 – no longer certifying*	*USA*	*Sustainable Travel International (not-for-profit)*		*Y*	*https://sustainabletravel.org*
10	*Mountain IDEAL: Sustainable Destination*	*Mountain resort destinations*	*2017*	*USA*	*Partnership between Sustainable Travel International, the Town of Vail, and Walking Mountains Science Center*		*Y*	*https://sustainabletravel.org/ mountain-destination-standard/*
11	*Panama Tourism Sustainability Standard*	*Regulatory framework for hotels, tour guides, land and marine transportation providers, restaurants, tour operators and community-based tourism enterprises*	*2017*	*Panama*	*Sustainable Travel International*	*National protected area services concessions law-making compliance mandatory for any businesses operating within protected areas. It has also been endorsed by the Ministry of Trade and Industry*	*N*	*http://www.atp.gob.pa/ programas/norma-de -sostenibilidad-turistica & https://sustainabletravel.org/ places/panama/developing-a -sustainability-standard-for -tourism-enterprises-in-panama/*
12	Blue Certified Sustainable Scuba Diving	Dive operators and dive resorts		USA	Ocean First Institute (OFI) (not-for-profit)		N	https://www.bluecertified.org/ certification

#	Name	Scope of certification	Year est.	Country of origin	Ownership	Operator	GSTC	Website
13	Actively Green Business Certification	Businesses of any type can participate		USA	Walking Mountains Science Center (not-for-profit)	Sustainable Travel International	N	https://www.walkingmountains.org/project/actively-green/
14	Seychelles Sustainable Tourism Label	Applicable to hotels of all sizes	2011	Seychelles	Ministry of Tourism, Civil Aviation, Ports and Marine	Sustainable Travel International	Y	http://www.sstl.sc
15	Green Key	Accommodation providers; camping; restaurants & catering services; attractions; activities	Late 1990s	Denmark	Green Key Global (not-for-profit)		Y	https://www.greenkey.global
16	Green Seal	Hotel and lodging properties; industrial cleaning services; restaurants and food services	1989	USA	Green Seal (not-for-profit)		N	https://www.greenseal.org/certification/
17	*Mexican Regulación NMX-AA-133-SCFI-2006: Ecoturismo Sustentable*	*Regulatory*	*2006*	*Mexico*	*Secretaría de Medio Ambiente y Recursos Naturales (GOV)*		*N*	*http://legismex.mty.itesm.mx/normas/aa/nmx-aa-133-scfi-2013.pdf*
18	Green Pearl Unique Places	Green and eco friendly accommodation providers; camping; restaurants & catering services; attractions; destinations	2012	Germany	Green Pearls (for profit)		N	https://www.greenpearls.com
19	*EU Ecolabel*	*Accommodations*	*1992*	*EU*	*European Commission (GOV)*		*N*	*http://ec.europa.eu/environment/ecolabel/index_en.htm*
20	GREAT Green Deal (GGD)	Tour operators, travel agents, intermediaries; transport & mobility services; accommodation providers; restaurants & catering services; attractions	2010	Guatemala	Certifica (private consulting firm with representation in Guatemala and El Salvador)		Y	http://www.sellosverdes.com

#	Name	Scope of certification	Year est.	Country of origin	Ownership	Operator	GSTC	Website
21	Rainforest Alliance Certified Seal	Hotels, restaurants and inbound tour operators	2000	USA	Rainforest Alliance (NY) (not-for-profit)	NEPCon (authorized since 2018 Denmark, not-for-profit)	Y	https://www.nepcon.org/certification/tourism/nepcon-sustainable-tourism-certification-services
22	**Smart Voyager**	**Medium and small hotels and sites; eco-friendly accommodation (eco lodges); local food and beverages (restaurants/bars)**	**2000**	**Ecuador**	**Conservación y Desarrollo (not-for-profit)**		N	**http://www.smartvoyager.org/sample-page/**
23	Biosphere Responsible Tourism	Accommodations as well as restaurants, amusement parks, golf courses, attractions, and entire destinations	1995	Guatemala	Responsible Tourism Institute (RTI) (GOV)		Y	https://www.biospheretourism.com/en/biosphere-certification/83#bloque-400
24	Blue Flag	Transport & mobility services; attractions; activities; destinations	1987	Denmark	Foundation for Environmental Education (FEE) (not-for-profit)		N	https://www.blueflag.global
25	Green Tourism	Tour operators, travel agents, intermediaries; transport & mobility services; accommodation providers; camping; restaurants & catering services; attractions; activities; destinations	1997	UK	Green Business UK (private consulting company, for profit)		N	https://www.green-tourism.com/pages/home
26	QualityCoast Destination	Attractions and destinations	2007	Netherlands	Coastal & Marine Union - EUCC (not-for-profit)		N	http://www.qualitycoast.info/?page_id=110
27	TourCert	Tour operators, travel agents, intermediaries; accommodation providers; destinations	2004	Germany	TourCert Certification Council (consulting company, for profit)		Y	https://www.tourcert.org/en/

#	Name	Scope of certification	Year est.	Country of origin	Ownership	Operator	GSTC	Website
28	Green Destinations Certification Program	Destinations	2018	Netherlands	Green Destinations (not-for-profit)		Y	http://greendestinations.org/awards-certification/
29	ECOTEL Certification	Accommodation providers	1994 Unsure if still operates	USA	HVS International (for profit)		N	
30	Certified Green Hotel	Accommodation providers		Germany	Association of German Travel Management (VDR) (for profit)		N	https://www.certified.de
31	Fair Trade Tourism	Accommodation providers; restaurants, catering services; activities; attractions	2003	South Africa	Fair Trade Tourism (not-for-profit)		Y	http://www.fairtrade.travel/home/
32	*Responsible Tourism Tanzania*	*Accommodation providers*	*2011*	*Tanzania*	*Responsible Tourism Tanzania (not-for-profit)*		*N*	*https://www.rttz.org*
33	Green Star Hotels	Accommodation providers	2012	Egypt	AGEG Consultants e.G. (private consulting company, for profit)		Y	http://www.greenstarhotel.org
34	Hoteles mas Verdes	Accommodation providers	2012	Argentina	Tourism Hotels Association (not-for-profit)		Y	http://www.hotelesmasverdes.com.ar/quienes-somos/

Note: Programs in **bold** are Ecotourism Certification Programs. Programs in *italic* are Sustainable Tourism Certification Programs. Programs in roman are Hybrid Tourism Certification Programs.

Sources: Global Ecotourism Network (2019); Global Sustainable Tourism Council (GSTC) (2019); Hamele and Núñez (2016).

26. Case study research for sustainable tourism: towards inclusive community-based tourism

Regis Musavengane and Darlington Muzeza

CASE STUDY UNDERPINNINGS: DEFINITIONS AND CHARACTERISTICS

Calls for sustainable development are growing due to a number of contemporary phenomena, including, but not limited to, climate change, urbanization, and increasing inequality. Tourism is not immune to the call, and there is a need for sustainable tourism through inclusive or participatory approaches. The birth of sustainable tourism led to the emergence of several 'new' tourism approaches and forms such as pro-poor tourism, community-based tourism, green tourism, inclusive tourism and peace through tourism. Researchers are therefore encouraged to adopt participatory research approaches to ensure equal participation and fair representation of the populace or community members. The case study approach has been widely accepted as a suitable participatory research approach.

A case study can be defined "as an empirical inquiry that investigates a contemporary phenomenon within its real-life context; when the boundaries between phenomenon and context are not evident; and in which multiple sources of evidence are used" (Yin, 1984, p. 23). Mesec (1998, p. 383) defined it "as a description and analysis of an individual matter or case ... with the purpose to identify variables, structures, forms and orders of interaction between the participants in the situation (theoretical purpose), or, to assess the performance of work or progress in development (practical purpose)". Sagadin (1991, p. 31) states that a "case study is used when we analyse and describe ... a group of people ... individual institutions or a problem (or several problems), process, phenomenon or event in a particular institution, etc. in detail".

The case study approach is most ideal when one seeks answers to the 'why' and 'how' related questions (Yin, 2009). For example, in explanatory research, a case study enables an investigation of causal relationships. For instance, how is 'A' related to 'B' or why is there a change in 'B' if 'A' is altered? A case study approach can also be used when a holistic understanding is needed, as it facilitates a holistic perspective on causality since it examines the case as a specific whole (George and Bennett, 2005). Furthermore, case studies are mostly preferred when there are multiple factors that seem to contribute to a certain effect or event. Thus, the case study can facilitate the investigation of causal complexities. Case studies can also be used to obtain answers to process-related questions because the use of multiple data sources supports the retrospective investigation of events.

From the above definitions, it can be deduced that there is an agreement of real-life engagement in case studies. Due to this, the case study method provides data of particular units which enables researchers to closely examine specifics within a small geographical area. Based

475

on our wide experience in community-based tourism, and as noted by Gomm et al. (2000) common features of the case study include:

1. In-depth study of a small number of cases facilitates in observing the events, collecting data, analysing information, and reporting the results over a long period.
2. Data are collected and analysed about a large number of features of each case.
3. Cases are studied in their real-life context; understanding how the case influences and is influenced by its context is often of central interest to case researchers.
4. Cases are naturally occurring in the sense that they are not manipulated as in an experiment.
5. The use of multiple sources of data including interviews, observation, archival documents and even physical artefacts to allow triangulation of findings.

Furthermore, the US General Accounting Office (GAO) (1990) provides a classification of six types of case studies; some of which will be discussed in detail below:

1. Illustrative – the case study dwells much in realism and is descriptive, provides detailed analysis using in-depth examples on programs and policies.
2. Exploratory – it is also descriptive; however, it does not have clear answers. It generates hypotheses that will be used later for further investigations.
3. Critical instance – this examines a single occurrence. Oftentimes the case will be unique and/or serves as a critical test of an assertion about a strategy, problem or program.
4. Program implementation – it is most ideal for operational purposes and applied at several sites. It is normative in nature, meaning it focuses on evaluations.
5. Program effects – this is the case study that focuses on the cause and effect approach where multi-site and multi-method assessments are used.
6. Cumulative – this collates findings from different case studies to respond to an evaluation question, whether descriptive, normative or cause-and-effect.

CASE STUDY CATEGORIES

Having outlined the definitions of case studies and common features, it is important to know how they are categorized and when to use a particular type of case study. Yin (1984) noted three case study categories, namely exploratory, descriptive and explanatory. First, exploratory case study seeks to explore a phenomenon in the data to pursue the point(s) of interest to the researcher. For example, a community-based tourism researcher may conduct an exploratory case study on the participation of community members in the decision-making process of their community game reserve. The researcher may ask general questions such as, "Does the game reserve have a policy on inclusion of community members in decision-making?", and "If so, is it being implemented?" If it is being implemented, "How often do you include community members? Do they all participate or there is representation?" If there is representation, "How do you select the representatives?" These general questions are meant to create an opportunity for the researcher to examine deeply a specific phenomenon. This may require undertaking prior fieldwork and small-scale data collection before proposing research questions or hypotheses. This will further assist in the preparation of a framework of the study. McDonough and

McDonough (1997) classify the pilot study as an example of an exploratory case study and essential to determine the research protocol to follow.

Second, descriptive case studies describe the characteristics of phenomena which occur within the data set. For instance, what different participatory strategies are used by the managers to involve community members in the game reserve decision-making process? Such studies tend to help to generate differences between individual cases (Gerring, 2004). It should be the goal of the researcher to describe the data as they occur. Thus, descriptive case studies are mainly presented in a narrative form as opposed to descriptive (McDonough and McDonough, 1997). The challenge faced with researchers adopting the descriptive case study is the failure to develop a strong descriptive theory to support the description of the phenomenon or case/story. This will consequently cause problems during the project as there is a high possibility of a lack of rigour in the description.

Third, explanatory case studies closely examine the data at both surface and deep level to establish the phenomenon in the data. For example, a researcher may ask the reason as to why the game reserve management used a *representation* strategy in involving community members in the decision-making process. Based on the data, a theory is then formulated and tested by the researcher. Furthermore, explanatory case studies may be used to investigate causal relationships to investigate a particular phenomenon in complex cases and where a large number of cases are involved. The three main theories to explain these complex phenomenon are: a knowledge-driven theory, a problem-solving theory, and a social-interaction theory (Yin and Moore, 1987). The knowledge-driven theory states that the conservation or community-based tourism product we see is a result of ideas and discoveries from basic research. The same notions apply to problem-solving theory. However, in this theory, products are not a result of research but are obtained from external sources. Lastly, the social interaction theory suggests that social networks and interactions are key in developing tourism products and solving complex problems associated with collaborative management of natural resources.

ADVANTAGES AND DISADVANTAGES OF CASE STUDY

Case studies have many advantages and disadvantages. It is therefore important to look at them as you consider choosing the appropriate approach for community-based tourism research.

Advantages

Adaptability: First, case studies are regarded as having strength in their adaptability to different types of research questions (Yin, 2009). The questions can be open or closed. Case studies further allow the obtaining of data from multiple sources which allows triangulation of findings. This will aid in-depth analysis of a specific phenomenon, particularly in situations where there are a high number of variables of interest.

Conceptual validity (CV): CV refers to the identification and measurement of specific indicators that present the concepts envisaged to be measured by the researcher (Starman, 2013). Many community-based tourism researchers or social scientists are interested in understanding issues such as democracy, inclusiveness, exclusion, power-play and corruption. Often, these concepts are difficult to measure; it is imperative for researchers to undertake a contextualized comparison, which automatically searches for analytically equivalent phenomena even if they are expressed in different terms and contexts. It can be difficult to obtain the salient details of these contextual factors in quantitative research, but much easier in qualitative, in particular case studies.

Deriving new hypotheses: inductive studies are common in community-based tourism, where researchers have to develop assumptions or hypotheses to form the basis of research. Case studies appear to be very suitable for serving the heuristic purpose of identifying specific variables to establish 'new' hypotheses. Furthermore, case studies are more suitable in analysing complex events qualitatively because they do not require many cases nor do they have a limit of variables. Case studies can lead to the identification of new hypotheses as open-ended interviews provide an opportunity to identify omitted variables.

Exploring causal mechanisms: cause and effect analysis is important to establish the relationship between variables. Case studies tend to examine the causation or linkages between variables in individual cases in detail. With case studies, it will be possible to identify any unexpected aspect of the operation of a particular causal mechanism. It is important to note that quantitative research can also identify causality; however, it is incapable of taking into account contextual factors other than those that are codified within the variables being measured; in this situation, many additional variables that might also be contextually important are missing.

Disadvantages

Regardless of the fact that case studies offer a number of advantages, they also have their own disadvantages. Researchers have to know these and devise plans in advance on how to mitigate these possible drawbacks. Disadvantages include:

- *Generalization* – results are difficult to generalize to a wider population
- *Subjective* – researcher's own subjective feelings may influence the results
- *Replication* – difficult to replicate
- *Time* – Time consuming and the process can be costly.

CASE STUDY STEP-BY-STEP APPROACH FOR COMMUNITY-BASED TOURISM RESEARCH

The following six-step case study approach postulated by Yin (2009) can be used in community-based tourism. The steps are presented alongside practical community-based tourism examples undertaken by us, the authors, since the year 2013. It is our belief that these examples will help you to understand the practical steps for undertaking case study in community set-ups.

Step 1: Plan

Planning is critical in undertaking case studies, as it sets the path the study will follow. One of the most important considerations is to provide detailed explanation of methods to the respondents or subjects, and articulate a wide range of potential experiences participants may go through as a necessary measure to ensure that they are fully aware and informed of the processes (Haines, 2017). In many cases, ethical clearance is usually sought ahead of the study being implemented and all the social safeguards to protect participants or respondents should be satisfied. It is important also that thorough consideration is given to complex ethical issues related to the nature of participants' involvement, the research subject relevance and the design, recruitment, techniques of collection of data and portrayal of participants in the eventual case report. When dealing with vulnerable groups in a case study, central ethical issues concern adhering to informed consent, risk of harm mitigation to protect the participants, confidentiality and anonymity (see Box 26.1). This will ensure that statements are not attributed to specific named people, lest this causes problems for them. Avoiding conflict of interest must also be considered as part of a plan on how these ethical issues can be managed during case study research.

BOX 26.1 COMMUNITY-BASED TOURISM CASE STUDY ETHICAL CONSIDERATIONS

General Ethics Documentation for Case Study

Gathering data from human participants requires fair treatment and meeting ethical standards. Thus, full disclosure of research information to participants is a requirement, without coercion and taking into account their right to privacy. Obtain clearance from local authorities such as Rural District Councils, government institutions and non-governmental organizations including community leaders. The following two forms are essential:

(a) The participant information sheet (see Appendix A) – a short letter, written by the researcher to the participant informing him/her about the study.
(b) The formal consent form (see Appendix B) – a document that will be signed by participants who agree to become involved in the study. NB: this is NOT the same as the letter of permission.

Ethical Consideration for the Vulnerable

(a) Low income groups

Oftentimes, necessity threatens ethical principles in case study research. People with minimal access to resources tend to be more vulnerable in the face of researchers or sponsors who can meet their point of need. It is therefore unethical to exclude participants on the basis of unmet or met needs, as this will increase disparity.

Tools to overcome challenges surrounding vulnerable communities:

• Select groups, communities and individuals on a scientific basis, not because their economic or social status makes them more submissive.
• Always remember that it is not burdensome to undertake research in low-income communities compared to other communities.
• Race, ethnicity, economic or social characteristics should not be used as inclusion or exclusion criteria. Overrepresentation should be justified.

- Fair selection of the subjects should be done. For example, one should not be turned away on the basis that she/he has higher income regardless of meeting the criteria.
- Real expectations should be clear to participants. Furnish them with adequate information to avoid over expectation and avoid unrealistic promises. For example, information on the duration of the study, who will benefit at the end, what will happen at the end of the study, what are the risks involved in participating and not participating in the study.

(b) Low literacy population

Most people in rural communities where community-based tourism is vibrant have low literacy levels. Literacy is described as the ability to understand a short, simple sentence without assistance and ability to read and write. If one has a low literacy level it poses communication challenges.

Tools to overcome low literacy challenges:

- Always remember that low literacy does not translate to poor intelligence.
- Employ teaching and learning strategies, where possible.
- Teach-back strategy – whereby the researcher presents the study to the potential participants and asks them to remember and explain in their own words what they learned.

(c) Subordinate subjects

A subordinate subject is a person with a lower job title, position or rank at an organization or community than the researcher or investigator who will perform or promote the research. Subordinates may feel uneasy to refuse to participate as it may affect their job evaluations. Moreover, their recruitment may be the result of undue influence or coercion.

Tools for selecting subordinate subjects:

- Explain to subordinates that participation is optional and acceptance or rejection to participate will not have an influence in future practices or endeavours. In other words, the principle of respect for persons should be upheld, such that they can act autonomously.
- Provide potential subjects with enough information, including specific aims, anticipated benefits, and possible risks.
- When recruiting subjects, superiors shall not directly request subordinates to sign participation forms. Instead, recruit a neutral person to do the task.
- Guarantee confidentiality of data.

Identification of the research questions or other rationales for doing a case study are done at this stage. At this point, the researcher has to understand the strengths and limitations of the study (see above). When stating the research objectives the researcher should ensure that the objectives are SMART (i.e. specific, measurable, attainable, realistic and time-bound). Clearly defining the research problem is probably the most important step in the entire tourism research project.

During this planning stage, researchers should ensure that there is alignment between research questions and the case study method. There are several factors influencing the choice of the research method to adopt in a specific case study. The most notable include:

1. The type of research question
2. The control an investigator has over actual behavioural events, and
3. The focus on contemporary as opposed to historical phenomena (Yin, 2009).

These factors point to the fact that case study may not be as simple as it may appear at face value. Hence the importance for researchers to embrace the complexities of doing case study research. The main challenge is for researchers to be independent and undertake the study without bias. It is therefore important to situate the researcher in the study. An extract in Box 26.2 can serve as an example of how researchers can situate themselves in community-based tourism research in relation to their race.

BOX 26.2 SITUATING THE RESEARCHERS AND THEIR RACE IN THE STUDY: SOMKHANDA GAME RESERVE, SOUTH AFRICA

The first author was an external researcher, while the second author was an internal researcher involved in the operations of the conservation organization managing the reserve. It was therefore imperative to clarify the roles of the researchers in the study and how their emic and etic perspectives did, or did not, influence the data analysis and findings.

The race of an interviewer has a high probability to affect interview responses, as respondents tend to adjust their responses to suit or satisfy the expectations of the interviewer (Januszka et al., 2007). This may lead to bias, whether in a focus group, survey or one-to-one interview. In this case study, the first author (Black African) negotiated access to the community through community leaders and the Somkhanda Game Reserve founder. It is important to point out that the first author was involved to a greater extent in the interviewing process. He interviewed and held focus group meetings with them as the respondents would feel more comfortable sharing details with a fellow Black person due to past negative experiences between Blacks and Whites during Apartheid. The second author, a White male, interviewed most of the White respondents, who were mainly in management at the Somkhanda Game Reserve.

Both researchers took notes before and during the interview and observation processes. Some of these notes described what was being observed directly (emic notes), while others detailed the feelings being observed (etic notes) (Gay and Airasian, 2003). The emic notes largely focused on what the researchers observed and recorded on their voice recorders and in their research diaries. Their cultural values and backgrounds influenced their feelings and eventually their etic notes. This assisted the researchers to make sense of, or analyse the views of, the respondents objectively. Recording both emic and etic notes enriched their deep understanding of what transpired during the interviews. Combining the cultural perspectives of both authors (Black African and White) brought diversity and a balance to the analysis of the role of social capital in building community resilience in a land reformed community.

Source: Musavengane and Kloppers (2020).

Step 2: Design

The second step in the qualitative case study for community-based tourism is the research design. It aims at defining the unit of analysis and the likely cases to be studied. It involves developing propositions and identifying underlying issues anticipated in the study. This is the stage where the researcher also identifies the case design (i.e. single, multiple, holistic or embedded) and develops procedures to enhance and maintain the quality of the case study design. Research design logically links the research questions to the research conclusions through the steps undertaken during data collection and data analysis.

The *first step* in the research design is the formulation of appropriate research questions that shape the structure of the study. At this stage, the researcher should clearly define what the 'cases' in their case study will be, for example, whether they are individuals, households, organizations, events and so on. The researcher's cases form the unit of analysis for the study (Yin, 2009). The researcher's research questions should also clarify what aspects of the cases are of interest; it will not be feasible to investigate every aspect of the chosen cases.

The *second step* in the research design is selecting cases. At this stage two main decisions are made, what cases and how many cases to study. Reservations have been made by some practitioners and authors on the use of single cases. Main concerns are on issues about the representativeness of the chosen case, the extent to which generalizability is possible and the vulnerability to confirmation bias, the tendency for the collection or analysis of data to be biased to confirm the researcher's preconceived opinion. The risk may be too visible or exposed when researchers are doing the case study at their organizations or communities. It is also difficult to carry out a comparative analysis with a single case study. Some of the reasons suggested by Yin (2009) for single-case design include:

1. That the case is critical in some way (e.g. in theory testing)
2. That it is either unique or typical, or
3. That it is revelatory (previously inaccessible to researchers).

When using a single case it is important to enhance the reliability and validity of the data by strengthening the data collection process and techniques.

Apart from single cases, multiple cases which are more compelling and robust can be used. Multiple cases allow for cross-case comparison analysis. Another option is to adopt a research design that focuses on a single case study with various departments or sub-units to attend to (Yin, 2009). For example, the case study might be of a single community-based tourism project but could analyse the experience of individual projects within the overall project. The projects, therefore, become the unit of analysis for the research.

Individual cases may be selected based on *convenience*, *purpose*, and *probability* (see Table 26.1).

The *third step* of the research design is to prepare a case study protocol. A case study protocol should be done before embarking on the field research. It is a written statement of what the researcher aims to achieve and how he/she is planning to achieve it; in other words, it is a sort of a project plan for the researcher's case study fieldwork. Specifically, the case study protocol provides the linkages between the researcher's research questions, the data required to obtain the answers to those questions, and the data collection and analysis plan. When preparing the protocol the researcher should be able to anticipate potential problems in the proposed research and devise possible mitigation approaches. The aim is to enhance systematic data

Table 26.1   Instance selection in case studies

Selection basis	When to use and what questions it can answer
Convenience	The case was selected because it was expedient for data collection purposes.
Purpose:	The reason for selecting the case:
Bracketing	What is happening at extremes? What explains such differences?
Best Cases	What accounts for an effective programme?
Worst Cases	Why isn't the programme working?
Cluster	How do different types of programmes compare with each other?
Representative	Instances chosen to represent important variations.
Typical	Instance chosen to represent a typical case.
Special Interest	Instances chosen based on an unusual/special attribute.
Probability	What is happening in the programme as a whole, and why?

Source: GAO (1990, p. 25).

Table 26.2   Case study protocol topics

Topic	Contents
Overview	A statement of the overall aims of the research.
Field procedures	The procedures to be adopted during the field research, including how to gain access, how to capture data, time plan for data collection, etc. for each case.
Research questions	The specific research questions should be stated, including clear links to the theory/literature where appropriate.
Data collection matrix	A matrix (table) can be used to show the types of evidence to be collected, along with their relationships to each other and the research questions identified above.
Data analysis and case study reports	How you will analyse individual cases, conduct cross-case analysis and create the case study reports.

Source: Based on Remenyi et al. (1998) and Yin (2009).

collection during the research process, whilst leaving room for the researcher's flexibility to address emerging issues during fieldwork. A case protocol is mostly useful in team-based projects for easy coordination of activities within a team, especially if there are a number of sites for data collection. Table 26.2 shows typical headings for a case study protocol.

Step 3: Prepare

The prepare stage focuses on sharpening the research skills of the case study researcher or investigator. Since cases differ from each other, at this stage training for a specific case study is provided. Specific training is needed in developing a case study protocol, conducting a pilot case, and gaining any relevant approvals (Yin, 2009). At this preparation stage, the case study composition team should be established; also relevant issues in the case study design are undertaken at this stage. The researcher should also endeavour to address any such issues before starting the data collection stage.

As noted by Yin (2009), the researcher should familiarize himself/herself with the study domain to understand the key issues relevant to the study. This said, the researcher should:

- Know the reasons why the study is being done;
- Know the critical issues that will be sought in the specific case;
- Be able to establish anticipated empirical variations;

- Be able to interpret the information in real-time and be flexible to adjust data collection activities to suit the case study.

During the preparation stage it is critical to undertake pilot case studies to refine the "data collection plans with respect to both the content of the data and the procedures to be followed" (Yin, 2009, p. 92). Pilot study reports should outline the strengths and weaknesses of the study design and flag areas that need to be looked at again. Furthermore, the researcher should obtain ethical clearance from potential respondents and representative organizations. An agreement regarding any limitations on the disclosure of data, identities, and findings should be highlighted.

Step 4: Collect

When a case study protocol is clear, the researcher may proceed to the collect stage to gather data. It is imperative to create a case study database as varied data may be obtained from multiple sources of evidence and it helps to maintain a chain of evidence which is auditable (GAO, 1990; Miles and Huberman, 1994; Yin, 2009). Case studies allow researchers to collect direct evidence, and data are analysed as they become available. The emerging results will then shape the next data collection step to be undertaken (Dooley, 2002). At this data collection stage, the researcher must guard against bias which may emanate from personal values and assumptions, which can unduly influence data collection and analysis. It is therefore important to take into account the potential influences of the researchers on the case study research process as well as preconceived ideas as to the response/results that will be obtained (see Table 26.1).

   Case study data may be collected through *documents*, *archival records*, *interviews*, *direct observations*, and *physical artefacts* (Yin, 2009). As much as document analysis is good, the researchers should always be cautious when reviewing documents as they may not always reflect the accurate situation on the ground due to outdated policies or documentation. However, archival records tend to be deemed more reliable as they are mainly used for record-keeping. In this regard, having a case study database allows researchers to develop an audit trail from data collection through analysis to conclusions. A case study database may include:

- Interview transcripts
- Investigator notes
- Documentary evidence
- Preliminary analyses.

Having a case study database enhances the reliability of the study. All items in the database should be categorized, indexed, dated and cross-referenced to facilitate easy retrieval.

   Case study data can be collected through multiple approaches to enable triangulation and the search of areas of convergence and divergence in the study. The most common approach to obtain data in a case study is through interviews (see Table 26.3).

   Interviews can be *structured*, *semi-structured*, or *unstructured*:

- *Structured interviews* involve the use of predefined questions, with a limited set of response categories to obtain data from respondents. The responses are coded by the interviewer based on an already established coding scheme (Miles and Huberman, 1994).

Table 26.3   *Interview process*

Step	Description
Orientation	Introductions and exchange of contact details.
	Description of the study and the interview process.
	Clarification of any expectations regarding non-attribution, sharing of data, the consent to
	participate, and any other issues relevant to participation.
Information gathering	The interviewer uses a questionnaire to guide the interview and to record responses.
Closing	The interviewer reviews the key points, any issues, and/or action items, and confirms accuracy
	with the respondent. The interviewee is invited to provide feedback on the interview process. The
	interviewer thanks the interviewee and seeks permission for any future contact.

Source: Kasunic (2010, p. 77).

- *Semi-structured interviews,* or focused interviews, can be more flexible and allow the researcher to better understand the perspective of the interviewees by refocusing the questions, or prompting for more information, if something interesting or novel emerges.
- *Unstructured interviews* do not have predefined answer categories. They utilize open-ended questions, thus allowing for even more flexibility. While such interviews are least efficient, they may generate rich data and uncover surprising/unexpected evidence (Daymon and Holloway, 2002). It is recommended for interviewers to mainly use probe questions, which start with "How ...?" and cannot be answered with a "yes" or a "no", in unstructured interviews.

Regarding the number of interviews to undertake, it depends on the number of study units and the phenomena under investigation, the scope of the study and timeframe. Nevertheless, in community-based tourism, for a case study to be deemed suitable, it is recommended to have more than 15 respondents/participants. Where possible two interviewers will be ideal to enhance the authenticity of the results as it will be more effective to compare notes and establish common themes. Common interview pitfalls include:

1. Misinterpretation/misunderstanding of questions and answers (perhaps due to personal prejudices or convictions);
2. Leading/loaded questions and interjecting comments that can bias the response;
3. Listening only to what is easy to understand or what the researcher wants to hear based on preconceptions;
4. Misinterpretation or translation can lead to collection of inaccurate data or wrong interpretation of data;
5. Making assumptions about what the interviewee may answer based on prior responses; and
6. Posing of why questions may create defensiveness on the part of the interviewees.

A number of ways that researchers can be good interviewers include:

1. Interviewers should avoid reading questions but try and memorize the first few and refer to the instrument only occasionally;
2. Interviewers should use eye contact and a confident manner to set the tone for the interview and help establish rapport with the respondent;
3. When tempted to omit a question because they think they already know the answer, interviewers should confirm their assumptions with the interviewee;

Table 26.4   *Do's and don'ts for the interviewer*

Do's	• Focus on the primary objective of the meeting. • Ask every question. • Manage time so that all questions are covered during the interview. • Record responses on the interview form. • Do not rely on an audio recording device.
Don'ts	• Allow personal stories to take up valuable time. • Diverge too far from the questionnaire. • Allow your personal interests to become part of the discussion.

Source: Kasunic (2010, p. 83).

4. When brief or ambiguous answers are provided, the interviewer should try to elicit more detail. The strategies that can be used are: silent probe (i.e. pause and wait), overt encouragement (e.g. saying "uh-huh" or "okay"), asking for elaboration, asking for clarification, repetition (verify understanding by paraphrasing interviewee responses).

Table 26.4 shows the do's and don'ts of the researcher/interviewer.

In addition to the interview, the interviewer should undertake a review of any actions and issues that were identified during the meeting. Upon completion of the interview, researchers should discuss it as soon as possible to compare impressions and identify any potential misunderstandings.

In collecting data, the researchers may consider using the Schutte Scale tool.

Schutte Scale: Understanding how it works – practical application

The use of the Schutte Scale is important because the researcher can examine complex aspects such as attitudes, perceptions, preferences and behaviour of community members and stakeholders. The Schutte Scale (see Figure 26.1) is used by participants to convey a message to the researcher. The Schutte Scale will have numbers on the side viewable to the researcher and on the side of the participant it has quantities in non-numeral form but weights. In other words, it is designed such that one side with numeric calibrations faces the interviewer and the other side that is dotted faces the respondent as shown in the figure. The respondent (interviewee) holds the Schutte Scale such that the dotted side faces the respondent when questions are asked. The more the level of satisfaction or top priority something is, the more the indicator is moved towards the denser-filled dots on the instrument. The less important something is, the more the indicator is moved towards the less dense-dot section of the instrument. The interviewer records the preferences of each respondent by simply tabulating numbers indicated on the side facing him or her from the respondents.

As a guide, for example, questions that can be best answered using the Schutte Scale are:

1. What is your perception about local participation in the Great Limpopo Transfrontier Park (GLTP) establishment consultation process for sustainable wildlife management and integrative tourism development to benefit communities?
2. What are your attitudes (positive or negative) about your participation and representation in the GLTP governance?
3. What is your level of satisfaction concerning community involvement in the GLTP's biodiversity planning, governance and project implementation?

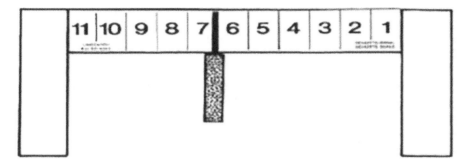

The side that faces the researcher (1)

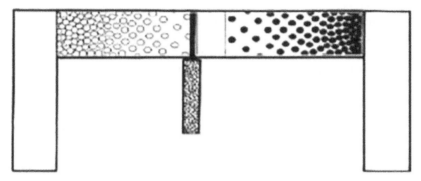

The side that faces the interviewee (2)

Source: Adapted and applied in the field with permission from Schutte (2000, p. 12).

Figure 26.1   The Schutte Scale instrument

According to Schutte (2000, p. 12), the instrument allows ranking of issues without having to weigh items against each other, which is a further advantage that enables community develop-ment practitioners, tourism and conservation planners to obtain valuable qualitative data. The Schutte Scale provides a number of advantages to the researcher. First, it is regarded as a flex-ible instrument malleable enough for use in interdisciplinary research to obtain community perspectives. Schutte (2000) noted that applying the technique is relatively cheap, and presents a reliable picture of the actual needs of the target community. Essentially, on a comparative basis, less time and money is needed than in door-to-door surveys. Moreover, the procedure is simple such that minimal training is required. The trainees immediately participate in the discussions using the Schutte Scale, and no doubt, it also gives the community members a sense of ownership of the process and the exercise encourages alertness such that individuals do not lose track of the discussion process. Furthermore, Schutte (2000) highlighted that the instrument is suitable for data collection that helps to determine priorities of communities, which can be used as projective data of the overall community's perceptions.

Moreover, respondents in the same geographical proximity can express not only their own opinions but respond on behalf of other people from the same neighbourhood. Ultimately, the technique produces statistical data, which helps in collecting, tabulating and analysing local attitudes and feelings to complement household survey questionnaire responses where variables would have been covered by other scale measurements. Generally sensitive aspects such as perceptions and feelings of people regarding skewed benefit streams between the communities and state-driven enterprises, are fluid and sometimes very difficult to obtain from the community members including their validation from questionnaires in a scale of 'strongly agreeing, agreeing and not agreeing' on given varying responses. The Schutte Scale addresses that discrepancy by ensuring that the community participants provide immediate follow-up responses to questions by the researcher in the case study on particular issues of interest being investigated.

While the Schutte Scale proves to be effective, it requires a little more time in terms of mobilizing people of the same gender or age group, and training is a necessity, which can be a lengthy process especially where the researcher has very limited time to execute the process, and also where literacy levels are low to comprehend the procedure of using the instrument. In cases where the case study community members are not proactive, it can be difficult to bring the group of people under one station for discussions. The Schutte Scale technique merges the process of participation and prioritization of community needs.

Step 5: Analyse

In the context of case studies, "data analysis consists of examining, categorising, tabulating, testing, or otherwise recombining evidence to draw empirically-based conclusions" (Yin, 2009, p. 126). Although the process may be guided by a prior theory (Perry, 1998), research-ers should be open-minded to adjust the theoretical misconceptions based on actual findings. In analysing case study evidence in community-based tourism the following techniques can be used: *pattern matching, explanation building, time-series analysis, logic models*, and *cross-case analysis* (Yin, 2009).

Pattern matching involves the comparison of empirically observed patterns with predicted ones to establish any variances or gaps. It is critical to have a detailed record of such predic-tions and actual results. If the differences in rival patterns/effects are greater it will be easier to perform the matching, and the results will be more convincing. It is also important to note that confirmations of counterintuitive predictions will be more convincing than confirmations of commonsensical predictions (Campbell, 1975).

The *explanation building* case study analytical approach depends on building explanations about the case to show the linkages or divergence. Explaining can be done by building a set of causal links about *how* or *why* something happened (Miles and Huberman, 1994). It is an iterative process which requires researchers to make initial predictions, which they will then use as a comparison with the case study evidence. Then, depending on the variances, the initial predictions are adjusted and compared against any additional evidence and/or cases. The process is repeated until a satisfactory match is attained. It is important to note that the strengths of a case study are in "the ability to trace changes over time" (Yin, 2009, p. 145).

Time-series analysis focuses on changes over some time period. It can also be regarded as a type of pattern matching, involves temporal patterns, and may involve statistical analysis techniques (e.g. regression analysis). Chronological analysis of events may involve any of the following rules: event X must always be followed by event Y on a contingency basis, event X must always occur before event Y, event X can only follow event Y after a prescribed interval of time, and certain time periods in a case study may be marked by classes of events that differ substantially from those of other time periods (Yin, 2009).

Logic models are used to explain the logic between events over a specific period of time. They can be described as a cross between pattern matching and time-series analysis. This involves a comparison between predicted cause–effect of events with the empirically observed evidence. Such logic models, which may be represented as *influence diagrams* (*causal maps*), can be used to causally model competing explanations.

Cross-case analysis/synthesis applies to multiple cases and can involve any of the techniques described above.

In addition to the above, the *observe, think, test, and revise* (OTTR) concept is central to case study data collection and analysis (GAO, 1990). In summary, during and after the field-work where *observations* take place, the researcher *thinks* deeply on the meaning of information collected and tries to make sense of it in terms of what it may imply. The thinking process will lead to the generation of new types of information required to confirm or rule out existing interpretations. The additional information collected during the *test* phase when examined may lead to *revisions* of initial interpretations. Such *revisions* may, in turn, lead to another *test* phase. When plausible explanations can be developed or when there is no unexplained data or no possible further interpretations possible, the process can be stopped. Thus, "in case study methods, causality is established through the internal consistency and plausibility of explanation, derived additively through the OTTR sequence" (GAO, 1990, p. 70).

Coding is also a critical step in qualitative data analysis. It involves breaking the data into manageable pieces which the researcher then reconstructs to reflect a view of reality (Beekhuyzen et al., 2010). First, the researcher has to read the interview transcripts, observational notes, and/or any other relevant documents, which may lead to the development of preliminary notes or memos that can then be used to formulate initial categories, themes and relationships. Coding is an iterative and incremental process that may be performed at differing levels of abstraction:

1. *Descriptive coding* is mainly done before conducting interviews and observations. It relates to the broad topics that the researcher may wish to develop (Morse and Richards, 2002).
2. *Topic coding* is undertaken after data collection. It pertains to issues that generally only become apparent during data analysis (Beekhuyzen et al., 2010).
3. *Analytical coding* involves arranging the coded data into a more abstract framework with categories that are generally more abstract than words in interview transcripts.

Box 26.3 shows a typical example of a step-by-step coding process done in a community-based project at Somkhanda Game Reserve in KwaZulu Natal, South Africa.

BOX 26.3 DATA CODING AT SOMKHANDA GAME RESERVE

Data were thematically analysed to bring out the linkages between the community and resilience in the Gumbi community, specifically at the Somkhanda Game Reserve (SGR). The interview transcripts were analysed and data were coded to derive key issues. Coding

Table 26.5   Major categories of the Somkhanda Game Reserve community resilience

Major categories	Associated concepts
Governance shocks	Inclusion, exclusion, transparency, power, elite and the minority, judicial laws, traditional policies, feedback/communication
Financial shocks	Salaries, funding, technological advancement, armoury to protect animals, income generation, amenities
Skills shocks	Experience, exposure to conservation, qualifications, lack of management ideas, monitoring dangerous game, tracking, training, game rangers empowerment, skills transfer

refers to "categorising segments of data with a short name that simultaneously summarises and accounts for each piece" (Charmaz, 2014, p. 43). Three main shocks emerged as key community resilience themes: governance, financial and skills. Table 26.5 shows the major results of the focused coding analysis of data on community resilience at the Somkhanda Game Reserve.

Table 26.5 shows three superordinate and 29 subordinate categories emerging from the analysis of the resilience of SGR stakeholders. The superordinate categories include governance shocks, financial shocks and skills shocks. Each superordinate has between 8 and 12 sub-categories associated with them. The dominant category most frequently referred to by respondents during interviewing was 'governance shocks'. Here the participants' language reflected descriptions, assumptions and reports about governance. Across the three superordinate categories, the subordinate categories were ranked in terms of frequency of mention during the interviewing process. The descriptive codes were drawn from the subordinate categories, and were based on what outcomes the community or Somkhanda Game Reserve received from conservation activities. The researchers assigned each unit of data its own unique code. A pattern emerged naturally due to repetition and consistencies in frequency of mentions of specific issues about community conservation. Coding patterns were characterized by similarity, difference, frequency, sequence, correspondence and causation. The key code words and phrases (see right side in Table 26.5) were then integrated to establish a theme (see left side in Table 26.5), which is an outcome of coding (Charmaz, 2014).

Affective coding methods were adopted to enable the researchers to investigate the subjective qualities of the participants' experiences with regards to conservation at the Somkhanda Game Reserve. As land reform is a sensitive issue in South Africa, the affective methods assisted the researchers to investigate the emotions, values and conflicts within the community. The authors used: (i) emotional coding to label the emotion recalled or experienced; (ii) value coding to assess the participants' integrated values, attitudes and belief systems; and (iii) versus coding, which acknowledges that people are always in conflict. The codes identified power-play issues. Combined, these codes assisted the researchers to understand the extent of community resilience in the management and governance of the Somkhanda Game Reserve.

Source: Musavengane and Kloppers (2020).

Step 6: Share

The share stage focuses on how to communicate synthesized data or information. To effectively communicate, it requires the researchers to clearly define the audience, compose textual and visual materials, and display enough evidence for a reader to reach his/her conclusions (Yin, 2009). GAO (1990) provides a detailed checklist for reviewing case study reports (see https://www.gao.gov/special.pubs/10_1_9.pdf).

Common case study drawbacks encountered by researchers at this stage include:

- Potential overgeneralization
- Inadequate interpretation
- Unintegrated narrative
- Results not adequately related to research questions, and
- Not enough evidence (i.e. raw data) being presented.

These can be avoided by reporting all relevant facts and assumptions. It is better to over-report than under-report. The use of direct quotations from key informants or participants is encouraged to support and stress the main points (Eisenhardt and Graebner, 2007; Musavengane and Kloppers, 2020). To contextualize the findings and demonstrate novelty, the findings should be supported by the literature, and the social and historical background of the research settings (Dooley, 2002). This is very important in community-based tourism where social and historical issues strongly dominate.

Before sharing the research report it is important to identify the audience. A single report cannot reach everyone at once as the needs of the audiences vary. More versions of the case study report may be required if effective communication is to be to reach more than one audience.

IMPLICATIONS OF THE APPROACH

The broad elements of a case study approach are derived from a variety of sources outlined in this chapter. A number of strands emerge. In many cases, the empirical case approach can be affected by internal political dynamics and social grouping. In other instances, poverty and social status of the people have a bearing on the levels of participation at the micro-level of the community. For example, those with low status can feel inferior to actively participate and they can be overshadowed by those with higher status in the community. Therefore, in a case study, it is important to mobilize the participants at the household-level to muster sufficient participation of community members of varying social, economic and political backgrounds to achieve inclusive contributions to the study. Thus, the approach demands an understanding of the dynamics of the community and its households within which the case study is carried out.

The question of who can participate in a case study is crucial to addressing the issue of the success of the research project. In many cases, those with low status lack social networks and education and lack confidence to actively participate, share their knowledge and contribute meaningfully to the discourses. However, it is important in a case study to value all contributions regardless of the social status of participants. This chapter implores respecting community knowledge rooted in indigenous knowledge systems. Although the case study approach contributes to the understanding of important issues, the participation of people should be voluntary and is dependent on the willingness of the participants who are involved. Ethically, they should not be coerced into certain actions and involvement in the research. Their consent always matters. In instances where the community members are not keen to participate, it prolongs the time needed to accomplish the study, which in most cases, can be a costly process to the researcher. Therefore, there is a need to prepare adequately in terms of the resources and the anticipated time needed to ensure the case study community is sufficiently covered in term of researching a phenomenon. Consequently, in scenario planning for a case study, the researcher should take these critical research behavioural risks of the people in the community into consideration for a successful case study to be completed.

Essentially, the quieter community members tend to hold back information whilst the vocal and more confident than the others tend to step forward to speak out during research. This has the potential to affect the gathering of diverse views. In other instances, where the political processes are closely monitored and controlled because of what community members may say about their government, participants' discussions are constrained by fear to express themselves. Thus, it is imperative to navigate the political terrain through key-informant interview processes in which individual members can open up to reveal details that ordinarily are difficult to obtain when they discuss as a group. As an example, Muzeza (2013) posits that the context, content and articulation of the Great Limpopo Transfrontier Park conservation governance in respect of Makuleke and Sengwe communities in South Africa and Zimbabwe respectively, showed that local political leadership determined what should be said as opposed to community members participating and expressing themselves. In discussions, the local Councillors and Community Property Association would try to guide what the people would say (Muzeza, 2013). However, employing covert semi-structured key-informant discussions with community members also helps to gain insights especially on matters of government governance and management of projects with a bearing on the community (Muzeza, 2013).

The researcher, therefore, needs to be innovative to involve all the members to avoid the pitfalls of leaving out key information from the participants as a result of local politics. Such innovation is important to improve the validity, reliability and objectivity of information obtained through a case study approach. The message here is that there should be enough evidence to ensure that the entire community is covered without marginalizing the individual(s) and subgroup(s) within it, since every community member, regardless of their position, is important (Ruddal, 1999, p. 49). The case study research approach is important to understand community perspectives, and members of each community studied should be involved regardless of social relationships and power dynamics in that community.

CONCLUSIONS

Case study research is a complex exercise. It requires patience. Research skills in scenario planning, coupled with sufficient resources and finding the right entry point into a case study area is dependent on the researcher's ability to negotiate the 'way into' the community. Essentially, flexibility to adapt and appreciate the local culture and networks among the subjects being studied is important to find a way into the community. In complex and insecure research areas, communities and violent social groups, researchers are encouraged to take precautions and adhere to local security protocols to ensure the safety of the researcher and the community members being studied. The benefits of case study research are immense once the procedures and methodologies, as outlined in this chapter, are followed. As much as no community is value-free and incident-free, the researcher should be versatile to overcome challenges that impede obtaining the information. One needs to be innovative to ensure the research is accomplished. Ideally, one should be able to manage local relationships and leverage those relationships as social capital to get things done within set timelines. This type of research involves planning and putting in place sufficient resources. It is suggested that participation in a case study is not only important in terms of getting the views from people, but also for gaining access into the field to practically obtain information from the community being studied. Fundamentally, the case study approach allows, amongst other things, for critical events, interventions, policy developments and programme-based service reforms to be properly studied in detail in their political, social and economic real-life contexts and the people in the study engaged to contribute to the discourse. Although the case study approach has numerous advantages in the research process in that it presents real-life situations and data and provides better insights into the detailed behaviours of the subjects of being studied, it is also criticized for its inability to generalize the results especially in areas where one group dominates the process of research. The case study method has always been criticized for its lack of rigour, and the tendency for a researcher thereof, to have a biased interpretation of the information that is obtained. It is important, therefore, to establish the grounds for testing reliability, validity and generality of the information obtained from the subjects so that the findings are not subjected to scepticism after the results are made available to the public. Thus, the sample should be sufficient, and the subjects participate during the research. Notwithstanding these criticisms, researchers continue to deploy the case study method particularly in studies of real-life situations, on matters of public opinions of communities and more importantly, on matters governing social issues and problems in society.

REFERENCES

Beekhuyzen, J., Nielsen, S. and von Hellens, L. (2010) The Nvivo looking glass: Seeing the data through the analysis. Paper presented at the 5th Conference on Qualitative Research in IT, Brisbane, Australia.

Campbell, D. T. (1975) "Degrees of freedom" and the case study. *Comparative Political Studies*, 8(2), 178–193.

Charmaz, K. (2014) *Constructing Grounded Theory* (2nd ed.). London: Sage.

Daymon, C. and Holloway, I. (2002) *Qualitative Research Methods in Public Relations and Marketing Communications*. New York: Routledge.

Dooley, L. M. (2002) Case study research and theory building. *Advances in Developing Human Resources*, 4(3), 335–354.

Eisenhardt, K. M. and Graebner, M. E. (2007) Theory building from cases: Opportunities and challenges. *Academy of Management Journal*, 50(1), 25–32.

Gay, L. R. and Airasian, P. (2003) *Educational Research: Competencies for Analysis and Applications* (7th ed.). Upper Saddle River, NJ: Merrill Prentice Hall.

General Accounting Office (GAO) (1990) *Case Study Evaluations*. Washington, DC: GAO.

George, A. L. and Bennett, A. (2005) *Case Studies and Theory Development in the Social Sciences*. Cambridge, MA: MIT Press.

Gerring, J. (2004) What is a case study and what is it good for? *American Political Science Review*, 98(2), 341–354.

Gomm, R., Hammersley, M. and Foster, P. (eds.) (2000) *Case Study Method*. London: Sage.

Haines, D. (2017) Ethical considerations in qualitative case study research recruiting participants with profound intellectual disabilities. *Research Ethics*, 13(3–4), 219–232.

Januszka, C. M., Lora, A. C., Wollard, K. K. and Rocco, T. S. (2007) Investigating race and ethnicity on data collection and analysis. In S. M. Nielsen and M. S. Plakhotnik (eds.), *Proceedings of the Sixth Annual College of Education Research Conference: Urban and International Education Section* (pp. 36–42). Miami: Florida International University. http://coeweb.fiu.edu/research_conference/.

Kasunic, M. (2010) Measurement and analysis infrastructure diagnostic, version 1.0: Method definition document. Online. https://www.sei.cmu.edu/reports/10tr035.pdf 02/02/2020.

McDonough, J. and McDonough, S. (1997) *Research Methods for English Language Teachers*. London: Arnold.

Mesec, B. (1998) *Uvod v kvalitativno raziskovanje v socialnem delu*. Ljubljana: Visokašola za socialno delo.

Miles, M. B. and Huberman, A. M. (1994) *Qualitative Data Analysis: An Expanded Sourcebook*. Thousand Oaks, CA: Sage.

Morse, J. and Richards, L. (2002) *Readme First for a User's Guide to Qualitative Methods*. London: Sage.

Musavengane, R. and Kloppers, R. (2020) Social capital: An investment towards community resilience in the collaborative natural resources management of community-based tourism schemes. *Tourism Management Perspectives*, 100654. doi:10.1016/j.tmp.2020.100654.

Muzeza, D. (2013) *The Impact of Institutions of Governance on Communities' Livelihoods and Sustainable Conservation in The Great Limpopo Transfrontier Park (GLTP): The Study of Makuleke and Sengwe Communities*. http://etd.cput.ac.za/bitstream/handle/20.500.11838/806/210227028_Muzeza_D_2013.pdf?sequence=1&isAllowed=y.

Perry, C. (1998) Process of a case study methodology for postgraduate research in marketing. *European Journal of Marketing*, 32(9–10), 785–802.

Remenyi, D., Williams, B., Money, A. and Swartz, E. (1998) *Doing Research in Business and Management: An Introduction to Process and Method*. London: Sage.

Ruddal, C. (1999) West Myagdi community health programme, Nepal. In I. Smout (ed.), *NGO Experience of Water Supply and Sanitation* (pp. 48–49). London: WELL.

Sagadin, J. (1991) *Razprave iz pedagoške metodologije*. Ljubljana: Znanstveni inštitut Filozofske fakultete.

Schutte, D. (2000) Cape Peninsula University of Technology notes: A short overview of development theories. Cape Peninsula University of Technology.

Starman, A. B. (2013) The case study as a type of qualitative research. *Journal of Contemporary Educational Studies*, 1, 28–43.

Yin, R. K. (1984) *Case Study Research: Design and Methods*. Beverly Hills, CA: Sage.

Yin, R. K. (2009) *Doing Case Study Research* (4th ed.). Thousand Oaks, CA: Sage.

Yin, R. and Moore, G. (1987) The use of advanced technologies in special education. *Journal of Learning Disabilities*, 20(1), 60–63.

APPENDIX A: THE PARTICIPANT INFORMATION SHEET

This should not be more than one page. The following headings serve as guidelines in preparing the information sheet:

1. Salutation or a polite greeting to the potential participant.
2. Self-introduction – who are you and what is your role as a researcher.
3. The research title of your project (some prefer to have this as number 1).
4. Statement on the aims and rationale (potential/direct benefits) of the study.
5. Call or invitation to the participant to participate in the study – use a friendly tone.
6. A sentence of how or why they were selected.
7. An explanation of what specific involvement in the study will require potential participants to do (procedures, duration, place, when).
8. To avoid ambiguity or misunderstanding, a statement clarifying that the research does not involve payment is necessary to avoid over expectation.
9. A statement on voluntary participation should be added. Where necessary, further state that refusal to participate will not involve any penalty or withdrawal of any benefits currently enjoyed (i.e. access to game park resources). Failure to clarify this, and the research will face the risk of accusation for obtaining consent by force/duress/coercion.
10. Add a statement to guarantee anonymity (not to reveal the identity of the person) and confidentiality (how you are going to use the information). However, in the case of focus groups, immediately state that confidentiality and anonymity cannot be guaranteed as there will be many people.
11. State that participants may not answer if they are uncomfortable and may withdraw from participating freely at no cost of any sort.
12. If necessary, state any foreseeable risks that participants should expect during the study.
13. If there are possibilities to arouse participant's feelings of past trauma (for example, in some communities, where issues of land and social injustice are raised) details on counselling services and costs should be included.
14. A statement on data security and management should be added. In other words, how you are going to use, secure, retain, reuse and get rid of the data safely.

NB: All this should fit in one page – Do not exceed a page. All the best!

APPENDIX B: CONSENT FORM FOR RECORDED INTERVIEWS

The following contents should be contained in the consent form:

1. A statement explaining that they have been provided full details of the research.
2. A short list summarizing what they have been told (for example, promises, risks etc.).
3. A clear statement on what participants are agreeing or consenting to, by getting involved in the research (for example, agreeing to be interviewed / to be observed while working / to complete the questionnaire).
4. Consent to retain, destroy or reuse data.
5. Provide a section for signature and date.

Example of a consent form

Thank you for your interest in participating in this research. Before you agree to take part, please read the participant information sheet [*provided separately*]. If you have any questions regarding the information sheet or explanations provided, please ask the researcher before you decide whether to participate. You will be given a copy of this consent form to keep for future reference.

Participant's statement:
I confirm that:

I have read the participant information sheet and understand the purpose of the research.
I understand that if I decide I no longer wish to take part in this research I can notify the researcher involved and withdraw within one month after the interview.
I understand that the information I submit, including anonymized direct quotes, may be included in any resulting report.
I understand that my participation will be audio recorded for accuracy and I consent to the use of this material as part of the project.
I agree the project named above has been explained to me to my satisfaction and I agree to take part in this research.

Name (optional):
Signature:
Date:
If you would like to receive a copy of any resulting report, please enter your email address below.
Email:

27. Establishing and managing research programmes in tourism destinations: the case of South African National Parks

Liandi Slabbert

WHERE THIS TOOLKIT CAN BE USED IN PRACTICE

The increased focus on tourism and visitation in protected areas as a strategy to fund conservation and improve the livelihoods of local people is expected to continue (McCool and Khumalo, 2015). This puts further pressure on park and tourism managers already expected to display a good understanding of a wide range of management issues, including environmental, social, legal and financial (Dudley et al., 2018) as they bring into consideration the potential of the area, its conservation imperative and heritage significance, the capacity of local entities to implement tourism, as well as visitor expectations (McCool, 2006). At the same time though, experts have noticed a decline in the internal research capacities of conservation agencies around the world (Roux et al., 2019). How then, with limited resources available, can protected areas and other tourism destinations acquire the knowledge necessary to inform decision-making in this changing landscape of tourism?

This chapter, written from a practitioner's point of view, reflects on the past challenges and the recent progress made in the development, coordination, management, and implementation of tourism research to guide management decision-making, in the context of a tourism destination and protected area agency with limited research capacity. It provides a toolkit for promoting and managing tourism research that is aligned with a responsible tourism strategy of an organization. Where sustainable tourism is considered a set of principles based on the fundamentals of sustainability (Buckley, 2012; Mihalic, 2016), responsible tourism builds on these foundational strategies and policies and adds a layer of appropriate behaviour, of "acting responsibly in terms of one's own actions, and moreover, in the management and operation of business" (Leslie, 2012, p. 20). Responsible tourism therefore represents the transition towards actual tourism based on more sustainable values (Mihalic, 2016).

For purposes of this chapter, responsible tourism is framed within the Cape Town Declaration on Responsible Tourism in Destinations (2002), of tourism that (i) reduces negative economic, ecological, and social impacts; (ii) creates better economic benefits for local people and improves the welfare of host communities; (iii) includes local people in decisions that affect their lives and life chances; (iv) contributes positively to the conservation of natural and cultural heritage; (v) provides more enjoyable experiences for tourists through more meaningful connections with local people, and improved knowledge of local cultural, social and ecological issues; (vi) offers equitable access to tourists with disabilities, the elderly, and families with young children; and (vii) is culturally sensitive, engenders respect between tourists and hosts, and builds local pride and confidence.

While the context presented in this case study is that of tourism in protected areas, which may be of particular interest to nature-based tourism destinations, the toolkit also provides practical advice on managing a tourism research programme in general for other tourism destinations to consider.

TOURISM AND SOUTH AFRICAN NATIONAL PARKS

For a tourism provider to stay competitive in the global arena of the twenty-first century, it needs to demonstrate an ability to attract visitors over long timeframes by providing satisfactory experiences (McCool, 2006). The vision of the South African National Parks, "A world class system of sustainable national parks reconnecting and inspiring society", alludes to one of its mandates, of creating destinations for nature-based tourism in a manner that is not harmful to the environment and that is to the benefit of current and future generations (SANParks, 2018).

SANParks, being the largest state run tourism provider and enjoying high visitation rates from both international and domestic tourists, is a major player in the tourism industry in South Africa. The agency self-manages a total of 2,310 accommodation units representing 7,143 beds along with 1,459 campsites catering for 8,784 camping guests in 19 national parks, situated in six different provinces across South Africa (De Wet, 2020). Two of its national parks, namely Table Mountain National Park and Kruger National Park feature as top tourist attractions in the country (SA-Venues.com, 2017; TourismTattler.com, 2013; Travelstart Online Travel Operations, 2018). Kruger National Park is further regarded as one of the best sustainable tourism destinations in the world (Edgell, 2020). In 2011, SANParks formulated its Responsible Tourism Strategy, outlining its commitment towards the principles of responsible tourism, to ensure tourism development makes a positive contribution towards local communities and the conservation of natural and cultural heritage, is compatible with the environment in which it operates, and provides quality visitor experiences (SANParks, 2011; SANParks, 2013).

Income from its tourism business continues to be the cornerstone for growth and sustainability of the organization, financially supporting its biodiversity and conservation objectives (SANParks, 2018). Growing the tourism income stream requires diversification of the tourism product to attract new target markets, while still catering for the traditional visitor to ensure SANParks remains competitive as a tourism provider. In its Responsible Tourism Strategy (SANParks, 2011), the agency states that SANParks as a "destination", has entered the space between consolidation and stagnation, when assessed against the theoretical framework of Butler's (1980) Tourism Area Life Cycle (TALC) model (Figure 27.1). Stagnation is visible in parks such as Kruger National Park, while some of the smaller parks are still in the developmental phase.

Aside from market maturation, SANParks was also presented with the challenge of government funding moving from day-to-day operational funding to one-off, project based, grant funding. This, coupled with a projected increase in operational costs presented a serious threat which required targeted and well managed responsible interventions. By implementing responsible tourism management and principles, the organization hopes to continue to benefit from enhanced income levels, improved tourism offerings, more efficient management practices, and higher levels of local involvement and benefits flowing to local communities (SANParks,

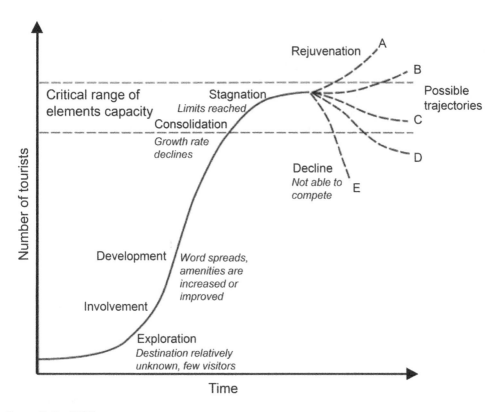

Source: Butler (1980).

Figure 27.1   Butler's Tourism Area Life Cycle model

2011). As the organization's Tourism Development and Marketing division continued with the implementation of its approved strategic plans, a need was identified for more appropriate research to inform the responsible development and implementation thereof.

Increased Focus on Tourism Research

Against the backdrop of an increasing and varied demand for recreational opportunities on public lands, and the uncertainty and complexity involved in the decisions that accompany the provision and management of such opportunities, managers of public lands are increasingly expected to base decisions on scientific evidence (McCool et al., 2007).

SANParks, through its Scientific Services unit within the Conservation Services division, has an established record of conducting and facilitating scientific research since the 1950s (van Wilgen et al., 2016), fuelled by a strong team of embedded researchers (Carruthers, 2017). Up until recent years, however, there was limited focus on the social and business sciences and in particular tourism research, mainly due to capacity limitations and the lack of a formal research strategy to guide and direct tourism research priorities for SANParks. The lack of focus on social and business research was, and in many cases still is, a familiar challenge among protected areas (Dudley et al., 2018; Eagles, 2014; Gruby et al., 2016; Hallstrom et al., 2019). The changing landscape of tourism within protected areas, emphasized by the increase in public–private partnerships and other agreements between private tour operators and protected area managers adds to the complexity of protected area management. A full comprehension of the nature and diversity of visitor expectations and experiences and appropriate partnerships is as necessary for the responsible management of PAs as is understanding the biodiversity and biophysical processes occurring within the area (McCool, 2006).

In 2011, SANParks moved forward with the formulation of a research framework to integrate tourism research into the adaptive management policies of the agency. Following an initial stakeholder workshop and discussions between Scientific Services and the Tourism Executive at that time, a framework was defined, based on a social-ecological systems understanding of tourism in national parks, and the need for more strategic and evidence-based decision-making in tourism at SANParks was emphasized.

A few years later, however, the implementation of the framework had shown little progress (Biggs et al., 2014) resulting in the Tourism division's research needs remaining unfulfilled. Contributing factors include the absence of a structured approach to promote closer collaboration between Scientific Services, Tourism and Park Management to overcome the barriers created by the divergent views held by each of the stakeholder groups (Biggs et al., 2014). Another major challenge was the turnaround time involved in gaining approval from SANParks to conduct research, which frustrated tourism researchers who questioned the relevance of commentary from scientists outside of their academic fields. This, coupled with the long lead times accompanying postgraduate academic research, obstructed the provision of actionable research in a timely manner to inform management decision-making. When information is not available to park managers, or does not reach them in time, an organization runs the risk of decisions being based on personal opinions and/or political motives, or highly influenced by resource constraints, instead of being based on insights generated through sound research. A lack of information on tourists' preferences, values and behaviour also constrains an organization's ability to identify and consider alternative management practices (Wardell and Moore, 2005).

Then there was also the disunity between the research interests of academic researchers and the needs of the organization. Without dedicated tourism research resources in SANParks to actively drive and incentivize key tourism intelligence needs, the implementation of the research framework would have remained an afterthought. Third, more of a business-oriented approach with a focus on the responsible development, marketing and management of tourism products and experiences was needed to equip managers with tools required to navigate the complexities encountered in protected area contexts (McCool and Khumalo, 2015). This is necessary to grow and operate tourism business in protected areas to ensure a sustainable future for all stakeholders reliant on revenue generation while still upholding protected area objectives. Research themes and topics in the agenda that emulated such a way of thinking was limited. For example, very little attention was given to market and product development initiatives, an important element for the future sustainability of the tourism business of SANParks.

To address these challenges, SANParks established a tourism research function within the Visitor Services unit, housed within the Tourism Development & Marketing division. Since 2015, SANParks has begun to actively promote and facilitate tourism, marketing and business-related research in national parks through its Tourism Research Strategy.

SANPARKS TOURISM RESEARCH STRATEGY

Tourism Research Objectives

In support of the SANParks Responsible Tourism Strategy, the Visitor Services unit promotes, conducts, facilitates and manages tourism research in order to reach five key objectives:

1. Enhance understanding, and management, of the visitor and the visitor experience;
2. Grow and sustain revenues through identifying and targeting appropriate markets and products;
3. Assist the organization in conducting business in a responsible and sustainable manner;
4. Better defining the value of nature-based tourism to society and the economy;
5. On a practical level, assist tourism operations to become more efficient.

The SANParks Tourism Research Strategy discussed in this section is described along two main components:

1. The Tourism Research Protocol, including a description of the research process, the research project review process, the guiding principles by which SANParks abides, and the various research mechanisms used to implement research projects;
2. The Tourism Research Agenda.

The Tourism Research Protocol (TRP) is the driving force behind the implementation of the Tourism Research Agenda (TRA) which aims to address SANParks' tourism research needs, ultimately equipping managers and practitioners with better information to make informed, evidence-based decisions. Practical examples of projects that have informed management decision-making are provided throughout the chapter.

Tourism Research Protocol (TRP)

In 2015, the TRP was drafted to guide the Visitor Services unit's "way of work" in implementing tourism research. Key to the successful implementation of the protocol is a shared understanding amongst all parties of the mechanisms and processes by which tourism research is carried out and the guiding principles it strives towards, in the context of SANParks' mandate.

The main objectives of the protocol are:

1. To provide the organization with a framework that will guide the execution of the tourism research strategy;
2. To define the process by which knowledge gaps in tourism and marketing are identified;
3. To promote alignment of the TRA with the SANParks Responsible Tourism Strategy;
4. To provide clear principles and values that will guide the organization and its research partners in conducting rigorous and ethical tourism research.

The TRP contains a description of the research cycle, a set of guiding principles, a list of research mechanisms used as facilitators of research, and the research project review process. Each is discussed in turn.

Research cycle and project review process

Research is an ongoing process with many subtasks associated with it. Figure 27.2 depicts how the research cycle typically plays out in the SANParks context – in particular, how research projects move from needs identification to dissemination and implementation of results. Practically, this is not a single process occurring in a circular fashion from start to finish and concluded in a specific timeframe. Instead, when viewed through the lens of a research programme where requests for research are raised throughout the year, multiple projects commence at different times and progress at varying speeds, each component could be viewed as an ongoing task, perhaps with the exception of the setting of the TRA which is refreshed every four years.

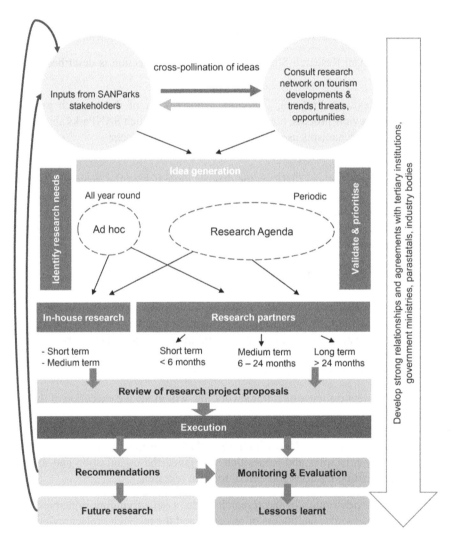

Figure 27.2   SANParks tourism research cycle

Table 27.1   Rating criteria used for tourism research projects

(A) Alignment to management objectives	Research concept is concerned with addressing specific management objectives as determined by Tourism, Parks and Conservation Services.
(B) Alignment to Responsible Tourism Strategy	Research concept is concerned with tourism that maximizes benefits to local communities, minimizes negative social or environmental impacts, and helps local people conserve fragile cultures, habitats, and species.
(C) Directive was received from a tourism manager	Research was requested directly from a tourism manager.
(D) Of national importance	Project is of national importance.
(E) Urgency of request	Findings and recommendations are expected in less than six months.

The process starts with the generation of ideas through ongoing collaboration between multiple stakeholders. Inputs from the heads of the Tourism Development and Marketing division, park and hospitality managers, scientists and other Conservation Services divisional staff provide guidance to the Visitor Services unit as to the extent and priority of research needs. Ideas for future research are also generated through engaging with an external research network. Participants in this network include public or private research partners, government and industry bodies, and other thought leaders in the tourism industry. This research network is a valuable source of insight into new developments, threats and opportunities in the industry and other major economic, social, political and technological forces that influence tourism business.

From idea generation, a research need is identified, either through (i) the periodic formulation of the TRA or (ii) ad hoc workshops, meetings and informal discussions with managers and practitioners of SANParks. Validation and prioritization of research takes place next with the Visitor Services unit applying a rating criteria to identify priority projects to be implemented in a specific financial year:

- For a project to be given a priority rating of 3 (highest priority), a minimum of three out of the five conditions (A, B, C, D or E) set out in Table 27.1 should be met.
- Projects meeting two out of the five conditions are assigned a rating of 2 (medium priority).
- Projects meeting condition D, considered of national importance, are assigned a minimum priority of 2 (medium).
- Projects meeting only one of the three conditions (A, B, or C) are assigned a (low) priority rating of 1.
- All other projects are given a rating of 0, including those meeting the requirement of E only.

Apart from the topic's priority rating, the Visitor Services team also takes into consideration the available financial and human resources required to implement a project before communicating it to researchers. High priority projects take precedence when it comes to the allocation of financial and logistical support provided by the Visitor Services unit to researchers.

Next, appropriate research partners and internal research staff are informed of the research priorities. They then, according to their own research interests and availability, respond by developing a research concept note or a brief project proposal. The Visitor Services team will perform an initial screening of the research brief to determine its appropriateness and preliminarily approve the concept if satisfied. The researcher(s) then develops a full research proposal with details on the objectives, methodology, timelines and costs associated with the project.

All tourism research projects, whether commissioned by SANParks or submitted ad hoc by a researcher wanting to conduct research in a national park for academic purposes, are subjected to a project review process before approval is granted. The purpose of the review process is:

- To ensure that the proposed research addresses the knowledge gaps of SANParks.
- To ensure the research approach, methodology and design is appropriate for achieving the planned objectives.
- To ensure that the research objectives are attainable within the SANParks context.
- For the internal requestor of the research to confirm that the researcher or research partner organization has correctly understood the directive.

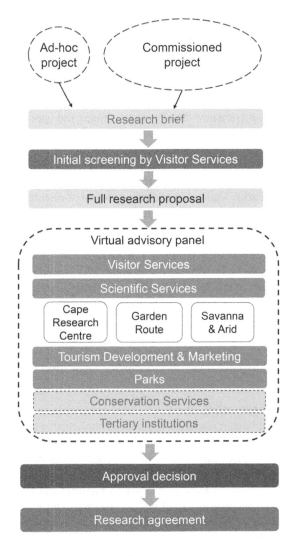

Figure 27.3   SANParks tourism research project review process

- To reduce bias or subjectivity in the research approach by giving practitioners an opportunity to comment and provide inputs.
- To promote quality research.
- To increase the chances of the research outcomes realizing into actionable recommendations for SANParks to use in decision-making at policy level.

A virtual tourism research advisory panel, consisting of members with a diverse range of experiences, is employed to review research proposals. The review process takes place virtually, through email correspondence and is dynamic as members with relevant expertise or interests are invited to comment on a particular research proposal. This virtual review process reduced turnaround times for the approval of projects from months to two or three weeks where full proposals were provided. The advisory panel pulls resources from a pool of specialists and practitioners from the different departments and institutions (Figure 27.3). Once a project is approved, the lead researcher signs a research agreement with SANParks, to ensure the conditions under which approval is granted are adhered to.

The research commences with logistical support provided by the Visitor Services unit as and when required. Results are disseminated to appropriate SANParks managers and practitioners through emails, workshops and presentations. Recommendations by researchers are put forward to managers for implementation, monitored, and lessons learnt from implementation noted. Ideas for future research are often created from the recommendations of researchers and fed back into the research cycle loop.

Guiding principles
In the TRP, the Visitor Services unit stipulates the following guiding principles which tourism research should aim to strive for:

- Tourism research projects should be implemented in keeping with the philosophies of SANParks, the national government's Department of Environment, Forestry and Fisheries and relevant international conservation organizations operating in South Africa.
- Research that aligns closely with SANParks' strategic objectives and more specifically, the SANParks Responsible Tourism Strategy, as well as the goals set out by the Tourism Development and Marketing division shall be prioritized.
- Research should be conducted in an open and transparent manner. Findings and recommendations proposed to management should be based on the nature of what was studied.
- The researcher should be flexible and adaptable, but still follow a robust methodology so as to ensure credibility.
- The identification of research needs in SANParks is an ongoing process.
- An investment of human and financial resources will be necessary if SANParks wishes to reap the rewards from tourism research.
- Academic researchers will be required to provide proof of ethical clearance from their respective tertiary institution prior to commencement of fieldwork.
- Researchers conducting market and social research shall adhere to the global codes of ethical practice and professional standards set out in the Code on Market and Social Research developed jointly by the International Chamber of Commerce (ICC) and the European Society for Opinion and Market Research (ESOMAR), and undersigned by and endorsed by the South African Marketing Research Association. This includes the

requirement that research involving human participants shall obtain informed consent from participants.

- Market research and visitor surveys should take cognizance of the needs of different demographic visitors and where appropriate, research designs should be developed to focus on specific target groups.
- It should be acknowledged that tourism research success is dependent on the environment, cultures and politics within the organization.
- There is no single solution to a research problem. Knowledge is always changing. SANParks works with complexity and accepts that knowledge will always be partial, that we have to make decisions based on incomplete information and that we use the techniques of reflective learning or strategic adaptive management to monitor and refine implementation of current best information.

Research mechanisms

With limited human resources to conduct tourism research, SANParks relies heavily on its research partners to execute its TRA, driving the organization closer towards achieving its Responsible Tourism Strategy objectives. The establishment of such a research network is an ongoing effort and involves the identification of mutual interests between SANParks and a potential research partner. Considering the multidisciplinary nature of protected areas tourism research, partnerships with a range of institutions and organizations involved in various aspects of the study field is preferable. The Visitor Services unit uses four main mechanisms to implement its TRA. Each is discussed briefly and practical examples of projects that have made a meaningful contribution towards management decision-making provided.

Memorandums of Understanding with tertiary institutions

One of the main mechanisms used as an enabler of research partnerships is the establishment of research agreements in the form of Memorandums of Understanding (MoUs) with tertiary institutions. MoUs facilitate the cross-pollination of ideas between industry and academia at levels normally not possible for organizations with highly constrained financial resources. Having strong relationships with research partners has contributed towards SANParks' tourism objectives in numerous ways. It has assisted SANParks with the identification and validation of opportunities for the diversification of tourism products and services in national parks; indicated ways in which national park experiences could be enhanced; brought to light tourism development initiatives that could generate income and employment for local people; improved the organization's understanding of the impact of current and potential tourism developments on the biodiversity conservation efforts of SANParks; and provided management with insight that informed park planning and business planning processes. Over the years 2015 to 2019, SANParks expanded the number of MoUs from two to ten, of which 70 per cent are with local South African tertiary institutions.

The MOU agreements typically span a three or five year period, which allows for medium to long term planning of research projects that suit the timeframes of academic research.

The purpose of putting agreements in place is to:

- Acknowledge an ongoing and strategic relationship between institutions for long term engagements.

- Facilitate cooperation between the relevant parties based upon the principles of mutual benefit.
- Establish a broad framework for research collaboration activities to:
  - *Promote quality research that can be sustained;*
  - *Endeavour to empower students from the tertiary institution by the provision of practical experience in the field of tourism research.*
- The identification of opportunities to enhance SANParks' business and operational strategies, models and practices.
- Provide guidelines as to the issue of intellectual property rights coming forth from research engagements.
- To ensure compliance with SANParks rules and regulations for conduct in its national parks.

If managed correctly, MoU agreements can be highly effective in promoting closer alignment between tertiary institutions' research interests and a destination organization's key intelligence needs. Many projects driven through this mechanism have directly influenced SANParks' management strategies and practices.

In 2015, were it not for the MoU between SANParks and the University of Pretoria and funding received from the Global Environmental Facility (GEF) and the United Nations Environment Programme, the Visitor Services unit would not have been in a position to respond to a request from the SANParks Board in a timely fashion. In the wake of one of the biggest poaching wars in history, the unit was instructed to conduct research into the impact of rhino poaching on tourist experiences. The study outcomes (Lubbe et al., 2019) produced evidence of rhino poaching and anti-poaching initiatives impacting negatively on tourism, potentially affecting future visitation to parks. The results were presented back to the then Minister of Environmental Affairs.

In 2017, SANParks joined forces with the University of Queensland's Business School to conduct a stakeholder perception study to inform the Kruger National Park's (KNP) Traffic Management Plan. In recent years, incidences of congestion in the south of the KNP, particularly at the park's entrance gates, picnic sites and at major wildlife sightings, have become a regular occurrence during peak visitation periods. Different types of visitors travel in or through the park, including day visitors, overnight visitors, guests from tourism accommodation establishments near the Park, tour operators, service delivery vehicles, military and other operational vehicles, staff of KNP and other private companies, and taxi operators who assist with transporting staff to and from their respective workplaces every day. The sometimes diverging interests and requirements from each user group made the development of universally accepted traffic management policies and practices challenging. It was decided that a broad collaborative approach was needed to deal with stakeholder divergence. Focus group methodology was used by the researchers to first solicit the major traffic-related problems in KNP, as perceived by seven different user groups, together with suggestions of practical solutions to address each of the major problems. This was followed by two rounds of a Delphi survey to converge opinions towards consensus and led to a list of negotiated stakeholder solutions and recommendations, supported by most user groups.

External individual researchers

The second mechanism which has a long history of success in SANParks is providing opportunities to individual researchers to conduct research in national parks, subject to the approval of a project proposal. Most researchers are Masters or PhD students with an interest in working in one or multiple national parks; however, the Visitor Services unit also allows undergraduate projects to be conducted. In some cases, the researcher approaches SANParks, already with a specific topic and methodology in mind, which may or may not be suited to the context of SANParks. It is then up to the Visitor Services unit to determine the degree to which the research scope aligns to the SANParks Responsible Tourism Strategy objectives and whether what is being proposed is practically implementable.

For example, a PhD student from the University of Johannesburg investigated the potential contribution of geotourism towards social sustainability at KNP. Another PhD candidate from the same institution is modelling a visitor satisfaction index for SANParks.

Two undergraduate student projects are worth mentioning as well. In 2019, a student from the University of Pretoria's Industrial and Systems Engineering Department put forward a conceptual model for the scheduling and staffing of maintenance and technical services in tourist rest camps in the Kruger National Park. Most rest camps currently work on a three-book system which requires reception, housekeeping and maintenance teams to log the complaints received or requests for maintenance in three separate paper-based books, one for each team. The books are rotated between the three teams and maintenance tends to the issues recorded in the book in their possession. The system makes coordination and status updates of maintenance issues challenging and results in delayed response times. The model proposes a computerized system to record, track and manage maintenance issues, replacing the three-book paper-based system and helps maintenance teams prioritize critical issues that require urgent attention.

A student from the Nelson Mandela University looked into the impact of the 2015–16 droughts on tourism operations within the Garden Route National Park and found there were several impacts linked to the different ecological infrastructure used for tourism. The findings can be used for risk mitigation in long term planning related to tourism and recreation revenue generation.

In-house research

The third mechanism used to further the TRA is in-house research conducted by the Visitor Services unit – primarily through internet-mediated questionnaires for purposes of enhancing its understanding of the current market's needs, interests and opinions which inform various types of management decisions.

To better understand the matching potential of different visitor segment needs and the unique proposition of each national park, the unit concluded two large sample studies in 2016 and 2018, as part of its Visitor Segmentation Programme. The camping diversification study involved an online survey (n = 3,524) of SANParks' camping guests to collect demographic and behavioural attributes, including motivation for camping, travel group size, travel behaviour, destination requirements, preferences towards various facilities and destinations and perceptions of SANParks' pricing. Another segmentation study of overnight visitors, concluded in 2018 (n = 6,023), included both camping and non-camping guests and revealed a number of different profiles of overnight visitors, the determinants behind each group's destination choice, whether visitors consider themselves ecotourists or not and a range of other aspects which informed marketing and product development plans.

Procurement of research services through a bid process

Last, but not least, SANParks puts large projects out on a formal bid process to the open market, in accordance with SANParks' supply chain management policies. These happen on an ad hoc basis and usually involve time-sensitive research needs prioritized by executive management.

In 2016, SANParks partnered with two consumer market research companies to conduct research on South African National Parks as a tourist destination from the perspective of the so-called *non-traditional market* – domestic tourists from demographically underrepresented groups who could afford to go on an annual holiday but not yet considering SANParks in their basket of destination choices. As part of its Responsible Tourism initiatives, SANParks is driven towards attracting more black guests to national parks. A need was identified for research to inform management on how this market could be approached and persuaded to visit parks, along with insights into which product diversification initiatives might contribute more to sustainable future growth levels from this market. The findings indicated there was a general lack of awareness of the SANParks conservation mandate and of its tourism offerings. Most participants, who have not visited national parks, were not open to the experience and anticipated boredom due to various misperceptions about SANParks. They were reluctant to switch holiday destinations as they felt they risked disappointment. However, most were willing to test it on a weekend basis. The findings further pointed towards a mismatch between what this market expects from an ideal holiday, and that which SANParks can offer them – national parks were not associated with fun! The findings were no doubt an eye-opener to SANParks and pointed towards numerous barriers that needed to be overcome (misperceptions being a major one) before SANParks would realize substantial growth from this market.

All four mechanisms discussed above have been employed to drive the Tourism Research Agenda.

SANParks Tourism Research Agenda

The themes and topics addressed through SANParks' tourism research have evolved considerably since the development of the first tourism research framework in 2011, most notably in terms of the diversity of themes and topics investigated. The diversification of topics was greatly stimulated by the expansion in the number of partnerships over the past five financial years as tertiary institutions with varying research interests and skills sets have come aboard.

The task of gathering and identifying knowledge gaps is a continuous process that takes place in the natural flow of business throughout the year. Although the SANParks TRA is viewed as a living document, every four years, the Visitor Services unit facilitates the process of formally updating it by consulting with key internal and external stakeholders (Figure 27.2). Through a series of workshops, consultations and online correspondence with stakeholders, an initial list of research requirements is validated, categorized and prioritized. Research topics for short, medium and long term research are considered and categorized according to the rating criteria discussed earlier. The current SANParks TRA for the period 2018 to 2021 with its themes and topics is provided below as an illustration of the breadth of subjects covered and its linkages to the SANParks Responsible Tourism Strategy objectives.

Theme 1: Market and product development; sales, marketing and branding strategies
This theme addresses topics such as market analysis, market segmentation, visitor typologies, and competitive analysis; product development and product diversification; improving the SANParks tourism brand; diversifying the profile of visitors; increasing the relevance of SANParks as a destination to future generations; sales, distribution and marketing models for nature-based tourism; econometric models for tourist demand in parks and pricing strategies.

Theme 2: Visitor management and visitor interpretation
Crowding and vehicle traffic congestion are major challenges in Table Mountain National Park and Kruger National Park respectively and require substantial research to inform appropriate visitor management strategies and practices. To increase the quality of the visitor experience, research that evaluates tourists' interpretive experiences (and assets) in various parks is necessary, along with insights that guide the development of new interpretive products and services. Furthermore, research to inform strategies that induce mindfulness towards the environment, communities and other visitors is also required.

Theme 3: Responsible tourism
While many of the topics covered in other themes in the TRA touch on both responsible tourism and sustainability practices, its importance in the overall strategy of SANParks warrants it being treated as a theme on its own. This category therefore caters for projects with a strong and definite responsible tourism focus.

Researchers from four tertiary institutions (University of Pretoria, University of South Africa, North West University and Edith Cowen University) combined efforts to study sustainable tourism development and responsible tourism practices in selected South African national parks. The project commenced with a measurement of visitor expectations and experiences against sustainability assessment outcomes (Morrison-Saunders et al., 2019), and branched into further assessments of the contribution of environmental impact assessment (EIA) to responsible tourism (Pope et al., 2019).

Theme 4: Sustainable tourism practices
This theme investigates how the tourism business could become more environmentally sustainable in practical day-to-day tourism operations in areas such as waste management and energy usage. It also covers theories and interventions that could bring about behavioural change amongst both visitors and staff of national parks to support environmental sustainability. Also covered are investigations into ways to avoid, minimize and mitigate tourism's contribution towards climate change and vice versa, the impact of climate variability on tourism.

Theme 5: Biodiversity and tourism
The delicate relationship between biodiversity and tourism is explored under this theme with topics such as the impact of tourism on biodiversity and the natural environment in general, the impact of poaching on tourism, and the impact of biodiversity on tourism.

In 2017, the Visitor Services unit asked visitors whether they would be willing to contribute towards an additional fee imposed on visitors to the seven parks that have rhino, in order to fund much-needed anti-poaching technology and operations. The introduction of the fee was supported by the majority of visitors who also indicated a preferred method of payment and amount they were willing to contribute. The fee was subsequently implemented as a ring-fenced reserve and today forms an important source of additional funding.

Theme 6: Operations

This research theme seeks to find ways to make tourism operations more efficient by reducing the cost of tourism operations, improving the professional competencies of staff, improved management of tourism infrastructure and enhancing customer satisfaction levels through service excellence.

Theme 7: Value of parks

The value of parks theme seeks to measure and understand the contribution of national parks to local economies, community benefit and socio-economic conditions, and to human well-being in general. While a few projects have touched on these subjects, more work needs to be done to investigate tourism opportunities that benefit communities and learn from case studies of successful implementation of community centred tourism.

One of the key projects launched in 2019 explores how visitation to national parks contributes to human well-being. The research, conducted by the Tshwane University of Technology's Department of Nature Conservation, seeks to find the deeper meanings members of society attach to the feelings and emotions experienced when visiting parks, and how long such positive effects typically last.

Concerted efforts to establish and grow a tourism research function in SANParks have led to an increased understanding of many of the sub-themes of tourism research; however, in some areas, critical knowledge gaps still remain. The Visitor Services unit continues to target these by strengthening research partnerships.

CHALLENGES, OPPORTUNITIES AND LESSONS LEARNT

The Utilization of New Knowledge by Practitioners

Perhaps the greatest challenge for SANParks' tourism research function in recent years has not been a shortage of research but the absorption of research findings and recommendations into management strategies and practices. The problem of knowledge utilization is internationally recognized, well studied (Ottoson, 2009; Rich, 1997; Xiao and Smith, 2007), and in the context of protected areas tourism, involves much complexity (McCool, 2012). In SANParks, research results often go unnoticed and recommendations are lost as already overworked managers and practitioners struggle to find the time to work through additional documents during the normal flow of business. In many cases, researchers merely dump research outputs onto practitioners, assuming they will be taken further, as described by McCool (2012) as the "hypodermic needle" approach, before moving on to the next research problem.

A joint effort is required from researchers and the Visitor Services unit to (1) disseminate research findings to practitioners in a format and language they understand; (2) clearly outline the practical implications to their work; (3) meet face-to-face with practitioners to discuss the implications of the research results; and (4) where feasible, become involved in the implementation of recommendations, in doing so gaining a better understanding of the on-the-ground challenges facing practitioners, providing further guidance and potentially conducting more research as the process unfolds. While the Visitor Services unit tries to facilitate such efforts by arranging workshops and presentations between internal staff and researchers, at least for projects considered high priority, limited staff makes this a monumental task.

Raising awareness of the research findings at a senior executive level can lead to recommended actions being delegated to specific teams or functions within the organization. Roles and responsibilities need to be assigned and recommended actions preferably included into the key performance indicators of the parties responsible.

Funding Challenges

While a lot can be gained by tapping into the freely available research capacity of tertiary institutions (such as self-funded Masters or PhD students), this approach can make a valuable but limited contribution towards driving a tourism destination's research agenda. This is because students and their supervisors will have their own agenda and interests and need to adhere to academic requirements and timelines, which might not align closely to the needs of an organization. Most tourism destinations cannot wait two to five years for research results to be published before moving forward with business decisions. Nonetheless, some topics require in-depth and thorough investigations that can only come from strong theory-based, academically sound research and should be encouraged to run its course. A commitment towards funding for commissioned research, through research partnerships and procurement procedures, is vital if a tourism destination wants research to influence its business decisions at all levels.

Some research projects, particularly those with a considerably large scope or methods that involve long periods of data collection, may require a significant amount of time to initiate in year one and execute during years that follow. There is therefore a need for funding commitments that span across multiple financial years. Currently, the budget process of SANParks, in accordance with the government's public finance laws, does not allow for the carry-over of budget from one year to the next. The result is often a delay in the continuation of projects at the start of the financial year when the Tourism division awaits confirmation of budget. This can influence trust levels between SANParks and its research partners and lead to unnecessary delays in the implementation of larger, more complex projects when budgets for consecutive years cannot be guaranteed.

Fragmented Approach to Responsible Tourism Research

Even though most of the tourism research conducted in national parks in South Africa aligns with the agency's Responsible Tourism Strategy in some way, research efforts strengthening SANParks' responsible tourism strategies and practices are still conducted in a fragmented fashion, often only focusing on one or two dimensions of responsible tourism. More research that incorporates a holistic view of SANParks' vision with respect to responsible and sustainable tourism and how that could translate to the various functions and activities within its tourism operations is needed.

Matching Demand and Supply of Knowledge Resources

Given the Visitor Services unit's reliance on research partners to execute the TRA, successfully advancing SANParks' tourism research priority themes and topics depends heavily on the unit's ability to match the organization's research needs with the research skills and interests of its partner researchers. Engaging with research networks and individual researchers (including students) early on in the research cycle is essential in order to identify and fully tap into the research interest synergies between external producers of knowledge and that of a tourism destination. Making use of independent third party researchers either through MoU agreements or individual research projects is not just a useful mechanism by which research capacity can be acquired cost-effectively, but also increases the objectivity and credibility of research conducted.

Internet-Mediated Data Collection

Internet-mediated surveys provide a cost-effective way of gathering opinions, perspectives and preferences from tourism stakeholders in a timely manner. The organization's database of overnight accommodation bookings, along with pre-bookings of day visits to parks has made it possible to reach a large part of its constituency fairly easy and in a timely manner. Conducting visitor surveys in this manner has reduced the seasonality bias often encountered in fieldwork conducted in the park. Most researchers have limited time to collect data from visitors to a national park and may find that the profile and behaviour of visitors differ depending on whether data is collected during peak or off-peak seasons. Internet-mediated surveys reduce this bias as tourists who have visited parks during different times of the year can be reached.

Nevertheless, research methodology should not be guided by convenience and cost measures alone as some projects require face-to-face interviews or observations to ensure validity and reliability of the data. Tourism destinations should further realize that the profile of respondents to online surveys would, at best, match the profile of clients from the booking database and not necessarily the profile of those who actually visit the destination. In the case of Kruger National Park for example, roughly 30 per cent of visitors are international tourists (SANParks, 2020), some of whom do not book directly with SANParks but utilize third parties. These individuals' particulars would therefore not be included in the client database and they may therefore be underrepresented in the research sample. Internet-mediated data collection is a useful tool, but the objectives of a research project should be carefully considered before it is chosen as the preferred data collection strategy. The utilization of client databases for market research should also be done in accordance with international and local laws pertaining to the protection of personal information.

IMPLICATIONS OF ADOPTING THIS TOURISM RESEARCH STRATEGY

The SANParks Tourism Research Strategy, through its Tourism Research Protocol and accompanying Tourism Research Agenda provides a structured approach for tourism destinations wanting to advance their research efforts to better inform responsible tourism management decisions. The toolkit, consisting of guidelines, processes, research mechanisms and list of research themes and topics, can be adopted and adjusted by other tourism destinations to suit different contexts and priorities.

The processes described in this chapter were designed to encourage a balanced approach to prioritizing research topics and allocation of research budget, promoting alignment to the organization's overall strategic objectives and its Responsible Tourism Strategy. The solution towards better utilization of research discussed earlier, is not just confined to improving dissemination and engagement efforts between practitioners and researchers. It starts with the identification of research needs and knowing which research topics are 'nice to have' and which have a high probability of influencing a tourism destination's policy decisions. Tourism destinations with limited capacity to execute research recommendations should be mindful of the consequences of taking on too many research projects at the same time, or simply allowing projects that seem like a good idea but which have limited to no strategic intent to continue, the biggest consequence perhaps being wasted resources that could have been channelled to underfunded projects elsewhere in an organization. Even projects self-funded by university students have implications on the human resources of an organization. In all cases, the potential value to be gained from the research should be weighed against the investment in time and resources before a decision is made to approve a project. The criteria rating used by SANParks may serve as a guideline for such decisions.

The Tourism Research Protocol was further designed to promote fairness and transparency in the way the unit approves research projects. Having a standard project review process in place creates trust between research partners and decreases uncertainty among researchers on what it takes for a research project to be approved. Providing opportunity to experts from various departments of an organization to provide inputs into research proposals helps secure internal support towards research efforts and keeps managers informed of the level and types of intelligence that will become available to them in the future. It also reduces bias in project approval decisions.

Tourism destinations considering setting up their own research strategy would require at least some level of dedicated resources to accelerate progress. A resource in the form of a tourism research champion with close ties to both the tourism business and industry and academic researchers is preferable. In the case of SANParks, although the organization identified tourism as a neglected area of research and had the best intention of changing that status, it had no dedicated staff that proactively gathered and promoted the tourism business' key intelligence needs amongst researchers. Without an advocate that understands the business needs and challenges of managers, any research strategy will have difficulty gaining traction. Tourism destinations may also benefit from considering the variety of research mechanisms described in this chapter to serve their research needs, particularly where research budgets are constrained.

CONCLUSION

Nature-based tourism destinations such as a protected area carry out their mandate in an environment characterized by constant change, complexity and great uncertainty, against a backdrop of great expectations from society (McCool and Khumalo, 2015). Research will remain a valuable component towards the sustainable development and management of tourism. Destinations should effectively steer research efforts towards evidence-based decision-making by developing policy-relevant research agendas and prioritizing projects that align closely to these. Even organizations with limited resources can find ways to fill their knowledge gaps by collaborating closely with the academic research community. Investment in some internal research capacity ensures knowledge gaps are adequately identified and contextualized within a balanced framework of research needs, and research outputs are fed back into policy decisions.

REFERENCES

Biggs, D., Swemmer, L., Phillips, G., Stevens, J., Freitag, S. and Grant, R. (2014) The development of a tourism research framework by South African National Parks to inform management. *Koedoe*, 56(2), 1–9.

Buckley, R. (2012) Sustainable tourism: Research and reality. *Annals of Tourism Research*, 39(2), 528–546.

Butler, R. W. (1980) The concept of a tourist area cycle of evolution: Implications for management of resources. *The Canadian Geographer/Lengyel Géographe Canadien*, 24(1), 5–12.

Cape Town Declaration on Responsible Tourism in Destinations (2002). http://responsibletourismpartnership.org/CapeTown.htm.

Carruthers J. (2017) *National Park Science: A Century of Research in South Africa*. Cambridge: Cambridge University Press.

De Wet, D. (dries.dewet@sanparks.org) (2020) RE: SANParks tourism capacity. [Email to:] Slabbert, L. (liandi.slabbert@sanparks.org) 2020-02-20.

Dudley, N., Hockings, M., Stolton, S., Amend, T., Badola, R., Bianco, M., Chettri, N., Cook, C., McGeoch, M., Day, J. C., Dearden, P., Edwards, M., Nogue, S., Ferraro, P., Foden, W., Gambino, R., Gaston, K. J., Hayward, N., Hickey, V., Irving, J., Jeffries, B., Karapetyan, A., Kettunen, M., Laestadius, L., Laffoley, D., Nguyen, D., Lham, D., Lichtenstein, G., Makombo, J., Marshall, N., Paxton, M., Rao, M., Reichelt, R., Rivas, J., Roux, D., Rutte, C., Sadovoy, Y., Schreckenberg, K., Sovinc, A., Sutyrina, S., Utomo, A., Vallauri, D., Vedeld, P. O., Verschuuren, B., Waithaka, J., Woodley, S., Wyborn, C. and Zhang, Y. (2018) Priorities for protected area research. *Parks*, 24(1), 35–50.

Eagles, P. F. J. (2014) Research priorities in park tourism. *Journal of Sustainable Tourism*, 22(4), 528–549.

Edgell Sr, D. L. (2020) *Managing Sustainable Tourism* (3rd ed.). Abingdon: Routledge.

Gruby, R. L., Gray, N. J., Campbell, L. M. and Acton, L. (2016) Toward a social science research agenda for large marine protected areas. *Conservation Letters*, 9(3), 153–163.

Hallstrom, L. K., Hvenegaard, G., Gould, J. and Joubert, B. (2019) Prioritizing research questions for protected area agencies: A case study of provincial parks in Alberta, Canada. *Journal of Park & Recreation Administration*, 37(3).

Leslie, D. (ed.) (2012) *Responsible Tourism: Concepts, Theory and Practice*. Wallingford: CABI.

Lubbe, B. A., Du Preez, E. A., Douglas, A. and Fairer-Wessels, F. (2019) The impact of rhino poaching on tourist experiences and future visitation to National Parks in South Africa. *Current Issues in Tourism*, 22(1), 8–15.

McCool, S. F. (2006) Managing for visitor experiences in protected areas: Promising opportunities and fundamental challenges. *Parks*, 16(2), 3–9.

McCool, S. F. (2012) Potential roles of research in enhancing the performance of management in securing high quality visitor experiences in wilderness. In D. N. Cole (ed.), *Wilderness Visitor Experiences: Progress in Research and Management*; 4–7 April 2011; Missoula, MT. Proc. RMRS-P-66 (pp. 179–187). Fort Collins, CO: US Department of Agriculture, Forest Service, Rocky Mountain Research Station.

McCool, S. F., Clark, R. N. and Stankey, G. H. (2007) *An Assessment of Frameworks Useful for Public Land Recreation Planning*. General Technical Report-Pacific Northwest Research Station, USDA Forest Service: PNW-GTR-705.

McCool, S. F. and Khumalo, K. E. (2015) Empowering managers: Enhancing the performance of protected area tourism managers in the twenty-first century. *Tourism Recreation Research*, 40(2), 169–180.

Mihalic, T. (2016) Sustainable-responsible tourism discourse: Towards 'responsustable' tourism. *Journal of Cleaner Production*, 111, 461–470.

Morrison-Saunders, A., Hughes, M., Pope, J., Douglas, A. and Wessels, J. A. (2019) Understanding visitor expectations for responsible tourism in an iconic national park: Differences between local and international visitors. *Journal of Ecotourism*, 18(3), 284–294.

Ottoson, J. M. (2009) Knowledge-for-action theories in evaluation: Knowledge utilization, diffusion, implementation, transfer, and translation. *New Directions for Evaluation*, 124, 7–20.

Pope, J., Wessels, J. A., Douglas, A., Hughes, M. and Morrison-Saunders, A. (2019) The potential contribution of environmental impact assessment (EIA) to responsible tourism: The case of the Kruger National Park. *Tourism Management Perspectives*, 32, 100557.

Rich, R. F. (1997) Measuring knowledge utilization: Processes and outcomes. *Knowledge and Policy*, 10(3), 11–24.

Roux, D. J., Kingsford, R. T., Cook, C. N., Carruthers, J., Dickson, K. and Hockings, M. (2019) The case for embedding researchers in conservation agencies. *Conservation Biology*, 33(6), 1266–1274.

SANParks (2011) *Responsible Tourism in SANParks 2012 to 2022 Strategy*. Pretoria.

SANParks (2013) *Strategic Plan for Commercialisation*. Pretoria.

SANParks (2018) *5-Year Strategic Plan 2019/20 – 2023/24 & Annual Performance Plan 2019/20*. Pretoria. https://www.sanparks.org/assets/docs/about/annual_performance_plan_2019-2020.pdf.

SANParks (2020) *Visitor Statistics: Q4 Demographics April 2019 – March 2020*. Pretoria.

SA-Venues.com (2017) And the most visited attractions in South Africa are … [Online]. http://blog.sa-venues.com/attractions/most-visited-tourist-attractions-south-africa/.

TourismTattler.com (2013) Top 5 attractions in South Africa [Online]. https://www.tourismtattler.com/news/trade-news/top-5-attractions-in-south-africa/6778.

Travelstart Online Travel Operations (2018) 50 Top tourist attractions in South Africa – Travelstart.co.za [Online]. http://www.travelstart.co.za/blog/50-top-tourist-attractions-in-south-africa/.

van Wilgen, B. W., Boshoff, N., Smit, I. P., Solano-Fernandez, S. and Van der Walt, L. (2016) A bibliometric analysis to illustrate the role of an embedded research capability in South African National Parks. *Scientometrics*, 107(1), 185–212.

Wardell, M. J. and Moore, S. A. (2005) *Collection, Storage and Application of Visitor Use Data in Protected Areas: Guiding Principles and Case Studies*. Gold Coast, Queensland: CRC for Sustainable Tourism.

Xiao, H. and Smith, S. L. J. (2007) The use of tourism knowledge: Research propositions. *Annals of Tourism Research*, 34(2), 310–331.

Index

Printed and bound by CPI Group (UK) Ltd, Croydon, CR0 4YY

16/04/2025

14658392-0004